Ethics of Human Rights

A. Reis Monteiro

Ethics of Human Rights

Springer

A. Reis Monteiro
University of Lisbon
Portugal

ISBN 978-3-319-03565-9 ISBN 978-3-319-03566-6 (eBook)
DOI 10.1007/978-3-319-03566-6
Springer Cham Heidelberg New York Dordrecht London

Library of Congress Control Number: 2013957487

Printed on acid-free paper

Springer is part of Springer Science+Business Media (www.springer.com)

To a life's loves…

Acknowledgments

I'm deeply indebted to Professor Joseph Betz for the role he played in the publication of this study. He is Emeritus Professor at Villanova University (Pennsylvania), where the Center for Peace and Justice Education recently renamed its 'Solidarity Award' the 'Joseph M. Betz Solidarity Award'. In addition to his very generous and stimulating appraisal of this manuscript, he provided comments and suggestions that greatly contributed to its improvement. Moreover, he recommended the manuscript for linguistic revision by two doctoral students, Daniel Wood and Yong Dou (Michael) Kim. Daniel and Michael not only have provided competent and careful editing work, but also added valued commentaries as learned readers. I express to them my great appreciation and gratitude for their generosity. I wish also to thank Neil Olivier, Senior Publishing Editor, for his helpful mediating role. Diana Nijenhuijzen, Senior Editorial Assistant, was a kind interlocutor too.

The elaboration of this essay has benefited from research stays at the Erik Castrén Institute of International Law and Human Rights (ECI), in Helsinki, and at the *Ludwig Boltzmann Institut für Menschenrechte* (BIM), in Vienna. I'm grateful to Dr. Sanna Villikka (Executive Director of ECI) and to Prof. Dr. Hannes Tretter (Administrative Director of BIM) for their welcome and assistance. The research stays were supported by a sabbatical grant from the Foundation for Science and Technology (Portugal).

Preliminary Observations

1. There is a great diversity among languages and authors concerning the use of capital or lower case letters (as some quotations in this book by themselves document). Some are minimalist, other are maximalist. This writing takes the following criterion: to respect, as a rule, the options of the quoted authors but to use capital letters for highlighting certain concepts (Ethics of Human Rights, Rule of Law, for example), to distinguish between different semantic uses of a term (such as 'state' and State, 'law' and Law), or to designate disciplines of knowledge.
2. As the form of the bibliographical references is concerned, they are manifold and may be confusing, especially when quotations include quotations. This writing follows basically the *Chicago Manual of Style,* but no standard style is a bible and adaptations may be needed. Notes inside quotations are suppressed, as usual, and inside double quotation marks may be changed into single quotation marks. When an author is cited for the first time, his or her first name is referred to in full.
3. Nowadays, the Internet serves as an increasingly valuable, easily accessible and frequently unavoidable documental source[1]. In this writing, when an exclusively electronic source is quoted, it is, as a rule, referred to only as footnote: without access date, if originated from an electronic site institutionally stable; indicating month and year of access, if the presumption of stability is uncertain. Anyway, there are no immortal links... their volatility is great (but it is always possible to try to find the documents elsewhere, if they remain available on the WEB). When a document included in the references is available electronically too, its source is mentioned.
4. The use of acronyms is rather pragmatic. A list of frequent acronyms in writings on human rights is included, but only the most frequent are used in this study, following a context criterion, as no uniform criterion would be advisable. Their first appearance is accompanied, as usual, by the full denomination.

[1] As evidenced, for example, by *Conducting Research in International Human Rights Law–Legal Research Guide Series–Specialized Research Guide # 8*, George Washington University, Law School, Jacob Burns Law Library, 2012. (www.law.gwu.edu/Library/Research/Documents/Guides/Human%20Rights%20Guide%20(2013).pdf)

5. While the manuscript strives to use gender inclusive language, historical expressions such 'rights of man' are retained, without attempting to *amend* history, and the options of the quoted authors are respected.
6. Each chapter begins with an abstract and includes its own references.

Contents

1 Introduction ... 1
References ... 14

Part I Ethics And Human Rights

2 Overview of Ethical Thought ... 19
2.1 Ethics ... 19
2.2 Metaethics ... 22
2.3 Normative Ethics ... 27
2.4 Ethical Epistemology ... 33
References ... 40

3 Historical and Theoretical Rising of Human Rights and Their International Codification and Protection ... 45
3.1 Natural Law and Natural Rights ... 45
3.2 First Declarations and the Constitutionalization of Human Rights ... 57
3.3 Internationalization and Codification of Human Rights ... 68
3.3.1 Beginnings ... 68
3.3.2 Advent of the United Nations (1941–1945) ... 78
3.3.3 United Nations Charter and Human Rights (1945) ... 81
3.3.4 Commission on Human Rights (1946) ... 85
3.3.5 Drafting of the Universal Declaration of Human Rights (1947–1948) ... 87
3.3.6 Drafting of the International Covenants on Human Rights (1949–1966) ... 103
3.3.7 Other Core Human Rights Treaties ... 109
3.3.8 New Human Rights ... 112
3.4 Human Rights Protection ... 116
3.4.1 Universal Level ... 116
3.4.2 Regional Level ... 130
3.4.3 National Level ... 135

3.4.4 Case Law 143
3.4.5 NGOs 148
References 152

Part II Human Rights: Common Ethics of Humankind

4 Ethics of Recognition 161
4.1 Terminological and Conceptual Remarks 161
4.2 The Ethical Significance of Human Rights 167
4.3 The Foundational Question 173
4.4 Stakes of Recognition 185
4.5 Legal Recognition 191
References 195

5 Human Dignity Principle 199
5.1 Conceptual Origins 199
5.2 The Kantian Moment 203
5.3 Juridification 212
5.3.1 International Human Rights Law 212
5.3.2 Constitutional Law 218
5.4 Case Law 222
5.4.1 Dignity and Freedom of Speech 226
5.4.2 Dignity and Privacy 228
5.4.3 Dignity and Sexuality 229
5.4.4 Dignity and Abortion 231
5.4.5 Dignity and Corporal Punishment 233
5.4.6 Dignity and the Treatment of Prisoners 237
5.4.7 Dignity and the Death Penalty 239
5.4.8 Dignity of Life 241
5.4.9 Dignity in Death 243
5.5 Some Conclusions 245
5.5.1 Dignity is a Term with Manifold Uses 246
5.5.2 Human Dignity is a Right and a Principle 249
5.5.3 Human Dignity is Multidimensional 255
5.5.4 Human Dignity is Violable, Vulnerable and Variable 272
5.6 An Account of Human Worth 277
5.6.1 Human Worth Consists in the Perfectibility of the Human Species that Demands the Perfecting of Human Beings 279
5.6.2 The Perfectibility of the Human Species is Rooted in its Semiotic Nature that is the Source of Human Beings' Aptitude to the Liberty of Rationality 283
5.6.3 The Perfecting of Human Beings Should Consist in the Cultivation of Their Semiotic Seeds that Require Human Rights' Protection and Provisions 290
5.6.4 Right to Education: Key for the Human Perfecting 295

5.6.5 Neurobiological Insights 303
5.7 Synthesis: Human Worth, Dignity and Rights 311
References 322

6 **Other Principles** 327
6.1 Life and Liberty 327
6.2 Equality and Diversity 329
6.3 Non-discrimination 332
6.4 Tolerance and Solidarity 335
6.5 Democracy, Development and Peace 337
6.6 Common Responsibility of Humankind 346
References 350

Part III Human Rights Revolution

7 **A Changed and Changing Legal Landscape** 355
7.1 Revolution 355
7.2 Rebirth of International and Constitutional Law 358
7.3 Refounding the Rule of Law and Rethinking Democracy 365
7.4 New Law of Humanity? 375
References 385

8 **Answering Some Questions** 389
8.1 Are Human Rights Cultural Fruits Whose Colors and Flavors are Exclusively Western? 389
8.2 Are Human Rights Individualistic, Neglecting the Corresponding Duties to Others and Community? 399
8.3 Is the Ethical Universality of Human Rights Compatible with the Cultural Diversity of the World? 409
8.4 Today, What About the *Faith* in Human Rights Proclaimed in the United Nations Charter and the Universal Declaration of Human Rights? 415
References 420

9 **Conclusion** 423
References 438

Appendices 441
A Glossary Relating to Human Rights 441
A Chronology of Human Rights 485
Summary 494
Internet Resources 502
Selected Bibliography 503
Additional Bibliography Not Quoted in the Present Study 505

Index 507

Some Acronyms Used in Writings on Human Rights and Other Used in This Study

ACHR	American Convention on Human Rights
ACP	African, Caribbean and Pacific States
ACHPR	African Charter on Human and Peoples' Rights
AHRC	Asian Human Rights Commission
AIDS	Acquired immunodeficiency syndrome
ALI	American Law Institute
ASEAN	Association of Southeast Asian Nations
AU	African Union
CAT	Convention against torture and other cruel, inhuman or degrading treatment or punishment
CAT-OP	Optional protocol to the CAT
CCPR	Human Rights Committee
CED	Committee on enforced disappearances
CEDAW	Convention on the elimination of all forms of discrimination against women
CEDAW-OP	Optional protocol to the CEDAW
CERD	Committee on the elimination of racial discrimination
CESCR	Committee on economic, social and cultural rights
CHR	Commission on human rights
CIS	Commonwealth of Independent States
CMW	Committee on the protection of the rights of all migrant workers and members of their families
CoAT	Committee against torture
CoEDAW	Committee on the elimination of all forms of discrimination against women
CoRC	Committee on the rights of the child
CoRPD	Committee on the rights of persons with disabilities
CPED	International Convention for the protection of all persons from enforced disappearance
CRC	Convention on the rights of the child
CRC-OP1	Optional protocol to the CRC on the involvement of children in armed conflict

CRC-OP2	Optional protocol to the CRC on the sale of children, child prostitution and child pornography
CRC-OP3	Optional protocol to the CRC on a communications procedure
CRPD	Convention on the rights of persons with disabilities
CSCE	Conference on security and cooperation in Europe
CSW	Commission on the status of women
DPKO	Department of peace-keeping operations
ECHR	European Convention on Human Rights (Convention for the protection of human rights and fundamental freedoms)
ECOSOC	Economic and Social Council (United Nations)
ECPT	European Convention for the prevention of torture and inhuman or degrading treatment or punishment
EIA	Environmental impact assessment
ESC	European Social Charter
EU	European Union
EU Charter	Charter of Fundamental Rights of the European Union
FAO	Food and Agriculture Organization
GATS	General Agreement on Trade in Services
GATT	General Agreement on Tariffs and Trade
GC	General comment
GDP	Gross domestic product
GG	*Grundgesetz* (German Basic Law or Constitution)
GNP	Gross national product
GPG	Global public good
HABITAT	Centre for human settlement (United Nations)
HDI	Human Development Index
HDP	Human Dignity Principle
HIPC	Heavily indebted poor country
HIV	Human immunodeficiency virus
HPI	Human Poverty Index
HRC	Human Rights Council
IBRD	International Bank for Reconstruction and Development
ICC	International Criminal Court
ICCPR	International Covenant on Civil and Political Rights
ICCPR-OP1	Optional protocol to the ICCPR on individual complaints
ICCPR-OP2	Second optional protocol to the ICCPR, aiming at the abolition of the death penalty
ICERD	International Convention on the Elimination of All Forms of Racial Discrimination
ICESCR	International Covenant on Economic, Social and Cultural Rights
ICESCR-OP	Optional protocol to the ICESCR
ICJ	International Court of Justice
ICPRMW	International Convention on the Protection of the Rights of All Migrant Workers and Members of Their Families
ICRC	International Committee of the Red Cross

IGO	Intergovernmental Organization
IHL	International humanitarian law
IHRL	International human rights law
ILO	International Labor Organization
IMF	International Monetary Fund
IOM	International Organization for Migration
LDC	Least developed countries
MDGs	Millennium development goals
MC	Multinational Corporation
NGO	Non-Governmental Organization
NHRI	National Human Rights Institution
OAS	Organization of American States
OAU	Organization of African Unity
OCHA	Office for the coordination of humanitarian affairs
ODA	Official development assistance
OECD	Organization for Economic Cooperation and Development
OHCHR	Office of the High Commissioner for Human Rights
OIC	Organisation of Islamic Cooperation
OP	Optional protocol
OSCE	Organization for Security and Cooperation in Europe
PCIJ	Permanent Court of International Justice
PG	Public good
PPP	Purchasing power parity
SAFHR	South Asia Forum for Human Rights
SPT	Subcommittee on prevention of torture
TMB	Treaty Monitoring Body
TNC	Transnational Corporation
UDHR	Universal Declaration of Human Rights
UK	United Kingdom
UN	United Nations
UNCED	United Nations Conference on Environment and Development
UNCTAD	United Nations Conference on Trade and Development
UNDEF	United Nations Democracy Fund
UNDP	United Nations Development Program
UNDRO	United Nations Disaster Relief Office
UNEP	United Nations Environment Program
UNESCO	United Nations Educational, Scientific and Cultural Organization
UNFPA	United Nations Population Fund
UNHCHR	United Nations High Commissioner for Human Rights
UNHCR	United Nations High Commissioner for Refugees
UNHRP	United Nations Housing Rights Program
UNICEF	United Nations Children's Fund
UNIFEM	United Nations Development Fund for Women
UNOG	United Nations Office at Geneva
UNRRA	United Nations Relief and Rehabilitation Administration

USA United States of America
UPR Universal Periodic Review
VCLT Vienna Convention on the Law of Treaties
WFP World Food Program
WHO World Health Organization
WTO World Trade Organization

Chapter 1
Introduction

Abstract This introduction justifies the relevance of this volume and presents its purpose, structure, content and methodology.

The study that follows is a long journey focused on the ethical significance of human rights. Its scope and rationale are reflected in its three-part structure. It aims at contributing to a universal culture of human rights with deep roots and wide horizons. While not discussing every viewpoint quoted, nor elaborating on too specific matters, it touches on much of the typical syllabus of a human rights course and also explores emerging issues.

This study consists principally of normative research, drawing on International Human Rights Law as it currently stands and functions. The study combines different approaches but takes a predominantly juridical one. Its extended legal and jurisprudential content, as well as the communicative and argumentative rationality peculiar to the normative field, require broad quotations from a variety of sources.

During the last decades, international initiatives were launched with the purpose of identifying universal values.

For example, in 1987, the United Nations Educational, Scientific and Cultural Organization (UNESCO) published a Report commanded to The Club of Roma[1]. Its title was *In search of a wisdom for the world—The role of ethical values in education—A collective investigation of the Club of Rome* (*February-October* 1986). Prepared by Bertrand Schneider, General-Secretary of the Club of Rome, it was the outcome of a broad consultation and debate, including a Symposium in the Royaumont Foundation (France) in June 1986. The Symposium adopted a Declaration that affirmed:

---

[1] The Club of Rome was founded by an Italian manufacturer (Aurelio Peccei) and a Scottish scientist (Alexander King). As informs its electronic site:

> The Club of Rome was founded in 1968 as an informal association of independent leading personalities from politics, business and science, men and women who are long-term thinkers interested in contributing in a systemic interdisciplinary and holistic manner to a better world. The Club of Rome members share a common concern for the future of humanity and the planet. (www.clubofrome.org/eng/about/3)

A. Reis Monteiro, *Ethics of Human Rights*, DOI 10.1007/978-3-319-03566-6_1,

> We believe that amongst the emerging universal values, stress should be laid upon:
>
> - the respect of cultural diversity;
> - the respect of the richness of genetic and biological heritage;
> - protection of environmental quality;
> - the prevention of adverse man-made long-term effects on climate.
>
> [...]
>
> Values such as collective human survival, the primacy and protection of human life, the preservation of nature and the dignity of humankind, justice, freedom and equity, already form the nucleus of universally accepted values [...]. (UNESCO 1987, p. 15)

In 1999, the results of the Universal Ethics Project (UNESCO) were published in the report *A Common Framework for the Ethics of the twenty-first Century*. It affirmed: "The symptoms of uncertainty and crisis that mark this *fin-de-siècle* are, in an important sense, a reflection of the inability of nation states to deal effectively with the new historical situation" (Kim 1999, p. 8). According to the Report: "A necessary first step is to make an inventory of ethical values and principles which have been proposed in many declarations and studies" (p. 34), in order to answer to the "global problems which humanity faces in common" (p. 40). The vectors of the ethical framework should be the relation with nature, human fulfillment, the relation between the individual and the community, and justice.

In 1993, a Declaration Toward a Global Ethic was adopted by the Parliament of the World's Religions, in Chicago, where representatives of more than 120 religions met[2]. The Declaration reads:

> We women and men of various religions and regions of Earth therefore address all people, religious and non-religious. We wish to express the following convictions which we hold in common:
>
> - We all have a responsibility for a better global order.
> - Our involvement for the sake of human rights, freedom, justice, peace, and the preservation of Earth is absolutely necessary.
> - Our different religious and cultural traditions must not prevent our common involvement in opposing all forms of inhumanity and working for greater humaneness.
> - The principles expressed in this Global Ethic can be affirmed by all persons with ethical convictions, whether religiously grounded or not.
> - As religious and spiritual persons we base our lives on an Ultimate Reality, and draw spiritual power and hope therefrom, in trust, in prayer or meditation, in word or silence. We have a special responsibility for the welfare of all humanity and care for the planet Earth. We do not consider ourselves better than other women and men, but we trust that the ancient wisdom of our religions can point the way for the future.

In 1995, the Commission on Global Governance published the Report *Our Global Neighborhood*[3]. It reads (Chapter Two – Values for the Global Neighborhood):

> We believe that all humanity could uphold the core values of respect for life, liberty, justice and equity, mutual respect, caring, and integrity.
>
> [...]

[2] www.parliamentofreligions.org/_includes/FCKcontent/File/TowardsAGlobalEthic.pdf.

[3] The Commission on Global Governance, established in 1993, was an initiative of Willy Brandt, former West German Chancellor. It is composed of 28 selected personalities. (www.globalgovernancewatch.org/authors/-commission-on-global-governance)

> The global ethic we envisage would help humanize the impersonal workings of bureaucracies and markets and constrain the competitive and self-serving instincts of individuals and groups. [...]
> During the past fifty years, the world has made great progress in elaborating universal human rights. [...] They provide an important starting point for a global ethic, but they need to be supplemented in two important ways.
> First, as presently conceived, rights are almost entirely defined in terms of the relationship between people and governments. We believe it is now important to begin to think of rights in broader terms by recognizing that governments are only one source of threats to human rights and, at the same time, that more and more often, government action alone will not be sufficient to protect many human rights. This means that all citizens, as individuals and as members of different private groups and associations, should accept the obligation to recognize and help protect the rights of others.
> Second, rights need to be joined with responsibilities. [...]
> We therefore urge the international community to unite in support of a global ethic of common rights and shared responsibilities.

In 2001, the participants in an experts' meeting on 'Ethics for the twenty-first Century' convened by UNESCO on 21–22 September, in Paris[4], agreed on the need for a Universal Ethics—the 'Globalization of Ethics', integrating universality and diversity—and also agreed upon the need to promote the reflection about contemporary ethical problems, especially through philosophical problematization and education.

This is also the concern of the Humanist Movement. It is a collection of organizations that propose a New Humanism, also known as Universalist Humanism[5].

Humanitas is the Latin translation of the Greek word *Paideia* (education). As noted the Italian scientist, thinker and writer Salvatore Puledda (1943–2001), a preeminent advocate of the Universalist Humanism:

> In a confluence rich in meanings, *humanitas* came to indicate the formation and development, through education, of those qualities that make an individual a truly *human* being, that rescue 'humanity' from its natural condition and differentiate it from the barbarian. With the concept of *humanitas* the Romans wished to denote a cultural operation: the construction of the individual, the citizen, who lives and acts within human society. (Puledda 1997, p. 4)

The Latin word *humanista* appeared in Italy during the first half of the sixteenth century, meaning "a man of letters who dedicates himself to the *studia humanitatis*" (p. 3).

The term *humanism*, however, is an invention of the nineteenth century. It was coined by the German pedagogue Friedrich I. niethammer who published a book, in 1808, titled *Der Streit des Philanthropinismus und Humanismus in der Theorie des Erziehungs-Unterrichts unserer Zeit* (The dispute between philanthropism and humanism in the theory of education-instruction of our time). Ever since, Humanism became associated with the Renaissance.

[4] http://unesdoc.unesco.org/images/0012/001246/124626f.pdf.

[5] The founder of the Humanist Movement was the Argentine writer Mario Rodríguez Cobos (1938–2010), known as Silo, in 1969, in Punta de Vacas, mountain of Andes, close to the border of Argentina and Chile.

In Puledda's opinion, "humanist currents, which have appeared since the beginning of Western civilization, have displayed a behavior that is wave-like—appearing in certain periods and later fading from view, only to reappear once again". This occurred with the first one, Greco-Roman Humanism, which submerged during the Middle Ages until the Renaissance (p. 2). However:

> By the end of the Renaissance, with the birth of the experimental sciences and the development of rationalist and mechanistic philosophies, the human being came to be interpreted as a purely natural phenomenon. Thus began the decline of humanism as a philosophical vision affirming a central position or uniqueness for the human being in the world of nature. (p. 60)

In the twentieth century, the term 'humanism' revived. Recall, for instance, the First Humanist Society of New York, founded in 1929 by Charles F. Potter (1885–1962), whose advisory board included Julian Huxley, John Dewey, Albert Einstein, and Thomas Mann[6]; the *Humanist Manifesto* (1933); Jacques Maritain's *Humanisme Intégrale* (*Integral Humanism* 1937); Jean-Paul Sartre's *L'Existentialisme est un humanisme* (translated as *Existentialism* 1946); Martin Heidegger's *Brief über den 'Humanismus'* (Letter on Humanism 1947); Howard M. Jones' *American Humanism: Its Meaning for World Survival* (1957); Corliss Lamont's *The Philosophy of Humanism* (1993).

According to Puledda: "The meaning of the word *humanism* appears lost today, as with the Tower of Babel, in a confusion of tongues and interpretations" (p. 59). In his opinion: "Of modern currents of thought, structuralism has taken perhaps the most determinedly anti-humanist stance" (p. 40)[7]. The New Humanism serves to counter "an eclipse of humanism" and "our loss of the sense of what it is to be human" (p. 2). It considers that Humanism is not a purely European and temporally limited phenomenon, but an *approach* and *attitude* towards personal and community life to be found in different cultures in different historical eras. It is an appeal to *transcendence*, a *project*, inherent in human nature as nature in motion. Consequently, "it is the common heritage of all the cultures of the Earth. And it is in this sense that such a humanism can be spoken of as a *universal humanism*" (p. 63). Giving a talk on 4 January 1998 in Buenos Aires, Silo said:

> What is the humanist movement today? Is it perhaps a refuge in the face of the general crisis of the system in which we live? Is it a sustained critique of a world that is becoming more dehumanized day by day? Is it a new language and a new paradigm, a new interpretation of

[6] In 1933, Charles Potter and his wife Clara C. Potter, published *Humanism: A New Religion*.

[7] Struturalism "attempted to develop research strategies that would throw light on the constant, systematic relationships that they believed existed within human behavior, individual and collective, and that they called 'structures'" (Puledda 1997, p. 41). The concept of 'structure' comes from Ferdinand de Saussure's (1857–1913) *Course in General Linguistics* (1915) that introduced the use of the 'structural method' to the study of language. However, the term never appears in the *Course*, 'system' being used instead. Its spread to the other human sciences is due mainly to the Russian linguist Roman Jakobson (1896–1982) who the anthropologist Claude Lévi-Strauss (1908–2009) met in New York. Lévi-Strauss "might be considered the 'father' of structuralism" (p. 43), having proposed that human cultures be studied as structures of verbal and nonverbal languages, so reducing Anthropology to a Semiotics.

> the world and a new landscape? Does it represent an ideological or political current, a new aesthetic, a new scale of values? Is it a new spirituality, destined to redeem subjectivity and diversity through concrete action? Is the Movement perhaps the expression of the struggle in support of the dispossessed, the abandoned, and the persecuted? Or is it a manifestation of those who feel the monstrosity inherent in human beings not having the same rights and the same opportunities?
> The Movement is all that and much more. It is the practical expression of the ideal of humanizing the Earth and the aspiration of moving towards a Universal Human Nation. It is the seed of a new culture in this civilization that is becoming planetary, and which will have to change its course, accepting and valuing diversity and giving equal rights and identical opportunities to all human beings, because of the dignity that they deserve by the simple fact of their having been born.[8]

In other words, the Universalist Humanism is a Human Rights Humanism. It professes the central value and dignity of each human being and the liberty and the equality of all human beings, recognizes cultural and personal diversity, and rejects all forms of discrimination and violence.

Human rights are also highly prized in the document *The Search for Universal Ethics: A New Look at Natural Law* published by the International Theological Commission (Vatican) in 2008[8]. It reads:

> 1. Are there objective moral values capable of bringing people together and securing peace and happiness for them? What are they? How are they recognized? How are they realized in the life of individuals and of the community? These questions about good and evil, questions which always return, are today more urgent than ever, in as much as people are more aware of forming a single community in the world. The great problems that present themselves to human beings now bear an international, planetary dimension, since the development of the techniques of communication favors a growing interaction between persons, societies, and cultures. [...] The rapid developments in biotechnology, which threaten the very identity of the human being (genetic manipulation, cloning, etc.), urgently demand an ethical and political reflection of universal breadth. In this context, the search for common ethical values becomes once more a current issue.
> [...]
> 115. ... Since the Second World War, nations of all the world have been able to make a universal declaration of human rights, which implicitly suggests that the source of inalienable human rights is found in the dignity of every human person. The present contribution has no other aim than helping to reflect on this source of personal and collective morality.

The Universal Declaration of Human Rights (UDHR) was an unprecedented proclamation of common moral values. During its drafting process, the Colombian representative (Augusto Ramirez Moreno) said, at the 90th meeting of the Third Committee of the General Assembly of the United Nations (UN), on 1 October 1948 (A/C.3/SR.90)[9], that its results "should be of great significance, even though they might be merely the seed of a tree which would bear fruit at a much later time" (see subsection 3.3.5). The tree has become the International Human Rights Law (IHRL) (see Glossary)[10].

---

[8] www.humanistmovement.net/.

[9] The documents related to the history of the UDHR drafting quoted in this study are available at: www.un.org/depts/dhl/udhr.

[10] "The concept of 'international human rights norm' is broad, and it overlaps with rights protected under other areas of international and domestic law, including international humanitarian law, international criminal law, international environmental law, development law, labor law, refugee

In 1970, the UN General Assembly stated in the Declaration on the Occasion of its Twenty-Fifth Anniversary[11]: "The international conventions and declarations concluded under its auspices give expression to the moral conscience of mankind and represent humanitarian standards for all members of the international community". As Manfred Nowak (2003) wrote: "As long as international law is understood as the only normative basis for international relations, human rights will hold their ground as the only universally recognized and legally codified system of values" (p. 33). Alexander Kiss (2006) noted: "Several human rights treaties explicitly proclaim that they are based on ethical foundations" (p. 16). The Recommendation concerning Education for International Understanding, Co-operation and Peace and Education relating to Human Rights and Fundamental Freedoms, adopted by UNESCO in 1974[12], refers expressly to the Ethics of Human Rights when it recommends to Member States (para. 33):

> (a) provide teachers with motivations for their subsequent work: commitment to the *ethics of human rights* [italics added] and to the aim of changing society, so that human rights are applied in practice; a grasp of the fundamental unity of mankind; ability to instill appreciation of the riches which the diversity of cultures can bestow on every individual, group or nation;

This Recommendation's long denomination reflects, in itself, a diplomatic ideological balance during the Cold War, when human rights were a battle-ground between West (giving priority to civil and political rights, as well as to democracy) and East (giving priority to economic, social and cultural rights, as well as to the peaceful coexistence)[13].

In the post-Cold War era, the *ideology of human rights* became the prevailing ethical discourse, as Alain Badiou rightly noted (1993, Introduction). A striking proof of "the ideological hegemony of human rights" (Freeman 2004, p. 306) is that "no government dares to dissent from the ideology of human rights today" (Henkin 1978, p. 28), even if that means no more than "the homage that vice pays to virtue" (p. 137). Mary Glendon (2001) remarks that the "most impressive advances" (p. 236) of human rights were the end of *Apartheid* and of the Communist Block. She notes:

> The fact that nations and interest groups increasingly seek to cast their agendas or justify their actions in terms of human rights is one measure of the success of the human rights

---

and asylum law, constitutional law, domestic criminal law and procedure, and even the law of the sea" (Edwards 2010, p. 152).

[11] http://daccessdds.un.org/doc/RESOLUTION/GEN/NR0/348/92/PDF/NR034892.pdf?OpenElement.

[12] http://portal.unesco.org/en/ev.php-URL_ID=13088andURL_DO=DO_TOPICandURL_SECTION=201.html.

[13] These diverging views go back to the UDHR drafting process. For example, at the second session of the Commission on Human Rights (CHR), in December 1947, the United Kingdom (UK) representative (Lord Charles Dukeston) said that: "The world needed free men and not well-fed slaves. Therefore, in developing human rights, it was necessary to begin by proclaiming freedom of speech, freedom of association and freedom of thought". On the contrary, the Ukrainian Soviet Socialist Republic representative (Klekovkin) defended that the economic, social and cultural rights "were the foundation of all other rights" (E/CN.4/SR.42).

> idea. Nearly every international dispute today sooner or later implicates human rights; nearly every exercise of military force claims some humanitarian justification. (p. xviii)

Furthermore, the respect for human rights became a conditionality. "Conditionality—Sia S. Åkermark (2009) explains—means the inclusion of clauses in loan agreements, arrangements and programs of the World Bank, IMF [International Monetary Fund] and other economic organizations (including the European Union) that make disbursement of money conditional upon certain actions to be performed or results to be achieved by the beneficiary" (p. 359)[14].

Having as backdrop "a spectacular widening of the field of juridicity" in contemporary societies (Chevallier 2008, p. 389), the expansion and deepening of the idea and ideal of human rights have been one of the most important facts of the second half of the twentieth century—*The Age of Rights* (Louis Henkin 1990; Norberto Bobbio 1990). Highlighting "the impressive expansion of the human rights notion", more than three decades ago, René Cassin (1976) gave this example: "Nowadays, the relationships between the husband and wife, parents and children, are examined in the light of human rights" (p. 326, 327). Tom Campbell (2006) concludes:

> Rights currently enjoy a highly favorable reputation. The discourse of rights is pervasive and popular in politics, law and morality. There is scarcely any position, opinion, claim, criticism or aspiration relating to social and political life that is not asserted and affirmed using the term 'rights'. Indeed, there is little chance that any cause will be taken seriously in the contemporary world that cannot be expressed as a demand for the recognition or enforcement of rights of one sort or another. It is not enough to hold that a proposal will lead to an improvement in wellbeing or a reduction in suffering, unless it can also be presented as a recognition of someone's rights, preferably their human rights.

The rights discourse is "a language of high normative force [...] because they express the great moral significance of every individual human being. A society that is based on rights is believed to manifest and affirm the dignity of each and every human life as something that is deserving of the highest respect" (p. 3). Behind a rights approach to morality and politics is "the moral imperative [...] to secure and protect in a concrete way the treasured freedoms, interests and capacities from which rights derive their justifications" (p. 85). Summing up, Claudio Corradetti (2012) writes: "Never before has the appeal to human rights been as pervasive as it is today" (p. xiii). This appeal comes, in particular, from the critics of the dominant and aggressive wave of Globalization.

Globalization is a term that has been used in social sciences since the 1960s and by economists since the 1980s, but the rhetoric of world globalization expanded in the 1990s. It is not an entirely new phenomenon, but has roots in ancient and modern times. Ancient empires, especially the Roman Empire, as well as the 'discovering' of new continents and peoples by the Portuguese and Spanish sailors, in

[14] Regarding the European Union (EU): "Since the early 1999s, the EC [European Community] systematically included a so-called human rights clause in its trade and cooperation agreements concluded with third countries, including so-called association's agreements" (Rosas 2009, p. 466).

the fifteenth and sixteenth centuries, were globalizing too (see Ferri 2005)[15]. Karl Marx (1818–1883) and Friedrich Engels (1820–1895) wrote: "Modern industry has established the world market, for which the discovery of America paved the way" (as cit. in Spring 2000, p. 40).

However, the new Era of Globalization is an unprecedented and complex phenomenon that contracts time and space by the dissolution of borders and the interconnection of people and countries. It has scientific-technological, economic/financial, socio-cultural and ethical-political vectors, amounting to a refoundation of Civilization (see Brunsvick and Danzin 1998). It originates in the generalization of the applications of scientific and technological innovations in all of the domains of human life, which have extraordinarily accelerated the mobility of people, services and goods. The Internet is the symbol of such a revolution of the new technologies of information and communication that, from the beginning of the 1990s, involved the world in an ever extending worldwide interconnectivity. So a networking has also been favoured by the end of the Cold War and the fall of the Berlin Wall. As wrote Koichirō Matsuura (2004), UNESCO's former General-Director (1999–2009), Globalization created "an entirely new territory, where our old navigation tools became obsolete" (p. 9). The vertiginous transformation of the world it caused is comparable to a *fast-forward* film, while our reacting capacity remains in *slow motion*.

Globalization is a process and the result of that process. The process is complex, inexorable, irreversible, like other civilizational mutations. The result is ambivalent, as every great technical innovations are. So far, the balance between its inclusive and exclusive effects is globally negative. While increasing world economic wealth, it aggravated the gap between the wealthy and the poor. The globalizing wave has been ridden by neo-liberalism, the dominating economic ideology for over three decades.

The neo-liberal 'decalogue' was the improperly called *Washington Consensus*, an expression used in 1989 by the economist John Williamson that summarized in ten recommendations the dominant thought in the United States Department of the Treasury, the World Bank and the IMF, of which the World Trade Organization (WTO) also became an instrument, as of 1995. Other powerful neo-liberalism actors are the Multinational Corporations (MCs), which control world trade and manage world wealth to a great extent.

Neo-liberalism presents itself as the economic ideology of the 'free world', advantageous for everybody and for democracy, but its flag is not human freedom. Alain Renaut (2004) observes that the "neo-liberal drift" of the classic liberalism is devoted "to the mission of liberating the market, tending to skip politics" (p. 25). It is a macroeconomic dictatorship whose commandments are the deregulation and privatisation of whatever can generate profit. Its world is a market without borders nor scruples nor sense of the Common Good, through the weakening and submission of States and the people's instrumentation. It is an "ultra-liberal financial and deregulated globalization", as affirms an important report prepared for the French

[15] The idea of world globalization is present in the Roman historian Polybe (200–125 BC).

President (Védrine 2007, paras. 3 and 19). It is an economic fundamentalism that reduces human horizons, remarks Gérard Mendel (2002), to "a simple economic productivism" (p. 184), and people to the mere condition of manpower and consumers. It is not at all concerned with the fundamental needs of the great majority of the world population. On the contrary, its productive effectiveness is brutally destructive for human beings and their environment. Jeremy Fox (2001) said: "Neo-liberalism is, in its essence, a system designed to serve the rich" (p. 38, 39).

Summing up, neo-liberal Globalization is limited, unbalanced, inhuman and unsustainable:

- *Limited*, because it has a principally economic-financial content.
- *Unbalanced*, because it is geographically asymmetric, dominated by the most powerful economies.
- *Inhuman*, because it has been an instrument that intensified the oppression of the strongest over the weakest, worsening the most expanded violation and cause of violations of human rights: poverty and extreme poverty.
- *Unsustainable*, because besides its human costs, the malfunction of neo-liberalism is illustrated by the crisis generated by the turbulences of the world financial system, disturbing the neo-liberal illusion.

Neo-liberal Globalization gave rise to a global movement, not of insane opposition to it, but of struggle for another kind of Globalization. As Joseph E. Stiglitz (2006), Nobel Prize in Economics in 2001, wrote, so far "there is a democratic deficit in the way that globalization has been managed", because we have failed, at international level, "to develop the democratic political institutions that are required if we are to make globalization work—to ensure that the power of the global market economy leads to the improvement of the lives of most of the people of the world, not just the richest in the richest countries" (p. 276). It is a matter, in particular, of the International Community providing *collectively* "an array of global public goods—from global peace to global health, to preserving the global environment, to global knowledge" (p. 281). In effect:

> Globalization does not have to be bad for the environment, increase inequality, weaken cultural diversity, and advance corporate interests at the expense of the well-being of ordinary citizens. [...]
> I hope that this book will help to change mindsets—as those in the developed world see more clearly some of the consequences of the policies that their governments have undertaken. I hope it will convince many, in all countries, that 'another world is possible'. Even more: that 'another world is necessary and inevitable'. [...]
> The globalization debate has become so intense because so much is at stake—not just economic well-being, but the very nature of our societies, even perhaps the very survival of society as we have known it. (p. XV, 24, 288)

The 1999 United Nations Development Program (UNDP) *Human Development Report*[16] was dedicated to 'Globalization with a human face'. How can we humanize Globalization in order to realize its promises and to avert its dangers? The Report's answer was (p. 2):

---

[16] http://hdr.undp.org/en/media/HDR_1999_EN.pdf.

The challenge of globalization in the new century is [...] globalization with:

- *Ethics*—less violation of human rights, not more.
- *Equity—less disparity within and between nations, not more.*
- *Inclusion—less marginalization of people and countries, not more.*
- *Human security—less instability of societies and less vulnerability of people, not more.*
- *Sustainability*—less environmental destruction, not more.
- *Development—less poverty and deprivation, not more.*

Indeed, the direction of Globalization depends upon the kind of development undergirding its dynamic: A merely economic growth pursuing the exploitation and oppression, or a development consistent with the 'human right' to development, as recognized in the Declaration on the Right to Development (UN 1986)[17], and reaffirmed by the Vienna Declaration and Programme of Action adopted by the World Conference on Human Rights (1993)[18]?

The United Nations Millennium Declaration[19], solemnly proclaimed on 8 September 2000 by the Heads of State and Government gathered at the UN Headquarters, in New York, reads: "We believe that the central challenge we face today is to ensure that globalization becomes a positive force for all the world's people" (para. 5). A priority should be "to free our fellow men, women and children from the abject and dehumanizing conditions of extreme poverty, to which more than a billion of them are currently subjected. We are committed to making the right to development a reality for everyone and to freeing the entire human race from want" (para. 11).

The struggle for another Globalization is, therefore, the struggle for a Globalization harmonizing ethical and other values, public and private interests, progress and economic growth with ecological sustainability, human safety and social justice. In other words, the alternative to neo-liberal Globalization is the Globalization of Human Rights.

'Human right' is an "essentially contested concept"[20], however. Philosophers are right in remaining "concerned by the question of the philosophical foundations

---

[17] www.ohchr.org/Documents/Issues/Development/RTD_booklet_en.pdf.

[18] www.ohchr.org/Documents/Events/OHCHR20/VDPA_booklet_English.pdf.

[19] www.un.org/millennium/declaration/ares552e.htm.

[20] This idea was introduced by Walter B. Gallie (1956) in an essay that reads:

> In order to count as essentially contested, in the sense just illustrated, a concept must possess the four following characteristics: (I) it must be appraisive in the sense that it signifies or accredits some kind of valued achievement. (II) This achievement must be of an internally complex character, for all that its worth is attributed to it as a whole. (III) Any explanation of its worth must therefore include reference to the respective contributions of its various parts or features; [...] In fine, the accredited achievement is initially variously describable. (IV) The accredited achievement must be of a kind that admits of considerable modification in the light of changing circumstances; and such modification cannot be prescribed or predicted in advance. For convenience I shall call the concept of any such achievement 'open' in character. These seem to me to be the four most important necessary conditions to which any essentially contested concept must comply.
>
> [...]
>
> More simply, to use an essentially contested concept means to use it against other uses and to recognize that one's own use of it has to be maintained against these other uses. Still more simply, to use an essentially contested concept means to use it both aggressively and defensively. (p. 171, 172)

of human rights", without "epistemological complacency", Andrew Fagan (2005) observes. There is an immense literature on human rights. Nonetheless, as James Griffin (2008) rightly points out, human rights discourse "is much too well established" and IHRL has "its own perfectly coherent conception of a human right" (p. 19, 203). Referring to the purpose of the authors of the founding legal texts proclaiming human rights in the aftermath of the Second World War, he writes:

> There is not the slightest doubt which is the more important, more noble ambition. My aim is, at best, a contribution to their much larger aim. But then the drafters were not interested in arriving at a narrow list of human rights with impeccable semantic credentials. They were interested in an ampler list, in a way the ampler the better, with some claim to being, or decent prospects of becoming, a standard that crossed cultures, religions, borders, and power blocs. And so they made use, without too much worry, of a deeply obscure, largely undefined notion of 'the dignity of the human person'. [...] The rights on their lists, even if it turned out that they were not all strictly speaking *human* rights, have become, once embodied in treaties, basic international *legal* rights. That is a status hardly to be scorned. (p. 202, 203)

This study is a long journey focused on the ethical significance of human rights, from an International Law and IHRL perspective. It aims at contributing to a universal culture of human rights[21]. A culture of human rights with deep roots and wide horizons needs broad information and answers to most questions that human rights imply or arouse, such as: Which are the main theoretical problems and what is the epistemological specificity of the moral field? Where do the human dignity and human rights ideas come from? Who were the greatest protagonists of their theoretical elaboration? Why did they inspire political revolutions? How did they become universal values? Are there legal definitions of human dignity and human right? In what does the human worth underlying the recognition of human dignity and rights consist? Which are the most far-reaching contemporary outcomes of the human rights movement? What are the present major human rights debates and challenges?

The study's purpose, scope and rationale are reflected in its three-part structure, namely:

- Part I (Ethics and Human Rights) begins with a general introduction and overview of ethical thought, including an approach to Ethical Epistemology. Thereafter is presented an outlook of the dawning of the human rights idea and ideal, until their expansion during the second half of the twentieth century. This entails mentioning and quoting the great classical and modern philosophical references, common to every historical and theoretical approach to human rights, as well as some contemporary ones. The drafting of the International Bill of Human Rights—composed of the 1948 Universal Declaration and the 1966 International Covenants—deserves to be summarized, providing a taste of the historical climate that made possible such an ethical achievement. Two main facts stand out from these analyses:

[21] According to Campbell (2006), "a society may be said to have a 'rights culture', when its members think of themselves in terms of their rights and interact with each other on the basis of their perceived rights and duties" (p. 123).

- The human rights ideal is born from the "resistance to despotism, oppression, and humiliation" (Habermas 2012, p. 65).
- The human rights idea "has evolved out of earlier notions of natural law and natural rights" (Pogge 2001, p. 189).

• Part II (Human Rights: Common Ethics of Humankind) begins with some terminological and conceptual remarks, highlights the essential ethical dimension of human rights, and includes an approach to the question of their foundation/justification. Thereafter, the origins, evolution and juridification of the concept of human dignity are traced, and the jurisprudential uses of the Human Dignity Principle (HDP) are illustrated. As it means the consecration of the human worth, an interdisciplinary account of the latter is submitted. Thereafter, other principles of the Ethics of Human Rights are identified and justified. This central part may be so summed up:

  - The Ethics of Human Rights is best understood as an Ethics of Recognition of human worth, dignity and rights.
  - The human worth consists in the perfectibility of the human species, rooted in its semiotic nature, to be accomplished through the perfecting of human beings.
  - The HDP is the bedrock of the IHRL architecture designed to protecting and enhancing the human worth.

• Part III (Human Rights Revolution) points out the main legal and political influences of IHRL on International and Constitutional Law, on the conceptions of Rule of Law and democracy, as well as on the vision of Humanity as a global rights-holder in space and time. Further historical and conceptual developments address the most frequent and debated criticisms of human rights, namely: their alleged western-centrism, individualism, neglect of duties, incompatibility with cultural diversity, and impotence. To conclude, the human stature of the Big Five drafters of the UDHR is highlighted, as well as the priority that should be given to human rights education. Some appendices add to this volume's purpose, scope and usefulness.

To be up to its ambition, the study enters the rainforest of the literature on human rights. While not intending to provide a detailed description of the present human rights landscape, it includes much of the content of the typical syllabus for a human rights course.

Fons Coomans, Fred Grünfeld and Menno Kamminga convened an international conference to examine methodological questions in the field of human rights research. It took place at Maastricht University (Netherlands), under the auspices of the Maastricht Centre for Human Rights, in November 2007, and the best papers were published in 2009. In an article summarizing the Conference's key findings, they note: "Human rights research encompasses a very broad range of topics and approaches. [...] Although human rights scholarship is often regarded as the exclusive province of lawyers, it covers a much wider range of disciplines". However, there is "a methodological deficit in human rights scholarship" that affects "legal research more than research performed by social scientists" (Coomans et al. 2010,

p. 181). In their opinion, it is due to the lack of formal training in methodology, in particular. As a consequence, many articles contain no explicit information on the method used. Other shortcomings are related to "a tendency by authors from all [Social Sciences] disciplines to rely on secondary rather than primary sources"; to the fact that "some human rights lawyers display an excessive deference towards the case law from international human rights bodies" (p. 182); as well as because "human rights scholars often know which conclusions they want to arrive at before they begin their research". This results in "a marked absence of *internal* critical reflection among human rights scholars" (p. 183).

Trying to find an explanation of "such poor methodological standards in human rights scholarship", the authors submitted:

> Our hypothesis is that human rights scholars tend to passionately believe that human rights are positive. Many of the scholars are activists or former activists in the field of human rights. Although seldom stated, the explicit aim of their research is to contribute to improve respect for human rights standards. (p. 182)

They further suggest:

> Arguably, the description of a work's methodology is the most interesting and revealing part of any academic paper (or research proposal).
> A description of the research project's method should not be confused with a description of the sources of information. [...]
> The methodology cannot be derived from the table of contents. Rather, the methodology requires a detailed description of the steps taken by the researcher to travel from the problem statement to the conclusion.
> There is no single, preferred research method, nor is there a typical, preferred method for carrying out research in the field of human rights. [...] A combination of methods, if expertly employed, may produce more reliable results.
> The method chosen for a research project should flow logically from the project's research question.
> [...]
> Normative research projects in the field of human rights must clearly distinguish the law as it is (*lex lata*) from the law as it should be in the opinion of the author (*lex ferenda*). (p. 184, 185)

This volume consists principally of normative research, taking IHRL as it is and functions. It draws mainly on primary sources and combines different approaches, but takes mostly a juridical one. Its extended legal and jurisprudential content, as well as the communicative and argumentative rationality peculiar to the normative field, require broad quotations from a variety of sources that should be allowed to speak for themselves. While not discussing every viewpoint quoted for the sake of a comprehensive culture of human rights, the quotations are the indispensable stuff of a reasoning driven by confrontation of arguments and the search for consensus. Indeed, while making a case for the high ethical value and liberating power of the human rights ideal, objections, controversies and uncertainties are not at all overlooked, new approaches are proposed and emerging issues are explored. Moreover, capturing debates' nuances and supporting less consensual interpretations imply some unavoidable but useful and dialectical redundancy. It is a matter of spiral dialectic, that is, the same concept being approached, under different lights, in different contexts. If we intend to explore an idea, "dialectic is the only inquiry that travels this road" and allows "proceeding to the first principle itself", said Plato (427–347 BC) (1997, 533d).

The simplicity and elegance of the Einstein's formula $E = mc^2$ is out of reach for the epistemology of the human and social sciences, which, rather, resembles the architectural and pictorial profusion of the medieval Catholic Cathedrals or Buddhist Temples...

References

Åkermark, S. 2009. Human rights, globalization, trade and development. In *International protection of human rights: A textbook*, ed. C. Krause and M. Scheinin, 343–362. Turku/Åbo: Åbo Akademi University, Institute for Human Rights.

Badiou, A. 1993. *L'éthique—essai sur la conscience du mal*. Paris: Hatier.

Bobbio, N. 1990. *A era dos direitos* ('L'età dei Diritti', trad. de Carlos Nelson Coutinho). Rio de Janeiro: Editora Campos (1992).

Brunsvick, Y., and A. Danzin. 1998. *Naissance d'une civilisation—Le choc de la mondialisation (Préface de Jean Favier, Postface de Federico Mayor)*. Paris: Éditions UNESCO.

Campbell, T. 2006. *Rights—A critical introduction*. London: Routledge.

Cassin, R. 1976. Les droits de l'homme. In Académie de Droit International, *Recueil des Cours/Collected Courses of the Hague Academy of Internationl Law—1974—Tome 140 de la collection*, 221–231. Leiden: Martinus Nijhoff Publishers.

Chevallier, J. 2008. État de Droit. In *Dictionnaire des Droits de l'Homme*, ed. J. Andriantsimbazovina et al. (Sous la direction de), 388–390. Paris: PUF.

Commission on Global Governance. 1995. *Our global neighborhood—report of the commission on global governance*. New York: Oxford University Press.

Coomans, F., F. Grünfeld, and M. Kamminga. 2010. Methods of human rights research: A primer. *Human Rights Quaterly* 32:179–186.

Corradetti, C. ed. 2012. *Philosophical dimensions of human rights—some contemporary views*. Dordrecht: Springer Science+Business Media B. V.

Edwards, G. 2010. Attributes of successful human rights non-governmental organizations (NGOs)—Sixty years after the 1948 universal declaration of human rights. In *An Introduction to International Human Rights Law*, ed. A. Chowdhury, and Md. Bhuiyan, 145–218. Leiden: Brill. http://therights.files.wordpress.com/2012/07/an_introduction_to_international.pdf. Accessed Sept 2013.

Fagan, A. 2005. Human rights. In *Internet Encyclopedia of Philosophy*. www.iep.utm.edu/hum-rts. Accessed July 2013.

Ferri, L. (Textes choisis et présentés par). 2005. *De Sénèque à Lévi-Strauss—ils racontent la mondialisation*. Paris: Éditions Saint-Simon.

Fox, J. 2001. *Chomsky and globalisation*. Cambridge: Icon Books (2002).

Freeman, M. 2004. The problem of secularism in human rights theory. *Human Rights Quartely* 26:375–400.

Gallie, W. 1956. 'Essentially contested concepts'. *Proceedings of the Aristotelian society* 56:167–198. http://commonsenseatheism.com/wp-content/uploads/2011/05/Gallie-Essentially-Contested-Concepts.pdf. Accessed July 2013.

Glendon, M. 2001. *A world made new—Eleanor roosevelt and the universal declaration of human rights*. New York: Random House, Trade Paperbacks

Griffin, J. 2008. *On human rights*. New York: Oxford University Press.

Habermas, J. 2012. Chapter 4—The concept of human dignity and the realistic utopia of human rights. In *Philosophical dimensions of human rights—Some contemporary views*, ed. C. Corradetti, , 63–79. Dordrecht: Springer Science+Business Media B. V.

Henkin, L. 1978. *The rights of man today*. London: Stevens and Sons.
Henkin, L. 1990. *Recueil des Cours/Collected Courses of the Hague Academy of International Law, 1989, IV, Tome 216 de la collection. International Law: Politics, Values and Functions—General Course on Public International Law*. Dordrecht: Martinus Nijhoff Publishers.
Kim, Y. 1999. *A common framework for the ethics of the 21th century*. Paris: UNESCO, Division of Philosophy and Ethics. http://unesdoc.unesco.org/images/0011/001176/117622eo.pdf. Accessed July 2013.
Kiss, A.-Ch. 2006. International human rights treaties: A special category of international treaty? In *The status of international treaties on human rights*, ed. AAVV, 11–29. Strasbourg: Council of Europe Publishing, Venice Commission.
Matsuura, K. 2004. Préface. In Jérôme Bindé (Sous la direction de), *Où vont les valeurs—Entretiens du XXIe siècle II*, 9–11. Paris : UNESCO/Albin Michel.
Mendel, G. 2002. *Une histoire de l'autorité—Permanences et variations*. Paris: La Découverte/Poche (2003).
Nowak, M. 2003. *Introduction to international human rights regime*. Leiden: Martinus Nijhoff Publishers.
Plato (ed. by J. Cooper, & D. Hutchinson). 1997. *Plato—Complete works*. Indianapolis: Hackeht Publishing Company.
Pogge, W. 2001. How should human rights be conceived? In *The philosophy of human rights*, ed. P. Hayden, 187–210. St. Paul: Paragon House.
Puledda, S. 1997. *On Being Human—Interpretations of Humanism from the Renaissance to the Present* (Andrew Hurley, Transl., with a Forward by Mikhail Gorbachev). Cardiff: Latitude Press, New Humanism Series. www.leonalado.org/en/node/4018. Accessed Sept 2013.
Renaut, A. 2004. *Qu'est-ce qu'une politique juste?—Essai sur la question du meilleur régime*. Paris: Grasset, Livre de Poche-4386
Rosas, A. 2009. The European union and fundamental rights/human rights. In *International protection of human rights: A textbook*, eds. C. Krause and M. Scheinin, 443–474. Turku/Åbo: Åbo Akademi University, Institute for Human Rights.
Spring, J. 2000. *The universal right to education—justification, definition, and guidelines*. Mahwah: Lawrence Erlbaum Associates, Publishers
Stiglitz, J. 2006. *Making globalization work*. New Cork: W. W. Norton & Company.
UNESCO. 1987. *In search of a wisdom for the world—The role of ethical values in Education—A collective investigation of the Club of Rome (February-October 1986)—report by Bertrand Schneider*. Paris: UNESCO, Bureau of Studies and Programming. http://unesdoc.unesco.org/images/0007/000767/076756eb.pdf. Accessed July 2013.
Védrine, H. 2007. *Rapport pour le Président de la République sur la France et la Mondialisation*. http://medias.lemonde.fr/mmpub/edt/doc/20070905/951341_rapport_d-hubert_vedrine.pdf. Accessed Sept 2013.

Part I
Ethics And Human Rights

Chapter 2
Overview of Ethical Thought

Abstract This overview of ethical thought has a merely introductory character. It does not enter into discussions of philosophical views.

Axiology or Theory of Value is the discipline addressing values in general; it comprises the study of what makes things desirable. Metaethics, Normative Ethics and Applied Ethics constitute the current main divisions in the field of ethical studies. In the history of Western Philosophy there are three main Normative Ethics theories: Virtue Ethics, Consequentialist Ethics, and Deontological Ethics.

Rationality is traditionally equated with experimental or mathematical scientificity, and Epistemology is currently often defined as the study of knowledge as justified true belief. Ethical or Moral Epistemology is concerned with moral beliefs. Reason being theoretical and practical, unique and multiple, valid belief is a broader epistemological category and seemingly more accurate than true belief, as it encompasses all kinds of beliefs and agreed reasons for justifying them.

2.1 Ethics

Axiology or Theory of Value is the discipline that studies values, in general, what makes things desirable[1]. According to Charles W. Morris (1901–1979): "Since the life process depends on the selection or rejection of certain objects or situations, preferential behavior (positive or negative) is a basic phenomenon of life. I have proposed that axiology (as the study of 'value') be considered as the study of preferential behavior" (1964, p. 17). He called a "value situation" any situation in which preferential behavior occurs.

> A 'value situation' [...] is inherently relational, involving an action of (positive or negative) preferential behavior by some agent to something or other. [...]

[1] The term 'Axiology' stems from Greek αξια (worth) and *logos* (science/discourse). The term was first used in a book title by Eduard von Hartmann in *Grundriss der Axiologie* (Outline of Axiology, 1909). It "originally meant the worth of something, chiefly in the economic sense of exchange value, as in the work of the 18th-century political economist Adam Smith. A broad extension of the meaning of value to wider areas of philosophical interest occurred during the nineteenth century under the influence of a variety of thinkers and schools" (Encyclopedia Britannica 2012).

A. Reis Monteiro, *Ethics of Human Rights*, DOI 10.1007/978-3-319-03566-6_2,

> So conceived, values are 'objectively relative'; that is, they are properties of objects (in a wide sense of this term) relative to preferential behavior. [...]
> Such a view avoids the ancient dispute among value theorists as to whether values are 'subjective' or 'objective'—for they are envisaged as properties of objects (or properties of properties of objects) relative to a 'subject' (conceived of as responding by preferential behavior). Hence, they involve both subjects (agents) and objects. The relations of objects to agents (or 'subjects') are no less 'objective' than the relations of objects to other objects. (p. 18)

Values are manifold[2]. Some, such as wealth and power, are instrumental for reaching other ones. Other values have instrumental and intrinsic senses (as means and ends), such as health and knowledge. Moral values are goals for human life, such as compassion, happiness and justice. They are concerned with good and evil, right and wrong, regulating the behaviors and relations between human beings and giving sense to their individual and collective lives. In every society, there are moral values commanding obligations and interdictions, often supported by myths. Individuals have to make moral choices and take decisions in their everyday lives. Moral sensitivity means, in particular, the conscience of how our actions may affect other people, and being concerned with their suffering.

Morality is a universal phenomenon, but moral values are historically, culturally, socially and individually variable, and may vary radically. The world never was as Voltaire saw it when he quietly said: "There is a sole morals as there is a sole geometry" (cit. in Bindé 2004, p. 14). There are obsolete, lasting and emerging values. For example, thinkers as preeminent as Plato, Aristotle (384–322 BC) and St. Augustine (354–430) deemed slavery natural and necessary. Religious intolerance was a theological imperative giving rise to the establishment of the Catholic Inquisition, in the Middle Ages. In nineteenth century, several Popes severely condemned the 'evils' of 'modernism', liberalism and socialism. The most famous document of the Catholic resistance to moral, intellectual and political advancements was the *Syllabus*[3] attached to the Encyclical *Quanta cura* of Pope Pius IX (1864)[4], which anathematized the modern 'errors' in 80 statements. Before, Pope Gregory XVI had condemned, in Encyclical *Mirari vos* (1832)[5], "the unbridled lust for freedom", the "liberty of conscience", the "immoderate freedom of opinion, license of free speech, and desire for novelty", which were "a pestilence more deadly to the state than any other". The "freedom to publish" was said "harmful and never sufficiently denounced".

[2] A research into the meaning of the term 'value', conducted in 1971, identified 171 definitions. They had in common only the fact of considering values as factors of the judgments and behaviors concerning the Good, the Truth and the Beautiful (see Elchardus 1998, p. 103).

[3] www.ewtn.com/library/PAPALDOC/P9SYLL.HTM

[4] www.papalencyclicals.net/Pius09/p9quanta.htm
Encyclical or Encyclical Charter (a term first used perhaps by Pope Benedict XIV in the eighteenth century) is a doctrinal document issued by a Pope.

[5] www.papalencyclicals.net/Greg16/g16mirar.htm

Morals and Ethics are terms etymologically synonymous, with Latin (*mos*) and Greek (*ethos*, *êthos*) etymologies, respectively[6]. Both refer to 'right' or 'wrong' conduct, to custom or way of being. Ethics designated the part of Philosophy concerned with human behavior. Aristotle "may be deemed to be creator of the expression and of the concept of moral theory as a distinct discipline" (Ricoeur 2004, p. 136). The Stoic philosophers made it the core of wisdom. George W. F. Hegel (1770–1831) distinguished between Ethics (*Sittlichkeit*) and Morals (*Moralität*), applying the former to the concrete rules and behaviors, and the latter to the reflection on the moral values. These days, many authors view the relation between Ethics and Morals differently. For example, in the opinion of Paul Ricoeur (1913–2005), "ethics is more fundamental than morals" (1994, p. 16). We should "distinguish between ethics and morals, to reserve the term ethics for every questioning preceding the introduction of the moral law idea, and to call moral all that, in the field of good and evil, refers to laws, norms, imperatives" (1990, p. 62). Jacqueline Russ (1994) also considered justified and useful this distinction between Ethics and Morals: "The first one is more theoretical than the second one, intended to be more concerned with a reflection on the foundations of the latter". Ethics denotes, "not a morals, namely a set of rules particular to a culture, but rather a 'meta-morals', a doctrine situated beyond morals [...], deconstructing and founding, stating principles or ultimate foundations" (p. 5, 6).

Therefore, the following distinction may be made:

- Morals denotes the *what* of values (which they are), that is, a set of values and norms concerning the right and wrong individual behaviors within a given human community. A moral judgment is one of approving or condemning decisions and behaviors in the light of common values.
- Ethics or Moral Philosophy is the theory of morality, that is, the reflection on the *why* of moral values, on the principles of good and evil, pointing to a worldwide horizon. It is a term with a rather intellectual and universal meaning, without the frequent religious and conservative connotation of the term Morals. One says, for instance, 'Ethics of Human Righs', and not 'Morals of Human Rights'.

While the moral phenomenon is as old as humankind itself, the origins of a systematic ethical thought go back to relatively recent times. The *Vedas* (meaning religious wisdom), which are the foundational texts of Hinduism, are considered the oldest known Moral Philosophy. In the Western world, it is born in Classical Greece, in the fifth–forth centuries BC, with Socrates (469–399 BC), Plato and Aristotle, whose thought is rooted in the wisdom of earlier thinkers known as the 'Seven Sages', one of whom was Pythagoras (sixth century BC). In the opinion of Ricoeur (2004), Aristotle "may be deemed to be creator of the expression and of the concept of moral theory as a distinct discipline" (p. 136).

At present, the ethical field of studies is usually divided into three main areas: Metaethics, Normative Ethics, and Applied Ethics. The latter has dramatically grown in importance during the second half of the twentieth century. It is concerned with specific and controversial moral issues such as stem cell research, in vitro

[6] It was Cicero (106–43 BC) who translated the Greek term *ethos* with the Latin term *moralis*.

fertilization, human cloning, abortion, euthanasia, death penalty, homosexuality, environmental ethics, animals' rights, etc. Although some of these issues will be later mentioned as Case Law issues, they are too varied and vast to be introduced here. We are considering the principal stakes of Metaethics and Normative Ethics.

2.2 Metaethics

Metaethics is a term coined in the first half of the twentieth century. Its Greek etymology means 'after' or 'beyond' (*meta*) ethics. It addresses the most general moral questions, such as: Is there a specific human moral sense? Where do moral values come from? Have they an objective, absolute, universal and eternal existence, or result from social conventions, being particular, relative, and changeable? Do moral judgments and behaviors have a rational basis or are they merely expressions of emotions? Why should I be moral, if I am not compelled to act on given moral standards?

The major ethical questions are as old as philosophical inquiry and revive at times of cultural destabilization and ideological unrest. It is out of the scope of this study to give an account of the present variety of answers to them. Only the first one is next briefly approached (The epistemological question is addressed in sect. 2.4).

Aristotle (2000) wrote that "it is a characteristic of man that he alone has any sense of good and evil, of just and unjust". Being so, "when perfected, [he] is the best of animals, but, when separated from law and justice, he is the worst of all; since armed injustice is the more dangerous, and he is equipped at birth with the arms of intelligence and with moral qualities which he may use for the worst ends" (1253a, p. 12, pp. 15–16). That is why José-Luis Aranguren (1909–1996) concluded that the human being "may be defined as a moral animal, rather than as rational animal" (1990, p. 99). This is also why morality may be considered the highest cultural expression of the human species, and "the most important subject on earth" (Pojman 2000, p. 40). The *soul* of cultures are their moral values, crystallized in traditions and religious and other texts. They became "part of the mechanism of change and evolution", and "progress has been increasingly concerned with values—intellectual, aesthetic, emotional and moral" (Huxley 1946, p. 11, 14). Consequently, wrote René Descartes (1596–1650) in the Letter-Preface of his *Principes de la Philosophie* (Principles of Philosophy 1644), Ethics is "the highest and most perfect science", as it presupposes the knowledge of all others[7]. Also "Kant put morality much higher than [every other] science" (Fischl 1968, p. 315, 316).

[7] *Ainsi toute la philosophie est comme un arbre, dont les racines sont la métaphysique, le tronc est la physique, et les branches qui sortent de ce tronc sont toutes les autres sciences, qui se réduisent à trois principales, à savoir la médecine, la mécanique et la morale; j'entends la plus haute et la plus parfaite morale, qui présupposant une entière connaissance des autres sciences, est le dernier degré de la sagesse.* (www.ac-nice.fr/philo/textes/Descartes-LettrePreface.htm)

Morality has biological roots. In 1975, the entomologist Edward O. Wilson published *Sociobiology—The New Synthesis*. The term was not new, but the thing's definition was: "the systematic study of the biological basis of all social behavior". Sociobiology envisaged the unification of the biological study of social behaviors in the whole animal world, including human beings. The book gave rise to a heated controversy[8]. In 2001, John Alcock published *The Triumph of Sociobiology*. It became amply integrated into the larger field of the behavioral sciences. Its researches have diluted frontiers between the animal and the human worlds.

The term 'moral sense' was first used by the 3rd Earl of Shaftesbury (1671–1713). Following David Hume (1711–1776) and Charles Darwin (1809–1882), there is a moral sense common to human beings and other animals. Darwin believed that all in the human species had arisen from its biological evolution, including social, rational, moral and esthetical aptitudes. He wrote in Chapter III of *The descent of man, and selection in relation to sex* (1871)[9]: "The moral sense perhaps affords the best and highest distinction between man and the lower animals". Nevertheless: "Besides love and sympathy, animals exhibit other qualities which in us would be called moral; and I agree with Agassiz that dogs possess something very like a conscience". In Frans de Waal's opinion, the base of moral sense is compassion or empathy, that is, the capacity to put oneself in another's place and suffer by a kind of emotional contagion. It is common to human beings and other higher animal species, such as apes, dolphins and dogs. Even altruistic behaviors and the moral sentiment of equity may be observed in animals. "Philosophers have surrounded the sense of equity with all kinds of complex rational justifications, but it probably rests on simple sentiments. At the risk of shocking some people, I would say that these sentiments act both in some animals and in the human being" (in Journet 2012, p. 30).

As Monique Canto-Sperber and Ruwen Ogien (2004) write: "The evolutionist account is very broad and there is no reason for not being applied to the morality's institution, more precisely to the emergence, persistence and importance, in human life, of behaviors called 'moral' (concern with justice, altruism, etc.) and of moral sentiments (shame, culpability, indignation, etc.)" (p. 62, 63). In fact, neurobiological research—by means of images of the human brain's activity and comparative studies of damaged persons' brains and other experiments—proves the influence of emotions on moral judgments and decisions, which activate archaic parts of the human brain, allowing the conclusion that they originate in the instinctive social behavior of mammals. They may be a heritage of that evolution stage. There is so,

[8] "The violence of reactions against Wilson's proposals, going as far as physical aggression, [...] is level to the *enjeux* some people believe to detect in the development of the human Sociobiology: at best an attempt to establish a diktat of the biological sciences over the human sciences, at worst a resurgence of the social darwinism's and eugenics' nauseous ideas. [...] The debate quickly moves to the political stage. Lewontin and Gould see in the Sociobiology an intellectual manipulation aiming at bridling the social progress by protecting the interests of the higher social classes and the domination exerted by the white race" (Cézilly 2007, p. 40).

[9] www.gutenberg.org/files/34967/34967.txt

perhaps, an animal proto-moral. Anyway, between the fact of the biological roots of human morality and pretentions to reduce the latter to the former, there is a gulf that Behavioral Ethology is not prepared to nullify (so far, at least). Following Nicolas Baumard:

> There are many explanations for the emergence of morals.. [...]
> The two main evolutionist theories, one continuist and other altruist, are not able to account for the morals' logic. They do not succeed in explaining why the moral sense rests on a specific logic of equity.
> [...]
> My approach starts from observing that, in the human beings' life, cooperation holds a central place. [...] This was the context where morals evolved, because it provided a comparative advantage to those able to it. [...]
> According to this theory that I call mutualistic, morals' function is to regulate the individual interactions so that they are equitable [...]. As one sees, this theory meets the intuition of the social contract philosophies [...]. It may be said that morals exists because it is advantageous, in the final analysis. [...]
> Human beings are by nature equipped not only with social sentiments but with a specific moral sense too. (in Journet 2012, p. 15, 17, 18, 19)

In Jean-Michel Besnier's (2004) opinion: "Only those beings able to distance themselves from situations they are confronted to are moral. [...] If, in animals, there is something like a moral sense, it is not different from the vision, the tact or the smell senses, which all living beings possess" (ib. p. 82). Pascal Picq (2004) concluded: "There is, therefore, no natural morals, but rather natural foundations of morals, which are to be found in animals closer to us. We have a base to affirm that they have no morals, especially because they cannot speak about morality. This does not prevent them from having notions of right and wrong regarding others" (ib. p. 30). Patrick Tort (2004) explained:

> Tendentially, the extension of sympathy to the whole mankind and, in the final analysis, the humanity's sense towards animals, replace the old warlike conducts or dominating brutality. That is what I called, in 1983, *evolution reversed effect*, introducing into evolution, not a breach but rather a *breach effect*, deriving from applying its own law to natural selection (disappearance of the old forms). Natural selection selects then the *civilization*, which *opposes* to natural selection. (ib. p. 43)

For Yvon Quiniou (2004), Möbius strip (or ring)[10] is the metaphor of the "evolution reverse effect", explaining the progressive emergence of the human moral behavior through natural selection of social instincts (ib. p. 41). According to Waal (2004):

> We may distinguish two levels in human morals. That of moral emotions or sentiments: sympathy, empathy, reciprocity, fears of punishment. We share this level with some other animals. That of moral judgment: it is the level of good and evil, of language, of reasoning, of logic, of social consensus. Here, it appears a greater discontinuity; this is, undoubtedly, a

[10] Möbius strip is a surface with two meeting faces, forming a sole one. It is got by jointing the two ends of a strip, after twisting one of them. This effect was discovered by two mathematicians simultaneously and independently from one another, in nineteenth century—August Ferdinand Möbius (1790–1868) and Johann Benedikt Listing (1808–1882)—but lasted associated to the name of the former.

> specifically human level of morality. Let us say, to conclude, that human morals is founded in social emotions and that we find these social emotions in other animals. (ib. p. 11)

Consequently: "I do not claim that chimpanzees are full moral beings, because it seems that they are not able to reason about good and evil" (p. 31).

> Even if animals other than ourselves act in ways tantamount to moral behavior, their behavior does not necessarily rest on deliberations of the kind we engage in. It is hard to believe that animals weigh their own interests against the rights of others, that they develop a vision of the greater good of society, or that they feel lifelong guilt about something they should not have done. Members of some species may reach tacit consensus about what kind of behavior to tolerate or inhibit in their midst, but without language the principles behind such decisions cannot be conceptualized, let alone debated. (as cit. in Rolston III 2008, p. 148)

Holmes Rolston III (2008), reviewing a number of research data on what makes human beings unique, concluded that "there is nowhere in animal behavior the capacity to be reflectively ethical. After a careful survey of behavior, Helmut Kummer concludes, 'It seems at present that morality has no specific functional equivalents among our animal relatives'" (p. 140, 148).

Following Karl-Otto Apel (1988), the moral conscience originated from the need of *homo faber*—an animal without instinctive mechanisms of self-control—to take control of his transformation and destruction powers. That is why the central problem of the human morality lies "in the question of the relation of *homo sapiens* to *homo faber*, in other words, in the question of knowing whether man can compensate, by means of his ethical reason, its constituent lack of instinct" (p. 25). In Éric Weil's (1989) opinion:

> Morals is considered as the result of two primitive and irreducible tendencies: the fear of need and the desire of taking maximum profit of the work's products, by eliminating violence among men belonging to the same community; morals is the way of life of beings needing each other for their satisfactions, but also remaining potentially violent. (p. 745)

In this connection, Richard Taylor, after remarking that to say that human beings are rational or cognitive is leaving "entirely out of account the most important fact about men, that they are desiderative or conative beings as well", that "men have needs, desires, and goals", proposes an account of the origin of the distinction between good and evil. If we imagine the world as inhabited by just one sentient being, "certain things in the world do acquire the aspect of good and evil. Those things are good that this one being finds satisfying to his needs and desires, and those bad to which he reacts in the opposite way". If another similar being comes on stage, with which the former begins to interact, a conflict may arouse between the two. In order so they can peacefully cohabit, there is a need of "*rules*, using the notion of rules in an extremely broad sense that encompasses any regular and predictable behavior". Notions of right and wrong then appear. "Right is simply the adherence to rule, and wrong is violation of it" (in Pojman 2000, p. 142…152).

The neuroscientist António Damásio (2010) pointed out that the central value for every organism is survival. Also for human beings, the "biological value is the root" of all meanings of 'value' we find in a standard dictionary (p. 48). The management of life, its regulation or *homeostasis*, is "the primary function of human brains", even though it is not "their most distinctive feature" (p. 63). There is a basic biological homeostasis, entirely automated, which began in unicellular living creatures, and an added "sociocultural homeostasis" (p. 27), with a complexity peculiar to organisms possessing "brain, mind, and consciousness" (p. 44), making them able to deliberate. The sociocultural homeostasis consists of cultural devices for life regulation such as the normative, political, economic systems, science, technology, art, etc., by means of which "consciousness optimized life regulation. The self in each conscious mind is the first representative of individual life-regulation mechanisms, the guardian and curator of biological value" (p. 183).

Damásio observes "the sameness that hallmarks the repertoire of human behavior", due to the "genomic unconscious" formed of "the colossal number of instructions that are contained in our genome and that guide the construction of the organism with the distinctive features of our phenotype, in both body proper and brain, and that further assist with the operation of the organism" (p. 278, 279). Emotions are complex programs of action, "unlearned, automated, and predictably stable", originated "in natural selection and in the resulting genomic instructions", which participate in life regulation. There are "so-called universal emotions (fear, anger, sadness, happiness, disgust, and surprise [...]. Such emotions are present even in cultures that lack distinctive names for the emotions. We owe to Charles Darwin the early recognition of this universality, not only in humans but in animals" (p. 123). Social emotions are another major group of emotions.

> Examples of the main social emotions easily justify the label: *compassion, embarrassment, shame, guilt, contempt, jealousy, envy, pride, admiration*. [...] The physiological operation of the social emotions is in no way different from that of other emotions. [...] But there are some noteworthy differences. Most social emotions are of recent evolutionary vintage, and some may be exclusively human. This seems to be the case with admiration and with the variety of compassion that focuses on the mental and social pain of others rather than on physical pain. Many species, primates and the great apes in particular, exhibit forerunners of some social emotions. Compassion for physical predicaments, embarrassment, envy, and pride are good examples. Capuchin monkeys certainly appear to react to perceived injustices. Social emotions incorporate a number of moral principles and form a natural grounding for ethical systems. (p. 125, 126)

The need and dilemmas of human morality have frequently been literary themes. For example, *Brave New World* (1931), by Aldous Huxley (1894–1963), "highlights the paradox of freedom and welfare better than any political philosophy book" (Pojman 2000, p. xiii). *Lord of the Flies* (1954), by William Golding (1911–1993), Nobel Literature Prize in 1983, "is like a picture worth a thousand arguments about why we need morality". It is a counterpoint of *The Choral Island*, a classical work of literature for children, published by Michael Ballantyne (1825–1894) in 1858, in which human nature is described as essentially good. In *Sophie's Choice* (1978), William Styron (1925–2006) evokes the drama of having to choose between two evils, during the Holocaust.

2.3 Normative Ethics

Normative Ethics is concerned with moral principles/standards/norms on right and wrong, which are considered necessary to guide human conduct. A central question is whether there is a fundamental universal moral principle.

Following the above mentioned document of the International Theological Commission (2008)[11], every human being "discovers that he is fundamentally a moral being, capable of perceiving and of expressing the call that, as we saw, is found within all cultures: 'to do good and avoid evil'. [...] This first precept is known naturally, immediately, with the practical reason, just as the principle of non-contradiction" (para. 39). There is a more precise and probably more universal principle of morality, however: it is the Golden Rule that is a principle of reciprocity and compassion, with both positive and negative formulations, namely: 'Do unto others as you would have them do unto you', and 'Do not do unto others what you would not have them do unto you'. The second one is sometimes named Silver Rule. Another formulation commands: 'Treat others in the way that they wish to be treated'. In R. M. MacIver's view:

> This is the only rule that stands by itself in the light of its own reason, the only rule that can stand by itself in the naked, warring universe, in the face of the contending values of men and groups.
> What makes it so? [...] It prescribes a mode of behaving, not a goal of action. On the level of goals, of *final* values, there is irreconcilable conflict. (in Pojman 2000, p. 333)

Although 'Golden Rule' is a term that appeared relatively recently—it goes back to the seventeenth century, when it was, for the first time, the subject of an entire book (*The Golden Rule* 1688) by John Goodman (1625–1690)—its command is millenary, having "appeared in the fifth century BC in all cultural and religious areas of the world" (Roy 2012, p. 12)[12]. There are Confucian, Buddhist, Hinduist, Jewish, Christian and Islamic versions of it[13]. For example, it is to be found in biblical texts (Tobit 4:15; Leviticus 19:18; Matthew 7:12; Luke 6:31, and 10:27). Tobit 4:15 reads: "Do not do to anyone what you do not want done to you".

In China, Confucius (around 551–479 BC)[14] and Mencius (372–289 BC) were the most prominent representatives of a tradition of thought going back to more than 2500 years. Confucianism is a reinterpretation of very old traditions. The teachings of Confucius consisted mainly in sayings and aphorisms, usually in reply to ques-

[11] www.pathsoflove.com/universal-ethics-natural-law.html

[12] The author informs that in the nineteenth century some people wanted to erect a monument to the Golden Rule at Central Park, New York (p. 15).

[13] www.newworldencyclopedia.org/entry/Golden_Rule

[14] Confucius or Kong Qiu was a teacher known as Kongzi, Master Kong, and to later followers as Kong Fuzi, "our Master Kong". He was contemporary of other great moral philosopher of ancient China, Laozi, best known for his thought about the Dao ('Way' or the Supreme Principle), based on the traditional Chinese virtues of simplicity and sincerity.

tions of disciples aiming at becoming better persons, superior men. They were recorded by his students in *The Analects*"[15]. For example (15.24, and also 5.12, 12.2):

> Zigong asked, "Is there a single saying that one may put into practice all one's life?"
> The Master said, "That would be 'reciprocity': That which you do not desire, do not do to others".

According to Joseph Chan (2005):

> The Confucian ethical tradition is a system of human relationships based on virtue of *ren*. The moral ideal for each individual is the attainment of *ren*—the highest and most perfect virtue. *Ren* is a human quality, an expression of humanity, which can be manifested in a wide range of dispositions from personal reflection and critical examination of one's life to respect, concern and care for others. In dealing with oneself, *ren* requires us to 'overcome the self through observing the rites' (*The Analects*, Book XII: 1). In dealing with others, *ren* asks us to practise the art of *shu*—'do not impose on others what we ourselves do not desire' (*The Analects*, Book XII: 2), an ethics of sympathy and reciprocity similar to the Golden Rule in other traditional religions and Kantian tradition. (p. 56)

Jean-Jacques Rousseau (1712–1778) wrote (1751) in Preface to *Discours sur l'origine et fondements de l'inégalité parmi les hommes* (Discourse on the Origin and Basis of Inequality Among Men):

> … contemplating the first and most simple operations of the human soul, I think I can perceive in it two principles prior to reason, one of them deeply interesting us in our own welfare and preservation, and the other exciting a natural repugnance at seeing any other sensible being, and particularly any of our own species, suffer pain or death. (p. 46, 47)

The two principles are love of self and compassion. Love of self is not to be confused with *amour-propre*.

> Love of self is a natural feeling which leads every animal to look to its own preservation, and which, guided in man by reason and modified by compassion, creates humanity and virtue. *Amour-propre* is a purely relative and factitious feeling, which arises in the state of society, leads each individual to make more of himself than of any other, causes all the mutual damage men inflict one on another, and is the real source of the 'sense of honor'.

Compassion "is a disposition suitable to creatures so weak and subject to so many evils as we certainly are. […] Such is the pure emotion of nature, prior to all kinds of reflection! Such is the force of natural compassion, which the greatest depravity of morale has as yet hardly been able to destroy!" (p. 73, 74).

Love of self and compassion or piety are two fundamental concepts of Rousseau's thought (see Trousson and Eigeldinger 1996, p. 33, 725), but compassion is "the first relative sentiment which touches the human heart according to the order of nature", as we read in *Émile* Book IV (1762, p. 220). According to Lévi-Strauss (1963), Rousseau was the "father of Anthropology" notably for having considered compassion (*pitié*) the essential faculty of the human being that "is at the same time natural and cultural, affective and rational, animal and human".

---

[15] www.indiana.edu/~p374/Analects_of_Confucius_(Eno-2012).pdf

Following Gertrud Himmelfarb (2002), it was the English philosophers, especially Adam Smith (1723–1790), who made compassion/sympathy "the central theme of their moral philosophy" (p. 69)[16].

Bertrand Russell (1872–1970) held that sympathy was the primordial source of human morality: "Almost every individual that has ever existed, so far as history is aware, has had a profound horror of certain kind of acts. [...] Sympathy is the universalizing force in ethics; I mean sympathy as an emotion, not as a theoretical principle" (1938, p. 198, 203).

The Golden Rule was invoked in Article 6 of the *Déclaration des droits de l'homme et du citoyen* (Declaration of the Rights of Man and of the Citizen) preceding the 1793 French Constitution (never applied)[17]: "Liberty is the power that belongs to man to do whatever is not injurious to the rights of others; it has nature for its principle, justice for its rule, law for its defense; its moral limit is in this maxim: Do not do to another that which you do not wish should be done to you".

The Golden Rule's universality and topicality are highlighted in two important documents referred to in Introduction: Declaration Toward a Global Ethic[18], and The Search for Universal Ethics: A New Look at Natural Law[19].

In Waal's opinion (2004), the Golden Rule includes "the two pillars of human morality that are reciprocity and empathy" (p. 9).

Compassion/sympathy/empathy or pity—are terms translating the Aristotelian word *eleos*, but some authors distinguish them according to their selfless meaning[20]. The fact that compassion is a spontaneous feeling does not exclude a reflex or calculation of interested reciprocity: I'm affected by the suffering of others inasmuch as I imagine being in their situation, suffering what they are suffering.

Another ethical principle is the Golden Mean that commands a 'middle way' between two extremes (deficiency and excess). It is an ancient precept too, existing in

---

[16] He considered *The Theory of Moral Sentiments* (1759) more important than *The Wealth of Nations* (1776).

[17] www.columbia.edu/~iw6/docs/dec1793.html

[18] "There is a principle which is found and has persisted in many religious and ethical traditions of humankind for thousands of years: What you do not wish done to yourself, do not do to others. Or in positive terms: What you wish done to yourself, do to others! This should be the irrevocable, unconditional norm for all areas of life, for families and communities, for races, nations, and religions". (www.parliamentofreligions.org/_includes/FCKcontent/File/TowardsAGlobalEthic.pdf)

[19] "In the different cultures, people have progressively elaborated and developed traditions of wisdom in which they express and transmit their vision of the world, as also their reflected perception of the place that the human being occupies in society and in the world. [...] The form and the extension of these traditions can vary considerably. Still they are witnesses to the existence of a patrimony of moral values common to all people, beyond the manner in which such values are justified within a particular vision of the world. For example, the 'golden rule' ('Do not do to anyone what you do not want done to you' [Tobit 4:15]) is found, in one form or another, in the majority of the wisdom traditions" (para. 12). (www.pathsoflove.com/universal-ethics-natural-law.html)

[20] Lynn Hunt (2008) explains: "I have used the term 'empathy' because though it entered English only in the twentieth century, it better captures the active will to identify with others. Sympathy now often signifies pity, which can imply condescension, a feeling incompatible with a true feeling of equality" (p. 65).

various traditions. *Doctrine of the Mean* is the name of a text attributed to the only grandson of Confucius. Buddha proposed a "middle path" between self-indulgence and self-renunciation. The same idea was expressed in the inscription on the front of the temple at Delphos, in Ancient Greece: 'Nothing in Excess'. It is also at the heart of the Aristotelian Virtue Ethics.

Virtue Ethics is one of the three main Normative Ethics theories in history of Western Philosophy. The other two are Consequentialist Ethics and Deontological Ethics.

Virtue Ethics is the oldest type, varieties of which exist in diverse cultures. Its focus is what sort of people we should strive to be, emphasizing personal perfection. It highlights the importance of the moral character to be developed mainly by moral education, through the cultivation of virtues such as Plato's four cardinal or basic virtues (prudence, courage, temperance, and justice) and the Christian three theological virtues (faith, hope, and charity). A good life is a virtuous life. A virtuous person is a good and admirable person. Examples of highly virtuous persons were people like Confucius, Socrates, Christ, Mahatma Gandhi, Martin Luther King Jr. or Nelson Mandela. In the Western world, the most influential theory of Virtue Ethics was Aristotle's.

For Aristotle (2000), virtue (*aretê*) is a character trait, so that "for men of preeminent virtue there is no law—they are themselves a law" (III.13, 1284a). It is not then an isolated attitude, but rather a *disposition* or *tendency* to reason or act in a certain way. Virtues are good habits that regulate human emotions. Considering that every human activity aims at a kind of good, Aristotle (1925) searched to know in what the good of human beings consists (Book I.4, 1095a6). The highest good should be toward which one aims in itself, not as a means to reach other ones. This "supreme good" is *eudaimonia* (translated as 'happiness' or 'wellbeing' or 'human flourishing'). "Happiness, then, is found to be something perfect and self-sufficient, being the end to which our actions are directed" (1097b2-21). It consists in "an activity of soul in accordance with virtue, or if there are more kinds of virtue than one, in accordance with the best and most perfect kind" (1097b22, 1098a8-27). Which is it? "If happiness is an activity in accordance with virtue, it is reasonable to assume that it is in accordance with the highest virtue, and this will be the virtue of the best part of us. [...] We have already said that it is a contemplative activity [...which is] the only activity that is appreciated for its own sake" (1177a5-25, 1177a25-b13). In other words, what is distinctive about human beings is the capacity to reason. Their ultimate goal should be, therefore, to develop their reasoning powers. Accordingly, there is a conceptual link between, *virtue*, *eudaimonia* and *phronêsis* (practical knowledge), which are the main Aristotelian ethical concepts.

As "in order to be a good man one must first have been brought up in the right way and trained in the right habits" (1179b29-1180a15), Aristotle (1953) wrote, education plays a paramount role. Nevertheless: "In the great majority of states matters of this kind have been completely neglected, and every man lives his life as he likes, 'laying down the law for wife and children', like Cyclopes" (1180a16-b1). Therefore, the ethical investigation should enter the political field, "so that our philosophy of human conduct may be as complete as possible" (1181b10-23), i.e. concerned with private and public education.

The idea of virtue was incorporated into Christian Morals, and Virtue Ethics remained the dominant Western ethical tradition—a kind of *default Ethics*—until the eighteenth century, when ethical thought began to focus on what one ought to do, rather than on what kind of person one should be. As Griffin (2008) observed: "From the eighteenth century to the present, most philosophers, dazzled by the success of natural scientists, pre-eminently Newton, went in search of highly systematic theory. Moral philosophers sought the reduction of all our varied moral thought to one principle, or to a small number of them" (p. 74). It was the attempt both of the Consequentialist Ethics and of the Deontological Ethics, called deontic or action-based because they focus entirely upon action.

Consequentialist Ethics takes the observable results or consequences or behaviors as the primary criterion by which to assess moral actions[21]. It is also called Teleological Ethics (from the Greek word *telos* that means 'end'). It implies a kind of cost-benefit analysis, for balancing both the good and bad consequences of an action. Its simplest form is Utilitarianism, following which the morality of behaviors depends upon its utility for general wellbeing. "The maxim that the right act is the act that produces the greatest happiness for the greatest number summarises the classic utilitarian moral theory" (Campbell 2006, p. 40). Francis Hutcheson (1694–1746) had already proposed a similar principle of goodness: "That action is best which procures the greatest happiness for the greatest number". However, the very intellectual father of Utilitarianism was Jeremy Bentham (1748–1832). Its second most influential thinker was John Stuart Mill (1806–1873), with his essay *Utilitarianism* (1861). Bentham wrote at the beginning of *An Introduction to the Principles of Morals and Legislation* (1789)[22]:

> I. Nature has placed mankind under the governance of two sovereign masters, *pain* and *pleasure*. [...]
> II. The principle of utility is the foundation of the present work. [...] By the principle of utility is meant that principle which approves or disapproves of every action whatsoever, according to the tendency it appears to have to augment or diminish the happiness of the party whose interest is in question; or, what is the same thing in other words, to promote or to oppose that happiness.

Peter Singer concluded: "Never before had a complete, detailed system of ethics been so consistently constructed from a single fundamental ethical principle" (Encyclopedia Britannica 2012—Ethics).

Deontological Ethics is concerned with precise rules of conduct to be followed, such as "don't kill" or "don't steal", irrespective of their consequences. It found its best-known proponent in Kant (see sect. 5.2). Kantian Ethics is an Ethics of Duty (the Greek term *deon* means 'duty'). In his opinion, actions resulting from desires cannot be free. Human actions possess moral worth to the extent that they

[21] Consequentialism is a term coined probably by Gertrude Elizabeth Margaret Anscombe (1919–2001) in her article "Modern Moral Philosophy" (1958).

[22] www.efm.bris.ac.uk/het/bentham/morals.pdf

are commanded by duty for its own sake. He agreed with Samuel von Pufendorf (1632–1694), following whom there are moral duties to oneself and others. The most absolute one is the "categorical imperative" that commands to act irrespective of one's personal desires and of consequences. Kantian Moral Philosophy remains highly influential to this day. In the Western world, the most common moral thought is, in general, deontological, in line with the Jewish-Christian tradition (the Ten Commandments have a deontological content: Some behaviors are always wrong).

Summing up, "a deontological approach calls for doing certain things on principle or because they are inherently right, whereas a teleological approach advocates that certain kinds of actions are right because of the goodness of their consequences" (Encyclopedia Britannica 2012—Normative Ethics). The debate between Consequentialist and Deontological Ethics gave rise to number of rival views in both camps.

All three types of Normative Ethics have weaknesses and are insufficient. None is a complete and satisfying theory. Virtue Ethics does not propose a universal moral ideal. Consequentialist Ethics does not preclude sacrificing individuals to the interests of groups. Deontological Ethics cares more about universality than about the good of each human being. Human morality is a matter of being and doing. The virtuous person possesses dispositions or tendencies making her able to act rightly in every situation, but guiding moral norms are needed. However, consequentialism and deontologism may clash with broadly shared moral convictions and conscience. No principle can replace individual wisdom and judgment. Even compassion/sympathy/empathy or pity are not as natural and universal as often believed, as daily news from around the world cruelly witness[23]. Neomi Rao (2011) cites Isaiah Berlin according to whom "the belief that some single formula can in principle be found whereby all the diverse ends of men can be harmoniously realized is demonstrably false" (p. 269, note 356). There is no moral algorithm.

Around the middle of the twentieth century, Virtue Ethics reflourished in Western Philosophy[24], focusing on the complex mindset demanded by the practical wisdom of the virtuous person, rather than seeking a one-size-fits-all moral principle. As a consequence, it emphasizes the importance of moral education, understood as character education, as Plato and Aristotle did.

James Fieser (2009) wrote:

> Arriving at a short list of representative normative principles is itself a challenging task. [...] The following principles are the ones most commonly appealed to in applied ethical discussions:
> *Personal benefit*: acknowledge the extent to which an action produces beneficial consequences for the individual in question.
> *Social benefit*: acknowledge the extent to which an action produces beneficial consequences for society.

---

[23] "The capacity for empathy is universal because it is rooted in the biology of the brain". However: "Ambivalence about the power of empathy can be found from the mid-eighteenth century onward, and it was expressed even by those who undertook to explain its operation" (Hunt 2008, p. 39, 210).

[24] Its revival is frequently referred to Anscombe article above referred to.

> *Principle of benevolence*: help those in need.
> *Principle of paternalism*: assist others in pursuing their best interests when they cannot do so themselves.
> *Principle of harm*: do not harm others.
> *Principle of honesty*: do not deceive others.
> *Principle of lawfulness*: do not violate the law.
> *Principle of autonomy*: acknowledge a person's freedom over his/her actions or physical body.
> *Principle of justice*: acknowledge a person's right to due process, fair compensation for harm done, and fair distribution of benefits.
> *Rights*: acknowledge a person's rights to life, information, privacy, free expression, and safety.
> The above principles represent a spectrum of traditional normative principles and are derived from both consequentialist and duty-based approaches. The first two principles, personal benefit and social benefit, are consequentialist since they appeal to the consequences of an action as it affects the individual or society. The remaining principles are duty-based. The principles of benevolence, paternalism, harm, honesty, and lawfulness are based on duties we have toward others. The principles of autonomy, justice, and the various rights are based on moral rights.

Let us now have a look to ethical epistemology.

2.4 Ethical Epistemology

According to the term's Greek etymology, epistemology means the science/study/theory (*logos*) of knowledge (*episteme*). Epistemology is concerned with the origin, nature and limits of human knowledge. As reads the presentation of Plato's (1997) *Theaetetus* by John M. Cooper:

> Plato has much to say in other dialogues about knowledge, but this is his only sustained inquiry into the question: 'What is knowledge?' As such, it is the founding document of what has come to be known as 'epistemology', as one of the branches of philosophy: its influence on Greek epistemology—in Aristotle and the Stoics particularly—is strongly marked. [...]
> The American logician and philosopher C. S. Peirce counted it, along with *Parmenides*, as Plato's greatest work, and more recently it has attracted favorable attention from such major philosophers as Ludwig Wittgenstein and Gilbert Ryle.

There are different uses of the verb 'to know': to know that... to know why... to know how... to know where... to know whether... to know someone... Epistemology has mostly focused on *knowing that*, i.e. propositional knowledge, expressed by declarative sentences describing facts or states of affairs. It encompasses a variety of knowledge, but all require *belief*, a central epistemological concept. It is not sufficient for knowledge, however. If knowledge exists only about objective, factual things, a belief must be true, i.e. describe how things really are. Yet not all true beliefs constitute knowledge. It is still needed that it be justified, i.e. based on reasoning and evidence, not the result of hazard or chance. Justification is the reason for holding a belief. Consequently, to qualify as knowledge, a belief must be both *true and justified*. Anyway, truth and justification are two independent conditions. A belief can be unjustified yet true, and be justified yet false (see Truncellito 2007).

The assumption has prevailed that science is value free, and that subjectivity is an obstacle to objectivity.

> The view in the natural sciences—in physics, chemistry and biology—was, until recently, that true knowledge is attainable and provides an accurate and objective report on the world: knowledge is a mental representation of the way the world really is. [...] According to this point of view, a true statement is one that corresponds to reality; falsity is a result of error, ignorance or deliberate distortion on the part of the scientist. There was an acceptance of David Hume's (1772) assertion that there is a fundamental gulf between statements of fact and judgments of value. (John Scott, as cit. in Letherby et al. 2012, p. 13, 14)[25]

This causes "the worst of all epistemological crimes", namely, "to define quantitative methods (however well or badly used) with objectivity and qualitative methods (however well or badly used) with subjectivity" (Letherby, ib. p. 76). Gayle Letherby proposes a third way called *theorized subjectivity*, following which: "All social research involves individuals—both researchers and respondents—who have subjectivities, who make subjectivities. Theorized subjectivity acknowledges that research is a subjective, power-laden, emotional, embodied experience, but does not see this as a disadvantage, just as how it is" (ib. p. 80). As Letherby, Scott and Malcolm Williams write:

> ... the values and subjectivity of the scientist, far from being extraneous to science, are integral elements in its claims to objectivity and expertise, accountability and value.
> Our descriptions of the world are always partial, selected and filtered by our perceptual apparatus, by the assumptions that we bring to our observations, and by the particular perspective or standpoint from which we view the world. The ways in which we interpret these observations and formulate them into statements that can be communicated with others are, furthermore, dependent on the particular language that we use. Both our perceptions of the world and our descriptions of those perceptions are linguistically mediated. [...] In all of these respects, then, observations are to be regarded as *cultural* constructions that depend also on the physical perceptual apparatus that we, by virtue of our 'natural' human characteristics, bring to our observations. (ib. p. 6, 7)

[25] Alvin Goldman (2007) described "the central components of the traditional conception" of epistemology as follows:

> First, in traditional epistemology the epistemic agents are exclusively individual human beings. Second, mainstream epistemology is heavily invested in the study of several concepts of epistemic evaluation or normativity, including justifiedness, rationality, and knowledge. Traditional epistemology is concerned with how individuals can acquire knowledge or maintain justified or rational credal states. Third, it is assumed that the evaluative/normative standards of rationality and justifiedness are not merely conventional or relativistic in a pejorative sense, but have some sort of universal, objective validity. Fourth, the central notions of epistemic attainment—certainly knowledge and possibly justification—either entail or are linked to truth. [...] Finally, mainstream epistemology typically assumes that truth is an objective, largely mind-independent, affair. Let us call these assumptions the core assumptions of mainstream epistemology.

Knowledge is, therefore, always physically *embodied* and historically, culturally and socially *embedded*. Before focusing on Ethical or Moral Epistemology, let us mention some subsets of Epistemology.

Social Epistemology (a term first used in the 1950s) is a cross-disciplinary field of studies approaching knowledge as intrinsically social. In 1987, the journal *Synthese* published a special issue on 'social epistemology' that included two of the authors now best known in the field: Alvin Goldman and Steve Fuller. Fuller founded, in the same year, the journal *Social Epistemology: a journal of knowledge, culture, and policy*. In 2004, the journal *Episteme: a journal of social epistemology* was founded[26].

Virtue Epistemology, rather than focusing on what the knower knows, turns its attention to the knower him/herself. "The question, for virtue epistemology, is not so much what knowledge is as what it is to be a good knower" (Kotzee 2013, p. 157; see also Greco and Turri 2011).

Naturalized Epistemology is a movement in the direction of its becoming scientific[27].

Ethical or Moral Epistemology is concerned with the epistemic or conceptual nature of moral beliefs. It falls under the study of Metaethics.

While truth and falsity are the basic categories of scientific knowledge, the basic moral categories are those of right and wrong. If knowledge requires truth, and truth presupposes an objective, factual reality, there cannot be moral knowledge unless moral values are objective, i.e. susceptible to truth or falsity in the ordinary way. If no such a moral knowledge is viable, how can their validity be established?

---

[26] According to Goldman (2006), the current editor of *Episteme*:

> Social epistemology is the study of the social dimensions of knowledge or information. There is little consensus, however, on what the term 'knowledge' comprehends, what is the scope of the 'social', or what the style or purpose of the study should be. According to some writers, social epistemology should retain the same general mission as classical epistemology, revamped in the recognition that classical epistemology was too individualistic.

He continues:

> Proponents of the anti-classical approach have little or no use for concepts like truth and justification. In addressing the social dimensions of knowledge, they understand 'knowledge' as simply what is believed, or what beliefs are 'institutionalized' in this or that community, culture, or context. They seek to identify the social forces and influences responsible for knowledge production so conceived. Social epistemology is theoretically significant because of the central role of society in the knowledge-forming process. It also has practical importance because of its possible role in the redesign of information-related social institutions.

[27] It is so described by Richard Feldman (2012):

> Naturalized epistemology is best seen as a cluster of views according to which epistemology is closely connected to natural science. Some advocates of naturalized epistemology emphasize methodological issues, arguing that epistemologists must make use of results from the sciences that study human reasoning in pursuing epistemological questions. The most extreme view along these lines recommends replacing traditional epistemology with the psychological study of how we reason. A more modest view recommends that philosophers make use of results from sciences studying cognition to resolve epistemological issues.

Aristotle is deemed to have been the first to develop the idea that there exists a rationality peculiar to human deliberations, decisions and behaviors, which search for justifications. As we know, he distinguished between two main kinds of knowledge: theoretical knowledge (*episteme*), aiming at the truth, and practical knowledge (*phronesis*), aiming at a wisdom about what kind of person to be and how to act at a given moment and situation. As he wrote (1925), "it is the mark of an educated man to look for precision in each class of things just so far as the nature of the subject admits; it is evidently equally foolish to accept probable reasoning from a mathematician and to demand from a rhetorician demonstrative proofs" (1094b12-1095a6). Accordingly:

> Scientific knowledge is judgment about things that are universal and necessary; and the conclusions of demonstration, and all scientific knowledge, follow from first principles (for scientific knowledge involves proof). [...]
> Practical wisdom on the other hand is concerned with things human and things about which it is possible to deliberate [...] but no one deliberates about things invariable, or about things which have not an end which is a good that can be brought about by action. [...] Nor is practical wisdom concerned with universals only—it must also recognize the particulars; for it is practical, and practice is concerned with particulars. (1140b30, 1141a33-b21)

Therefore, as Ricoeur (1994) highlighted, "what we call human sciences belongs to an intelligibility regime irreducible to that of nature sciences".

> [T]he whole of the human knowledge achieves in different ways the reason project following multiple regions of intelligibility, so configuring reason as an archipelago of small islands of intelligibility obeying to different rules. [...] So the word 'reason' may be kept as a term unique to say that common horizon constituting in some way the eschatology of knowledge. To become aware of that multiple functioning of the intelligibility and unique of reason is, I think, to accede to a maturity higher than that the positivistic trend of the 'unity of science' intends to support. (p. 31, 32)[28]

As a consequence, Raymond Boudon (1934–2013) rightly asked: "Can the notion of rationality itself mean something other than behaviors based on reasons?" (as cit. in Pierrot 2003, p. 32). In fact, human action has its source in the will that is motivated by some kind of good to be reached, which becomes 'reason to act'. So understood, every human action is reasonable, that is, moved by whatever reason to act, concerning basic or moral goods (see Zambrano 2012). Consequently:

> ... it is obvious that Science is not to be taken in the narrow sense in which it is sometimes employed in the English-speaking countries, as denoting the Mathematical and the Natural Sciences only, but as broadly as possible, to cover all the primarily intellectual activities of man, the whole range of knowledge and learning. This, then, includes the Natural Sciences, the Social Sciences, and the Humanities – in the logical German terminology, *Naturwissenschaft, Sozialwissenschaft,* and *Geisteswissenschaft.* (Huxley 1946, p. 26)

The necessity and possibility of an ethical rationality is addressed, for example, by Karl-Otto Apel and Jürgen Habermas.

[28] Howard Gardner, psychologist and professor of sciences of cognition and of education at Harvard University, has proposed a theory of "multiple intelligences" since 1983.

According to Apel (1988):

> We are facing a dilemma:
> ... *on the one hand*, the need of an ethics of the responsibility with solidarity, having the force of an intersubjective obligation and engaging the whole humankind regarding the consequences the human activities and conflicts may generate, has never been so urgent as at present. [...] *On the other hand*, the rational foundation of an intersubjectively valid ethics has never been so apparently difficult as at present; the reason is that modern science was the first to take possession of the concept of rational foundation, intersubjectively valid, and did it in the sense of axiological neutrality; (p. 134)

The result of this was a dualism: "on the one hand, an instrumental reason, axiologically neutral, and on the other hand, concerning the ultimate values or norms, a decision in conscience, irrational" (p. 27). Here is "the present ideological misery of the Western system of complementary" between science and morality. In fact, "*objective* science and *subjective liberty* and the *responsibility* of the scientists presuppose themselves reciprocally" (p. 145). Rationality is never dissociable from morality, because scientific research itself "is not only a question of the *subject-object relation* of the cognitive act, but also, simultaneously and always, a question of the *relation between subjects*, peculiar to communication and interaction between members of a scientific community", which "has to presuppose an ethics of an *ideal community of communication* concerning the *relation between subjects* that is complementary to the relation *subject-object*" (1992b, p. 16). The validity of a "macroethics" transcending the limitations of the conventional moral—that is to say both of the (interpersonal) microethics and of the (social) mesoethics—and guaranteeing, at the same time, the pluralism of differences compatible with essential universal values depends, however, upon the possibility of a "rational consensus" achieved by argumentation (Apel 1992a, 1992b). This "*consensual and communicative rationality*" is possible and necessary "to overcome the scientist blockade of rationality" (1988, p. 149).

Habermas (1983) also considered the "empiristic reductions" and the positivist monopoly of the "rationality concept" (p. 98) as a "pathology of the modern conscience" (p. 65). Such reductions exclude practico-moral questions from rational discussion for not being able to be held true within the epistemological framework of positivist rationality. He distinguished two types of rational activities: those aiming at success (through organized means) and those turned to inter-understanding. The first ones constitute the instrumental activity (over objects) and the strategic activity (of manipulation to gain power over people). The second one is a communicative activity aiming at a common adhesion to conclusions by means of a rational argumentation according to rules and without violence. The fundamental rule is the recognition of the 'other' as a person. In Habermas' view, the basis of an ethics of discussion is formed by two hypotheses: the first one considers that "the normative exigencies of validity have a cognitive sense and may be treated *as* exigencies of truth"; the second one requires "a real discussion to found in reason norms and precepts" (p. 89), "because the legitimization of norms (differently from the justification of propositions) is not a communicative matter by accident, but *by essence*" (p. 91). Experimental and demonstrative rationality has as a counterpoint an intersubjective and argumentative rationality, that is, "the rational nucleus that is lying down in the moral agreement produced by argumentation" (p. 94).

Following Anders Bordum (2005): "It has often been said that discourse ethics as developed by Jürgen Habermas can be understood as a dialogical continuation of the monological ethics developed by Immanuel Kant (1724–1804), as it was formulated in the categorical imperative in *Grounding for the Metaphysics of Morals* (McCarthy 1978, p. 326; Honneth 2003, p. 310)" (p. 851). Objecting to Kant that his approach is monological and formal, Habermas sought "to give it a new dialogical (intersubjective) and procedural foundation", making "the communicative turn within philosophy" by moving "the locus of knowledge from persons to the communication taking place between persons" (p. 868).

> Jürgen Habermas takes over Kant's ambition of finding a valid moral point of view, from where moral judgments can be tested regarding their validity. This idea that moral judgments can be valid or invalid, shared by Kant and Habermas, is often in the vocabulary of meta-ethics called moral cognitivism. The concept of moral cognitivism is used when ethics and morality are internally connected to concepts like reason, rationality, justification, knowledge, truth, and validity. Habermas insists that moral judgments have a rational basis with an appeal to reason and can be justified accordingly. He claims an analogy between the validity determination of truth (objective knowledge) and rightness claims (valid moral judgments). If knowledge is defined as intersubjectively justified true beliefs, then moral validity may be defined in analogy as intersubjectively justified right beliefs. To Habermas, normative validity about what is right is analogous to what is true (Habermas 1991, p. 76).

Consequently: "The validity of norms stems from the universal recognition they merit (Habermas 2003, p. 109, 229)", for being produced by a rational consensus resulting from a rational discourse based on valid arguments (p. 865, 866, 867)[29].

Another major theorist of the communicative and argumentative rationality was Chaïm Perelman (1912–1984). Having noticed that "there is not a logic specific to value judgments", he found it "in a very old discipline, at present forgotten and despised, namely Rhetoric, the old art of persuading and convincing" that Greeks considered as the technique by excellence. If the validity of its logic is denied, culture, "insomuch as it consists in affirmations that are not tautological or controlled by experience, would be nothing more than irrational doing" (1977, p. 9).

Perelman's "New Rhetoric" is a "philosophy of the reasonable", a "logic of the preferable", that is, enlarging the notion of proof to "rhetorical proofs" peculiar to value judgments concerning convictions and preferences. Values are its main field, but the "empire of Rhetoric" stretches to "every discourse not pretending to impersonal validity" (p. 177). According to Michel Meyer (1985), Rhetoric is not simply complementary to the theory of demonstration but rather a new discourse of the method of the rational and of the reasonable. For Eugène Dupréel (1925), convention is the form of what "should be most cherished and precious for us,

[29] "That a solution be reasonable means that one may justify it with attractive reasons; put another way, that it is a solution able to arouse a rational consensus. There are good arguments to suppose that the best way to reach such reasons consists in finding them through democratic dialogue. Democratic deliberation provides a minimum of respect not to be despised at all: as a rule, every human being is recognized as a valid speaker" (Cianciardo 2012, p. 29, 30).

our common values". The principle of the theory of convention is "the *principle of diverse reasons*", its nucleus being "the agreement of spirits" (p. 95, 96). Argumentation may be then considered as the discourse of the method of the uses, not of the demonstrative reason (whose proofs are imposing by themselves), but of the argumentative reason (whose reasons are proposed). Law is the expression of the power and duty of agreeing that makes human being the remedy and the creator of itself (p. 112). According to Ricoeur (1990), it is the rule that, as a neutral term mediating "the intersubjective relation between two positions of liberty [...] takes, at the ethical level, the same position as the object between two subjects. [...] The role of interdiction is to protect values against each one's arbitrariness" (p. 64, 66).

Emmanuel Levinas (1906–1995) argued that the primacy of inter-human relations over the cognitive-instrumental relation with nature makes ethical rationality the "prime rationality". After asking whether "the entry of someone into the re-presentation of others [...] is the sole—and original and ultimate—rationality of thought and of discourse", source of the sense and justification of knowledge, considered "the face of the other man obliging the I" as "the founding inter-human" rationality. The "*re-presentation*" is expression of "a rationality of an already derived order" (1993, p. 454...456). Levinas' Ethics was qualified by Jacques Derrida (1930–2004) as "an ethics of ethics" or "metaethics" (as cit. in Kovak 1993, p. 188).

In Plato's *Theaetetus*, Socrates concluded: "So, it seems, the answer to the question 'What is knowledge?' will be 'Correct judgment accompanied by *knowledge* of differentness'—for this is what we are asked to understand by the 'addition of an account'" (210). Before, he had told Theaetetus "that if you get hold of the *difference* [italics added] that distinguishes a thing from everything else, then, so some people say, you will have got an account of it" (208d). In the light of the foregoing, the difference of Ethical Epistemology may be summarized as follows:

- Rationality is the quality of what is rational. It refers to reason, a term with two main meanings:
  - Reason is the faculty distinguishing human beings from other animal species. That is why they were defined as 'rational animals'.
  - Reason means justification, foundation, cause. To act rationally is, thefore, to act based on 'reasons'.
- The faculty of reason may be described as a capacity to think, to imagine, to discover hidden relations, to draw conclusions, to assess, concerning the truth and the efficiency, the good and the preferable, etc., including the ability to communicate by means of abstract and especially linguistic signs, but also through other sounds and through gestures, colors, figures, etc.
- Rationality is traditionally equated with experimental or mathematical scientificity, and epistemology is currently defined as the study of knowledge as justified true belief. So understood, moral judgments cannot be rationally justified and universalized as they have not a cognitive content able to be proved or falsified. Values are so beyond rational justification because they are considered nothing more than subjective emotional expressions.

- If human beings are rational and moral animals, according to the classical definition (see Chapter 5), it is not rational to exclude from rationality aspects of their lives as fundamental and far-reaching as their moral values, feelings and behaviors are.
- To begin with, it should be noted that between scientific knowledge and moral values exists an unavoidable relationship: There is no scientific knowledge dissociated from moral values, nor moral values dissociated from knowledge. That is why the progress of sciences may be made difficult or stimulated by the moral and ideological climate surrounding it, and why moral progress is inevitably influenced by the state of knowledge regarding moral matters. We may still ask whether an absolute rationality, above every intersubjectivity and normativity, is conceivable.
- The scope of rationality includes any beliefs (not only the true ones) and their justifications by convincing reasons (not only experimental or mathematical). Considering that human relations are weaved by verbal communication—which is the form of human communication by excellence—by means of which human beings are able to think, act, interact and collaborate, there is a communicative, argumentative rationality, amounting to a logic of the reasonable and the preferable. Inter-recognition and argumentation are epistemological devices apt for the production of consensus validating norms needed to regulate the human interindividual, social and international relations.
- Reason is, therefore, theoretical and practical, unique and multiple. Theoretical reason searches for truths to understanding and transforming the world. Practical reason deals, in particular, with choices and decisions relating to moral values giving sense to the human life and allowing for the human coexistence. The validity resulting from well-regulated intersubjective communication appears as analogous, concerning relations between subjects, of truth, regarding the relation subject-object.
- As a consequence, valid belief seems to be a broader epistemological category and more accurate than true belief, as it encompasses all kinds of beliefs and reasons for justifying them, so embracing scientific knowledge universally true and moral values universally agreed.

After quickly sketching this landscape of ethical thought and characterizing its specific epistemology, we are entering this study's highway—the human rights idea and ideal as an historical advancement of the human moral conscience.

References

Apel, K.-O. 1988. *Discussion et responsabilité—1. L'Éthique après Kant* ('Diskurs und Verantwortung. Das Problem des Übergangs zur postkonventionnellen Moral', trad. par Christian Bouchindhomme, Marianne Charrière et Rainer Rochlitz). Paris: Les Éditions du Cerf (1996).

Apel, K.-O. 1992a. L'impératif moral. *Le Courier de l'Unesco*, 13–17.

Apel, K.-O. 1992b. A necessidade, a aparente dificuldade e a efectiva possibilidade de uma macroética planetária da (para a) humanidade (Trad. de António Fernando Cascais). *Revista de Comunicação e Linguagens*, *15/16*, Julho, 11–26.

Aranguren, J.-L. 1990. A Razão na Ética. In *Balanço do século—Ciclo de Conferências promovido pelo Presidente da República*, ed. AAVV, 95–101. Lisboa: Imprensa Nacional-Casa da Moeda.
Aristotle. 1925. *The Nicomachean Ethics* (David Ross, Trans. and Introd., Revised by J. L. Ackrill and J. O. Urmson). Oxford: University Press (1928).
Aristotle. 1953. Ethics (J. A. K. Thomson, Trans.). London: Penguin Books (1976).
Aristotle. 2000. Politics (B. Jowett, Trans., with Introduction, Analysis and Index by H. W. C. Davis). Mineola. New York: Dover Publications, Incl.
Besnier, J.-M. 2004. La brute et l'imbécile. *Sciences et Avenir—Hors-Série, N° 139*, 82.
Bindé, J. (Sous la direction de). 2004. *Où vont les valeurs—Entretiens du XXIe siècle II*. Paris: UNESCO/Albin Michel.
Bordum, A. 2005. Immanuel Kant, Jürgen Habermas and the categorical imperative. *Philosophy and Social Criticism* 31 (7): 851–874.
Campbell, T. 2006. *Rights—A critical introduction*. London and New York: Routledge.
Canto-Sperber, M., and R. Ogien. 2004. *La Philosophie Morale*. Paris: PUF, Que sais-je?-3696.
Cézilly, F. 2007. Le point de vue des gènes. *Sciences et Avenir—Hors-Série N°152*, 38–41.
Chan, J. 2005. Confucianism and human rights. In *The essentials of human rights*, R. Smith and Ch. Anker eds., 55–57. London: Hodder Arnold.
Cianciardo, J. 2012. La paradoja de la irrelevancia moral del Gobierno y del Derecho—Una aproximación desde el pensamiento de Carlos Nino. In *Razón jurídica y razón moral—Estudio sobre la valoración ética en el Derecho*, eds. J. Cianciardo et al., 1–30. México: Editorial Porrúa, Universidad Austral, Facultad de Derecho.
Damásio, A. 2010. *Self comes to mind: Constructing the conscious brain*. New York: Pantheon Books.
Dupréel, E. 1925. Convention et raison. In *L'homme et la rhétorique—L'école de Bruxelles*, ed. A. Lempereur (Sous la direction de), 89–116. Paris: Méridiens Klincksieck (1990).
Elchardus, M. 1998. The recent rediscovery of the value of values. Lessons for the schools. *Colóquio/Educação e Sociedade N 3—Nova Série*, Junho, 103–130.
Encyclopedia Britannica. 2012. *Encyclopedia britannica ultimate reference suite. [DVD]*. Chicago: Encyclopedia Britannica.
Feldman, R. 2012. Naturalized Epistemology. In *The Stanford Encyclopedia of Philosophy* (Summer 2012 Edition), ed. E. Zalta. (http://plato.stanford.edu/archives/sum2012/entries/epistemology-naturalized).
Fieser, J. 2009. Ethics. In *Internet encyclopedia of philosophy*. www.iep.utm.edu/ethics/print. Accessed July 2013.
Fischl, J. 1968. *Manual de Historia de la Filosofía* ('Geschichte der Philosophie', trad. de Daniel Ruiz Bueno). Barcelona: Editorial Herder (1980).
Goldman, A. 2006. Social Epistemology. In *The stanford encyclopedia of philosophy* (Summer 2010 Edition), ed. E. Zalta. (http://plato.stanford.edu/archives/sum2010/entries/epistemology-social).
Goldman, A. 2007. Why social epistemology is real epistemology (Stirling Conference on Social Epistemology, 8/31/07). www.philosophy.stir.ac.uk/postgraduate/documents/GoldmanSEPaper.pdf. July 2013.
Greco, J., and J. Turri 2011. Virtue Epistemology. In *The stanford encyclopedia of philosophy* (Winter 2011 Edition), ed. E. Zalta. (http://plato.stanford.edu/archives/win2011/entries/epistemology-virtue).
Griffin, J. 2008. *On human rights*. New York: Oxford University Press.
Habermas, J. 1983. *Morale and Communication—Conscience morale et activité communicationnelle* ('Moralbewusstsein und Kommunicatives Handeln', traduction et introduction par Christian Bouchindhomme). Paris: CERF, Passages (1986).
Himmelfarb, G. 2002. A ideia de compaixão: o iluminismo inglês contra o iluminismo francês. *Nova Cidadania, Ano III, Nº 12*, 62–75.
Hunt, L. 2008. *Inventing human rights—A history*. New York: W. W. Norton and Company Ltd.

Huxley, J. 1946. *UNESCO—Its purpose and its philosophy*. Preparatory Commission of the United Nations Educational, Scientific and Cultural Organisation, 62 p. http://unesdoc.unesco.org/images/0006/000681/068197eo.pdf.

Journet, N. (Sous la direction de). 2012. *La Morale—Éthique et sciences humaines*. Auxerre: Sciences Humaines Éditions.

Kotzee, B. 2013. Introduction: Education, social epistemology and virtue epistemology. *Journal of Philosophy of Education* 47 (2). http://onlinelibrary.wiley.com/doi/10.1111/1467-9752.12033/pdf. Accessed July 2013.

Kovak, E. 1993. L'Intrigue éthique. In AAVV, *Emmanuel Levinas—L'éthique comme philosophie première (Actes du colloque de Cerisy-la-Salle sous, 23 août—2 septembre 1986)*, 177–192. Paris: Les Éditions du Cerf.

Letherby, G., J. Scott, and M. Williams 2012. *Objectivity and subjectivity in social research*. Los Angeles: SAGE.

Levinas, E. 1993. Diachronie et représentation. In *Emmanuel Levinas—L'éthique comme philosophie première (Actes du colloque de Cerisy-la-Salle sous, 23 août—2 septembre 1986)*, eds. J. Greisch and J. Rolland (Sous la direction de), 447–468. Paris: Les Éditions du Cerf, La nuit surveillée.

Lévi-Strauss, C. 1963. Rousseau, père de l'anthropologie. *Courrier de l'UNESCO, XVI, 3*.

Meyer, M. 1985. Pour une rhétorique de la raison/Les figures de l'humain. In *L'homme et la rhétorique—L'école de Bruxelles*, ed. A. Lempereur (Sous la direction de), 153–165, 187–206. Paris: Méridiens Klincksieck (1990).

Morris, Ch. 1964. *Signification and significance—A study of the relations of signs and values*. Cambridge: The M.I.T Press.

Perelman, Ch. 1977. *L'empire rhétorique-Rhétorique et argumentation*. Paris: Librairie Philosophique J. Vrin.

Picq, P. 2004. Une innovation évolutive. *Sciences et Avenir—Hors-Série, N° 139*, 26–30.

Pierrot, A. 2003. Sens et rationalité à l'école. Quelques réflexions librement inspirées de Wittgenstein. *Revue Française de Pédagogie, n° 143*, 31–41.

Plato (Ed. by J. Cooper, & D. Hutchinson). 1997. *Plato—Complete Works*. Indianapolis: Hackeht Publishing Company.

Pojman, L. 2000. *The moral life—An introductory reader in ethics and literature* (2th edition). New York, Oxford: Oxford University Press (2004).

Quiniou, Y. 2004. L'émergence de la morale. *Sciences et Avenir—Hors-Série, N° 139*, 39–42.

Rao, N. 2011. Three concepts of dignity in constitutional law. *Notre Dame Law Review 86* (1): 183–271. George Mason Law and Economics Research Paper No. 11–20.

Ricœur, P. 1990. Avant la loi morale: l'éthique. In *Encyclopedia Universalis—Symposium: Les enjeux*, 62–66.

Ricœur, P. 1994. Entretien. In *Éthique et responsabilité—Paul Ricoeur*, ed. AAVV, 11–34. Neuchâtel: Éditions de la Baconnière.

Ricœur, P. 2004. *Parcours de la reconnaissance*. Paris: Gallimard, Folio Essais-459.

Rolston III, H. 2008. Human uniqueness and human dignity: Persons in nature and the nature of persons. In *Human dignity and bioethics—Essays commissioned by the president's council on bioethics*, ed. AAVV, 129–153. Washington, D. C.

Rousseau, J.-J. 1751. *The social contract and the discourses* (G. D. H. Cole, Trans., revised and augmented by J. H. Brumfitt, & J. C. Hall, with an Introduction by A. Ryan). New York: Everyman Library (1993).

Roy, O. 2012. La règle d'or, maxime universelle. *Sciences Humaines—Un siècle de philosophie—Une bibliothèque idéale, N° 29*, 12–15.

Russ, J. 1994. *La pensée éthique contemporaine*. Paris: PUF, Que-sais-je?-2834.

Russell, B. 1938. *Power—A new social analysis*. London: Routledge.

Tort, P. 2004. La généalogie darwinienne de la morale. *Sciences et Avenir—Hors-Série, N° 139*, 43.

Trousson, R., and F. Eigeldinger (Sous la direction de). 1996. *Dictionnaire de Jean-Jacques Rousseau*. Paris: Honoré Champion.

Truncellito, D. 2007. Epistemology. In *Internet Encyclopedia of Philosophy*. (www.iep.utm.edu/epistemo).
Waal, F. 2004. L'émotion morale. *Sciences et Avenir—Hors-Série, N° 139*, 8–11.
Weil, É. 1989. Morale. In *Encyclopedia Universalis—Corpus* 15:743–751.
Zambrano, P. 2012. El Derecho como razón excluyente para la acción—Una aproximación desde la teoría iusnaturalista del Derecho de John Finnis. In *Razón jurídica y razón moral—Estudio sobre la valoración ética en el Derecho*, J. Cianciardo et al., 71–115. México: Editorial Porrúa, Universidad Austral, Facultad de Derecho.

Chapter 3
Historical and Theoretical Rising of Human Rights and Their International Codification and Protection

Abstract This chapter offers a synthesis of the history of the advent and elaboration of the idea of human rights, as well as of their international juridification and protection.

Although the term 'human rights' appeared only in modern times, the corresponding sentiment and ideal are likely as ancient and cross-cultural as human suffering itself. Natural Law and natural rights were major ground-breaking insights in the genealogy of human rights, whose modern era began with the American and French Revolutions and Declarations of Rights. The new era of international recognition and protection of human rights began with the establishment of the Organization of the United Nations, in 1945, and the proclamation of the Universal Declaration of Human Rights in 1948.

The protection of human rights has two faces, like the god Janus: one turned to the outside, to International Law, the other turned to the inside, to domestic legal orders. They are thus protected at universal, regional and national levels. Moreover, human rights are a general responsibility as well, epitomized by the Non-Governmental Organizations movement. An educated world public opinion may be considered their ultimate protection.

Keywords Natural law · Natural rights · United Nations · Universal Declaration of Human Rights · International human rights law · Protection

3.1 Natural Law and Natural Rights

"Natural law was a fundamental concept of pre-modern western political philosophy" (Campbell 2006, p. 5), but whether there is a natural, unwritten higher Law to which all written positive Law should conform in order to be legitimate and obeyed—this remains a central problem of the Legal Philosophy.

For those believing in Natural Law or 'Law of Nature' (*jus natural* or *lex naturalis*, in Latin), it is a higher Law inherent to the whole Universe or *Cosmos* that includes principles or standards of good and evil, right and wrong, against which

A. Reis Monteiro, *Ethics of Human Rights*, DOI 10.1007/978-3-319-03566-6_3,

all moral and legal norms are to be assessed. Being based on nature, not on culture or customs:

- Natural Law is permanent and universal, unlike positive Law, i.e. the human-made Law, the Law created by a State, varying from society to society and changing over time.
- All human beings are able to access and act in accordance with it, for being endowed with the faculty of reason.

The feeling and belief in the correspondence between what is 'natural' and what is 'right' go back to the most ancient of times. However, as the meaning of nature is variable in the course of time, the history of the idea of Natural Law presents a variety of theories too. There are religious and secular versions of it.

Following the *Vedas*, the basic principle of the universe is the principle of *Ritam*, from which derives the Western notion of right. Truth and right are linked, so that there is a moral order somehow built into the universe.

In the Western world, although the term 'natural law' appeared, for the first time, perhaps in the sixteenth century, the idea is generally associated with a passage from Sophocles' *Antigone* (fifth century BC)[1]. King Creon orders that the body of Polyneices, Antigone's brother, be left "unburied, a corpse for birds and dogs to eat, a ghastly sight of shame", because he died fighting "the city of his fathers and the shrines of his fathers' gods". Antigone disobeys and gives a burial to her brother. When Creon asks 'And thou didst indeed dare to transgress that law?' she answers:

> Yes, for it was not Zeus that had published me that edict; not such are the laws set among men by the justice who dwells with the gods below; nor deemed I that thy decrees were of such force, that a mortal could override the unwritten and unfailing statutes of heaven. For their life is not of to-day or yesterday, but from all time, and no man knows when they were first put forth.

The first Greek philosophers, in particular Socrates, Plato and Aristotle, made a distinction between *φύσις* (nature) and *νόμος* (norm, customary or conventional). In the *Republic*, Plato refers to "a whole city established according to nature" (1997, p. 428e). The first philosophical concept of Natural Law is generally attributed to Aristotle (1953) and his distinction between:

> … two sorts of political justice, one natural and the other legal. The natural is that which has the same validity everywhere and does not depend upon acceptance; the legal is that which in the first place can take one form or another indifferently […]. Similarly laws that are not natural but man-made are not the same everywhere, because forms of government are not the same either. (1134b24–1135a8)

[1] http://classics.mit.edu/Sophocles/antigone.pl.txt.

The Greco-Roman Stoicism, notably that of Cicero and Seneca, explored the idea of Natural Law even further[2]. It posits an eternal, trans-historical, trans-cultural, universal, rational order underlying all legal systems, according to whose fundamental moral principles human beings should live. Human laws are valid to the extent that they reflect the eternal laws governing the whole *Cosmos*.

According to Rosenbaum (1980): "The Stoics were the foremost contributors to a natural law theory. In their philosophy, nature was conceived as a universal system of rules both physical, such as the law of gravity, and ethical, such as the obligation of all rational beings to respect one another as equals" (p. 10).

> Perhaps the most important legacy of Stoicism, however, is its conviction that all human beings share the capacity to reason. [...] The belief that the capacity to reason is common to all humans was also important because from it the Stoics drew the implication that there is a universal moral law, which all people are capable of appreciating [...]. The Stoics thus strengthened the tradition that regarded the universality of reason as the basis on which to reject ethical relativism. (Encyclopedia Britannica 2012)

The belief in the universality of reason would be the most influential in shaping the modern conception of human rights. It may not be a mere coincidence that the Stoic universalism is also a contemporary of the advent of empires[3]. And it was not by chance that the revolutionary triumph of the idea of human rights emerged contemporaneously with the 'Age of Reason' and 'Enlightenment', in the eighteenth century, whose core value was individual autonomy.

Stoic Philosophy greatly influenced Christian thinkers. While Stoics grounded equality between human beings on their common capacity to reason, the Christian doctrine introduced a new sense of the equal moral status of all human beings by preaching that they are created in the image of God. St. Paul said in the *Epistle to the Romans*[4]: "for when Gentiles who don't have the law do by nature the things of the law, these, not having the law, are a law to themselves" (2.14–15). According to St. Augustine, the first human creatures lived under the Natural Law, in the Garden of Eden, before original sin.

---

[2] Cicero, De Republica, Book III:

> *Est quidem vera lex recta ratio naturae congruens, diffusa in omnis, constans, sempiterna, quae vocet ad officium iubendo, vetando e fraude deterreat; quae tamen neque probos frustra iubet aut vetat nec improbos iubendo aut vetando movet. Huic legi nec abrogari fas est, neque derogari aliquid ex hac licet neque tota abrogari potest.*
> (There is a true law, a right reason, conformable to nature, universal, unchangeable, eternal, whose commands urge us to duty, and whose prohibitions restrain us from evil. Whether it enjoins or forbids, the good respect its injunctions, and the wicked treat them with indifference. This law cannot be contradicted by any other law, and is not liable either to derogation or abrogation.)
> (http://files.libertyfund.org/files/546/Cicero_0044-01_EBk_v6.0.pdf)

The *recta ratio* corresponds to the Greek *orthos logos*.

[3] The Stoic universalism bears on the idea of Globalization as well, which is found in the Roman historian Polybe in the second century BC, as above said.

[4] http://ebible.org/web/Romans.htm.

Roman Law drew a distinction between *jus naturale* and *jus civile*. The former encompasses common universal principles of justice, with which all legal codes—regardless of time or place—are expected to comply. The latter is particular to a society and variable from society to society, as Aristotle wrote. The idea is so explained in Gaius' *Institutes* (about 160)[5]:

> The laws of every people governed by statutes and customs are partly peculiar to itself, partly common to all mankind. The rules established by a given state for its own members are peculiar to itself, and are called *jus civile*; the rules constituted by natural reason for all are observed by all nations alike, and are called *jus gentium*.

Following the *Iustiniani Institutiones*[6], part of the *Corpus Iuris Civilis* of the Emperor Justinian Code (529–535), intended as a sort of legal textbook for Law schools, *jus naturale* is "that law which nature teaches to all animals. For this law does not belong exclusively to the human race, but belongs to all animals, whether of the earth, the air, or the water"[7]. Its laws, "which all nations observe alike, being established by a divine providence, remain ever fixed and immutable". On the contrary, "the laws which every state has enacted undergo frequent changes, either by the tacit consent of the people or by a new law being subsequently passed"[8]. According to the Natural Law: "The maxims of law are these: to live honesty, to hurt no one, to give everyone his due"[9].

In the twelfth century, the jurist Gratian, an Italian monk and author of the legal textbook known as the *Decretum Gratiani* (or *Concordia discordantium canonum* or *Concordantia discordantium canonum*), equated Natural Law with Divine Law, that is, with the Old and the New Testament revealed Law. Tierney (2004) remarked that:

> ... the most important feature of the twelfth-century renaissance was a great revival of legal studies, centered at first in Italy at Bologna. This was a new civilization, emerging after centuries of near-anarchy. Medieval people valued their rights but, in a still turbulent age, they also felt a need for more adequate systems of law. First, around 1100, came a recovery of the whole corpus of Roman law, then an immensely influential codification of church law in the work known as Gratian's *Decretum* (c. 1140).
> [...]
> Gratian's *Decretum* was not just a compendium of twelfth-century rules and regulations. It reached back to the church Fathers and the early councils of the church; it presented the juridical life of the church in the world for a thousand years, all included in one volume and equipped with a critical commentary. Medieval intellectuals found the work fascinating and they flocked to the great law schools of Bologna to study it. Soon dozens, then hundreds,

[5] http://files.libertyfund.org/files/1154/Gaius_0533_EBk_v6.0.pdf.

[6] For Latin text: http://web.upmf-grenoble.fr/Haiti/Cours/Ak/.
For English translation: http://classes.maxwell.syr.edu/His381/InstitutesofJustinian.htm#Book I.

[7] *Ius naturale est quod natura omnia animalia docuit. Nam ius istud non humani generis proprium est, sed omnium animalium, quae in caelo, quae in terra, quae in mari nascuntur.*

[8] *Sed naturalia quidem iura, quae apud omnes gentes peraeque servantur, divina quadam providentia constituta, semper firma atque immutabilia permanent: ea vero quae ipsa sibi quaeque civitas constituit, saepe mutari solent vel tacito consensu populi vel alia postea lege lata.*

[9] *Iuris praecepta sunt haec: honeste vivere, alterum non laedere, suum cuique tribuere.*

of commentaries on the *Decretum* were written—nearly all of them still unpublished and accessible only in medieval manuscripts.

In the first half of the thirteenth century, Latin translations of Aristotle gave rise to the rediscovery of his writings, which would dominate the later Middle Ages. Its influence impregnated the thought of St. Thomas Aquinas (1224/25–1274), "the most prominent thinker of the natural law tradition" (Encyclopedia Britannica 2012). Aquinas' Theology, exposed in his landmark *Summa Theologiae or Summa Theologica*, was, to a great extent, a Christianization of Aristotelian Philosophy (he referred to Aristotle as *The Philosopher*). The Encyclical of Pope Leo XIII *Æterni Patris* (1879) declared the thought of Aquinas to be the Theology best suited to the Christian world view.

According to Aquinas' theorization, the source of Law, in general, is the reason of a ruler, aiming at the wellbeing of a community. Since God is the Creator of the world, the Divine Law is the eternal idea by which the whole creation—the world and the human beings—is ordered. Natural Law is the Eternal Law imprinted in the created world. However, while nonrational beings are entirely determined by this Law, human beings are able to know it partially by reason and to act freely on it. Being naturally knowable, it is universally binding.

Natural Law entails levels of precepts. According to the Thomistic theory of Natural Law, the most basic, shared with the natural world, commands the preservation of our life (and the reproduction of it). The most general command is: "Good is to be done and pursued, and evil is to be avoided". From that, others may be derived. Laws can be divided into divine, natural and human types:

- *Divine laws* are those written in the Bible and conveyed by the Catholic Church doctrine.
- *Natural laws* are those which are inscribed in physical and human nature, being discoverable through the use of reason common to all human beings.
- *Positive laws* are human laws, changeable from people to people, as well as over time.

As a result of the unique capacities of human beings, and their infinite desire to know and to love, their destiny is not confined to this world[10].

According to Jacques Maritain (1882–1973)—the greatest interpreter of Aquinas' thought in the twentieth century (see Viola 1984)—Natural Law is known by a natural inclination or disposition, a kind of co-naturality (a central Thomistic concept), and not conceptually, by way of rational deduction. It is, therefore indemonstrable, more instinctive than reflexive, but not irrational. It concerns only the first principles of morality, which are immutable and within everyone's reach. However, co-naturality of knowledge concerning good and evil does not mean that it is evident for everybody, in all eras. It depends upon cultural circumstances and the evolving of moral conscience. Consequently, Natural Law is, at the same time, eternal-immutable and historical-relative. Its historicity and relativity explain mistakes and wrongdoings, such as social divisions and discriminations, including

[10] www.aquinasonline.com/Topics/natlaw.html.

slavery. As reads the document of International Theological Commission (2008)[11], mentioned above:

> 59 …moral science cannot furnish an agent subject with a norm that may be applied adequately and almost automatically to concrete situations; only the conscience of the subject, the judgment of his practical reason, can formulate the immediate norm of action. But at the same time it can never abandon the conscience to mere subjectivity: the subject needs to acquire the intellectual and affective dispositions that permit it to open itself to moral truth in such a way that its judgment may be adequate. Natural law cannot, therefore, be presented as an already established set of rules that impose themselves *a priori* on the moral subject, but is a source of objective inspiration for his process, eminently personal, of making a decision.

During the seventeenth century, Natural Law theories began to secularize, breaking with the Aristotelian-Thomist conception. The Dutch legal philosopher and diplomat Hugo Grotius (1583–1645) went so far as to affirm that Natural Law is independent of God, to the extent that "even the will of an omnipotent being cannot change or abrogate" it, and "would maintain its objective validity even if we should assume the impossible, that there is no God or that he does not care for human affairs" (*De Jure Belli ac Pacis*) (On the Law of War and Peace 1625). Grotius made Natural Law the source of International Law (especially in relation to the freedom of the seas and the theory of just war)[12]. Moreover, it is an expression of 'right reason' that:

> … includes the power of judging what is right, which is defined by Grotius as one of the moral qualities or powers essential to human nature. Grotius described these powers as 'rights', an interpretation that was to have a profound effect on later philosophers. In this way Grotius helped initiate modern thinking about human rights by associating rationality with the idea that each person possesses rights simply by being human. (Hayden 2001, p. 4)

In Germany, Pufendorf—the first holder of a chair in Natural Law in a German university—developed Grotius' conception of Natural Law in his *De Jure Naturae et Gentium* (On Natural and Civil Law 1672), a work that was reprinted more than 60 times until the mid-eighteenth century and that was translated into almost all European languages. He sustained "the subjection of the legislator to the higher law of human nature and of reason" (as cit. in Trindade 2006, p. 255). Grotius and Pufendorf's translations into French by Jean Barbeyrac, thereafter translated into English, proved to be greatly influential.

In England, Thomas Hobbes (1588–1679) "is probably the writer most responsible for inaugurating modern social and political philosophy", notably with *Leviathan* (1651), by initiating "an important tradition of ethical and political theory known as *contractarianism* that is modified and extended by Locke, Rousseau and Kant" (Hayden 2001, p. 57, 58). *Contractarian theory* posits a pre-social *state of nature*, without laws, where each one was free to do what one wants, a state that

---

[11] www.pathsoflove.com/universal-ethics-natural-law.html.

[12] "International law is a product of natural law, that is, it has grown and developed from the workings of the moral impulses and needs of mankind by a sort of instinctive growth, as well as by edicts or decrees or authoritative pronouncements" (United Nations War Crimes Commission 1948, p. 8).

succeeded the peaceful and happy existence in the biblical Garden of Eden. It was a state of "continual fear and danger of violent death, and here the life of people was solitary, poor, nasty, brutish, and short" (*Leviathan*, Chap. XIII, Of the natural condition of mankind as concerning their felicity and misery)[13].

According to Hobbes, to overcome such a savage and dangerous state, people agreed to a *social contract* that consisted in surrendering their unlimited freedom and other natural rights, including the right to resistance, to an absolute sovereign who should guarantee their security. This sovereign remains subject to the commands of God and the laws of nature, however. Hobbes identified 19 laws of nature in *Leviathan* (Chaps. XIV and XV). Robert R. Williams commented: "If it is not an actual historical period, the 'state of nature' is a heuristic methodological fiction for sorting out the emergence of social rationality and the replacement of custom and tradition by the rule of law" (Williams 1997, p. 96).

John Locke (1632–1704) "used the theory of natural law as a foundation for a theory of natural rights" and "to justify the supremacy of parliamentary government" (Rosenbaum 1980, p. 12), especially in *Two Treatises of Government* (1689), his major political writing. Like Hobbes, he imagined a pre-political *state of nature* but, differently from him, the voluntary transfer of natural rights to the sovereign is partial rather than absolute. While putting consent as the contractual political basis of a society—"the consent of the society, over whom nobody can have a power to make laws but by their own consent, and by authority received from them"—he affirmed: "A man [...] cannot subject himself to the arbitrary power of another" (Chap. XI, p. 135). One is born "with a title to perfect freedom and an uncontrolled enjoyment of all the rights and privileges of the law of Nature, equally with any other man". They are "his property—that is, his life, liberty, and estate" (Chap. VII, p. 87). They are rights existing prior to and independently of any given political society. Their respect and protection should be the purpose and the criterion of the legitimacy of political power. Their persistent disregard and contempt legitimize the rebellion of the citizens against the rulers.

As far as naturalism in Montesquieu (1689–1755) is concerned, Michael Zuckert (2004) wrote:

> Montesquieu is normally not seen as a thinker of either natural law or of natural rights. Even though surveys of these topics seldom include him, he does speak of natural law with some frequency. One of the French terms that he uses is *droit naturel*, a phrase that can also be translated as natural right. Nonetheless, the contexts in which Montesquieu uses this phrase suggest natural law rather than natural right as the preferred translation. In accord with that observation, Montesquieu hardly ever speaks of natural rights (*droits naturels*) in the plural; when speaking of the natural law in the plural, he regularly speaks of *lois*, a word that does not have the same ambiguity as *droit*.

Nevertheless, in *De l'esprit des lois* (The Spirit of the Laws 1748)[14], he endorsed the Lockean conception of rights. Like Hobbes, Locke, and others, he begins with the state of nature, but his version of it is rather like that of Rousseau, i.e. it was a state

[13] www.gutenberg.org/files/3207/3207-h/3207-h.htm.

[14] http://files.libertyfund.org/files/837/Montesquieu_0171-01_EBk_v6.0.pdf.

of peace and not of war. Human beings' feeling of weakness, and their biological needs, including sexual attraction, brought them into proximity with one another. Social degeneration was a later phenomenon[15].

Montesquieu builds on Locke who called natural rights property rights, based on self-ownership. "A self-ownership understanding of rights was by his time a well-established motif within political philosophy" (id.). He recognized a natural right of self-preservation that implies "a right to kill in case of natural defense" (Book X, Chap. II).

Rousseau also advanced the theory of the *Social Contract* (1762). The will of the majority is the general will (*la volonté générale*), synonymous with the Law. The Natural Law idea resonates in these words of Rousseau (1751), concluding his *Discours sur les sciences et les arts* (Discourse on Sciences and Arts 1751): "Virtue! sublime science of simple minds, are such industry and preparation needed if we are to know you? Are not your principles graven on every heart? Need we do more, to learn your laws, than examine ourselves and listen to the voice of conscience, when the passions are silent?" (p. 29)

Towards the end of the eighteenth century, the attractiveness of Natural Law theories was declining, for many reasons, in particular because of the rise of the legal positivism which became dominant during the nineteenth through the mid-twentieth centuries. According to it, Law is only the one created or *posited* by the State. It is the Law as it is, rather than the Law as it should be. Morals and Law ought, therefore, to be kept separate. The historic context of the legal positivism was the empiricist, scientist and materialist climate of the nineteenth century.

Hume is deemed to have paved the way to the legal positivist turn in his *Treatise of Human Nature* (1739), where he attacked the *is-ought fallacy* consisting in the attempt to deduce an *ought* from an *is*[16]. The most prominent pioneers of legal positivism were Bentham and John Austin (1790–1859). Bentham's critique of Natural Law greatly influenced Austin, commonly considered the founder of contemporary legal positivism, notably in his *Province of Jurisprudence Determined* (1832). In the twentieth century, Hans Kelsen (1981–1973) and Herbert L. A. Hart (1907–1992) were two preeminent legal positivists. The Nazi crimes committed in accordance with the *positive* Nazi Law prompted the resurgence of Natural Law theory. The Nuremberg Trials, though never referring to it, have consecrated the principle

---

[15] "Every society, then, faces three forms of the state of war: war with other societies, war among members of the society, war between government and the members of society. In response to these three dimensions of war arise three forms of positive law: the law of nations (*droit des gens*) to deal with relations among societies; the civil law (*droit civil*) to deal with 'the relation that all citizens have with one another'; and political (public) law (*droit politique*) to deal with 'the relation between those who govern and those who are governed. [...] Far from there being a deep continuity between social and pre-social humanity, Montesquieu claims that the move into society results in a near erasure of the original human nature. As he says in the preface, man is 'that flexible being [...]'" (id.).

[16] George E. Moore (1873–1958) defined the 'naturalistic fallacy' as any attempt to define the good in terms of some natural thing, such as pleasure (but also in terms of something supernatural, such as "God's will").

following which every individual must disobey laws which are clearly violating higher moral principles (see Mirabella 2011). As Perelman (1980) observed: "The renaissance of natural law theories in contemporary legal philosophy is certainly in great part the consequence of the failure of positivism" (p. 47).

Blandine Barret-Kriegel (1989) referred to "the strange riddle of natural law" that "implies the existence of an order simultaneously logical and axiological crossing the world" (p. 39, 40). Janos Tóth (1972) called Natural Law "a boat within which a certain conception of justice crossed the times, adapting to the demands of each era, but keeping some fundamental values" (p. 71). In Henri Batiffol's opinion, it is "a corpse we never end to re-bury" (as cit. in Goyard-Fabre 1988, p. 9). As reads the *History of the United Nations War Crimes Commission and the Development of the Laws of War*, Natural Law "has never meant more than the innate sense of right and wrong possessed by all decent-minded human beings" (United Nations War Crimes Commission 1948, p. 16). Antônio C. Trindade (2006) described this phenomenon as "[t]he eternal return or 'rebirth' of jusnaturalism" (p. 265).

The tension between Natural Law and Positive Law remains. Nowadays, there are attempts to elaborate a new Natural Law theory[17].

Louis Henkin (1917–2010) remarked: "Perhaps the most striking philosophical development in recent decades is the quiescence of positivism and the reanimation of natural law and natural rights [...] escaping and bridging the dichotomy of natural and positive law" (1978, p. 19, 23). According to Justin Kissangoula (2008): "The codification of the natural rights of man means the development of the legal positivism over the corpse of jusnaturalism" (p. 572).

The foregoing made clear that natural rights are an offspring of Natural Law. When did the concept really emerge? This is a debated issue.

Campbell (2006) observes: "Rights talk emerged in the medieval period with the notion of natural rights, a by-product of the idea of natural law" (p. 5). However, as Fagan (2005) remarks: "Many attempts have been made to identify the 'first' theorist of human or natural rights in the Middle Ages".

At stake are mainly the two meanings of 'natural right' in late medieval scholasticism, based on two senses of the Latin word *jus*: one *objective* (*id quod justum est*: what is just or right), the other *subjective* (*facultas* or *potestas*: the faculty or power someone holds). How did the subjective meaning emerge from the objective one?

Williams (2004) pointed to "a common historical misunderstanding, namely that a single, unified rights tradition can be traced from the earliest theories of the rights of man to contemporary rights claims, and that this theory originated with Thomas Hobbes" (p. 49). In some authors' opinion, St. Thomas Aquinas' doctrine on Natural Law already embodies the idea of 'natural rights' (without the expression). Nonetheless, according to Griffin (2008), while the origins of the modern concept of Natural Law go back to Middle Ages, different is the case of the modern concept of natural rights.

[17] Their most known authors are John Finnis (Australian, but based in Oxford), Germain Grisez, Robert P. George (USA), and Joseph Boyle (Canada).

> Aquinas had much to say about natural law and the natural right, but it is a matter of dispute whether he had our modern concept of a natural right.
> Indeed, the term 'natural right', in our modern sense, though it first appeared in the late Middle Ages, did not itself gain wide use until the seventeenth and eighteenth centuries. (p. 9)

In the opinion of Michel Villey, the fourteenth century Franciscan philosopher William of Ockham was the first to create a doctrine of subjective rights, by associating, for the first time, *jus* (right) and *potestas* or *libertas* (subjective power). However, Brian Tierney (2004) found that "such language was common in juridical writings—especially among the medieval canonists—for more than a century before Ockham". Tierney "came to think that the jurists of the twelfth century, especially the church lawyers, played an important innovatory role". The subjective meaning of *jus* emerged "from the twelfth century down to around 1500", when an unforeseen event "redirected the course of human rights thinking for the future". Such an event was "the European encounter with America and the great debate that it stirred up about the rights of American Indians among Spanish scholars, especially Vitoria and Las Casas and, on the other side, Sepúlveda". He remarks that the first chapters of the *Decretum* included several different usages of *jus naturale*. The early medieval canonists realized that one of them was subjective in nature and developed it into the meaning of natural rights as a concept included in an "adequate concept of natural justice". What *natural rights*?

"The first one, a very radical one, was a right of the destitute poor to the necessities of life, even if this meant appropriating for themselves the surplus property of the rich". This principle of extreme necessity is found in the *Ordinary Gloss* to the *Decretum* (D. 5 c.). Towards the end of the thirteenth century, jurists began to argue that the right to appear and defend oneself before a Court of Law was also a natural right, as was the presumption of innocence. Another development, during the thirteenth century, was the recognition of natural rights as belonging to all peoples, Christian or infidels, a doctrine applied by sixteenth century theologians to the indigenous populations of America against their Spanish conquerors.

Following Tierney, the achievement of the Decretists was not to formulate a coherent theory of natural rights, but rather to create "a language within which a doctrine of rights could be expressed by generations of later thinkers. Their definitions of *jus* as 'faculty' or 'power' were repeated frequently by jurists and political theorists down to the time of Grotius". It was the debates over Franciscan poverty, from the 1250s to the 1340s, that inspired the contribution of Ockham to the emergence of subjective rights. Tierney mentions another medieval figure, Jean Gerson, a great French theologian who, around 1400, defined right as "a faculty or power belonging to anyone according to right reason".

Around 1500, the debate about natural rights going on in the schools of Paris was too arid, metaphysical, and far removed from real life, but the European encounter with the American continent gave it a modern topicality and historical resonance by arousing this question: Do American indigenous peoples have natural rights too?

As above mentioned, the great debate took place in Spain, with the Second Scholastic, whose best known representatives are Francisco de Vitoria (1486?–1546)—

commonly regarded as the founder of the 'School of Salamanca'—and Francisco Suárez (1548–1617). The School of Salamanca was a School of Law at the Pontifical University of Salamanca where learned theologians and lawyers played a significant role in the creation of modern International Law, as well in the elaboration of the natural rights doctrine.

Suárez used in his *Tractatus de legibus ac Deo legislatore in decem libri distributus* (1613, several times reprinted), the formula *ex natura rei omnes homines nascuntur liberi* (all human beings are born free by nature), later taken over by the Declarations of Rights. Native peoples are, therefore, human beings with rights too. However, the protagonist of this universalistic doctrine was Bartolomé de las Casas (1474/1484–1566). According to Paolo Carozza (2003): "The modern idea of human rights had a period of gestation lasting millennia. But it would be fair to say—even if it is not commonly recognized—that this birth was in the encounter between sixteenth century Spanish Neo-Scholasticism and the New World. If the encounter embodied in a single person, it would be Bartolommeo de Las Casas", whose *History of the Indies* is an account of the cruelty of the Spanish *conquistadores* (p. 289). "Perhaps in no other time or place has a single man's life and work so deeply embodied the cry for justice of a whole continent" (p. 291), so that Simon Bolivar, the *Libertador* (Liberator), suggested naming the new capital city of a future Pan-American Union "Las Casas" (p. 296).

Arguing for the equal rights of the 'Indians', Las Casas famously stated: "All the races of the world are men, and of all men and of each individual there is but one definition, and this is that they are rational. All have understanding and will and free choice, as all are made in the image and likeness of God. [...] Thus the entire human race is one" (as cit. p. 293). During the famous Valladolid debates, in 1550 and 1551, Las Casas affirmed, against Juan Ginès Sepúlveda, who considered the 'Indians' to be beast-like and 'natural slaves': "They are our brothers, and Christ gave His life for them" (p. 293). In the opinion of Tierney (2004): "It was truly a doctrine of *human* rights that Las Casas presented". This may be considered a watershed in the history of the idea of human rights. Virpi Mäkinen (2008) commented:

> According to Tierney and Brett, the 'School of Salamanca' represents the final phase of the medieval tradition of natural rights thought. Human rights became the focus of the writings of the Spanish scholastics because of the practical questions sent to them by the missionaries in the New World: the humanity of the Native Americans and their right to elect or reject the missionaries' offering of Christianity. The Spanish scholastics defended the rights of the Indians and justified it with the novel ideas of natural liberty.
> [...]
> The importance of the Spanish scholastics for the emergence of Western rights theories is at least twofold. First, they focused especially on human rights, pointing out the free choice of the individual and his autonomy or 'self-mastery'. [...] Second, they had a great impact on the early-modern figures of natural rights, such as Hugo Grotius, Thomas Hobbes, John Locke and Samuel Pufendorf. (p. 107, 115)

Summing up: Grotius and Pufendorf—preeminent representatives of the modern school of Natural Law, as we saw—deepened the process of its secularization. Hobbes' hypothesis of a *state of nature* and of the *social contract* paved the way to the theories of natural rights developed in the seventeenth and eighteenth centuries, when the protection of natural rights became progressively the principle of legitimacy of political power.

> The religious, scientific, and political revolutions of the sixteenth and seventeenth centuries initiated a momentous shift in thinking about the nature of human beings and the character of a just social order. [...] These events resulted in the development of democratic governments founded on the rights of man rather than the divine right of kings. (Hayden 2001, p. 3)

According to Hunt (2008), Jacques Burlamaqui "synthesized the various seventeenth-century natural law writings in *The Principles of Natural Law* (1747)", which became "a kind of textbook of natural law and natural rights in the last half of the eighteenth century. [...] Burlamaqui's work fed a more general revival of natural law and natural rights theories across Western Europe and the North American colonies. [...] Grotius, Pufendorf, and Burlamaqui were all well known to American revolutionaries, such as Jefferson and Madison, who read in the law" (p. 118). The most frequently cited was Locke, however. The *Second Treatise of Government*[18] is often considered as the first fully developed natural rights theory[19]. The French Revolution was mostly influenced by Rousseau whose *Social Contract* (1762) also drew upon the idea of the state of nature. In this connection, Campbell (2006) noted:

> The revolutionary implications of Locke and Rousseau were developed and applied in the blunt and stirring rhetoric of the republican activist Thomas Paine, an Englishman who emigrated to the United States, which matched the mood of both the newly independent American colonies and the post-revolutionary regimes in France. Paine [...] captured the radical political implications of demanding that governments respect universal rights and declaring that they gain legitimacy only through obtaining the consent of the governed [...]. (p. 7)

Jorn Rusen observed: "By conceiving of nature as meta-political authority of legitimation and critique, Classical Antiquity created the intellectual preconditions for reflecting on political rule in terms of human rights" (as cit. in Hansungule 2010, p. 9).

Fagan (2005) concluded: "It is perhaps best to examine the development of the theory of human rights as an incremental process. Various thinkers contributed important dimensions to its history without necessarily enunciating the idea in its final form or perhaps even appreciating the wider significance of their particular contributions".

The idea of natural rights prompted the rising of the liberating human rights flag that may be said to meet one of the famous Karl Marx's *Theses on Feuerbach* first published as an appendix to *Ludwig Feuerbach and the End of Classical German Philosophy* (1888)[20]. Thesis XI (engraved on Marx's tombstone) reads: "The philosophers have only interpreted the world, in various ways; the point is to change it". The American and French Revolutions and their Declarations of Rights "rep-

---

[18] www.earlymoderntexts.com/pdf/lockseco.pdf.

[19] Waldron (2009a) remarked: "The epitome of natural rights theory is John Locke's political philosophy in the second of his *Two Treatises of Government*" (p. 7).

[20] www.marxists.org/archive/marx/works/1845/theses/theses.htm.

resented a fundamental break with 2,000 years of Western theory and practice", as stresses Jack Donnelly (2009, p. 21), contributing to "a broad transformation of modern societies towards more individual-centered and universalistic systems of social, political, and ethical life. [...] And through the idea and practice of human rights, we have tried to construct societies worthy of truly human beings" (p. 12).

We are proceeding to see how the human rights history went on.

3.2 First Declarations and the Constitutionalization of Human Rights

When did the history of human rights really begin?

While the term 'human rights' appeared only in modern times, their sentiment is likely as ancient and cross-cultural as human suffering. It is tied with the history of justice and Law, as Ramcharan (2008) points out:

> Although the idea of human rights has seen great intellectual fermentation in Western philosophy and practice since the Magna Carta of 1215, this intellectual activity drew on earlier ideas of law, justice, and humanity from ancient civilizations. Justice is undoubtedly the fundamental basis and yardstick for determining the content and implementation of human rights. The quest for justice in Babylon, China, India, Egypt, wider Mesopotamia, Persia, and Sumeria long predated that drive in Western civilization. [...]
> Law has been traced to ancient scripts such as the Codex Ur-Nammu, the Sumerian Codex, the Babylonian Codex Lipit-Ishtar, Codex Eshnunna, and the Code of Hammurabi, significantly predating the development of the idea of law in Western civilizations. The ideas of law and justice were not Western ideas in their inception. Rather they are part of the patrimony of humankind, and different civilizations have contributed to them.
> [...]
> All societies have seen struggles for what is now known as human rights, and the seeds of the human rights idea are scattered in different parts of the world. Some experts have traced instances of workers' and women's rights to ancient Egypt. Elements of humanitarian law have been traced to practices in Africa and Asia. Societies have cross-fertilized and shared ideas, and some societies have taken ideas further in different historical epochs. It is a matter of historical record that the Greek philosophers owed debts to Babylon and Egypt. The philosophies of Socrates, Plato, and Aristotle drew and built on intellectual strands in ancient civilizations. (p. xxii, 2, 3)

Some documents are generally highlighted as historical landmarks:

- Code of Hammurabi (Babylon, eighteenth century BC)[21]
- Biblical Decalogue (thirteenth century BC)[22]

---

[21] http://avalon.law.yale.edu/ancient/hamframe.asp.

[22] www.jewishvirtuallibrary.org/jsource/judaica/ejud_0002_0005_0_05021.html.

During the UDHR drafting, at the 98th meeting of the Third Committee of the UN General Assembly, on 9 October 1948 (A/C.3/SR.98), the Argentina representative (Enrique V. Corominas) said: "It could properly be said that the Ten Commandments were the first declaration of human rights" (see Subsect. 3.3.5).

- Cyrus Charter (Persia, sixth century BC)[23]
- Constitution of Medina [24]
- Magna Carta or The Great Charter of Liberties of England (1215)[25]
- Petition of Rights (England, 1628)[26]
- Habeas Corpus Act (England, 1679)[27]
- Bill of Rights (England, 1689)[28]

The Code of Hammurabi[29], the oldest legal code known today (but based upon other unknown texts), preserved on a large black stone containing 282 clauses, affirmed that the Code established "laws of justice" and that the king "brought about the well-being of the oppressed" and ruled "to further the well-being of mankind". The Cyrus Charter[30] declared: "I prevent slavery and my governors and subordinates are obliged to prohibit exchanging men and women as slaves within their own ruling domains. Such a traditions should be exterminated the world over".

Consequently, as Jean-Bernard Marie (1985) wrote, "it would be in vain to search for a 'birth certificate' of human rights, duly filled with date and place [...], the *claim* for human rights was made always, everywhere" (p. 7). They have emerged slowly as a dawn, from the night of the times, from East and West. They are a conquest of all epochs, fruits of the "thousand flowers of culture", as said Robert Badinter (1990, p. 183) and illustrates the anthology *Birthright of Man* published by UNESCO (Hersch 1969). They are a heritage accumulated by millennia of material, moral, intellectual, scientific, artistic, legal and political progresses of Humankind. The human rights history is a tapestry woven with many lines and many colors by many artisans, resounding cries and impregnated with blood of countless victims of cruelties and injustices. They juridified a demand that is, following Ricoeur:

> ... older than any philosophical formulation [...]. At every age and in every culture, a complaint, a cry, a proverb, a song, a tale, a treaty of wisdom said the message: if the human rights concept is not universal, the fact remains that all human beings, in all cultures, feel the need, the expectation, the sense of these rights. The demand has always been that 'something is due to the human being only for being human'. (as cit. in Ponton 1990, p. 20)

In Bates' (2010) view, if the history of human rights begins with the idea that every human being possesses 'natural rights', their origins go back to the Greek Stoicism. If it begins with the first measures to protecting individuals against the political

[23] http://pt.scribd.com/doc/24498206/Cyrus-Charter-of-Human-Rights-Cylinder.

[24] http://deenrc.files.wordpress.com/2008/03/constitution_madina.pdf.

The Constitution of Medina of 622 AD said to have been drafted by Prophet Muhammad and which constituted formal agreement between all signifiticant tribes and families of Yathrib later known as Medina, including Muslims, Jews and Pagans, is probably the first constitution or treaty which entertained diverse human rights (Hansungule 2010, p. 24).

[25] www.britannia.com/history/docs/magna2.html.

[26] www.britannia.com/history/docs/petition.html.

[27] www.constitution.org/eng/habcorpa.htm.

[28] www.britannia.com/history/docs/rights.html.

[29] On display in Louvre Museum, Paris.

[30] Kept in British Museum, London. A replica is kept at the UN Headquarters in New York.

power, their starting point was the Magna Carta (1215). "The enduring significance of the Magna Carta, and other similar documents of this age, for the history of human rights, lies in the fact that it has come to be seen as a starting point—the beginning of the limitation of absolute and arbitrary power of the sovereign" (p. 19). The Declarations of Rights proclaimed during the last decades of the eighteenth century gave "a precise name to that claim and began defining its content and outlook: in that sense, they gave rise to the modern notion of human rights as it continuously developed until nowadays" (Marie 1985, p. 7).

According to Hunt (2008), Richard Price's pamphlet Observations on the Nature of Civil Liberty, the Principles of Government, and the Justice and Policy of the War with America (1776):

> ... put 'the natural rights of mankind', 'the rights of human nature', and especially 'the unalienable rights of human nature' on the agenda in Europe. As one author clearly recognized, the crucial question was this: 'Whether there are inherent rights in Human Nature, so connected with the will, that such rights cannot be alienated'. (p. 123)

The terminology evolved. "While English speakers continued to prefer 'natural rights' or just plain 'rights' throughout the eighteenth century, the French invented a new expression in the 1760s—'rights of man' (*droits de l'homme*)". The term "gained currency in French after its appearance in Rousseau's *Social Contract* of 1762" (p. 23, 24). In English, 'rights of man' was hard to find before 1789. Even though not defined, the term meant something like 'natural rights'. *Human rights* is a term first used perhaps by Thomas Paine (1737–1809) in his English translation of the 1789 French Declaration of the Rights of Man and of the Citizen (see Rosenbaum 1980, p. 9)[31]. Another term was 'rights of humanity'. One of its earliest uses was in 1734. In Rousseau's *Émile* (1762) one reads (Book V): "Sophy, [...] do not hope to make me forget the rights of humanity; they are even more sacred in my eyes than your own rights; I will never renounce them for you". Later, Rousseau said that "he does not want to write books; if ever he did so, it would not be to pay court to those in authority, but to establish the rights of humanity" (p. 484, 506).

In sum, "rights talk was gathering momentum after the 1760s. 'Natural rights', now supplemented by 'the rights of mankind', 'the rights of humanity', and 'the rights of man' became common currency" (Hunt 2008, p. 125).

Hunt's essay is devoted to answering the question: "How then do we account for the sudden crystallization of human rights claims at the end of the eighteenth century?" (p. 20). She argues for the thesis "that any account of historical change must in the end account for the alteration of individual minds. For human rights to become self-evident, ordinary people had to have new understandings that came from new kinds of feelings" (p. 34). In effect, this is "the most important quality of human rights: they required a certain widely shared 'interior feeling'" (p. 27). They "could only flourish when people learned to think of others as their equals,

[31] Thomas W. Pogge (2001) noted: "The adjective 'human'—unlike 'natural'—does not suggest an ontological status independent of any and all human efforts, decisions, (re)cognition. It does not rule out such a status either. Rather, it avoids these metaphysical and metaethical issues by implying nothing about them one way or the other" (p. 191).

as like them in some fundamental fashion" (p. 58). This is the meaning of empathy or sympathy. "Sympathy or sensibility—the latter term was much more common in French—had a broad cultural resonance on both sides of the Atlantic in the last half of the eighteenth century". The first novel written by an American, published in 1789, bared the title *The Power of Sympathy* (p. 66). Epistolary novels played a unique role in creating the emotional climate favorable to a new sensitivity to the human rights idea, in Hunt's opinion. Their rising "coincides chronologically with the birth of human rights. The epistolary novel surged as a genre between the 1760s and 1780s and then rather mysteriously died out in the 1790s" (p. 40). They:

> ... taught their readers nothing less than a new psychology and in the process laid the foundations for a new social and political order. [...] Novels made the point that all people are fundamentally similar because of their inner feelings [...]. Can it be coincidental that the three greatest novels of psychological identification of the eighteenth century—Richardson's *Pamela* (1740) and *Clarissa* (1747–48) and Rousseau's *Julie* (1761)—were published in the period that immediately preceded the appearance of the concept of 'the rights of man'? (p. 39)

She further explained: "The novel made up of letters could produce such striking psychological effects because its narrative form facilitated the development of a 'character', that is, a person with an inner self" (p. 43). The 'devouring' of novels had so disturbing effects in minds that they entered onto the Papal Index of Forbidden Books. In 1755, a "Catholic cleric, abbé Armand-Pierre Jacquin, wrote a 400-page work to show that reading novels undermined morality, religion, and all the principles of social order" (p. 51).

The new moral sensitivity was put to the test by the *Affaire Calas*, in France. In 1762, in Toulouse, a Court convicted Jean Calas, a 64-year-old Calvinist, of murdering his son to prevent him from converting to Catholicism. He was sentenced to death by breaking on the wheel, after enduring a torture known as the 'preliminary question', designed to get those already convicted to name their accomplices. The *Affaire Calas* caused Voltaire (1694–1778) writing the *Traité sur la tolérance à l'occasion de la mort de Jean Calas* (Treatise on Tolerance on the Occasion of the Death of Jean Calas 1763)[32], in an age "when Enlightenment had made such progress!", ending with "A prayer to God". Voltaire exclaims: "May all men remember that they are brothers! May they abhor the tyranny which would imprison the soul [...]. But let us use the moment of our earthly existence to praise, in a thousand different but equal languages, from Siam to California, Thy goodness which has given us this moment". Voltaire used the term 'human right', especially in Chap. 6 that bears the title "On intolerance as natural law or human right".

[32] http://books.google.pt/books?id=hnZNwHWdB-UC&printsec=frontcover&hl=pt-PT#v=onepage&q&f=false; in French: http://athena.unige.ch/athena/voltaire/voltaire_traite_tolerance.html.

The *Affaire Calas* was revised in 1765 by a 50-judge panel that reversed Calas' conviction, and the Government paid the family an indemnity.

The *Affaire Calas* marked a turning point. "Seeing him repeatedly affirm his innocence during his torments, the people of Toulouse began to feel compassion and to repent of their earlier unreasoning suspicion of the Calvinist" (Hunt 2008, p. 99). Hunt notes:

> As with human rights more generally, new attitudes about both torture and humane punishment first crystallized in the 1760s, not only in France but elsewhere in Europe and in the American colonies. [...]
> The conversion of elites to the new views of pain and punishment took place in stages between the early 1760s and the end of the 1780s. [...]
> During the second half of the 1760s, five new books appeared advocating criminal law reform. In the 1780s, in contrast, thirty-nine such books were published.
> [...]
> The campaign for penal reform thus became ever more closely associated with the general defense of human rights. (p. 75, 98, 104, 106)

Cesare Beccaria's (1738–1794) *Crimes and Punishments* (1764), in particular, "helped valorize the new language of sentiment" (p. 81). Although it was included in the Papal Index of Forbidden Books in 1766, it was printed, reprinted and translated into many languages.

Moreover: "Eighteenth-century novels reflected a deeper cultural preoccupation with autonomy" (p. 60). Indeed: "In each novel, everything comes back to the heroine's desire for independence" (p. 59). Explaining why "the ideas of autonomy and equality, along with human rights, [...] only gained influence in the eighteenth century", Hunt writes:

> Two related but distinct qualities were involved: the ability to reason and the independence to decide for oneself. Both had to be present if an individual was to be morally autonomous. [...] If the proponents of universal, equal, and natural human rights automatically excluded some categories of people from exercising those rights, it was primarily because they viewed them as less than fully capable of moral autonomy.
> [...]
> The Enlightenment's emphasis on individual autonomy grew out of the seventeenth-century revolution in political thinking started by Hugo Grotius and John Locke. They had argued that the autonomous male entering into a social compact with other such individuals was the only possible foundation of legitimate political authority. If authority justified by divine right, Scripture, and history was to be replaced by a contract between autonomous men, then boys had to be taught to think for themselves. Educational theory, shaped most influentially by Locke and Rousseau, therefore shifted from an emphasis on obedience enforced through punishment to the careful cultivation of reason as the chief instrument of independence. (p. 27, 28, 60)

That was the cultural climate when human rights were first proclaimed.

> The equality, universality, and naturalness of rights gained direct political expression for the first time in the American Declaration of Independence of 1776 and the French Declaration of the Rights of Man and Citizen of 1789. [...]
> In other words, sometime between 1689 and 1776 rights that had been viewed most often as the rights of a particular people—freeborn English men, for example—were transformed into human rights, universal natural rights, what the French called *les droits de l'homme* or 'the rights of man'. (p. 21, 22)

'Declaration of Rights' is the beginning of the "positivisation of Natural Rights" (Arslan 1999, p. 201). They were included in the United States' Constitutions[33].

The greatest influence in shaping American Constitutionalism was Montesquieu's *The Spirit of the Laws*[34], whose most famous and influential part was Book XI Chap. VI (Of the Constitution of England), where he presented his theory of separation of powers. It begins as follows: "In every government there are three sorts of power: the legislative; the executive in respect to things dependent on the law of nations; and the executive in regard to matters that depend on the civil law". Zuckert (2004) noted:

> *The Spirit of the Laws*, published about forty years before the constitutional convention met, was the beginning point for all serious thinking about political construction in late eighteenth century America. The prominence of Montesquieu at the time has been well documented. In his citation analysis of eighteenth century political writings in America, Donald Lutz discovered that Montesquieu was the single most widely cited political thinker of the entire founding era.

According to James Madison, called the "father of the Constitution", it was a "system without a Precedent" (as cit. ib.). While Montesquieu was the first to formulate the judicial power as a conceptually distinct power, one of the convention's adaptations of Madison's adaptations of Montesquieu—and likely the greatest political innovation of the American constitutional order—was the USA's Supreme Court profile.

> These American modifications in the Montesquieuan blueprint have proved to be among the most widely imitated features of the American constitution. There are almost as many countries that have instituted constitutional courts modeled more or less on the U.S. Supreme Court as there are brands of cola aiming to be Coke. If ability to spawn imitators is a sign of success, then the U.S. Supreme Court is surely a great success.

The first American Constitution was that of Virginia, which formulated, for the first time, a list of rights. The Virginia Declaration of Rights, adopted on 12 June 1776, which echoed Locke almost verbatim, stated (Article 1):

---

[33] In regard to the word 'Declaration', Hunt observes:

> The history of the word 'declaration' gives a first indication of the shift in sovereignty. The English word 'declaration' comes from the French *déclaration*. [...]
> In other words, the act of declaring was linked to sovereignty. [...]
> In 1776 and 1789, the words 'charter', 'petition', and 'bill' seemed inadequate to the task of guaranteeing rights (the same would be true in 1948). 'Petition' and 'bill' both implied a request or appeal to a higher power (a bill was originally 'a petition to the sovereign'), and 'charter' often meant an old document or deed. 'Declaration' had less of a musty, submissive air. Moreover, unlike 'petition', 'bill', or even 'charter', 'declaration' could signify the intent to seize sovereignty. [...]
> The acts of declaring were at once backward- and forward-looking. In each case, the declarees claimed to be confirming rights that already existed and were unquestionable. But in so doing they effected a revolution in sovereignty and created an entirely new basis for government. [...] Even while claiming these rights already existed and they were merely defending them, the deputies created something radically new: governments justified by their guarantee of universal rights. (p. 114, 115, 116)

[34] http://files.libertyfund.org/files/837/Montesquieu_0171-01_EBk_v6.0.pdf.

> That all men are by nature equally free and independent, and have certain inherent rights, of which, when they enter into a state of society, they cannot, by any compact, deprive or divest their posterity; namely, the enjoyment of life and liberty, with the means of acquiring and possessing property, and pursuing and obtaining happiness and safety.[35]

Thomas Jefferson (1743–1826) used the Virginia Declaration of Rights to draft the first part of the American Declaration of Independence (The unanimous Declaration of the 13 United States of America) proclaimed on 4 July 1776[36] that stated: "We hold these truths to be self-evident, that all men are created equal, that they are endowed by their Creator with certain unalienable Rights, that among these are Life, Liberty and the pursuit of Happiness". It was also the basis of the first Ten Amendments to the United States' Constitution of 1787, which were adopted on 15 December 1791[37].

In France, the National Assembly adopted the *Déclaration des droits de l'homme et du citoyen* (Declaration of the Rights of Man and of the Citizen) on 26 August 1789[38]. "As a consequence, the use of rights language increased dramatically after 1789. Evidence for this surge can be found readily in the number of titles in English using the word 'rights': it quadrupled in the 1790s (418) as compared to the 1780s (95) or any previous decade during the eighteenth century" (Hunt 2008, p. 135). In Alain Touraine's (1992) opinion, the French Declaration is "the supreme creation of modern political philosophy" (p. 74). It summarized political contractualism, namely: Human beings possess natural rights prior to life in society, which the State must protect. The ethical-legal individualism triumphant in the French Revolution is condensed in its two first Articles:

---

[35] http://constitution.org/bor/vir_bor.htm.

[36] www.ushistory.org/declaration/document/.

[37] www.ushistory.org/documents/amendments.htm.

[38] www.hrcr.org/docs/frenchdec.html: and www.textes.justice.gouv.fr/textes-fondamentaux-10086/droits-de-lhomme-et-libertes-fondamentales-10087/declaration-des-droits-de-lhomme-et-du-citoyen-de-1789-10116.html, and: www.hrcr.org/docs/frenchdec.html

The American Declaration of Independence was highly influential in France, where nine different translations were made between 1776 and 1783.

In 1788, facing bankruptcy caused, to a great extent, by the participation in the American War of Independence, Louis XVI agreed to convoke the Estates-General, which had last met in 1614. The three Estates should elect delegates and write up lists of grievances. A number of them "referred to 'the inalienable rights of man', 'the imprescriptible rights of free men', 'the rights and the dignity of man and the citizen', or 'the rights of enlightened and free men', but 'rights of man' predominated" (Hunt 2008, p. 128). The Estates-General opened on 5 May 1789. On 17 June, the deputies of the Third Estate unilaterally pronounced themselves members of a National Assembly. They were eventually joined by the two other Estates. On 6 July, a Committee on the Constitution was set up, and on 9 July it announced that it would begin with the drafting of a Declaration of rights. Lafayette and Condorcet had already prepared draft Declarations. On 14 July, the attack of the Bastille (*Prise de la Bastille*) occured. The deputies devoted six days to the debate (20–24 August, and 26 August). "Exhausted by the discussion of articles and amendments, on 27 August the Assembly voted to postpone any further discussion until after drawing up a new constitution. They never reopened the question. In this somewhat backhanded fashion, the Declaration of the Rights of Man and Citizen took its definitive shape" (p. 131). On 5 October, under a great popular pressure, Louis XVI gave his formal approval to the Declaration.

1. Men are born and remain free and equal in rights. Social distinctions may be founded only upon the general good.
2. The aim of all political association is the preservation of the natural and imprescriptible rights of man. These rights are liberty, property, security, and resistance to oppression.

The individualism of the 1789 French Declaration meant a New Law celebrated as the rising of a new era. Hegel said, in *Vorlesungen über die Philosophie der Geschichte* (Lessons on the Philosophy of History, 1837), that the French Revolution was a "magnificent dawn", because "the principle of the liberty of will made the most of itself against the existing Law", making possible the constitutional reconstruction of the State (in Monchablon 1989, p. 168, 169). Jules Michelet (1798–1874) wrote in the Preface to *Histoire de la Révolution Française* (History of the French Revolution 1847): "Our parents [...] found the arbitrary in heaven and in earth, and began the Law", by proclaiming "the right of the individual" (ib. p. 176, 177). Victor Hugo (1802–1885) exclaimed in *William Shakespeare* (1864): "yes, we are your children, Revolution" (ib. p. 213). Jean Jaurès (1859–1914) wrote in *La justice dans l'humanité* (Justice in humanity 1902) that:

> ... it is the French Revolution's credit to have proclaimed that in every individual humankind had the same inherent excellence, the same dignity and rights, and when it proclaimed this symbol of justice, when it declared that governments, societies, should be submitted to rules drawn from this idea of human right, the Revolution did more than shaping a new world, it created a new philosophy of history.

In the Conclusion of *Histoire Socialiste de la Révolution Française* (Socialist History of the French Revolution 1903), he noticed that, in spite of everything, "the new Law took definite possession of history" (ib. p. 229, 227).

Louis A. Saint-Just (1767–1794) said in *L'esprit de la Révolution et de la constitution* (The Spirit of the Revolution and of the Constitution 1791): "The rights of man would have been the ruin of Athens or Lacedemonia: there, one knew only the beloved homeland, each one forgot himself for it. The rights of man made France stronger, here the homeland forgets itself for their children" (ib. p. 81). Before, Anne R. J. Turgot (1727–1781) had written in *Seconde Lettre sur la Tolérance* (Second Letter on Tolerance, 1754): "Governments got too used to sacrifice always the happiness of the individuals to alleged rights of society. It is forgotten that society is made for the individuals, that it is instituted only to protecting the rights of everyone, securing compliance with all reciprocal duties" (ib. p. 57).

A controversy on the historical priority between the American and French Declarations of Rights involved Georg Jellineck and Émile Boutmy, at the beginning of the twentieth century. In this regard, Henkin (1978) remarked: "Americans tend to think of human rights as their special gift to the world [... but] the French revolution and declaration were probably more influential than ours in spreading them in many parts of the world" (p. 13). Lord Acton (John Emerich Edward Dalberg-Acton, first Baron Acton, 1834–1902), an English historian, said that the French Declaration "outweighs libraries, and is stronger than all the armies of Napoleon" (as cit. ib. p. xii)[39].

[39] Lord Acton is the author of the famous phrase: "All power tends to corrupt, and absolute power corrupts absolutely".

Towards the end of the eighteenth century, the concept of natural rights (droits naturels) had acquired a secularized content and the formula was progressively replaced by 'rights of man' (*droits de l'homme*) and 'human rights', though the French Declaration still reads "*droits naturels, inaliénables et sacrés de l'homme*" (Preamble), "*droits naturels et imprescriptibles de l'homme*" (Article II), "*droits naturels de chaque homme*" (Article IV). Henkin pointed out:

> The American and French revolutions, and the declarations that expressed the principles that inspired them, took 'natural rights' and made them secular, rational, universal, individual, democratic, and radical. For divine foundations for the rights of man they substituted (or perhaps only added) a social-contractual base. (p. 5)

Like Natural Law theory, the discourse of natural/human rights attracted much criticism from different sides.

Edmund Burke (1729–1797) scorned the "chaff and rags, and paltry, blurred shreds of paper about the rights of man", in *Reflections on the Revolution in France* (1790)[40], affirming that "their abstract perfection is their practical defect [...] and in proportion as they are metaphysically true, they are morally and politically false".

Bentham famously wrote in *Anarchical Fallacies* (1843)[41], regarding "the nothingness of the laws of nature and the rights of man that have been grounded on them":

> *Natural rights* is simple nonsense: natural and imprescriptible rights, rhetorical nonsense—nonsense upon stilts. But this rhetorical nonsense ends in the old strain of mischievous nonsense: for immediately a list of these pretended natural rights is given, and those are so expressed as to present to view legal rights. And of these rights, whatever they are, there is not, it seems, any one of which any government *can*, upon any occasion whatever, abrogate the smallest particle.
>
> [...]
>
> Right, the substantive right, is the child of law: from real laws come real rights; but from imaginary laws, from laws of nature, fancied and invented by poets, rhetoricians, and dealers in moral and intellectual poisons, come imaginary rights, a bastard brood of monsters, 'gorgons and chimaeras dire'. And thus it is that from legal rights, the offspring of law, and friends of peace, come anti-legal rights, the mortal enemies of law, the subverters of government, and the assassins of security.

Joseph-Marie, Comte de Maistre (1753–1821) wrote in *Considérations sur la France* (Considerations on France 1796)[42]:

> The 1795 [the French] constitution, like its predecessors, was made for man. But there is no such thing as man in the world. During my life, I have seen Frenchmen, Italians, Russians, and so on; thanks to Montesquieu, I even know that one can be Persian; but I must say, as for man, I have never come across him anywhere; if he exists, he is completely unknown to me.

[40] www.gutenberg.org/files/15679/15679-h/15679-h.htm.

[41] www.law.georgetown.edu/faculty/lpw/documents/Bentham_Anarchical_Fallacies.pdf.

[42] http://maistre.ath.cx:8000/considerations_on_france.

Karl Marx's (1818–1883) criticism in *On the Jewish Question* (1844)[43] is well known too:

> Let us examine, for a moment, the so-called rights of man—to be precise, the rights of man in their authentic form, in the form which they have among those who discovered them, the North Americans and the French. [...]
> The *droits de l'homme*, the rights of man, are, as such, distinct from the *droits du citoyen*, the rights of the citizen. Who is *homme* as distinct from *citoyen*? None other than the *member of civil society*. Why is the member of civil society called 'man', simply man; why are his rights called the *rights of man*? How is this fact to be explained? From the relationship between the political state and civil society, from the nature of political emancipation.
> Above all, we note the fact that the so-called rights of man, the *droits de l'homme* as distinct from the *droits du citoyen*, are nothing but the rights of a *member of civil society*—i.e. the rights of egoistic man, of man separated from other men and from the community.

One reason for the criticism of natural rights was, no doubt, the excesses of the French Revolution, often attributed to the 1789 Declaration. It was reflected in the popularization of the expression "the tyranny of the majority". Another one was the "chameleon-like character" of the idea of natural right. Jeremy Waldron (2009a) notes: "It could be used to defend economic liberty against government attempts to redress inequality, or it could be used to condemn existing inequalities of social conditions and to argue for a natural right to subsistence for the poor" (p. 23). It was used by both sides in the slavery controversy, from the 1780s to the 1860s.

Henkin (1978) pointed out: "Thomas Paine had proclaimed constitutionalism as *the* right of man and as the foundation of all rights of man", and "constitutionalism became identified with respect for individual rights" (p. 135, 32). Paine even qualified the American Constitution as a "political Bible"[44]. Indeed, as Nowak (2003) noted: "Human rights in the legal sense have only been in existence since the establishment of constitutions, in other words, the development of human rights is closely linked with the era of constitutionalism" (p. 7).

> As a rule, constitutions consist of two distinct parts: a formal and a material one. The formal part contains rules concerning the highest bodies within the state, procedures of and the appointment of such bodies, as well as the main structural principles of the state [...]. The material part lays down the values, aims and objectives professed by the state [...] as well as fundamental rights. (p. 8)

The 1787 American Constitution, with the 1791 Bill of Rights, and the French 1791 Constitution, with the 1789 Declaration in its Preamble, were the historical beginnings of the "age of constitutions" (Henkin 1978, p. 32). After the end of the Napoleonic Empire and the Vienna Peace Conference (1815), a constitutional movement started in Europe. As for France, the 1793 Constitution was introduced by a new Declaration, more extensive than the 1789 one (35 Articles, instead of 17). The Preamble of the French 1848 Constitution[45], drawn up by the National Constituent Assembly elected following the revolution of February 1848, which created the

---

[43] www.marxists.org/archive/marx/works/1844/jewish-question/.

[44] *West's Encyclopedia of American Law*: www.answers.com/topic/natural-law.

[45] www.assemblee-nationale.fr/histoire/constitutions/constitution-deuxieme-republique.asp.

Second Republic (terminated by a *Coup d'État* in 1851), adopted "as principle Liberty, Equality and Fraternity" (Preamble). In the Preamble of the 1946 Constitution, "the people of France proclaim anew that each human being, without distinction of race, religion or creed, possesses sacred and inalienable rights. They solemnly reaffirm the rights and freedoms of man and the citizen enshrined in the Declaration of Rights of 1789 and the fundamental principles acknowledged in the laws of the Republic"[46].

The twentieth century saw the constitutional rise of economic, social and cultural rights. In this respect, Christian Tomuschat (2008) wrote:

> During the whole of the nineteenth century, national constitutions did not depart from that line. Invariably the catalogues of human rights, which were progressively deemed to constitute a necessary component of a modern constitutional text, were confined to classical freedoms. In that sense, the Belgian Constitution of 1831, which had a considerable influence on constitutional developments all over Europe, lists the well-known freedoms in Articles 4–23, without embarking on new paths. Prussia largely adopted that model in enacting its Constitution in 1850.
> Only since the beginning of the twentieth century have civil liberties lost their monopoly as constituting the only class of fundamental rights acknowledged at a constitutional level. (p. 27)

The 1917 Constitution of the Mexican United States[47] recognized a broad set of economic, social and cultural rights. The Declaration of Rights of the Working and Exploited People[48], drafted by Lenin and adopted by the Third All-Russian Congress of Soviets in January 1918, reflected the achievements of the Great October Socialist Revolution[49]. It was included in the Constitution of the Russia Soviet Federative Socialist Republic adopted by the Fifth All-Russia Congress of Soviets on 10 July 1918. The 1919 Constitution of the German Reich (known as the Weimar Constitution)[50] recognized civil, political, economic, social and cultural rights.

More than 80 % of the Constitutions adopted between 1778 and 1948 included provisions concerning human rights (see Bates 2010, p. 25), but the concrete advancements were not far-reaching[51]. Between 1949 and 1975, the percentage rose to 93 %. This tendency grew in the 1990s with the new constitutional texts of the States members of the former Union of the Soviet Socialist Republics (USSR) and Eastern Bloc.

---

[46] www.conseil-constitutionnel.fr/conseil-constitutionnel/root/bank_mm/anglais/cst3.pdf.

[47] www.latinamericanstudies.org/mexico/1917-Constitution.htm.

[48] www.marx2mao.com/Lenin/DRWP18.html.

[49] www.marxists.org/history/ussr/government/constitution/1918/article1.htm.

[50] www.zum.de/psm/weimar/weimar_vve.php.

[51] For example, in France, Olympe de Gouges drafted in 1791 a *Déclaration des droits de la femme et de la citoyenne* (Declaration of the Rights of Woman and the Female Citizen), but was guillotined on 3 November 1793. In the USA, slavery was permitted for long decades and it was a crime to assist run-away slaves. The Supreme Court decided, in 1857 (Case *Dred Scott v Sandford*), that the *Bill of Rights* protected the right to property of slaves … which were not addressed by the constitutional guarantees. The abolition of slavery happened only after a civil war, new amendments to the Federal Constitution and the *Emancipation Proclamation* of President Lincoln, in 1863. However, racial discrimination was not legally abolished before the 1950s.

Following Giovanni Bognetti (2003), two phases may be distinguished in the history of the Western Constitutionalism:

> In the *nineteenth century*, the state model prevailing on both sides of the Atlantic was the *classical liberal model*. The legal system was composed of relatively few stable norms, some of which were modified from time to time by special legislation. These norms were meant to be interpreted narrowly. They would define and protect the autonomy of the individual in all areas of social life, in particular the economy, culture and politics. [...]
> The *twentieth century* witnessed the advent and the expansion of the model of the *interventionist state*. The progress of the new model was primarily connected with the industrialization of society. [...]
> All new written constitutions dating from the period following World War II phrased the guarantees of fundamental rights in ways that reflected the new interventionist model. It is important to notice that the new interventionist model has been adopted in two different versions: a version which is more responsive to the old idea of individual freedom (the neo-liberal version), and a version which is more open to the values of social solidarity (a version that may be called 'democratic-social').

At international level, the situation was rather contradictory, as Nowak (2003) notices:

> International law provided that prisoners of war had a right to be protected from torture and to be treated with human dignity, yet by the same token states could go as far as committing genocide on 'their own' people without interference or reaction from outsiders. [...] This double standard of morals was the result of the dogma of state sovereignty and the international principle of non-interference in national matters. (p. 14, 15)

It took the "twentieth-century moral catastrophe" (Habermas 2012, p. 64) to fully revive the idea of Natural Law and natural rights. The "barbarous acts which have outraged the conscience of mankind", as reads the UDHR (second preambular paragraph)[52], "definitively paved the way for a new understanding of the relationship between the individual, the state, and the international community. [...] It had been learned during the horrendous years from 1933 to 1945 that a state apparatus can turn into a killing machine" (Tomuschat 2008, p. 22). The internationalization of the human rights protection became a moral and political imperative.

3.3 Internationalization and Codification of Human Rights

3.3.1 Beginnings

Following Schabas (2000):

> International law's role in the protection of national, racial, ethnic and religious groups from persecution can be traced to the Peace of Westphalia of 1648, which provided certain guarantees for religious minorities. [...] These concerns with the rights of national, eth-

[52] www.un.org/en/documents/udhr/.

nic and religious groups evolved into a doctrine of humanitarian intervention which was invoked to justify military activity on some occasions during the nineteenth century.

The author adds: "International human rights law can also trace its origins to the law of armed conflict or international humanitarian law" (p. 15) whose codification began in the nineteenth century[53].

In effect, the international protection of human rights was already envisaged by the protection of religious, linguistic and national minorities clauses progressively included in some treaties, such as those of Oliva (1660), Nimègue (1678), Passarowitz (1718) and Vienna (1815). Religious freedom was probably the first human right internationally protected, but its recognition was not general. It implies the recognition of other freedoms, such as freedom of association, of assembly and of expression.

In the nineteenth century, the international protection of human rights was advanced by the formal ban of slavery and slave trade, probably as old as the human species. Slavery was abolished in the British Empire in 1834, but it was illegal in England since 1772. The General Act of the African Conference signed in Berlin on 26 February 1885 was a landmark in the struggle against it. Other steps on the way of the internationalization of the human rights protection were the first initiatives towards the abolishment of the death penalty (Portugal did it in 1867), the diplomatic protection of citizens abroad, the humanitarian intervention[54] and the creation of the International Red Cross Committee in 1863, which gave rise to the International Humanitarian Law (IHL) or Geneva Law (see Glossary).

Meanwhile, after its flourishing in the seventeenth and eighteenth centuries—culminating in the American and French Revolutions and Declarations—the term natural/human rights fell into general oblivion during the nineteenth century. Following Hunt (2008): "The long gap in the history of human rights, from their initial formulation in the American and French Revolutions to the United Nations' Universal Declaration in 1948" (p. 176) was to a great extent due to the taking over of nationalism, but other factors also contributed, in particular the rising of legal positivism, according to which, as we know, Law is only the written, positive Law enacted by State[55]. In addition: "Thinkers like Hegel, Comte, Marx, Weber, and Freud, became more interested in social processes and structures, rather than

[53] Michelo Hansungule (2010) notes:

> The ancient Indian concept of human rights and humanitarian laws based on wars and regulated humanitarian laws to be adopted before, during and after war. The yardstick to measure human rights during ancient period was mostly conducted in the field of battle. The ancient writings contained rules of warfare that were laid down in the legal texts such as *Manusmriti* or the code of *Manu* (200 BC to AD 100), the *Mahabharat* (1000 BC), Kautilya's *Arthastra* (300 BC) and Sukranitisar of *Sukracharya*. (p. 24)

[54] Humanitarian intervention "represented, until the First World War, the sole kind of international protection of human rights" (Vasak 1976, p. 343). It meant that a foreigner could be entitled to better treatment than a national.

[55] Although the 1848 French Constitution, for instance, refers in Article 3 to *des droits et des devoirs antérieurs et supérieurs aux lois positives* [rights and duties previous and higher than positive laws].

individual rights, and increased nationalism also shifted the emphasis away from the individual and to the nation" (Encyclopedia Britannica 2012). Notwithstanding: "Through the nineteenth and early twentieth centuries, benevolent societies had kept the flame of universal human rights burning as nations turned in upon themselves" (Hunt 2008, p. 205).

The revival of the idea of human rights began slowly after the First World War as a reaction against the ideologies and practices of totalitarian regimes, namely those of Stalin and Hitler. The League of Nations played a significant role.

During the drafting of the Covenant of the League of Nations adopted in 1919, in Versailles (France)[56], in the aftermath of the First World War, human rights matters were discussed, especially non-discrimination. The American President Woodrow Wilson proposed to include in the Covenant an obligation of all League members to respect religious freedom and to refrain from discrimination on the basis of religion. The UK delegate (Lord Robert Cecil) proposed to give the Council of the League a right of intervention against States adopting a policy of religious intolerance. For the USA this went too far. The Japanese delegate (Baron Makino) proposed to extend the non-discrimination clause to discrimination on the basis of race or nationality against foreigners who would be nationals of League members. The USA and the UK did not accept. As a result, no provision on the matter was agreed upon and the Covenant did not formally mention human rights. However, it dealt with many human rights matters, in particular two Articles (22 and 23) related to its Mandate System, which was an international control mechanism, as well as to its system for the protection of minorities.

The 'minority clauses'—to protecting the members of linguistic, religious or racial minorities—were included in peace treaties with Austria, Bulgaria, Hungary and Turkey (not with Germany), in particular treaties with Czechoslovakia, Greece, Poland, Romania and Yugoslavia, and in declarations which Albania, Estonia, Finland, Latvia and Lithuania had to make for being admitted into the League of Nations. Similar clauses were included in two bilateral treaties, namely between Germany and Poland, regarding Upper Silesia, and between Germany and Lithuania regarding the Memel Territory. The Council of the League of Nations was assigned certain supervisory powers concerning the minority clauses, including receiving petitions relating to the minority clauses directly addressed to it by members of a minority[57].

The minority clauses regime was not limited to the members of minorities as such. It consisted of three categories of obligations: protection of life and liberty of all inhabitants of the country or region concerned; guarantee to all nationals of equality before the Law; special guarantees for nationals belonging to minorities, such as the use of their language and the right to establish social and religious institutions. Jan H. Burgers (1992) commented:

---

[56] www.dshs.wa.gov/pdf/oip/AboriginalRights/ch15.pdf.

[57] "The first time that the individual was given a remedy which would permit him to take action on the international scene to protect his rights, including the right to education, was after the First World War, under the Minority Treaties" (Al-Samman 1987, p. 47).

> Although the minority clauses only covered a handful of countries, they were of historical significance as unprecedented limitations on national sovereignty under international law. [...] In 1925 some states bound by minority clauses proposed in the Assembly of the League the elaboration of a general convention among all League members determining their obligations towards minorities. This proposal was rejected. The same happened to similar proposals in 1930 and 1932. (p. 450)

The Mandates Commission (Article 22 of the Covenant) was "an indisputable achievement" (Verdoodt 1964, p. 37). An Office precursor of the present UN High Commissioner for Refugees was also created. In 1922, the Permanent Court of International Justice was established that also dealt with matters related to human rights concerning the enforcement of the minorities' treaties. In 1924, a Temporary Slavery Commission of Experts was set up. In 1926, a Slavery Convention was adopted (amended in 1953 by the Supplementary Convention on the Abolition of Slavery). In 1932, an Advisory Committee of Experts on Slavery was established. The League pushed forward the international protection of human rights notably with the establishment (Part XIII, Sect. I, of the Covenant) of the International Labor Organization (ILO), first named International Labor Office.

The League of Nations failed for many reasons[58]. The fact that the USA and the USSR kept outside was its original weakness. The principle of unanimity in decision-making contributed too. Its weakening entered an irreversible course in the 1930s, when several States withdrew, including Germany. The context-pretext of Germany withdrawing was a petition submitted to the Council of the League on 12 May 1933, a few months after Hitler had come into power on 30 January, by Franz Bernheim, a 32 year old German national of Jewish descent. He had been a resident of Gleiwitz in Upper Silesia and then temporarily staying in Prague, and had been discharged by a German business because all Jewish employees had to be dismissed. The petition was based on the 1922 German-Polish Convention regarding Upper Silesia (Article 147).

The Council discussed the petition during its session of 22 May to 6 June 1933. A compromise was reached with the payment of 1,600 marks to the petitioner. This and other cases raised matters of principle, however, which were discussed in the Assembly of the League during its regular annual session that lasted from 25 September to 11 October. The Nazi Minister Joseph Gœbbels suddenly arrived as a German Delegation member, but did not take the floor. He only gave a long speech for an audience of invited journalists in a Geneva hotel, on 27 September, and then went back to Germany. Also the German Delegation took no part in the general debate in the plenary Assembly. Cassin (1887–1976), who was a member of the French Delegation to the Assembly of the League, testified:

> The day when the Assembly dared to invoke the general principles authorizing the legally organized international community to protect human rights, even in a field not covered by this or that special minority treaty, Hitler alleged the absolute sovereignty of the Third Reich over its nationals to refuse to the League of Nations any control right and, on 14 October 1933, withdrew from it. (in Verdoodt 1964, p. 37)

[58] The League of Nations ceased to exist on 20 April 1946.

In a doctoral thesis on *Les droits internationaux de l'homme* (The international rights of man), submitted during the same year at the University of Paris, its author (Gramain 1933) remarked that the International Law "did not yet achievè to impose on States, regarding their own nationals, the minimal legal treatment it imposes regarding national minorities" (p. 26). In his opinion: "Solidarity, interdependence, the new basis of the International Law, creates a common juridical conscience". Burgers (1992) remarked: "While in the period between the First and the Second World Wars most governments were unwilling to accept obligations under international law regarding the treatment of their own citizens, a far more positive attitude developed among the scholars of international law" (p. 450) and many freedom-loving intellectuals. Let us see.

Alejandro Álvarez (1868–1960) was a Chilean jurist co-founder and Secretary-General of the American Institute of International Law in 1912 (active until 1938), with James Brown Scott, both of whom attempted to foster better relations between the USA and Latin America. In 1917, he submitted to this Institute a draft declaration on the fundamentals of future international law that included a section on "international rights of the individual".

André Nicolayevitch Mandelstam (1869–1949)—"the principal champion of international protection for human rights in the period after Versailles" (p. 451)—was a Russian jurist and former diplomat under the Tsarist Government. He emigrated to Paris, after the 1917 Russian Revolution, and devoted himself to the study and teaching of International Law. In 1921, he proposed to the *Institut de Droit International* (International Law Institute), founded in 1873 in Belgium, the creation of a commission to study the protection of minorities and of human rights in general, of which he was rapporteur.

Antoine F. Frangulis (1888–1975), another member of the Paris *immigrés* community, was a Greek jurist and diplomat who had represented his country at the League of Nations from 1920 to 1922. In 1926, he founded the *Académie Diplomatique Internationale* (International Diplomatic Academy), together with Álvarez, among others. One of the first initiatives of the Academy was to set up a commission to study the question of the protection of human rights, of which Frangulis and Mandelstam were members. On 28 November 1928, the Academy adopted a resolution taking as starting point the first and the second category of the obligations laid down in the minorities clauses. The resolution, considering:

> That the international protection of the Rights of Man and of the citizen, consecrated by the minorities' treaties, corresponds to the juridical feeling of the contemporary world;
> [...]
> Takes the vow of the establishment of a world convention, under the patronage of the League of Nations, securing the protection and the respect of said rights.

Mandelstam had submitted a similar proposal to the International Law Institute that was adopted on 12 October 1929, at its plenary session in Briarcliff Lodge, close to New York, titled *Déclaration des droits internationaux de l'homme* (Declaration of the International Rights of Man)[59], consisting of a Preamble and six Articles. Considering:

> that the juridical conscience of the civilized world demands the recognition to individual of rights out of reach by the State;
> that the Declarations of Rights inscribed in a great number of Constitutions and especially in the American and French Declarations of the end of the 18th century have not addressed only the citizen, but the man too;
> [...]
> that it is important to extend to the whole world the international recognition of human rights;

the *Déclaration des droits internationaux de l'homme* proclaimed the rights to life, liberty, property, freedom of religion, use of the mother tong, non-discrimination, real equality and nationality. The New York meeting was chaired by Albert de Geouffre de la Pradelle, the Director of the *Institut des Hautes Études Internationales* founded in 1920 in Paris by himself, Álvarez and Paul Fauchille. In this regard, Tomuschat (2008) notes:

> One of the few exceptions to the intellectual aridity of the 20 years between the end of World War I and the outbreak of World War II was the *Déclaration des droits internationaux de l'homme*, adopted by the Institute of International Law at its New York session on 12 October 1929. This declaration marked a resolute departure from the traditional stance according to which the relationship between a state and its citizens was a matter of domestic law, not to be interfered with from outside, neither by third states nor by institutions of the international community. Yet its preamble is more courageous than its operative part. (p. 21)

On 11 November 1931, on the basis of a report by Mandelstam, the Council of the International Federation of Leagues for the Defense of the Rights of Man and of the Citizen adopted a resolution endorsing the New York Declaration. The Assembly of the International Union of Associations for the League of Nations, meeting in Montreux from 3 to 7 June 1933, also discussed the matter, again on the basis of a proposal submitted by Mandelstam, and a special committee of seven members was charged to examine on what bases a draft convention on international guarantees for human rights could be established. Mandelstam was a member of this committee, which also included, among others, the French Jacques Dumas, the Belgian Henri Rolin, and the French George Scelle (later coopted).

Dumas gave a course, in 1937, at The Hague Academy of International Law on 'The international guarantee of human rights'. He said that "man is the subject *par excellence* of International Law", that "human rights" are the principle, inspiration and purpose of every Law (Dumas 1937, p. 5). "This is increasingly the point of view of the great theorists of International Law", who "teach that man is the sole and supreme end of every Law" (p. 7). Rolin was delegate in the San Francisco Conference, in 1945, having proposed that the UN Charter should open with the words "We, the peoples". In 1968, he became President of the European Court of Human Rights.

---

[59] www.idi-iil.org/idiF/resolutionsF/1929_nyork_03_fr.pdf.

Participating in the Assembly of the League of Nations during its regular annual session, from 25 September to 11 October 1933, as delegate for Haiti, Frangulis tabled a draft resolution, on behalf of the President of Haiti, Stenio Vincent, according to which a worldwide convention on human rights should be prepared under the auspices of the League. Several delegations resumed the idea of generalization of the protection of minorities. All proposals were referred to a sub-committee. The plenary Assembly adopted unanimously only part of a draft resolution, on 11 October, the last day of its session. The monthly journal *La Revue Diplomatique* reproduced the text of Frangulis' speech of 30 September under the headline 'The rights of man and of the citizen before the fourteenth Assembly of the League of Nations', affirming that he had been named in Geneva "the delegate of the rights of man" (Burgers 1992, p. 459). At the Assembly session of 1934, he submitted a brief Haitian draft resolution calling for the convening of a conference and the generalization of the human rights protection, but it found insufficient support.

In July 1936, the French *Ligue des Droits de l'Homme* (League of Human Rights) adopted at its congress held in Dijon a text named *Complément à la Déclaration des Droits de l'Homme* (Complement to the Declaration of the Rights of Man and of the Citizen, 1789 and 1793)[60], consisting of a Preamble and 14 Articles. It is a largely unknown but innovating text, which would be one of the references of the UDHR drafting, through Cassin (who participated in the Congress of Dijon as a member of the *Ligue*). Article 1 of the *Complément* is revealing of a pioneering vision of the protection of human rights:

> The rights of the human being do not admit any distinction of sex, race, nation, religion or opinions. They are inalienable and imprescriptible rights, tied to the human person; they should be always respected, in any situation, and guaranteed against every kind of political and social oppression. The international protection of human rights should be universally organized and guaranteed, so that no State could refuse the exercise of such rights to a single human being living within its territory.

In spite of all efforts and initiatives, the disregard for the human rights idea prevailing during the nineteenth century continued during the decades after the First World War, mainly in Europe, as Burgers found. In the Netherlands, for instance, "the gigantic subject index of the Royal Library in The Hague had no entry for human rights up to the year 1980!" (Burgers 1992, p. 460)

> In Latin America, the human rights idea was held in esteem by the influential anti-clericalist current which continued to pay homage to the spiritual legacy of the Enlightenment. In the United States, the idea was kept alive, at least on a theoretical level, as an essential element of the national heritage. Nevertheless, I sometimes get the impression that even in the United States the human rights concept went almost out of circulation. This is illustrated by three American dictionaries I consulted [...]. (ib.)

In the UK, the Association for Education in Citizenship, led by Sir Ernest Simon, organized a conference in July 1937 on 'The Challenge to Democracy' which was addressed by 12 notable speakers (whose speeches were published in book form).

[60] www.ldh-france.org/1936-COMPLEMENT-DE-LA-LDH-A-LA.

It was inspired by the belief in human rights, but the concept was never explicitly mentioned.

In 1940, the book *Freedom: Its Meaning*, consisting of contributions by 19 distinguished thinkers such as Henri Bergson, Benedetto Croce, John Dewey, Albert Einstein, Thomas Mann, Jacques Maritain, Bertrand Russell, and A. N. Whitehead was published.

> This can really be considered a representative sample of freedom-loving western intellectuals in the 1930s. Significantly, in the book's index containing over six hundred entries, including one for 'human nature', there are no entries for 'human rights', 'rights of man' or 'fundamental freedoms'. Although all the articles deal with the concept of freedom, most contributors do not mention the human rights concept at all. Two American authors mention it in passing. Maritain uses at least the term 'human rights' [...]. Only the geneticist Haldane deals at some length with such freedoms as freedom of movement, freedom to communicate, political freedom and religious liberty. None of the contributors calls for a reassertion of the human rights idea as a rallying cry for the defense of freedom against the totalitarian menace. (p. 461)

The human rights idea did not play a significant role in the clandestine documents of the French Resistance of 1940–1944 during the German occupation either. Burgers concluded:

> Whereas before the Second World War the idea of giving human rights an international status was only advocated by some limited circles without meeting a meaningful political response, during the war it finally broke through to the mainstream of public discussion. A flood of publications developed on this issue, mostly in the United States. We may assume that much of it was triggered by Wells' Rights of Man campaign and further stimulated by Roosevelt's battle-cry of the Four Freedoms. (p. 471)

Herbert G. Wells (1866–1946) wrote on 23 October 1939 a letter to *The Times* referring to "the extensive demand for a statement of War Aims on the part of young and old, who want to know more precisely what we are fighting for". He said in his letter:

> At various rises in the history of our communities, beginning with Magna Carta and going through various Bills of Rights, Declarations of the Rights of Man and so forth, it has been our custom to produce a specific declaration of the broad principles on which our public and social life is based.... The present time seems peculiarly suitable for such a restatement of the spirit in which we face life in general and the present combat in particular.... In conjunction with a few friends I have drafted a trial statement of the rights of man brought up to date. I think that this statement may serve to put the War Aims discussion upon a new and more hopeful footing. (as cit. ib. p. 464)

The letter included his draft 'Declaration of Rights', consisting of a short Preamble and ten Articles. Various personalities had contributed to the draft.

The Times refused to open its pages for a Great Debate, but the *Daily Herald* agreed to serve as forum for the discussion. A drafting committee was formed that included Wells, Norman Angell (recipient of the 1933 Nobel Peace Prize), John Orr (who after the war became the Director-General of the UN Director-General of the FAO (UN Food and Agriculture Organization), Viscount Sankey (a former Lord Chancellor, i.e. president of the House of Lords), Francis Williams (the editor of the *Daily Herald*), among others. Wells wrote texts in several periodicals and included the draft in his books published in 1940 *The New World Order* and *The Commonsense of War and Peace*. He sent the draft Declaration to many people he knew, including the American President Franklin Delano Roosevelt (1882–1945), who answered on 9 November 1939. They knew each other, as Wells had lunched more than once with Roosevelt and his wife Eleanor Roosevelt in the White House (Roosevelt was also an early member of the International Diplomatic Academy).

The final version of the Declaration as elaborated by the drafting committee—with a long Preamble and ten Clauses—was published in the *Daily Herald* under the title 'The Rights of Man' from 5 to 24 February 1940, with comments by distinguished persons continuing up to 1 March. The Declaration was later referred to as the 'Sankey Declaration' (for it not being linked too closely with Wells' name). It was spread internationally too. Reactions were received, among others, from Mahatma Gandhi (1869–1948), Jawaharlal Nehru (1889–1964), Chaim Weizmann (1874–1952) and Jan Christiaan Smuts (1870–1950), who in 1945 drafted the Preamble of the UN Charter.

Meanwhile, other initiatives were taken and books published, such as:

- On 14 April 1941, Wilfred Parsons S.J proposed 'An International Bill of Rights' to the Catholic Association for International Peace.
- On 3 June 1942, Rollin McNitt, honorary Dean of the Law School of Southwestern University (Los Angeles) proposed an 'International Declaration of Human Rights'.
- In July, a special legal subcommittee for studying the problems of postwar international organization, set up by the USA Department, presented a preliminary draft and in December 1942 a final draft of an International Bill of Rights.
- Still in 1942, Jacques Maritain published *Les Droits de l'Homme et la Loi Naturelle* (The Rights of Man and the Natural Law, New York).
- In 1943, Irving A. Isaacs published *The International Bill of Rights and Permanent Peace Concordance* (under the aegis of The International Bill of Rights Committee of the Twentieth Century Association, Boston).
- In 1943, Hersch Lauterpacht expounded his draft of an international bill of rights in a public lecture at the University of Cambridge, and 2 years later published the booklet *An International Bill of the Rights of Man* (New York).
- In February 1944, the American Law Institute (ALI, established in 1923), which represented different cultures of the world, made public a *Statement of Essential Human Rights* drafted by a committee of lawyers from 24 countries set up in 1942.
- In May 1944, the Fourth Report of the Commission to Study the Organization of Peace titled *International Safeguard of Human Rights* proposed:

> ... that measures be taken to safeguard human rights throughout the world by (1) convening without delay a United Nations Conference on Human Rights to examine the problem, (2) promulgating, as a result of this conference, an international bill of rights, (3) establishing at the conference a permanent United Nations Commission on Human Rights for the purpose of further developing the standards of human rights and the methods for their protection, (4) seeking the incorporation of major civil rights in national constitutions and

promoting effective means of enforcement in each nation, (5) recognizing the right of individuals or groups, under prescribed limitations, to petition the Human Rights Commission, after exhausting local remedies, in order to call attention to violations.

All this is only the tip of the iceberg, as Burgers (1992) observed, quoting René Brunet, a French ex-Minister and ex-delegate to the League of Nations, who in 1947 noted a:

> ... vast movement of public opinion which, born in England and the United States nearly at the beginning of the hostilities, grew incessantly in force and in scope as the war rolled on. Hundreds of political, scholarly and religious organizations have, by their publications, appeals, manifestations and interventions, spread and impressed the idea that the protection of human rights should be part of the war aims of the Allied Powers, and that the future peace would not be complete if it would not consecrate the principle of international protection of human rights in all States and if it would not guarantee this protection in an effective manner. (p. 474)

Summing up: The recognition of religious freedom, the abolishment of slavery and the slave trade, the protection of the rights of aliens, the humanitarian intervention, the IHL, the protection of minorities and of the rights of workers were steps towards the internationalization of the protection of human rights. However, a Second World War was tragically the 'price' to pay for the taboo of States' omnipotent sovereignty to be definitely challenged[61]. As a document of the European Movement (1949) read:

> Many attempts have been made to extend the rule of law beyond the limits of national frontiers. In the political sphere these have been directed chiefly towards the object of preventing war or of restricting its horrors. On the other hand the idea of restraining a government from perpetrating acts of oppression upon its own citizens was, until recent years, not seriously considered. So long as the tyrant—or his modern counterpart, the totalitarian state—confined his activities to his own national territory, no other country claimed the right to object or interfere. [...]
> It needed the shock of the Nuremberg trials, with their unbelievable revelations of infamy and human degradation, to awaken the conscience of the civilized world. (p. 3)[62]

A new era should begin with the establishment of the Organization of the United Nations, "created to meet the claims coming from the depths of the human conscience" (Cassin 1951, p. 253).

---

[61] The First World War had caused the killing of 18 million persons, soldiers and civil. The number of mortal victims of the Second World War reached about 60 million and caused tens of millions of displaced and refugee peoples.

[62] The International Military Tribunal at Nuremberg (see below) quoted figures according to which, at Auschwitz, at least 2,500,000 prisoners died in the gas chambers, and 500,000 died of disease and starvation. As noted the United Nations War Crimes Commission (1948), "the poison gas used caused excruciating agony before death" (p. 15). Following Adolf Eichmann, the policy of exterminating the Jews resulted in the killing of 6,000,000 Jews, of whom 4,000,000 in the extermination camps. A commandant of Auschwitz said before the Tribunal of Hoess: "It took from 3 to 15 minutes to kill the people in the death chamber, depending upon climatic conditions. [...] After the bodies were removed, our special commandos took off the rings and extracted the gold from the teeth of the corpses" (p. 15).

3.3.2 *Advent of the United Nations (1941–1945)*

In a speech in Chicago (the 'Quarantine Speech' in October 1937), USA President Roosevelt (from 1933 to 1945) had stated that it would be desirable to create a universal peace organization more effective than the League of Nations. Later, he suggested the term 'United Nations'. The shaping of the Organization of the United Nations began in 1941, with the Atlantic Conference, and concluded with the Conference of San Francisco in 1945.

After Japan's attack on Pearl Harbour, on 7 December 1941, the USA resolved to enter the current World War. On 14 August, Roosevelt and Winston Churchill (1874–1965), Prime Minister of the UK (1940–1945 and 1951–1955), met together at the Atlantic Conference "somewhere at sea", in Newfoundland (Canada). They made known "certain common principles in the national policies of their respective countries on which they base[d] their hopes for a better future for the world". Their Joint Declaration of principles became known as the Atlantic Charter[63], "often regarded as a kind of birth-certificate of the United Nations" (Simma 1998, p. 7).

On 1 January 1942, the representatives of 26 States fighting against the Axis Powers (the alliance between Germany, Italy and Japan) signed the Declaration by the United Nations[64] in Washington D. C., subscribing to the "common program of purposes and principles" of the Atlantic Charter. It was the first time the term 'United Nations' was used at an international level.

On 30 October 1943, the Foreign Ministers of the USA, the UK, the USSR, and the Chinese Ambassador to Moscow issued, in that city, the Declaration of Four Nations on General Security[65]. They recognized "the necessity of establishing at the earliest practicable date a general international organization, based on the principle of the sovereign equality of all peace-loving States, and open to membership by all such States, large and small, for the maintenance of international peace and security". The term 'Charter' was, for the first time, applied to the constitutional document of the envisaged Organization. On 5 November, the USA Senate adopted the so-called Connally Resolution and voted in favor of the establishment of an international authority after the war by a majority of 85 to 5 (see Simma, ib. p. 5).

Other summits took place in Cairo (on 26 November 1943) and in Tehran (on 1 December 1943), and other international conferences on special problems led to the establishment of some UN specialized agencies[66]:

- An Agreement was signed in Washington on 9 November 1943 by representatives of 44 nations, creating the United Nations Relief and Rehabilitation Administration (UNRRA) that was the first of the UN agencies formally to come into being.

---

[63] http://avalon.law.yale.edu/wwii/atlantic.asp.

[64] http://avalon.law.yale.edu/20th_century/decade03.asp.

[65] http://avalon.law.yale.edu/wwii/moscow.asp.

[66] A specialized agency is an international organization brought into the UN system under Articles 57 and 63 of the Charter.

- The United Nations Conference on Food and Agriculture, held in Hot Springs, Virginia, from 18 May to 3 June 1943, set up an Interim Commission on Food and Agriculture to draw up the Constitution of the Food and Agriculture Organization of the United Nations (FAO) that came into being when its Constitution was signed on 16 October 1945.
- The United Nations Conference for the Establishment of an Educational, Scientific and Cultural Organization (UNESCO), held in London from 1 to 16 November 1945, drew up its Constitution according to plans drafted by the Conference of Allied Ministers of Education in London in October 1942.
- The United Nations Monetary and Financial Conference, held in Bretton Woods, New Hampshire, from 1 to 22 July 1944, prepared the draft Agreement of the International Monetary Fund (IMF) and the draft Agreement of the International Bank for Reconstruction and Development (IBRD), now best known as the World Bank. The Agreements came into force on 27 December 1945.
- The International Civil Aviation Conference, held in Chicago from 1 November to 7 December 1944, drafted a Convention on International Civil Aviation and an Interim Agreement on International Civil Aviation. The Interim International Civil Aviation Organization came into being on 15 August 1945.

The first step towards the creation of the general international organization announced in the Moscow Declaration took place in 1944, from 21 August to 28 September, with the Dumbarton Oaks Conversations, close to Washington, between the representatives of the USSR, the UK and the USA. The second phase of the meeting, from 29 September to 7 October, was joined by representatives of China[67]. Following the Proposals for the Establishment of a General International Organization[68], made public on 9 October 1944: "There should be established an international organization under the title of 'The United Nations', the Charter of which should contain provisions necessary to give effect to the proposals which follow".

In 1945, Roosevelt, Churchill and Josef Stalin (1878–1953) met in Yalta, Crimea (USSR), from 3 to 11 February. According to the Yalta Agreement[69], the Big Three decided: "That a United Nations conference on the proposed world organization should be summoned for Wednesday, 25 April 1945, and should be held in the United States of America". It was agreed that the basis of the Charter of the Organization should be the proposals "made public last October as a result of the Dumbarton Oaks conference and which have now been supplemented" by new provisions. These concerned the structure and powers of the Security Council that should be the Organization's executive organ.

The Dumbarton Oaks Proposals were discussed by the nations of the world, especially in an Inter-American Conference held in Mexico City from 21 February

---

[67] "This division into two separate conferences was due to the fact that the Soviet Union maintained a strictly reserved attitude vis-à-vis the Chiang Kai-shek government and did not accept it as a conference partner" (Simma 1998, p. 8).

[68] www.udhr.org/history/dumbarto.htm.

[69] www.u-s-history.com/pages/h2066.html.

to 8 March 1945, and in a British Commonwealth Conference held in London from 4 to 13 April 1945.

On 5 March 1945, the USA Administration, on behalf of itself and the other sponsoring Governments, invited the Governments that had signed or adhered to the United Nations Declaration and had declared war against Germany or Japan to send representatives to the San Francisco Conference, officially known as the United Nations Conference on International Organization. It began on 25 April, having been attended by about 300 official delegates, supported by a large number of technical staff, from 50 nations. It was chaired by the USA Secretary of State Edward R. Stettinius, and the opening ceremony took place at the San Francisco Opera House.

The UN Charter[70] was unanimously adopted on 25 June 1945, at the final plenary session of the Conference, attended by USA President Harry S. Truman (1884–1972), who succeeded Franklin Roosevelt, died on 12 April from a cerebral haemorrhage in Warm Springs, Georgia. It was signed on the following day, in the Veterans War Memorial Building. It was arranged that China should be accorded the honour of being the first to sign, followed by the USSR, the UK and France. The other participating countries signed in alphabetical order. The USA, as host country, signed last, but was the first signatory to deposit its instrument of ratification on 8 August 1945, after the Senate had given its consent by an overwhelming majority of 89 to 2 votes.

The USA Department of State had not overlooked the importance of a campaign for the new Organization addressed to public opinion and to Congress. The right of veto in the Security Council granted by the UN Charter to the great powers contributed to weaken resistances in the Senate (and from the USSR too). As far as public opinion was concerned, it was much favourable to USA participation in an international organization aimed at protecting the values so shockingly scorned during the war. The 42 North American Non-Governmental Organizations (NGOs) invited to San Francisco as consultants of the USA Delegation played a great role in that.

The UN Charter came into force on 24 October 1945, when the five permanent members of the Security Council (USA, UK, France, USSR and China) and a majority of the other signatory States had deposited their ratifications with the USA Government, as provided under Article 110.3 of the Charter.

On 26 June 1945, an agreement on Interim Arrangements that established a Preparatory Commission that held its first meeting on 27 June in San Francisco was also signed. It was decided that an Executive Committee should carry on the work of the Commission in London. Its first meeting was held on 16 August. On 3 October, the Executive Committee decided, by a vote of 9 in favour, with 3 against and 2 abstaining, that "the permanent headquarters of the United Nations be located in the United States of America". Later, in February 1946, an Inspection Group recommended that the permanent headquarters should be established: (1) near to

[70] http://treaties.un.org/doc/Publication/CTC/uncharter.pdf.

New York City, and (2) in the North Stamford—Greenwich district[71]. "In December 1946 the General Assembly accepted a gift of $ 8.5 million from John D. Rockefeller, Jr. (1874–1960) to buy the tract of land on the East River in New York where the UN building now stands" (Glendon 2001, p. 54).

3.3.3 *United Nations Charter and Human Rights (1945)*

On 6 January 1941, in his State of the Union Address[72], President Roosevelt said:

> In the future days, which we seek to make secure, we look forward to a world founded upon four essential human freedoms.
> The first is freedom of speech and expression—everywhere in the world.
> The second is freedom of every person to worship God in his own way—everywhere in the world.

---

[71] The *Yearbook of the United Nations 1946–1947* informs:

> Notwithstanding the Executive Committee's recommendation that the headquarters be located in the United States, the whole question was reopened in the Preparatory Commission, many representatives expressing themselves in favour of Europe as the seat of the headquarters of the United Nations. A lengthy debate ensued, involving points of substance as well as procedure.
> In favour of establishing the United Nations headquarters in Europe it was argued that Europe was the most important potential centre of international unrest. The United Nations should be located where the need for action to maintain peace and security was greatest. [...] Europe was the cultural centre of a large part of the world; it was a natural centre of communications and was closer to the capitals of the majority of the Members of the United Nations than the United States.
> Another argument in favour of Europe as against the United States considered of major importance was that the United Nations should not be located in the territory of one of the major powers, in particular one of the five permanent members of the Security Council. [...] On the other hand the presence of the United Nations on its territory might embarrass a permanent member of the Security Council and limit its freedom of action. The headquarters of the United Nations, therefore, should be established in a small country unaffected by major political and international issues. [...]
> In favour of establishing the headquarters of the United Nations in America it was maintained that Europe was not the only centre of international difficulties and that other areas such as the Pacific or South America should not be neglected. [...] The League of Nations had failed despite the fact that it was located in Europe. A new start toward world peace should be made in a new atmosphere. [...] Finally, the location of the headquarters of the United Nations in the United States would help to ensure the support of the American people for the United Nations, which was an important factor in its success.

In this regard, it should be recalled that, although the USA President Woodrow Wilson had played a significant role in establishing the League of Nations, in 1919, the USA never joined, because Wilson was not able to convince the Senate to ratify the Covenant of the League of Nations.

For further details on the origins of the Organization of the United Nations, see p. 1–50 of the *Yearbook*: http://unyearbook.un.org/unyearbook.html?name=isysadvsearch.html.

[72] http://americanrhetoric.com/speeches/fdrthefourfreedoms.htm.

> The third is freedom from want, which, translated into world terms, means economic understandings which will secure to every nation a healthy peacetime life for its inhabitants—everywhere in the world.
> The fourth is freedom from fear, which, translated into world terms, means a world-wide reduction of armaments to such a point and in such a thorough fashion that no nation will be in a position to commit an act of physical aggression against any neighbour—anywhere in the world.
> That is no vision of a distant millennium. It is a definite basis for a kind of world attainable in our own time and generation.

In the Atlantic Charter (1941), the sixth principle addressed the establishment of a peace "which will afford assurance that all the men in all the lands may live out their lives in freedom from fear and want".

In the Declaration by the United Nations (1942), the conviction had been proclaimed that the struggle and victory over the "savage and brutal forces seeking to subjugate the world" was "essential to defend life, liberty, independence and religious freedom and to preserve human rights and justice".

In his State of the Union Address, on 11 January 1944, sometimes referred to as the 'Second Bill of Rights', Roosevelt said[73]:

> This Republic had its beginning, and grew to its present strength, under the protection of certain inalienable political rights—among them the right of free speech, free press, free worship, trial by jury, freedom from unreasonable searches and seizures. They were our rights to life and liberty.
> As our nation has grown in size and stature, however—as our industrial economy expanded—these political rights proved inadequate to assure us equality in the pursuit of happiness.
> We have come to a clear realization of the fact that true individual freedom cannot exist without economic security and independence. 'Necessitous men are not free men'. People who are hungry and out of a job are the stuff of which dictatorships are made.
> In our day these economic truths have become accepted as self-evident. We have accepted, so to speak, a second Bill of Rights under which a new basis of security and prosperity can be established for all—regardless of station, race, or creed.
> Among these are:
>
> - The right to a useful and remunerative job in the industries or shops or farms or mines of the nation;
> - The right to earn enough to provide adequate food and clothing and recreation;
> - The right of every farmer to raise and sell his products at a return which will give him and his family a decent living;
> - The right of every businessman, large and small, to trade in an atmosphere of freedom from unfair competition and domination by monopolies at home or abroad;
> - The right of every family to a decent home;
> - The right to adequate medical care and the opportunity to achieve and enjoy good health;
> - The right to adequate protection from the economic fears of old age, sickness, accident, and unemployment;
> - The right to a good education.
>
> All of these rights spell security. And after this war is won we must be prepared to move forward, in the implementation of these rights, to new goals of human happiness and well-being.

[73] www.ushistory.org/documents/economic_bill_of_rights.htm.

America's own rightful place in the world depends in large part upon how fully these and similar rights have been carried into practice for our citizens.

Not surprisingly, at the Dumbarton Oaks Conversations President Roosevelt deemed essential that human rights are mentioned "*somewhere in the document*" (as cit. in Samnøy 1993, p. 13), but neither the UK delegation nor the USSR delegation agreed. It was eventually decided that the Proposals for the Establishment of a General International Organization (1944) should include a mention to them in Chap. IX—Sect. A:

1. With a view to the creation of conditions of stability and well-being which are necessary for peaceful and friendly relations among nations, the Organization should facilitate solutions of international economic, social and other humanitarian problems and promote respect for human rights and fundamental freedoms. Responsibility for the discharge of this function should be vested in the General Assembly and, under the authority of the General Assembly, in an Economic and Social Council.

At San Francisco, every effort for the UN Charter to contain a Bill of Rights or, at least, a strong engagement with human rights protection was made, mainly by Latin–American States and NGOs.

The Inter-American Conference on Problems of War and Peace, meeting in Chapultepec (Mexico City), from 21 February to 8 March 1945, adopted a resolution recalling the engagement of the Declaration by the United Nations (1942) regarding the protection of human rights, and stressed the need to define them, as well as the correspondent duties, in a Convention. Furthermore, it required the Inter-American Juridical Committee to prepare a draft American Declaration of the Rights and Duties of Man, while the Charter of the Organization of American States (OAS) was being elaborated. The OAS Charter was adopted on 30 April 1948 by the Ninth International Conference of American States, held in Bogota, Colombia, and signed by 21 Latin–American Republics and the USA. Its headquarters are in Washington. The American Declaration of the Rights and Duties of Man was adopted on 2 May[74].

In San Francisco, Panamanian Minister of Foreign Affairs Ricardo J. Alfaro (1882–1971), former President of Panama and now delegate to the Conference, proposed to be included in the UN Charter the above mentioned Statement of Essential Human Rights[75] sponsored by the ALI. The proposal was supported by Chile, Cuba and México. The lobbying to improve the human rights profile in the Charter also counted with the presence and initiatives of the near 50 NGOs, mostly coming from the USA. They included organizations in the fields of law, education and labor, church groups, women's associations and civic organizations such as the American Association for the United Nations. Among their representatives were several key spokesmen of the human rights movement, such as Judge Proskauer of the American Jewish Committee, Frederick Nolde of the joint Committee on Religious Liberty, and James Shotwell who was chosen as chairman of the consultants.

---

[74] www.cidh.oas.org/Basicos/English/Basic2.american%20Declaration.htm.

[75] www.jstor.org/discover/10.2307/1025050?uid=3738880anduid=2129anduid=2anduid=70anduid=4andsid=47698954934967.

The best results of this lobbying for human rights were the raising of the Economic and Social Council (ECOSOC), whose scope included the human rights, to the category of one of the UN principal organs (Article 7.1 of the Charter), greatly due to Australian Foreign Minister Herbert V. Evatt, and the inclusion in the Charter of more references to human rights. The greatest achievement, however, was the joint proposal of the delegations of the USA, UK, USSR and China, presented on 4 May—the deadline for the submission of formal amendments to the Dumbarton Oaks Proposals—for the establishment by the ECOSOC of a Commission on Human Rights. It must be credited to a letter of 21 NGOs presented to the head of the American Delegation and President of the Conference (Secretary of State Stettinius), during a decisive meeting on 2 May. Glendon informs: "The last speaker, Clark Eichelberger of the American Association for the United Nations, had a specific request. It was especially important, he said, for the United Nations to set up a *commission* on human rights", and "the United States made a single exception to its opposition to the naming of special commissions in the Charter. It would agree to a Human Rights Commission" (Glendon 2001, p. 17). This support was crucial for the normative status of human rights in the UN Charter that conferred on ECOSOC the competence "to set up commissions in economic and social fields and for the promotion of the human rights" (Article 68). The Commission on Human Rights was thus the only Commission specifically suggested in the Charter.

The efforts to improve the human rights profile in the UN Charter were favoured by the first reports and photographs from the concentration camps. In this regard, on 15 April 1945 the legendary CBS reporter Edward R. Murrow, after visiting the *Buchenwald Lager*, said to his listeners:

> [This] will not be pleasant listening. If you're at lunch, or if you have no appetite to hear what Germans have done, now is a good time to switch off the radio, for I propose to tell you about Buchenwald.
> [...]
> I pray you to believe what I have said about Buchenwald. I have reported what I saw and heard, but only part of it. For most of it, I have no words. (Facing History and Ourselves Foundation 2010, p. 110, 113)

In the course of May, the media brought many reports about what the Allied forces had found in the concentration camps. For example, photographs of piles of corpses in *Bergen-Belsen Lager*. This was only the beginning of the coming to light of the full scale of the horrors perpetrated by Nazism and also Stalinism.

The UN Charter was the first universal treaty to proclaim the principle of the human rights respect. It includes seven references to human rights, even though it does not use the terms 'protection' or 'guarantee' (a proposal of New Zealand to include the obligation of all members "to preserve, protect and promote human rights" was not adopted), but only such terms as 'promote' and 'encourage' by means of 'studies' and 'recommendations'. The Preamble reads:

> We, the peoples of the United Nations, determined to save succeeding generations from the scourge of war, which twice in our lifetime has brought untold sorrow to mankind, and to reaffirm faith in fundamental human rights, in the dignity and worth of the human person, in the equal rights of men and women and of nations large and small.

One of the purposes of the UN, according to the Charter, consists in "promoting and encouraging respect for human rights and for fundamental freedoms for all without distinction as to race, sex, language, or religion" (Article 1.3), reflecting Roosevelt's conviction that the respect of human rights is a necessary condition of peace. It also refers to human rights in other provisions (Articles 13.1.b, 55.c, 62.2, 68 and 76.c).

The Yearbook of the United Nations 1948–1949 recorded (p. 524):

> Committee I/1 of the Conference, which was charged with the task of considering the Preamble, Purposes and Principles of the Charter, received the idea [of a Bill of Rights] with sympathy, but decided that 'the present Conference, if only for lack of time, could not proceed to realize such a draft in an international contract. The Organization, once formed, could better proceed to consider the suggestion and to deal effectively with it through a special commission or by some other method. The Committee recommends that the General Assembly consider the proposal and give it effect'.

At the Closing Session of the San Francisco Conference, at the Opera House, on 26 June 1945, USA President Truman stated:

> Under this document we have good reason to expect the framing of an international bill of rights, acceptable to all the nations involved. That bill of rights will be as much a part of international life as our own Bill of Rights is a part of our Constitution. The Charter is dedicated to the achievement and observance of human rights and fundamental freedoms. Unless we can attain those objectives for all men and women everywhere—without regard to race, language or religion—we cannot have permanent peace and security.
> With this Charter the world can begin to look forward to the time when all worthy human beings may be permitted to live decently as free people.[76]

Glendon (2001) remarks:

> The human rights project was peripheral, launched as a concession to small countries and in response to the demands of numerous religious and humanitarian associations that the Allies live up to their war rhetoric by providing assurances that the community of nations would never again countenance such massive violations of human dignity. Britain, China, France, the United States, and the Soviet Union did not expect these assurances to interfere with their national sovereignty. (p. xv–xvi)

3.3.4 Commission on Human Rights (1946)

The UN General Assembly held the first part of its first session from 10 January to 14 February 1946 in London (Central Hall, Westminster), as decided at the San Francisco Conference, pending the decision on the headquarters of the Organization. It elected the members of the ECOSOC on 12–14 January. At its first meeting, the ECOSOC created a 'Nuclear Commission on Human Rights', preparatory

[76] www.presidency.ucsb.edu/ws/?pid=12188.

of a Commission on Human Rights. According to the Resolution 5 (I) of 16 de February[77]:

> 2. The work of the Commission shall be directed towards submitting proposals, recommendations and reports to the Council regarding:
>
> a. an international bill of rights;
> b. international declarations or conventions on civil liberties, the status of women, freedom of information and similar matters;
> c. the protection of minorities;
> d. the prevention of discrimination on grounds of race, sex, language or religion.

Its Resolution 9 (II) of 21 June 1946[78] added to paragraph 2 a new sub-paragraph (e) as follows: "any other matter concerning human rights not covered by item (a), (b), (c), and (d)".

The Nuclear Commission was composed of nine members, not chosen as representatives of their Governments. Two of them should play a great influence during the *travaux préparatoires* (drafting process) of the UDHR: Eleanor Roosevelt, wife of the President Franklin Roosevelt (representative of the USA, who would be elected President of the Commission), and René Cassin (representative of France). It held a sole meeting, at Hunter College, New York (Bronx), from 29 April to 20 May 1946, but only six of the nine members attended. According to the respective Report (E/38/Rev.1, of 21 May)[79], it was unanimously recommended to the ECOSOC, among others, that it should instruct the Secretariat to "compile a yearbook, the first edition of which should contain all declarations and bills on human rights now in force in the various countries"[80]. The full Commission should include 18 members.

> With regard to the type of membership, it was generally felt that as the Economic and Social Council was elected by the governments represented in the General-Assembly, and as the Members of the Economic and Social Council, in their turn, represented governments, the Commission on Human Rights, appointed by the Council, should not again consist of representatives of governments. It was further emphasized that the Commission should consist of highly qualified persons. The Commission, by a majority, agreed to recommend that all members of the Commission on Human Rights should serve as non-governmental representatives, appointed by the Council out of a list of nominees submitted by the Member States of the United Nations.
> [...]
> The Commission agreed that the full Commission should determine the character of the bill which is to be drafted, as well as the content and the form of the bill (for instance, should it be a resolution by the Assembly of the United Nations or an appendix to the Charter, hav-

[77] http://daccess-dds-ny.un.org/doc/RESOLUTION/GEN/NR0/041/47/IMG/NR004147.pdf?OpenElement.

[78] http://daccess-dds-ny.un.org/doc/RESOLUTION/GEN/NR0/043/08/IMG/NR004308.pdf?OpenElement.

[79] http://daccess-dds-ny.un.org/doc/UNDOC/GEN/NG9/000/22/PDF/NG900022.pdf?OpenElement.

[80] As already said, the documents related to the history of the UDHR drafting quoted here are available at: www.un.org/depts/dhl/udhr.

ing to be integrated into the constitution of each Member Nation, or a convention between those States, or in any other form).

The ECOSOC discussed the Report of the Nuclear Commission at its second session, in New York, from 25 May to 21 June. It accepted the proposal that the Commission on Human Rights (CHR) should consist of 18 members, but was divided concerning the type of membership. It was eventually decided that their members should be representatives of States. The CHR was established on 21 June 1946 [(Resolution 9 (II)]. The Secretary-General was requested to make arrangements for the publication of a *Yearbook of the United Nations*. The ECOSOC also adopted on 21 July a Resolution proposed by the CHR under which the Secretary-General was requested to make arrangements for "the collection and publication of information concerning human rights arising from trials of war criminals, quislings and traitors, and in particular from the Nuremberg and Tokyo Trials"[81]. Later, at its third session (1948), the Commission would express the view that Court decisions should also be included in the *Yearbook* first edition, for being as important as provisions of Treaties, Constitutions and ordinary laws. The UN Secretariat created a Division of Human Rights, and John P. Humphrey (Canada) was named its first Director.

The CHR was elected at the third session of the ECOSOC, held from 11 September to 10 December. It was composed of representatives from Australia, Belgium, Byelorussian SSR (Soviet Socialist Republic), Chile, China, Egypt, France, India, Iran, Lebanon, Panama, Philippines, Ukrainian SSR (Soviet Socialist Republic), Union of Soviet Socialist Republics (USSR), UK, United States of America (USA), Uruguay, and Yugoslavia. Most of the commissioners were not lawyers.

3.3.5 Drafting of the Universal Declaration of Human Rights (1947–1948)

The elected CHR held its first session at the UN Interim Headquarters, in an old gyroscope factory at Lake Success, New York, from 27 January to 10 February 1947 (not attended by the delegates of Byelorussia and Ukraine). The Commission elected Eleanor Roosevelt as Chairman, Peng-chun Chang (representative of China) as Vice-Chairman, Charles Malik (representative of Lebanon) as Rapporteur or Secretary. Cassin missed the beginning of the session because of storms that had delayed his Atlantic Sea travelling. Roosevelt and Cassin were the oldest members (in their sixties) and Malik the youngest (in his forties). Roosevelt and Hansa Metha (representative of India), jurist and activist in the Indian independence movement, were the only women.

The CHR recommended to ECOSOC the establishment of two sub-commissions: a Sub-Commission on the Prevention of Discrimination and the Protection of Minorities, suggested by the USSR, and a Sub-Commission on Freedom of Information and the Press, suggested by the USA, the UK and France. "This was but the

[81] The United Nations War Crimes Commission had been constituted in 1943.

beginning of continual finger-pointing by American and Soviet UN representatives at the respective weaknesses of their countries" (Glendon 2001, p. 36).

> Other divisions were ominous, too—such as those between the philosophically inclined and the more practical-minded members; between representatives of small or weak nations and the major powers; and between proponents of enforceable instruments and supporters of a declaration of principles. [...]
> The disagreements, misunderstandings, personal quirks, national rivalries, and colonial resentment that surfaced within the Commission were not the only obstacles to effective collaboration: events unfolding in the world outside would further complicate the work ahead. (p. 43, 50)

After a long discussion on the form and content of the intended Bill of Rights, the CHR decided that the Chairman, together with the Vice-Chairman and the Rapporteur, should undertake the drafting of a text. However, this small group was not able to achieve the task, and the creation of a larger Drafting Committee was decided upon. The ECOSOC endorsed the CHR proposal to appointing a Drafting Committee consisting of eight of its members that should be convened prior to its second session to "prepare, on the basis of documentation supplied by the Secretariat, a preliminary draft of an international bill of human rights" [Resolution 46 (IV) of 28 March 1947]. The Secretariat was asked "to prepare a documented outline concerning an international bill of human rights". Furthermore, the ECOSOC decided upon the following timetable:

> a. That the draft prepared by the abovementioned drafting committee be submitted to the second session of the Commission on human rights, and
> b. That the draft as developed by the Commission on Human Rights be submitted to all State Members of the United Nations for their observations, suggestions and proposals; and
> c. That these observations, suggestions and proposals then be considered as a basis of a redraft, if necessary, by the drafting committee; and
> d. That the resulting draft then be submitted to the Commission on Human Rights for final consideration; and
> e. That the Council consider the proposed international bill of human rights as submitted by the Commission on Human Rights with a view to recommending an international bill of human rights to the General Assembly in 1948; [...]

Between February and June 1947, the Human Rights Division compiled a vast documentation on human rights forming a 408 pages volume, called *Documented Outline* (E/CN.4/AC.1/3/Add.l). It included an account of the human rights provisions in the Constitutions of 55 countries, only 14 of which were Western[82]. Other texts had been submitted by the delegations of several countries, including Chile, China, Cuba Ecuador, France, India, Panama, USA, UK, Chile, Cuba and Panama were the first States to submit a draft to the UN. The Panama draft was the same already

[82] Similar accounts existed: In 1929, A. Aulard and B. Mirkine-Guetzdvitch had published *Les Déclarations des Droits de l'Homme: Textes constitutionnels concernant les droits de l'homme et les guaranties des libertés individuelles dans tous les pays* (The Declarations of the Rights of Man: Constitutional texts regarding the rights of man and the individual guarantees in all countries) (Paris: Payot). The elaboration of the Statement of Essential Human Rights (ALI) included a survey of existing human rights clauses in national Constitutions.

proposad at the San Francisco Conference, prepared by the American Law Institute. The Chile draft was that prepared by the Inter-American Juridical Committee of the OAS. Still others came from varied origins, institutions and personalities, such as those above mentioned (subsection 3.3.1) and other proposals from the American Federation of Labor, the American Jewish Congress, the World Government Association, the American Association for the United Nations, etc.

Humphrey prepared a draft that he called *Draft Outline*, which "provided the drafting committee with a distillation of nearly 200 years of efforts to articulate the most basic human values in terms of rights" (Glendon 2001, p. 57). He wrote (1984) in his memoirs:

> It was therefore at the Lido Beach Hotel, where Jeanne [his wife] and I were living at the time, that, with some help from Émile Giraud, I prepared the first draft of the Universal Declaration of Human Rights.
> I was no Thomas Jefferson and, although a lawyer, I had practically no experience drafting documents. But since the Secretariat has collected a score of drafts, I had some models on which to work. One of them had been prepared by Gustavo Gutierrez and had probably inspired the draft declaration of the international duties and rights of the individual which Cuba had sponsored at the San Francisco Conference. [...] With two exceptions, all these texts came from English-speaking sources and all of them from the democratic West. The documentation which the secretariat brought ex post facto in support of my draft included texts extracted from the constitutions of many countries. But I did not have this before me when I prepared my draft.
> The best of the texts from which I worked was the one prepared by the American Law Institute, and I borrowed freely from it. This was the text that had been unsuccessfully sponsored by Panama at the San Francisco Conference and later in the General Assembly. It had been drafted in the United States during the war by a distinguished group representing many cultures, one of whom was Alfredo Alfaro, the Panamanian foreign minister [[83]].
> [...]
> The drafting committee used my text, officially known as the Secretariat Outline (a misnomer if there ever was one, since it was really a draft declaration) as the basis for its work. (p. 31, 32, 37)

The Drafting Committee held its first session from 9 to 25 June 1947, at Lake Success. On the table were the following documents, among others:

- Plan of the Draft Outline of an International Bill of Rights, prepared by the Secretariat (E/CN.4/AC.1/3/Add.2, 9 June 1947).
- Draft Outline of International Bill of Human Rights, prepared by the Division of Human Rights, with 48 Articles (E/CN.4/AC.1/3, 4 June 1947).

[83] In Louis Sohn's (1996) opinion: "The influence of this statement which represents the spirit of the times is often underestimated" (p. 53). Its Preamble reads:

> Upon the freedom of the individual depends the welfare of the people, the safety of the state and the peace of the world.
> [...]
> The function of the state is to promote conditions under which the individual can be most free.
> To express those freedoms to which every human being is entitled and to assure that all shall live under a government of the people, by the people and for the people, this declaration is made.

- Documented Outline (E/CN.4/AC.1/3/Add.1, 11 June, 1947) including:
  - Observations made by members to the Commission on Human Rights at its first session.
  - Draft international declarations or proposals submitted by Governments to the Commission on Human Rights: declarations from Chile, Cuba and Panama; proposals from India and USA.
  - Provisions related to human rights from 50 national Constitutions (more 5 non written Constitutions were referred to, as well as other provisions not directly related to any Article of the Draft).
  - Draft international declaration presented by the American Federation of Labor.

Each Article was followed by related Member States observations and constitutional provisions. "The fact that almost all of the articles in the Declaration were matched with existing constitutions adds a great deal to the authority and universality of the document" (Morsink 1999, p. 7).

The Drafting Committee decided "to take the Secretariat outline as a basis for discussion, referring to other documents when there appeared to be similarity between them" (E/CN.4/AC.1/SR.2). According to the session Report (E/CN.4/21, 1 July 1947):

> 12. Concerning the form which the Preliminary Draft might take, two views were put forward. In the opinion of some Representatives it was necessary that the Preliminary Draft, in the first instance, should take the form of a Declaration or Manifesto; others felt that it should be in the form of a Convention. It was agreed, however, by those who favored the Declaration form that the Declaration should be accompanied or followed by a Convention or Conventions on specific groups of rights. [...] The Drafting Committee, therefore, while recognizing that the decision as to the form of the Bill was a matter for the Commission, decide to attempt to prepare two documents, one a working paper in the form of a Preliminary Draft of a Declaration or manifesto setting forth general principles, and the second a working paper outlining a Draft Convention on those matters which the Committee felt might lend themselves to formulation as binding obligations.
> 13. The Committee established a temporary working group, composed of the representatives of France, Lebanon, and the United Kingdom, with the Chairman of the Committee as an ex officio member. It requested this working group:
>
> a. to suggest a logical rearrangement of the articles of the Draft Outline supplied by the Secretariat;
> b. to suggest a redraft of the various articles in the light of the discussions of the Drafting Committee; and
> c. to suggest to the Drafting Committee how the substance of the articles might be divided between a Declaration and a Convention.
>
> [...]
> 14. The temporary working group had three meetings, and after a general discussion decided to request Professor Cassin to undertake the writing of a draft Declaration based on those Articles in the Secretariat Outline which he considered should go into such a Declaration. [...]
> Professor Cassin produced a draft containing a Preamble and forty-four suggested Articles.
> [...]
> 17. The Drafting Committee accepted Professor Cassin's offer to prepare, on the basis of the discussion of his draft, a revised Draft Declaration. [...]

The Drafting Committee also devoted one meeting specifically to the question of implementation, and transmitted to the CHR a memorandum on the subject prepared by the Secretariat (E/CN.4/21, Annexes F, G, H).

Meanwhile, the UNESCO contributed with a worldwide consultation, decided by its first General Conference. According to a communication it addressed to the Chairman of the CHR (E/CN.4/78), on 16 December 1947, in order to meet "the difficult problem of the philosophical bases of human rights", the following initiative was taken: "A questionnaire on the philosophical bases of human rights was addressed to about 150 philosophers personally in various parts of the world, as well as to the National Educational, Scientific and Cultural Commissions, which constitute the liaison organs of UNESCO".

The Committee on the Theoretical Bases of Human Rights (sometimes also referred to as Committee on the Philosophic Principles of Human Rights), composed of leading intellectuals from different philosophical orientations and religious beliefs (such as Benedetto Croce and Jacques Maritain), met in January 1947 and sent in March to personalities worldwide, such as Mahatma Gandhi and Teilhard de Chardin, a "Memorandum and Questionnaire Circulated by UNESCO on the Theoretical Bases of Human Rights" (UNESCO 1948, Appendix I). In July, the Committee had received about 70 responses. In its Report with the title *The Grounds of an International Declaration of Human Rights* (Appendix II), the Committee concluded:

> Varied in cultures and built upon different institutions, the members of the United Nations have, nevertheless, certain great principles in common. […]
> The Committee […] is convinced that the philosophic problem involved in a declaration of human rights is not to achieve doctrinal consensus but rather to achieve agreement concerning rights, and also concerning action in the realization and defense of rights, which may be justified on highly divergent doctrinal grounds. […]
> They may be seen to be implicit in man's nature as an individual and as a member of society and to follow from the fundamental right to live.

Fifteen human rights were formulated. The CHR was not much interested in philosophical arguments, however.

The Report of the Drafting Committee was submitted to the CHR for consideration at its second session, held in Geneva from 2 to 17 December 1947, at the former headquarters of the League of Nations, in front of the Lake of Geneva. The Geneva meeting, "by all accounts, represented the high point of harmony for the group" (Glendon 2001, p. 83).

Implementation "was the most heated dispute of the Geneva meeting. […] The United Kingdom strongly opposed an international court or Charter amendments but was from the beginning the chief proponent of a covenant" (p. 84). Its draft became influential in drafting the 1950 European Convention on Human Rights and the 1966 International Covenant on Civil and Political Rights. The Belgian representative (Fernand Dehousse) made a proposal that resulted in the following decision (E/600)[84]:

[84] http://daccess-dds-ny.un.org/doc/UNDOC/GEN/GL9/011/01/PDF/GL901101.pdf?OpenElement.

> 18. Two titles were frequently used in respect of the documents in preparation, Declaration and Convention. The latter was to be entered into and ratified by Governments and not only to be discussed and adopted by the General Assembly.
> The question arose whether the term "Bill of Rights" was to be applied only to the Convention, or only to the Declaration, or to the two documents taken together. In its night meeting on 16 December 1947 the Commission decided:
>
> a. To apply the term 'International Bill of Human Rights', or, for brevity, 'Bill of Rights', to the entirety of documents in preparation: the Declaration, the Convention and the Measures of Implementation;
> b. To use the term 'Declaration' for the articles in Annex A of this Report;
> c. To call the Convention on Human Rights embodied in Annex B, 'The Covenant on Human Rights'; and
> d. To refer to the outcome of the suggestions embodied in Annex C as 'Measures for Implementation', regardless of whether these measures will eventually form part of the Covenant or not.

In addition:

> 16. In order to fulfill its mission, the Commission decided to set up three Working Groups immediately, to deal respectively with the problem of the Declaration, the Convention or Conventions, and Implementation. [...]
> 17. The Working Groups began their work immediately upon establishment, and met simultaneously. The Working Group on the Declaration met nine times, that on the Convention nine times and that on the question of Implementation seven times. [...]

The Working Group on the Declaration was chaired by Roosevelt, Cassin serving as Rapporteur. On the basis of the reports of the first two Working Groups, the Commission drafted a Declaration of Human Rights and a Covenant on Human Rights.

> 13. Taking into consideration the necessity for the Drafting Committee to be fully informed of the replies from the Governments before its next meeting on 3 May 1948, the Commission requested the Secretary-General (a) to transmit this Report to the Governments during the first week of January 1948; (b) to fix the date of 3 April 1948 as the time limit for the reception of the replies from Governments on the draft International Bill of Human Rights, and (c) to circulate these replies to the members of the Commission as soon as they are received.

Fourteen States sent comments on the Geneva Draft: Australia, Brazil, Canada, Egypt, France, India, Mexico, Netherlands, New Zealand, Norway, Pakistan, South Africa, Sweden, and USA.

The Drafting Committee met for its second session at Lake Success, from 3 to 21 May 1948. It considered, among others, the replies from 13 Governments on the 'Geneva drafts', as well as the just adopted American Declaration of the Rights and Duties of Man. It had time to redraft the Covenant, but not the entire Declaration, and no time to consider the question of Measures for Implementation.

The Drafting Committee Report (E/CN.4/95) was examined by the CHR meeting for its third session at Lake Success too, from 24 May to 18 June 1948 (E/800). "The most prolonged arguments of the Commission's third and final session involved the still thorny question of precisely how to frame the social and economic rights [...]. The disputes centred on their implementation and on their relation to traditional political and civil liberties" Glendon 2001, p. 115). The Declaration was redrafted, and Malik was asked by Roosevelt to prepare a preamble over the weekend of 11

June. He proposed a new provision that became Article 28. A reference was added to the UN Charter's purposes. The USSR representative made the following statement (E/CN.4/SR.81):

> Mr. PAVLOV (Union of Soviet Socialist Republics) stated that he would be unable to vote in favour of the Draft Declaration, which his delegation considered unsatisfactory. While it could not be said that the document contained nothing at all, since it did, in a somewhat vague way, repeat certain generally accepted democratic concepts of fundamental rights; but it did nothing to ensure respect for human rights. [...].
> The chief faults of the Draft Declaration the Commission was about to vote lay in the absence of any effective measures to combat Fascism and Nazism and to provide against the possibility of their re-appearance; the deletion of all references to democracy; the rejection of the original article 31 and hence the limitation of certain rights; the absence of any provision for the implementation of human rights; and the rejection of any specific definition of the rights and obligations of individuals to the State.
> Despite, however, the weak and inadequate document which was now before the Commission, the USSR delegation was confident that there would eventually emerge a Declaration which would effectively encourage the progress of democracy and the fight against Nazism and Fascism.
> Mr. PAVLOV asked to have his statement appended to the report of the Commission as an expression of the minority view.

The draft Declaration was adopted on 18 June by 12 votes to none, with four abstentions (USSR, Byelorussia, Ukraine and Yugoslavia).

The Commission did not have time to consider the draft Covenant and Measures for Implementation. The draft Declaration, together with the draft Covenant and several proposals on implementation (including the creation of an International Court of Human Rights), as prepared by the respective Drafting Groups, were transmitted to the ECOSOC (E/800). Glendon (2001) comments:

> As they launched their fragile paper boat upon the troubled seas of world politics in the summer of 1948, the civil war in China was nearing its end and fighting was about to resume in the Middle East. The Iron Curtain had descended around Eastern Europe, and the postwar alliance had definitely collapsed on June 24, when Stalin precipitated the gravest crisis since war's end by blockading all land and water traffic in and out of Berlin. (p. 121)

The ECOSOC (now chaired by Malik, elected in February) decided, at its seventh session, on 17 August 1948, that each of its members could make general statements on the CHR Report, on 25 and 26 August. According to the record of its 215th meeting (E/SR.215)[85], on 25 August, the representative of France (Cassin) remarked:

> The question before the Council was whether to wait until the whole task was finished, or to proceed by stages.
> ... There were two steps which it should take: (1) to transmit the Commission's Report with its annexes and appendix to the General Assembly, so that the latter could take a decision on it; and (2) to call a session of the Human Rights Commission early in 1949, so that it might complete as rapidly as possible both the draft Covenant and the proposed measures of implementation.

By rejecting "the alternative of all or nothing", Cassin "urged that the draft Declaration of Human Rights should be submitted to the Assembly". Recalling "that when

[85] http://daccess-dds-ny.un.org/doc/UNDOC/GEN/NL4/806/28/PDF/NL480628.pdf?OpenElement.

Germany had been questioned in the thirties, not far from the *Palais des Nations*, about her treatment of the German Jews, she had replied that every man was master in his own home", Cassin said:

> There must be no possibility that it could be said that the fate of nationals of any country did not interest the community of nations; for if any nation oppressed its subjects, it was obviously capable of extending oppression to its neighbors, and even further. That was the overriding reason why the Declaration of Human Rights should be voted on without the least delay.
> [...]
> A decision on the Declaration of Human Rights might hasten the completion of the International Bill of Human Rights as a whole. In order to achieve that aim, the Council might convene the Human Rights Commission at the beginning of 1949, when it would be stimulated in its work on the Covenant and on implementation by the debates on human rights which would have taken place in the General Assembly.

Different was the opinion of New Zealand representative (James Thorn):

> The Declaration should not be adopted until it had been reconsidered by the Commission in the light of detailed comments by governments. It might then be possible to present an acceptable draft to the 1949 Assembly.
> [...]
> If the Declaration were adopted by itself, there was less likelihood of a Covenant ever being concluded.

This point of view was reaffirmed in the General Assembly Third Committee. The Netherlands representative (Van der Mandele) agreed:

> The Netherlands delegation felt that a Declaration of Human Rights without a corresponding Covenant with provisions for implementation would have little meaning; it therefore considered that the Declaration should be referred back to the Commission [on Human Rights] for latter submission to the Council together with a draft Covenant and the proposals for its implementation.

On 26 August, the ECOSOC, owing to lack of time, decided unanimously "to transmit to the General Assembly the International Declaration of Human Rights draft submitted to the Council by the Commission on Human Rights in the Report of its third session (E/800), together with the remainder of this Report and the records of the proceedings of the Council at its seventh session on this subject" (E/SR.218)[86].

The UN General Assembly met for its third session, in Paris, from 21 September to 12 December 1948[87]. On 23 September, USA Secretary of State George Marshall called in a speech to the General Assembly:

> Let this third regular session of the General Assembly approve by an overwhelming majority the Declaration of Human Rights as a standard of conduct for all; and let us, as members

[86] http://daccess-dds-ny.un.org/doc/UNDOC/GEN/NL4/806/41/PDF/NL480641.pdf?OpenElement.

[87] "The UN General Assembly chose to hold its fall 1948 meeting in Paris in order, it was said, to conduct its business at a sensible remove from the final weeks of the American presidential election [...]. The tension between Russia and the United States may have played a role in the decision, too" (Glendon 2001, p. 130). At the time, the Papal Nuncio in Paris was the Cardinal Angelo Giuseppe Roncalli. Cassin wrote in his memoirs: "I received discreet personal encouragements from the Papal Nuncio Roncalli", who 10 years later would be elected Pope (John XXIII, 1958–1963) (p. 132).

> of the United Nations, conscious of our own shortcomings and imperfections, join our effort in good faith to live up to this high standard. [...] The people of the earth are anxiously watching our efforts here. We must not disappoint them. (as cit. in Glendon 2001, p. 135, 136)

On 24 September, at its 142th meeting, the Assembly presented the draft to its Third Committee (Social, Humanitarian and Cultural Questions), composed of representatives from all UN Member States, also chaired by Malik. It convened on 28 September and dedicated to the item its 88th to 105th, 107th to 116th, 119th to 134th, 137th to 167th, and 174th to 179th meetings, held from 30 September to 18 October, from 19 to 29 October, from 30 October to 12 November, from 15 to 30 November, and from 4 to 7 December 1948. At the Third Committee 89th meeting, on 30 September (A/C.3/SR.89), the New Zealand representative (A. M. Newlands) reaffirmed that:

> The draft Declaration before the Committee was only the first part of an International Bill of Human Rights. It had been prepared by only eighteen Member States. The Economic and Social Council, at its seventh session, had not had time to deal with it thoroughly, but had merely referred it to the General Assembly together with a statement of positions taken by its representatives. The New Zealand delegation felt that the draft Declaration was not yet a mature document, reflecting the views of all the Members of the United Nations. Not all Governments had as yet examined it in relation to their systems of law. A Declaration of Human Rights by fifty-eight States would be a great event; further study was required to make the document worthy of the occasion.
> [...]
> Mrs. Newlands hoped that the views of her delegation would be taken into account. She urged the Committee, after a thorough discussion, to refer the draft Declaration back to the Commission on Human Rights for further study in the light of additional comments by Governments. The Commission could also continue to work on the covenant, and both documents could be adopted by the General Assembly at its fourth session.

This argument was opposed by other delegations. For example, the Argentinean representative (Enrique V. Corominas) said that: "The members of the Committee were responsible to their people; they could not return from the current session empty-handed. They must respond to the civic and social aspirations of mankind and adopt the declaration of human rights for which the world was waiting". At the 91th meeting of the Third Committee, on 2 October (A/C.3/SR.91), the Belgian representative (Count Henry Carton de Wiart) said that "it was important to give to the waiting world a tangible proof of its activity and usefulness". After a general debate, the Third Committee decided, at its 94th meeting, on 5 October, by 41 votes to 3, with 7 abstentions, to consider only the draft Declaration, as the draft Covenant and Measures of Implementation were not yet in a state suitable for consideration.

Glendon (2001) notes: "Even Malik's heart must have sunk, however, when it took 6 days to get through Article 1" (p. 144)[88]. The debates kept slow, and after a whole month only three articles were approved. Then the speed increased until mid-November, when the provisions on economic, social and cultural rights began

---

[88] Nevertheless: "Perhaps only someone like Malik, from a small, newly independent country, could understand how important it was for every member state to have a sense of ownership with respect to the Declaration" (p. 143).

to be examined. The discussions lasted until 7 December. Thirty-four delegates had expressed their views.

On 15 November, the representative of France (Cassin) proposed the amendment of the title: "Substitute the word 'universal' for the word 'international'". It was approved with 17 votes for, 11 against, and 10 abstentions (A/C.3/339)[89]. The same proposal included the adoption of the phraseology of the UN Charter in the Preamble (that had been adopted in the 'Draft International Declaration of Rights' submitted by the Working Group of Drafting Committee (E/CN.4/AC.1/W.1): "We, the peoples of the United Nations". It was not approved.

As Humphrey (1984) reported: "At one o'clock in the night of 6 December, by roll call vote [29 to none, with 7 abstentions], the Third Committee adopted its draft of the Declaration and sent it on to the Assembly" (p. 71). According to the Third Committee Report (A/777), it decided to recommend for adoption by the General Assembly, together with the draft UDHR, four draft resolutions more, relating to "the right of petition", "the fate of minorities", "publicity to be given to the Universal Declaration of Human Rights", "the preparation of a draft Covenant and draft measures of implementation". A draft Resolution (A/C.3/407) submitted by the USSR representative (Alexander E. Bogomolov) during the Third Committee's 179th meeting, on 7 December 1948 (A/C.3/SR.179), requesting "the General Assembly to postpone the final adoption of the Declaration of Human Rights to the next session of the General Assembly", was rejected by 26 votes to 6, with 1 abstention.

The Third Committee Report was debated by the General Assembly at its 180th to 183th plenary meetings, on 9 and 10 December. Many of the 35 delegations that made statements resumed questions already raised during the Third Committee meetings. For example, the USSR representative submitted a draft Resolution (A/785/Rev.2) recommending again that the General Assembly postpone the adoption of the Declaration until its fourth regular session. The representatives of Byelorussian Soviet Socialist Republic, Czechoslovakia, Poland, Ukraine and Yugoslavia supported the USSR proposal. On the contrary, in the General Assembly's 183th plenary meeting, on 10 December (A/PV.183), the Ecuadoran representative (Jorge Carrera Andrade) took the following position:

> The delegation of Ecuador would not support any draft resolution recommending that the Declaration of Human Rights should be referred back to the Third Committee for redrafting. Such a delay would not improve the international atmosphere and would dash the

---

[89] Glendon (2001) comments:

> As soon as the committee wound up its review of the draft Declaration, a subcommittee on style chaired by Cassin began to put everything into final form. At this stage a few changes were made in the sequence of articles, and the title was officially changed to the 'Universal Declaration of Human Rights' from 'International Declaration of Human Rights'. The new title had been in casual use for some time, but Cassin, who proposed the official change, rightly considered the name to be of the utmost significance. The title 'Universal', he later wrote, meant that the Declaration was morally binding on everyone, not only on the governments that voted for its adoption. The Universal Declaration, in other words, was not an 'international' or 'intergovernmental' document; it was addressed to all humanity and founded on a unified conception of the human being. (p. 161)

hopes of the ordinary people of the world, who today were not only expecting the restoration of material ruins but that of human dignity as well.

The General Assembly proclaimed the Universal Declaration of Human Rights on 10 December 1948 [Resolution 217 A (III)], a little before midnight, by 48 votes to none against, with 8 abstentions: Byelorussia SSR (now Belarus), Czechoslovakia (now split into Czech Republic and Slovakia), Socialist Federal Republic of Yugoslavia (now dissolved, giving rise to several States: Bosnia and Herzegovina, Croatia, Montenegro, Serbia, Slovenia and The former Yugoslav Republic of Macedonia), Poland, Ukraine, the USSR (now dissolved, giving rise to several Sates), the South-African Union (or Union of South Africa, now Republic of South Africa) and Saudi Arabia. The abstentions were not due to disagreements on principles: The Eastern States considered the Declaration to be insufficient; the South-African Union disagreed on the inclusion of economic, social and cultural rights; Saudi Arabia formulated reservations to Article 16 (right to marriage without restrictions relating to religion) and to Article 18 (freedom of religion). The representatives from Honduras and Yemen were absent in the moment of the vote, but the Honduran Government made known, afterwards, that it would have voted favourably.

Humphrey (1984) considered the UDHR "the greatest achievement of the United Nations" (p. 76). It became the most translated document overall in the world, following the *Guinness Book of Records*. Over 300 language versions are available at the website of the Office of the High Commissioner for Human Rights (OHCHR).

Summing up: The UDHR drafting process took more than 2 years, if the establishment of the CHR is included. Eight stages may be distinguished:

1. 29 April to 20 May 1946: Meetings (in Hunter College, New York) of the 'Nuclear Commission' created by the ECOSOC to make recommendations about the terms of reference and membership of the CHR to be established.
2. 27 January to 10 February 1947: First Session of the CHR, in Lake Success (New York), UN Interim Headquarters.
3. 9 to 25 June 1947: First Session of the Drafting Committee, in Lake Success.
4. 2 to 17 December 1947: Second Session of the CHR, in Geneva (at the former headquarters of the League of Nations).
5. 3 to 21 May 1948: Second Session of the Drafting Committee, in Lake Success.
6. 24 May to 18 June 1948: Third Session of the CHR, in Lake Success.
7. 28 September to 7 December 1948: Meetings of the Third Committee of the UN General Assembly.
8. 9 and 10 December 1948: Plenary meetings of the UN General Assembly that proclaimed the UDHR.

During the drafting process:

- The Nuclear Commission held 18 meetings.
- The CHR held 81 meetings.
- The Drafting Committee held 44 meetings.
- The Third Committee held 85 meetings and about more 20 subcommittees meetings.
- The General Assembly held four plenary meetings.

The UDHR contains a Preamble and 30 Articles proclaiming about 40 rights. It provides a comprehensive statement of what human rights are, including both principal categories of rights: the classical civil and political liberties, including the right to asylum and the right to property (Articles 3–21), and 'new' economic, social and cultural rights (Articles 22–27). Explaining the content and structure of the Declaration in his course at The Hague Academy, Cassin (1951) said:

> We have compared the Universal Declaration to a vast portico of a temple, whose courtyard is formed by the Preamble that affirms the unity of the human family, and whose base is constituted by the general principles of liberty, equality, non-discrimination and brotherhood proclaimed in articles 1 and 2.
> The portico is supported by four columns equally important. The first one is that of the personal rights and freedoms (art. 3–11 included) [...].
> The second one concerns the rights of the individual in his or her relations with the groups of which he or she is member and to the things of the external world (art. 12–17 included) [...].
> The third pillar is that of the spiritual faculties, of the public freedoms and of the fundamental political rights (art. 18–21) [...].
> The fourth pillar, symmetrical with the first one, with an entirely new character at the international level and whose potential is not at all weaker than that of the other ones, is that of the economic, social and cultural rights (art. 22–27 included) [...].
> Over these four columns a frontispiece was needed to signing the ties existing between the individual and the society. Articles 28–30 affirm the need of a social international order where the personal rights and freedoms can reach their full effect. [...] Consequently, the Declaration is characterized by a continuing *élan* from the individual to the social. (p. 277...279)

During the 180th plenary meeting of the General Assembly, on 9 December 1948 (A/PV.180), when the draft Universal Declaration began to be discussed, Cassin said that: "The last war had taken on the character of a crusade for human rights" and the UDHR was "a world milestone in the long struggle for human rights". He still affirmed that:

> In common with the 1789 Declaration, it was founded upon the great principles of liberty, equality and fraternity [...]. The Declaration rests on four fundamental pillars: personal rights, relationships between man and his fellow men, public liberties and fundamental political rights, and economic and social rights. [...A]rticle 30 was one of the keystones of the Declaration. [...]
> It should finally be pointed out that the four pillars of the Declaration were all of equal importance, and no hierarchy of rights could be established in the Declaration.
> To Mr. Cassin the chief novelty of the Declaration was its universality. [...]

At the same meeting, Eleanor Roosevelt said that "it was first and foremost a Declaration of the basic principles to serve as a common standard for all nations. It might well become the Magna Carta of all mankind"[90].

Hernan Santa Cruz (representative of Chile) witnessed:

> I perceived clearly that I was participating in a truly significant historic event in which a consensus had been reached as to the supreme value of the human person, a value that did

[90] Copies of the UN Charter and of the UDHR were deposited inside the cornerstone of the UN Headquarters, in New York.

> not originate in the decision of a worldly power, but rather in the fact of existing—which gave rise to the inalienable right to live free from want and oppression and to fully develop one's personality. (as cit. in Glendon 2001, p. 169)

As Tomuschat (2008) points out: "A new chapter of human history began" with the UDHR proclamation (p. 24). Glendon (2001) notes:

> Together with the Nuremberg Principles of international criminal law developed by the Allies in 1946 for the trials of German and Japanese war criminals and the 1948 Genocide Convention, the Universal Declaration of Human Rights became a pillar of a new international system under which a nation's treatment of its own citizens was no longer immune from outside scrutiny.
> [...]
> The Declaration marked a new chapter in a history that began with the great charters of humanity's first rights moment in the seventeenth and eighteenth centuries. [...] They proclaimed that all men were born free and equal and that the purpose of government was to protect man's natural liberties. They gave rise to the modern language of rights.
> From the outset, that language branched into two dialects. One, influenced by continental European thinkers, especially Rousseau, had more room for equality and 'fraternity' and tempered rights with duties and limits. It cast the state in a positive light as guarantor of rights and protector of the needy. [...]
> The Anglo-American dialect of rights language emphasized individual liberty and initiative more than equality or social solidarity and was infused with a greater mistrust of government. [...]
> When Latin American countries achieved independence in the nineteenth century, these two strains began to converge. (p. xvi, xvii)

The Universal Declaration's normative authority was a point of great debate, however.

Cassin (1951) had proposed that the Declaration be a legislative act of the UN and incorporated in its Charter. It could begin like it: "We, People of the United Nations..." (p. 279). In the ECOSOC's 215th meeting, on 25 August 1948 (E/SR.215), he affirmed:

> The Declaration of Human Rights was a complement of the Charter which could not be included therein because of the lengthy preparation it had required. It was a clarification of the Charter and a basic instrument of the United Nations, having all the legal force of such an instrument. No one could disregard with impunity the principles it proclaimed.

This was repeated during the Third Committee's 92th meeting, on 2 October (A/C.3/SR.92). He reaffirmed that the Declaration "could be considered as an authoritative interpretation of the Charter of the United Nations", and that States "are compelled by the terms of the Charter to recognize the competence of the main bodies of the United Nations". At the 180th plenary meeting of the General Assembly, on 9 December (A/PV.180), he said again that:

> The Declaration had a wide moral scope. Furthermore, while it was less powerful and binding than a convention, it had no less legal value, for it was contained in a resolution of the Assembly which was empowered to make recommendations; it was a development of the Charter which had brought human rights within the scope of positive international law.
> He expressed the hope that the 1948 Paris Assembly of the United Nations would, by the unanimity of its delegations, be known in history as the 'human rights Assembly'.

The representative of the Union of South Africa (Roland Andrews Egger) admitted, during the 182th plenary meeting of the General Assembly (A/PV.182), that as the UDHR "would probably be interpreted as an authoritative definition of fundamental rights and freedoms which had been left undefined in the Charter", such an interpretation implied that "Member States who voted for the draft Declaration would be bound in the same manner as if they had signed a convention embodying those principles".

A different opinion was expressed at the Third Committee 93th meeting, on 4 October (A/C.3/SR.92), by the UK representative (Christopher P. Mayhew):

> He did not agree with Professor Cassin that the Declaration could be considered to have legal authority as an interpretation of the relevant provisions of the Charter. No General Assembly resolution could establish legal obligations. The moral authority of the document that would be adopted by the Assembly, however, would serve as a guide to Governments in their efforts to guarantee human rights by legislation and through their administrative and legal practice.

In Sohn's (1982) view:

> Although some delegations emphasized that the Universal Declaration of Human Rights was not a treaty imposing legal obligations, others more boldly argued that it was more than an ordinary General Assembly resolution, that it was a continuation of the Charter and shared the dignity of that basic document. It merely expressed more forcefully rules that already were recognized by customary international law. Under the latter view, the Declaration would possess a binding character. [...]
> The Declaration thus is now considered to be an authoritative interpretation of the U.N. Charter, [...] has joined the Charter of the United Nations as part of the constitutional structure of the world community. The Declaration, as an authoritative listing of human rights, has become a basic component of international customary law, binding on all states, not only on members of the United Nations. Another revolutionary step thus has been taken in protecting human rights on a worldwide scale. (p. 15, 16, 17)

Notwithstanding, the Charter contained a provision that would remain a bone of contention for a long-time in regard to the international protection of human rights, namely: the principle of the national sovereignty (Article 2.7). Inherited from Article 15.8 of the Covenant of the League of Nations, Article 2.7 was so worded[91]:

> Nothing contained in the present Charter shall authorize the United Nations to intervene in matters which are essentially within the domestic jurisdiction of any state or shall require the Members to submit such matters to settlement under the present Charter; but this principle shall not prejudice the application of enforcement measures under Chap. VII[92].

[91] http://treaties.un.org/doc/Publication/CTC/uncharter.pdf.

[92] Bruno Simma (1998) commented that:

> ... the 'domestic jurisdiction reservation' was deemed important for a wide variety of reasons. Among the Latin American republics there was a strong fear of intervention by the powerful North American neighbor; the USA Congress was always eager to safeguard the unrestricted sovereignty of the USA over its domestic affairs; the Soviet Union was strongly resolved to protect the social and political order of socialism. After difficult and protracted negotiations, Art. 2(7) of the Charter emerged as an ambivalent compromise. (p. 12)

How could one reconcile the principle of the international protection of human rights with the principle of non-interference in the States' domestic affairs?

Examining this apparent contradiction, in his Course on "The International Protection of Human Rights" at The Hague Academy of International Law, in 1947, Lauterpacht (1948)—"one of the godfathers of international human rights" (Henkin 1978, p. 133)—said: "Undoubtedly, the limitation of Article 2, paragraph 7, is, because of its generality, the governing rule of the Charter. But that governing effect does not reach beyond its clearly and indisputably ascertainable terms" (p. 23). With the Charter, "the respect and observance of human rights have become a subject of international obligations in the legal sense of the term" (p. 26), as well as "one of the fundamental principles of the Charter" (p. 28). As a consequence: "There is no reason why commentators should transform the imperfections of the Charter into manifest absurdities" (p. 31). Even though Article 2.7 "constitutes a source of uncertainty", he concluded: "The reservation of domestic jurisdiction cannot accomplish the impossible and combine the acceptance of obligations with freedom from obligation" (p. 55).

During the Third Committee's 92th meeting, on 2 October 1948 (A/C.3/SR.92), Cassin said that:

> In his country's opinion, the United Nations' competence in the question of human rights was an established fact and the provisions of Article 2, paragraph 7 of the Charter, relating to matters within the domestic jurisdiction of Member States, could not be invoked against such competence when, by adoption of the Declaration, the question of human rights was a matter no longer of domestic, but of international concern.
> [...]
> Summing up, he stated that if the competence of the United Nations should be exercised with moderation, the United Nations should not nevertheless fail to be inflexible when human rights were violated.

In his Course on *La Déclaration universelle et la mise en œuvre des droits de l'homme* (The Universal Declaration and the Implementation of Human Rights), at the same Academy (1951), he affirmed: "We consider as psychologically and politically impossible to be presumed that Article 2§ 7, made a citadel of the States' sovereignties, closes all the human rights inside this citadel" (p. 253). And reaffirmed that the UDHR, having been proclaimed by a Resolution of the General Assembly, created "the legal obligation to cooperate with the action of the United Nations, formulated in Article 56 of the Charter". Moreover:

> The notion of human rights was certainly included, prior to the United Nations Charter, among 'the general principles of law recognized by civilized nations' that the Permanent Court of Hague applies in regulating the international disputes, according to Article 38 of its Statute. It may even be said that the Charter made the respect of those rights, in general, a positive rule of conventional International Law. (p. 293, 294)

In this respect, it is often mentioned the response given by the UN Legal Adviser to a request of the CHR regarding the UDHR, in 1962[93]:

---

[93] http://portal.unesco.org/en/ev.php-URL_ID=23772andURL_DO=DO_TOPICandURL_SECTION=201.html.

In United Nations practice, a 'declaration' is a formal and solemn instrument, suitable for rare occasions when principles of great and lasting importance are being enunciated, such as the Declaration of Human Rights. A recommendation is less formal.
Apart from the distinction just indicated, there is probably no difference between a 'recommendation' and a 'declaration' in United Nations practice as far as strict legal principle is concerned. A 'declaration' or a 'recommendation' is adopted by resolution of a United Nations organ. As such it cannot be made binding upon Member States, in the sense that a treaty or convention is binding upon the parties to it, purely by the device of terming it a 'declaration' rather than a 'recommendation'. However, in view of the greater solemnity and significance of a 'declaration', it may be considered to impact, on behalf of the organ adopting it, a strong expectation that Members of the international community will abide by it. Consequently, in so far as the expectation is gradually justified by State practice, a declaration may by custom become recognized as laying down Rules binding upon States.
In conclusion, it may be said that in United Nations practice, a 'declaration' is a solemn instrument resorted to only in very rare cases relating to matters of major and lasting importance where maximum compliance is expected.
(Report of the Commission on Human Rights, United Nations document E/3616/Rev. 1, paragraph 105, eighteenth session, Economic and Social Council, 19 March—14 April 1962, United Nations, New York)

As a result of their repeated invocation in the UN texts and in many constitutional texts, some of the UDHR's provisions have become legally binding rules of Customary International Law. In some commentators' opinion, the entire Declaration possesses this status. In any case, the Universal Declaration has been "a powerful factor of creation or of acceleration of the Customary International Law concerning human rights" (Nations Unies 1995, p. 28). Moreover, a number of human rights in the UDHR may be said to have the character of *jus cogens* (see Glossary). In some of its Advisory Opinions, the International Court of Justice (ICJ)[94] considered some of its provisions, at least, to be obligatory (see Schutter 2009a, p. 43, 44).

On 16 November 1950, at the 315th meeting of the Third Committee, during the fifth session of the General Assembly, the USA proposed (A/C.3/L.102) that Governments of Member States designate 10 December as the United Nations Human Rights Day. The proposal was adopted. The General Assembly [Resolution 423(V), 4 December]:

Considering that the Declaration marks a distinct forward step in the march of human progress,
[...]

1. Invites all States and interested organizations to adopt 10 December of each year as Human Rights Day [...].

[94] The ICJ succeeded the Permanent Court of International Justice created by the League of Nations in 1921. It is composed of 15 Judges, elected by the General Assembly and the Security Council, which can request its Advisory Opinion. Only States can accede to it. Its jurisdiction is optional, but the Decisions are binding for the disputing States (Article 92 and Article 94.1 of the UN Charter).

2. Invites all States to report annually through the Secretary-General concerning the observance of Human Rights Day.[95]

According to the CHR third session's Report (E/800): "The Commission recommended to the Economic and Social Council that a meeting of the Commission be held early in 1949 for the completion of the Covenant and the measures of implementation" (para. 17). On the same day of the UDHR adoption, the General Assembly passed a Resolution [217(III)E] requesting the ECOSOC "to ask the Commission on Human Rights to continue to give priority in its work to the preparation of a draft Covenant on Human Rights and draft measures of implementation". This was transmitted to the Commission by the ECOSOC at its eighth session, on 9 February 1949 [191 (VIII)].

The drafting process of the enforceable legal instruments that would complete the International Bill of Human Rights is briefly presented below.

3.3.6 Drafting of the International Covenants on Human Rights (1949–1966)

- *1949*
  The CHR held its fifth session from 9 May to 20 June 1949. It decided to proceed according to the General Assembly Resolution. Having concluded the draft Covenant and the draft Measures of Implementation (but without considering additional articles, including articles on economic, social and cultural rights), it requested the Secretary-General to transmit them to Member States for comments. The drafts would be revised, taking into account the States' comments, at its sixth session. The revised texts should be sent to the ECOSOC to be submitted to the fifth session of the General Assembly.

- *1950*
  The CHR revised the draft Covenant during its sixth session, from 27 March to 19 May 1950 (E/1618 and Corr. 1 and Add. 1) and considered the question of implementation, taking into consideration the comments of Governments. After

---

[95] Meanwhile, according to the *Yearbook of the United Nations 1948–1949*:

> In order to carry out the above resolution [of the Third Committee, concerning the publicity to be given to the Universal Declaration], the United Nations began at once to develop a large-scale programme for disseminating the text of the Universal Declaration of Human Rights in various languages throughout the world, and for using every possible medium of publicity on behalf of this document. With the active co-operation of Member Governments, UNESCO and important non-governmental organizations, it was possible, during 1949, to prepare and disseminate the text of the Universal Declaration in fourteen languages in addition to the five official languages of the United Nations. The fourteen additional languages in which the Declaration was available at the end of 1949 were: Basque, Danish, Dutch, Esperanto, Finnish, German, Japanese, Norwegian, Portuguese, Sinhalese, Swedish, Tagalog, Tamil and Turkish. (p. 537)
> (http://unyearbook.un.org/unyearbook.html?name=isysadvsearch.html).

the revision of the first 18 Articles, it decided that a Human Rights Committee (CCPR) should be established as a permanent body. It would receive complaints by States Parties to the Covenant that another State Party was not giving effect to any provision thereof. The Commission drafted articles on the establishment, composition and competence of the CCPR. In respect of proposals on economic, social and cultural rights, it decided that they would be addressed by additional covenants and measures. These and other decisions were transmitted to the ECOSOC for consideration at its eleventh session, from 3 July to 16 August 1950. The ECOSOC concluded that further progress could not be made until policy decisions were taken by the General Assembly on certain matters [Resolution 303 I (XI) of 9 August 1950], namely: the adequacy of the first 18 articles; the desirability of including articles on economic, social and cultural rights, as well as of special articles on the application of the Covenant to Federal States and to Non-Self-Governing and Trust Territories; and the adequacy of the articles relating to implementation. Member States were requested to submit comments on the draft Covenant.

At the General Assembly fifth session that took place from 19 September to 15 December 1950, the question of the draft Covenant and Measures of Implementation was considered. The drafts were discussed by the Third Committee at its 287th to 316th and 318th meetings, from 18 October to 1 November, and at the Assembly 317th plenary meeting, on 4 December 1950. The Assembly decided, among other things [Resolution 421 (V) of 4 December 1950][96], that the draft articles proposed by the Commission should be revised and additional rights be added. Considering that "the enjoyment of civil and political freedoms and of economic, social and cultural rights are interconnected and interdependent", and that "when deprived of economic, social and cultural rights man does not represent the human person whom the Universal Declaration regards as the ideal of the free man", it requested the Commission "to include in the draft covenant a clear expression of economic, social and cultural rights in a manner which relates them to the civic and political freedoms proclaimed by the draft covenant". Regarding the question of implementation, the Commission was requested "to proceed with the consideration of provisions, to be inserted in the draft covenant or in separate protocols, for the receipt and examination of petitions from individuals and organizations with respect to alleged violations of the covenant".

- *1951*

  At its twelfth session, from 20 February to 21 March 1951, the ECOSOC transmitted to the CHR the General Assembly decisions, and invited the specialized agencies (ILO, UNESCO and WHO) to participate in the work of the Commission relating to economic, social and cultural rights [Resolution 349 (XII) of 23 February 1951].

  The Commission held its seventh session in New York, from 16 April to 19 May. It drafted 14 articles on economic, social and cultural rights, formulated ten

[96] http://daccess-dds-ny.un.org/doc/RESOLUTION/GEN/NR0/060/19/IMG/NR006019.pdf?OpenElement.

articles on Measures of Implementation, and revised the provisions concerning the CCPR. The question of including economic, social and cultural rights in the draft Covenant was much debated, because of their implementation particulars. According to a Document prepared by the Secretary-General to the General Assembly[97]:

> The question of drafting *one* or two covenants was intimately related to the question of implementation. If no measures of implementation were to be formulated, it would make little difference whether one or two covenants were to be drafted. Generally speaking, civil and political rights were thought to be 'legal' rights and could best be implemented by the creation of a good offices committee, while economic, social and cultural rights were thought to be 'program' rights and could best be implemented by the establishment of a system of periodic reports. Since the rights could be divided into two broad categories, which should be subject to different procedures of implementation, it would be both logical and convenient to formulate two separate covenants.

A proposal recommending to ECOSOC that the General Assembly be requested to reconsider its decision to include economic, social and cultural rights in the same Covenant with civil and political rights was not adopted, but the ECOSOC, at its thirteenth session, from 30 July to 21 September 1951, after considering the Report of the Commission, invited "the General Assembly to reconsider its decision in resolution 421 (V), Sect. E, to include in one covenant articles on economic, social and cultural rights, together with articles on civil and political rights" [Resolution 384 (XIII) of 29 August 1951].

The General Assembly debated the matter at its sixth session, held from 6 November 1951 to 5 February 1952. The Third Committee devoted 40 meetings to the question of the draft Covenant and Measures of Implementation, which were also discussed at two plenary meetings of the General Assembly. According to the *Yearbook of the United Nations 1951* (p. 482)[98]:

> Those who spoke in favor of reaffirming the Assembly's decision included the representatives of: Afghanistan, Argentina, the Byelorussian SSR, Chile, Cuba, Czechoslovakia, the Dominican Republic, Ecuador, El Salvador, Ethiopia, Guatemala, Haiti, Iraq, Israel, Mexico, Poland, Syria, the Ukrainian SSR, the USSR, Uruguay and Yugoslavia.
> [...]
> It was claimed by the representatives of Guatemala and the USSR that economic, social and cultural rights were capable of precise definition and that it was possible to include in one instrument the various categories of rights and the measures of implementation pertaining to them, without robbing the covenant of the necessary clarity and precision. The representatives of Chile and Mexico stated that the measures of implementation could be mapped out for both types of rights and that, even if this were not so, the covenant could contain provisions on different measures of implementation applying to different rights.
> Other representatives, however, including those of Australia, Belgium, Brazil, Canada, China, Denmark, Greece, India, Liberia, the Netherlands, New Zealand, the United States and Venezuela, spoke in favor of not inserting in one instrument provisions both on political and civil rights and on economic, social and cultural rights. These members stated that, while civil and political rights could be protected by appropriate legislative or administra-

[97] www2.ohchr.org/english/issues/opinion/articles1920_iccpr/docs/A-2929.pdf.

[98] www.unhcr.org/4e1ee76b0.pdf.

tive measures, the realization of economic, social and cultural rights could only be achieved progressively, because their protection depended on economic and social conditions.

- *1952*
  On 4 February 1952, the General Assembly, overturned its previous decision and [Resolution 543 (VI)]:

  1. Requests the Economic and Social Council to ask the Commission on Human Rights to draft two Covenants on Human Rights, to be submitted simultaneously for the consideration of the General Assembly at its seventh session, one to contain civil and political rights and the other to contain economic, social and cultural rights, in order that the General Assembly may approve the two Covenants simultaneously and open them at the same time for signature, the two Covenants to contain, in order to emphasize the unity of the aim in view and to ensure respect for and observance of human rights, as many similar provisions as possible, particularly in so far as the reports to be submitted by States on the implementation of those rights are concerned;

  The Assembly still decided, among other things, that an article providing that "all peoples shall have the right to self-determination" [Resolution 545 (VI)] should be included in the Covenants.
  The CHR held its eighth session from 14 April to 14 June 1952. It started to work on two Covenants, taking into consideration the instructions of the General Assembly and the ECOSOC, as well as the comments of Governments and Specialized Agencies. It adopted a preamble and 15 articles for the draft Covenant on Economic, Social and Cultural Rights and a preamble and 18 articles for the draft Covenant on Civil and Political Rights. A proposal asking the General Assembly to reverse its Resolution 543 (VI) on the drafting of two separate Covenants was not adopted.
  The Commission having not been able to conclude its tasks, the ECOSOC instructed it to complete the work on the Covenants at its next session [Resolution 440 (XIV)].

- *1953*
  The CHR met for its ninth session from 7 April to 30 May 1953. Following the decision of the General Assembly and the instructions of the ECOSOC, it proceeded with the work of drafting the Covenants and Measures of Implementation, but did not have time to conclude its agenda. The ECOSOC requested it to complete the work at its tenth session in 1954, transmitted the draft Covenants to the General Assembly, and invited Member States, Specialized Agencies and NGOs to submit comments [Resolution 501 B (XVI)]. A new proposal asking the General Assembly to reconsider its Resolution 543 (VI) was rejected again.

- *1954*
  The CHR completed the drafting of the Covenants at its tenth session, from 23 February to 18 April 1954 (E/2573), which were transmitted by the ECOSOC to the General Assembly without further debate [Resolution 545B I (XVII) of 29 July 1954].
  In the same year, at its ninth session, the General Assembly held a first reading of the draft Covenants and recommended that, during the tenth session, the Third Committee should give priority to their discussion.

- *1955*
  At the tenth session, held between 11 October and 11 November, between 21 and 30 November and on 2 December 1955, the Third Committee dedicated 39 meetings to the reading of the draft Covenants.

- *1956*
  The Third Committee continued the article-by-article discussion of the draft Covenants, during 40 meetings, from 13 to 21 December 1956, and from 3 to 21 January 1957.
  Because of the political climate prevailing then, the reading advanced slowly and continued from 1955 to 1963, until the seventeenth session of the General Assembly[99].

- *1966*
  The heavy agenda of the General Assembly caused the topic to be deferred to 1966, when the Third Committee eventually completed the drafting and adoption of the two Covenants and the Optional Protocol to the Covenant on Civil and Political Rights (A/6564). They were adopted by the General Assembly on 16 December 1966 [Resolution 2200 A (XXI)]: the International Covenant on Civil and Political Rights (ICCPR), essentially codifying and developing the provisions of Articles 3 to 21 of the UDHR, was adopted with a vote of 106 to 0; the Optional Protocol enabling the Committee established by the Covenant to receive individual communications claiming to be victims of violations of any of the rights set forth in it (ICCPR-OP1) was adopted by a vote of 66 to 2, with 38 abstentions; the International Covenant on Economic, Social and Cultural Rights (ICESCR), essentially codifying and developing the provisions of Articles 22 to 27 of the UDHR, was adopted with a vote of 105 to 0[100]. In accordance with their respective provisions, the ICESCR entered into force on 3 January 1976, and the ICCPR, together with its Protocol, entered into force on 23 March 1976[101].

The two Covenants have a similar structure and similar wording in some of their provisions. The Preambles affirm the interdependence of all human rights. Part I of both Covenants recognizes the right of all peoples to self-determination and to freely dispose of their natural wealth and resources. Part II contains general provisions prohibiting discrimination and affirming the equal rights of men and women. Part III elaborates on the substantive provisions. The ICCPR does not include the right to property and the right to asylum, but includes additional rights, such as the

[99] It should be noted that between 1945 and 1960 more than 40 territories achieved independence. By 1967, 57% of the UN 127 States Members were Asian and African States (representing a quarter of the inhabitants of the planet). This transformation of the world's political geography shifted the balance of power in the General Assembly and had significant influence in the Covenants' drafting. Meanwhile, 29 new Asian-African independent States met in Bandung (Indonesia) for their first conference, in 1955. The Bandung Conference paved the way to the so-called Non-Aligned Movement, the first summit of which took place in 1961, in Belgrade (Yugoslavia).

[100] www.un.org/documents/instruments/docs_en.asp?year=1969.

[101] Humphrey (1989) observed that the title of the ICCPR is a misnomer, for most of the rights enunciated in it are both citizens' and aliens' rights. The only rights limited to citizens are those mentioned in Article 25, which are also the only rights exclusively political.

rights of detainees and the protection of minorities. According to the above mentioned Document prepared by the Secretary-General to the General Assembly:

> There were two schools of thought regarding the manner in which articles on substantive rights should be drafted. One school held that each article should be a brief clause of a general character; another school was of the opinion that each right, its scope and substance, its limitations, as well as the obligations of the State in respect thereof, should be drafted with the greatest possible precision.
> [...]
> It was clear that each of the two schools had exerted its influence on the drafting of the substantive articles. Some articles were formulated in a very general manner, while others were drawn up in elaborate terms.
> It was realized, of course, that the logic of neither school could be carried to its extreme: the covenants should not be a second edition of the Universal Declaration of Human Rights, nor could they be a compendium of all civil and criminal codes and all social and educational laws.[102]

A second Optional Protocol to the ICCPR (ICCPR-OP2), aiming at the abolition of the death penalty, was adopted in 1989 and entered into force in 1991.

In 1985, the ECOSOC established the Committee on Economic, Social and Cultural Rights (CESCR) (Resolution 1985/17 of 28 May). In 2008, an Optional Protocol to the ICESCR was adopted, enabling the CESCR to receive and consider individual communications. This new instrument, recognizing "the justiciability of economic, social and cultural rights in the international sphere, on an equal footing with civil and political rights" (Courtis 2012), provides for three mechanisms:

- A procedure for communications, allowing individuals and groups of individuals to present complaints before the CESCR.
- An inter-state communications procedure, allowing a State Party to submit communications to the CESCR (dependent upon a formal acceptation by States).
- An inquiry procedure, allowing the CESCR to conduct an inquiry based on grave or systematic violations of the ICESCR by a State Party[103].

---

[102] www2.ohchr.org/english/issues/opinion/articles1920_iccpr/docs/A-2929.pdf.

[103] www2.ohchr.org/english/law/docs/a.RES.63.117_en.pdf

It was in 1991 that the CESCR initiated the debate on whether to draft an Optional Protocol to the Covenant. A draft Protocol was finalized in 1996 and submitted to the CHR in 1997. Between 1998 and 2001, Governments and several organizations submitted comments. In 2001, the CHR appointed an Independent Expert on the Question of an Optional Protocol to the International Covenant on Economic, Social and Cultural Rights. In 2002, the Commission established an open-ended Working Group to study options regarding the elaboration of the Optional Protocol. The Working Group met three times (2004, 2005 and 2006). In 2006, its mandate was extended for a period of 2 years.

Concluded on 4 April 2008, the Optional Protocol draft was adopted by the UN General Assembly, without a vote, on 10 December 2008. On 24 September 2009, it was opened for signature in the Treaty Event, at the UN Headquarters, in New York. It was then signed by 29 States, the first of which was Portugal (see Albuquerque 2010).

An Australian Report on a research project observes that "many of the objections to the recognition of ESCR [economic, social and cultural rights] as 'real' human rights capable of judicial enforcement reflect an analysis that is out of date and that fails to reflect the significant advances

The 1948 Universal Declaration and the 1966 International Covenants, with their Protocols, form the so-called International Bill of Human Rights that is the IHRL's most general normative framework.

3.3.7 Other Core Human Rights Treaties

The UDHR became progressively "the source of inspiration and has been the basis for the United Nations in making advances in standard setting as contained in the existing international human rights instruments", as reads the Preamble of the Declaration and Programme of Action adopted by the World Conference on Human Rights in 1993, in Vienna[104]. In addition to the two 1966 International Covenants, there are currently seven more core human rights treaties, with some protocols[105].

- International Convention on the Elimination of All Forms of Racial Discrimination (ICERD), 1965.
- Convention on the Elimination of All Forms of Discrimination against Women (CEDAW), 1979.
- Convention against Torture and Other Cruel, Inhuman or Degrading Treatment or Punishment (CAT), 1984.
- Convention on the Rights of the Child (CRC), 1989[106].
- International Convention on the Protection of the Rights of All Migrant Workers and Members of Their Families (ICPRMW), 1990.
- Convention on the Rights of Persons with Disabilities (CRPD), 2006[107].
- International Convention for the Protection of All Persons from Enforced Disappearance (CPED), 2006.

In addition to the three Optional Protocols to the 1966 International Covenants, there are six more Optional Protocols establishing complaints procedures or providing additional rights:

---

that have been made in scholarly analysis, international practice, and domestic litigation in relation to ESCR". In fact: "It is clear that, while certain aspects of ESCR are subject to obligations of progressive realization, all ESCR have dimensions that are capable of immediate implementation. These include in particular the obligations of non-discrimination, to ensure a core minimum level of enjoyment of ESCR, and to take concrete and targeted steps towards full realization of the rights". That is why, "far from being unusual, legal protection of ESCR—including judicial enforcement—is common in countries on all continents, with differing legal systems, and at different stages of development", especially "in South Africa, which is frequently seen as showing the way in which justiciable guarantees of ESCR can provide meaningful protection without undermining the appropriate division of powers between the different branches of government" (p. 12, 13, 14). (http://regnet.anu.edu.au/sites/default/files/u82/ACTESCR_project_final_report.pdf).

[104] http://daccess-dds-ny.un.org/doc/UNDOC/GEN/G93/142/33/PDF/G9314233.pdf?OpenElement.

[105] www2.ohchr.org/english/law/.

[106] The CRC is the ever most rapidly ratified human rights treaty.

[107] This is the second treaty most rapidly ratified (after the CRC).

- Optional Protocol to the CEDAW establishing a complaints procedure (CEDAW-OP), 1999.
- Optional Protocol to the CRC on the involvement of children in armed conflict (CRC-OP1), 2000.
- Optional Protocol to the CRC on the sale of children, child prostitution and child pornography (CRC-OP2), 2000.
- Optional Protocol to the CAT establishing a system of independent inspection of places of detention (CAT-OP), 2002.
- Optional Protocol to the CRPD establishing a complaints procedure (CRPD-OP), 2006.
- Optional Protocol to the CRC establishing a complaints procedure (CRC-OP3), 2011.

This is the most general framework of the IHRL, the normative *corpus* of which encompasses instruments adopted at universal level (UN) and at regional level (European, American and African). They may have conventional nature (being binding) or declaratory nature (not binding); general content (encompassing all or a set of rights) or categorical content (concerning the rights of a more vulnerable category of people) or specific content (regarding a sole right).

A 2002 UN publication recorded 97 instruments on human rights, 53 of which having a conventional nature, and 44 having a non-conventional nature[108]. This is not a complete compilation, however. It includes instruments adopted by UNESCO and ILO, in particular, but not all of them (ILO adopted around 200 Conventions and about as many Recommendations on different aspects of the right to work).

Another branch of International Law closely related to IHRL is IHL (International Humanitarian Law) that aims at 'humanizing' the means of warfare, and protecting persons who are not, or no longer, taking part in armed conflicts (see Glossary).

Two international Conferences convened to commemorate two anniversaries of the UDHR deserve to be mentioned:

- The International Conference on Human Rights that met in Tehran from 22 April to 13 May 1968, with the participation of 84 States. It adopted a Proclamation

[108] *Human Rights—A Compilation of International Instruments*, 2002 (www.ohchr.org/Documents/Publications/Compilation2en.pdf)
With respect to the normative value of the non-binding instruments, in the Introduction to that publication it is noted that "such instruments have an undeniable moral force and provide practical guidance to States in their conduct. The value of such instruments rests on their recognition and acceptance by a large number of States and, even without binding effect, they may be seen as declaratory of broadly accepted goals and principles within the international community".
Trindade (2006) observes: "Resolutions of international organizations have a specificity of their own, being distinct from other categories of 'sources' enumerated in Article 38 of the ICJ (International Court of Justice) Statute. Significantly, the silence, about them, of that provision has not impeded the ICJ to take them promptly and properly into account" (p. 166). In Andrew Clapham's (2009) view: "The resolutions and declarations can develop customary international law, may provide pertinent interpretations of treaty obligations, and often represent the universal standards which are used throughout the human rights movement to hold states and non-state actors accountable" (p. 80).

and 29 Resolutions (apart from 18 especially addressed to the United Nations bodies).
- The World Conference on Human Rights that met in Vienna from 14 to 25 June 1993 (above mentioned). Prepared by regional Conferences, it gathered about 7000 people, among them representatives of more than 170 States and of about 800 NGOs. It adopted a Declaration and Programme of Action that, according to a UN publication (1995), "should be considered as the arrival point of a long process and the starting point of a new adventure in the service of human rights [...], the reference document of the policies and activities of the international community for the future" (p. 97, 103).

On the occasion of the 20th anniversary of this Conference, was organised an international expert conference entitled 'Vienna + 20: Advancing the Protection of Human Rights', in Vienna, on 27–28 June 2013, in cooperation with the OHCHR. According to the Conference Report[109]:

> Overall, participants expressed their concerns about the significant implementation gap between the high aspirations of the universal human rights system and the sobering reality on the ground. It was pointed out, in particular, that the lack of accountability for human rights violations today goes beyond States and increasingly applies to other powerful actors, including inter-governmental organisations, transnational corporations and other non-state duty bearers.

Within the international regional framework, there are three major instruments:

- European Convention on Human Rights (ECHR), adopted by the Council of Europe in 1950, now with 14 Protocols[110]
- American Convention on Human Rights (ACHR), also known as Pact of San José de Costa Rica, adopted by an Inter-American Specialized Conference in 1969, now with 2 Protocols[111]
- African Charter on Human and Peoples' Rights (ACHPR), also known as Banjul Charter, adopted by the former Organization of African Unity (OAU) in 1981, now with two Protocols[112].

The strength of IHRL depends on it being incorporated into the domestic law, and the sanction of its breaches (by action or omission) depends on the will and power of the organized International Community.

Henkin (1990) concluded: "The move from State values to human values represented by the new international law of human rights [...] contributed to a universal human rights culture which has been slowly taking root around the world" (p. 273). In 1947, in his Course at The Hague Academy of International Law, Lauterpacht (1948) said that "an International Bill of Human Rights [...] may, by finally consti-

[109] www.ohchr.org/Documents/Events/OHCHR20/ConferenceReport.pdf.

[110] www.echr.coe.int/NR/rdonlyres/D5CC24A7-DC13-4318-B457-5C9014916D7A/0/ENG_CONV.pdf.

[111] www.echr.coe.int/NR/rdonlyres/D5CC24A7-DC13-4318-B457-5C9014916D7A/0/ENG_CONV.pdf.

[112] www.wunrn.com/reference/pdf/American_convention_Human_Rights.PDF.

tuting the individual a subject of the international commonwealth, prove to be the first decisive step in the evolution of the Federation of the World which must, till accomplished, be regarded as the primary goal of humanity" (p. 105).

3.3.8 New Human Rights

The history of the juridification of human rights is frequently put in terms of 'generations'.

Following the denominations of the 1966 International Covenants, there are five categories of human rights: civil, political, economic, social and cultural. The civil and political rights are often called 'first generation' rights or 'liberty rights'. They are mainly rights against the State, proclaimed by the eighteenth century Declarations and progressively incorporated into the constitutional texts, becoming a cornerstone of the liberal democracies. In the course of the nineteenth and first half of the twentieth centuries, the economic and social transformations made clear the insufficiency of those rights, and economic, social and cultural rights emerged, such as the right to work and the right to education. They are often called 'second generation' rights or 'equality rights'. They were forwarded especially by the socialist ideologies and entered the Constitutional Law principally after the First World War[113]. Milestones in their development were the 1917 Mexican Constitution, the 1919 German Constitution (Weimar) and the 1936 Soviet Constitution[114]. They were included in the UDHR.

Since the late 1960s, a 'third generation' of human rights took the floor. They were called 'solidarity rights' or 'new human rights' (so were called the social, economic and cultural rights too, when the Universal Declaration was being drafted). Their promotion owes much to Karel Vasak who, in 1979, in his Opening Lesson of the Tenth Session of the Summer Course of the *Institut International des Droits de l'Homme* (International Institute of Human Rights) (Strasbourg), under the title "For the third generation of human rights: the rights of solidarity", said that they are new because they respond to new problems and aspirations. "Rights of liberty, rights of equality, rights of fraternity and of solidarity: here are the three generations of the human adventure" (Vasak 1979).

At the same Course, Jean Rivero (1979) also addressed "The problem of the 'new' human rights", but in a divergent way. In his opinion, they are rights not fitting into the scheme following which every human right is defined by determining its right-holders, object and duty-bearers. Are they individual or collective? If collective, what

---

[113] However: "The Bern Convention of 1906 prohibiting night-shift work by women can be seen as the first multilateral convention meant to safeguard social rights. [...] Remarkable as it may seem, therefore, while the classic human rights had been acknowledged long before social rights, the latter were first embodied in international regulations" (Sepúlveda et al. 2004, p. 5).

[114] Cassin observed during the CHR third session: "It was noteworthy that all States which had rewritten their constitutions during the past 30 years had given special and separate attention to economic and social rights" (E/CN.4/SR.72).

collectivities are the respective holders? Their object is generally imprecise and even impossible. Regarding the duty-bearers, they are undetermined (against whom, for instance, can one claim the right to peace?) and are opposable to the rights-holders themselves. Furthermore, it was argued too, the terms 'generation' and 'new' may be interpreted as suggesting that the older ones became less important.

The matter was debated in a Colloquium on the New Human Rights convened by UNESCO in 1980, in Mexico City, from 12 to 15 August, following a Resolution (3/1.1/1) of its General Conference. It was prepared by experts' studies on the right to communicate, the right to be different, the right to a healthy environment, the right to peace, the right to development and the right to the common heritage of mankind. According to the Final Report, the following opinions were expressed, among others:

- The right to communication is not new, strictly speaking, as it derives from rights already recognized. It is an extension of the right to information, which is its more important element. "The right to information is a particularly sensitive political issue. It can even be claimed that political regimes can be categorized according to their performance with regard to information" (UNESCO 1980, p. 5).
- The right to be different is "truly a new right" (p. 11). It was recognized for the first time in the Declaration on Race and Racial Prejudice (UNESCO 1978). However, it may be connected to existing rights, such as the right to life and the freedoms of thought, conscience, religion, etc. To that extent, it is "more a principle for the interpretation of existing human rights than an actual new right" (p. 13).
- The right to a healthy environment is indisputably new. Everyone is both its right-holder and duty-bearer. "It is today widely accepted that a healthy and balanced environment is vital to respect for human dignity and the exercise of individual rights and freedoms" (p. 14)[115].
- The right to peace has its foundation in the UN Charter, having been subsequently reaffirmed in a number of international instruments. Peace may be considered as the *raison d'être* (reason of being) of International Law. "From a human rights perspective, the struggle to achieve peace is very closely associated with the struggle against all forms of massive and flagrant violations of human rights" (p. 21).
- The right to development has an evolving content. "Originally, the concept of development appeared to be closely linked to the much-debated notion of 'economic growth'; today, the concept has become more independent and 'development' is a multi-dimensional notion, or even better, one of 'fullness'" (p. 23).

[115] The most comprehensive international statement on environmental rights to date is the *Draft Declaration of Principles on Human Rights and the Environment* (1994) appended to the Report of the UN Special Rapporteur on Human Rights and the Environment, presented to the Sub-Commission on Prevention of Discrimination and Protection of Minorities. (www.unhchr.ch/Huridocda/Huridoca.nsf/0/eeab2b6937bccaa18025675c005779c3).

- The right to the common heritage of mankind is concerned with common goods, indivisible, such as the space and the sea bed. "States are the direct beneficiaries of this right, and through States, individuals" (p. 28).

The individual and collective dimensions of these rights were time and again restated. Other ideas were expressed, such as: The human being is the final addressee of any legal order; human rights are dynamic; the new human rights may be considered as new dimensions or syntheses of existing rights; participation is essential for their implementation. It may be argued that the basis for the third generation of human rights is provided in UDHR Article 28 that reads: "Everyone is entitled to a social and international order in which the rights and freedoms set forth in this Declaration can be fully realized". ACHPR does recognize the right to development, the right to peace and the right to a health environment (Articles 22–24), but this is an isolated advancement in conventional International Law.

Asbjørn Eide and Allan Rosas (2001) comments:

> It has been asserted that economic, social and cultural rights constitute a 'second generation' of human rights, the first generation being civil and political rights, and the later or a third generation of solidarity rights has been added, such as the right to self-determination and the right to development. [...] The editors of this volume, however, do not adhere to the notion of 'generations'. The history of the evolution of human rights at the national level does not make it possible to place the emergence of different human rights into clear-cut stages. Efforts to do so would in any case make it necessary to distinguish also between civil and political rights, since political rights were accepted as human rights much later than some of the civil rights, in some countries even later than economic and social rights. [...] Trade union rights and property rights are often mentioned as rights which are difficult to classify according the two-fold distinction. (p. 4)

In Martin Scheinin's (2009a) view:

> In the international discourse on human rights, reference is often made to a 'third generation' of human rights, supplementing the more traditional categorization into civil and political v. economic, social and cultural rights. These third-generation rights are described as 'rights of solidarity', and include rights such as the right to peace, the right to development and environmental rights.
>
> [...]
>
> While they are disputed as true human rights per se, they at least relate to a number of internationally recognized human rights. The right to development can, in fact, be seen as an umbrella concept and a policy-oriented programme, which covers most of the existing human rights, including civil and political rights. The right to peace can be tackled in the context of the right to life. The right to a satisfactory environment can be broken down into more specific environmental rights which can be dealt with in the context of rights such as the protection against inhumane and degrading treatment, and the right to privacy, the right to health, the right to participate in public affairs, the right to property, etc. (p. 25)

In this respect, Nowak (2001) remarked:

> Modern human rights terminology usually distinguishes three generations of human rights: the first generation of civil and political rights, the second generation of economic, social and cultural rights, and the third generation of solidarity or group rights.
>
> Since all human rights are interdependent, indivisible and interrelated, the theory of three generations does not, of course, imply any hierarchy of lower and higher stages in the development of human rights law. Nevertheless, this theory provides a vivid illustration

> [of] how the major categories of human rights emerged in political philosophy as well as in the history of national constitutions and international law. In addition, the assignment to any of the three generations may assist in interpreting the exact scope of the right in question, the precise legal claims of the respective holder of the right as well as the corresponding obligations of the State.

However: "Certain rights, such as the right to own property or the right to strike and form trade unions may qualify as both civil or political and economic rights and, therefore, fall into two generations" (p. 252).

The 'generations' terminology is not accurate. While the classic freedoms have been acknowledged long before social rights, the latter internationalized first. Following Ramcharan (2008): "Rights cannot be separated into generational categories except as academic classifications for the purposes of teaching or research" (p. 4).

While the human rights division into 'generations' remains controversial, the principle of the indivisibility and interdependence of all human rights is a cornerstone of the IHRL (see Glossary), meaning that human rights have equal legal status and cannot be ranked in a hierarchy. Indeed, human dignity is not divisible. "Human dignity, which is one and the same everywhere and for everyone, grounds the *indivisibility* of all categories of human rights" (Habermas 2012, p. 67).

> So, for example, a child who is unable to receive necessary medical care (the right to the highest attainable standard of health) will have difficulty in learning at school (the right to education) and, as an adult, will have difficulty in finding a fulfilling job (the right to work), in expressing her or his views (the right to freedom of expression), in contributing to political life (the right to vote) and so on. These rights are interdependent, relying on the enjoyment of one for the enjoyment of others. (APF 2012, p. 8)

The principle of the human rights indivisibility is encapsulated in the UDHR second preambular paragraph: "...the advent of a world in which human beings shall enjoy freedom of speech and belief and freedom from fear and want has been proclaimed the highest aspiration of the common people". These words pay tribute to Roosevelt who affirmed in the above quoted 'Second Bill of Rights' (1944): "We have come to a clear realization of the fact that that true individual freedom cannot exist without economic security and independence. 'Necessitous men are not free men'"[116].

CEDAW (1979) was the first human rights treaty to encompass all categories of human rights. This holistic articulation was taken up by ACHPR (1981), CRC (1989), ICPRMW (1990), and the Charter of Fundamental Rights of the European Union (EU Charter 2000). The Vienna Declaration and Programme of Action (1993) reaffirmed:

> 5. All human rights are universal, indivisible and interdependent and interrelated. The international community must treat human rights globally in a fair and equal manner, on the same footing, and with the same emphasis. While the significance of national and regional particularities and various historical, cultural and religious backgrounds must be borne in mind, it is the duty of States, regardless of their political, economic and cultural systems, to promote and protect all human rights and fundamental freedoms.

[116] www.ushistory.org/documents/economic_bill_of_rights.htm.

The human rights indivisibility is epitomized by the right to life meaningfully and broadly understood (see below). To stress the unity of all human rights, their traditional categories are often mentioned in alphabetical order: civil, cultural, economic, political and social.

Sohn (1982) concluded:

> The new group of human rights has been given a variety of names: the third generation of human rights; rights of solidarity; collective rights, or rights of every human being and of all human beings taken collectively; synthetic rights; consolidated rights; communal rights; rights of the peoples, or populist or popular rights; joint rights of individuals and other groups, or rights exercised by individuals separately and jointly; and new rights or new dimensions of existing rights. [...]
> Perhaps these new concepts can be the equivalent of the Dutch boy's finger that at the last minute plugged the hole in the dike. We are in a desperate situation; we need to be brave. As Virgil said, '*audentes fortuna juvat*': fortune helps the daring. In the field of human rights we have had two successful revolutions; we should have the courage to begin a third. (p. 61, 63, 64)

Indeed, the Humankind destiny is "to move forward [...] to new goals of human happiness and well-being", as affirmed President Roosevelt in his 'Second Bill of Rights' (1944).

3.4 Human Rights Protection

Where there is a right, there must be a remedy, a Latin adage says (*Ubi ius ibi remedium*). "The principle that every right must be accompanied by the availability of an effective remedy is a general principle of law that exists across all legal systems and is enshrined in Article 8 of the Universal Declaration on Human Rights" (Schutter et al. 2012, p. 1160). Rights and obligations are two sides of the same coin.

There are universal and regional systems/regimes of human rights.

3.4.1 Universal Level

In 1946, as we saw, on the basis of Articles 7.2 and 68 of the UN Charter, the ECOSOC established the CHR as the main body for human rights promotion and protection within the UN system, and authorized it to create a subsidiary organ: the Sub-Commission on Prevention of Discrimination and Protection of Minorities (renamed Sub-Commission on the Promotion and Protection of Human Rights in 1999), composed of independent experts. The CHR did not assume authority to deal with complaints of human rights violations, however.

The establishment of an International Penal Tribunal was admitted in the UN Convention on the Prevention and Punishment of the Crime of Genocide (1948)[117],

[117] www2.ohchr.org/english/law/genocide.htm.

whose Article VI reads: "Persons charged with genocide or any of the other acts enumerated in article III shall be tried by a competent tribunal of the State in the territory of which the act was committed, or by such international penal tribunal as may have jurisdiction with respect to those Contracting Parties which shall have accepted its jurisdiction". This possibility was never implemented.

In 1951, Uruguay submitted to the CHR (Seventh Session, E/CN.4/549) a proposal on the Establishment of an Office of the United Nations High Commissioner (Attorney-General) for Human Rights[118], but the idea was not considered. It was resumed in the 1960s. By its Resolution 2062 (XX) on the 'Creation of the post of United Nations High Commissioner for Human Rights' (16 December 1965), the General Assembly requested the ECOSOC to transmit the proposal to the CHR for study. A draft was prepared by a working group in which Costa Rica played a major role. It was transmitted to the General Assembly but was not discussed.

In 1967, the ECOSOC authorized the CHR to deal with violations of human rights in some countries [Resolution 1235 (XLII), of 6 June 1967], abandoning the doctrine of no competence in addressing human rights violations. So was created the first 'Charter-based' human rights procedure to review human rights violations.

In 1970, the Commission was authorized to receive and inquire into complaints of "consistent patterns of gross and reliably attested violations of all human rights and all fundamental freedoms" [Resolution 1503 (XLVIII), of 27 May 1970].

In 1982, the former Division of Human Rights was replaced with a Centre for Human Rights, based in Geneva, with an Office in New York.

In 1989, responding to a request from Trinidad and Tobago, the General Assembly asked the UN International Law Commission to resume work on establishment of an International Criminal Court.

In the 1990s, gross and systematic violations of the IHL and the IHRL led the UN Security Council to the establishment of two *ad hoc* Tribunals: the International Criminal Tribunal for Former Yugoslavia (S/RES/827, 1993), based in The Hague (Netherlands), and the International Criminal Tribunal for Rwanda (S/RES/955, 1994), based in Arusha (Tanzania). In 2002, a similar Court was set up by Agreement between the United Nations and the Government of Sierra Leone on the Establishment of a Special Court for Sierra Leone, Freetown.

In 1994, the International Law Commission submitted a draft Statute for an International Criminal Court to the General Assembly. In 1998, a UN Diplomatic Conference of Plenipotentiaries on the Establishment of an International Criminal Court met in Rome, from 15 June to 17 July, to adopt the Statute of the Court drafted by a Preparatory Committee on the Establishment of an International Criminal Court that met since 1996 (A/CONF.183/9 of 17 July 1998)[119]. The Rome Statute of the International Criminal Court (ICC) entered into force on 1 July 2002. The Court, composed of 18 Judges, sits at The Hague (Netherlands).

The ICC Statute, affirming that the individual is no more only holder of international rights but is also internationally accountable of "the most serious crimes

[118] www2.ohchr.org/english/issues/opinion/articles1920_iccpr/docs/A-2929.pdf.

[119] http://untreaty.un.org/cod/icc/statute/romefra.htm.

of concern to the international community as a whole" (Article 5), culminated an evolution started with the International Military Tribunal at Nuremberg.

The principle of individual responsibility had already been explicitly embodied in the Kellogg-Briand Pact (1928), based on the distinction between just and unjust war.

During the Moscow Conference, in October 1943, Roosevelt, Churchill and Stalin, "speaking in the interest of the 32 United Nations", signed a Statement on Atrocities, according to which lists of the war criminals should be compiled "in order they may be judged and punished"[120]. In the same month, the United Nations War Crimes Commission was constituted at a meeting held at the British Foreign Office in London. "It should investigate and record the evidence of war crimes, identifying where possible the individuals responsible" (United Nations War Crimes Commission 1948, p. 3). Over 36,800 were listed.

On 8 August 1945, the Government of the United States of America, the Provisional Government of the French Republic, the Government of the United Kingdom of Great Britain and Northern Ireland and the Government of the Union of Soviet Socialist Republics signed, in London, an Agreement for the Prosecution and Punishment of the Major War Criminals of the European Axis[121]. Annexed, it included the Charter of an International Military Tribunal. It was constituted by one judge and one associate judge from each of the four Great Powers. Only the Russian members were military judges, however. The trials of the 23 major war criminals (political and military leaders) were held at Nuremberg between 20 November 1945 and 1 October 1946. An International Military Tribunal for the Far East was established at Tokyo by the Special Proclamation of 19 January 1946 of Supreme Commander for the Allied Powers, General D. McArthur. It was made up of 11 Justices from 11 Allied nations: Australia, Canada, China, France, Great Britain, India, the Netherlands, New Zealand, the Philippines, the Soviet Union and the United States of America. The trials lasted two and a half years (from May 1946 to November 1948). Other war criminals were tried in the victims' countries[122].

According to the Charter of the International Military Tribunal at Nuremberg:

> Article 7
> The official position of defendants, whether as Heads of State or responsible officials in Government Departments, shall not be considered as freeing them from responsibility or mitigating punishment.
>
> Article 8
> The fact that the Defendant acted pursuant to order of his Government or of a superior shall not free him from responsibility, but may be considered in mitigation of punishment if the Tribunal determines that justice so requires.

[120] http://avalon.law.yale.edu/wwii/moscow.asp.

[121] http://avalon.law.yale.edu/imt/imtconst.asp.

[122] From the autumn of 1945 until the spring of 1948, about 1,000 cases were tried in the European continent, involving about 2,700 'minor' criminals. A comparable number of war criminals were tried in the Far Eastern region.

Also according to the Charter of the International Military Tribunal for the Far East, at Tokyo (Article 6)[123]:

> Neither the official position, at any time, of an accused, nor the fact that an accused acted pursuant to order of his government or of a superior shall, of itself, be sufficient to free such accused from responsibility for any crime with which he is charged, but such circumstances may be considered in mitigation of punishment if the Tribunal determines that justice so requires.

As was to be expected, the defense of the war criminals invoked both the doctrine of acts of State and that of immunity of State actors. It was also objected that an International Tribunal is incapable of applying the international laws of war to individuals, because International Law is binding only on the States as such. However, the London Charter "not only authoritatively rendered aggressive war an international crime, but made it in addition a crime *punishable* by an international tribunal" (United Nations War Crimes Commission 1948, p. 246). The Nuremberg Tribunal considered that the London Charter was the expression of International Law existing at the time of its creation, and that a violation of the laws of war is both an international and a national crime. It stated:

> It was submitted that international law is concerned with the actions of sovereign States, and provides no punishment for individuals; and further, and where the act in question is an act of State, those who carry it out are not personally responsible, but are protected by the doctrine of the sovereignty of the State. In the opinion of the Tribunal, both these submissions must be rejected. [...]
> ... the very essence of the Charter is that individuals have international duties which transcend the national obligations of obedience imposed by the individual state. He who violates the laws of war cannot obtain immunity while acting in pursuance of the authority of the state if the state in authorizing action moves outside its competence under international law. (as cit. ib. p. 272)

The Nuremberg Tribunal further stressed: "Crimes against international law are committed by men, not by abstract entities, and only by punishing individuals who commit such crimes can the provisions of international law be enforced" (p. 9)[124]. The United Nations War Crimes Commission remarked: "The irrelevance of the doctrines of acts of States and of immunity of State administrators, and the principle of individual penal responsibility of the latter in contemporary international law, received the highest judicial sanction at the trials of the Nazi war criminals at

---

[123] www.jus.uio.no/english/services/library/treaties/04/4-06/military-tribunal-far-east.xml.

[124] In a Report submitted to the President of the United States in June 1945, Justice Robert H. Jackson, the United States Chief of Councel in the prosecution of European Axis criminals, had referred to:

> ... the obsolete doctrine that a head of State is immune from legal liability. There is more than a suspicion that this idea is a relic of the doctrine of the divine right of Kings. [...] We do not accept the paradox that legal responsibility should be the least where power is the greatest. We stand on the principle of responsible government declared some three centuries ago to King James by Lord Chief Justice Coke, who proclaimed that even King is still 'under God and the law'. (as cit. ib. p. 271)

Nuremberg" (p. 269)[125]. The Convention against Torture and Other Cruel, Inhuman or Degrading Treatment or Punishment[126] provides (Article 2.3): "An order from a superior officer or a public authority may not be invoked as a justification of torture".

Coming back to the ICC Statute, it includes only three references to human rights (Articles 21.3; 36.3.b.ii; 69.7), but they lie at the core of its mission. In Schabas' (2009) opinion: "Diplomats drafting the Statute at Rome were anxious than any suggestions that the Court was an institution involved in the promotion and protection of human rights might discourage support" (p. 657).

In any case, following the first paragraph of the Preamble of the Vienna Declaration and Programme of Action[127], "the promotion and protection of human rights is a matter of priority for the international community". They are addressed by a variety of mechanisms established at universal and regional levels[128].

The UN Charter established six principal organs: General Assembly, Security Council, ECOSOC, Trusteeship Council, ICJ, and Secretariat.

The General Assembly consists of all UN Member States (193, as of September 2013). It meets for its annual session from September to December, in New York, but may meet at other times to consider specific issues. It decides by a majority vote, every Member State having one vote regardless of its geographical size, population amount, wealth or any other factor. Most matters are decided by a simple majority, but some "special" matters require stronger majorities. However, while it is a universal Parliament, its decisions have no legal force (except for the treaties adopted within its framework).

The General Assembly membership is organized into five regional groupings, namely:

- African Group (54 States)
- Asian Group (54 States)
- Latin American and the Caribbean Group (33 States)

[125] Very surprising is that Goebbels himself had written in an article published in the German press on 28 May 1944: "No international law of warfare is in existence which provides that a soldier who has committed a mean crime can escape punishment by pleading as his defence that he followed the commands of his superiors. This holds particularly true if those commands are contrary to all human ethics and opposed to the well-established international use of warfare" (as cit. ib. p. 288).

[126] www.ohchr.org/EN/ProfessionalInterest/Pages/CAT.aspx.

[127] http://daccess-dds-ny.un.org/doc/UNDOC/GEN/G93/142/33/PDF/G9314233.pdf?OpenElement.

[128] Partsch (1991) referred to them as follows:

> The function of promotion and protection of human rights, at international and regional level, is entrusted to a *great number* of very differentiated organs. They are own and statutory bodies of the organizations, specialized conventional bodies, permanent or *ad hoc* bodies created for this effect. They distinguish themselves according to a great number of criteria: permanence, composition (government representatives or experts), according to their procedure methods (conciliatory, almost-judicial or judicial; public or confidential) and, finally, according to the character of the act concluding their works (conciliation, friendly solution, recommendation, obligatory decision or judgement, accompanied or not of sanctions). (p. 482)

- Western European and Others Group (29 States)
- Eastern European Group (23 States)

The General Assembly has six committees, namely:

- First Committee (Disarmament and International Security Committee)
- Second Committee (Economic and Financial Committee)
- Third Committee (Social, Humanitarian and Cultural Committee)
- Fourth Committee (Special Political and Decolonization Committee)
- Fifth Committee (Administrative and Budgetary Committee)
- Sixth Committee (Legal Committee)

Each Committee is made up of representatives of all the UN Member States. The Third Committee addresses most human rights issues. It adopts and recommends that the General Assembly adopt resolutions, and considers the report of the Human Rights Council (HRC).

The Security Council is composed of 15 members, five of which with permanent seats, namely: USA, UK, Russia, France and China, which have the power of veto. The other ten members are elected for terms of 2 years (five each year), on a regional basis, by an absolute majority of the General Assembly. Its decisions require nine members to vote in favor, with no permanent member voting against. The Security Council is the only UN organ empowered to make legally enforceable decisions, including authorizing the lawful use of force (but has no executive or military power independently of States).

ECOSOC has 54 members, elected by the General Assembly for three-year terms. The Trusteeship Council was set up to supervise the administration of Trust Territories placed under the International Trusteeship System. A month after the last remaining United Nations trust territory—Palau—became independent, on 1 October 1994, the Trusteeship Council suspended operation. The ICJ has a separate Statute (annexed to the UN Charter). The Secretariat, headed by the Secretary-General, has currently a staff of around 7,500 members, originating from 170 countries. Its principal offices sit in New York, Geneva, Vienna and Nairobi, but there are other regional offices.

According to the UN Charter, human rights are one of the three pillars of the organization, alongside peace and development. Each of them is under the responsibility of a Council, namely:

- Security Council for international peace.
- Economic and Social Council (ECOSOC) for development.
- Human Rights Council (HRC), not directly based on the Charter[129].

The UN's universal system for human rights protection is made up of a twofold set of mechanisms: Charter-based and Treaty-based. The distinction between them

[129] Proposals for it being included as a principal organ too did not succeed, because that would require amending the UN Charter.

"is between those mechanisms that have grown up under the UN Charter and therefore apply to all Member States and those that are based on the human rights treaties and thus apply to the States Parties to the relevant treaties. This distinction is also sometimes described as the difference between non-conventional protection and conventional protection" (Clapham 2009, p. 79).

UN Charter-based Mechanisms The principal UN human rights body is the HRC that replaced the CHR, whose sixty-second and final session took place in Geneva from 13 to 27 March (E/2006/23-E/CN.4/2006/122)[130]. It was established by the UN General Assembly (A/RES/60/251 of 15 March 2006)[131] as a subsidiary body reporting directly to it. It is entrusted with a broad mandate. *Inter alia*, it "should address situations of violations of human rights, including gross and systematic violations, and make recommendations thereon. It should also promote effective coordination and the mainstreaming of human rights within the United Nations system" (para. 3). Its work "shall be guided by the principles of universality, impartiality, objectivity and non-selectivity, constructive international dialogue and cooperation, with a view to enhancing the promotion and protection of all human rights, civil, political, economic, social and cultural rights, including the right to development" (para. 4).

The HRC is composed of 47 representatives of the UN Members States. They were elected on 9 May 2006 by an absolute majority of the General Assembly, the voting being secret, on the basis of equitable geographical distribution. Its composition is representative of the five UN geographical regions, namely:

- African Group (13 States)
- Asian Group (13 States)
- Latin America and Caribbean Group (8 States)
- Western European and Others Group (7 States)
- Eastern European Group (6 States)[132]

The HRC is based in the UN headquarters in Geneva (*Palais des Nations*) and should meet in regular sessions three times a year, for at least 10 weeks. Special sessions may be requested by one-third of its members. The sessions are almost always held in public. The first session was held from 19 to 30 June 2006, having adopted the following operating principles: universality, impartiality, objectivity, non-selectiveness, constructive dialogue and cooperation, predictability, flexibility, transparency, accountability, balance, inclusive/comprehensive, gender perspective, implementation and follow-up of decisions. It set up an Advisory Committee, composed of 18 experts, in replacement of the Sub-Commission on the Promotion and

[130] www2.ohchr.org/english/bodies/chr/docs/English.pdf.

[131] www2.ohchr.org/english/bodies/hrcouncil/docs/A.RES.60.251_En.pdf.

[132] "The Western European and Others Group and the East European Group had proportionally more members and the African Group and the Asian Group had proportionally fewer members in the Commission than in the HRC. The change from the Commission to the Council therefore has led to significantly different results in voting on resolutions and, as a consequence, significant differences in the content of resolutions" (APF 2012, p. 29).

Protection of Human Rights. Moreover, it created three working groups: one to develop the modalities of the universal periodic review mechanism for monitoring Member States' fulfillment of their human rights obligations (see below); the second one to make recommendations for reviewing, improving and rationalizing existing mandates and mechanisms; and the third one to make proposals on the Council's agenda, annual program of work, methods of work and rules of procedure. The first session of the HRC was marked by approval of the International Convention for the Protection of All Persons from Enforced Disappearances, and of the Declaration on the Rights of Indigenous Peoples, to be adopted by the UN General Assembly.

According to the General Assembly decision, the HRC should, in particular (5.e):

> Undertake a universal periodic review, based on objective and reliable information, of the fulfilment by each State of its human rights obligations and commitments in a manner which ensures universality of coverage and equal treatment with respect to all States; the review shall be a cooperative mechanism, based on an interactive dialogue, with the full involvement of the country concerned and with consideration given to its capacity-building needs; such a mechanism shall complement and not duplicate the work of treaty bodies;

The Universal Periodic Review (UPR) is the greatest novelty brought by the HRC. The first cycle was accomplished between 2007 and 2011. The second one began in June 2012 and will take four and a half years.

The UPR addresses universal and State-specific obligations, i.e. those common to all UN Member States by virtue of their membership, and those based on the treaties each State is party to. The obligations derived from IHL and International Customary Law are also taken into account.

Each State's review is undertaken by a working group formed by HRC members. It is prepared by a 'troika' of three rapporteurs chosen from the HRC members from different regional groups, and includes five phases: documentation, interactive dialogue, UPR report and recommendations, HRC plenary debate and adoption of the report, follow up. During the second UPR cycle, the HRC working group will have three sessions a year, each of 2 weeks, 14 States being reviewed at each session.

Being conducted by only States' representatives, the UPR is a political process rather than a legal one.

When establishing the HRC, the UN General Assembly decided that the new body should maintain the '1503 Procedure' that does not deal with individual complaints and is confidential. Under this Procedure, complaints are dealt with by two working groups, namely:

- Working Group on Communications, consisting of five independent experts from the HRC Advisory Committee.
- Working Group on Situations, consisting of the representatives of five States, one from each regional grouping

Another mechanism of the HRC is the 'Special Procedures' created by the former CHR. The Special Procedures consist in independent human rights experts being appointed to undertake specific mandates that may be a 'thematic mandate', i.e. to deal with a specific human rights issue, or a 'country mandate', i.e. to deal with the human rights situation in a specific country. Thematic mandates are usually created for a period of 3 years and can be renewed for the same period. Country mandates are usually created and renewed on an annual basis. As of 1 October 2013, there are 37 thematic and 14 country mandates.

Mandate holders can be individuals or groups of five members, one from each of the five UN geographical regions. The independent experts serve on a voluntary basis, being unpaid except for expenses, and are appointed after a selection procedure following criteria that include, in particular, expertise and personal integrity.

The independent experts were named Special Rapporteur, Independent Expert or Special Representative, but now they are generally called Special Rapporteur. The groups are called Working Groups. The mandates' working methods include undertaking studies, conducting country visits, receiving and investigating complaints from alleged victims of human rights violations, issuing urgent action requests, and annually reporting on their activities.

Being Charter-based mechanisms, the action of the Special Procedures is not dependent upon a State being party in any relevant human rights instrument. It can be activated even if a State has not ratified any relevant human rights instrument, and it is not necessary to have exhausted domestic remedies to accede to the Special Procedures. Therefore:

> The universal scope of special procedures and their easy accessibility are particularly valuable in a world where many States are not covered by specific regional system of protection of human rights; may not have ratified all the UN core international human rights instruments, or may have ratified them only partially (with reservations or accepting limited monitoring procedures). (Domínguez-Redondo 2010, p. 140)

There are other permanent HRC mechanisms for undertaking studies. They are its Advisory Committee, the Social Forum, the Forum on Minority Issues, the Working Group of Experts on People of African Descent, and the Expert Mechanism on the Rights of Indigenous Peoples. The HRC Advisory Committee is a think tank that meets twice a year, usually for 5 days in January and 5 days in August. In addition, there are temporary mechanisms, such as special commissions of inquiry and *ad hoc* working groups. An example of a special commission is the independent international commission of inquiry on the Syrian Arab Republic. Examples of working groups are those established for preparing a new international human rights instrument. They are intergovernmental, open-ended, and there is usually no deadline for their task being concluded. All these mechanisms meet and work in public sessions.

Treaty-based Mechanisms As already said, the UN Treaty-based system is concerned with States' commitments and obligations created by the core human rights treaties to which they are parties. Each one is supervised by a Committee known as the Treaty Monitoring Body (TMB), created by the treaty itself, except for ICESCR, whose Committee was established by a decision of the ECOSOC (Resolution 1985/17 of 28 May 1985), as we know[133]. Their membership varies from 10 to 23 members. In spite of being elected by the States Parties to the particular treaty, their members are independent human rights experts, not States' representatives, serving

[133] www.ohchr.org/EN/HRBodies/CESCR/Pages/CESCRIndex.aspx.

in their personal capacities. They are elected for a term of 4 years, with half the number of each one being elected each 2 years. The provisions for their election include, in addition to recognized competence and high moral character, equitable geographical distribution and representation of the different forms of civilization and of the principal legal systems. Consequently, in contrast with the HRC, these are legal bodies, not political.

The TMBs are the following ones:

- Committee on the Elimination of Racial Discrimination (CERD, 18 members), monitoring the implementation of the ICERD (1965).
- Human Rights Committee (CCPR, 18 members), monitoring the implementation of the ICPCR (1966).
- Committee on Economic, Social and Cultural Rights (CESCR, 18 members), monitoring the implementation of the (ICESCR (1966)[134].
- Committee on the Elimination of Discrimination against Women (CoEDAW, 23 members), monitoring the implementation of the CEDAW (1979).
- Committee against Torture (CoAT, 10 members), monitoring the implementation of the CAT (1984).
- Committee on the Rights of the Child (CoRC, 18 members), monitoring the implementation of the CRC (1989).
- Committee on Migrant Workers (CMW, 14 members), monitoring the implementation of the ICPRMW (1990).
- Committee on the Rights of Persons with Disabilities (CoRPD, 18 members), monitoring the implementation of the CRPD (2006).
- Committee on Enforced Disappearances (CED, 10 members), monitoring the implementation of the CPED (2006).

There is also a Subcommittee on Prevention of Torture (SPT, 25 members) established by the Optional Protocol to Convention against Torture and Other Cruel, Inhuman or Degrading Treatment or Punishment (CAT-OP).

They meet in Geneva for two or three sessions each year, each session consisting of 2 or 3 weeks. The CCPR and the CoEDAW usually hold one of their annual sessions in New York. They report to the General Assembly (with the exception of the CESCR, which reports to the ECOSOC).

As all States are parties to at least one of the core human rights treaties, the Treaty-based system applies universally too.

The TMBs' mandate includes:

- Examining the reports the States Parties undertake to send, in accordance with the treaties' provisions.

  The Reports System is the softest and most common international procedure to monitoring States' compliance with their human rights obligations. It originated in an ECOSOC resolution in 1956. The idea was incorporated into the

[134] The CESCR and the European Committee of Social Rights are the two international organs exclusively concerned with economic, social and cultural rights.

1965 ICERD, the two 1966 International Covenants and other core international human rights treaties. The Reports System consists in each State Party submitting a comprehensive initial report to the Committee within 1 or 2 years of the treaty entering into force for it, setting out the legal, administrative and judicial measures taken to give effect to the treaty, and also mentioning the difficulties encountered in implementing the rights concerned. Thereafter, the reporting obligation is periodical, usually every 4 or 5 years (with the exception of the CPED).

To assist the States Parties in the preparation of their reports, the TMBs (all but the SPT) have issued guidelines. To assist the States Parties in the preparation of their reports, the TMBs (all but the SPT) have issued guidelines. In 2005, the TMBs "harmonized" their guidelines, so that now the reports consist of two parts: a Common Core Document with basic information about the State constitutional, legal and political systems, as well as general demographic statistics; and a treaty-specific document.

On the basis of the State Party report and other information available (received especially from UN agencies, IGOs, NGOs, etc.), all TMBs formulate, usually at a pre-sessional working group, a list of issues and questions which is transmitted to the State Party in advance of the session at which its report will be considered. This list provides the framework for the constructive dialogue with the State Party's delegation. The delegation may respond to the issues and questions orally during the session, but some Committees encourage the State Party to submit written responses to the list of issues in advance, allowing the dialogue to move more quickly to specificities. The list of issues is particularly important for TMBs facing a backlog of reports awaiting consideration as it provides a source of up-to-date information for the Committee with regard to a State whose report may have been awaiting consideration for as much as 2 years. Lists of issues are published as official documents and are available on the TMBs' database. Written responses are not published as official documents but are also available on the TMBs' database. The review of the State Party's report ends with Concluding Observations and recommendations by the Committee. The TMBs have begun to introduce procedures to ensure follow-up to their Concluding Observations. Following a recommendation of the meeting of Chairpersons in 2010, a working group on follow-up was established.

While most States report regularly, even if they are often behind in doing so, overdue reports or not submitting reports at all are widespread malpractices among States. In this case, the States' performance can be examined in their absence.

- Receiving and examining complaints or 'communications' (as they are generally referred to in the international human rights system) from individuals on alleged violations by States Parties of the human rights whose respect they supervise (all but the SPT).

  Complaints may also be brought by third parties on behalf of individuals who have given their written consent or are incapable of giving such consent. However, States concerned must have expressly recognized the competence of the

Committee in this regard. The Special Procedures can accept complaints that are already being investigated by other UN mechanisms, and a complaint can be made to more than one Special Procedure at the same time, if its subject matter justifies it. In this case, the Special Procedures implicated may decide to act jointly.

Some treaties established an inter-State complaints procedure. They include: ICCPR (Article 41), ICESCR (Article 10 of the Optional Protocol), CAT (Article 21), ICPRMW (Article 74), CPED (Article 32), and CRC (Article 12 of the Optional Protocol on a communications procedure). There are two inter-state complaints procedures within the framework of the ILO, too. Some human rights treaties address disputes between State Parties concerning their interpretation or application. The inter-States procedure applies only to States Parties who have made a declaration accepting the competence of the Committee in this regard. However, it has never been used, owing to its political implications. The Contracting States are reluctant to have recourse to it. It is "understandable that states might anyway wish to refrain from using such an elephant of a procedure that can only give birth to such a mouse of an outcome" (Rodley 2009, p. 125). If needed, States prefer to have recourse to the ICJ (see Schabas 2009, p. 638). On the contrary, the European inter-state mechanism has been used in cases such as *Ireland v. The United Kingdom* (1978), *Denmark v. Turkey* (2000) and *Cyprus v. Turkey* (2001).

While the complaints procedures of the HRC and the Special Procedures are universal, insofar as they apply to all UN Member States, the TMBs' procedures apply only to States Parties to the relevant treaties that have accepted the complaint jurisdiction of the respective Committee. They differ from one to another, but none is a judicial process providing an enforceable remedy for victims. They have certain common requirements of admissibility, however. To be admissible, international complaints must, in particular:

- not be anonymous, not be an abuse of the right to individual complaint and not be incompatible with the provisions of the treaty;
- have exhausted domestic remedies (unless they are cumbersome, unreasonably prolonged or ineffective);
- not be under investigation by another international body.

• Conducting country inquiries and/or visits, if they receive reliable information on serious, grave or systematic violations of the particular treaty.

The Committees empowered with this competence include: CoAT (CAT Article 20), CoEDAW (Article 8 of the Optional Protocol to the CEDAW), CoRPD (Article 6 of the Optional Protocol to the CRPD), CED (CPED Article 33), CESCR (Article 11 of the Optional Protocol to the ICESCR), and CoRC (Article 13 of the Optional Protocol to the CRC on a communications procedure). Inquiries may only be undertaken with respect to States Parties who have made a declaration accepting the competence of the Committee in this regard, with the exception of inquiries by the CED, for which State Parties automatically accept the Committee's competence when they ratify the Convention.

Each Committee can also take urgent action, before a case is considered, in order to prevent any irreparable harm, such as the execution of a death sentence or the deportation of an individual facing a risk of torture.

In addition, the TMBs play an interpreting role accomplished by issuing General Comments (GCs) or General Recommendations[135]. They are documents elaborating on the content of the relevant human rights instruments with the purpose to assist the States Parties in fulfilling their obligations. The TMBs are, in fact, the most authoritative interpreters of the treaties under their monitoring responsibility.

The practice of the 'General Discussion Day' (during a day of the regular sessions of a Committee) on an article, a right or issue arising under the treaty is also relevant for the 'normative development' of human rights. It is usually open to external participants and may lead to drafting of a new GC. In Scheinin's (2009a) view, the most important role of the Committees is "their capacity to contribute towards the concretization and evolution of international human rights law" (p. 619).

The human rights treaties being separate and free-standing, the TMBs do not function as an integrated system. They are interdependent and complementary, however. Hence the increasing awareness of the need to improve the coordination and harmonization of the monitoring procedures. In 1983, The UN General Assembly called on the TMBs' Chairpersons to meet in order to discuss how to enhance their work. The first meeting took place in 1984 and has occurred annually since then. The Annual Chairpersons Meeting takes place in Geneva, normally in May. They strive to make the system more effective, in particular by streamlining their procedures. In 2005, the United Nations High Commissioner for Human Rights (UNHCHR) suggested the possibility of merging all Committees into a single permanent body, but the idea did not meet with general acceptance. In 2012, the UNHCHR published the Report *Strengthening the United Nations human rights treaty body system* (Pillay 2012).

The UNHCHR was established by the UN General Assembly in 1993, following a recommendation of the World Conference on Human Rights held in Vienna in the same year. The High Commissioner is the principal UN official concerned with human rights, playing a leading role in the UN human rights system, under the authority of the Secretary-General. The Office of the UNHCHR (OHCHR) is seated in Geneva, having a little branch in New York and being present in over 50 countries. It absorbed the Centre for Human Rights and provides secretariat services for all the UN activities in the field of human rights. Its Human Rights Treaties Division supports the TMBs in particular. A complaint may be sent to the OHCHR that refers it to the most appropriate mechanism.

Besides the principal UN organs and bodies, many other UN agencies and partners are involved in the promotion and protection of human rights[136]. UNESCO,

[135] The CCPR, the CESCR, the CoAT, the CoRC, the CMW, the CED and the CoRPD issue General Comments. The CERD and the CoEDAW issue General Recommendations.

[136] See: www2.ohchr.org/english/bodies/.

ILO, FAO, and the World Health Organization (WHO), in particular, are "specialized agencies" of the UN system for the protection of specific human rights. For example, UNESCO's Executive Board laid down a procedure for the examination of complaints concerning alleged violations of human rights in the Organization's fields of competence. They are considered by one of UNESCO's permanent subsidiary organs: the Committee on Conventions and Recommendations. The ILO has set up the International Labour Conference Committee on the Application of Standards, the Committee of Experts on the Application of Conventions and Recommendations, and the Committee on Freedom of Association.

The 2005 United Nations World Summit adopted the concept of *Responsibility to Protect* (R2P) (A/RES/60/1)[137]. It is so worded:

> 138. Each individual State has the responsibility to protect its populations from genocide, war crimes, ethnic cleansing and crimes against humanity. This responsibility entails the prevention of such crimes, including their incitement, through appropriate and necessary means. We accept that responsibility and will act in accordance with it. [...]
> 139. The international community, through the United Nations, also has the responsibility to use appropriate diplomatic, humanitarian and other peaceful means, in accordance with Chapters VI and VIII of the Charter, to help to protect populations from genocide, war crimes, ethnic cleansing and crimes against humanity. In this context, we are prepared to take collective action, in a timely and decisive manner, through the Security Council, in accordance with the Charter, including Chapter VII, on a case-by-case basis and in cooperation with relevant regional organizations as appropriate, should peaceful means be inadequate and national authorities are manifestly failing to protect their populations from genocide, war crimes, ethnic cleansing and crimes against humanity.

Still in 2005, the General Assembly adopted the Basic Principles and Guidelines on the Right to a Remedy and Reparation for Victims of Gross Violations of International Human Rights Law and Serious Violations of International Humanitarian Law[138]. "The guidelines provide a superb encapsulation of the thrust of the human rights idea in the contemporary world" (Ramcharan 2008, p. 7).

In 1997, the Secretary-General launched a Program for Reform of the United Nations calling to mainstream human rights into all programmes and activities of the Organization. For instance, the comprehensive approach to UN strategies for peace and security now incorporates human rights components into all peace-keeping operations, with the participation of the OHCHR in training peace-keeping personnel or establishing a human rights presence after the peace-keeping mandate.

---

[137] http://daccess-dds-ny.un.org/doc/UNDOC/GEN/N05/487/60/PDF/N0548760.pdf?OpenElement

This concept was adopted on the basis of the work of the Independent International Commission on Intervention and State Sovereignty (ICISS), established by the Canadian Government in September 2000, based on a wide process of consultation. The Commission presented two documents published in December 2001 under the title 'The Responsibility to Protect': the first one was focused on the redefinition of the notion of 'State sovereignty', the second on the expansion of some central concepts drawn from the first. According to the Commission, the principle of sovereignty should imply both the respect of State's sovereignty and of citizens' dignity and fundamental rights, as well as internal and external responsibility.

[138] www2.ohchr.org/english/law/remedy.htm.

The UN action in the field of human rights further includes the proclamation of International Days, Years and Decades, and campaigns of information and education.

The action taken by the UN concerning the protection and promotion of human rights is, therefore, "based on the triangular connection existing between codification, implementation of the instruments and information/education" (Martenson 1990, p. 3).

3.4.2 Regional Level

At the regional level, standards and supervisory mechanisms have also been developed in the European, American and African contexts.

The ECHR instituted the oldest, most developed and most effective regional system. The European Convention constitutes "the most accomplished expression of the specificity of the International Human Rights Law", for having given conventional form to the "revolutionary advance in the legal position of the individual" (Friedmann, W.) (Velu and Ergec 1990, p. 35). Indeed, it was the first treaty to include formally a large set of human rights and to grant to individuals the right to bring complaints for their human rights violations before international bodies, namely the European Commission of Human Rights and the European Court of Human Rights (merged into a permanent Court since 1 November 1998). The Court may be acceded to by individuals and groups, besides States. There is also, since 1999, a European Commissioner on Human Rights, whose mandate concerns principally information and education regarding human rights. The ECHR is supplemented with the European Social Charter (adopted in 1961, in force since 1965 and revised in 1996) whose scope covers economic and social rights (see Schutter 2009b). More than 200 treaties have been adopted within the framework of the Council of Europe, most of them relating to human rights. They include the European Convention for the Prevention of Torture and Inhuman or Degrading Treatment or Punishment (1987), the Framework Convention on National Minorities (1994), the Convention for the Protection of Human Rights and Dignity of the Human Being with regard to the Application of Biology and Medicine: Convention on Human Rights and Biomedicine (1997) and the Council of Europe Convention on Action against Trafficking in Human Beings (2005).

Three other Intergovernmental Organizations (IGOs) should be mentioned in the European region: the European Union (EU) and the Organization for Security and Co-operation in Europe (OSCE).

The EU was designed to prevent the possibility of another war in Europe. It is an IGO unique in the world, founded on the Rule of Law and committed to prosperity and peace. It adopted the EU Charter, solemnly signed and proclaimed at the European Council meeting held in Nice (France) on 7 December 2000, not primarily directed to the Member States, but to the EU Institutions. It embodies all categories of rights, including some group and recent rights not addressed by other general instruments, such as those concerning the elderly and consumers. Moreover, most rights are recognized also to non-citizens of the EU. The Treaty of Lisbon amending the Treaty on European Union and the Treaty Establishing the European Community, adopted in Lisbon (Portugal), on 18 October 2007, guarantees the enforcement of the Charter. Article 6.2 of its consolidated version provided that the EU could adhere to the ECHR. Article 17 of the Protocol 14 to the ECHR (now Article 59.2 of the Convention) formalized such a possibility, so allowing communications to the European Court alleging violations of human rights by the EU as such. There has also been a European Union Agency for Fundamental Rights since 2007.

OSCE is the largest regional security organization in the world. It gathers 56 States, including all States of the former Eastern Bloc. Its approach to security is very comprehensive, dealing with a wide range of security-related issues, including human rights and democratization. It was first established as Conference for Security and Co-operation in Europe (CSCE), which began on 3 July 1973 and closed on 1 August 1975, in Helsinki, with the Helsinki Final Act signed by 35 States. Its purpose was to set up a platform for dialogue and cooperation between the Western and Eastern ideological fields, during the Cold War. It was the first European Conference with the participation of all Continent's States but Albania. The Helsinki Final Act recognized the inviolability of the post-war frontiers (so meeting the USSR's interests) and included the protection of human rights (so satisfying the Western claims). The CSCE transformed into the OSCE in 1994, entering in effect on 1 January 1995.

A third European IGO is the Commonwealth of Independent States (CIS). It was created in 1991 by the Russian Federation, the Republic of Belarus and Ukraine, being later joined by all Republics of the former USSR (except for the Baltic States). In 1995, the CIS adopted a Convention on Human Rights and Fundamental Freedoms that entered into force in 1998.

The American system for the protection of human rights was created by the OAS Charter and the ACHR (1969). It includes the Inter-American Commission on Human Rights and the Inter-American Court of Human Rights. The Commission was originally a Charter-based body that the American Convention transformed into a Treaty-body. Therefore, as an OAS Charter organ its mandate is concerned with all OAS Member States; as a Convention organ it is limited to States Parties to Convention. It plays thus a 'dual role': it can consider communications alleging violations of rights contained under the ACHR and also under the American Declaration of Human Rights. This means that those States that are members of the OAS but are not parties to the ACHR, such as the United States of America (that only signed it), can be monitored by the Commission for their compliance with the Declaration. It can refer a case to the Court, provided that the State concerned has accepted its jurisdiction.

The ACHR has been complemented by the Protocol of San Salvador on economic, social and cultural rights (1988) and the Protocol to abolish the death penalty (1990). Other Inter-American Conventions include: Convention to Prevent and Punish Torture (1985), Convention on the Forced Disappearances of Persons (1994), Convention on the Prevention, Punishment and Eradication of Violence against Women (1995) and Inter-American Convention on the Elimination of All

Forms of Discrimination against Persons with Disabilities (1999). In 2012, the OAS adopted a Social Charter of the Americas.

The African system was created by the ACHPR (1981) that established an African Commission of Human and Peoples' Rights. In 1998, a Protocol to the African Charter on Human and Peoples' Rights on the Establishment of an African Court on Human and Peoples' Rights was adopted. The African Court on Human and Peoples' Rights later merged with the African Court of Justice, giving origin, in 2008, to the African Court of Justice and Human Rights. Two other protocols were adopted: Protocol on the Rights of Women in Africa (2003) and Protocol on the Statute of the African Court of Justice and Human Rights (2008). Other African instruments include: the Convention Governing the Specific Aspects of Refugee Problems in Africa (1969) and the African Charter on the Rights and Welfare of the Child (1990). It is noteworthy that the ACHPR incorporates all category of human rights, includes individual duties and has been ratified by all 54 member States of the AU.

In the Asian and Pacific region there is not yet a human rights system. One obstacle is the huge diversity of Asia. According to Joshua Castellino: "It can be argued that there are at least five distinct sub-regions within the continent, in terms of geography, cultural ethos and regional identity" (in Smith and Anker 2005, p. 16). Sub-regional mechanisms are emerging, however. The Southeast Asia sub-region is the most advanced.

Within the framework of the Association of Southeast Asian Nations (ASEAN)[139], founded in 1967, the Asia–Pacific region States have been meeting regularly since 1982, assisted by the UN Program of technical cooperation and advisory services in human rights field. In 1993, the 26th ASEAN Foreign Ministers Meeting, held in Singapore (23–24 July), approved a Joint Communiqué where "they agreed that ASEAN should also consider the establishment of an appropriate regional mechanism on human rights". In 1996, the informal Working Group for an ASEAN Human Rights Mechanism was established, composed of individuals and groups from official and private sectors, with a secretariat in Manila (Philippines). In July 2000, the Working Group submitted a draft Agreement on the Establishment of the ASEAN Human Rights Commission. In 2009, ASEAN created the Asian Intergovernmental Commission on Human Rights (AICHR). It is a consultative body with ten members appointed for a three-year term by the ASEAN Member States, one from each State. There is also a Commission on the Promotion and Protection of the Rights of Women and Children, similar to the AICHR.

On 18 November 2012, on the occasion of the 21st ASEAN Summit in Phnom Penh, Cambodja, the Asian Human Rights Declaration was adopted[140]. However, its language the UNHCHR considered not to be consistent with international standards.

[139] www.asean.org/asean/about-asean.

[140] http://asean2012.mfa.gov.kh/pdf_view.php?article=328andlg=en.

The West Asia sub-region is part of the Arabic-speaking States, grouped together in the League of Arab States[141], established in 1945, in Cairo, now with 22 Member States. It established an Arab Commission for Human Rights, in 1968, and adopted the Arab Charter of Human Rights in 1994, which was not ratified by any Member of the League of Arab States. It was revised in 2004, establishing a new Commission, and entered into force in 2008. It contains provisions not consistent with the IHRL, including the application of the death penalty for children, the treatment of women and non-citizens, and equating Zionism with racism (contrary to the General Assembly Resolution 46/86, which rejects that Zionism is a form of racism and racial discrimination) (see Rishmawi 2009). There is a Charter on the Rights of the Arab Child (1983).

The Organisation of Islamic Cooperation (OIC), formerly Organization of the Islamic Conference, with a membership of 57 States in four continents (the second largest IGO after the United Nations), established an Independent Permanent Human Rights Commission, with a consultative and promotional mandate[142]. According to the Charter adopted in 2008 to replace the Charter of the Organisation of the Islamic Conference (Article 15)[143]:

> The Independent Permanent Commission on Human Rights shall promote the civil, political, social and economic rights enshrined in the organisation's covenants and declarations and in universally agreed human rights instruments, in conformity with Islamic values.

The declarations and covenants are the Cairo Declaration on Human Rights in Islam (1990)[144] and the Covenant of the Rights of the Child in Islam (2004)[145].

Meanwhile, several human rights declarations were adopted in in the Asia–Pacific region. "On the Occasion of the Commemoration of the 50th Anniversary of Universal Declaration of Human Rights" (1998), *Our Common Humanity—Asian Human Rights Charter—A Peoples' Charter*[146] was adopted in Kwangju, South Korea. It was developed over 3 years by the Asian Human Rights Commission together with more than 200 NGOs and numerous experts. Here are some significant highlights of this long Charter:

> 1.2 In particular the marketization and globalization of economies are changing the balance between the private and the public, the state and the international community, and worsening the situation of the poor and the disadvantaged. These changes threaten many valued aspects of life, the result of the dehumanizing effects of technology, the material orientation of the market, and the destruction of the community. [...]
> 1.5 ... Authoritarianism has in many states been raised to the level of national ideology, with the deprivation of the rights and freedoms of their citizens, which are denounced as

[141] www.lasportal.org/wps/portal/las_en/home_page/!ut/p/c5/04_SB8K8xLLM9MSSzPy8xBz9CP0os3gXy8CgMJMgYwOLYFdLA08jF09_X28jIwN_E6B8JG55C3MCuoNT8_TDQXbiNwMkb4ADOBro-3nk56bqF-RGVHjqOioCAKQoUKM!/dl3/d3/L2dBISEvZ0FBIS9nQSEh/.

[142] www.oicun.org/75/20120607051141117.html.

[143] www.oic-oci.org/english/charter/OIC%20Charter-new-en.pdf.

[144] www.arabhumanrights.org/publications/regional/islamic/cairo-declaration-islam-93e.pdf.

[145] www.oic-oci.org/english/convenion/Rights%20of%20the%20Child%20In%20Islam%20E.pdf.

[146] www.hurights.or.jp/archives/other_documents/#ConferenceDeclarations.

foreign ideas inappropriate to the religious and cultural traditions of Asia. Instead there is the exhortation of spurious theories of "Asian Values" which are a thin disguise for their authoritarianism. Not surprisingly, Asia, of all the major regions of the world, is without a regional official charter or other regional arrangements for the protection of rights and freedoms.

1.7 Our commitment to rights is not due to any abstract ideological reasons. We believe that respect for human rights provides the basis for a just, humane and caring society. A regime of rights is premised on the belief that we are all inherently equal and have an equal right to live in dignity. [...]

2.4 Widespread poverty, even in states which have achieved a high rate of economic development, is a principal cause of the violation of rights. Poverty deprives individuals, families, and communities of their rights and promotes prostitution, child labor, slavery, sale of human organs, and the mutilation of the body to enhance the capacity to beg. [...]

2.5 The responsibility for the protection of rights is both international and domestic. The international community has agreed upon norms and institutions that should govern the practice of human rights. The peoples of Asia support international measures for the protection of rights. State sovereignty cannot be used as an excuse to evade international norms or ignore international institutions.

2.6 On the other hand, international responsibility cannot be used for the selective chastisement or punishment of particular states; or for the privileging of one set of rights over others. Some fundamental causes of the violation of human rights lie in the inequities of the international world economic and political order. The radical transformation and democratization of the world order is a necessary condition for the global enjoyment of human rights. [...]

2.8 The capacity of the international community and states to promote and protect rights has been weakened by processes of globalization as more and more power over economic and social policy and activities has moved from states to business corporations. States are increasingly held hostage by financial and other corporations to implement narrow and short sighted economic policies which cause so much misery to so many people, while increasing the wealth of the few. Business corporations are responsible for numerous violations of rights, particularly those of workers, women and indigenous peoples.

2.9 Economic development must be sustainable. We must protect the environment against the avarice and depredations of commercial enterprises to ensure that the quality of life does not decline just as the gross national product increases. Technology must liberate, not enslave human beings. Natural resources must be used in a manner consistent with our obligation to future generations. We must never forget that we are merely temporary custodians of the resources of nature. Nor should we forget that these resources are given to all human kind, and consequently we have a joint responsibility for their responsible, fair and equitable use.

6.2 The plurality of cultural identities in Asia is not contrary to the universality of human rights but rather as so many cultural manifestations of human dignity enriching universal norms. At the same time we Asian peoples must eliminate those features in our cultures which are contrary to the universal principles of human rights. We must transcend the traditional concept of the family based on patriarchal traditions so as to retrieve in each of our cultural traditions, the diversity of family norms which guarantee women's human rights. We must be bold in reinterpreting our religious beliefs which support gender inequality. We must also eliminate discriminations based on caste, ethnic origins, occupation, place of origin and others, while enhancing in our respective cultures all values related to mutual tolerance and mutual support. We must stop practices which sacrifice the individual to the collectivity or to the powerful, and thus renew our communal and national solidarity.

6.3 The freedom of religion and conscience is particularly important in Asia where most people are deeply religious. Religion is a source of comfort and solace in the midst of poverty and oppression. Many find their primary identity in religion. However religious fundamentalism is also a cause of divisions and conflict. Religious tolerance is essential for the enjoyment of the right of conscience of others, which includes the right to change one's belief.

The protection of human rights has two faces, like the god Janus: one turned to the outside, to International Law, the other one turned to the inside, to domestic legal orders. Although the protection of human rights is not the sole and exclusive responsibility of States, the primary responsibility rests with them.

3.4.3 National Level

As the Vienna Declaration and Programme of Action recalled, the promotion and protection of human rights "is the first responsibility of Governments" (I-1). The Declaration on the Right and Responsibility of Individuals, Groups and Organs of Society to Promote and Protect Universally Recognized Human Rights and Fundamental Freedoms (UN 1998) repeats:

> Article 2
> 1. Each State has a prime responsibility and duty to protect, promote and implement all human rights and fundamental freedoms, inter alia, by adopting such steps as may be necessary to create all conditions necessary in the social, economic, political and other fields, as well as the legal guarantees required to ensure that all persons under its jurisdiction, individually and in association with others, are able to enjoy all those rights and freedoms in practice.
> [...]
> Article 3
> Domestic law consistent with the Charter of the United Nations and other international obligations of the State in the field of human rights and fundamental freedoms is the juridical framework within which human rights and fundamental freedoms should be implemented and enjoyed and within which all activities referred to in the present Declaration for the promotion, protection and effective realization of those rights and freedoms should be conducted.

States—the authors and the first addressees of the International Law that they have engaged to comply with—are legally and politically the main entities responsible for all human rights both vertically (concerning the State-citizens relations) and horizontally (concerning the citizens-citizens relations). Indeed, while the IHRL addresses in the first place the relations between State and individuals, the State also has a duty to protect each one's rights against other individuals, for instance, against homicide. The obligation of protection against third parties—individuals or private entities—is provided by the ICCPR (Article 2.1). It was recalled by the CCPR in its GC 31 (CCPR/C/21/Rev.1/Add. 13, 26 May 2004, para. 8)[147], and affirmed by the European Court of Human Rights too. The Protocol 7 to the ECHR (Article 5) refers to that horizontal dimension in connection with the equal rights of husband and wife.

The States' first obligation, when they become parties to international human rights instruments, is to bring domestic Law into line with those instruments. However, the relation between International Law and domestic legal systems varies. Two ways may be distinguished: dualist and monist. Following the first one, International Law and domestic legal orders are different systems and the enforcement

[147] www.unhchr.ch/tbs/doc.nsf/0/58f5d4646e861359c1256ff600533f5f?Opendocument.

of international norms depends on their being transformed into domestic Law. Following the second one, the norms of a treaty duly ratified become automatically part of the domestic Law, without need of any legal transformation. The rank of treaties may be supra-constitutional, constitutional, infra-constitutional but superior to laws, or equivalent to laws. Ineke Boerefijn (2009) observes:

> Much has been written on the various methods that can be applied to implement international law in the domestic system. The traditional distinction between dualist and monist systems—whereby under the former international and national law are two separate systems and under the latter the two form one system—is somewhat outdated, and the reality is more complex. There are various degrees of monism and dualism. More recent writings distinguish between various implementation methods that can coexist. (p. 577)

Regarding the incorporation of International Law into domestic legal orders, the CCPR said in its GC 31[148]:

> 13. Article 2, paragraph 2, requires that States Parties take the necessary steps to give effect to the Covenant rights in the domestic order. It follows that, unless Covenant rights are already protected by their domestic laws or practices, States Parties are required on ratification to make such changes to domestic laws and practices as are necessary to ensure their conformity with the Covenant. Where there are inconsistencies between domestic law and the Covenant, article 2 requires that the domestic law or practice be changed to meet the standards imposed by the Covenant's substantive guarantees. Article 2 allows a State Party to pursue this in accordance with its own domestic constitutional structure and accordingly does not require that the Covenant be directly applicable in the courts, by incorporation of the Covenant into national law. The Committee takes the view, however, that Covenant guarantees may receive enhanced protection in those States where the Covenant is automatically or through specific incorporation part of the domestic legal order. The Committee invites those States Parties in which the Covenant does not form part of the domestic legal order to consider incorporation of the Covenant to render it part of domestic law to facilitate full realization of Covenant rights as required by article 2.

This point of view is shared by other UN Committees.

As the economic, social and cultural rights, in particular, are concerned, the CESCR dedicated GC 3 (1990)[149] to the nature of obligations of States Parties in the respective Covenant, in accordance with Article 2.1. Using the terminology of the UN International Law Commission, the Committee started affirming that States have "obligations of conduct and obligations of result". Some of them "are of immediate effect", such as those concerning the principle of non-discrimination (para. 1), and "to take steps" (para. 2). According to the Committee, "a minimum core obligation to ensure the satisfaction of, at the very least, minimum essential levels of each of the rights is incumbent upon every State party" (para. 10). The GC 12 (E/C.12/1999)[150] states that every human right "imposes three types or levels of obligations on States parties: the obligations to *respect*, to *protect* and to *fulfil*. In turn, the obligation to *fulfil* incorporates both an obligation to *facilitate* and an obligation to *provide*" (para. 15).

- The obligation to respect means to ensure that none public official acts against the human rights recognized and protected by the relevant particular treaty.

[148] http://daccess-dds-ny.un.org/doc/UNDOC/GEN/G04/419/56/PDF/G0441956.pdf?OpenElement.

[149] www.unhchr.ch/tbs/doc.nsf/0/94bdbaf59b43a424c12563ed0052b664?Opendocument.

[150] www.unhchr.ch/tbs/doc.nsf/0/3d02758c707031d58025677f003b73b9.

- The obligation to protect means to take action to ensure that nobody violates the human rights recognized and protected by the relevant treaty.
- The obligation to fulfill means to take action to ensure that the human rights recognized and protected by the relevant treaty are enjoyed by everybody within its jurisdiction.

Scheinin (2009a) observes:

> One important source of inspiration for this typology was Asbjorn Eide's 1987 Special Rapporteur's report on the right to food. [... It] combines other typologies, such as the dichotomies *positive and negative* obligations, or *obligations of conduct and result*. In short, the state obligation to respect entails the negative (or passive) obligation not to violate a human right. [...]
> To relate these categorizations to the more traditional distinction between negative and positive state obligations, one can say that the duty to respect closely corresponds to negative obligations, and the other dimensions (protect and fulfil) to positive state obligations. It is typical for economic and social rights that positive state obligations have a major role in their implementation. (p. 27, 28)

The IHRL does not forbid provision by non-State actors of the public services the human rights require, to the extent that the most important is that human rights are satisfied, but the first responsibility rests always with States in case of decentralization, delegation or privatization. Although public-private partnerships, for instance, may be positive, State's responsibility for protecting and fulfilling human rights can never be privatized. In this regard, the CoRC unequivocally stated in GC 5[151]:

> 20 The Committee welcomes the incorporation of the Convention into domestic law, which is the traditional approach to the implementation of international human rights instruments in some but not all States. Incorporation should mean that the provisions of the Convention can be directly invoked before the courts and applied by national authorities and that the Convention will prevail where there is a conflict with domestic legislation or common practice. Incorporation by itself does not avoid the need to ensure that all relevant domestic law, including any local or customary law, is brought into compliance with the Convention. In case of any conflict in legislation, predominance should always be given to the Convention, in the light of article 27 of the Vienna Convention on the Law of Treaties. Where a State delegates powers to legislate to federated regional or territorial governments, it must also require these subsidiary governments to legislate within the framework of the Convention and to ensure effective implementation (see also paragraphs 40 et seq. below).
> 44. The Committee emphasizes that enabling the private sector to provide services, run institutions and so on does not in any way lessen the State's obligation to ensure for all children within its jurisdiction the full recognition and realization of all rights in the Convention (arts. 2 (1) and 3 (2)).

States have extraterritorial obligations too.

On 26–28 September 2011, the Maastricht Principles on Extraterritorial Obligations of States in the area of Economic, Social and Cultural Rights were adopted by a group of 40 experts in International Law and human rights from all regions of the world, including current and former members of the TMBs, regional human rights bodies, former and current UN Special Rapporteurs, along with scholars and legal advisers of leading NGOs. They were convened by the International Commission

[151] www.unhchr.ch/tbs/doc.nsf/(symbol)/CRC.GC.2003.5.En.

of Jurists and Maastricht University. According to Salomon and Seiderman (2012), two participants, the new Maastricht Principles address the following questions:

> What are a state's human rights obligations when it engages in conduct that carries human rights consequences for the inhabitants of another state? What obligations do states have to contribute to the global realization of human rights, such as the rights to food, to healthcare, and to an adequate standard of living, of persons residing in a territory outside their own? How is international human rights law evolving so as to remain efficacious under conditions of globalization?

The 2011 Maastricht Principles are composed of a Preamble and 44 Principles. They are driven by the concept of international cooperation. Some highlights of a Commentary to them are next presented:

- The Preamble states:

> The human rights of individuals, groups and peoples are affected by and dependent on the extraterritorial acts and omissions of States. The advent of economic globalization in particular, has meant that States and other global actors exert considerable influence on the realization of economic, social and cultural rights across the world.
> [...]
> States have repeatedly committed themselves to realizing the economic, social and cultural rights of everyone.
> [...]
> Drawn from international law, these Principles aim to clarify the content of extraterritorial State obligations to realize economic, social and cultural rights with a view to advancing and giving full effect to the object of the Charter of the United Nations and international human rights. (Schutter et al. 2012, p. 1085, 1086)

- International cooperation is a UN Charter principle.

> Under Article 56 of the UN Charter: "All Members pledge themselves to take joint and separate action in cooperation with the Organization" to achieve the purposes set out in Article 55 of the Charter. Such purposes include: "universal respect for, and observance of, human rights and fundamental freedoms for all without distinction as to race, sex, language, or religion". (p. 1091)

This principle was taken up by number of international instruments, such as the UDHR (Articles 22 and 28), the ICESCR (Article 2.1) and the CRC (Article 4 and other). The UN Millennium Declaration[152] states: "We recognize that, in addition to our separate responsibilities to our individual societies, we have a collective responsibility to uphold the principles of human dignity, equality and equity at the global level" (I.2). The CESCR emphasized that, "in accordance with Articles 55 and 56 of the Charter of the United Nations, with well-established principles of international law, and with the provisions of the Covenant itself, international cooperation for development and thus for the realization of economic, social and cultural rights is an obligation of all States" (p. 1146).

- International cooperation is a broad concept.

> International cooperation must be understood broadly to include the development of international rules to establish an enabling environment for the realization of human rights and the provision of financial or technical assistance. It also includes an obligation to refrain

[152] www.un.org/en/development/devagenda/millennium.shtml.

from nullifying or impairing human rights in other countries and to ensure that non-state actors whose conduct the state is in a position to influence are prohibited from impairing the enjoyment of such rights. (p. 1104)

- Is there a right to international cooperation?

Despite its provision in binding international instruments, disagreement persists as to the legally binding nature of the obligation of international cooperation as expressed in the International Covenant on Economic, Social and Cultural Rights. Neither the drafting history of the Covenant nor subsequent state practice provides a definitive answer. When negotiating what came to be Article 2 (1) of the International Covenant on Economic, Social and Cultural Rights, the drafters agreed that international cooperation and assistance was necessary to realize economic, social, and cultural rights, but they disagreed whether it could be claimed as a right. No vote was conducted to decide between these competing views and to reflect one of the contending views in the text. The issue was reopened in recent years, when the Optional Protocol to the Covenant was negotiated. During those negotiations, some industrialized countries accepted the moral responsibility of international cooperation, but argued that the Covenant does not impose legally binding obligations in regard to economic, social, and cultural rights internationally. However, that interpretation is far from unanimous among states. There are disagreements as to the scope of the duty and its precise implications while, conversely, there is broad agreement that the Covenant imposes at least some extraterritorial obligations in the area of economic, social, and cultural rights. (p. 1094)

- Anyway, the international protection of human rights implies extraterritorial jurisdiction that is supported in general International Law.

Several human rights treaties require states to ensure human rights to all people within their jurisdiction. When used to refer to the scope of application of human rights and comparable treaties, the term "jurisdiction" refers to the territory and people over which a state has factual control, power, or authority. [...] In addition, the preservation of human rights is in the interest of all states, even in the absence of any specific link between the state and the situation where human rights are violated: they are owed *erga omnes*. Thus, while the beneficiaries of human rights obligations are the rights-holders who are under a state's authority and control, the legal obligations to ensure the rights in question are owed to the international community as a whole. (p. 1102, 1103)
The *erga omnes* character of human rights may justify allowing the exercise by states of extraterritorial jurisdiction, even in conditions that might otherwise not be permissible, where such exercise seeks to promote such rights. [...] Under the principle of universality, certain heinous crimes may be prosecuted by any state, acting in the name of the international community, where the crime meets with universal reprobation. It is on this basis that, since time immemorial, piracy could be combated by all states: the pirate was seen as the *hostis humanis generis*, the enemy of the human race, which all states are considered to have a right to prosecute and punish. The international crimes for which treaties impose the principle *aut dedere, aut judicare*, or that are recognized as international crimes—requiring that all states contribute to their prevention and repression by investigating and prosecuting such crimes where the author is found on their territory unless the suspected author is extradited—also require the exercise of universal jurisdiction. International crimes justifying the exercise of universal jurisdiction include war crimes, crimes against humanity, genocide, torture, and enforced disappearances. In prosecuting these crimes, states are not seen to act exclusively in their own interest; they act as agents of the international community. The same applies to violations of *jus cogens* norms (peremptory norms of international law), because these norms serve the interests of the international community and the compliance that all states have a legal interest in. (p. 1142, 1143, 1144)

- The extraterritorial jurisdiction includes a number of States' functions.

  ... even under the narrowest understanding of such functions, they should comprise law enforcement activities and those of armed forces, the provision of basic infrastructure, certain essential public services such as water and electricity, and traditionally public functions of the state such as education and health. These functions may be considered to constitute elements of governmental authority for which the state should be held responsible, even if it has chosen to delegate these functions to private entities. (p. 1111)
  The duty to regulate the conduct of private groups or individuals, including legal persons, in order to ensure that such conduct shall not result in violating the human rights of others is well established in international human rights law. [...] The duty of the state to protect human rights by regulating the conduct of private actors extends to situations where such conduct may lead to violations of human rights in the territory of another state. (p. 1134, 1135)
  Specifically, in regard to corporations the Committee on Economic, Social and Cultural Rights has further stated that: "States Parties should also take steps to prevent human rights contraventions abroad by corporations that have their main seat under their jurisdiction, without infringing the sovereignty or diminishing the obligations of host states under the Covenant." (p. 1137)

- Each State's responsibilities for the protection of human rights continue when it becomes member of an international organization.

  Each state has a duty to ensure that the international organization which the state establishes or of which it becomes a member complies with the pre-existing human rights obligations of that state in the exercise of the powers that organization has been delegated. For instance, the European Court of Human Rights has noted that while the European Convention on Human Rights "does not exclude the transfer of competences to international organizations," this is "provided that Convention rights continue to be 'secured.' Member States' responsibility therefore continues even after such a transfer".
  This rule follows from the prohibition on entering into treaties that are incompatible with pre-existing treaty obligations in violation of the obligatory nature of treaties, pacta sunt servanda. This is well established in international human rights law. (p. 1119, 1120)

- IGOs are also bound by IHRL.

  Although stipulated in multilateral treaties that are binding on the states parties, a wide range of human rights has acquired a customary status in international law, and international organizations are therefore bound to exercise the powers they have been delegated in compliance with the requirements that they impose. Human rights may also be considered to form part of the "general principles of law recognized by civilized nations" within the meaning of Article 38 (1) (c) of the Statute of the International Court of Justice. The constitutions of several international organizations include human rights obligations, in particular the UN. Thus, the UN, including its specialized agencies, is necessarily bound by the human rights obligations contained in Articles 1 (3) and 55 of the UN Charter.
  [...]
  The UN Sub-Commission on Promotion and Protection of Human Rights has asserted the centrality and primacy of human rights obligations in all areas, including international trade and investment. The special rapporteurs of the Sub-Commission on Human Rights on globalization and its impact on the full enjoyment of human rights noted that, "[the] primacy of human rights law over all other regimes of international law is a basic and fundamental principle that should not be departed from." (p. 1121, 1123)

- International embargoes and similar measures should not undermine human rights protection.

  Article 103 of the UN Charter provides that states' obligations under the UN Charter prevail over states' obligations under any other international agreements. However, this cannot be interpreted to mean that the UN Security Council can adopt measures that set aside human rights obligations. As noted by the Committee on Economic, Social and Cultural Rights, even when the Security Council is acting under Chapter VII of the Charter, "those provisions of the Charter that relate to human rights (Articles 1, 55 and 56) must still be considered to be fully applicable in such cases".
  [...]
  The Committee on Economic, Social and Cultural Rights has stated in its General Comments on the rights to water, food, and health that states should refrain at all times from imposing embargoes or similar measures that prevent the supply of water, food, and health care, as well as goods and services essential for securing these rights; denial of access to such rights should never be used as an instrument of political and economic pressure. Such obligations almost certainly apply to other economic, social, and cultural rights, such as the rights to sanitation and to education. (p. 1132, 1133)

The Supreme Court of the Netherlands found in *The State of the Netherlands v. Hasan Nuhanovic*[153] and *The State of the Netherlands v. Mehida Mustafic-Mujic et al.*[154] (6 September 2013) that States can be held responsible for the conduct of international peacekeepers[155]. It is "the first time an individual government has

[153] www.rechtspraak.nl/Organisatie/Hoge-Raad/OverDeHogeRaad/publicaties/Documents/12%20 03324.pdf.

[154] www.rechtspraak.nl/Organisatie/Hoge-Raad/OverDeHogeRaad/publicaties/Documents/12%20 03329.pdf.

[155] The Cases are summarized in the website of the American Society of International Law as follows:

> The Supreme Court of the Netherlands (the Court) has issued two judgments upholding separate judgments of the Hague Court of Appeal finding the Dutch State (the State) responsible for the death of certain Muslims from Srebrenica. According to the press release, both cases concern the actions of the Dutch battalion (Dutchbat), part of the United Nations Protection Force, immediately after the fall of the Srebrenica enclave on July 11, 1995. In the first case, Hasan Nuhanovic, a United Nations employee in the Dutchbat compound in Potocari, was on the list of local personnel who could be evacuated with Dutchbat. Though his father, mother, and brother had also sought refuge in the compound, they were forced to leave because they were not on the list. They were ultimately murdered by the Bosnian-Serb army or related paramilitary groups. In the second case, Rizo Mustafic, an electrician working under Dutchbat authority in the Potocari compound, along with his wife and children was forced to leave the compound because the family was not on the list. Mustafic was subsequently murdered by the Bosnian-Serb army or related paramilitary groups.
> Both Hasan Nuhanovic and the family of Rizo Mustafic brought separate suits against the State, arguing that Dutchbat had acted wrongfully in sending their family members away from the compound. Though the District Court rejected both plaintiffs' applications for relief on the ground that Dutchbat's conduct was exclusively attributable to the United Nations, the Court of Appeal set aside the lower court judgments on the ground that the State was responsible for the wrongful conduct of Dutchbat. The Court found that public international law allowed conduct to be attributed to the State because it had effective control over Dutchbat's conduct, and further that such conduct was wrongful. According to the press release, the Court also rejected the State's argument in favor of judicial restraint,

been held to account for the conduct of its peacekeeping troops under a UN mandate"—said Jezerca Tigani, Deputy Europe and Central Asia Programme Director at Amnesty International[156]. In the Judgment of *The State of the Netherlands v. Hasan Nuhanovic* the Supreme Court said:

> 3.17.1 Part 5 submits that any assessment of Dutchbat's disputed conduct by reference to the legal principles implicit in articles 2 and 3 ECHR and articles 6 and 7 ICCPR is prevented by the fact that the State did not have jurisdiction as referred to in article 1 ECHR and article 2(1) ICCPR either in Srebrenica or in the compound in Potočari. This submission fails.
> 3.17.2 According to the case law of the European Court of Human Righs (ECtHR), the possibility is not excluded that a Contracting State may, in exceptional circumstances, have the jurisdiction referred to in article 1 ECHR even outside its territory [...].
> 3.17.3 In this case Dutchbat's presence in Srebrenica and in the compound in Potočari resulted from the participation of the Netherlands in UNPROFOR, and UNPROFOR derived its right to take action in Srebrenica from the Agreement on the status of the United Nations Protection Force in Bosnia and Herzegovina concluded between the United Nations and Bosnia and Herzegovina [...]. This means that the State was competent, through Dutchbat, to exercise jurisdiction within the meaning of article 1 ECHR in the compound.

Another way to foster the protection of human rights is the establishment of National Human Rights Institutions (NHRIs). They exist since late 1970s. In 1991, their first international meeting, in Paris, adopted the 'Principles relating to the Status of National Institutions' (Paris Principles)[157] that were endorsed by the CHR and the UN General Assembly in 1993 (Resolution 48/134). According to the Paris Principles, such institutions should have a strong legal basis, "competence to promote and protect human rights", and "as broad a mandate as possible". The Resolution includes 'Additional principles concerning the status of commissions with quasi-jurisdictional competence' that provides: "A national institution may be authorized to hear and consider complaints and petitions concerning individual situations". The CESCR dedicated the GC 10 (E/C.12/1998/25)[158] to 'The role of national human rights institutions in the protection of economic, social and cultural rights'; the CoRC dedicated the GC 2 (CRC/GC/2002/2)[159] to 'The role of independent national human rights institutions in the protection and promotion of the rights of the child'; and the Committee on the Elimination of Racial Discrimination adopted the 'General recommendation XVII (42) on the establishment of national institutions to facilitate the implementation of the Convention'[160]. The Council of Europe adopted

---

reasoning that "there would be virtually no scope for the courts to assess the conduct of a troop contingent in the context of a peace mission. According to the Supreme Court, this is unacceptable. However, a court that assesses the conduct of a troop contingent in retrospect must make allowance for the fact that the decisions in question were taken under great pressure in a war situation.
(Retrieved September 2013 from: www.asil.org/ilib130913.cfm).

[156] Retrieved September 2013 from:/www.amnesty.org/en/news/netherlands-supreme-court-hands-down-historic-judgment-over-srebrenica-genocide-2013-09-06.

[157] www2.ohchr.org/english/law/parisprinciples.htm.

[158] www.unhchr.ch/tbs/doc.nsf/0/af81bf2fed39cec1802566d50052f53b?Opendocument.

[159] www.unhchr.ch/tbs/doc.nsf/(symbol)/CRC.GC.2002.2.En?OpenDocument.

[160] www.rwi.lu.se/pdf/publications/gccerd.pdf.

in 1997 the 'Recommendation N° R(97)14 on the establishment of independent national institutions for the promotion and protection of human rights'[161].

NHRIs have varying denominations and powers. They may be named Commission, Ombudsman (a masculine name now often replaced with the neutral *Ombudsperson*)[162], Mediator, *Defensor del Pueblo*, *Provedor de Justiça*, etc. They may even have the rank of a Ministry or a Secretary of State. There are more than 100 such institutions, half of them corresponding to the Paris Principles. The EU created an *Ombudsperson* in 1994. Within the OHCHR there is an International Coordination Committee of National Institutions for the Promotion and Protection of Human Rights, as well as a Sub-Committee on Accreditation[163].

Summing up: "The primacy of the state in the protection and fulfilment of internationally guaranteed human rights is the fundamental starting point of international human rights law" (Byrnes and Renshaw 2010, p. 498). International protection is auxiliary and subsidiary of the national protection, by means of cooperation or intervention.

3.4.4 Case Law

The normative content of human rights is to a large extent defined by their jurisprudential interpretation. Given the evolving nature of the Law and the openness of the concept of 'human right', the legal instruments have to be interpreted following a teleological approach in order to bring up to date their letter.

There is not yet a veritable Case Law on human rights at universal level. The ICJ hardly mentioned human rights in its early decades when, as Schabas (2009) remarked, it was mainly "a club of former legal advisors and ambassadors", without "judges with a human rights pedigree" (p. 641). Christopher McCrudden (2008) noted that human rights were mentioned, for the first time, by one of its members in an individual opinion, in 1947 (p. 682). According to a UN publication, it pronounced 16 decisions relevant for the protection of human rights that "permitted, in some extent, to define the international law concerning the human rights" (Nations Unies 1995, p. 13, 510).

The Decisions ('Views') adopted by the CCPR, after examining individual communications concerning alleged violations of the respective Covenant by the States Parties to its Optional Protocol, are often qualified as 'quasi-jurisprudence'. It may be considered, in Scheinin's (2006) opinion, "as various forms of 'subsequent practice' in the meaning of VCLT [Vienna Convention on the Law of Treaties] article 31(3)(b)—at least in the vast majority of instances where no formal objection is made by states parties" (p. 52). In Tomuschat's (2008) opinion, "the general com-

[161] https://wcd.coe.int/com.instranet.InstraServlet?command=com.instranet.CmdBlobGetand%20InstranetImage=567349%20%20andSecMode=1andDocId=578706andUsage=2.

[162] The first *Ombudsman* goes back to 1809, in Sweden.

[163] www.ohchr.org/en/countries/nhri/pages/nhrimain.aspx.

ments and recommendations of the monitoring bodies acquire an ever-growing weight" (p. 39).

The only true international jurisprudence addressing human rights is that of the jurisdictional bodies established by the regional systems of protection. The most abundant and influential has been pronounced by the European Court of Human Rights that has developed jurisprudential principles such as: positive obligations, effective protection, implicit rights, evolving interpretation, not abuse of rights, subsidiarity, proportionality, margin of appreciation, legality, Rule of Law, fair procedure, and democracy (see Lawson 2009, pp. 411–117; Greer 2010, pp. 470–471)[164].

The establishment of a Universal Court of Human Rights is an aspiration as old as the UDHR.

At the 1946 Paris Peace Conference, the head of the Australian Delegation (Foreign Minister Herbert V. Evatt) had already proposed the creation of an International Court of Human Rights, as he recalled during the 181th plenary meeting of the General Assembly, on 10 December 1948 (A/PV.181), when the draft UDHR began to be discussed.

In answer to the 'Memorandum and Questionnaire Circulated by UNESCO on the Theoretical Bases of Human Rights', in 1947, there were more or less explicit references to it. For example: "The corollary to a world charter of human rights is therefore the creation of some world authority" (Kabir 1948, p. 194).

During the first session of the CHR, the Australian representative (Colonel William Roy Hodgson) had submitted a detailed draft resolution for the establishment of an International Court of Human Rights (E/CN.4/15). "Colonel William Roy Hodgson of Australia and Mrs. Mehta were adamant that an international bill of rights would be meaningless without some machinery for enforcement" (Glendon 2001, p. 38).

According to the Report of the CHR second session, in December 1947, in Geneva (E/600), the Working Group on Implementation, considering that the right to petition "*shall be open not only to States, but also to associations, individuals and groups*" (para. 36), agreed that a "Standing Committee composed of not less than five independent (non-government) men and women shall be established" that should "receive petitions from individuals, groups, associations or States" (para. 37). It should be permanent, composed of experts, and its function is, "essentially, one of conciliation, not of arbitration, and still less of final decision" (para. 41). A specialized agency could also be established to be called the International Human Rights Organization.

[164] These principles may be expanded as follows: Pre-eminence of Law; Primacy of International Law; Primacy of the most up to date norm and of the most favourable interpretation; Human rights subjectivity, universality, reciprocity and culturality; Indivisibility and interdependence of everyone's human rights; Non-discrimination, inclusion and, if needed, affirmative action; Priority of children and women rights; Primacy of State responsibility; International Community subsidiary responsibility; Everyone's responsibility; Correlation between human rights, democracy, development and peace; International cooperation; Human rights open-ended concept and evolving content; etc.

Based on the Australian plan, the Working Group prepared a draft Statute for an International Court of Human Rights (the term 'Court' was generally preferred to 'Tribunal') (E/CN.4/AC.1/27). Following its Report:

> The Working Group was unanimous in admitting the principle of a right of appeal to an International Court, but some representatives (those of Australia, Belgium and Iran) demanded the creation of a new Court, whilst others (the representatives of India and the United Kingdom observer), on the other hand, favored the employment of the present International Court of Justice. There were also two variants of the latter view. One favored and one opposed the creation under Article 26 of its Statute of a special Chamber of this Court, to deal with human rights. There were also different opinions as to whether final decisions (in other words, binding decisions), or merely advisory opinions should be obtained from the present Court. (para. 49)

The alternative as between the present Court and a new Court was discussed during two meetings of the Working Group. "After a voting, it was decided in favor of a Court as the final guarantor of human rights, of a new Court, empowered to pronounce final and binding decisions" (para. 50). In this regard, it was pointed to the terms of UN Charter Article 95: "Nothing in the present Charter shall prevent Members of the United Nations from entrusting the solution of their differences to other tribunals by virtue of agreements already in existence or which may be concluded in the future" (para. 56). A proposal to create the post of an Attorney-General for the International Court on Human Rights was not discussed, as that was a role within the scope of the of the CHR. The Commission, at its third session, in May-June 1948, in Lake Success (E/800), did not have time to consider the question of "implementation". In fact, as had said Santa Cruz at the Drafting Committee first session, in June 1946, "an international tribunal at this stage was utopian and something for the future" (E/CN.4/AC.a/SR.11).

In 1968, Sean McBride asked: "Will not it already be a time to think of creating a Universal Court of Human Rights similar to the European Court of Human Rights, which should be competent to decide on all violations of human rights?" (1968, p. V).

In 1989, the Final Report of the Colloquium *Universalité des droits de l'homme dans un monde pluraliste* (The human rights universality in a pluralistic world) that took place in Strasbourg stated: "We all want a World Court of Human Rights" (Badinter 1990, p. 188).

In 2004, Stefan Trechsel, former President of the (former) European Commission of Human Rights, concluded ("to my great regret"), that: "Realistically speaking, the creation of a world court for human rights is, at the present time, neither desirable, nor necessary, nor probable" (2004, para. 70). Notwithstanding:

> Since the entry into force of the 1998 Rome Statute of the International Criminal Court, developments in the field of international criminal law have been rapid and in many ways affect the international protection of human rights. The discussion on a future world court of human rights is still at an early stage but promising signals are coming from various corners of the world, suggesting that when there is momentum, we may again witness amazingly quick progress. (Krause and Scheinin 2009, p. ix)

Riedel (2009) notes too:

> A new communications procedure in the ICESCR context will soon be in operation, raising the expectations for ultimately judicial procedures in the field of human rights, such as the creation of a world court on human rights. The experience with the long drawn-out process of establishing an International Criminal Court might serve as a model: propagation of its institution for decades seemed utopian, yet eventually it came into being. (p. 149)

Scheinin (2009b) remarks elsewhere:

> The multitude of regional and international human rights instruments and monitoring mechanisms, coupled with the rapid evolution of international criminal law, may be paving the way for the future establishment of a world court of human rights. [...] With a proper design a world court of human rights could also help to remedy one of the greatest shortcomings of the present-day human rights architecture, namely the fact that only governments of nation states are held to account through the monitoring mechanisms of existing human rights treaties. A world court could—and should—be designed so as to provide monitoring of and accountability for human rights violations also in respect of other centres of power, such as intergovernmental organizations, international institutions and even transnational corporations. (p. 620)

Indeed, a recent challenge to the protection of human rights is the "changing configuration of the public-private divide in human rights ordering" (Steiner, Alston, and Goodman 2008, p. vi). According to Krause and Scheinin (2009a):

> ... globalization, with the emergence of other actors besides states as world-level agents that affect the lives of individuals in ways that traditionally were thought to be a monopoly of states, through trade, services, investments and other means, has put into question the very concept of human rights as a body of vertical norms between the state and the individual. If human rights are rights of the individual, should it not be for anyone who has the power to affect the enjoyment of those rights to be obliged to respect them? (p. ix)

After noticing the existence "of the intensified debate on new subjects of the international community, including intergovernmental organizations, multinational corporations, terrorist networks and non-governmental organizations", Åkermark (2009) wrote. "Around the year 2000 there occurred a clear shift in public debates in favour of recognizing the duties of private enterprise in environmental and social affairs and the fight against poverty" (p. 347, 353). In 2000, the UN launched the *Global Compact* so defined in the respective electronic site: "The UN Global Compact is a strategic policy initiative for businesses that are committed to aligning their operations and strategies with ten universally accepted principles in the areas of human rights, labour, environment and anti-corruption"[165]. It addresses especially transnational corporations "which a growing body of doctrine is willing, for well understandable reasons, to consider as subjects of international law, since they are active participants in the international legal process: in order to impose human rights obligations on such private non-state actors, these obligations must have their source elsewhere than in treaties, which only states may ratify" (Schutter 2009a, p. 45, 46).

In 2005, the CHR established the mandate of a 'Special Representative of the Secretary-General on the issue of transnational corporations and other business en-

[165] www.unglobalcompact.org/AboutTheGC/index.html.

See: *A guide for Business—How to Develop a Human Rights Policy* (www.ohchr.org/Documents/Publications/DevelopHumanRightsPolicy_en.pdf).

terprises with regard to human rights' (Resolution 2005/69). In 2011, the Special Representative (John Ruggie) proposed to the HRC Guiding Principles on Business and Human Rights: Implementing the United Nations 'Protect, Respect and Remedy' Framework[166]. They were adopted unanimously. In this connection, the CESCR affirms in the GC 18 on 'The right to work' (E/C.12/GC/18, 2005)[167]:

> 52. While only States are parties to the Covenant and are thus ultimately accountable for compliance with it, all members of society—individuals, local communities, trade unions, civil society and private sector organizations—have responsibilities regarding the realization of the right to work. States parties should provide an environment facilitating the discharge of these obligations. Private enterprises—national and multinational—while not bound by the Covenant, have a particular role to play in job creation, hiring policies and non-discriminatory access to work. They should conduct their activities on the basis of legislation, administrative measures, codes of conduct and other appropriate measures promoting respect for the right to work, agreed between the government and civil society. Such measures should recognize the labor standards elaborated by the ILO and aim at increasing the awareness and responsibility of enterprises in the realization of the right to work.

Tomuschat (2008) commented: "To advocate such a third-party effect of human rights amounts to an almost revolutionary step" (p. 108).

As Judge Rosalyn Higgins, President of the ICJ, pointed out: "The plethora of judicial and quasi-judicial bodies operating in the field of human rights does pose the risk of divergent jurisprudence"[168]. Moreover, only when it shall become possible for everyone to complain before a Universal Court for human rights violations the individual will be "truly consecrated as subject of the International Law" (Cohen-Jonathan 2001, p. 161). This points to a long-term contradiction, as Habermas (2012) remarks:

> On the one hand, human rights could acquire the quality of enforceable rights only within a particular political community—that is, within a nation-state. On the other hand, human rights are connected with a universalistic claim to validity, which points beyond all national boundaries. This contradiction would find a reasonable solution only in a constitutionalized world society (not necessarily with the characteristics of a world republic). (p. 74)

3.4.5 NGOs

Human rights are also a general responsibility, as proclaims the long title of the Declaration on the Right and Responsibility of Individuals, Groups and Organs of Society to Promote and Protect Universally Recognized Human Rights and Fundamental Freedoms (UN 1998)[169], known as the 'Declaration on Human Rights

[166] www.ohchr.org/documents/issues/business/A.HRC.17.31.pdf.

[167] www.unhchr.ch/tbs/doc.nsf/898586b1dc7b4043c1256a450044f331/493bee38093458c0c1257 1140029367c/$FILE/G0640313.pdf.

[168] www.echr.coe.int/NR/rdonlyres/38D1E6A5-DE24-42BD-BC3D-45CCCC8A7F8A/0/300120 09PresidentHigginsHearing_eng_.pdf.

[169] This Declaration has its origins in a Working Group established by the CHR in 1984. In order to support the 1998 Declaration, the CHR adopted a Resolution (2000/61) requesting "the Secretary-

Defenders'. This Declaration meets the wording of the last paragraph of the UDHR Preamble, according to which "every individual and every organ of society, keeping this Declaration constantly in mind, shall strive by teaching and education to promote respect for these rights and freedoms". A militant way of assuming the individual responsibility for the promotion and protection of human rights is the creation and participation in the work of NGOs.

There is agreement neither on a definition of NGO nor on what constitutes a human rights NGO and how to categorize them. George Edwards (2010) provides the following working definition: "An NGO is a private, independent, non-profit, goal-oriented group not founded or controlled by a government". The term "may encompass research institutes, churches and other religious groups, cooperatives, literary or scientific organizations, credit unions, foundations, girl and boy scouts, sporting groups, service organizations" (p. 148). Regarding human rights NGOs, "stakeholders in the international human rights law arena universally agree that human rights NGOs are meant to protect internationally recognized human rights at local, national, sub-regional, regional and global levels". Following Laurie Wiseberg (1996):

> A 'pure type' human rights NGO is one established specifically to do human rights work. Such groups may have a universal focus, like Amnesty International or Human Rights Internet (HRI) in Canada, or a regional or country-specific one, like the Inter-American Institute for Human Rights (IIDH) in Costa Rica or the Peoples' Union for Civil Liberties (PUCL) in India. It may have a mandate that is broad, like that of the Human Rights Watch Committees in New York, or narrowly focused on one issue, like the Minority Rights Group (MRG) in the UK or Defense for Children International (DCI) in Switzerland. All of these groups exist solely to do human rights work. By way of contrast, trade unions, churches or professional associations were created for other purposes, although they may devote substantial resources to the defense of human rights. (p. xxxv, note 42)

In Edwards' (2010) opinion, "successful human rights NGOs" distinguished themselves by the following ten overlapping and not exhaustive characteristics: mission; adherence to human rights principles; legality; independence; funding; non-profit status and commitment to service; transparency and accountability; adaptability and

---

General to appoint, for a period of three years, a special representative who shall report on the situation of human rights defenders in all parts of the world and on possible means to enhance their protection in full compliance with the Declaration" (para. 3).

The CESCR remembered in its GC 14 (2000) in respect of "The right to the highest attainable standard of health (art. 12)" (E/C.12/2000/4):

> 42. While only States are parties to the Covenant and thus ultimately accountable for compliance with it, all members of society—individuals, including health professionals, families, local communities, intergovernmental and non-governmental organizations, civil society organizations, as well as the private business sector—have responsibilities regarding the realization of the right to health. State parties should therefore provide an environment which facilitates the discharge of these responsibilities.
> (www.unhchr.ch/tbs/doc.nsf/(symbol)/E.C.12.2000.4.En)

International organizations are subjects of International Law, with obligations, as said the ICJ, but most human rights treaties do not provide for their becoming Parties, with few exceptions, such as the Convention on the Rights of Persons with Disabilities (UN, 2006) and its Protocol.

responsiveness; cooperative and collaborative nature; and competence and reliability (p. 147).

The early NGOs:

> ... included the British and Foreign Anti-Slavery Society (1839), the International Committee of the Red Cross (1863), the International Worker's Association (1864), the International Peace Bureau (1892), the Union of International Associations (1907), the Federal Council of Churches (1908), the American Jewish Committee (1906), and the French-based League for Human Rights (1898). (p. 150)[170]

After the Second World War, they multiplied, forming a network of unceasing pressure over States and the International Community, if needed by *naming, blaming and shaming* when this appears to be "the only way in which recalcitrant States can be encouraged to implement human rights within their jurisdictions" (Castellino 2010, p. 39). According to Wiseberg (1996):

> It was in the late 1970s that the human rights movement grew significantly and became an increasingly influential international actor. Between the factors that contributed to it, let us mention the following ones:
>
> - The coup against Salvador Allende Government in Chile in 1973 and the Latin American military dictatorships.
> - The Helsinki Final Act agreed in the Conference on Security and Cooperation in Europe in 1975.
> - The development of a liberation theology in the wake of the Catholic Vatican II (1961).
> - The awarding of the Nobel Peace Prize to Amnesty International in 1977.
> - The end of the Vietnam War.
> - The entering into force of the human rights International Covenants in 1976.
> - The human rights agenda of the USA President Carter, in 1977. (p. xxvii)

In the author's opinion:

> As we approach the end of this century, there has been a significant paradigm shift. [...]
> The paradigm shift has been occasioned by at least five significant developments. First has been the erosion of the concept of State sovereignty. [...]
> The second and related development leading to the paradigm shift has been the phenomenon of 'globalization'—the fact key issues and problems that once were national now defy national solutions. [...] Together with the third development—the shrinkage of the globe brought about by the technological revolution in communication—and the fourth development—the end of the Cold War—this has caused States to turn increasingly to the United Nations for solutions to planetary crises. [...]
> What, however, is clear is that the United Nations, which remains an inter-governmental, not supranational, actor, cannot do it alone. [...] Thus the fifth development, and a critical one, has been the development of a worldwide and vibrant human rights movement, exposing and denouncing human rights violations, lobbying governments and IGOs, extending legal and humanitarian aid to victims, helping to draft protective legislation, devising legal remedies, educating government and civil society about human rights standards, and building links of solidarity across the globe. (p. xix, xx)

[170] "International consciousness against slavery, led by William Wilberforce is considered by many to be the first real human rights struggle on the basis that it posited the inherent dignity and worth of every human being, including that of the slaves" (Castellino 2010, p. 39).

NGOs have consultative status with the main IGOs, especially with UN. They were already consulted under the League of Nations, but the UN Charter was the first UN document to use the term 'non-governmental organization'[171]. Article 71 provided the legal bases for NGOs to receive UN consultative status. On 14 February 1946, the General Assembly adopted the Resolution 4 (1) on 'Representation of Non-Governmental Bodies on the Economic and Social Council'[172]. On 21 of June, the ECOSOC established the Committee on Non-Governmental Organizations by its Resolution 3(II). This Committee's terms of reference were set out in ECOSOC's Resolution 288 B (X) of 27 February 1950. The rules were revised by its Resolution 1296 (XLIV) of 23 May 1968. The current terms of reference are set out in ECOSOC's Resolution 1996/31 of 25 July 1996[173]. It distinguishes between three categories of NGOs:

> 22. Organizations that are concerned with most of the activities of the Council and its subsidiary bodies [...].
> 23. Organizations that have a special competence in, and are concerned specifically with, only a few of the fields of activity covered by the Council and its subsidiary bodies [...].
> 24. Other organizations that do not have general or special consultative status but that the Council, or the Secretary-General of the United Nations in consultation with the Council or its Committee on Non-Governmental Organizations, considers can make occasional and useful contributions to the work of the Council or its subsidiary bodies or other United Nations bodies within their competence shall be included in a list (to be known as the Roster). This list may also include organizations in consultative status or a similar relationship with a specialized agency or a United Nations body.

At present, about 4,000 NGOs are accredited by the ECOSOC[174]. As we saw, they contributed greatly to the strengthening of the human rights profile in the UN Charter, to the drafting of the UDHR and to virtually all, if not all, of the UN's major international human rights instruments. More than 800 were present at the Vienna World Conference on Human Rights (1993) and about 2,500 participated in a Forum parallel to the Conference. About 200 were present during the Rome ICC Treaty Conference (1998), coordinated by the Coalition for the International Criminal Court, a network of 2,500 NGOs. Several NGOs and preeminent human rights activists were awarded Nobel Peace Prizes, such as: International Committee of the Red Cross (1917, 1944, 1963), Amnesty International (1977), *Médecins Sans Frontières* (1999), Rigoberta Menchú Tum (1992), Aung San Suu Kyi (1991), Mother Teresa (1979), Shirin Ebadi[175].

There are the OHCHR's Civil Society Section, the United Nations Non-Governmental Liaison Service (NGLS)[176], the Conference of Non-Governmental Organiza-

[171] There is a European Convention on the Recognition of the Legal Personality of International Non-Governmental Organisations, adopted in 1986. (http://conventions.coe.int/Treaty/en/Treaties/Html/124.htm).

[172] http://daccess-dds-ny.un.org/doc/RESOLUTION/GEN/NR0/032/55/IMG/NR003255.pdf?OpenElement.

[173] www.un.org/documents/ecosoc/res/1996/eres1996-31.htm.

[174] See: http://esa.un.org/coordination/ngo/new/index.asp?page=intro.

[175] See: http://nobelprize.org/nobel_prizes/peace/laureates/index.html.

[176] www.un-ngls.org/spip.php?page=sommaire.

tions in consultative relationship with the UN (CoNGO) founded in 1948[177], as well as a World Association of Non-Governmental Organizations (WANGO) founded in 2000[178]. In the same year, the CHR passed a resolution pursuant to which a UN Special Representative on the Situation of Human Rights Defenders was appointed[179]. In 2001, the Front Line Defenders was founded, which is an International Foundation for the Protection of Human Rights Defenders[180].

The role of NGOs is praised in the Vienna Declaration and Program of Action (I.38):

> The World Conference on Human Rights recognizes the important role of non-governmental organizations in the promotion of all human rights and in humanitarian activities at national, regional and international levels. The World Conference on Human Rights appreciates their contribution to increasing public awareness of human rights issues, to the conduct of education, training and research in this field, and to the promotion and protection of all human rights and fundamental freedoms. While recognizing that the primary responsibility for standard-setting lies with States, the conference also appreciates the contribution of non-governmental organizations to this process. In this respect, the World Conference on Human Rights emphasizes the importance of continued dialogue and cooperation between Governments and non-governmental organizations.

These words may be interpreted as "the implicit recognition of a right of regarding [*droit de regard*] of the organizations of citizens on the behavior of States" and of their loss of the "monopoly of elaboration of Law", as wrote Sophie Bessis. Indeed, "never had the organizations representatives of the civil society been so closely associated to the preparation of a world conference. [...] The NGOs appeared then simultaneously as actors and revealing the new fractures that are recomposing the new world landscape"[181].

Trindade (2006), in his General Course on Public International Law at The Hague Academy of International Law, in 2005, after stressing that "individuals and non-governmental organizations (NGOs) assume nowadays an increasingly relevant role in the formation itself of *opinio juris communis*" (see Glossary), observes:

> In recent years, they [NGOs] have been entitled to present on a regular basis their *amici curiae* [see Glossary] before international tribunals such as the Inter-American and the European Courts of Human Rights, and the *ad hoc* International Criminal tribunals for the former Yugoslavia and for Rwanda.
> In recent years, individuals and NGOs have effectively participated in the *travaux préparatoires* [elaboration] of certain international treaties, or influenced them, such as, for example, the 1984 UN Convention against Torture and its 2002 Optional Protocol, the 1989 UN Convention on the Rights of the Child [...].
> Individuals, NGOs and other entities of civil society come, thus, to act in the process of formation as well as application of international norms. [...] In sum, the very process of formation and application of the norms of International Law ceases to be a monopoly of the States. (p. 262, 263, 264)

---

[177] www.ngocongo.org/.

[178] www.wango.org/.

[179] See: www.ohchr.org/EN/issues/SRHRDefenders/Pages/SRHRDefendersindex.aspx.

[180] www.frontlinedefenders.org/about-front-line#sthash.c8mlaoF7.dpuf.

[181] Sophie Bessis, "La percée des ONG", *Le Courrier de l'UNESCO*, 1994, Mars, 12–14.

Campbell (2006) remarks: "The natural rights tradition and its successors, the Enlightenment 'rights of man', and the modern human rights movement, all focus primarily on the role of the state, with some ambivalence as to whether the state is the grand defender or the great danger to human rights" (p. 122). Here is the paradox of human rights protection: they are born against State, but need protection and provisions from State. States should be their major guarantors and promoters, but they are frequently also their prime violators. The legal approach to human rights protection—through Parliaments, Public Administration, Courts, etc.—is not the sole one. The most effective protection is not necessarily the most coercive. An educated world public opinion is the ultimate protection of human rights as a Common Ethics of Humankind.

References

Åkermark, S. 2009. Human rights, globalization, trade and development. In *International protection of human rights: a Textbook*, ed. C. Krause and M. Scheinin, 343–362. Turku/Åbo: Åbo Akademi University, Institute for Human Rights.

Al-Samman, S. 1987. *The right to education as a human right in international law—a thesis submitted for the degree of doctor of philosophy*. University of Manchester: Faculty of Law.

Albuquerque, C. 2010. Chronicle of an announced birth: The coming into life of the optional protocol to the international covenant on economic, social and cultural rights—the missing piece of the international bill of human rights. *Human Rights Quartely* 32:144–178.

APF (Asia Pacific Forum of National Human Rights Institutions). 2012. *international human rights and the international human rights system—a manual for national human rights institutions*. Sidney. www.asiapacificforum.net/support/resources/training/int-hr-systems/downloads/resources/international-human-rights-and-the-international-human-rights-system-a-manual-for-nhris-2012. Accessed Sept 2013.

Aristotle. 1953. *Ethics* (J. Thomson, Trans.). London: Penguin Books (1976).

Arslan, Z. 1999. Taking rights less seriously: Postmodernism and human rights. *Res Publica* 5:195–215. www.philosophy.ru/library/pdf/234617.pdf. Accessed July 2013.

Badinter, R. 1990. Rapport final. In *Universalité des droits de l'homme dans un monde pluraliste—Actes du Colloque organisé par le Conseil de l'Europe en collaboration avec l'Institut international des droits de l'homme, Strasbourg, 17–19 avril 1989*, 181–188. Strasbourg: Conseil de l'Europe/Éditions N. P. Engel.

Barret-Kriegel, B. 1989. *Les droits de l'homme et le droit naturel*. Paris: Quadrige/PUF.

Bates, E. 2010. History. In *International human rights law*, ed D. Moeckli, S. Shah, and S. Sivakumaran, 18–38. Oxford: Oxford University Press.

Byrnes, A., and C. Renshaw 2010. Within state. In *International human rights law*, ed D. Moeckli, S. Shah, and S. Sivakumaran, 498–517. Oxford: Oxford University Press.

Boerefijn, I. 2009. International human rights in national law. In *International protection of human rights: a textbook*, ed. C. Krause and M. Scheinin, 577–599. Turku/Åbo: Åbo Akademi University, Institute for Human Rights.

Bognetti, G. 2003. The concept of human dignity in European and U. S. Constitutionalism. In European Commission for Democracy through Law (Venice Commission), *European and U. S. Constitutionalism. Proceedings of the UniDem Seminar organised in Göttingen on 23–24 May 2003 in co-operation with the Institute of International Law, University of Göttingen, and Yale Law School*.
Now in print: Bognetti, G. 2005. The concept of human dignity in European and US constitutionalism. In *European and US Constitutionalism*, 85–107. Cambridge: Cambridge

University Press. Cambridge Books Online. Web. 24 June 2013. http://dx.doi.org/10.1017/CBO9780511493904.007.

Burgers, J. 1992. The road to San Francisco: The revival of the human rights idea in the twentieth century. *Human Rights Quarterly* 14 (4): 447–477. http://humanrightsinitiative.ucdavis.edu/files/2012/10/burgerroadtosf.pdf. Accessed July 2013.

Campbell, T. 2006. *Rights—a critical introduction*. London: Routledge.

Carozza, P. 2003. From conquest to constitutions: Retrieving a latin American Tradition of the idea of human rights. *Human Rights Quarterly* 25:281–313. http://ssrn.com/abstract=984953. Accessed July 2013.

Cassin, R. 1951. La Déclaration universelle et la mise en œuvre des droits de l'homme. In *Recueil des Cours—1951, II, Tome 79 de la Collection*, ed. Académie de droit international, 237–367. Paris: Librairie du Recueil Sirey.

Castellino, J. 2010. Civil and political rights. In *An introduction to international human rights law*, ed. A. Chowdhury and Md. Bhuiyan, 31–49. Leiden: Brill. http://therights.files.wordpress.com/2012/07/an_introduction_to_international.pdf. Accessed Sept 2013.

Clapham, A. 2009. United Nations charter-based protection of human rights. In *International protection of human rights: a Textbook*, ed. C. Krause and M. Scheinin, 79–103. Turku/Åbo: Åbo Akademi University, Institute for Human Rights.

Cohen-Jonathan, G. 2001. Les droits de l'homme, une valeur internationale. *Droits fondamentaux, n° 1*, juillet-décembre, 157–164. (www.droits-fondamentaux.org).

Courtis, Ch. 2012. The optional protocol to the international covenant on economic, social and cultural rights: A new instrument to address human rights violations. *Global Policy* 3 (4, November):484–487. http://onlinelibrary.wiley.com/doi/10.1111/j.1758–5899.2012.00200.x/pdf. Accessed July 2013.

Domínguez-Redondo, E. 2010. Role of the UN in the promotion and protection of human rights. In *An introduction to international human rights law*, ed. A. Chowdhury and Md. Bhuiyan, 119–144. Leiden: Brill. http://therights.files.wordpress.com/2012/07/an_introduction_to_international.pdf. Accessed Sept 2013.

Donnelly, J. 2009. Human dignity and human rights. *Swiss initiative to commemorate the 60th anniversary of the UDHR—protecting dignity: An agenda for human rights—research project on human dignity*. www.udhr60.ch/report/donnelly-HumanDignity_0609.pdf. Accessed July 2013.

Dumas, J. 1937. La sauvegarde internationale des droits de l'homme. In *Académie de Droit International—Recueil des Cours—I Tome 59 de la Collection*, 5–18. Paris: Recueil Sirey.

Edwards, G. 2010. Attributes of successful human rights Non-Governmental Organizations (NGOs)—Sixty Years After the 1948 Universal Declaration of Human Rights. In *An introduction to international human rights law*, ed. A. Chowdhury and Md. Bhuiyan, 145–218. Leiden: Brill. http://therights.files.wordpress.com/2012/07/an_introduction_to_international.pdf. Accessed Sept 2013.

Eide, A., and A. Rosas 2001. 1. Economic, social and cultural rights: A universal challenge. In *Economic, social and cultural rights—a textbook*, ed. A. Eide, C. Krause, and A. Rosas, 3–7. The Hague: Kluwer Law International.

Encyclopedia Britannica. 2012. *Encyclopedia britannica ultimate reference suite*. [DVD]. Chicago: Encyclopedia Britannica.

European Movement. 1949. *European convention on human rights—submitted by the european movement to the committee of ministeres of the council of Europe, INF/5/E/R.*

Facing History and Ourselves Foundation. (2010). *Fundamental freedoms—eleanor roosevelt and the universal declaration of human rights*. Brookline:The Making History Series.

Fagan, A. 2005. Human Rights. In *Internet Encyclopedia of Philosophy*. www.iep.utm.edu/hum-rts. Accessed July 2013.

Glendon, M. 2001. *A world made new—eleanor roosevelt and the universal declaration of human rights*. New York: Random House, Trade Paperbacks.

Goyard-Fabre, S. 1988. Les deux jusnaturalismes ou l'inversion des enjeux politiques. *Cahiers de Philosophie Politique et Juridique—Des théories du droit naturel, N° 11*, 9–42. Centre de Publications de l'Université de Caen.

Gramain, P. 1933. *Les droits internationaux de l'homme*. Paris: Les Éditions Internationales.
Greer, S. 2010. Europe. In *International human rights law*, ed D. Moeckli, S. Shah, and S. Sivakumaran, 454–478. Oxford: Oxford University Press.
Griffin, J. 2008. *On human rights*. New York: Oxford University Press.
Habermas, J. 2012. Chapter 4—the concept of human dignity and the realistic utopia of human rights. In *Philosophical dimensions of human rights—some contemporary views*, ed. C. Corradetti, 63–79. Dordrecht: Springer Science+Business Media B. V.
Hansungule, M. 2010. The historical development of international human rights law. In *An introduction to international human rights law*, ed. A. Chowdhury and Md. Bhuiyan, 1–30. Leiden: Brill. http://therights.files.wordpress.com/2012/07/an_introduction_to_international.pdf. Accessed Sept 2013.
Hayden, P. 2001. *The philosophy of human rights*. St. Paul: Paragon House.
Henkin, L. 1978. *The rights of man today*. London: Stevens and Sons.
Henkin, L. 1990. *Recueil des Cours/Collected Courses of the Hague Academy of International Law, 1989, IV, Tome 216 de la collection. International Law: Politics, Values and Functions—General Course on Public International Law*. Dordrecht: Martinus Nijhoff Publishers.
Hersch, J. (A selection of texts prepared under the direction of). 1969. *Birthright of Man*. New York: UNESCO/UNIPUB Inc.
Humphrey, J. 1984. *Human rights and the united nations—a great adventure*. New York: Transnational Publishers.
Humphrey, J. 1989. *No Distant Millennium: The International Law of Human Rights*. Paris: UNESCO.
Hunt, L. 2008. *Inventing human rights—a history*. New York: W. W. Norton and Company Ltd.
Kabir, H. 1948. The rights of man and the islamic tradition. In UNESCO, *Human rights—comments and interpretations—A symposium edited by UNESCO, with an Introduction by Jacques Maritain*. http://unesdoc.unesco.org/images/0015/001550/155042eb.pdf. Accessed July 2013.
Kissangoula, J. 2008. Jusnaturalisme. In *Dictionnaire des Droits de l'Homme*, ed J. Andriantsimbazovina, et al. (Sous la direction de), 570–573. Paris: PUF.
Krause, C., and M. Scheinin 2009. Preface. In *International protection of human rights: a Textbook*, ed. C. Krause and M. Scheinin, ix–x. Turku/Åbo: Åbo Akademi University, Institute for Human Rights.
Lauterpacht, H. 1948. The international protection of human rights. In *Recueil des Cours—1947, I—Tome 70 de la Collection*, ed. Académie de Droit International, 5–108. Paris: Recueil Sirey.
Lawson, R. 2009. The European convention on human rights. In *International protection of human rights: a Textbook*, ed. C. Krause and M. Scheinin, 389–424. Turku/Åbo: Åbo Akademi University, Institute for Human Rights.
MacBride, S. 1968. Introduction: La signification de l'année des droits de l'homme. *Revue de la Commission Internationale des Juristes (Numéro spécial: 1968—Année internationale des droits de l'homme, Première partie), Tome VIII, N°2*, III–XII.
Mäkinen, V. 2008. The evolution of natural rights, 1100–1500. In *COLLeGIUM: Studies across disciplines in the humanities and social sciences, volume 4: Universalism in international law and political philosophy*, 105–119. Helsinki: Helsinki Collegium for Advanced Studies. https://helda.helsinki.fi/bitstream/handle/10138/25778/06_makinen_2008_4.pdf?sequence=1. Accessed July 2013.
Marie, J.-B. 1985. *Les droits de l'homme ou 'Les choses de la vie' démocratique*. Strasbourg, Conseil de l'Europe, Direction des droits de l'homme.
Martenson, J. 1990. Introduction. *Bulletin des Droits de l'Homme—Mise en œuvre des instruments internationaux des droits de l'homme, 89/1.*
McCrudden, Ch. 2008. Human dignity and judicial interpretation of human rights. *The European Journal of International Law* 19 (4):655–724.
Mirabella, D. 2011. The death and resurrection of natural law. *The Western Australian Jurist* 2:251–260.
Monchablon, A. (Coord. de) 1989. *L'esprit de 1789 et des droits de l'homme—Textes et documents (1725–1986)—Préface de Claude Nicolet*. Paris: Coédition CNDP/Larousse.

Morsink, J. 1999. *The universal declaration of human rights: Origins, drafting, and intent*. Philadelphia: University of Pennsylvania Press.
Nations Unies. 1995. *Les Nations Unies et les droits de l'homme—1945–1995—Avec une introduction de Boutros Boutros-Ghali, Secrétaire général de l'Organisation des Nations Unies*. New York: Nations Unies, Département de l'information, Série Livres bleus des Nations Unies, Volume VII.
Nowak, M. 2001. The right to education. In *Economic, social and cultural rights—a textbook*, ed. A. Eide, C. Krause, and A. Rosas, 245–271. The Hague: Kluwer Law International.
Nowak, M. 2003. *Introduction to international human rights regime*. Leiden: Martinus Nijhoff Publishers.
Partsch, J. 1991. La mise en œuvre des droits de l'homme par l'UNESCO—Remarques sur un système particulier. In *Annuaire Français de Droit International*, 482–506. Paris: Éditions du Centre National de la Recherche Scientifique, XXXVI.
Perelman, Ch. 1980. Can the rights of man be founded? In *The philosophy of human rights—international perspectives*, ed. A. S. Rosenbaum, 45–51. Greenwood Press.
Pillay, N. 2012. *Strengthening the United Nations human rights treaty body system—A report by the United Nations High Commissioner for human rights*. United Nations—Human Rights: Office of the High Commissioner. www2.ohchr.org/english/bodies/HRTD/docs/HCReportTB-Strengthening.pdf. Accessed July 2013.
Plato (Ed. by J. Cooper, & D. Hutchinson). 1997. *Plato—complete works*. Indianapolis: Hackeht Publishing Company.
Pogge, W. 2001. How should human rights be conceived? In *The philosophy of human rights*, ed. P. Hayden, 187–210. St. Paul: Paragon House.
Ponton, L. 1990. *Philosophie et droits de l'homme de Kant à Levinas*. Paris: J. Vrin.
Ramcharan, B. 2008. *Contemporary human rights ideas*. London: Routledge.
Riedel, E. 2009. Economic, social and cultural rights. In *International protection of human rights: a Textbook*, ed. C. Krause and M. Scheinin, 129–149. Turku/Åbo: Åbo Akademi University, Institute for Human Rights.
Rishmawi, M. 2009. The revised Arab charter on human rights. In *International protection of human rights: a Textbook*, ed. C. Krause and M. Scheinin, 529–545. Turku/Åbo: Åbo Akademi University, Institute for Human Rights.
Rivero, J. 1979. Le problème des 'nouveaux' droits de l'homme. In *Documents de la 10e Session d'enseignement de l'Institut International des Droits de l'Homme*. Strasbourg, 2–27 juillet.
Rodley, N. 2009. Civil and political rights. In *International protection of human rights: a Textbook*, ed. C. Krause and M. Scheinin, 105–128. Turku/Åbo: Åbo Akademi University, Institute for Human Rights.
Rosenbaum, A. ed. 1980. *The philosophy of human rights—international perspectives*. Greenwood Press.
Rousseau, J.-J. 1751. *The social contract and the discourses* (G. D. H. Cole, Trans., revised and augmented by J. H. Brumfitt, & J. C. Hall, with an Introduction by A. Ryan). New York: Everyman Library (1993).
Rousseau, J.-J. 1762. *Émile* (Barbara Foxley, Trans., Introdution by P. Jimack). J. M. Dent, London, Charles E. Tuttle, Vermont: Everyman Library (2004).
Salomon, M., and I. Seiderman 2012. Human rights norms for a globalized world: The maastricht principles on extraterritorial obligations of states in the area of economic, social and cultural rights. *Global Policy* 3 (4):458–462. http://onlinelibrary.wiley.com/doi/10.1111/j.1758-5899.2012.00206.x/pdf. Accessed July 2013.
Samnøy, Å. 1993. *Human rights as international consensus—the making of the universal declaration of human rights—1945–1948*. Bergen: Chr. Michelsen Institute, Report.
Schabas, W. 2000. *Genocide in international law—the crimes of crimes*. Cambridge: University Press.
Schabas, W. 2009. International tribunals. In *International protection of human rights: a Textbook*, ed. C. Krause and M. Scheinin, 637–663. Turku/Åbo: Åbo Akademi University, Institute for Human Rights.

Scheinin, M. 2006. Human rights treaties and the Vienna Convention on the Law of treaties: Conflict or harmony? In *The status of international treaties on human rights*, ed AAVV, 43–54. Strasbourg: Council of Europe Publishing, Venice Commission.

Scheinin, M. 2009a. Characteristics of human rights norms. In *International protection of human rights: a Textbook*, ed. C. Krause and M. Scheinin, 19–37. Turku/Åbo: Åbo Akademi University, Institute for Human Rights.

Scheinin, M. 2009b. International mechanisms and procedures for monitoring. In *International protection of human rights: a Textbook*, ed. C. Krause and M. Scheinin, 601–620. Turku/Åbo: Åbo Akademi University, Institute for Human Rights.

Schutter, O. 2009a. The status of human rights in international law. In *International protection of human rights: a Textbook*, ed. C. Krause and M. Scheinin, 39–58. Turku/Åbo: Åbo Akademi University, Institute for Human Rights.

Schutter, O. 2009b. The European social charter. In *International protection of human rights: a Textbook*, ed. C. Krause and M. Scheinin, 425–442. Turku/Åbo: Åbo Akademi University, Institute for Human Rights.

Schutter, O., A. Eide, A. Khalfan, M. Orellana, M. Salomon, and I. Seidermanf 2012. Commentary to the maastricht principles on extraterritorial obligations of states in the area of economic, social and cultural rights. *Human Rights Quartely* 34:1084–1169. www2.lse.ac.uk/humanRights/articlesAndTranscripts/2012/HRQMaastricht.pdf. Accessed July 2013.

Sepúlveda, M, Th. Van Banning, G. Gudmundsdottir, Ch. Chamoun, and W. Van Genugten 2004. *Human rights reference hanbook*. 3rd. revised ed. Costa Rica: University for Peace. www.hrc.upeace.org/files/human%20rights%20reference%20handbook.pdf.

Simma, B. 1998. *The charter of the united nations—a commentary*. Oxford: Oxford University Press.

Smith, R., and Ch. Anker 2005. *Human rights*. London: Hodder Arnold.

Sohn, L. 1982. The new international law: Protection of the rights of individuals rather than states. *American University Law Review* 32 (1):1–64. www.wcl.american.edu/journal/lawrev/32/sohn.pdf. Accessed July 2013.

Sohn, L. 1996. The contribution of latin American lawyers to the development of the United Nations concept of human rights and economic and social justice. In *The Modern World of Human Rights 7 El Mundo Moderno de los Derechos Humanos—Essays in Honour of/ Ensayos en Honor de Thomas Bürgenthal*, ed. AAVV, 33–56. San José de Costa Rica: Instituto Interamericano de Derechos Humanos.

Steiner, H., Ph. Alston, and R. Goodman 2008. *International human rights in context—law, politics, morals*. 3rd ed. New York: Oxford University Press.

Tierney, B. 2004. The idea of natural rights—origins and persistence. *Nordwestern Journal of International Human Rights* 2. http://scholarlycommons.law.northwestern.edu/cgi/viewcontent.cgi?article=1005 & context=njihr. Accessed July 2013.

Tomuschat, Ch. 2008. *Human rights—between idealism and realism*. Oxford: Oxford University Press, Collected Courses of the Academy of European Law, XIII/1.

Tóth, J. 1972. Les droits de l'homme et la théorie du droit. In *René Cassin Amicorum Discipulorumque Liber—IV. Méthodologie des Droits de l'Homme*, ed. AAVV, 69–90. Paris: Éditions Pedone, Institut International des Droits de l'Homme, 'Jura Hominis ac Civis'.

Touraine, A. 1992. *Critique de la modernité*. Paris: Fayard.

Trechsel, S. 2004. A world court for human rights? *Northwestern Journal of International Human Rights* 1 (1), Article 3. http://scholarlycommons.law.northwestern.edu/cgi/viewcontent.cgi?article=1002 & context=njihr. Accessed Sept 2013.

Trindade, A. 2006. International law for humankind: Towards a new *jus gentium*—general course on public international law. In *Recueil des Cours/ Collected Courses of The Hague Academy of International Law—2005—Tome 316 de la Collection*, ed. Académie de Droit International. Leiden: Martinus Nijhoff Publishers.

UNESCO. 1948. *Human rights—comments and interpretations—a symposium edited by UNESCO, with an Introduction by Jacques Maritain*. http://unesdoc.unesco.org/images/0015/001550/155042eb.pdf. Accessed July 2013.

UNESCO. 1980. Colloquium on the new human rights. Matias Romero Institute of Diplomatic Studies of the Secretariat for External Affairs of Mexico. http://unesdoc.unesco.org/images/0004/000453/045394eo.pdf. Accessed July 2013.
United Nations War Crimes Commission. 1948. *History of the United Nations war crimes commission and the development of the laws of war*. London: His Majesty's Stationery Office. www.cisd.soas.ac.uk/documents/un-war-crimes-project-history-of-the-unwcc,5243951 7,p2. Accessed Sept 2013.
Vasak, K. 1976. Le droit international des droits de l'homme. In *Recueil des Cours, 1974, IV, Tome 140 de la collection*, ed. Académie de Droit International, 333–415. Leyde: A. W. Sijthoff.
Vasak, K. 1979. Pour les droits de l'homme de la troisième génération: les droits de solidarité. *Documents de la 10e Session d'enseignement de l'Institut International des Droits de l'Homme*, Strasbourg, 2–27 juillet.
Velu, J., and R. Ergec 1990. *La Convention européenne des droits de l'homme*. Bruxelles: Bruylant.
Verdoodt, A. 1964. *Naissance et signification de la Déclaration universelle des droits de l'homme (Préface de René Cassin)*. Louvain-Paris: Éditions Nauwelaerts.
Viola, F. 1984. La connaissance de la loi naturelle dans la pensée de Jacques Maritain (traduit de l'italien par G. et C. Brazzola). *Nova et Vetera* 3:204–228.
Waldron, J. 2009a. The decline of natural law. New York University, School of Law, Public Law and Legal Theory Research Papers Series, Working Paper N° 09–38. http://ssrn.com/abstract=1416966. Accessed July 2013.
Williams, R. 1997. *Hegel's ethics of recognition*. Berkeley: University of California Press.
Williams, Th. 2004. Francisco de Vitoria and the Pre-Hobbesian Roots of Natural Rights Theory. *Alpha Omega* VII (1):47–59.
Wiseberg, L. 1996. Introductory essay. In *Encyclopedia of Human Rights*, ed. E. Lawson and M. Bertucci, xix–xxxviii. Washington: Taylor & Francis.
Zuckert, M. 2004. Natural rights and modern constitutionalism. *Northwestern Journal of International Human Rights* 2(1), Article 4. http://scholarlycommons.law.northwestern.edu/njihr/vol2/iss1/4. Accessed July 2013.

Part II
Human Rights: Common Ethics of Humankind

Chapter 4
Ethics of Recognition

Abstract This chapter, after some terminological and conceptual clarifications, highlights the ethical essence of human rights, summarizes the philosophical debate on their foundation/justification, and argues that they are best understood as an Ethics of Recognition.

The main rights theories are the 'Will Theory' and the 'Interest Theory'. International Human Rights Law does not provide any definition of 'human right' (nor do national Laws). According to the most common definition, a human right is a right every person possesses simply by virtue of being human. Human rights are then rights with deep ethical significance. They have become a Common Ethics of Humankind.

There are three main accounts of human dignity and rights foundation/justification: Naturalism, Self-evidence and Consensus. I submit that human rights originated from a double Historical Consensus: (1) consensus of religious traditions and philosophical wisdom and (2) consensus laid down in the legal human rights instruments adopted by the International Community. It means their recognition—a topical and multi-purpose concept, with anthropological, political, juridical, psychological, etc, stakes. The Ethics of Human Rights is probably best understood as an Ethics of Recognition of the worth, dignity and rights of every and each human being.

4.1 Terminological and Conceptual Remarks

The use of the expression *droits de l'homme* (rights of man or human rights) instead of *droits naturels* (natural rights) began in the 1760s in France, as we saw. After the 1789 Declaration, the translation 'rights of man' entered the English language. 'Human rights' is a term first used perhaps by Thomas Paine in his translation of the French Declaration.

At the 13th meeting of the Drafting Committee first session, on 20 June 1947 (E/CN.4/AC.1/SR.13), the Soviet representative (Vladimir M. Koretsky):

> ... also pointed out that members seemed to have accepted the expression "all men", on the understanding that all persons were included. However, he thought that this implied an historical reflection on the mastery of men over women, and that the phrase should be modified in some way to make it clear that all human beings were included. He was opposed to such historical atavisms which precluded from an understanding that men were only one half of the human species and not the whole human species.

A. Reis Monteiro, *Ethics of Human Rights*, DOI 10.1007/978-3-319-03566-6_4,

The Australian representative (Ralph Lindsay Harry) "said he believed the problem, insoluble; he could find no other word to replace 'men'. He added that in the Charter itself reference was made to 'mankind' and not to 'mankind and womankind'". Eleanor Roosevelt (Chairman) "pointed out that it had become customary to say 'mankind' and mean both men and women without differentiation. She herself had no objection to the use of the word in this manner".

At the 34th meeting of the CHR second session, in Geneva, on 12 December 1947 (E/CN.4/SR.34), when discussing the draft of Article 1, Hansa Mehta (India) "said she did not like the wording 'all men' or 'and should act towards one another like brothers', because it was out of date and could be interpreted to exclude women. Roosevelt replied again that the word 'men' was generally accepted to include all human beings". Later, Metha observed that "Article 1 was the only place in the Declaration where the expression 'men' appeared. She wished to have this changed to 'human beings' or 'persons'". Supported by Bodil Gertrud Begtrup, the representative from Denmark, the change was eventually introduced during the CHR third session, at Lake Success (May–June 1948).

According to the *Yearbook of the United Nations*[1], the matter returned during the 10th session of the Third Committee of the UN General Assembly, held between 11 October and 2 December 1955, during the discussion of the draft International Covenants. A joint amendment submitted by Brazil, Bolivia, Costa Rica, the Dominican Republic and Greece "would replace the words 'free men' in the third paragraph of both preambles by the words 'free human beings'. It was explained that while the phrase 'free men' could hardly be misinterpreted so as to exclude women, it was preferable to use a more general term which clearly covered persons of both sexes. The amendment was adopted by a roll-call vote of 50 to none, with 6 abstentions" (p. 154).

In this respect, the *Yearbook of the United Nations*[2] reported that, at the 409th meeting of the Third Committee on 29 January 1952, a draft resolution by Mexico was discussed (A/C.3/L.194) concerning the adoption in Spanish of the terms 'derechos humanos' in the Covenants, instead of 'derechos del hombre'. The Mexican representative noted that the UN Charter used the words 'derechos humanos'. The draft resolution was supported by representatives of many States. They argued that the words 'derechos del hombre' reflected somewhat obsolete individualistic ideas. "The representative of France, however, felt that the expression 'derechos del hombre' exactly because of its individualistic meaning expressed better the principles of the Universal Declaration". After two drafting changes proposed by the representatives of Lebanon and the USSR, the Mexican draft resolution was adopted by a roll-call vote of 36 to none, with 9 abstentions. It was also adopted by the UN Assembly at its 375th plenary meeting by 45 votes to none, with 10 abstentions. It read:

> Whereas in the Spanish text of the United Nations Charter, Articles 1, 13, 55, 62, 68 and 76 refer to 'derechos humanos' and not to 'derechos del hombre'.

[1] http://unyearbook.un.org/unyearbook.html?name=isysadvsearch.html.

[2] www.unhcr.org/4e1ee76b0.pdf.

> Whereas the content and purpose of the Universal Declaration of Human Rights and of the draft Covenant have a wide significance which is not covered in Spanish by the term 'derechos del hombre',
> Taking into account the fact that, in the general discussion on this matter in the Third Committee during the sixth session of the General Assembly, prominent representatives of Spanish-American countries expressed their preference for the term employed in the Charter,
> The General Assembly
> Decides that, in future, in all United Nations working documents and publications in Spanish, and in the Universal Declaration and draft Covenant, the words 'derechos humanos' shall be used instead of the words 'derechos del hombre', used at present (p. 491).

Although 'human rights' is the most common term in International Law, the most used in constitutional texts is 'fundamental rights', consecrated by the 1919 German Constitution of Weimar, the title for Part II of which was 'Fundamental rights and obligations of Germans' (*Zweiter Hauptteil—Grundrechte und Grundpflichten der Deutschen*)[3].

There is also the term 'fundamental freedoms', frequently associated with 'human rights'. It appears five times in the UN Charter, two times in the UDHR, two times in the ICESCR and one time in the ICCPR. The complete title of the ECHR is, as we know, European Convention for the Protection of Human Rights and Fundamental Freedoms. There is no agreed conceptual distinction between human rights and fundamental freedoms, as Marc Bossuyt (1975) observed:

> Of course, we should see no significant difference between fundamental rights and fundamental freedoms, as that is a usual distinction in the current language not covering very different realities. Indeed, these freedoms are rights and these rights are freedoms! The expression 'freedom of thought' is nothing more than an abbreviation of the expression 'right to freedom of thought'. The right to life is not obviously the right to get to life, but the right to freedom of living. Concerning the right to freedom, it is no need to say that it is both a freedom and a right.
> These freedoms are rights because they represent 'legally protected interests'. In this respect, it is important to clearly distinguish the two elements constitutive of every subjective right, namely the interest, on the one hand, and the legal protection, on the other one. The interest corresponds to the matter addressed by this legal protection or, in other words, to the material content of the subjective right concerned (p. 802).

By contrast, the French *libertés publiques* and the American 'civil rights' are restrictive terms that do not cover all human rights[4].

'Right' is a word used in a variety of senses, somethimes confusing. Two main meanings can be distinguished: (1) rectitude or righteousness, meaning to do the right thing, and (2) entitlement, meaning the ability to claim something. There are social/moral rights derived "from the accepted customs and practices whose violation attracts general criticism", and legal rights derived from legal rules (Campbell 2006, p. 28). A rule is a social norm stating that, "in a certain type of situation, a certain category of person (P) may, may not, or must, or must not, do a certain type

[3] www.documentarchiv.de/wr/wrv.html.

[4] Civil rights/liberties refer primarily to those human rights which are laid down in the USA Constitution. The American Civil Liberties Union is an ONG active since the 1920s. (www.aclu.org).

of action (A)" (p. 27). If they are mandatory (non-optional), they are legal rules, conferring private power rights that are "normative powers of individuals to affect the legal position of other individuals"[5]. Legal rights, "with their correlative duties, always require a rationale that is sufficiently powerful to justify the element of coercion that is present to some degree within all legal systems" (p. 82, 83). They are always based on common moral values. "Law is nothing more than the minimum ethics", said the German legal philosopher Georg Jellinek (1851–1911)[6].

Horacio Spector (2009) noticed that "philosophers and legal theorists still disagree about the correct analysis of 'rights', both moral and legal" (p. 355). Two main accounts are the 'Will Theory' (or 'choice' or 'power' theory) and the 'Interest Theory' (or 'benefit' or 'wellbeing' theory). The first "was introduced in Anglo-American legal theory by H. L. A. Hart under the name of 'Choice Theory', but it was defended by a number of German jurists in the nineteenth century with its roots going back to Kant (Simmonds 1998, p. 179)" (p. 359). The second account (the 'Interest Theory'), first suggested by Bentham, was formulated as the 'Benefit Theory'. The German legal scholar Caspar Rudolf von Jhering (1818–1892) gave it the most well-known formulation when he famously defined 'right' as a "legally protected interest". Following Spector (2009), both theories "can each account for various features of rights, but neither of them is totally satisfactory. The controversy has now been running for decades and seems irresolvable" (p. 355). According to the view of 'value pluralism' (proposed by Isaiah Berlin), values are inherently plural and incommensurable; therefore, they cannot be hierarchized[7].

Spector observes that, from the seventeenth to the nineteenth centuries, the prevailing paradigm of moral and legal rights was that of individual autonomy, epitomized by Kant's Moral Philosophy. In the second half of the nineteenth century, a new paradigm emerged, centered on subjective interests, especially those of politically influential groups, such as unionized workers. "Yet, the old paradigm did not vanish. Rather, both paradigms started to clash in legal and moral thought". As a consequence, "the difference in value paradigms explains the radical semantic

[5] It should be noted that rights might not be confined to human beings (or groups). It is a matter of debate, for instance, whether rights may be also ascribed to animals, not capable of reason and autonomy or free agency, or to other non-human entities.

[6] "Das Recht ist nichts anderes als das ethische Minimum" (*Die sozialethische Bedeutung von Recht, Unrecht und Strafe*, 2. Aufl., Berlin 1908, S. 45).(www.jura.uni-wuerzburg.de/fileadmin/02160100/Lehrveranstaltungen/SS_2006/Rechts-_und_Staatsphilosophie_II/Materialien/B._Recht_und_soziale_Normen/jellinek_recht_als_ethisches_minimum.pdf).

[7] Campbell (2006) summarizes:

> According to the will theory of rights, rights are explained in terms of our capacity for choice and agency through the action of the will. Rights on this account enable the rights-holder to control through correlative obligations on others how such others may act towards the rights-holder. According to the interest theory of rights, rights are explained in terms of the fact that human (and perhaps other) beings are capable of having interests. On this account rights secure through correlative obligations the protection and advancement of the interests of the rights-holder. [...]
> We have to conclude that neither approach can explain the full panoply and variety of rights that feature in standard right discourse (p. 43, 46).

variation of the term right as deployed in the paradigm of individual autonomy and the paradigm of subjective interests". The meaning of 'rights' differs from the one to the other. "Today's normative language includes both terms but in ambiguous fashion" (p. 364). Contemporary Law embodies different kinds of rights. In Spector's opinion, however, there is "a common core that seems to be paradigm invariant. Right is conceptually tied to state or public enforceability" (p. 369). In this context, Habermas (2012) writes:

> The modern doctrines of morality and law that claim to rest on human reason alone share the concepts of individual autonomy and equal respect for everyone. This common foundation of morality and law often obscures the decisive difference that whereas morality imposes *duties* concerning others that pervade all spheres of action without exception, modern law creates well-defined *domains* of private choice for the pursuit of an individual life of one's own. Under the revolutionary premise that everything is permitted which is not explicitly prohibited, subjective rights rather than duties constitute the starting point for the construction of modern legal systems. The guiding principle for Hobbes, and for modern law generally, is that all persons are allowed to act or to refrain from acting as they wish within the confines of the law. Actors take a different perspective when, instead of following moral commands, they *make use of* their rights. A person in a *moral relation* asks herself what she owes to another person independently of her social relation to him—how well she knows him, how he behaves, and what she might expect from him. People who stand in a *legal relation* to one another are concerned about potential *claims* they expect others to make on them. In a legal community, the first person acquires obligations as a result of claims that a second person makes on her (p. 6, 70).

To hold a legal right is, therefore, a normative subjective stance, meaning that somebody is entitled to a liberty or claim, recognized and protected by written or positive Law, and that someone else (in the last instance some public authoritative body) is under a corresponding legal obligation, either negative (not acting against) or positive (doing something). This is what distinguishes legal rights from mere moral claims, as Campbell (2006) points out: the former imply "an authoritative remedial mechanism that is called into action to deal with alleged rights violations". There is thus a "close, almost logical, connection between rights and remedies", so that rights "without remedies are not rights at all" (p. 89). In his opinion: "All this may be summed up by saying that the rule of positive law is an essential part of any acceptable rights régime and is capable of giving a special place to those rights we choose to designate as human rights" (p. 102). Human rights "are at the heart of the very idea of rights" (p. 39). They "are based on core moral values, such as autonomy and wellbeing" (p. 81).

As IHRL does not provide any definition of 'human right' (nor do national Laws), "visions may vary considerably as to what is understood by human rights" (Tomuschat 2008, p. 1). Griffin (2008), after noting the "undeterminateness" and "nearly criterionless" of the notion of human right (p. 2, 14), rightly understands, as mentioned in Introduction, that the purpose of its philosophical problematization is not the same as that which inspired the drafters of the legal texts proclaiming them in the aftermath of the Second World War. However, the philosophical question remains "to identify a sense for the term 'human right'" (p. 38). If most recognized human rights "are acceptable, [...] there are some that are not, and several that are at least debatable" (p. 194). Griffin noticed that their popularity and appeal tend to transfer into human right all that is morally important, but not all things good or important for one's well-being and happiness can be claimed as human rights. In addition, there are goods that Law cannot guarantee (love, for example). "Human rights do not exhaust the whole moral domain; they do not exhaust even the whole domain of justice and fairness" (p. 41).

Following the most common definition, 'human right' is a right one possesses simply for being human. It is a legal right recognized to every member of the human species, without discrimination, irrespective of ethnical, cultural, religious, political or other membership, of gender, age, handicap or of whatever circumstances. Human rights are therefore universal and qualified as imprescriptible and inalienable:

- *Universal,* because they are held by every human being everywhere in the world and in all situations.
- *Imprescriptible,* because they are 'natural', inextinguishable, not capable of being lost.
- *Inalienable,* because they are inherent in the human dignity, ethically indisposable, not capable of being transferred, renounced or expropriated.

'Imprescriptible' and 'inalienable' are terms of the 18th century Declarations, but only the second one subsists in IHRL, subsuming the idea of imprescriptibility. The metaphysical notion of 'human nature', innate essence, immutable, was replaced with the historical idea of 'human dignity' recognized and consecrated by universal or universalizable consensus.

Human rights are the answer to the following question: What do human beings need to live free "from fear and want" (UDHR)?

Defining the normative content of a human right is to determine its right-holders, object and duty-bearers.

- *Right-holders* of human rights are, by definition, "every human being", "all persons", "everyone", "anyone", except when a legal instrument addresses a particular, more vulnerable category of persons (children or women, for example). Another exception regards the political rights of children the exercise of which is subjected to a minimum age. 'Collective rights' derive from individual rights (see Glossary).
- The *object* of a human right is that to which the right-holder is entitled. It should be something precise and obtainable, however difficult to implement and enforce.
- *Duty-bearers* are mainly States, individually and collectively, but human rights have a horizontal dimension, too: they create (passive or active) duties between individuals. Moreover, each individual has duties towards his or her own human dignity and the species' dignity.

While right-holders and duty-bearers are largely the same for all human rights, and some principles also apply to every human right (notably the principle of non-discrimination), each right entails unique norms that constitute its specific 'core content'. There is still the concept of 'minimum core content' that means a level below which a State may not descend in complying with its obligations, regardless of economic constraints or other circumstances (see Young 2008).

It should be noted, however, that a distinction must be made between entitlement and the ability to exercise human rights. A child, for example, is entitled to all human rights but only progressively becomes able to exercise them autonomously. In addition, many human rights may be subject to reservations or declarations of interpretation, as well as legitimately restricted and even temporally suspended, in certain situations and under strict conditions. Only a few are qualified as non-derogable (see Glossary).

Human rights are, therefore, by definition, subjective rights with deep ethical significance.

4.2 The Ethical Significance of Human Rights

René Maheu (1972), UNESCO's Director-General from 1962 to 1974, wrote: "Law is the dialectic by means of which man forces himself to a best he invents", and the idea of human rights "introduces into the heart of history the principle of an indefinite surpassing of the man by man" (p. 317). This is a dense and beautiful vision of Law and of human rights' ethical scope.

According to the above mentioned document of the International Theological Commission (2008)[8], the human being is "fundamentally a moral being". Eleanor Roosevelt, in her speech to the UN General Assembly on 9 December 1948, cited these words of Gladstone Murray: "The central fact is that man is fundamentally a moral being"[9]. That is why, as Amartya Sen (2004) wrote, "proclamations of human rights are to be seen as articulations of ethical demands" (p. 320).

Even though the UDHR legal status was not consensual, as we saw, its moral value was prized by many representatives of the UN Member States when it was drafted and adopted. The American representative (Willard L. Thorp) affirmed during the ECOSOC 215th meeting, on 25 August 1948 (E/SR.215), that: "It was his firm hope that, at some future date, historians would be able to rank the Declaration before the Council among those great documents of history". At the ECOSOC 218th meeting, on 26 August (E/SR.215), the Chilean representative (Hernan Santa Cruz) stated that: "The Declaration was far from perfect, but it contained the essence of the ideals of the United Nations". So "it would have a future moral force". At the Third Committee 90th meeting, on 1 October (A/C.3/SR.90), the Pakistani representative (Shaista S. Ikramullah) affirmed that: "It was imperative that the peoples of the world should recognize the existence of a code of civilized behavior which would apply not only in international relations but also in domestic affairs. It was her hope that the Declaration would mark a turning-point in history". The Ecuadorian representative (Jorge Carrera Andrade) declared that: "The International Declaration of Human Rights was the most important document of the century, and, indeed, was a major expression of the human conscience".

[8] www.pathsoflove.com/universal-ethics-natural-law.html.

[9] www.americanrhetoric.com/speeches/eleanorrooseveltdeclarationhumanrights.htm.

By presenting the draft Declaration at the 180th plenary meeting of the General Assembly, on 9 December (A/PV.180), the Rapporteur of the Third Committee (Émile Saint-Lot) stated that: "It is perhaps not perfect, but it was the greatest effort yet made by mankind to give society new legal and moral foundations". In Cassin's opinion: "The Declaration was the most vigorous and the most urgently needed of humanity's protests against oppression", having "a wide moral scope". The Netherlandish representative (J. H. van Roijen) declared that: "Although the Declaration was not legally binding on Governments, it should have great moral force". During the 181th plenary meeting, on 10 December (A/PV.181), when the draft UDHR began to be discussed, the British representative (Ernest Davies) "stressed the fact that the preparation of the draft Declaration was a milestone on the road of human progress". The Belgian representative (Count Henry Carton de Wiart) declared that "the Declaration not only had an unprecedented moral value, it had also the beginnings of a legal value". At the 182th plenary meeting, on 10 December (A/PV.182), the Canadian representative (L. B. Pearson) also expressed the hope "that it would mark a milestone in humanity's upward march". The Paraguayan representative (Carlos A. Vasconcellos) said that it "would not, as if by a magic wand, end all the ills that afflicted humanity", but "would be regarded as a beacon in the history of mankind". At the General Assembly 183th plenary meeting, its President (Herbert V. Evat) declared that it "was a step forward in a great evolutionary process". In sum, as the Colombian representative (Augusto Ramírez Moreno) had affirmed at the Third Committee 90th meeting, on 1 October (A/C.3/SR.90), already quoted in Introduction, the results of the drafting process "should be of great significance, even though they might be merely the seed of a tree which would bear fruit at a much later time".

As a consequence, human rights "codify universal values and establish procedures to enable every human being to live a life of dignity" (Pillay 2012, p. 94). They "circumscribe precisely that part (and only that part) of morality which *can* be translated into the medium of coercive law and become political reality in the robust shape of effective civil rights" (Habermas 2012, p. 68). Human rights hold, therefore, an ethical-legal Janus face since they possess an ethical content with legal form and force.

It might be said that the history of human rights is the history of the invention of the Human Being by human beings. The Human Being is the ethical subject transcending empirical subjects—cultural, national, social, familial, psychological, etc. subjects—circumscribed by their roots, belongings, circumstances and other particularities. Human rights, by adding a universal moral heritage to the genetic heritage of the human species and to particular cultural heritages, vest every human being with an ethical identity. The Ethics of Human Rights expresses the essence of the evolution of the moral and juridical conscience of Humankind, concentrating the juice of the best fruits of its cultural diversity. It is an intercultural and universal Ethics with political, economic, pedagogical and other requirements.

In short: Human rights have an ethical meaning because their source and purpose are the worth and dignity of each and every human being. They constitute "an ethics legally sanctioned" (Rivero 1988, p. 638).

As a consequence, human rights are "the common property of all mankind", as the Bolivian representative (Eduardo Anze Matienzo) said during the 90th meeting of the General Assembly Third Committee, on 1 October 1948 (A/C.3/SR.90). They are a "general heritage of mankind", said Cassin (1972, p. 405), a "common heritage of the mankind" personified in every human being as both "a being unique and the essence of the species", affirmed Federico Mayor, former Director-General of UNESCO[10]. The International Theological Commission (2008)[11] also refers to "the existence of a patrimony of moral values common to all people, beyond the manner in which such values are justified within a particular vision of the world" (para. 12).

The idea that human rights are a common ethical heritage echoes throughout many texts adopted by the International Community. For example:

- The UDHR was proclaimed "as a common standard of achievement for all peoples and all nations", as reads its Preamble. Two years after its proclamation, Cassin (1951) affirmed, by concluding his course at The Hague Academy of International Law on 'The Universal Declaration and the Implementation of Human Rights', that it is constructed "over the unity of the human family and offers, in spite of its unavoidable imperfections, the basis of an ethics without which the universal society could not organize itself at moral, political, legal and even economic levels" (p. 360).
- In 1968, the Tehran International Conference on Human Rights adopted a Resolution on the 'Education of youth in the respect for human rights and fundamental freedoms' (Resolution XX)[12], which affirmed "that the principles set forth in the Universal Declaration of Human Rights represent ethics common to all members of the international community".
- In his address at the opening of the 1993 Vienna World Conference on Human Rights, then UN Secretary-General (Boutros Boutros-Ghali) said:

> In sum, what I mean to say, with all solemnity, is that the human rights we are about to discuss here at Vienna are not the lowest common denominator among all nations, but rather what I should like to describe as the 'irreducible human element', in other words, the quintessential values through which we affirm together that we are a single human community! (Nations Unies 1995, p. 441).

Human rights are, therefore, a *Common.*

According to the report *The State of the Commons*, published by the Tomales Bay Institute in 2003[13], "*commons, common assets, common property* and *common wealth*" are terms that "refer to the same thing in slightly different ways".

> *Commons* is the generic term. It embraces all the creations of nature and society that we inherit jointly and freely, and hold in trust for future generations.
> [...]

[10] "Les droits de l'homme: Patrimoine de l'humanité", *Le Courrier de l'UNESCO*, 1994, Mars, p. 8.

[11] www.pathsoflove.com/universal-ethics-natural-law.html.

[12] http://untreaty.un.org/cod/avl/pdf/ha/fatchr/Final_Act_of_TehranConf.pdf.

[13] www.onthecommons.org; see also www.iasc-commons.org.

> The Romans distinguished between three types of property: *res privatae*, *res publicae* and *res communes*. The first consisted of things capable of being possessed by an individual or family. The second consisted of things built and set aside for public use by the state, such as public buildings and roads. The third consisted of natural things used by all, such as air, water and wild animals.
> [...]
> The most useful way to understand the commons today is as the sum of all we inherit together and should pass on, undiminished, to our heirs.
> In this way of viewing things, the economy is divided between the market and the commons. The market encompasses private things (which we mostly manage for short-term monetary gain), while the commons comprises shared things (which we manage, or should manage, for shared long-term life enhancement).
> The boundaries between the market and the commons shift over time. (p. 3, 4)

At the dawn of the twenty-first century, the balance between the market and the Commons is in dangerous disruption.

> At one time the commons was vastly larger than the market. Today, however, the commons is in grave danger because the market relentlessly attacks it.
> The market assault comes from two sides. With one hand, the market takes valuable stuff from the commons and privatizes it. Historians have called this 'enclosure'. With its other hand, the market dumps wastes and side-effects into the commons and says, 'It's your problem'. Economists call this 'externalizing'.
> Much that is called 'growth' today is actually a form of cannibalization in which the market diminishes the commons that ultimately sustains it.
> The state's role is to nurture both the commons and the market, and to maintain a healthy balance between them. This balancing role is essential to prevent humanity from devouring its own nest. Unfortunately, in recent years, the state has abandoned a balancing role and become a single-minded champion of the market (p. 5).

This is one of the greatest political and civic challenges for the present time. "Despite the many benefits it brings, the market is like a runaway steam engine. It has no internal governor to tell it when to stop depleting the commons that sustains it" (p. 6).

In a warning to Humankind, some 1700 of the world's leading scientists, including the majority of Nobel laureates in the sciences, stated in November 1992: "A great change in our stewardship of the earth and the life on it is required, if vast human misery is to be avoided and our global home on this planet is not to be irretrievably mutilated"[14].

The Commons supply means for living and struggling against diseases, for improving quality of life and making societies more just and peaceful, for communicating and traveling, for knowing and dreaming, etc. They are both natural and cultural: air, water, knowledge, values, even quiet, etc; the Internet is one of the most recent.

Another name for the Commons is 'Public Goods' (PGs). A PG is something possessing such great value for everyone and the human community that it must be collectively guaranteed. Human communities have always needed PGs, that is, resources and services benefiting all their members, which nobody can or want to provide in isolation. Collective security, for instance, is a need for every society in every time. The concept is not new: The economic theory of PGs goes back to the 1950s. They are defined in opposition to 'private goods', which are charac-

[14] www.ucsusa.org/about/1992-world-scientists.html.

terized by two properties: excludability (they are not at everyone's disposal) and rivalry (their consumption by some people may reduce the possibility for other people to consume them). On the other hand, PGs exhibit the opposite properties: non-excludability (they are, in principle, accessible by everyone) and non-rivalry (their consumption by some people does not prevent other people from consuming them). There are also 'pure' and 'impure' PGs. The first possess the two properties aforementioned (but are scarce); the second exhibit a combination of them. The public or private nature of a good is seldom an intrinsic quality and may change depending on its scarcity, social demand, technological evolution, etc. For example, there were times when the maintenance of fire was a vital PG for human groups.

PGs may be local, national, regional or global. A 'Global Public Good' (GPG) is a good that, by nature, concerns every human being and all peoples of the world, or the guarantee of which exceeds, by its characteristics, the capacity of each State, crossing national frontiers. This notion gained international visibility in 1999 as an effect of a publication[15] whose main author (Inge Kaul), economist and sociologist, was Director of the UNDP Office of Development Studies. In the same year, the UNDP *Human Development Report* (1999) referred to GPGs in these terms: "At the national level, public goods have been recognized as vital when the market has neither the incentive nor the mechanisms to meet a public need. With growing globalization, international public goods are now needed for similar reasons". Quoting the aforementioned publication, it observed:

> In business and civil society the number of transnational actors has been growing. And these actors are placing more pressure on governments to harmonize policy—such as standardizing market rules for banking supervision or recognizing universal human rights. These trends turn many national public goods and bads into global public goods and bads—and place global concerns, notably those about the natural global commons, on national policy agendas. So, the number of global public goods—non-rival and non-excludable—is growing. Non-rivalry means that one person's consumption of a good does not detract from another's enjoyment of it. Non-excludability means that it is difficult and costly, if not impossible, to prevent a person from enjoying a public good once it exists. Peace is one such non-rival, non-excludable public good (p. 111).

If the notion of GPG is recent, the reality it denotes is not. GPGs include international agreements for regulation of telecommunications and civil aviation, for example, as well as the common natural elements, such as oceans, and the cultural creations declared the World Heritage of Mankind. GPGs caused by global evils are, for instance, the protection of the ozone layer, international financial stability and the fight against terrorism. What were once national PGs are becoming increasingly GPGs, requiring international protection.

Henkin (1978) said that "the promotion and protection of individual rights are a public good" (p. 2). Being the Common Ethics of Humanity, human rights should be considered the highest goods. As a consequence, GPGs may be divided into two main categories:

[15] Kaul, I., Grunberg, I., and Stern, M. (Ed.). (1999). *Global Public Goods: International Cooperation in the twenty-first Century*. New York: Oxford University Press.

- *GPGs with ethical substance*
  These are the goods inherent in the quality of being human, mostly the human genome and human rights, whose respect, protection and realization rest mainly with the responsibility of States, individually and collectively.
  - The Universal Declaration on the Human Genome and Human Rights (UN, 1997)[16] stated: "The human genome underlies the fundamental unity of all members of the human family, as well as the recognition of their inherent dignity and diversity. In a symbolic sense, it is the heritage of humanity" (Article 1).
  - The UDHR (UN, 1948)[17] was proclaimed, as we know, "the highest aspiration of the common people [...] a common understanding [...] a common standard of achievement for all peoples and all nations" (Preamble).
  - The Vienna Declaration and Programme of Action (World Conference on Human Rights, 1993)[18] stated: "Human rights and fundamental freedoms are the birthright [*inhérents* in French, *patrimonio inato* in Spanish] of all human beings; their protection and promotion is the first responsibility of Governments" (I-1).
  - The Millennium Declaration (UN, 2000)[19] reaffirmed the "commitment to the purposes and principles of the Charter of the United Nations, which have proved timeless and universal" (para. 3). They include "respect for human rights and fundamental freedoms, respect for the equal rights of all without distinction as to race, sex, language or religion" (para. 4).

- *GPGs instrumental in nature*
  These are manifold goods necessary to the protection and realization of the ethical ones. They are:
  - Institutional, such as the UN System and other the IGOs.
  - Normative, related to the agreements regulating the international communication and cooperation, such as those aiming at technical standardization.
  - Scientific, related to the knowledge accumulated by sciences, which spreads especially by means of school systems.
  - Technological, related to the countless applications of the scientific knowledge, such as telephone, radio, TV, Internet, other new technologies of information and communication, etc.
  - Preventive, related to prevention and struggle against global public bads, such as prevention of conflicts and epidemics, the struggle against poverty and transmissible diseases, as well as collective security.

---

[16] www.unesco.org/new/en/social-and-human-sciences/themes/bioethics/human-genome-and-human-rights/.

[17] www.un.org/en/documents/udhr/.

[18] www.unhchr.ch/huridocda/huridoca.nsf/(symbol)/a.conf.157.23.en.

[19] www.un.org/millennium/declaration/ares552e.htm.

- Environmental, related to the rationality of the exploitation of the natural resources and the preservation of ecological balances, such as the economy of water and protection of biodiversity.
- Aesthetic, related to the natural beauties and the material and immaterial creations of the genius of peoples, the protection of which is addressed by normative instruments adopted within the UNESCO framework, such as: Convention Concerning the Protection of the World Cultural and Natural Heritage (1972), Recommendation on the Safeguarding of Traditional Culture and Folklore (1989), Convention on the Protection of the Underwater Cultural Heritage (2001), Universal Declaration on Cultural Diversity (2001), Convention for the Safeguarding of Intangible Cultural Heritage (2003), Convention on the Protection and Promotion of the Diversity of Cultural Expressions (2005).

The UN General Assembly stated in a Resolution on the UDHR Sixtieth Anniversary, adopted on 10 December 2008 (A/RES/63/116)[20]: "In an ever-changing world, the Universal Declaration of Human Rights remains a relevant ethical compass that guides us in addressing the challenges we face today".

The specificity of ethical rationality was addressed earlier. The philosophical problem of conceptualizing 'human right' was also pointed out above. The question of the foundation/justification of human rights remains open, too.

4.3 The Foundational Question

UDHR Preamble and Article 1 borrow from the Enlightenment language. *Born*, *inherent*, *imprescriptible*, *inalienable*—are eighteenth century terms. First chapter of Rousseau's *Social Contract* begins with the sentence: "Man is born free, yet everywhere he is in chains". First Article of the 1789 French Declaration begins by stating: "Men are born free and remain free and equal in rights". UDHR Article 1 begins by proclaiming: "All human beings are born free and equal in dignity and rights". This was not at all understood as denying, as Johannes Morsink (1999) notes, "that gross inequalities existed everywhere". *Born* "was left standing by itself as an intentional reminder of the eighteenth-century approach to human rights as rights inherent in human nature, however that being or nature is construed" (p. 293). In his opinion:

> ... this inherence view is the most natural way to read the opening phrases of the declaration. [...] People have moral rights which constrain the behavior of others and those rights are inherent in them in that they are not the result of extraneous acts of governments, legislatures, courts, or even social conventions. The drafters believed that people start life already possessing certain moral rights, the right to life being just one of them. (p. 294, 295)

[20] http://daccess-dds-ny.un.org/doc/UNDOC/GEN/N08/477/75/PDF/N0847775.pdf?OpenElement.

During the CHR first session (Lake Success), in January-February 1947 (E/CN.4/SR.7), Peng-chun Chang said that: "At present time, it was necessary to affirm and enlarge the differences existing between man and animal. A standard should be established with a view to elevating the concept of man's dignity and emphasizing the respect of man". At the 98th meeting of the UN General Assembly Third Committee, on 9 October 1948 (A/C.3/SR.98), he said: "The eighteenth century thinkers, whose work had led to the proclamation of the principles of liberty, equality and fraternity in France and, in the United States, to the Declaration of Independence, had realized that although man was largely animal, there was a part of him which distinguished him from animals". Charles Malik, at the second meeting of the Drafting Committee (Lake Success), on 11 June 1947 (E/CN.4/AC.1/SR.2):

> … stated that in his opinion the Secretariat document did not contain a sufficient reference to the dignity of man. This, he felt, ought to be made the basic woof of the Preamble. He stated that the four points enumerated in the suggestions for Preamble made by the Secretariat were excellent ones but that even when all were considered together they somehow failed to bring out what is distinctive, fundamental and human about man.

At the 95th meeting of the Third Committee, on 6 October 1948 (A/C.3/SR.95), the Cuban representative (Guy Pérez-Cisneros) said that: "Article 1 was almost like a *credo* of the whole of the Declaration and he felt it should be used as a foreword to the final document". At the 96th meeting, on 7 October (A/C.3/SR.96), René Cassin affirmed that: "The Declaration had to begin with a statement of the framework within which all the rights that followed were contained; article 1 represented that framework". As a consequence, the Uruguayan representative (Jiménez de Aréchaga) "suggested that Article 1 should be modified and that it should stand neither as article 1 nor as a part of the preamble but should be given a special position before Article 1; it would thus serve as a basis for interpretation of the subsequent provisions". The Greek representative (Rozakis) also "drew attention to the solemnity of the statement in the first sentence of draft Article 1 which seemed to summarize the whole contents of the draft Declaration. In order not to weaken the effect of that statement, he proposed that it should be separated from the second sentence and that the latter should be included as an additional paragraph under draft article which referred to duties".

With regard to the differences existing between man and animal underlying human dignity, Article 1 of the draft of the temporary Working Group set up by the Drafting Committee (E/CN.4/AC.1/W.1) read: "All men are brothers. Being endowed with reason, members of one family, they are free and possess equal dignity and rights". At the 8th meeting of the Drafting Committee first session, on 17 June 1947 (E/CN.4/AC.1/SR.8), Chang said, referring to the draft Article 1, "that there should be added to the idea of 'reason', the idea which in a literal translation from the Chinese would be 'two-man-mindedness'. The English equivalent might be 'sympathy' or 'consciousness of his fellow men'. This new idea, he felt, might well be included as an essential human attribute". At the 13th meeting, the British representative (Geoffrey Wilson) proposed the expression "endowed with reason and conscience", and Malik "supported the proposal of the representative of the United Kingdom defining man as a being 'endowed with reason and conscience'"

(E/CN.4/AC.1/SR.13). Article 1 of the draft of the Drafting Committee submitted to the CHR, as included in its Report (E/CN.4/21), read: "All men are brothers. Being endowed with reason and conscience, they are members of one family. They are free, and possess equal dignity and rights". The expression "endowed with reason and conscience" echoes the classical and Kantian characterizations of the human being.

During the debates on the draft Declaration in the Third Committee, in October-December 1948 (A/C.3/254), Article 1 gave rise to long discussions and twelve amendments proposals; nine of them included the expression "endowed with reason and conscience". At the 99th meeting, on 11 October (A/C.3/SR.99), the Syrian representative (Abdul Rahman Kayaly) said that "the words 'endowed with reason and conscience' should be retained as they served to differentiate man from the animals". Following the Lebanese representative (Karim Azkoul): "If, however, reason and conscience were the distinguishing characteristics of man as distinct from animals, then nothing could change man's essential right to freedom and equality". Glendon (2001) comments: "A word emblematic of an entire worldview and way of life, *ren* has no precise counterpart in English. [...] Chang's suggestion was accepted, but his idea was rendered awkwardly by adding the words 'and conscience' after 'reason'" (p. 67).

Following Morsink (1999): "The majority of the drafters had come to see the phrase 'endowed with reason and conscience' as problematic because they did not see the need to pinpoint the locus of human rights other than to affirm, as does the first sentence of Article 1, that people are born with them". However, "many of them kept the phrase in to please Malik, who in addition to being a member of the inner core of drafters also happened to be the chair of the Third Committee proceedings" (p. 299). In his opinion, the terms 'reason' and 'conscience' should not be understood "in a narrow essentialist way", but in "an epistemological one" (p. 296). They were not viewed by most of the drafters "as (ontological) foundation stones for the possession of human rights. Instead, they saw these two human capacities as (epistemic) vehicles by which we can come to know that people have human rights". As a consequence, we should act towards one another "in a spirit of brotherhood" (p. 283).

More heated were the discussions concerning the source of the uniquely human attributes. The American Declaration of Independence refers to the "Creator", and the 1789 French Declaration to "the Supreme Being". Artice 1 of the draft Declaration approved at the CHR second session (Geneva), in December 1947, as included in its Report (E/600), read: "All men are born free and equal in dignity and rights. They are endowed by nature with reason and conscience, and should act towards one another like brothers". This wording resulted from a joint proposal of the Philippine and French representatives in the Working Group on the Declaration, set up by the Commission. The words "by nature" were retained in Article 1 of the draft approved at the CHR third session (Lake Success), in May-June 1948, as included in its Report (E/800): "All human beings are born free and equal in dignity and rights. They are endowed by nature with reason and conscience, and should act towards one another in a spirit of brotherhood". At the ECOSOC 215th meeting, on 25 August (E/SR.215), the Netherlandish representative (Van der Mandele) affirmed that his Government "deeply appreciated the proposal submitted by the Lebanese Delegation, that [...] the Declaration should recognize the Creator as the source of certain inalienable rights, and regretted that that proposal had not been accepted by the Commission".

At the Third Committee's 92th meeting, on 2 October (A/C.3/SR.92), the Brazilian representative (Belarmino Austregésilo de Athayde) affirmed that the Declaration "should include, in the preamble, a reference to God as the absolute origin of the rights of man and of all rights", so reflecting "the religious faith of the greater part of humanity", and proposed amending the second sentence of the second part of Article 1 to read: "Created in the image and likeness of God, they are endowed with reason and conscience, and should act towards one another in a spirit of brotherhood" (A/C.3/215). At the 98th meeting, on 9 October (A/C.3/SR.98), the Argentinian representative (Enrique V. Corominas) "warmly supported the Brazilian amendment" that "would give to Article 1 an element of universality, a breath of the divine". He added: "It could properly be said that the Ten Commandments were the first declaration of human rights". The Bolivian representative (Eduardo Anze Matienzo) affirmed that: "The common factor in mankind and the most realistic basis for human understanding was the belief in a Supreme Being and that belief should therefore be mentioned in the Declaration of Human Rights". On 4 October, the Netherlandish representative had proposed inserting the following text in the first paragraph of the Preamble, after the words "human family": "based on man's divine origin and immortal destiny" (A/C.3/219).

Meanwhile, at the 96th meeting, on 7 October (A/C.3/SR.96), the Belgian representative (Count Henry Carton de Wiart), considering that "by nature" were words that "might be ambiguous and lead to long, philosophical arguments", had proposed their deletion. The Uruguayan representative (Jiménez de Aréchaga) also:

> ... said that rights were derived from the nature of man and not from the acts of States. As it stood, the article could give rise to objections on dogmatic grounds. It might be thought to imply nature as distinct from God. No reference to godhead should be made in a United Nations document, for the philosophy on which the United Nations was based should be universal. The Declaration was a legal document and therefore no transcendental source of rights should be stated.

The Cuban representative (Guy Pérez-Cisneros) agreed "that there should be no question of implying that nature, as opposed to God, was the source of man's reason and conscience".

At the 99th meeting, on 11 October (A/C.3/SR.99), after the Brazilian representative had withdrawn his country's amendment (that included a reference to God), the Chilean representative (Hernan Santa Cruz) said that the words "by nature" should also be deleted "and no mention should be made of the origin of man's reason and conscience". In his opinion, "article 1 should be confined to an enunciation of the essential attributes of man". The French representative (Salomon Grumbach) said that he:

> ... agreed with the representative of China (98th meeting) that it was useless to attempt to reach agreement with regard to man's origin, and that such controversial issues should be avoided. The Committee's essential aim was to reach agreement on fundamental principles which could be put into practice. That attitude would be endorsed by believers and non-believers alike. The great Catholic, Jacques Maritain, had stated in relation to that very

> question that the nations should try to reach agreement on a declaration of human rights, but that it was useless to try to reach agreement on the origin of those rights. It had been that agreement on practical fundamental rights which had kept the leaders of his country strong and united during the terrible years of the occupation.

After being discussed for six days, the draft UDHR Article 1 was adopted at the Third Committee 100th meeting (A/C.3/SR.100), on 12 October, without the words "by nature", by 26 votes to none, with 8 abstentions. It stated (A/777): "All human beings are born free and equal in dignity and rights. They are endowed with reason and conscience and should act towards one another in a spirit of brotherhood". A compromise was so reached without having recourse to voting on a so sensible matter. As Cassin later wrote, this "allowed the Committee to take no positions on the nature of man and of society and to avoid metaphysical controversies, notably the conflicting doctrines of spiritualists, rationalists, and materialists regarding the origin of the rights of man" (as cit. in Morsink 1999, p. 287).

However, at the 180th plenary meeting of the UN General Assembly (A/PV.180), on 9 December, the Netherlandish representative (J. H. van Roijen) still "regretted that man's divine origin and immortal destiny had not been mentioned in the Declaration, for the fount of those rights was the Supreme Being, who laid a great responsibility on those who claimed them. [...] The solemn Declaration it was proposed to adopt might have had, as its foundation, the recognition of the lofty origin of those rights". At the 181th plenary meeting, on 10 December (A/PV.181), the Belgian representative (Count Henry Carton de Wiart) affirmed too: "It would no doubt have been desirable to acknowledge the real basis of the equality of rights, namely, the common origin and destiny of all men".

The theoretical question of the foundation/justification of human rights became less pronounced as the IHRL expanded. Nevertheless, it remains alive. In Michael Freeman's (2004) opinion: "The most fundamental problem of contemporary human rights theory is that, while the concept of human rights seems necessary to oppose abuses of power, there is no consensus on its religious and philosophical foundations" (p. 392).

According to Norberto Bobbio (1990): "There are three ways to found values: to deduce them from an objective constant given as, for instance, human nature; to consider them as truths evident in themselves; and eventually discovering that, in a determined historical period, they are, in general, accepted (just the proof of consensus)" (p. 26). I submit that there are three main accounts of human rights' foundation/justification: Naturalism, Self-evidence, Consensus, as addressed below.

The naturalistic hypothesis is the most traditional foundation/justification for human rights. Its most authoritative contemporary restatement is the aforementioned document of the International Theological Commission (2008)[21]. After referring to the "[c]ontemporary attempts to define a universal ethic" (para. 5), and "the ethical foundation of human rights" in particular (para. 6), it affirms:

> 9. Aware of the current positions on the table in this question, in this document we intend to invite all who ask themselves about the ultimate foundations of ethics and of the juridical and political order, to consider the resources that a renewed presentation of the teaching

[21] www.pathsoflove.com/universal-ethics-natural-law.html.

> of the natural law contains. This affirms in substance that human beings and human communities are capable, by the light of reason, of knowing the fundamental guidelines for moral action in conformity with the very nature of the human subject, and of expressing them in a normative manner, in the form of precepts or commandments. Such fundamental precepts, objective and universal, are needed to found and to inspire the ensemble of the moral, juridical, and political determinations that regulate the life of man and of society. They constitute a permanent, decisive authority and assure the dignity of the human person in the face of fluctuations of ideology.

Afterwards, it observes: "The idea of the natural moral law takes up numerous elements common to humanity's great wisdom traditions, both religious and philosophical" (para. 11). According to Catholic teaching, whose main doctrinal source remains Aquinas' *Summa Theologiae*:

> 39. Every human being who attains to consciousness and responsibility experiences an interior call to do good. He discovers that he is fundamentally a moral being, capable of perceiving and of expressing the call that, as was saw, is found within all cultures: 'to do good and avoid evil'. On this precept are based all the other precepts of the natural law. This first precept is known naturally, immediately, with the practical reason, just as the principle of non-contradiction (the intellect cannot simultaneously and in the same respect affirm and deny the same thing of one subject), which is at the base of all speculative reasoning, is gathered intuitively, naturally, with the theoretical reason, when the subject comprehends the sense of the terms employed.

Consequently: "The concept of natural law presupposes the idea that nature is for man the bearer of an ethical message and establishes an implicit moral norm which human reason actualizes" (para. 69). Nevertheless, from the point of view of the Catholic Church, the justification of natural law should take into account "the metaphysical dimension of reality" that "allows one to comprehend that the universe does not have in itself its own ultimate reason for being, and manifests the fundamental structure of reality: the distinction between God, subsistent being itself, and other beings placed by him in existence" (para. 62).

Summing up:

> 113. ... We call natural law the foundation of a universal ethics which we seek to derive from the observation of and reflection on our common human nature. It is the moral law inscribed in the heart of men and of which humanity should always become more aware as it advances in history. This natural law is not at all static in its expression; it does not consist in a list of definitive and immutable precepts. It is a source of inspiration that always springs up in the search for an objective foundation for a universal ethics.
> 114. ... The concept of natural law is therefore above all philosophical, and as such, allows a dialogue that, with respect for the religious convictions of each, appeals to what is universally human in every human being. An exchange on the level of reason is possible when it is a matter of experience and of saying what is common to all men endowed with reason and of establishing the requirements of life in society.
> 115. The detection of the natural law answers to the search of a humanity that always endeavours to give itself rules for moral life and life in society. [...]

So understood, Natural Law "answers to the requirement of grounding human rights in reason" (para. 35).

The idea of Natural Law then presupposes a 'human nature' where the seeds or principles of morality are inscribed. This would be "the best of their universal validity if truly the human nature existed and—as Bobbio (1990) wrote—admitting its existence as a constant and immutable given, we could know it in its essence". However, "the history of [Natural Law] shows that human nature has been interpreted in the most different ways and the appeal to nature served to justify systems of even diverging values. What is the fundamental human right according to human being's nature? The right of the strongest, as Spinoza alleged, or the right to freedom, as Kant argued?" (p. 26). In this connection, Holmes Rolston III (2008) quoted Ortega y Gasset: "Man, in a word, has no nature; what he has is...history", and commented: "José Ortega y Gasset pinpoints, with emphasis, the human idiographic uniqueness" (p. 139).

As Kant (1803) said, "good ends" are "those which are necessarily approved by everyone, and which may at the same time be the aim of every one" (p. 20). In Bobbio's (1990) opinion:

> With the argument of consensus, the proof of intersubjectivity replaces the proof of objectivity, considered as impossible or extremely uncertain. Of course, it is about a historical foundation and, as such, not absolute: but that historical foundation of consensus is the sole capable of being factually demonstrated. The Universal Declaration of Human Rights may be welcomed as the greatest historical proof given, so far, of the *consensus omnium Gentium* [overall consensus] on a determined system of values (p. 27).[22]

Naturalism and Consensus are the basis of the "four schools of thought on human rights" identified by Marie-Bénédicte Dembour (2010b) as "ideal-types" (p. 2–4):

- "natural scholars" conceive of human rights as *given*,
- "deliberative scholars" conceive of human rights as *agreed upon*.

She explains:

> The natural school embraces the most common and well-known definition of human rights: a definition that identifies human rights as those rights one possesses simply by being a human being. This definition, where human rights are viewed as given, can be considered the credo of the natural school. [...] The natural school has traditionally represented the heart of the human rights orthodoxy.
> The orthodoxy is increasingly moving, however, towards the deliberative school of thought, which conceives of human rights as political values that liberal societies *choose* to adopt. Deliberative scholars tend to reject the natural element on which the traditional orthodoxy bases human rights. For them, human rights come into existence through societal agreement. [...].

The two other schools are the "protest school" that conceives of human rights as a conquest (*fought for*), and "discourse school" that conceives of human rights as a language (*talked about*).

---

[22] In this respect, Trindade (2006) also pointed to:

> ... the new approach shifting the focus, on the process of formation of International Law, from individual consent to *consensus*. [...] This tendency was fostered by the formation of consensus in the Conferences of codification and progressive development of International Law. In this way, the old positivist posture of search for the consent of each State individually was challenged and overcome [... now being attributed] considerable importance to *opinion juris*, to the formation of which not only States but also international organizations contribute, [...as well as] entities of the organized civil society and of groups of individuals at international level. (p. 169, 171, 172)

> The protest school is concerned first and foremost with redressing injustice. For protest scholars, human rights articulate rightful claims made by or on behalf of the poor, the unprivileged, and the oppressed. Protest scholars look at human rights as claims and aspirations that allow the status quo to be contested in favor of the oppressed [...].
> The discourse school is characterized by its lack of reverence towards human rights. In its perspective, human rights exist only because people talk about them [...], but they do recognize that the language surrounding human rights has become a powerful language with which to express political claims [...] the prominent political ethical discourse of our time [...].

In another text (2010a), Dembour restated that the deliberative school "conceives of human rights as being agreed upon, the result of a consensus most evident in the development of international human rights law, rather than constituted as a universal given which exists outside social recognition" (p. 72). In effect, as Donnelly (2007) underlined, consensus, "rather than render human rights groundless, gives them multiple grounds" (p. 293). Elsewhere (2009) he noted: "As Jacques Maritain famously put it 'We agree about the rights but on condition no one asks us why' (UNESCO 1948, p. 10)—not because there is no good answer but because there are many different good answers (and each tradition remains committed to its own)" (p. 7).

Nevertheless, according to some authors, the foundation of human dignity and rights is a useless controversy: instead, they are axiomatic. The USA Declaration of Independence (1776) begins with the famous words: "We hold these truths to be self-evident... ". The 1789 French Declaration refers (in the Preamble) to the "*droits [...] sacrés de l'homme*". The UN Charter reaffirms (in the Preamble)—and the UDHR recalls (in the Preamble too)—"faith in fundamental human rights, in the dignity and worth of the human person, in the equal rights of men and women and of nations large and small"[23]. This is a foundational stance that, in Birnbacher's opinion, understands human dignity "as a kind of ultimate article of faith rather than as a principle open to rational debate", thus typically functioning as a 'conversation stopper' (as cit. in Hennette-Vauchez 2008, p. 1). Donnelly (2009) quoted other similar opinions: human dignity is a "foundational, declaratory, and undefined" principle (Beyleveld and Brownsword 1998, p. 663); "a bedrock concept that resists definition in terms of something else" (Weisstub 2002, p. 2); "a sort of axiom in the system or as a familiar and accepted principle of shared morality" (Harris and Sulston 2004, p. 797) (p. 81, 82). Canto-Sperber and Ogien (2004) observed that, in moral epistemology, "appeal to an 'intrinsic' value is supposed to serve as end point in the justification process", as it does not need to be further justified (p. 39).

Amitai Etzioni (2010), referring to the USA Declaration of Independence, argued that human rights possess "the axiomatic nature of self-evident precepts", which "indicates that they are inherently morally compelling rather than based on some empirical or logical exterior judgments" (p. 190).

> Attempts to base human rights on rationality, the social contract, or some kind of Kantian imperative are all approaches that invite often repeated criticisms, which need not be repeated here. An especially weak justification of the universality of human rights relies on

[23] The phrase 'faith in fundamental human rights' was included in the UN Charter following a South African proposal.

> the fact that a global normative consensus supports them. Actually, universal consensus on normative issues is extremely thin. [...] Although consensus is politically beneficial, it is morally dubious; many people can and do agree on positions that are not morally justified. [...] Human rights stand tall on their own. [...]. In sum, attempts to undergird human rights with constructions that need more support than the rights themselves are not beneficial. [...].
> Human rights are best recognized as one of the rare moral precepts whose normativity is self-evident. Human rights speak to us directly in a compelling manner, unmitigated by other causes. (p. 189, 190)

He further wrote:

> All systems of thought, whether mathematical, scientific, religious, or moral, require at least one starting point—a primary or axiomatic concept or assumption that we must take for granted. Many philosophers who are critical of the notion of self-evident moral claims may well agree that every moral argument ultimately draws on one or more a priori premises, that there are inevitably premises for which one cannot ask for further foundations—what Alvin Plantinga calls 'properly basic beliefs'.
> ... Other systems of thought employ nature or reason as their primary concept, fulfilling a role analogous to that played by God's commandments in religious systems. Every sustainable moral construction builds on a self-evident foundation. Human rights are the primary normative concept for the construction of international law and norms. (p. 193)[24]

In this regard, Hunt (2008) observes:

> Human rights are difficult to pin down because their definition, indeed their very existence, depends on emotions as much as on reason. The claim of self-evidence relies ultimately on an emotional appeal; it is convincing if it strikes a chord within each person. Moreover, we are most certain that a human right is at issue when we feel horrified by its violation. [...] This interior feeling is common both to the philosopher and to the man who has not reflected at all (p. 26)

She went on: "Despite their differences in language, the two eighteenth-century declarations both rested on a claim of self-evidence". However: "This claim of self-evidence, crucial to human rights even now, gives rise to a paradox: if equality of rights is so self-evident, then why this assertion did have to be made and why was it only made in specific times and places?". If the fact remains that the claim of self-evidence has been "crucial to the history of human rights" (p. 19), evidence changes historically. In his message to Congress on the State of the Union, on 11 January 1944 ('Second Bill of Rights')[25], Franklin Roosevelt said that the economic, social and cultural rights "have become accepted as self-evident". Bobbio (1990) remarked: "At present, who does not find it evident that one should not torture prisioners? Nevertheless, for millennia, torture was accepted and supported as a normal judiciary procedure" (p. 27). Alas, what show us this fact more than the concentration camps and the photographs of their museums, as well as pictures of the Abu Ghraib prison[26]?

[24] Fabre-Magnan (2008) also to note: "In the same way that both in hard sciences and in mathematics no logical-deductive reasoning is possible without a primordial not demonstrated and not discussed sentence, so the Law rests in indemonstrable truths that should be admitted by everyone" (p. 287).

[25] www.ushistory.org/documents/economic_bill_of_rights.htm.

[26] Such as those available at: www.antiwar.com/news/?articleid=8560.

In sum, there are no "ontologically 'real' or epistemologically 'true' rights"; they are construed, stresses Campbell (2006, p. 41). John Stuart Mill said that even truth is justified belief and belief is justified only if it has been subjected to free criticism. As Judge Oliver Wendell Holmes said in *Abrams v. United States* (USA Supreme Court 1919): "The best test of truth is the power of the idea to get itself accepted in the competition of the market", the marketplace in ideas (as cit. ib., p. 143). That is why freedom of speech is a "particularly sacrosanct human right" (p. 142), both ethically, as expression of the individual rationality and autonomy, and politically, as a cornerstone of the deliberative model of democracy.

> The object of deliberation, on this model, is to produce a reasoned consensus as to what is in the general interest, a consensus that is based on the best available evidence and the most thorough consideration of alternatives. [...] This approach is a development of the epistemology of achieving truth (or justified belief) through debate. (p. 146)

It meets the Kantian principle of universalisibility as the principle of ethical rationality.

In this connection, another concept should be called into play: Public Reason, a term that is not a recent invention. It is already found, for example, in Hobbes's *Leviathan*, in Rousseau's *Discourse on Political Economy*, in Jefferson's *Second Inaugural Address*, and in Kant's *What is Enlightenment?* In John Rawls' opinion, Public Reason includes public political values, the noncontroversial results of science and the higher Court's decisions[27]. It is a contested and evolving concept, however.

The ethical rationality of the consensus rising from debates underlies the UDHR's validity. Maritain (1951) reported the following:

> During one of the meetings of the French National Commission of UNESCO at which the Rights of Man were being discussed, someone was astonished that certain proponents of violently opposed ideologies had agreed on the draft of a list of rights. Yes, they replied, we agree on these rights, *providing we are not asked why*. With the 'Why', the dispute begins. (p. 77).

In effect, human rights "may be justified on highly divergent doctrinal grounds", as concluded the above quoted UNESCO Committee on the Theoretical Bases of Human Rights in its Report *The Grounds of an International Declaration of Human Rights* (1948). In this regard, Charles Taylor (2001), who mentions Maritain too, wrote:

> What would it mean to come to a genuine, unforced international consensus on human rights? I suppose it would be something like what John Rawls describes in his *Political Liberalism* as an "overlapping consensus". That is, different groups, countries, religious

[27] Following Sen:

> In this sense, the viability of human rights is linked with what John Rawls has called 'public reasoning'... This view of human rights in terms of social ethics and public reasoning contrasts with seeing human rights in primarily legal terms, either as consequences of humane legislation, or as precursors of legal rights. Human rights may well be reflected in legislation, and may also inspire legislation, but this is a further fact, rather than a defining characteristic of human rights themselves. (as cit. in Ramcharan 2008, p. 25).

> communities, civilizations, while holding incompatible fundamental views on theology, metaphysics, human nature, and so on, would come to an agreement on certain norms that ought to govern human behavior. Each would have its own way of justifying this from out of its profound background conception. We would agree on the norms, while disagreeing on why they were the norms. And we would be content to live in this consensus, undisturbed by the differences of profound underlying belief (p. 409, 410).

The role played by consensus in International Law is pointed out by Katharine Young (2008):

> The importance of consensus in international law is evidenced in the voluntarist structure of both treaties and customary international law. For general treaty regimes, consent precedes ratification and the acceptance of obligation. It also justifies the practice of allowing (certain) treaty reservations and a 'margin of appreciation' to constrain the application of international law in domestic legal systems. For customary international law, consensus is also a foundational feature. The positive sources of customary international law—*opinio juris* and state practice—are important precisely because they are proxies for consent, even if expressed tacitly. In permitting exceptions, custom again gives priority to consent, precluding customary law's application to persistently objecting states.
>
> Nonetheless, the centrality of consensus shifts with respect to human rights. For both treaty-based and customary human rights norms, the norm of consensus is secondary to the higher moral goals suggested by these conventions. For the obligations which flow from these moral goals, consent may be both constitutive and destructive. For example, while states' ratifications are required in order to establish obligations, the principal human rights treaties are purportedly universal in scope and there are limits to the reservations that countries can make in becoming parties. (p. 145)

Consensus is a term often used with respect to human rights too. IHRL may be said to be the ripening fruit of the "overwhelming trend toward consensus which is an expression of the juridical conscience of the world community" (T. O. Elias, as cit. in Trindade 2006, p. 196). I submit that human rights originated from a double Historical Consensus:

- Consensus of religious traditions and philosophical wisdom, condensed in the Golden Rule that is a principle of reciprocity and compassion, which epitomizes a moral heritage so culturally deeply shared that it seems to be natural, i. e. innate[28].
- Consensus laid down in the legal human rights instruments adopted by the International Community, with increasing influence of public opinion, giving rise to an expanding protection network[29].

---

[28] According to Olivier du Roy (2012), the Golden Rule "corresponds to a kind of moral maturity of the humankind", being "as a universal cultural datum, the foundation of a very 'natural law'" (p. 12).

[29] Ramcharan (2008) summarizes:

> The process of recognizing, declaring, or proclaiming rights at the national and international levels is essentially a normative one. To determine the existence of a right, one must enquire into whether it has been authoritatively recognized by a competent organ. In international law, human rights may be grounded in an international convention, an international declaration, international customary law, and the general principles of law recognized by nations. In addition, it can be determined by reference to judicial decisions and the academic work of experts. International law recognizes ordinary legal rights and human rights.

The Historical Consensus on human rights is a cultural, emotional, intersubjective, argumentative, political and international one. It is a virtuous consensus because it has universal ethical basis, namely: It is a consensus "as to the supreme value of the human person", as stated Hernan Santa Cruz, representative of Chile, during the UDHR drafting (as cit. in Glendon 2001, p. 169). If Natural Law continues to be resurrected in various incarnations, it is because it crystallizes and epitomizes in every instance the Historical Consensus on human rights' universal claims. Principles and precepts recognized by the universal moral conscience eventually merge with 'human nature' and qualify as 'Natural Law', though their conquest may have implied great suffering.

The foundational plurality of human rights is reflected in the UDHR that mentions, in its Preamble, "barbarous acts", "rebellion against tyranny and oppression", "faith", "common understanding", "common standard of achievement", "recognition", "rule of law". The unity of the foundational plurality of human rights may be illustrated with the metaphor of a four-faced head: Human rights have *natural*, *legal*, *national* and *international* faces. They may be said to be natural insofar as they are believed to be inherent in every human being; they are legal because they are vested with the form and force of written Law; they are national because, besides several of them having originated from many countries' Constitutions, their implementation and protection depend principally upon States; they are international because they have been recognized and developed by the International Community that is also co-responsible for their protection and promotion. Bobbio (1990) expressed this plurality as follows:

> We are tempted to describe the development process culminating in the Universal Declaration also in a different way, using the traditional categories of Natural and Positive Law: human rights are born as universal natural rights, develop as particular positive laws, and eventually reach their full realization as universal positive laws (p. 30).

Morsink (1999) asked: "What lies at the heart of the moral consensus about human rights that was born in the 1940s and has expanded ever since?" Here is the answer: "During the final General Assembly debate in December 1948 the drafters made it abundantly clear that the Declaration on which they were about to vote had been born out of the experience of the war that had just ended" (p. 36). Of the Holocaust, in particular, that was "nothing but applied biology", as said Rudolf Hess at a mass meeting in 1934, referring to National Socialism. It draws "the ultimate consequence of recognizing the importante of blood", wrote Hitler in *Mein Kampf* (as cit. ib., p. 38, 39)[30]. That is why, as the Ecuadoran representative (Jorge Carrera

---

Human rights possess one or more of certain qualitative characteristics: appurtenance to the human person or group; universality; essentiality to human life, security, survival, dignity, liberty, equality; essentiality for international order; essentiality in the conscience of humankind; and essentiality to protect vulnerable groups (p. 26).

[30] The Nuclear Commission had asked the ECOSOC, on 21 May 1946, "to instruct the Secretariat in its collection of data for the work of the Commission, to include information on the Nuremberg and Tokyo trials which might be important in the field of human rights" (E/38/Rev.1). The Report 'Information concerning human rights arising from trials of war criminals', prepared by the United Nations War Crimes Commission, was ready on 15 May 1948 (E/CN.4/W.19).

Andrade) pointed out, at the General Assembly 183th plenary meeting, on 10 December 1948 (A/PV.183), the after Second World War was about "the restoration" both "of material ruins" and "of human dignity".

The Historical Consensus founding human rights is about their recognition—a topical and multi-purpose concept.

4.4 Stakes of Recognition

Axel Honneth (2004) noted that, while the idea of recognition was always a part of Moral Philosophy, it has never been "the cornerstone of an ethics" (except for Hegel) (p. 1640). During the meeting of experts on 'Ethics for the 20th Century' organized by UNESCO in 2001, mentioned in Introduction, Honneth proposed an "Ethics of Recognition" as a substantive ethics (instead of a mere procedural one), because "every moral norm is linked to the recognition of the human being"[31]. By now an *Ethics of Recognition* (*Éthique de la Reconnaissance, Anerkennungsethik, Ética del Reconocimiento, Ética do Reconhecimento…*) has become a heuristic and inspiring idea.

It might be argued that human rights mean an Ethics of Recognition of common human dignity and inherent rights, including the real and legitimate individual, cultural and other differences. Let us begin by presenting the main stakes of human recognition.

Paul Ricoeur's (2004) last book traces the philosophical history of the idea of recognition. In his opinion, "the main conceptual revolution [occurred] at the level of the philosopheme, with the Hegelian theme of the struggle for recognition [*Anerkennung*], the horizon of which is 'being recognized'" (p. 25). Hegel also inscribed "the theme of recognition into the heart of political philosophy" (p. 284).

Since the 1980s, the heuristic power of the idea of recognition has been rediscovered and attracted a great deal of interest in the social sciences. Recognition has become a normative principle of the reinterpretation of morality and justice. Principally from the beginning of the 1990s, "claims formulated in recognition language" (Ferrarese 2008, p. 95) multiplied, giving rise to a "recognition rhetoric" (Payet and Battegay 2008, p. 25). One tries "to grasp the grammars of the human as grammars of recognition" (Bertram et al. 2007, p. 7). The most influential works of such a rediscovery were published in 1992, both taking their leads from Hegel's philosophy: *Multiculturalism and 'The Politics of Recognition'* by Charles Taylor, and *Kampf um Anerkennung—Zur moralischen Grammatik sozialer Konflikte* (The Struggle for Recognition: The Moral Grammar of Social Conflicts) by Honneth. According to Taylor, the emergence of the politics of recognition in the 1960s and 1970s—centered on gender, race, ethnicity—is a reaction to the oppressive assimilationism of Enlightenment universalism. "The politics of difference grows organically out

[31] http://unesdoc.unesco.org/images/0012/001246/124626f.pdf.

of the politics of universal dignity"[32]. Honneth engaged, on the other hand, in approaching the complexity of the concept of recognition (see McBride and Seglow 2009). His social theory has a psychological and moral basis. Self-esteem depends upon the value others recognize we have, so that recognition may be an ideological tool when it is used as a management device. Our relationships are crossed by expectations of recognition at the affective, social and legal levels. In Honneth's opinion, all social conflicts "should be understood as normative conflicts, as struggles for recognition"[33].

Nancy Fraser (2001), another well-known recognition theorist, summarized:

> For some time now, the forces of progressive politics have been divided into two camps. On one side stand the proponents of 'redistribution'. Drawing on long traditions of egalitarian, labor and socialist organizing, political actors aligned with this orientation seek a more just allocation of resources and goods. On the other side stand the proponents of 'recognition'. Drawing on newer visions of a 'difference-friendly' society, they seek a world where assimilation to majority or dominant cultural norms is no longer the price of equal respect. [...] The redistribution orientation has a distinguished philosophical pedigree, as egalitarian redistributive claims have supplied the paradigm case for most theorizing about social justice for the past 150 years. The recognition orientation has recently attracted the interest of political philosophers, however, some of whom are seeking to develop a new normative paradigm that puts recognition at its center (p. 21).

Fraser proposes to overcome the "false antitheses" of redistribution *or* recognition.

> Justice today requires *both* redistribution *and* recognition; neither alone is sufficient. As soon as one embraces this thesis, however, the question of how to combine them becomes pressing. I maintain that the emancipatory aspects of the two problematic need to be integrated in a single, comprehensive framework. The task, in part, is to devise an expanded conception of justice that can accommodate both defensible claims for social equality and defensible claims for the recognition of difference (p. 22).

Recognition is a more profound, anthropological phenomenon, however.

Giorgio Agamben (2002) affirmed, quoting Linnaeus (*Systema naturae* 1735), that "man posseses no specific identity other than that of being able to recognize himself. [...] *man is the animal that has to recognize himself as human to become human.* [...] He becomes himself only when he rises above the man" (p. 44, 45). This idea is illustrated by Jean-Pierre Néraudau (1984) with the Roman concept of *patria potestas* (possibly originating from India), defined by the Roman Law of the Twelve Tables (450 BC), whose most extreme expression was the *jus vitae necisque* (the right of life and death) of a father over his children. Néraudau comments: "The symbolic birth of a child, through his/her recognition by father, was accomplished later by means of social integration rites (frequent in the primitive civilizations), usually when he/she was given a name. 'Until then, all happened as if the child was not yet born, was not yet inscribed in the human condition framework', J. Cazeneuve remarks [quoted by Néraudau]" (p. 279).

---

[32] As quoted by Emmanuel Renault in Dossier 'Luttes pour la reconnaissance', *Sciences Humaines*, *172*, Juin 2006.

[33] Interview, ib.

Hegel distinguished three levels (*Stufen)* of the recognition of the human being: Family, Civil Society and State. Family is where, through love, human beings begin to matter for each other (interpersonal recognition). Located between the natural and the ethical dimensions of human existence, Family is the level of recognition grounded in feelings of consanguinity. Civil Society is the level of recognition grounded in moral and legal commonality (recognition between individuals and institutions). This is the field of individual needs and interests. The State represents the highest and most complex level of reciprocal recognition (general recognition). Human subjective freedom would be empty without citizens' objective freedom. Ludwig Siep, in a study entitled *Anerkennung als Prinzip der praktishen Philosophie* (Recognition as Principle of the Practical Philosophy 1978), distinguished only two levels: recognition between individuals and recognition between individuals and institutions (as cit. in Williams 1997, p. 21, 80). Regarding the first level, he distinguishes two forms of recognition: love and the struggle for recognition. Honneth proposes three models of recognition in his *Kampf um Anerkennung*: love, Law and social esteem, to which correspond so many forms of contempt. This correlation was considered by Ricoeur (2004) "the most important contribution of Honneth's work to the theory of recognition in its post-Hegelian phase" (p. 296).

Tzvetan Todorov (2013) comments:

> It is not by chance if Jean-Jacques Rousseau, Adam Smith and Georg Hegel emphasized recognition among all basic processes. This one is in effect exceptional in a double title. First by its content itself: it is that which, more than any other action, marks the entrance of the individual into specifically human existence. [...]
> Recognition includes obviously countless activities, in the most various aspects. Once having introduced such an 'inclusive' notion, one must wonder which are the reasons and forms of such a diversity. [...]
> Recognition concerns every sphere of our existence, and its different forms are not interchangeable: at the very most, they manage to bring some solace, if need be. I need to be acknowledged on the professional plane as well as in my personal relations, in love and in friendship [...] (p. 56, 57).

In fact, intersubjective and social recognition is a kaleidoscopic phenomenon.

Daily life is a theater, sometimes a drama, and sometimes even a tragedy, of games and scenes of tacit demands and struggles for recognition, at a variety of fields and stages. They vary in intensity, from the most disguised and discreet to the most ostentatious and imposing, from the most immoral to the most genial. As two psychotherapists wrote: "We have a psychological thirst for very particular stimuli called recognition signs. [...] That vital need of exchange with our emotional or social environment is as much important as to drink, to eat or to sleep" (Nunge and Mortera 1998, p. 77). Todorov (2013) distinguishes "two forms of recognition to which we all aspire, but in very different proportions. One may talk respectively of *recognition of conformity* and *recognition of distinction*" (italics added) (p. 58).

Recognition is both a need and desire. Desire is often synonymous with need, but while needs are fundamentally biological, common to other animals (such as hunger, thirst, sex), desires are specifically human. We don't say that a nonhuman animal has desires in the sense explained by Socrates in Plato's *Symposium* (1997): "So such a man or anyone else who has a desire desires what is not at hand and not present, what he does not have, and what he is not, and that of which he is in need; for such are the objects of desire and love" (200e).

Good and bad desires have always been distinguished. Aristotle (2000) said that desire "is a wild beast" (III.16, 1287a), which is why an ancient moral concern is how to control bad desires. In the seventeenth century, Hobbes reversed "the classical perspective of a power to be exercised over desires, which neglects the origin of power in desire's action" (Rabouin 1997, p. 188), when he wrote in *Leviathan* (1651): "So that in the first place, I put for a general inclination of all mankind, a perpetual and restless desire of power after power, that ceases only in death"[34]. Baruch Spinoza (1632–1677), his contemporary, conceived of an anthropologically totalizing view of desire: "*Desire* is the essence of the human being", it is the moving strength (*conatus*) of being, giving origin to "all efforts of human nature we call appetite, want, desire or impulse" (cit. ib., p. 170). Therefore, desire is not a *thing* determined by external causes. We simply *are* desire.

So understood, desire expresses a lack, but is not reducible to the need or the satisfaction of possession. It is essentially an infinite desire of being infinitely free. The human being is as much irreducible to its biological substratum as the Cathedral of Cologne to a chapter of Mineralogy.

In Françoise Dolto's (1908–1988) opinion (1994), it was Psychoanalysis that discovered "the difference between needs and desires" (p. 470). Indeed, Psychoanalysis sheded a unique light on the obscurity and mystery of desire. Jacques Lacan (1901–1981) recentered the Freudian theory in desire understood in the general and structural sense of "lacking of being", "metonymy of being" (as cit. in Rabouin 1997, p. 77, 149). Quoting Lacan, Roland Barthes (1915–1980) said (1977) that "the desire is to miss what one has—and to give what one has not" (p. 249). Psychoanalysis is then, in some ways, the "*science of what the human being lacks*" (Assoun 2003, p. 118). Consequently, Gaston Bachelard (1884–1962) wrote, "the human being is a creation of desire, not a creation of need" (as cit. ib., p. 221). Desire is "the surest emblem of the human" (Chebel 2000, p. 30).

Dolto concluded too: "I believe that the human being is a being of desire rather than of need. The human being is desire. This is my faith!" (in This 2002, p. 155, 156). The basis for love, for example, might be considered the desire of communication, since communication is desire for the other's desire and is most fundamentally a desire of recognition.

Following Hegel, being human "is being-recognized" (as cit. in Williams 1997, p. 101). Accordingly: "A human being counts simply because he is human, and not because he is a Jew, Catholic, Protestant, German, Italian, etc. [...] Therefore the imperative of right is: Be a person and respect others as persons" (as cit. ib., p. 135, 137). Williams comments: "In recognition, desire becomes sublimated to the ethical level. [...] When the other comes to count for me, then the threshold of the ethical is crossed; recognition is the medium in which and through which ethical life is constituted" (p. 72, 76, 77). In Hegel's opinion: "I am genuinely free only when the other is also free, and recognized as such by me" (cit. ib., p. 83). That is why, Wil-

[34] www.gutenberg.org/files/3207/3207-h/3207-h.htm.

liams remarks, "the themes of 'freedom', 'recognition', and 'ethics' are for Hegel not separable but inextricably interwined" (p. 6).

> This is the 'syllogism of recognition'; each term is both extreme and mean. Each self must serve as mediator for the other, while receiving in turn mediation—that is, recognition—from the other. Only through such reciprocal action can the self 'return' to itself out of its 'othered' state, by gaining itself in the other's recognition. Yet this syllogism contains a paradox: Recognition is both needed and yet cannot be coerced. [...] Affirmative self-recognition in the other cannot be coerced; it must be freely proffered by the other, who in turn must be allowed to be (p. 59).

The Family is the cradle of the first and most vital human recognition. For Hegel, marriage, whose principle is love, is essentially an ethical relation, more than a mere natural union or legal contract. In it, the woman ceases to be a simple object of the male's desire and becomes a being valuable on her own. "It is not nature, but rather freedom, that constitutes the basis of marriage", he wrote (as cit. ib., p. 223). Family is thus a unity of love-recognition that, through the intersubjectivity of marriage, realizes the transition from the biological to the ethical life.

The sociological realities of marriage do not reflect Hegelian objective idealism, but Family remains, in general, the place where each one of its members counts and is recognized, for the first time and forever, as a rule, only because he or she is a member. "Family is family! Blood is blood!" (Woody Allen, *Cassandra's Dream* 2007). Sophocles *Antigone*, which Hegel considered "the highest drama of the ancient or the modern period" (as cit. in Williams 1997, p. 191), said: "So for me to meet this doom is trifling grief; but if I had suffered my mother's son to lie in death an unburied corpse, that would have grieved me; for this, I am not grieved"[35].

Notwithstanding, Family is not always such a stronghold of recognition. Is there a purely natural human without a cultural mantle? The horrendous 'honor crimes' refute the idea that Family is a secure *natural sanctuary* of human love and recognition. In any case, the familial form of recognition is limited by the binding feelings of consanguinity.

Broader is the reciprocal recognition of the believers of a religion as a community of values and hope giving sense to life and death. As divine love does not depend upon reciprocity—the Christian God loves even the sinners—religion is a refuge for the most *un-recognized* and discriminated against human beings. The proliferation of sects and the proximity of their whorship places meet such feelings of lack and discrimination. Alain Caillé (2007) remarks:

> In the end, to be recognized in religious terms is to be considered as someone elected, that is, recognized, individually and/or collectively, by the *ultimate recognizer, the recognizer of all possible recognizers* that is the supreme divine figure, the Other generalized, the greatest and absolute other [*le tout grand tout autre*]. Is not that subject supposed to know absolutely beyond all knowledge? Religion is an answer to the enigmas and aporias of recognition (p. 190).

More extensive than familial recognition, commanded by the blood's voice, and than others' recognition preached by a religion, is the recognition of every suffering

[35] classics.mit.edu/Sophocles/antigone.html.

human being dictated only by an universal feeling of compassion (a term literally meaning 'suffering with'). It is a feeling that originates in imagining how we would suffer too, in the case of being at the place of the one who is suffering. Compassion for another human being, regardless of whoever he or she is, is in some way the 'natural' foundation of morals and the source of the Golden Rule. "Stated most often as a proverbial sentence or maxim, the golden rule is, more deeply, a fundamental anthropological structure or scheme, expressing the recognition of man by man" (Roy 2012, p. 15).

In addition to these more or less collective and moral kinds of recognition, there are interindividual and rather elective ways of the search for recognition that include friendship and love.

Friendship is a reciprocal affection that originates in a close relationship and affinity of feelings, of ideas or in similar psychological needs and character. It is lived in a relation of an affective exteriority immunized to the tensions and erosions of emotional daily intimacy, generally lacking the *Wings of Desire* (*Der Himmel über Berlin*, Wim Wenders).

The most famous philosophical text on love is Plato's *Symposium*. In Plato's (1997) *Phaedrus*, Socrates concluded: "Now, as everyone plainly knows, love is some kind of desire (237d). In Dieter Henrich's opinion, the concept of love is "the basic principle" of Hegel's thought (as cit. in Williams 1997, p. 208). In Hegel's opinion:

> Love has this significance, that I feel myself needy and incomplete. I am independent, and this independence is precisely that which, when I am in love, I find to be deficient. In love I don't want to be this independent person by myself. In love I negate my independence. This is the first moment [of love].
>
> The second moment is that I maintain and preserve myself in this negation, because I gain myself in another person. In her I have the intuition, the consciousness, that I count for something, in her I have worth and validity. But it is not only I who counts, she also counts for me. [...]
>
> Love is the most tremendous contradiction that the understanding cannot dissolve. (as cit. ib., p. 212, 213)[36]

Love is a vital and universal need. The 'emotional foods' are as necessary as the foods on which we feed. Love is "one of the most powerful dopes of our organism" (Fournier 2013, p. 6). That is why it is, perhaps, the most universal and lasting subject in history of literature and arts. There is a "universal library consecrated to love", observes Lucy Vincent (2004, p. 9). "All peoples sing songs of love, they write poems of love, they tell myths and legends founded on love, they play magic to provoke love and, in extreme cases, they commit suicide by disappointed love" (p. 107).

Love is a mysterious alchemy of emotions, but there is a "biology of the amorous condition" (p. 11). In particular, "neurobiology is sufficient to accounting for several phenomena typical of the amorous condition" (p. 90). For example, ocytocine is "the hormone of preference and of bonds" (p. 66), and dopamine is "the 'doping' of love" (p. 77). This amounts to a biology of recognition. "New meetings

[36] Poet Paul Éluard (1895–1952) said too: "Love is the human being unfinished" (*Quelques-uns des mots*, Some of the words, 1977).

always capture our attention, but the level of dopamine in brain only reaches the threshold necessary to our falling in love if there is 'recognition' and the liberation of dopamine that follows" (p. 79). Otherwise, "one may perhaps become friends, but not amorous" (p. 63). It has, therefore, the function of "assuring to a subject the presence of this other from whom he or she takes his or her own psychological substance, his or her profound I, and conscience of himself or herself. Hence his or her need of the 'other' so strong as that of water or oxygen" (p. 108). So that *qui se ressemble s'assemble* (those who resemble assemble).

By the light of this chemistry of recognition, there are the love-need of someone's sex and the love-desire of someone's desire. The first is a carnal love, limited to the "field of animality" (p. 10). In this sense, "to make love" may be considered, in some way, as the zero degree of love. The second may begin as a love-passion or romantic love, by "a shock of recognition, unattended and exhilarating" (p. 61), the duration of which "is estimated from 18 to 36 months" (p. 108), and continue "through a progressive recognition of oneself in another one" (p. 158), resulting in a love-marriage or love-family that may be broken by divorce. In many least happy cases, marriage is no more than a reciprocal arrangement better than loneliness. There is still the love-butterfly or Don Juan, peculiar to those always in need of new sensations and experiences of recognition. Vincent points out:

> To be sure, when we talk about love we think mainly of the 'great' love tying two sexual partners in a passionate manner for a period, after which it transforms itself in a profound complicity. Biology offers an evolutionist explanation for the first part of story; the second part, on the other hand, evokes a pure artifact of the human culture, a kind of 'super friendship' made unique by the passionate story lived up together, and reinforced by the regular liberation of ocytocine in sexual intercourse (p. 158).

Summing up, love-desire searches for the recognition by somebody, for the exclusivity of his or her desire. It is the desire to be unique to somebody who is unique to the individual who desires. Passion is its most profound, intense, turbulent and incandescent expression. It may be such a desperate desire that it may even cause murder or suicide.

In addition to the search for the exclusivity of recognition by somebody in erotic love or passion, each individual strives to deserve recognition for what he or she is able to imagine, to think or do (such is the recognition of the artistic and intellectual creators and of heroes).

The foregoing are pre-juridical or meta-juridical kinds of human recognition. Compassion, in particular, is perhaps the most universal ethical expression of inter-human recognition, commanded by the Golden Rule. However, it is not necessarily a compelling feeling, as the Holocaust or Shoah and the recent genocides cruelly illustrate. Legal recognition is needed to protect the most fundamental human values.

4.5 Legal Recognition

Recognition is a term with substantial juridical weight. The fields of its operation include Philosophy of Law, International Law, Civil Law, as well as IHRL.

Legal Philosophy's essential question is that of the nature of Law. It fundamentally concerns the problems of the validity or legitimacy of legal normativity—of its reasons for action—and its relationship with moral normativity, in the debate between Natural Law theorists and legal positivists. Natural Law theories hold that there is a higher Law to which every human written Law must conform. Consequently, there is a conceptual connection between Law and morality. It is in that sense that it may be argued that *Lex injusta non est lex* (unjust law is not law). Legal positivism, on the contrary, aims only at establishing the formal conditions of the validity of Law as technique of social regulation whose normative force is stronger than other types of normativity.

Hans Kelsen (*Pure Theory of Law*) and H. L. A. Hart (*The Concept of Law*) are two prominent representatives of legal positivism.

According to Kelsen, Law is a system of norms structured in levels (*Stufenbau*) with the higher norms commanding the creation of lower ones. The respect for such a hierarchy is the criterion for the validity of each norm, conceptually independent of the respective content. It presupposes the distinction between what *is* and what *ought to be*. The validity of the whole normative chain forming a system of Law depends on a basic norm (*Grundnorm*) that is a fictional historical first Constitution or aid to thought (*Denkbehelf*) serving "as an *epistemological* device for conceiving of the legal materials as valid legal norms" (Spaak 2005, p. 404). Its function is to avoid regression *ad infinitum*, similar to the Aristotelian First Cause or Unmoved Mover. Such independence from facts and from other normative fields confers on Law its normative purity.

Hart proposed a similar solution, but the *Grundnorm* is replaced with a somewhat obscure *Rule of Recognition*. In a pre-juridical society, all rules are customary ones. The Rule of Recognition is a customary or social rule that identifies and ranks the sources of Law according to certain criteria. In that sense, it is a rule about rules—about the validity of other ("primary") rules—included in the so-called "secondary rules", together with the "rules of change" (concerning the power to change the Law) and the "rules of adjudication" (concerning the power to apply the Law). "On Hart's theory, the rules of recognition, change and adjudication derive their content solely from consensus" (Shapiro 2009, p. 14). The Rule of Recognition constitutes, therefore, the ultimate normative source of a legal system to the extent that it secures its existence and determines its content.

In International Law, recognition concerns the legal existence of States or Governments. Kelsen wrote (1941):

> The term 'recognition' may be said to be comprised of two quite distinct acts: a political act and a legal act.
> The political act of recognition of a state or government means that the recognizing state is willing to enter into political and other relations with the recognized state or government, relations of the kind which normally exist between members of the family of nations. [...]
> The political act of recognition, since it has no legal effect whatsoever, is not constitutive for the legal existence of the recognized state or government. Political recognition presupposes the legal existence of a state or government to be recognized. [...]
> Entirely different from the political act is the legal act of recognition. Its real meaning has, so far, not been worked out clearly in the theory of international law. This is one of the reasons for the prevailing confusion. (p. 605, 606)

In national Law, the terms 'recognition' or 'acknowledgment' proliferate mainly in Civil Law, especially concerning Family Law. In the French Civil Code, for example, 'acknowledgment' appears more than forty times. In the Portuguese Civil Code, the term and the corresponding verb appear more than a hundred times. Recognition and the corresponding verb are frequently recurring terms in IHRL, too.

From the essential human desire of recognition Hegel concluded: "The absolute right is the right to have rights" (as cit. in Williams 1997, p. 240). The *right to have rights*—a contemporaneous slogan during the American Revolution—is also at the centre of the political thought of Hannah Arendt (1906–1975) that radically rejected the *jus naturalis* (doctrine of Natural Law). *Es gibt nur ein einziges Menschenrecht* (there is a sole human right)—was the title of a text she sent to her friend Hermann Broch in 1946 (published in 1949). Such a right is *ein Recht, Rechte zu haben* (a right to have rights). This idea is, in Peg Birmingham's (2006) opinion, her "most important contribution to political thought" (p. 1), which was articulated for the first time in *The Origins of Totalitarianism* (1951).

The Greek distinction between *zoé* (life) and *bios politicos* (political life) is fundamental in Arendt's thought. She recalled that, in Rome, the word *homo* designated someone who was nothing more than a man, being applied to the slave (a being without rights). That is why the right to citizenship must be considered as the first right, i. e. the right to a legal status in a political community. The Nazis deprived their victims of legal personhood before depriving them of life. Arendt observed: "It seems that a man who is nothing but a man has lost the very qualities which make it possible for other people to treat him as a fellow-man" (as cit. ib., p. 35).

Referring to Hegel's sentence 'The absolute right is the right to have rights', Williams (1997) comments in his interpretation of Hegel's Philosophy as an *Ethics of Recognition*: "This memorable sentence prompts a question: What is this absolute right and how is it secured? My proposal is that the absolute right is the right of recognition" (p. 240).

Human rights may be said to be the highest expression of the general need, desire and right to recognition.

UDHR first preambular paragraph states that "*recognition* [italics added] of the inherent dignity and of the equal and inalienable rights of all members of the human family is the foundation of freedom, justice and peace in the world". Morsink remarked:

> The word 'recognition' in the first recital aims at something that already exists and so fits the use of the phrases 'inherent dignity' and 'inalienable rights' also used in this recital.
> [...]
> The first paragraph [of the UN Charter] starts out not with an affirmation, but with a reaffirmation of faith in fundamental human rights. Like the word 'recognition' in the first recital of the Declaration this reaffirmation suggests that these fundamental human rights already exist and now need to be more firmly implemented to avoid the scourges of future wars. If we push these recognitions and reaffirmations as far back as we can, we must, of course, come to an original affirmation and an original cognition of these same rights (p. 319).

Commenting on the UDHR first preambular paragraph, too, Glendon (2001) highlighted:

> Equally noteworthy in the first clause is the word *recognition*. Prior to World War II, legal positivism (the view that there are no rights other than those granted by the laws of the state) flourished in the United States and Europe and was dogma in the Soviet Union. But legally sanctioned atrocities committed in Nazi Germany had caused many people to revaluate the proposition that there is no higher law by which the laws of nation-states can be judged. The declaration implicitly rejected the positivist position by stating that fundamental rights are recognized, rather than conferred (p. 176).

In the ICESCR, a frequent formula is: "The States Parties to the present Covenant *recognize* [italics added]..." And one of the rights recognized in the ICCPR is as follows: "Everyone shall have the *right to recognition* [italics added] everywhere as a person before the law" (Article 16).

Moreover, Rao (2011) pointed out, "the dignity of recognition as a constitutional right is a new value for a new time", focused not on freedom or liberty or a minimum standard of living, but rather "on the unique and subjective feelings of self-worth possessed by each individual and group" (p. 189). However, it "does not affect the underlying dignity of the individual, which persists whether or not it is recognized" (p. 244). It is rather "recognition for individual and group differences" (p. 248).

> Asserted on its own as a constitutional right, dignity as recognition is essentially distinct from inherent dignity. These two types of dignity emphasize different aspects of personhood. Inherent dignity focuses on the universal attribute of individuals as human agents, able to choose and direct their own lives. Recognition dignity focuses on the individual, but finds that the dignity of a person exists not only in making choices, but also in having those choices validated and accepted by the state and other members of the community (p. 267, 268).

Olivier Reboul (1992) underlined the fact that:

> ...humanity is not secured; it is a value, not a fact, a value that does not exist except through us, a dignity that is not about to know but 'to recognize', as much in others as in us, an equality that science is not at all able to prove but that is necessary to want before any proof. [...] Recognition of the humanity in each one is a value and is nothing other than a value. [...] Humanity, in that sense, is a cult, an act of belief in the human being (p. 90, 91).[37]

All in all, Julien Freund (1972) wrote, "every consistent thought concerning human rights has to start from this fundamental fact: they have not been established scientifically, but rather dogmatically", that is, "human rights are valuable because we recognize their validity" (p. 154, 163). In Griffin's (2008) opinion, the conception of 'human right' developed by IHRL was established "with something more in the nature of a rule of recognition" (p. 203). Habermas (2012) strongly states: "Human rights emerged from violent and sometimes even revolutionary struggles for recognition (see Honneth 1995)" (p. 73). Citizens "derive their self-respect from the fact that they are recognized by all other citizens as *subjects of equal actionable rights*" (p. 71). Steven Heyman concludes:

[37] As a representative of Human Rights Watch/Asia (Daniel S. Lev), said before the 1993 Vienna Conference, speaking in Jakarta: "The idea of universal human rights shares the recognition of one common humanity, and provides a minimum solution to deal with its miseries" (as cit. in Glendon 2001, p. 233).

> Recognition is the most fundamental right that individuals have, a right that lies at the basis of all their other rights. At the same time, mutual recognition is the bond that constitutes the political community. For these reasons, individuals have a duty to recognize one another as human beings and citizens (as cit. in Rao 2011, p. 251).

Whatever the *enjeux* or stakes of recognition—anthropological, cultural, political, psychological, etc.—human rights constitute, therefore, an Ethics of Recognition: for being human, for living and flourishing humanely, as well as for treating one another according to our common Humanity. It could be said that Human Dignity Principle (HDP) is for the IHRL a kind of Kelsenian *Grundnorm* that functions as a kind of Hartian *Rule of Recognition* of the human rights required for its protection and enhancement.

As a consequence, the following definition is proposed: The Ethics of Human Rights is an Ethics of Recognition of the worth, dignity and rights of each and every human being. While the HDP is paramount, some other human rights and values stand out as principles too: life, liberty, equality, diversity, non-discrimination, tolerance, solidarity, democracy, development, peace and the common responsibility of Humankind.

We are now presenting the ethical content of human rights.

References

Agamben, G. 2002. *L'ouvert – De l'homme et de l'animal* ('L'aperto. L'uomo e l'animale', trad. de l'italien par Joël Gayraud). Paris: Éditions Payot & Rivages.

Aristotle. 2000. *Politics* (B. Jowett, Trans., with Introduction, Analysis and Index by H. Davis). Mineola: Dover Publications, Incl.

Assoun, P.-L. 2003. *Lacan*. Paris: PUF.

Barthes, R. 1977. *Fragmentos de um discurso amoroso* ('Fragments d'un discours amoureux', trad. de Isabel Gonçalves). Lisboa: Edições 70.

Bertram, G. et al. (Textes réunis et présentés par). 2007. *Socialité et reconnaissance – Grammaires de l'humain*. Paris: L'Harmattan.

Birmingham, P. 2006. *Hannah arendt and human rights—the predicament of common responsibility*. Bloomington: Indiana University Press.

Bobbio, N. 1990. *A era dos direitos* ('L'età dei Diritti', trad. de Carlos Nelson Coutinho). Rio de Janeiro: Editora Campos (1992).

Bossuyt, M. 1975. La distinction juridique entre les droits civils et politiques et les droits économiques, sociaux et culturels. *Revue des droits de l'homme/Human rights journal – Droit international et Droit comparé/International and Comparative Law*. Vol. VIII-4, 783–820.

Caillé, A. (Sous la direction de). 2007. *La quête de reconnaissance – nouveau phénomène social total*. Paris: Éditions La Découverte.

Campbell, T. 2006. *Rights—a critical introduction*. London: Routledge.

Canto-Sperber, M., and Ogien, R. 2004. *La Philosophie Morale*. Paris: PUF, Que sais-je?–3696.

Cassin, R. 1951. La Déclaration universelle et la mise en œuvre des droits de l'homme. In Académie de droit international, *Recueil des Cours – 1951, II, Tome 79 de la Collection* 237–367. Paris: Librairie du Recueil Sirey.

Cassin, R. (1972). La Commission des Droits de l'Homme de l'ONU—1947–1971. In *Ganshof Van der Meersch—Studia ab discipulis amicisque in honorem egregii professoris edita – Tome Premier*, ed. AAVV and W. J. Miscellanea, 397–433. Bruxelles: Établissements Émile Bruylant/ Paris: Librairie Générale de Droit et de Jurisprudence.

Chebel, M. 2000. *Du désir*. Paris: Rivages poche (2003).

Dembour, M.-B. 2010a. Critiques. In *International Human Rights Law*, ed. D. Moeckli, S. Shah and S. Sivakumaran, 64–86. Oxford: Oxford University Press.
Dembour, M.-B. 2010b. What are human rights? Four schools of thought. *Human Rights Quartely* 32: 1–20.
Dolto, F. (Textes recueillis, annotés et présentés par Claude Halmos). 1994. *Les chemins de l'éducation*. Paris: Éditions Gallimard.
Donnelly, J. 2007. The relative universality of human rights. *Human Rights Quartely* 29: 281–306.
Donnelly, J. 2009. Human dignity and human rights. *Swiss Initiative to Commemorate the 60th anniversary of the UDHR—protecting dignity: An agenda for human rights—research project on human dignity*. www.udhr60.ch/report/donnelly-HumanDignity_0609.pdf. Accesses July 2013.
Etzioni, A. 2010. The normativivity of human rights is self-evident. *Human Rights Quartely* 32: 187–197.
Fabre-Magnan, M. 2008. Dignité humaine. In *Dictionnaire des Droits de l'Homme*, ed. Joël Andriantsimbazovina et al., 285–291. Paris: PUF.
Ferrarese, E. 2008. Pourquoi refuse-t-on la reconnaissance? Sur les effets de la reconnaissance institutionnelle. In *La reconnaissance à l'épreuve – Explorations socioanthropologiques*, ed. J.-P. Payet and A. Battegay (Dir.), 95–102. Villeneuve d'Ascq: Presses universitaires du Septentrion.
Fournier, M. 2013. On a tous besoin d'être aimés. *Sciences Humaines – Les Grands Dossiers – L'amour: un besoin vital, N° 32* (Septembre-Octobre-Novembre), 6–7.
Fraser, N. 2001. Recognition without ethics? *Theory, Culture and Society*, 18(2–3): 21–42.
Freeman, M. 2004. The problem of secularism in human rights theory. *Human Rights Quartely*, 26: 375–400.
Freund, J. 1972. Sociologie et Méthodologie. In AAVV. *René Cassin Amicorum Discipulorumque Liber – IV. Méthodologie des Droits de l'Homme*, 153–172. Paris: Éditions Pedone, Institut International des Droits de l'Homme, 'Jura Hominis ac Civis'.
Glendon, M. 2001. *A world made new—Eleanor Roosevelt and the universal declaration of human rights*. New York: Random House, Trade Paperbacks.
Griffin, J. 2008. *On human rights*. New York: Oxford University Press.
Habermas, J. 2012. Chapter 4—the concept of human dignity and the realistic Utopia of human rights. In *Philosophical dimensions of human rights—some contemporary views*, ed. C. Corradetti, 63–79. Dordrecht: Springer Science + Business Media B. V.
Henkin, L. 1978. *The rights of man today*. London: Stevens and Sons.
Hennette-Vauchez, S. 2008. A human dignitas? The contemporary principle of human dignity as a mere reappraisal of an ancient legal concept. European University Institute, Department of Law, EUI Working Papers, LAW 2008/18. http://cadmus.eui.eu/bitstream/handle/1814/9009/LAW_2008_18.pdf?sequence=1.Accessed July 2013.
Honneth, A. 2004. Reconnaissance. In *Dictionnaire d'Éthique et de Philosophie Morale – Tome 2*, ed. M. Canto-Sperber (Sous la direction de), 4ᵉ éd. 1640–1647. Paris: PUF.
Hunt, L. 2008. *Inventing human rights—a history*. New York: W. W. Norton and Company Ltd.
Kant, I. 1803. On education (Annette Churton, Transl., with an Introduction by C. A. Foley Rhys Davids, M. A.). Boston: D. C. Heath and Co., Publishers (1906). http://archive.org/details/kantoneducationu00kantuoft. Accessed July 2013.
Kelsen, H. 1941. Recognition in international law: Theoretical observations. *The American Journal of International Law*, 35(4): 605–616.
Maheu, R. 1972. Au service de l'esprit dans l'histoire. In *Dans l'esprit des hommes – UNESCO 1946–1971*, 313–352. Paris: UNESCO.
Maritain, J. 1951. *Man and the state*. Chicago: University of Chicago.
McBride, C., and J. Seglow. 2009. Introduction—recognition: Philosophy and politics. *European Journal of Political Theory* 8: 7–12.
Morsink, J. 1999. *The universal declaration of human rights: Origins, drafting, and intent*. Philadelphia: University of Pennsylvania Press.

Nations Unies 1995. *Les Nations Unies et les droits de l'homme – 1945–1995– Avec une introduction de Boutros Boutros-Ghali, Secrétaire général de l'Organisation des Nations Unies*. New York: Nations Unies, Département de l'information, Série Livres bleus des Nations Unies, Volume VII.

Néraudau, J.-P. 1984. *Être enfant à Rome*. Paris: Éditions Payot & Rivages (1996).

Nunge, O., and S. Mortera. 1998. *Satisfaire son besoin de reconnaissance – S'accepter et être accepté*. Saint-Julien-en-Genevois: Éditions Jouvence.

Payet, J.-P., and A. Battegay. 2008. La reconnaissance, un concept de philosophie politique à l'épreuve des sciences sociales. In *La reconnaissance à l'épreuve – Explorations socio-anthropologiques* (Recognition put to the test—Socio-anthropological explorations), ed. J.-P. Payet and A. Battegay, 23–42. Villeneuve d'Ascq: Presses Universitaires du Septentrion.

Pillay, N. 2012. *Strengthening the united nations human rights treaty body system—a report by the United Nations high commissioner for human rights*. United Nations—Human Rights: Office of the High Commissioner, 100. www2.ohchr.org/english/bodies/HRTD/docs/HCReportTB-Strengthening.pdf. Accesses July 2013.

Plato (Ed. by J. Cooper, & D. Hutchinson). 1997. *Plato—complete works*. Indianapolis: Hackeht Publishing Company.

Rabouin, D. (Textes choisis et présentés par). 1997. *Le désir*. Paris: GF Flammarion.

Ramcharan, B. 2008. *Contemporary human rights ideas*. London: Routledge.

Rao, N. 2011. Three concepts of dignity in constitutional law. *Notre Dame Law Review* 86(1): 183–271. George Mason Law and Economics Research Paper No. 11–20.

Reboul, O. 1992. *Les valeurs de l'éducation*. Paris: PUF.

Ricœur, P. 2004. *Parcours de la reconnaissance*. Paris: Gallimard, Folio Essais-459.

Rivero, J. 1988. Une éthique des droits de l'homme. In *Mélanges en l'honneur Phédon Vegleris – La crise des institutions de l'État, Tome premier*, ed. P. J. Pararas (Responsable de l'Édition), 627–638. Athènes: Editions Ant. N. Sakkoulas.

Rolston III, H. 2008. Human uniqueness and human dignity: Persons in nature and the nature of persons. In *Human dignity and bioethics—essays commissioned by the President's council on bioethics*, ed. AAVV, 129–153. Washington.

Roy, O. 2012. La règle d'or, maxime universelle. *Sciences Humaines – Un siècle de philosophie – Une bibliothèque idéale*, N° 29, 12–15.

Sen, A. 2004. Elements of a theory of human rights. *Philosophy and Public Affairs*, 32(4): 315–356. www.mit.edu/~shaslang/mprg/asenETHR.pdf. Accessed July 2013.

Shapiro, S. 2009. What is the rule of recognition (and does it exist)? In *The Rule of Recognition and the U.S. Constitution*, ed. M. Adler and K. Himma. Oxford University Press, Yale Law School, Public Law Working Paper No. 184. http://ssrn.com/abstract = 1304645. Accessed July 2013.

Spaak, T. 2005. Kelsen and Hart on the normativity of law. In *Perspectives on Jurisprudence: Essays in Honour of Jes Bjarup*, ed. P. Wahlgren, 397–414. http://ssrn.com/abstract = 922755. Accessed July 2013.

Spector, H. 2009. Value pluralism and the two concepts of rights. *RMM Vol. 0, Perspectives in Moral Science*, 355–371. www.rmm-journal.de/downloads/026_spector.pdf. Accessed July 2013.

Taylor, Ch. 2001. A world consensus on human rights? In *The philosophy of human rights*, ed. P. Hayden, 409–422. St. Paul: Paragon House.

This, B. 2002. Dolto et l'ange bleu – Entretien de Françoise Dolto avec Bernard This en juin 1980. *Le Coq-Héron*, 168, 2002/1, 139–157.

Todorov, T. 2013. Sous le regard des autres. *Sciences Humaines – Les Grands Dossiers – L'amour: un besoin vital*, N 32, 56–63.

Tomuschat, Ch. 2008. *Human rights—between idealism and realism*. Oxford: Oxford University Press, Collected Courses of the Academy of European Law, XIII/1.

Trindade, A. 2006. International law for humankind: Towards a new *Jus Gentium*—general course on public international law. In *Recueil des Cours/ Collected Courses of The Hague Academy*

of International Law – 2005– Tome 316 de la Collection, ed. Académie de Droit International. Leiden: Martinus Nijhoff Publishers.
UNDP. 1999. *Human development report*. New York: Oxford University Press. http://hdr.undp.org/en/media/HDR_1999_EN.pdf. Accessed July 2013.
UNESCO. 1948. *Human rights—comments and interpretations—a symposium edited by UNESCO, with an Introduction by Jacques Maritain*. http://unesdoc.unesco.org/images/0015/001550/155042eb.pdf. Accessed July 2013.
Vincent, L. 2004. *Comment devient-on amoureux*? Paris: Odile Jacob Poches.
Williams, R. 1997. *Hegel's ethics of recognition*. Berkeley: University of California Press.
Young, K. 2008. The minimum core of economic and social rights: A concept in search of content. *The Yale Journal of International Law*. 33:113, 113–175. www.yale.edu/yjil/PDFs/vol_33/Young%20Final.pdf. Accessed Oct 2013.

Chapter 5
Human Dignity Principle

Abstract This chapter presents an historical, philosophical, and jurisprudential approach to the Human Dignity Principle, as well as an interdisciplinary account of the human worth underlying human dignity and rights.

'Human dignity' is the core of Human Rights Philosophy and the bedrock of International Human Rights Law. There is no generally agreed legal definition of human dignity, any more than of human rights, but after the Second World War it became the foundational idea on which the different visions of human rights could agree when the United Nations Charter and the Universal Declaration of Human Rights were drafted.

In International Human Rights Law, besides 'human dignity', the most frequently used expression is probably 'dignity and worth of the human person'. Considering that human dignity is consubstantial to human worth, an account of human dignity should be a matter of answering the following principal question: In what does human worth consist? An interdisciplinary account of human worth is submitted, whose main operative categories are the human species' perfectibility, rooted in its semiotic nature, and human beings' perfecting, for which the right to education is key.

5.1 Conceptual Origins

Henkin pointed out: "The human rights idea and ideology begin with an *ur* value or principle (derived perhaps from Immanuel Kant), the principle of *human dignity*. Human rights discourse has rooted itself entirely in human dignity and finds its complete justification in that idea" (as cit. in Rao 2011, p. 191, note 20). Arthur Chaskalson observes[1]:

> Political leaders, jurists and philosophers have increasingly alluded to the dignity of the human person as a basic ideal so generally recognized as to require no independent support. It has acquired a resonance that leads it to be invoked widely as a legal and moral ground for protest against degrading and abusive treatment. No other ideal seems so clearly accepted as a universal social good.

[1] www.lrc.org.za/papers/419-the-third-bram-fischer-memorial-lecture-human-dignity-as-a-foundational-value-of-our-constitutional-order.

A. Reis Monteiro, *Ethics of Human Rights*, DOI 10.1007/978-3-319-03566-6_5,

Human dignity is indeed the core of Human Rights Philosophy and "the fundamental guiding principle of international human rights law enshrined in the Preambles to the Universal Declaration of Human Rights and both Covenants", as recalled the CESCR in GC 13 (E/C.12/1999/10, para. 41)[2]. The CoRC also recalled in its GC 8 (CRC/C/GC/8, 2007, para. 16)[3]: "The dignity of each and every individual is the fundamental guiding principle of international human rights law". In fact:

- The Preambles of the UN Charter and of the UDHR link human rights to human dignity.
- The 1996 International Covenants proclaim, in their Preambles, that human rights "derive from the inherent dignity of the human person".
- The Vienna Declaration and Program of Action (1993) reaffirms, in Preamble, that "all human rights derive from the dignity and worth inherent in the human person".
- The EU Charter Article 1 bears the title 'Human dignity' and states: "Human dignity is inviolable. It must be respected and protected". According to the Charter's official *Commentary*: "Article 1 is the foundation of all fundamental rights in the Charter. In the Convention [its drafting body] it was named several times the 'mother basic right'" (EU Network of Independent Experts on Fundamental Rights 2006, p. 23).

There is no generally agreed legal definition of 'human dignity', however, any more than that of 'human right'. A broad inquiry on it is, therefore, necessary. Let us begin by some useful etymological notes provided by Mette Lebech (2006) that show the historical ambivalence of the term:

- *Human* is related to *humus,* the Latin word for earth.
- *Dignity* comes from the Latin noun *decus,* meaning ornament, distinction, honour, glory. The impersonal verbal form *decet* is related to the Greek *δοκειν* (to seem or to show). The participle form *decens* survives in the English adjective 'decent'.
- The Latin term *dignitas* translated the Greek term *αχιομα* (axiom) that means something self-imposing, to be taken for granted, like a first principle.
- At the root of *axioma* is *αξια* that means worth, from which we also get the term axiology. In Aristotle, however, *αξια* means not what equalizes human beings but, rather, what distinguishes from one another.

In the Western world, the idea of human dignity has both philosophical and religious roots.

Donnelly observed that, in the ancient Greek and Roman world, the idea of a common Humanity was practically absent. We know the distinction between 'Hellenes' (the Greek term for 'Greeks' that is the Latin-derived name) and 'barbarians', as well as the distinction between Christians and heathens. A hierarchical vision

---

[2] www.unhchr.ch/tbs/doc.nsf/(Symbol)/ae1a0b126d068e868025683c003c8b3b#17%2F.

[3] www.unhchr.ch/tbs/doc.nsf/898586b1dc7b4043c1256a450044f331/6545c032cb57bff5c12571fc002e834d/$FILE/G0740771.pdf.

of the world prevailed in which only the best could reach public distinction and recognition. Aristotle (1925) noted that "not all specify the same sort of merit, but democrats identify it with the status of freeman, supporters of oligarchy with wealth (or with noble birth), and supporters of aristocracy with excellence" (Book V.3).

In the Roman Republic, *dignitas* was an attribute of those who commanded respect because of social standing, office, achievements or virtue. There was no fully equivalent term in classical Greece. Cicero is a great representative of the Greco-Roman Stoic Philosophy that highlighted the human rational and moral attributes. There is one passage in *De Officiis* (On Duties) that refers to "the superiority and dignity of our nature [*natura excellentia et dignitas*]" (Book I, XXX)[4]. However, as Habermas (2012) remarks, this was "a *collective* notion of *dignitas humana*", because:

> ... it was explained in terms of a distinguished ontological status of human beings in the cosmos, of the particular rank enjoyed by human beings vis-à-vis 'lower' forms of life in virtue of species-specific faculties, such as reason and reflection. The superior value of the species might have justified some kind of species protection but not the inviolability of the dignity of the individual person as a source of normative claims.
>
> Two decisive stages in the genealogy of the concept are still missing. First, universalization must be followed by individualization. The issue is the *worth of the individual* in the horizontal relations between different human beings, not the status of 'human beings' in the vertical relation to God or to 'lower' creatures on the evolutionary scale. Second, the relative superiority of humanity and its members must be replaced by the absolute worth of any person. The issue is the *unique worth* of each person. These two steps were taken in Europe when ideas from the Judeo-Christian tradition were appropriated by philosophy [...]. (p. 71, 72)

The Christian message introduced two fundamental ideas: that of inherent human dignity and that of equality between human beings. Human superiority was derived from the Christian narrative of divine creation of world. According to the Book of Genesis (1, pp. 26–27):

> Then God said: "Let us make humans in our image, after our likeness. Let them have dominion over the fish of the sea, the birds of the air, and the cattle, and over all the wild animals and all the creatures that crawl on the ground".

That is why man is the most perfect creature: He stands at the top of *The Great Chain of Being* (Walter Lovejoy 1936), in which the status of each link is defined by its respective ontological distance from the Creator. The Catechism of the Catholic Church teaches that among all visible creatures only man is "able to know and love his creator" and "the only creature on earth that God has willed for its own sake" (para. 356)[5].

Following Lebech (2006), Thomas Aquinas and Albert the Great in the thirteenth century refer to an anonymous scholastic Master who defined a person as "a subject

[4] Later, Cicero observes that "there are two orders of beauty: in the one, loveliness predominates; in the other, dignity; of these, we ought to regard loveliness as the attribute of woman, and dignity as the attribute of man" (Book I, XXXVI) (www.constitution.org/rom/de_officiis.htm).

[5] www.educationforjustice.org/free-files/HumanDignity09.pdf.

distinguished by dignity", but he also informs that Aquinas uses the expression *dignitas humana* only one time in the *Summa Theologiae*, in which he argues that human beings can lose their dignity if they do not remain rational and free. However, according to Daniel Sulmasy, Aquinas uses the term *dignitas* and its cognates 185 times (as cit. in Donnelly 2009, p. 19). In any case, a well-ordered society was one where every human being was in its proper place within the complex social hierarchy.

The fourteenth, fifteenth and sixteenth centuries were great times of *Renaissance* or *rebirth*. As we know, the Renaissance was a vast, multiform and complex cultural movement, beginning in Italy, which produced a radical—cultural, moral, political, etc.—transformation of Western Civilization. The world was no more a vale of suffering and tears because of the sin of Adam, as described in a work perhaps most representative of the medieval mentality: *De miseria conditionis humanæ* (On the Misery of the Human Condition) by Lothar of Segni who was later to become Pope Innocent III (about 1160–1216), one of the most powerful popes of the Middle Ages.

The Renaissance began by the rediscovery of the Greek and Roman *humanæ litteræ* (human writings) that was an *earthly* literature in contrast to the medieval *divinæ litteræ* (divine writings). This was Renaissance Humanism. "No matter how diverse the themes and subjects of the literature of humanism, all pointed to one common objective: the recovery of faith in the creativity of humankind and in humanity's capacity to transform the world and to forge its own destiny" (Puledda 1997, p. 5). In *Liber de Sapiente* (The Wise Man 1511) by French humanist Carolus Bovillus (Charles de Bouelles) (1479–1567), "the glorification of humankind reached perhaps its maximum expression" (p. 8).

Every Humanism, religious or lay, entails a more or less distinct definition of human 'nature' or 'essence' concerning what human beings 'are' and how they 'should be'. The Renaissance Humanism brought to the fore the idea of human dignity scorned during the Christian Middle Ages. Gianozzo Manetti (1396–1459), one of Humanism's major figures, published in 1452 *De dignitate et excellentia hominis* (On the Dignity and Excellence of Man). Pico della Mirandola's (1463–1496) *Oratio de Hominis Dignitate* (*Oration on the Dignity of Man* 1486)[6] is a *manifesto* of Renaissance Humanism.

> At last, the Supreme Maker decreed that this creature, to whom He could give nothing wholly his own, should have a share in the particular endowment of every other creature. Taking man, therefore, this creature of indeterminate image, He set him in the middle of the world and thus spoke to him:
> We have given you, O Adam, no visage proper to yourself, nor endowment properly your own, in order that whatever place, whatever form, whatever gifts you may, with premeditation, select, these same you may have and possess through your own judgment and decision. The nature of all other creatures is defined and restricted within laws which We have laid down; you, by contrast, impeded by no such restrictions, may, by your own free will, to whose custody We have assigned you, trace for yourself the lineaments of your own nature.

[6] The original title was simply *Oration*, an introduction to his 900 Theses. The longer title was added by the editor after Mirandola death (www.cscs.umich.edu/~crshalizi/Mirandola).

> I have placed you at the very center of the world, so that from that vantage point you may with greater ease glance round about you on all that the world contains. We have made you a creature neither of heaven nor of earth, neither mortal nor immortal, in order that you may, as the free and proud shaper of your own being, fashion yourself in the form you may prefer. It will be in your power to descend to the lower, brutish forms of life; you will be able, through your own decision, to rise again to the superior orders whose life is divine.

Therefore, the human being is seen not as possessing a fixed, immutable essence, but its dignity consists just in the anthropological openness and power of self-determination, that is, in the human beings' liberty to choose what they want to become. Mirandola does not use the terms 'dignity of man' or 'human dignity', however, as Lebech (2006) notes.

Referring to the *Grundgesetz Kommentar Bd I* 2nd edition (Dreier ed. 2004), Henk Botha (2009) remarks:

> Dreier is justifiably critical of a tendency in the academic literature to overlook the vast differences and discontinuities among ancient, medieval and modern conceptions of dignity. He points out that for stoic thinkers such as Cicero, human dignity was more of a duty than a right. He further argues that the Christian notion of man as *imago dei* [image of God] is closely bound up with the doctrine of original sin. For centuries, it was not viewed as an impediment to the institutionalization of grossly unequal social relations such as that between master and slave. Similarly, for a long time the commonality of the human species had to play second fiddle to the distinction between Christians, non-Christians and heretics. While Dreier does not deny the role of Christianity in the evolution of the idea of human dignity, he points out that Christian doctrine has by no means played an exclusive role in the institutionalization of dignity within the legal-political sphere, and that it has often impeded its realization. (p. 179, note 33)

Indeed, until the seventeenth and eighteenth centuries, there are very few examples of dignity being attributed not only to a few but to every human being[7]. Freedoms were privileges conferred upon individuals or groups by virtue of their rank or status. Nonetheless: "In the centuries after the Middle Ages, the concept of liberty became gradually separated from status and came to be seen not as a privilege but as a right of all human beings" (Sepúlveda et al. 2004, p. 1). Kant represents the climax of such an historic moral conquest in the history of Western Philosophy.

5.2 The Kantian Moment

Where the concept of dignity is concerned, almost all roads lead to Kant. "Although Kant's work continues to be dissected, contested, and reconfigured by contemporary philosophers, he is nevertheless considered by many to be 'the father of the modern concept of human dignity' [Giovanni Bognetti]" (Henry 2011, p. 36). The "canonical expression" (Habermas 2012, p. 64) of human dignity in Kant is a confluence of the most significant roots of the concept. The Enlightenment narrative of the conquest of autonomy culminated in his essay "What is Enlightenment?" He is:

[7] Leslie Henry (2011) notices: "The Colonial Laws of Massachusetts famously prohibited anyone but large landholders from wearing gold, silver, lace, silk, boots, ruffles, capes, or other signifiers of high social status" (p. 22, note 101).

> … the philosopher whose work is most commonly drawn upon in connection with rights-based approach to morality and politics. It is Kant's concepts of respecting people as ends in themselves and the dignity of autonomous beings that feature most prominently in justificatory rights discourse. The high, sometimes paramount, value many people place on autonomy is largely due to the powerful influence of Kant's conception of autonomy continues to exercise over moral and political thought […]. (Campbell 2006, p. 55)

Kant presented his vision of human dignity (*Menschenwürde, Würde der Menschheit, Würde der menschlichen Natur*) primarily in *Fundamental Principles of the Metaphysics of Morals* (FP)[8] that, despite its brevity, "is one of the greatest and most influential achievements in the history of philosophy" (Wood 1999, p. 12). In the Preface, Kant begins by justifying the need for a *Methaphysics of Morals* (MM) as the rational part of Ethics. In spite of its "discouraging title"—Kant wrote—it may be "presented in popular form": that is the purpose of the FP that consists in "the investigation and establishment of the supreme principle of morality".

According to Kant, human beings have a *twofold capacity/character/sense*, for belonging to two worlds: the sensible world and the intelligible world (the world of understanding). Hence a fundamental Kantian distinction in the MM, namely: the distinction between *homo phenomenon* and *homo noumenon*[9].

---

[8] The original German title is *Grundlegung zur Metaphysik der Sitten*. H. J. Paton translated it as *Groundwork of the Metaphysics of Morals*; James W. Ellington as *Grounding for the Metaphysics of Morals*; Lewis White Beck as *Foundations of the Metaphysics of Morals*; Thomas Kingsmill Abbott as *Fundamental Principles of the Metaphysic of Morals*. The latter is the source of the next quotations (www.gutenberg.org/cache/epub/5682/pg5682.html).

Regarding *The Metaphysics of Morals*, the electronic source is the translation by J. W. Semple, the title of which is *Metaphysic of Ethics* (http://philosophyfaculty.ucsd.edu/faculty/ctolley/texts/kant.html)

[9] Kant wrote in MM:

> Man regards himself, when conscious of a duty to himself, in a twofold capacity; first, as a sensible being, i. e. as a man, where he ranks only as one among other sorts of animals; but, second, he regards himself not only as an intelligent being, but as A VERY REASON (for the theoretic function of reason may perhaps be a property of animated matter), resident in a region inscrutable to sense, and manifesting itself only in morally practical relations, where that amazing quality of man's nature FREEDOM is revealed by the influence reason exerts upon the determination of the will.
> Mankind, then, as an intelligent physical being (*homo phenomenon*), is susceptible of voluntary determination to active conduct by the suggestions of his reason; but in all this the idea of obligation does not enter. The very same being, however, considered in respect of his personality (*homo noumenon*), i. e. cogitated as one invested with inward freedom, is a being capable of having obligation imposed upon him, and, in particular, of becoming obligated and beholden to himself, i.e. to the humanity subsisting in his person; and, so considered in this twofold character, mankind can acknowledge the obligations he stands under to himself, without incurring any contradiction, the notion MAN being now understood to be taken in a twofold sense. (Book I, Introduction, §3).

Cicero had made an analogous distinction:

> We must realize also that we are invested by Nature with two characters, as it were: one of these is universal, arising from the fact of our being all alike endowed with reason and with that superiority which lifts us above the brute. From this all morality and propriety are derived, and upon it depends the rational method of ascertaining our duty. The other

- Homo phenomenon is the human being regarded as a natural, physical, sensible and rational being, that is, an intelligent animal, "susceptible of voluntary determination to active conduct by the suggestions of his reason".
- Homo noumenon is the human being regarded as a rational and moral being, capable of "becoming obligated and beholden to himself, i.e. to the humanity subsisting in his person".

Kant (FP—Second Section):

> Everything in nature works according to laws. Rational beings alone have the faculty of acting according to the conception of laws, that is according to principles, i.e. have a will.

Kant (FP—Third Section):

> As a rational being, and consequently belonging to the intelligible world, man can never conceive the causality of his own will otherwise than on condition of the idea of freedom, for independence of the determinate causes of the sensible world (an independence which reason must always ascribe to itself) is freedom. Now the idea of freedom is inseparably connected with the conception of autonomy, and this again with the universal principle of morality which is ideally the foundation of all actions of rational beings, just as the law of nature is of all phenomena.

Kant (FP—First Section):

> Nothing can possibly be conceived in the world, or even out of it, which can be called good, without qualification, except a good will.

A good will is a will good in itself—unconditionally, absolutely good, pure and holy—that is, acting only from duty, not from desire, inclination, but independently, free from all influence of contingent grounds, acting from pure respect for the moral law. It is the sublimity and intrinsic dignity of duty that constitutes the moral worth of an action. When human behaviours are motivated by desires, emotions or external forces, they are not autonomous but heteronomous.

The will acts according to laws and maxims. Laws are objective principles of action, that is, they are valid for every rational being. Maxims are subjective principles of volition, on which a subject acts. Reason applied to action is practical reason, that is, reason determined by interests.

There are two ways of justifying an action: with reference to a purpose considered to be good or with reference to a self-evident good. So the commands of practical reason may be hypothetical or categorical imperatives. Hypothetical imperatives are those commanding something as means to something else; categorical imperatives are those commanding something as objectively necessary in itself, that is, without reference to any purpose. The latter are analogous to laws of nature and they are the principles of morality.

The supreme principle of morality may be presented in various formulations that include the following (FP):

---

character is the one that is assigned to individuals in particular. In the matter of physical endowment there are great differences: some, we see, excel in speed for the race, others in strength for wrestling; so in point of personal appearance, some have stateliness, others comeliness. (*De Officiis*, Book I, 107) (www.constitution.org/rom/de_officiis.htm).

> Act as if the maxim of thy will were to become, by thy adopting it, an universal law of nature.
> So act as to treat humanity, whether in thine own person or in that of any other, in every case as an end withal, never as means only.
> Act only on that maxim whereby thou canst at the same time will that it should become a universal law.

Kant refers to the second formulation as "the supreme limiting condition of every man's freedom of action". It is often called the dignity principle or principle of Humanity. According to Ricoeur (1991), it compensates for the "emptiness of the formalism" of the two others, being an expression of the Golden Rule (p. 261, 262), even though for Kant the Golden Rule was a "trivial maxim".

The three *formulae*, each one involving the two other, may be reduced to this supreme law or categorical imperative:

> 'Act always on such a maxim as thou canst at the same time will to be a universal law'; this is the sole condition under which a will can never contradict itself; and such an imperative is categorical.

Consequently, the ability to act autonomously allows human beings to obey only laws given to themselves by themselves and with universal validity, thus becoming legislating members of a kingdom of ends (in *mundus intelligibilis*).

Kant (FP—Second Section):

> It was seen that man was bound to laws by duty, but it was not observed that the laws to which he is subject are only those of his own giving, though at the same time they are universal, and that he is only bound to act in conformity with his own will; a will, however, which is designed by nature to give universal laws.
> By a kingdom I understand the union of different rational beings in a system by common laws. Now since it is by laws that ends are determined as regards their universal validity, hence, if we abstract from the personal differences of rational beings and likewise from all the content of their private ends, we shall be able to conceive all ends combined in a systematic whole (including both rational beings as ends in themselves, and also the special ends which each may propose to himself), that is to say, we can conceive a kingdom of ends, which on the preceding principles is possible.
> For all rational beings come under the law that each of them must treat itself and all others never merely as means, but in every case at the same time as ends in themselves. Hence results a systematic union of rational beings by common objective laws, i.e. a kingdom which may be called a kingdom of ends, since what these laws have in view is just the relation of these beings to one another as ends and means. It is certainly only an ideal.

The idea/ideal of a kingdom of ends gives rise to another well-known Kantian distinction between *price* and *dignity*[10]:

---

[10] Seneca also contrasted dignity with price in his *Epistles*: "Bodily goods are, to be sure, good for the body; but they are not absolutely good. There will indeed be some value [*pretium*] in them; but they will possess no genuine merit [*dignitas*], for they will differ greatly; some will be less, others greater". (www.stoics.com/seneca_epistles_book_2.html)

(Corporum autem bona corporibus quidem bona sunt, sed in totum non sunt bona; his pretium quidem erit aliquod, ceterum dignitas non erit; magnis inter se intervallis distabunt: alia minora, alia maiora erunt) (www.intratext.com/IXT/LAT0230/_P1Z.HTM).

Kant (FP—Second Section):

> In the kingdom of ends everything has either value or dignity. Whatever has a value can be replaced by something else which is equivalent; whatever, on the other hand, is above all value, and therefore admits of no equivalent, has a dignity.

Kant (FP—Third Section):

> What else then can freedom of the will be but autonomy, that is, the property of the will to be a law to itself? But the proposition: 'The will is in every action a law to itself' only expresses the principle: 'To act on no other maxim than that which can also have as an object itself as a universal law'. Now this is precisely the formula of the categorical imperative and is the principle of morality, so that a free will and a will subject to moral laws are one and the same.

Kant (MM—Book I, Introduction, § 11):

> Man, as a part of the physical system (*homo phenomenon*, animal rationale), is an animal of very little moment, and has but a common value with beasts, and the other products of the soil. Even that he is superior to those by force of his understanding, gives him only a higher external value in exchange, when brought to the market along with other cattle, and sold as wares.
> But man considered as a person, i. e. as the subject of ethico-active reason, is exalted beyond all price: for as such (*homo noumenon*), he cannot be taken for a bare means [...]: that is to say, he is invested with an internal dignity (an absolute worth) [...].

Kant (FP—Second Section):

> For then it is clear that he who transgresses the rights of men intends to use the person of others merely as a means, without considering that as rational beings they ought always to be esteemed also as ends.

Human beings are, therefore, endowed with freedom and the faculty of will. The attribute of freedom allows the will to be a kind of causality, as autonomy. The autonomy of the will is more than a psychological freedom. As the self-legislating power of human beings as members of a kingdom of ends, it is a *moral* freedom and, thus, the supreme principle of morality and the basis of our common human dignity.

Kant distinguished between inner worth and moral worth.

- *Inner worth* means the intrinsic human worth, related to the absolute dignity of being a member of Humanity, apart from any activity. "Humanity is itself a Dignity" (*Die Menschheit selbst ist eine Würde*) (MM, Book II, §38). The human being has, therefore, a duty "in respect of the dignity of our humanity".
- *Moral worth* refers to man's actions, which may violate "the dignity of humanity in his own person", by acting according to maxims grounded on non-universalizable laws.

The ultimate moral end of a human being is the perfection of virtue, and its greatest perfection is to do his or her duty for the duty's sake. Kant also distinguished between duties towards ourselves, and duties towards others, as well as between perfect and imperfect duties. A perfect duty is one which permits no exception. Not to commit suicide is an example of a perfect duty to oneself. Not to lie is an example of a perfect duty to others. An imperfect duty is, for example, to cultivate one's talent, which may perhaps not always be accomplished. In MM, Kant includes "three classical *formulae*" of the principles of Law according to Ulpian: *Honeste vive* (be an honest man), *Neminem lede* (do nobody wrong), *Suum cuique tribue* (give each man his own).

In sum, according to the classical and Kantian conception, the source of human dignity is the human worth that consists in the faculty of reason and capacity for autonomy, i.e. for rational free agency[11]. These are the distinctive attributes of human beings making them persons, that is, ends in themselves, which must never be treated merely as means. In other words, human beings are equally dignified as both rational and moral animals.

According to Beck: "Kant's most important discovery is that the law is not a mere restriction on freedom but is itself a product of freedom" (as cit. in Zaruk 2001, p. 53). In Étienne Balibar's (1989) opinion, in despite of the idealism, formalism and other criticisms of Kant's Moral Philosophy, the Kantian 'Copernican revolution' put the question about the subject "as a *juridical question* [...]: what we seek, under its name, is not the factual human being, subjected to diverse interior and exterior powers, but the juridical human being (who could be called the being human of human being or the being human in human being, which is also the non-empirical human being), whose autonomy corresponds to the position of an 'universal legislator'" (p. 30).

During the ninteenth century, while for Friedrich Nietzsche (1844–1900) "every human being [...] only has dignity in so far as he is a tool of the genius" (as cit. in McCrudden 2008, p. 661), the idea of human dignity inspired social and political movements, socialist or religious. These movements stressed the connection between dignity and economic-social conditions, highlighted by Friedrich Schiller (1759–1805) in *Würde des Menschen* (Dignity of Man 1796) in realistic terms: "Give him food and shelter,/When you have covered his nakedness, dignity will follow by itself" (as cit. ib. p. 701)[12]. The Catholic Church developed a social doctrine founded on human dignity, beginning with the encyclical by Pope Leo XIII (1810–1903) *Rerum Novarum*.

It seems undisputable, therefore, that the modern concept of human dignity evolved out of the inegalitarian Roman *dignitas*. According to Waldron (2009b), "the modern notion of *human* dignity involves an upwards equalization of rank, so that we now try to accord to every human being something of the dignity, rank, and expectation of respect that was formerly accorded to nobility" (p. 29). He writes:

> Some have suggested that the old connection between dignity and rank was superseded by a Judaeo-Christian notion of the dignity of humanity as such, and that this Judaeo-Christian notion is really quite different in character. I'm not convinced. I don't want to underesti-

---

[11] Recall that, as already quoted, Aristotle (2000) said that the human being "is equipped at birth with the arms of intelligence and with moral qualities which he may use for the worst ends" (1253a, 12, 15–16). Later, "the most important legacy of Stoicism" is perhaps "its conviction that all human beings share the capacity to reason" (Encyclopedia Britannica 2012).

[12] *Zu essen gebt ihm, zu wohnen, /Habt ihr die Blöße bedeckt, gibt sich die Würde von selbst.*

> mate the breach between Roman-Greek and Judaeo-Christian ideas, but I believe that as far as dignity is concerned the connotation of *ranking status* remained, and that what happened was that it was transvalued rather than superseded. (p. 24)

This is the thesis of James Whitman (2003), who deserves to be quoted at some length. Focusing on Germany and France, the dominant legal cultures of continental Europe, he argues:

> We cannot understand the pattern of 'dignity' in continental Europe today unless we begin with the forms of 'dignity' that existed in the aristocratic-monarchical orders of the *ancien regime* [ancient regime]. Of course, the 'dignity' of the *ancien régime* was not *human* dignity. Two hundred and fifty years ago or so [...], only high-status persons received respect and dignified treatment. [...] 'Human dignity', as we find it on the Continent today, has been formed by a pattern of leveling up, by an extension of formerly high-status treatment to all sectors of the population. [...] Strange as it may sound, there is in fact a genetic relation between the old, obnoxious forms of 'dignity' and the contemporary human forms. Continental Europe is a world in which former status privileges have been generalized. [...] In my view, the magnificent abstractions of Kant, with their talk of the categorical imperative, of treating persons as 'ends in themselves' and so on—these magnificent abstractions have little to do with the socio-historical reality of dignity in Europe. Nor is it only the importance of Kant that we should doubt. Many Europeans, of all nationalities, regard their law of 'human dignity' as the product of a reaction against Fascism and Nazism.

Narrowing his focus on the Law of criminal punishment, and comparing Europe and the USA, he goes on:

> The contrast only begins with the death penalty, reintroduced in the United States during exactly the period that it was definitively abolished in Europe. Prison sentences are far longer in the United States—probably something like five to ten times as long as sentences for comparable offences in Germany and France. [...] The widely-reported result is that American rates of imprisonment, which are the highest in the world, run at nearly ten times the per capita rate in Europe. A much wider range of offences is criminalised in the United States than in Europe.

Moreover:

> American criminal punishment is more *degrading*. Indeed, American criminal punishment is degrading in ways that the continental traditions have vigorously rejected. This is most obviously true in the case of certain notorious American practices, such as the use of chain gangs. But there are many other related phenomena that are far less well known. [... Continental systems] also have rules—very remarkable from the American point of view—requiring that inmates be treated with respect, in such things as forms of address: inmates are ordinarily to be addressed as '*Herr* so-and-so' or '*Monsieur* so-and-so'. [...] All of this conveys an important symbolic message: the message that offenders are to be treated like ordinary members of society, and not like status inferiors. [...] This helps us to understand why the prevalence of degradation in American punishment sustains the broad culture of American harshness. [...]
> As of roughly 1750, everywhere in Western Europe—as indeed, in all complex human societies—there were two classes of punishments: high-status punishments and low status punishments. These differences in the forms of punishment served everywhere as vivid markers of status differentiation. In the occident, the most familiar form of status-differentiation came in the practices of execution. Following a tradition that reached back into antiquity in the western world, high-status persons were beheaded, while low-status persons were

> ordinarily hanged. The forms of execution made for a peculiarly resonant symbol, as they always do, but they were only one aspect of a wider system of status differentiation. [...]
> The subsequent social history of punishment in continental Europe can be captured in a surprisingly simple formula. Over the last two and a half centuries, the high-status punishments have gradually driven the low-status punishments out. The commitment to ending the social practices of the *ancien régime* has expressed itself as a commitment to ending degradation in punishment. This has been a complex process of which I can only summarise broad outlines. Once again, the forms of execution offer the most symbolically resonant examples. After the French Revolution, as we all know, beheading, the old high-status form of execution, was generalised to all citizens in both France and (eventually) Germany. This was a potent symbol indeed of a kind of high-status egalitarianism, ghoulish though it may seem. In fact, it mattered a great deal for the shape of revolutionary equality on the continent that, by the latter part of the nineteenth century, the section on punishment in all continental penal codes began with a version of the phrase every person condemned to death shall be beheaded. For those who believe that the only question of "dignity" raised by the death penalty is whether we kill offenders or not, be advised: For a very long time, the principal question of dignity was how we killed them.
> [...]
> It is a world transformed since 1770 or 1870, or indeed since 1920, and what has transformed it is not just a redistribution of wealth. There has also been a redistribution of honour. Everyone—such at least is the ambition of the law—is supposed to count as a high-status person.

Let us now quote three authors—whose views are not only convergent but complementary too—to summarize the milestones of the genealogy of the idea of human dignity, and to introduce the approach to its legal significance and uses.

Antonio Pelé (2006)[13] identified "four stages of maturation of the human dignity plant":

- Greek-Roman Antiquity

  This was the stage of *seeds*, especially in the thought of Plato, Aristotle, Cicero and Seneca. There one finds "some properties that would be 'activated' in different historical, social and intellectual circumstances" (p. 222).

- Middle Ages and Renaissance

  This was the stage of *growth*, especially with the Renaissance discourse of *dignitas hominis* (dignity of man), as opposed to the medieval discourse of the *miseria hominis* (misery of man), with the idea of imperfection being replaced with the idea of indetermination. In the author's opinion, "for the first time in History, the value inherent to the human being was described by using systematically the 'dignitiy' concept" (p. 720).

- Seventeenth century

  This was the stage of *ramifications*, one Cartesian, another Pascalian and another legal. "The recognition of a value peculiar to the individual as a person began to be glimpsed as an essential criterion for the legitimacy of the Law and of the State" (p. 877).

[13] http://papers.ssrn.com/sol3/papers.cfm?abstract_id=1619983.

- Eighteenth century

  This was the stage of *flourishing*, especially with the Moral Philosophy of Kant that "discovered too 'early' the modern concept of human dignity characterized by the recognition of the autonomy inherent to the person, and the duty to treat her as an end". Kant intuited "the connection between the dignity of the person and the recognition of her rights, which the State should guarantee" (p. 1096, 1097).

Pelé begins by quoting A. N. Whitehead, according to whom the History of Civilization may be summarized as having been the progressive formation of the idea of human dignity. In his opinion, in European culture, it originated in the concept of the 'dignity of human nature', whose supremacy in relation to the animal world consists in reason, liberty and will. This conception was based on the presumption of the dualism between body and soul, both in the pagan and Christian worlds. The rational soul was thus the basis for the dignity of human nature. Dignity consisted in the soul controlling the body through reason. As not everybody was able to do that, several categories of human beings were excluded from the possession of human dignity, in particular slaves and the 'barbarians'. For different reasons, also women, children and old people had a diminished form of dignity. This amounted to their dehumanization in order to justify their exclusion. They had to accept the domination of those who were able to reach moral autonomy. The author concludes:

> We could so affirm that the construction of human dignity was based on a gigantic process of exclusion of various individuals from the circle of humanity [...]. However, in a quasi-paradoxical way, the consideration of the equality of dignity will proceed to extending to all individuals the characteristics that, before, identified the superiority of some over others. (p. 1105)

Adam Schulman highlighted four stages too:

> a. Classical antiquity: The word 'dignity' comes to us, via the Latin dignus and dignitas, from Greek and Roman antiquity, in whose literature it means something like 'worthiness for honor and esteem'. This classical notion of dignity as something rare and exceptional retains some of its power even in our egalitarian age [...]. But if dignity implies excellence and distinction, then to speak of 'human dignity' raises the question, what is it about human beings as such that we find distinctive and admirable, that raises them in our estimation above other animals? Is there some one attribute or capacity that makes man worthy of respect, such as reason, or conscience, or freedom? Or is it a complex of traits, no one of which is sufficient to earn our esteem?
> [...]
> b. Biblical religion: Another powerful source of a broader, shared notion of human dignity is the Biblical account of man as 'made in the image of God'.
> [...]
> c. Kantian moral philosophy: A daring attempt to set universal human dignity on a strictly rational foundation was made in the eighteenth century by the German philosopher Immanuel Kant. Kant's primary purpose was to show how moral freedom and responsibility could still be possible in a world governed by the laws of mathematical physics. For Kant, in agreement with the Stoics, dignity is the intrinsic worth that belongs to all human beings and to no other beings in the natural world.
> [...]
> d. 20th-century constitutions and international declarations: Finally [... the use of human dignity] in national constitutions and international declarations ratified in the aftermath of the Second World War. (in AAVV 2008, p. 6...12)

Nick Bostrom (2008) presents the following outlook:

> For many of the ancients, dignity was a kind of personal excellence that only a few possessed to any significant degree. Marcus Tullius Cicero (106–43 BC), a Roman following in the footsteps of the Athenian Stoics, attributed dignity to all men, describing it as both a characteristic (human rationality) and a requirement (to base one's life on this capacity for rationality).
> In Medieval Christianity, the dignity of man was based on the belief that God had created man in His image, allowing man to share some aspects of His divine reason and might. Theologians thought they saw man's dignity reflected in his upright posture, his free will, his immortal soul, and his location at the center of the universe. This dignity was viewed as an essential characteristic of the human being, possessed by each one of us, independent of social rank and personal excellence.
> … According to Kant (here partly echoing the Stoics), all persons have dignity, a kind of absolute value that is incomparable to any price or instrumental utility. Kant held that dignity is not a quantitative notion; we cannot have more or less of it. The ground of the dignity of persons is their capacity for reason and moral agency. […]
> The term 'human dignity' did not feature in any European declarations or constitutions in the 18th and 19th centuries. Dignity is to be found for the first time, albeit more or less in passing, in the German constitution drawn up in 1919 by the Weimar National Assembly, and its next appearance is in the corporate-fascist Portuguese constitution of 1933. Only in the aftermath of the Second World War does the concept's heyday begin. (p. 174, 175)

We are now starting on the way towards a broad legal and jurisprudential approach to the concept of human dignity.

5.3 Juridification

5.3.1 International Human Rights Law

The term 'dignity' referring to every human being does not feature, as above noted, in the American and French Declarations of the eighteenth century, although the idea may be seen implied in the famous passage of the USA Declaration of Independence (1776): "We hold these truths to be self-evident, that all men are created equal, that they are endowed by their Creator with certain unalienable rights, that among these are life, liberty and the pursuit of happiness". The term occurs one time in the 1789 French Declaration, but with its ancient meaning: "All citizens, being equal in the eyes of the law, are equally eligible to all *dignities* [emphasis added] and to all public positions and occupations, according to their abilities, and without distinction except that of their virtues and talents" (Article 6). This amounted somehow to a *republicanization* of the ancient *dignitas*, as Charles Renouvier (1815–1903) stressed in a text published in 1848, in which he affirmed that "Republic is a state which best reconciles the interests and the dignity of each individual with the interests and dignity of everyone" (as cit. in McCrudden 2008, p. 701).

In 1936, the *Complément à la Déclaration des Droits de l'Homme* (Complement to the Declaration of the Rights of Man and of the Citizen) adopted by the French League of Human Rights[14] referred to "the respect of personal dignity and of all civilizations" (Art. 10). The juridification of the idea of human dignity expanded only after the Second World War. It was mentioned in most proposals for an International Bill of Rights prepared during and after the war. For example, the draft Declaration on Human Rights sent by Cuba to ECOSOC, on 12 February 1946, stated that every human being shall have: "The right to life, to liberty, to personal security and to respect for his dignity as a human being". The International Bill of Rights proposed by the American Federation of Labor (1946) affirmed in its preamble that the "dynamic motive of a truly democratic society is to foster and enhance the worth and dignity of the individual human being" (cit. in McCrudden 2008, p. 666)[15]. Georges Gurvitch (1894–1965) proposed a Bill of Social Rights (1946) that referred to the protection of "liberty and human dignity" (ib.). The International Bill of Rights proposed by the UK (1947) referred in preamble to the "fundamental human rights and [...] the dignity and worth of the human person" (ib.). Also the Declaration Concerning the Aims and Purposes of the International Labor Organization (ILO)', a kind of Declaration of the rights of the worker adopted by the ILO's XXVIth General Conference, meeting in Philadelphia in May 1944 (Declaration of Philadelphia),[16] stated: "all human beings, irrespective of race, creed or sex, have the right to pursue both their material well-being and their spiritual development in conditions of freedom and dignity, of economic security and equal opportunity" (II.a).

The word "was so much in the political ether, as it were" (p. 671), that it comes without surprise that the UN Charter mentions, in Preamble, "the dignity and worth of the human person" as a foundational principle[17]. It was inserted following a suggestion by Field Marshal Jan Smuts, who led the South African Delegation to the San Francisco Conference (Glendon 2001, p. 144). The treaty establishing the UNESCO, adopted few months after the UN Charter (on 16 November 1945, London)[18], includes two references to the human dignity, in its Preamble: it refers to "the democratic principles of the dignity, equality and mutual respect of men", and states: "That the wide diffusion of culture, and the education of humanity for justice and liberty and peace are indispensable to the dignity of man".

McCrudden (2008) suggests that at the time of the drafting of the UN Charter and of the UDHR, a foundational idea on which the different visions of human rights could converge should have the following characteristics:

> It would need, probably, to be one (i) that gives a coherence to the concept of human rights so that the whole is greater than simply the sum of its parts, and not just a ragbag collection of separate unconnected rights, (ii) that is not rooted in any particular region of the globe and appeals across cultures, but is sensitive to difference, (iii) that places importance on the

[14] www.ldh-france.org/1936-COMPLEMENT-DE-LA-LDH-A-LA.

[15] www.ejil.org/pdfs/19/4/1658.pdf.

[16] www.ilo.org/ilolex/english/iloconst.htm.

[17] http://treaties.un.org/doc/Publication/CTC/uncharter.pdf.

[18] http://unesdoc.unesco.org/images/0013/001337/133729e.pdf#page=7.

> person rather than the attributes of any particular person, but that also places the individual within a social dimension, (iv) that is not dependent on human rights originating only from the exercise of state authority (not least because what the state gives the state can also take away), (v) that is non-ideological (in the sense that it transcends any particular conflicts, such as between capitalism and communism), (vi) that is humanistic (in the sense that it was not based on any particular set of religious principles or beliefs but is nevertheless consistent with them), and (vii) that is both timeless, in the sense that it embodies basic values that are not subject to change, and adaptable to changing ideas of what being human involves. (p. 677)

Such a Holy Grail was the Human Dignity Principle (HDP). It is the sole consensual principle upon which the IHRL developed.

The Secretariat Outline of an International Bill of Rights (E/CN.4/21) affirmed:

> The Preamble shall refer to the four freedoms and to the provisions of the Charter relating to human rights and shall enunciate the following principles:
> [...]
> 4. that there can be no human freedom or dignity unless war and the threat of war is abolished.

Humphrey's draft did not mention the term. As he (1984) explained:

> My own draft has carefully avoided any philosophical assertions which did not enunciate justifiable rights: if they have any place in the instrument it is in the preamble. [...] But the greatest harm which resulted from the introduction of unnecessary philosophical concepts was the needless controversy and useless debate they invited. (p. 44)

Cassin's draft mentioned human dignity as well in Article 1. According to Albert Verdoodt (1964), Cassin considered "indispensable, before defining concrete rights, as the right to life, to define values superior to life itself" (p. 79). However, at the ECOSOC 215th meeting, on 25 August 1948 (E/SR.215), the Brazilian representative (Ramiro Saraiva Guerreiro) observed that:

> His Government appreciated the advantage of adopting formulas to impress public opinion. Nevertheless, it saw no reason why a Declaration on Human Rights should be introduced by philosophical postulates taken from outdated theories of natural law. It considered that the Declaration on Human Rights might profitably omit article 1 altogether and begin with article 2.

At the Third Committee 98th meeting (A/C.3/SR.98), on 9 October 1948, Eleanor Roosevelt, referring to the word 'dignity', said that "the Commission had decided to include the expression in order to emphasize the inherent dignity of all mankind". Before, at the 91th meeting, on 2 October (A/C.3/SR.91), the Belgian representative (Count Henry Carton de Wiart) "stated that his country and his Government welcomed the draft Declaration of human rights, a document which gave full recognition to the 'dignity and worth of the human person'". During the 181th plenary meeting of the General Assembly, on 10 December (A/PV.181), he said that:

> The essential merit of that declaration was to emphasize the high dignity of the human person after the outrages to which men and women had been exposed during the recent war. It was essential that the dignity of the human person should be safeguarded against the recurrence of such acts and also against the excessive risks of individualism and of State control.

The International Bill of Human Rights (the UDHR and the 1966 International Covenants, with their Optional Protocols) refers to human dignity 14 times.

The UDHR refers to human dignity five times: twice in the Preamble, once in Article 1, and in Articles 22 and 23.3.

- According to the Preamble, "recognition of the inherent dignity and of the equal and inalienable rights of all members of the human family is the foundation of freedom, justice and peace in the world". It also recalls that "the peoples of the United Nations have in the Charter reaffirmed their faith in fundamental human rights, in the dignity and worth of the human person and in the equal rights of men and women and have determined to promote social progress and better standards of life in larger freedoms".
- Article 1 is said to contain the whole philosophy of human rights by stating: "All human beings are born free and equal in dignity and rights. They are endowed with reason and conscience and should act towards one another in a spirit of brotherhood".
- Article 22 states: "Everyone, as a member of society, has the right to social security and is entitled to realization, through national effort and international cooperation and in accordance with the organization and resources of each State, of the economic, social and cultural rights indispensable for his dignity and the free development of his personality".
- Article 23.3 provides: "Everyone who works has the right to just and favorable remuneration ensuring for himself and his family an existence worthy of human dignity, and supplemented, if necessary, by other means of social protection".

The ICCPR refers to human dignity three times. It affirms in the two first paragraphs of the Preamble:

> Considering that, in accordance with the principles proclaimed in the Charter of the United Nations, recognition of the inherent dignity and of the equal and inalienable rights of all members of the human family is the foundation of freedom, justice and peace in the world,
> Recognizing that these rights derive from the inherent dignity of the human person,

Article 10.1 affirms: "All persons deprived of their liberty shall be treated with humanity and with respect for the inherent dignity of the human person".

The ICCPR Second Optional Protocol aiming at the abolition of the death penalty (1989) mentions human dignity once (in the Preamble).

The ICESCR refers to human dignity three times, too (in the two first preambular paragraphs and in Article 13.1). The latter reads:

> The States Parties to the present Covenant recognize the right of everyone to education. They agree that education shall be directed to the full development of the human personality and the sense of its dignity, and shall strengthen the respect for human rights and fundamental freedoms.[19]

[19] www.ohchr.org/EN/ProfessionalInterest/Pages/CESCR.aspx.

The ICESCR Optional Protocol (2008) mentions human dignity twice (in the Preamble).

If we look at the other UN instruments that, with the International Bill of Human Rights, form *The Core International Human Rights Treaties*[20], we find the word 'dignity' in around 30 places[21].

In 1986, the UN General Assembly adopted a Resolution on 'Setting international standards in the field of human rights' (A/RES/41/120)[22] to propose "guidelines in developing international instruments in the field of human rights", such as: "Be of fundamental character and derive from the inherent dignity and worth of the human person".

In 1993, the Vienna Declaration and Program of Action underlined (Preamble) "that all human rights derive from the dignity and worth inherent in the human person, and that the human person is the central subject of human rights and fundamental freedoms, and consequently should be the principal beneficiary and should

---

[20] www2.ohchr.org/english/bodies/docs/OHCHR-FactSheet30.pdf; www.ohchr.org/Documents/Publications/newCoreTreatiesen.pdf.

[21] For example:

- International Convention on the Elimination of All Forms of Racial Discrimination (1965)
It recalls, in the Preamble, that "the Charter of the United Nations is based on the principles of the dignity and equality inherent in all human beings" (first paragraph); that "the Universal Declaration of Human Rights proclaims that all human beings are born free and equal in dignity and rights" (second paragraph); and mentions the aim of "securing understanding of and respect for the dignity of the human person" (fifth paragraph).
- Convention on the Elimination of All Forms of Discrimination against Women (1979)
It recalls, in the Preamble, that "the Charter of the United Nations reaffirms faith in fundamental human rights, in the dignity and worth of the human person" (first paragraph); that "all human beings are born free and equal in dignity and rights" (second paragraph); and that "discrimination against women violates the principles of equality of rights and respect for human dignity" (seventh paragraph).
- Convention on the Rights of the Child (1989)
In the Preamble, it recalls that "in accordance with the Charter of the United Nations, recognition of the inherent dignity and of the equal and inalienable rights of all members of the human family is the foundation of freedom, justice and peace in the world" (first paragraph); "that the peoples of the United Nations have, in the Charter, reaffirmed their faith in fundamental human rights and in the dignity and worth of the human person" (second paragraph); affirms that "the child should be fully prepared to live an individual life in society, and brought up in the spirit of the ideals proclaimed in the Charter of the United Nations, and in particular in the spirit of peace, dignity, tolerance, freedom, equality and solidarity" (seventh paragraph); in Article 23.1: "States Parties recognize that a mentally or physically disabled child should enjoy a full and decent life, in conditions which ensure dignity"; in accordance with Article 28.2: "States Parties shall take all appropriate measures to ensure that school discipline is administered in a manner consistent with the child's human dignity"; Article 37.c provides: "Every child deprived of liberty shall be treated with humanity and respect for the inherent dignity of the human person"; Article 39 commands that "recovery and reintegration" of a child victim "shall take place in an environment which fosters the health, self-respect and dignity of the child"; Article 40.1 recognizes "the right of every child alleged as, accused of, or recognized as having infringed the penal law to be treated in a manner consistent with the promotion of the child's sense of dignity and worth".

[22] http://daccess-dds-ny.un.org/doc/RESOLUTION/GEN/NR0/496/28/IMG/NR049628.pdf?OpenElement.

participate actively in the realization of these rights and freedoms". Among other references to the human dignity—related to the biomedical and life sciences, information technology (para. 11), gender-based violence and sexual harassment (para. 18), the treatment of indigenous peoples (para. 20)—it affirmed "that extreme poverty and social exclusion constitute a violation of human dignity" (para. 25), and emphasized "that one of the most atrocious violations against human dignity is the act of torture" (para. 55).

According to the common Article 3 of the 1949 four Geneva Conventions, "the following acts are and shall remain prohibited at any time and in any place whatsoever [...]: outrages upon personal dignity, in particular humiliating and degrading treatment"[23].

Human dignity has become a leitmotif of IHRL, being recalled in categorical and specific legal instruments dealing with slavery, forced labor, freedom from torture, treatment of those incarcerated, forced disappearances, violence against women, children, persons with disabilities, biomedical research, etc. Human dignity is the overarching principle of the emerging International Biomedical Law, in particular. In the Universal Declaration on the Human Genome and Human Rights (UNESCO 1997)[24], dignity appears fifteen times; in the International Declaration on Human Genetic Data (UNESCO 2003)[25], it appears eight times; in the Universal Declaration on Bioethics and Human Rights (UNESCO 2005)[26], it appears twelve times; in the Convention for the Protection of Human Rights and Dignity of the Human Being with regard to the Application of Biology and Medicine: Convention on Human Rights and Biomedicine (Council of Europe 1997)[27], it appears four times. It is also referred to several times in the Additional Protocols to this Convention: three times in the Additional Protocol 'On the Prohibition of Cloning Human Beings' (1998); five times in the Additional Protocol 'On Transplantation of Organs and Tissues of Human Beings' (2002); six times in the Additional Protocol 'Concerning Biomedical Research' (2005); and five times in the Additional Protocol 'Concerning Genetic Testing for Health Purpose' (2008).

At the regional level, human dignity is mentioned in the American Declaration of the Rights and Duties of Man (adopted in 1948, some months before the UDHR)[28];

[23] www.icrc.org/ihl.nsf/CONVPRES?OpenView.

[24] http://portal.unesco.org/en/ev.php-URL_ID=13177&URL_DO=DO_TOPIC&URL_SECTION=201.html.

[25] http://portal.unesco.org/en/ev.php-URL_ID=17720&URL_DO=DO_TOPIC&URL_SECTION=201.html.

[26] http://portal.unesco.org/en/ev.php-URL_ID=31058&URL_DO=DO_TOPIC&URL_SECTION=201.html.

[27] http://conventions.coe.int/Treaty/en/Treaties/html/164.htm.

[28] www.oas.org/dil/American_Declaration_of_the_Rights_and_Duties_of_Man.pdf.

in the ACHR (1969)[29]; in the ACHPR (1981)[30]; and in the Arab Charter on Human Rights (revised 2004)[31].

Surprisingly, the term 'dignity' does not feature in the ECHR[32]. Its most relevant provision relating to human dignity is Article 3 concerning the prohibition of torture and inhuman and degrading treatment and punishment. Notwithstanding, respect for human dignity and freedom is undoubtedly at the heart of the European system of human rights protection, as expressed the European Court of Human Rights in *Pretty v. The United Kingdom* (2002)[33]: "The very essence of the Convention is respect for human dignity and human freedom" (para. 65). Article 26 of the European Social Charter (1996)[34] bears the title: 'The right to dignity at work'. Human dignity features prominently in the EU Charter, as we know.

5.3.2 Constitutional Law

The humanistic meaning of 'dignity' began entering legal texts only during the first half of the twentieth century, when it was incorporated into several European and American Constitutions, such as that of Mexico (1917), Germany (1919), Finland (1919), Portugal (1933), Ireland (1937), and Cuba (1940). In the aftermath of the Second World War, three decades may be pointed out regarding the constitutionalization of human dignity:

- In the 1940s, the new Constitutions of Japan (1947)[35], Italy (1947)[36] and Germany (1949)[37]—the defeated States of the Second World War.
- In the 1970s, the new Constitutions of Greece (1975)[38], Portugal (1976)[39] and Spain (1978)[40]—resulting from the fall of dictatorships[41].

---

[29] www.oas.org/juridico/english/treaties/b-32.html.

[30] www.african-court.org/fileadmin/documents/Sources%20of%20Law/Banjul%20Charta/charte-ang.pdf.

[31] www1.umn.edu/humanrts/instree/loas2005.html?msource=UNWDEC19001andtr=yandauid=3337655.

[32] http://conventions.coe.int/treaty/en/Treaties/Html/005.htm.

[33] http://hudoc.echr.coe.int/sites/eng/pages/search.aspx#{"dmdocnumber":["698325"],"itemid":["001-60448"]}.

[34] http://conventions.coe.int/Treaty/en/Treaties/Html/163.htm.

[35] www.solon.org/Constitutions/Japan/English/english-Constitution.html.

[36] www.senato.it/documenti/repository/istituzione/costituzione_inglese.pdf.

[37] www.gesetze-im-internet.de/bundesrecht/gg/gesamt.pdf.

[38] www.hellenicparliament.gr/UserFiles/f3c70a23-7696-49db-9148-f24dce6a27c8/001-156%20aggliko.pdf.

[39] http://app.parlamento.pt/site_antigo/ingles/cons_leg/Constitution_VII_revisao_definitive.pdf.

[40] www.senado.es/constitu_i/indices/consti_ing.pdf.

[41] For example, the Portuguese Constitution states in its Article 1 (Portuguese Republic): "Portugal is a sovereign Republic, based on the dignity of the human person and the will of the people and committed to building a free, just and solidary society". A President of the Portuguese Constitutional Court noted:

- In the 1990s, the new Constitutions drafted in the Central and Eastern European countries—after the fall of the Berlin Wall (1989).

The *Grundgesetz* (Basic Law) for the Federal Republic of Germany (1949)[42] exerted a strong influence over the new Constitutions of the 1970s and the 1990s, and not only on the European continent. The *Verfassung des Deutschen Reiches* (Constitution of the German Empire) of 28 March 1849 (*Frankfurter Reichsverfassung* or *Paulskirchen-Verfassung*), which resulted from the first bourgeois revolution in Germany, mentioned the "Emperor's dignity" (*Würde des Reichsoberhauptes*)[43]. However, during its drafting, there were proposals aiming at the incorporation of a reference to human dignity For example (cit. in Bendor and Sachs 2011, p. 3):

> Society has to guarantee to everyone a life according to the dignity and the nature of man, therefore security of the person, freedom, resistance against oppression, the development of his talents and abilities, the means to easily acquire a competency, which ensures not only the necessities of life, but also a standing in society.
> A free people even in dealing with the criminal has to respect his human dignity.

The *Paulskirchen-Verfassung* never came into force, however.

The *Verfassung des Deutschen Reiches* of 11 August 1919 (*Weimarer Reichsverfassung*)[44]—the Weimar Constitution—the Second Part of which was dedicated to the "Basic rights and obligations of the Germans" (Articles 109–165), stated (Article 151): "The economy has to be organized based on the principles of justice, with the goal of achieving life in dignity for everyone [*Gewährleistung eines menschenwürdigen Daseins*]. Within these limits the economic liberty of the individual is to be secured"[45]. The respect for human dignity was provided in the Constitutions of three German *Bundesländer* (Federal States) before adoption of the *Bundesverfaßung* (Federal Constitution): Bavaria (1946), Hessen (1946) and Bremen (1947).

The *Grundgesetz* (GG) was prepared by a Constitutional Convention (*Verfassungskonvent*), a meeting of experts on Constitutional Law from eleven States of the Western German Zone and West Berlin in the island of *Herrenchiemsee*, in *Chiemsee* (a Bavarian lake), from 10 to 23 August 1948, and was drafted by the Parliamentary Council (*Parlamentarischer Rat*). It consecrates "Basic Rights" in Part I (Articles 1–19). Article 1.1 states: "The dignity of the human being is inviolable"

> As its position in the opening article of the Constitution suggests, this emphatic and categorical statement is one of great importance and significance. Its purpose and effect is clearly to make sure that the Portuguese Constitution is unequivocally stamped with this profoundly humanist and person-centred interpretation of the State—the State exists because of us rather than we because of the State—that characterises Western cultural tradition and its democratic constitutionalism. (in European Commission for Democracy through Law 1998, I.a).

[42] Official translation: www.btg-bestellservice.de/pdf/80201000.pdf.

[43] www.documentarchiv.de/nzjh/verfdr1848.htm.

[44] www.documentarchiv.de/wr/wrv.html.

[45] www.zum.de/psm/weimar/weimar_vve.php#Fifth Chapter: The Economy.

(*Die Würde des Menschen ist unantastbar*)[46]. According to Article 79.3: "Amendments to this Basic Law affecting the division of the Federation into *Länder*, their participation on principle in the legislative process, or the principles laid down in Articles 1 and 20 shall be inadmissible". As Brun-Otto Bryde (2005), former Judge of the German Federal Constitutional Court, notes:

> When German politicians drafted the Basic Law in 1949, their main inspiration was a negative one. They were not codifying the ideas of a successful revolution, but instead were reacting to the experience of totalitarian dictatorship.
> In reaction to the horrors of Nazi Germany, they based the new constitution on the principle of human dignity and the recognition of human rights, recognized in Article 1. In reaction to the abuse of state power, they were careful in drafting judicial safeguards against the abuse of state power, most notably creating an elaborate multi-tiered system of judicial review with a powerful Constitutional Court at the apex. [...]
> The drafters of the Basic Law reacted not only against dictatorship but also against what were seen to be the weaknesses of the Weimar Constitution. In addition to a new institutional arrangement, the position of fundamental rights was changed. In clear opposition to the most common reading of the Weimar Constitution, Article 1(3) states that '[t]he following fundamental rights shall bind the legislature, the executive, and the judiciary as directly enforceable law'. (p. 194)[47]

Franz J. Wetz (1998) underlined that "human dignity represents the highest legal value of our [German] Constitution and its supreme principle, with a value superior to all decisions of democratic majorities" (p. 11). Arthur Chaskalson, former President of the Constitutional Court of South Africa, remarked:

> Nowhere is the connection between human rights and dignity clearer than in German law. [...] The basic rights set out in the German constitution are preceded by a statement that 'the dignity of man shall be inviolable'. The enumerated rights that follow are interpreted and applied by the German Federal Constitutional Court in the context of the foundational value of dignity and the decisions of the German courts provide a prodigious jurisprudence of dignity.[48]

In Israel, according to the Proclamation of Independence, a Constituent Assembly should have prepared a Constitution by 1 October 1948, but the country does not have yet a formal written Constitution, because of lack of consensus between secular and religious political sides. Notwithstanding, there is a material Constitution composed of basic laws and other laws, in particular the two following ones:

---

[46] After an intense debate, it was agreed to avoid any religious or philosophical reference (God or Natural Law) to the sources of human dignity, although the influence of the Kantian Philosophy and of the Catholic doctrine seems indisputable.

[47] Henk Botha (2009) comments: "The prominence accorded to human dignity was a direct response to the terrors of National Socialism. The drafters of the Basic Law wished to stress that the dignity of the human person and not the "dignity of the state"—a notion which was central to National-Socialist attacks on the Weimar Constitution of 1919—was the foundation of the new constitutional order" (p. 178).

[48] www.lrc.org.za/papers/419-the-third-bram-fischer-memorial-lecture-human-dignity-as-a-foundational-value-of-our-constitutional-order.

- Basic Law: Human Dignity and Liberty (1992)[49] that states: "The purpose of this Basic Law is to protect human dignity and liberty, in order to establish in a Basic Law the values of the State of Israel as a Jewish and democratic state".
- Basic Law: Freedom of Occupation (1994)[50] that states as basic principles: "Fundamental human rights in Israel are founded upon the recognition of the value of the human being, the sanctity of human life, and the principle that all persons are free; these rights shall be upheld in the spirit of the principles set forth in the Declaration of the Establishment of the State of Israel".

These two pieces "instigated a 'constitutional revolution' in the protection of human rights in Israel", as Ariel Bendor and Michael Sachs (2011) highlighted, but, "in contrast with Germany, the right for human dignity, as are all other constitutional rights anchored in the Basic Laws, is not absolute but relative", not having any superior formal status over other rights (p. 16, 21). However, it serves as a guiding principle of interpretation of the Basic Laws, because human dignity is the source of human rights in general.

Other European countries included human dignity in their Constitutions. For instance, Belgium did it through a constitutional revision on 31 January 1994. In France, it was the Constitutional Council that, by its Decision n° 94-343/344 DC of 27 July 1994 regarding the constitutionality of the *Loi relative au respect du corps humain et loi relative au don et à l'utilisation des éléments et produits du corps humain, à l'assistance médicale à la procréation et au diagnostic prenatal*[51], said, referring to the first sentence in the Preamble to the 1946 Constitution, that "safeguarding human dignity against any form of enslavement and degradation is a principle with constitutional force"[52]. At present, all European Constitutions refer to human dignity.

In other continents, human dignity is also incorporated in many Constitutions[53], from Brazil (1988), Colombia (1991), to Namibia (1990), Ethiopia (1994), Madagascar (1998) and Afghanistan (2003). For example, the post-apartheid Constitution of the Republic of South Africa (1996)[54] provides in its Sect. 10 (Human dignity): "Everyone has inherent dignity and the right to have their dignity respected and pro-

---

[49] www.knesset.gov.il/laws/special/eng/basic3_eng.htm.

[50] www.knesset.gov.il/laws/special/eng/basic4_eng.htm.

[51] Respect for Human Body Act and Donation and Use of Parts and Products of the Human Body, Medically Assisted Reproduction and Prenatal Diagnosis Act.

(www.conseil-constitutionnel.fr/conseil-constitutionnel/root/bank/download/94343_344DCa94343dc.pdf).

[52] www.conseil-constitutionnel.fr/conseil-constitutionnel/francais/les-decisions/acces-par-date/decisions-depuis-1959/1994/94-343/344-dc/decision-n-94-343-344-dc-du-27-juillet-1994.10566.html.

Since the same year, Article 16 of the Civil Code provides the statement: "Legislation ensures the primacy of the person, prohibits any infringement of the latter's dignity and safeguards the respect of the human being from the outset of life" (http://195.83.177.9/upl/pdf/code_22.pdf).

[53] www.loc.gov/law/help/guide/nations.php.

[54] www.info.gov.za/documents/constitution/1996/index.htm.

tected". Other constitutional provisions refer to human dignity. For instance, Sect. 1.a states that the Republic of South Africa is "founded on the following values: Human dignity, the achievement of equality and the advancements of human rights and freedoms". Chaskalson comments: "The affirmation of [inherent] human dignity as a foundational value of the constitutional order places our legal order firmly in line with the development of constitutionalism in the aftermath of the second world war"[55].

The term 'dignity' does not figure in the USA Federal Constitution. Nevertheless, Leslie Henry (2011) notices: "For some commentators, dignity is nothing less than 'the premier value underlying the last 2 centuries of moral and political thought', an essential 'basis of human rights', and one of 'the great political values that define our constitutional morality'" (p. 4).

Following Botha (2009):

> 'Human dignity' has become an integral part of the vocabulary of comparative constitutionalism. Not only is the right to dignity proclaimed in national constitutions and international human rights instruments, but it is asserted with increasing frequency that dignity is the basis of all human rights and should be used as a guide to their interpretation. Dignity is invoked as a supreme value, an interpretive *Leitmotiv*, a basis for the limitation of rights and freedoms, and a guide to the principled resolution of constitutional value conflicts. In the view of some authors, dignity provides judicial review with a secure and legitimate basis. Consider, for instance, the claim made by a German law professor that dignity is the only absolute value in a world of relative values—a fixed star which provides orientation amidst life's uncertainties. [...] [H]uman dignity is central to the constitutions of many countries which have, over the past 60 years, emerged from dictatorship, oppression, totalitarianism, fascism, colonialism and discrimination. (p. 171, 172)

One may conclude, with Francis Delpérée, referring to the Belgian Constitution: "In short, human dignity is placed on a pedestal" (in European Commission for Democracy through Law 1998, II). It became the *alpha and omega* of Constitutional Law.

Stéphanie Hennette-Vauchez (2008) refers to "Western law's recently massive infatuation with the HDP", its "apotheosis in Western legal orders". She quotes Whitman, according to whom, "if we were looking for one phrase to capture the last fifty years of European legal history [...] we might call it the high era of 'dignity'". And highlights "the wideness of its consecration" at national, regional and international levels (p. 2, 3).

In countries whose Constitutions do not mention the HDP explicitly (or those who have no written Constitution), constitutional jurisprudence often derived it from constitutional or other fundamental provisions for many purposes.

5.4 Case Law

As the Report of the CHR third session, in May-June 1948, at Lake Success (E/800) reads, it "expressed the view that court decisions are fully as important as provisions of constitutions, ordinary laws and international treaties" (para. 21). Juris-

[55] www.lrc.org.za/papers/419-the-third-bram-fischer-memorial-lecture-human-dignity-as-a-foundational-value-of-our-constitutional-order.

prudence is even more important in Common Law countries. Steiner et al. (2008) remarked that "courts play a vital role in resolving human rights controversies and developing human rights norms, through constitutional and other bodies of law. [...] A whole field of comparative constitutional law that is worldwide in scope is emerging" (p. vii).

Here we provide an overview of international and constitutional Case Law regarding human dignity and rights.

According to McCrudden (2008), so far the ICJ "has not used the concept of human dignity in the human rights context" (p. 682). However, the Statutes of *ad hoc* International Criminal Courts and, in particular, the ICC Statute (1998)[56] refer to it. Article 8.2.a.ii of the latter (entitled: "Other serious violations of the laws and customs applicable in international armed conflict") includes: "Committing outrages upon personal dignity, in particular humiliating and degrading treatment" (Article 8.2.b.xxi).

Within the framework of the ECHR, human dignity has been invoked by its jurisdictional organs (the European Court and the former European Commission) in cases related to torture, the rights of prisoners, sexual orientation, etc. The European Court of Human Rights first referred to human dignity in its decision on *Tyrer v. The United Kingdom* (Application n° 5856/72, Judgment on 25 April 1978)[57], in which corporal punishment, administered as part of a judicial sentence, was held to be contrary to the European Convention Article 3.

The European Court of Justice mentioned human dignity several times, but only in 2001 acknowledged it as an objective principle of the Community Law, in its decision regarding Directive 98/44/EC of 6 July 1996 of the European Parliament and of the Council on the legal protection of biotechnological inventions. The Court said: "It is for the Court of Justice, in its review of the compatibility of acts of the institutions with the general principles of Community Law, to ensure that the fundamental right to human dignity and integrity is observed" (as cit. in EU Network of Independent Experts on Fundamental Rights 2006, p. 24)[58].

At the national level, the HDP has been broadly used by Constitutional and other similar Courts. Next is quoted the Case Law principally from the German Federal Constitutional Court, the Supreme Court of Israel, the USA Supreme Court, the Constitutional Court of South Africa, the Supreme Court of India, as well as of the European Court of Human Rights and the Inter-American Court of Human Rights.

Botha (2009) observed: "The scope and sophistication of the dignity jurisprudence of German courts—in particular the Federal Constitutional Court—and the depth of academic comment by German constitutional law scholars on the concept

---

[56] http://untreaty.un.org/cod/icc/statute/romefra.htm.

[57] http://cmiskp.echr.coe.int/tkp197/view.asp?action=htmlanddocumentId=695464andportal=hbkmandsource=externalbydocnumberandtable=F69A27FD8FB86142BF01C1166DEA398649.

[58] See also *Netherlands v. European Parliament and Council* (Case C-377/98, decision on 9 October 2001).
(http://eur-lex.europa.eu/smartapi/cgi/sga_doc?smartapi!celexplus!prod!CELEXnumdocandnumdoc=61998J0377andlg=EN)

and uses of dignity are unparalleled in any other country" (p. 173). This is due to the Judgment *BVerfGE 7, 198—Lüth* (1958)[59], a case that, in Bryde's (2005) opinion, "transformed the German legal system" (p. 198). The Court said:

> 1. Basic rights are primarily to protect the citizen against the state, but as enacted in the Constitution (GG) they also incorporate an objective scale of values which applies, as a matter of constitutional law, throughout the entire legal system.
> [...]
> 1. There is no doubt that the main purpose of basic rights is to protect the individual's sphere of freedom against encroachment by public power: they are the citizen's bulwark against the state. This emerges from both their development as a matter of intellectual history and their adoption into the constitutions of the various states as a matter of political history: it is true also of the basic rights in the Basic Law, which emphasizes the priority of human dignity against the power of the state by placing the section on basic rights at its head and by providing that the constitutional complaint (Verfassungsbeschwerde), the special legal device for vindicating these rights, lies only in respect of acts of the public power. But far from being a value-free system [...] the Constitution erects an objective system of values in its section on basic rights, and thus expresses and reinforces the validity of the basic rights [...]. This system of values, centring on the freedom of the human being to develop in society, must apply as a constitutional axiom throughout the whole legal system: it must direct and inform legislation, administration, and judicial decision. It naturally influences private law as well; no rule of private law may conflict with it, and all such rules must be construed in accordance with its spirit.

The German Federal Constitutional Court referred to human dignity in dozens of judgments. For example, in *VerfGE 12, 45, 1960* (*Prüfung des § 25 des Wehrpflichtgesetzes vom 21. Juli 1956 (BGBl. I S. 651)—Vorlage des Schleswig-Holsteinischen Verwaltungsgerichts*)[60]—a case concerning consciencious objection to military service—the Court said: "The Constitution regards the free human personality and its dignity as the highest value" (para. 26). In *BVerfGE 6, 32, 1957* (*Wilhelm E., Oberstadtdirektors i.R., gegen das Urteil des Bundesverwaltungsgerichts*)[61]—a case concerning the renovation of the passport of a politician—it said:

> 32. ... The Basic Law [...] erected a value-oriented order that limits public authority. This order guarantees the independence, self-determination, and dignity of man within the political community. [...] The highest principles of this order of values are protected against constitutional change. [...] Laws are not constitutional merely because they have been passed in conformity with procedural provisions. [...] They must be substantively compatible with the highest fundamental values of a free and democratic order as a constitutional order of values, and must also conform to unwritten fundamental constitutional principles as well as the fundamental decisions of the Basic Law, in particular the principles of the Rule of Law and the Social Welfare State [Grundsatz der Rechtsstaatlichkeit und dem Sozialstaatsprinzip].

In *BVerfGE 30, 173, 1971*[62]—a case concerning a satirical novel (*Mephisto*) describing the career of an actor during the Nazi regime and the infringement on

---

[59] www.verfassungsbeschwerde.info/L_th_Urteil_15_01_1958.pdf.

Translation:www.utexas.edu/law/academics/centers/transnational/work_new/german/case.php?i=1477.

[60] www.servat.unibe.ch/dfr/bv012045.html.

[61] www.servat.unibe.ch/dfr/bv006032.html.

[62] www.iuscomp.org/gla/judgments/tgcm/v710224.htm.

the publisher's right to freedom of art and speech—the Court repeated that human dignity is "the supreme and controlling value of the whole system of basic rights" (para. 5). In *BVerfGE 45, 187, 1977 (Lebenslange Freiheitsstrafe)*[63]—a case concerning a sentence to lifelong imprisonment—it affirmed: "Respect and protection of human dignity are among the constitutional principles of the Basic Law. The free human personality and her dignity represent the highest legal values within the constitutional order. [...] The state in all its forms has the duty to respect and to protect the dignity of human beings" (para. 143).

In Israel, the 'Basic Law: Human Dignity and Liberty' (1992) does not include rights such as freedom of speech, freedom of religion and conscience, right to equality, let alone rights such as the right to health and the right to education. The *Knesset* (Parliament) did not reach a wide consensus on a full catalogue of human rights. Nevertheless, the Israel Supreme Court used the right to dignity to expand the number of human rights therein recognized.

In USA, Henry (2011) concluded from "the first empirical study of the Supreme Court opinions that invoke dignity":

> Few words play a more central role in modern constitutional law without appearing in the Constitution than dignity. [...]
> The Supreme Court has invoked the term in connection with the First, Fourth, Fifth, Sixth, Eighth, Ninth, Eleventh, Fourteenth, and Fifteenth Amendments.
> [...]
> In the last 220 years, Supreme Court Justices have invoked the term in more than nine hundred opinions. Justices issued nearly half of these opinions after 1946, when the phrase 'human dignity' first appeared in a Supreme Court opinion, with more than one hundred opinions authored in the last twenty years alone. (p. 1, 4, 6, 9)

The Constitutional Court of South Africa said in *The State v. T Makwanyane and M Mchunu (CCT3/94) [1995] ZACC 3; 1995 (6) BCLR 665; 1995 (3) SA 391; [1996] 2 CHRLD 164; 1995 (2) SACR 1 (6 June 1995)*[64], a case concerning a death sentence for two murders:

> [144] The rights to life and dignity are the most important of all human rights, and the source of all other personal rights in Chapter Three. By committing ourselves to a society founded on the recognition of human rights we are required to value these two rights above all others. [...]
> [329] Respect for the dignity of all human beings is particularly important in South Africa. For apartheid was a denial of a common humanity. Black people were refused respect and dignity and thereby the dignity of all South Africans was diminished. The new constitution rejects this past and affirms the equal worth of all South Africans. Thus recognition and protection of human dignity is the touchstone of the new political order and is fundamental to the new constitution.

Rao (2011) distinguishes "Three Concepts of Dignity in Constitutional Law":

> First, in its most universal and open sense, dignity focuses on the inherent worth of each individual. Such dignity exists merely by virtue of a person's humanity and does not depend on intelligence, morality, or social status. [...]

---

63 www.servat.unibe.ch/dfr/bv045187.html, and: www.hrcr.org/safrica/dignity/45bverfge187.ht.

64 www.saflii.org/za/cases/ZACC/1995/3.pdf.

> Second, dignity can express and serve as the grounds for enforcing various substantive values. Unlike intrinsic dignity, substantive forms of dignity require living in a certain way. [...] Accordingly, such dignity may take a number of different forms. For example, a government policy may enforce a particular conception of dignity on individuals, a conception that accords with the community's view of what is dignified. Dignity in this sense depends on specific ideals of appropriateness and deems a person worthy or dignified to the extent that he conforms to such ideals. [...] Positive or substantive conceptions of dignity are also associated with social-welfare rights or protection by the state from poverty and violence. In this understanding, dignity demands that the government provide the basic conditions of wellbeing. [...]
>
> Finally, constitutional courts often associate dignity with recognition and respect. This dignity is rooted in a conception of the self as constituted by the broader community—a person's identity and worth depend on his relationship to society. Accordingly, respect for a person's dignity requires recognizing and validating individuals in their particularity. [...] These three concepts of dignity reflect different ways of thinking about what constitutes dignity as a legal matter. But the boundaries between these types of dignity are not impermeable, and constitutional courts will often use 'dignity' in overlapping ways. (p. 187, 189)

Botha (2009) summarizes:

> Reliance on human dignity serves a number of functions. In the first place, it often signals a break with a history of oppression, totalitarianism, colonialism and discrimination, and the wish to establish a new national or supranational order based on respect for human rights. Secondly, by invoking the inherent dignity and worth of the human person, the architects of a constitutional order or supranational human rights regime appeal to a higher law or transnational legal consensus, and thus seek to ground the protection of human rights in something more enduring than public opinion, which is seen as constantly shifting and sometimes fickle. Thirdly, in addition to the symbolic and foundational functions referred to above, constitutional appeals to human dignity have a legal significance which extends beyond the merely aspirational. Dignity is often entrenched as an individual right. It also has the status of an objective legal norm which serves as a guideline to the interpretation of ordinary law. Finally, to the extent that dignity is perceived to be at the centre of the constitutional value order and because dignity is closely related to other rights and values, such as freedom, equality and social solidarity, it is seen as a mechanism for the resolution of or mediation between conflicting constitutional values. Accordingly, dignity sometimes plays an important role in determining the proper boundaries of constitutionally protected rights and interests and in the balancing of conflicting interests. (p. 177)

We are now giving some examples of how the HDP was applied in cases concerning freedom of speech, privacy, sexuality, abortion, death penalty, treatment of prisoners, corporal punishment, dignity of life, dignity in death.

5.4.1 Dignity and Freedom of Speech

Concerning the freedom of speech, the above quoted judgment *BVerfGE 7, 198—Lüth* (1958) by the German Federal Constitutional Court was considered by Bryde (2005) to be "perhaps the most important case in the court's jurisprudence". Bryde summarized and commented:

> Lüth, director of the press office of the city-state of Hamburg and a victim of the Nazis, criticized as a private citizen the decision of the organizers of German Film Week in 1951 for including in their program a film by Veit Harlan, who had directed violently anti-Semitic films during the Third Reich. Lüth called for a boycott of Harlan's films by cinema owners and the public. Under German private law (§ 826 of the Civil Code-BGB), calling for a boycott of a business can be considered an actionable unethical infringement of commercial interests. Therefore the distributors of Harlan's films got an injunction against Lüth in the private law courts. Against these decisions Lüth brought a constitutional complaint to the new Federal Constitutional Court.
> The court had to chart unknown territory. Fundamental rights at that time were considered to have only the function to defend citizens against the state. Therefore it was unclear what role they could play in a conflict between private citizens. To solve this question, the Constitutional Court drew on Rudolf Smend's theory of the constitution as a system of values.
> [...]
> In this way the case could be solved: when interpreting what constitutes 'unethical behavior' in a commercial context in § 826 of the Civil Code, the civil courts should have taken the value of free speech, guaranteed in Article 5 of the Basic Law, as a 'guideline and inspiration'. Had they done so, they could not have found Lüth's behavior to be unethical. Failing to take the constitution into proper account, the civil law courts had violated Lüth's fundamental rights and therefore his constitutional complaint was successful.
> [...]
> By decreeing that all fields of law had to be interpreted in line with the constitution, and, more importantly, by assuming judicial control over this process, the Constitutional Court transformed the German legal system. (p. 197, 198)

The USA Supreme Court said in *Cohen v. California* (403 U.S. 15, 1971)[65], a case concerning the wearing of a jacket bearing the words 'Fuck the Draft' in a corridor of the Los Angeles Courthouse:

> The constitutional right of free expression is powerful medicine in a society as diverse and populous as ours. It is designed and intended to remove governmental restraints from the arena of public discussion, putting the decision as to what views shall be voiced largely into the hands of each of us, in the hope that use of such freedom will ultimately produce a more capable citizenry and more perfect polity and in the belief that no other approach would comport with the premise of individual dignity and choice upon which our political system rests.

The Court said in *Texas v. Johnson* (491 U.S. 397, 1989)[66], a case concerning the burning of a USA flag:

> We can imagine no more appropriate response to burning a flag than waving one's own, no better way to counter a flag burner's message than by saluting the flag that burns, no surer means of preserving the dignity even of the flag that burned than by—as one witness here did—according its remains a respectful burial. We do not consecrate the flag by punishing its desecration, for in doing so we dilute the freedom that this cherished emblem represents.

[65] http://supreme.justia.com/us/403/15/case.html.

[66] http://supreme.justia.com/us/491/397/case.html.

5.4.2 Dignity and Privacy

The German Federal Constitutional Court applied the HDP, together with the general right of autonomy and self-determination, for example, to protect professional confidential information in *BVerfGE 33, 367, 19 July 1972—Zeugnisverweigerungsrecht für Sozialarbeiter* (Professional Secret); to restrict State power in obtaining information about the personal data of citizens by way of the census in *BVerfGE 65, 1—Volkszählung, 15 December 1983* (Census Act); to condemn acoustic surveillance in the home in *1 BvR 2378/98, 1 BvR 1084/99, 3 March 2004—Akustische Wohnraumüberwachung* (Acoustic Surveillance)[67]. In the latter case, the Court said:

> [116] (1) This court has frequently expressed the view that it is inconsistent with the dignity of the individual for the state to treat him as an object.
> [...]
> [119] (2) ... The inviolability of the home is closely connected with the dignity of the individual and so is immediately related to the constitutional requirement that the exclusively private 'highly personal' sphere of a person's life be unconditionally safeguarded. When a person is at home, his right to be let alone must be especially assured.
> [120] A person cannot develop his personality unless he is able to express his inmost sentiments and feelings, his opinions, reflections and experiences—including non-verbal manifestations of emotions and sexuality—free from any fear that state agencies may be listening in. [...] The home is the 'last refuge' for the protection of human dignity. [...]

The German conception of a general right of personhood (*allgemeine Persönlichkeitsrecht*) relates to undefined freedoms, as the Constitutional Court said in *BVerfGE 54, 148 (Eppler 1980)*[68], a case concerning a politician's claim that his person had been offended: "Their function is, in the sense of the supreme constitutional principle of 'human dignity' (Art. 1, par.1 of the GG), to preserve the narrow personal life sphere and the conservation of its fundamental conditions, which are not encompassed by traditional concrete guarantees of freedom" (para. 13).

The USA Supreme Court, in *Rochin v. California* (342 U.S. 165, 1952)[69]—a case concerning forcing the petitioner, in a hospital, to vomit two capsules which were found to contain morphine, as evidence of his selling narcotics—qualified the case as "so brutal and so offensive to human dignity", and said that:

> ... we are compelled to conclude that the proceedings by which this conviction was obtained do more than offend some fastidious squeamishness or private sentimentalism about combatting crime too energetically. This is conduct that shocks the conscience. Illegally breaking into the privacy of the petitioner, the struggle to open his mouth and remove what was there, the forcible extraction of his stomach's contents—this course of proceeding by agents of government to obtain evidence is bound to offend even hardened sensibilities. They are methods too close to the rack and the screw to permit of constitutional differentiation. [...] Use of involuntary verbal confessions in State criminal trials is constitutionally obnoxious not only because of their unreliability. They are inadmissible under the Due Process Clause even though statements contained in them may be independently established as true. Coerced confessions offend the community's sense of fair play and decency. So here, to sanction the brutal conduct which, naturally enough, was condemned by the court whose

---

[67] www.utexas.edu/law/academics/centers/transnational/work_new/german/case.php?id=658.

[68] www.servat.unibe.ch/dfr/bv054148.html.

[69] http://supreme.justia.com/us/342/165/.

> judgment is before us would be to afford brutality the cloak of law. Nothing would be more calculated to discredit law, and thereby to brutalize the temper of a society.

In *Winston v. Lee* (470 U.S. 753, 1985)[70]—a case concerning an order directing a respondent to undergo a surgery to remove a bullet lodged under his left collarbone, asserting that the bullet would provide evidence of his being guilty or innocent of having wounded by gunshot a shopkeeper, during an attempted robbery, who apparently wounded the assailant—the Court affirmed:

> When conducted with the consent of the patient, surgery requiring general anesthesia is not necessarily demeaning or intrusive. In such a case, the surgeon is carrying out the patient's own will concerning the patient's body, and the patient's right to privacy is therefore preserved. [...]
> In weighing the various factors in this case, we therefore reach the same conclusion as the courts below. The operation sought will intrude substantially on respondent's protected interests. The medical risks of the operation, although apparently not extremely severe, are a subject of considerable dispute; the very uncertainty militates against finding the operation to be 'reasonable'. In addition, the intrusion on respondent's privacy interests entailed by the operation can only be characterized as severe. [...]
> The Fourth Amendment is a vital safeguard of the right of the citizen to be free from unreasonable governmental intrusions into any area in which he has a reasonable expectation of privacy.

The same Court said in *Hudson v. Michigan* (547 U.S. 586, 2006)[71]—a case concerning the Detroit police entering the petitioner's home for executing a search warrant for narcotics and weapons, in violation of the Fourth Amendment—that:

> ... the knock-and-announce rule protects those elements of privacy and dignity that can be destroyed by a sudden entrance. It gives residents the 'opportunity to prepare themselves for' the entry of the police. *Richards*, 520 U. S., at 393, n. 5. 'The brief interlude between announcement and entry with a warrant may be the opportunity that an individual has to pull on clothes or get out of bed.' *Ibid*. In other words, it assures the opportunity to collect oneself before answering the door.

The European Court of Human Rights, as noted Judge Higgins, President of the ICJ, "has developed the concept of self-determination in the sense of the family and the individual. Its case law has emphasized that the principle of self-determination forms the basis of the guarantees in Article 8 of the European Convention (Right to respect for private and family life)"[72].

5.4.3 *Dignity and Sexuality*

The USA Supreme Court said in *Lawrence et al. v. Texas* (539 U.S. 558, 2003)[73], a case concerning the validity of a Texas statute making homosexuality a crime:

> Liberty protects the person from unwarranted government intrusions into a dwelling or other private places. [...] Liberty presumes an autonomy of self that includes freedom of

[70] http://supreme.justia.com/us/470/753/case.html.

[71] http://supreme.justia.com/us/new-cases/04-1360.pdf.

[72] www.echr.coe.int/NR/rdonlyres/38D1E6A5-DE24-42BD-BC3D-45CCCC8A7F8A/0/30012009PresidentHigginsHearing_eng_.pdf.

[73] http://supreme.justia.com/us/539/558/case.html.

> thought, belief, expression, and certain intimate conduct. The instant case involves liberty of the person both in its spatial and in its more transcendent dimensions. [...]
> The liberty protected by the Constitution allows homosexual persons the right to choose to enter upon relationships in the confines of their homes and their own private lives and still retain their dignity as free persons. [...]
> The petitioners are entitled to respect for their private lives. The State cannot demean their existence or control their destiny by making their private sexual conduct a crime. [...]
> When homosexual conduct is made criminal by the law of the State, that declaration in and of itself is an invitation to subject homosexual persons to discrimination both in the public and in the private spheres.

The Constitutional Court of South Africa said in *National Coalition for Gay and Lesbian Equality and Another v Minister of Justice and Others (CCT11/98) [1998] ZACC 15; 1999 (1) SA 6; 1998 (12) BCLR 1517 (9 October 1998)*[74], a case also concerning homosexuality:

> [32] Privacy recognizes that we all have a right to a sphere of private intimacy and autonomy which allows us to establish and nurture human relationships without interference from the outside community. The way in which we give expression to our sexuality is at the core of this area of private intimacy. If, in expressing our sexuality, we act consensually and without harming one another, invasion of that precinct will be a breach of our privacy. Our society has a poor record of seeking to regulate the sexual expression of South Africans. In some cases, as in this one, the reason for the regulation was discriminatory; our law, for example, outlawed sexual relationships among people of different races. [...]
> [117] ... The expression of sexuality requires a partner, real or imagined. It is not for the state to choose or to arrange the choice of partner, but for the partners to choose themselves.

The Court said in *Minister of Home Affairs and Another v Fourie and Another (CCT 60/04) [2005] ZACC 19; 2006 (3) BCLR 355 (CC); 2006 (1) SA 524 (CC) (1 December 2005)*[75] and in *Lesbian and Gay Equality Project and Eighteen Others v Minister of Home Affairs (CCT 10/05) [2005] ZACC 20; 2006 (3) BCLR 355 (CC); 2006 (1) SA 524 (CC) (1 December 2005)*[76], two cases concerning the official recognition and registration of a homosexual relationship:

> [48] The way the words dignity, equality and privacy later came to be interpreted by this Court showed that they in fact turned out to be central to the way in which the exclusion of same-sex couples from marriage came to be evaluated. In a long line of cases, most of which were concerned with persons unable to get married because of their sexual orientation, this Court highlighted the significance for our equality jurisprudence of the concepts and values of human dignity, equality and freedom.

[74] www.saflii.org/za/cases/ZACC/1998/15.pdf.

[75] www.saflii.org/za/cases/ZACC/2005/19.pdf.

[76] www.saflii.org/za/cases/ZACC/2005/20.pdf.

5.4.4 Dignity and Abortion

The European Court of Human Rights, sitting as Grand Chamber[77], said in *Vo v. France (Application no. 53924/00, Judgment on 8 July 2004)*[78], a case concerning the conduct of a doctor who was found responsible for the death of a child *in utero*:

> 75. Unlike Article 4 of the American Convention on Human Rights, which provides that the right to life must be protected 'in general, from the moment of conception', Article 2 of the Convention is silent as to the temporal limitations of the right to life and, in particular, does not define 'everyone' ('toute personne') whose 'life' is protected by the Convention. The Court has yet to determine the issue of the 'beginning' of 'everyone's right to life' within the meaning of this provision and whether the unborn child has such a right. [...]
> 82. ... It follows that the issue of when the right to life begins comes within the margin of appreciation which the Court generally considers that States should enjoy in this sphere [...].
> 84. At European level, the Court observes that there is no consensus on the nature and status of the embryo and/or fetus (see paragraphs 39–40 above), although they are beginning to receive some protection in the light of scientific progress and the potential consequences of research into genetic engineering, medically assisted procreation or embryo experimentation. At best, it may be regarded as common ground between States that the embryo/fetus belongs to the human race. The potentiality of that being and its capacity to become a person [...] require protection in the name of human dignity, without making it a 'person' with the 'right to life' for the purposes of Article 2. [...]
> 85. Having regard to the foregoing, the Court is convinced that it is neither desirable, nor even possible as matters stand, to answer in the abstract the question whether the unborn child is a person for the purposes of Article 2 of the Convention ('personne' in the French text). [...]

The Court, sitting as Grand Chamber again, said in *Evans v. the United Kingdom (Application 6339/05, Judgment of 10 April 2007)*[79], a case concerning the legal

---

[77] As explains a Council of Europe document:

> A Chamber is composed of the President of the Section to which the case was assigned, the 'national judge' (the judge elected in respect of the State against which the application was lodged) and five other judges designated by the Section President in rotation.
> The Grand Chamber is comprised of the Court's President and Vice-Presidents, the Section Presidents and the national judge, together with other judges selected by drawing of lots. When it hears a case on referral, it does not include any judges who previously sat in the Chamber that first examined the case.
> [...]
> The initiation of proceedings before the Grand Chamber takes two different forms: referral [of the parties] and relinquishment [by a Chamber].
> (www.echr.coe.int/NR/rdonlyres/5C53ADA4-80F8-42CB-B8BD-CBBB781F42C8/0/ENG_50questions_Web.pdf).

[78] http://cmiskp.echr.coe.int/tkp197/view.asp?item=1andportal=hbkmandaction=htmlandhighlight=vo.%20-%7C%20v%20-%7C%20franceandsessionid=83237564andskin=hudoc-en.

[79] http://cmiskp.echr.coe.int/tkp197/view.asp?item=2andportal=hbkmandaction=htmlandhighlight=Evans%20-%7C%20v.%20-%7C%20United%20-%7C%20Kingdomandsessionid=83237209andskin=hudoc-en.

possibility of a woman's former partner to withdraw his consent to the storage and use by her of embryos created jointly by them:

> 56. The Grand Chamber, for the reasons given by the Chamber, finds that the embryos created by the applicant and J. do not have a right to life within the meaning of Article 2 of the Convention, and that there has not, therefore, been a violation of that provision.
> [...]
> 59. Given that there was no international or European consensus with regard to the regulation of IVF [in vitro fertilization] treatment, the use of embryos created by such treatment, or the point at which consent to the use of genetic material provided as part of IVF treatment might be withdrawn, and since the use of IVF treatment gave rise to sensitive moral and ethical issues against a background of fast-moving medical and scientific developments, the margin of appreciation to be afforded to the respondent State must be a wide one.

The German Federal Constitutional Court said in *BVerfGE 39, 1, 1975 (Schwangerschaftsabbruch I)*[80], a case concerning the interruption of pregnancy (*First Abortion Case*): "The protection of life of the child of the pregnant mother takes precedence as a matter of principle for the entire duration of the pregnancy over the right of the pregnant woman to self-determination and may not be placed in question for any particular time" (para. 3)[81].

The USA Supreme Court said in *Thornburgh v. Am. Coll. of Obstetricians* (476 U.S. 747, 1986)[82], a case concerning the validity of the Pennsylvania Abortion Control Act of 1982: "Few decisions are more personal and intimate, more properly private, or more basic to individual dignity and autonomy, than a woman's decision [...] whether to end her pregnancy. A woman's right to make that choice freely is fundamental". The Court said in *Planned Parenthood of Southeastern Pennsylvania et al. v. Casey, Governor of Pennsylvania et al.* (505 U.S. 833, 851, 1992)[83], a case concerning the same Act:

> Our law affords constitutional protection to personal decisions relating to marriage, procreation, contraception, family relationships, child rearing, and education. [...]
> These matters, involving the most intimate and personal choices a person may make in a lifetime, choices central to personal dignity and autonomy, are central to the liberty protected by the Fourteenth Amendment.
> At the heart of liberty is the right to define one's own concept of existence, of meaning, of the universe, and of the mystery of human life. Beliefs about these matters could not define the attributes of personhood were they formed under compulsion of the State.

80 http://groups.csail.mit.edu/mac/users/rauch/germandecision/german_abortion_decision2.html.

81 Botha (2009) remarks that:

> ... the recognition in Germany of the dignity of the unborn is often explained by South African lawyers as a uniquely German preoccupation which is rooted in Germany's particular history. In South Africa, the most innovative uses of dignity have come from an exploration of the intersections of dignity, equality and difference. This serves once again to confirm the influence of contingent historical factors on the shape and content given to dignity within a particular legal system. (p. 218)

82 http://supreme.justia.com/us/476/747/case.html.

83 http://supreme.justia.com/us/505/833/case.html.

However, the same Court said in *Gonzales v. Carhart et al.* (550 U.S. 05-380 and 05-1382, 2007)[84], another abortion case:

> Respect for human life finds an ultimate expression in the bond of love the mother has for her child. [...] Whether to have an abortion requires a difficult and painful moral decision. *Casey*, supra, at 852.853 (opinion of the Court). While we find no reliable data to measure the phenomenon, it seems unexceptionable to conclude some women come to regret their choice to abort the infant life they once created and sustained. [...] Severe depression and loss of esteem can follow. See *ibid*.

The Constitutional Court of South Africa held that a fetus is not a legal persona under the Constitution and that it does not enjoy the right to life. A woman holds the right to choose to have a pregnancy terminated in the circumstances and manner stated in the Choice of Termination and Pregnancy Act.

5.4.5 Dignity and Corporal Punishment

The European Court of Human Rights said in *Tyrer v. The United Kingdom* (Application n° 5856/72, Judgment on 25 April 1978)[85], a cases (above mentioned) concerning a pupil sentenced to three strokes of a birch whip in accordance with the relevant legislation, for having pleaded guilty before the local juvenile court to unlawful assault occasioning actual bodily harm to a senior pupil at his school:

> 33. ... The very nature of judicial corporal punishment is that it involves one human being inflicting physical violence on another human being. Furthermore, it is institutionalized violence that is in the present case violence permitted by the law, ordered by the judicial authorities of the State and carried out by the police authorities of the State (see paragraph 10 above). [...]
> The institutionalized character of this violence is further compounded by the whole aura of official procedure attending the punishment and by the fact that those inflicting it were total strangers to the offender. [...]
> 35. Accordingly, viewing these circumstances as a whole, the Court finds that the applicant was subjected to a punishment in which the element of humiliation attained the level inherent in the notion of 'degrading punishment' as explained at paragraph 30 above. The indignity of having the punishment administered over the bare posterior aggravated to some extent the degrading character of the applicant's punishment but it was not the only or determining factor.
> The Court therefore concludes that the judicial corporal punishment inflicted on the applicant amounted to degrading punishment within the meaning of Article 3 (art. 3) of the Convention.

The CoRC said in its first GC (CRC/GC/2001/1)[86]:

> 8. ... The Committee has repeatedly made clear in its concluding observations that the use of corporal punishment does not respect the inherent dignity of the child nor the strict limits

---

[84] http://supreme.justia.com/us/550/05-380/.

[85] http://cmiskp.echr.coe.int/tkp197/view.asp?action=htmlanddocumentId=695464andportal=hbkmandsource=externalbydocnumberandtable=F69A27FD8FB86142BF01C1166DEA398649.

[86] www.unhchr.ch/tbs/doc.nsf/(symbol)/CRC.GC.2001.1.En?OpenDocument.

on school discipline. Compliance with the values recognized in article 29 (1) [of the Convention on the Rights of the Child] clearly requires that schools be child-friendly in the fullest sense of the term and that they be consistent in all respects with the dignity of the child.

The same Committee said in the GC 8 (CRC/C/GC/8, 2007)[87]:

> 5. Since it began examining States parties' reports the Committee has recommended prohibition of all corporal punishment, in the family and other settings, to more than 130 States in all continents. The Committee is encouraged that a growing number of States are taking appropriate legislative and other measures to assert children's right to respect for their human dignity and physical integrity and to equal protection under the law. [...]
> 16. ... The dignity of each and every individual is the fundamental guiding principle of international human rights law.
> [...]
> 26. When the Committee on the Rights of the Child has raised eliminating corporal punishment with certain States during the examination of their reports, governmental representatives have sometimes suggested that some level of 'reasonable' or 'moderate' corporal punishment can be justified as in the 'best interests' of the child. [...] But interpretation of a child's best interests must be consistent with the whole Convention, including the obligation to protect children from all forms of violence and the requirement to give due weight to the child's views; it cannot be used to justify practices, including corporal punishment and other forms of cruel or degrading punishment, which conflict with the child's human dignity and right to physical integrity.
> 46. Children's developmental needs must be respected. Children learn from what adults do, not only from what adults say. When the adults to whom a child most closely relates use violence and humiliation in their relationship with the child, they are demonstrating disrespect for human rights and teaching a potent and dangerous lesson that these are legitimate ways to seek to resolve conflict or change behavior.

The CESCR said in the GC 13 (E/C.12/1999/10)[88]:

> In the Committee's view, corporal punishment is inconsistent with the fundamental guiding principle of international human rights law enshrined in the Preambles to the Universal Declaration of Human Rights and both Covenants: the dignity of the individual. Other aspects of school discipline may also be inconsistent with human dignity, such as public humiliation. Nor should any form of discipline breach other rights under the Covenant, such as the right to food. A State party is required to take measures to ensure that discipline which is inconsistent with the Covenant does not occur in any public or private educational institution within its jurisdiction. The Committee welcomes initiatives taken by some States parties which actively encourage schools to introduce 'positive', non-violent approaches to school discipline[89].

[87] www.unhchr.ch/tbs/doc.nsf/898586b1dc7b4043c1256a450044f331/6545c032cb57bff5c12571fc002e834d/$FILE/G0740771.pdf.

[88] www.unhchr.ch/tbs/doc.nsf/(Symbol)/ae1a0b126d068e868025683c003c8b3b#17%2F.

[89] Note 18 adds: "In formulating this paragraph, the Committee has taken note of the practice evolving elsewhere in the international human rights system, such as the interpretation given by the Committee on the Rights of the Child to article 28 (2) of the Convention on the Rights of the Child, as well as the Human Rights Committee's interpretation of article 7 of ICCPR". And note 19, regarding the HDP, reads: "The Committee notes that, although it is absent from article 26 (2) of the Declaration, the drafters of ICESCR expressly included the dignity of the human personality as one of the mandatory objectives to which all education is to be directed (art. 13 (1))".

The Inter-American Court of Human Rights said in its *Advisory Opinion OC-17/2002 of 28 August 2002 on the "Juridical Condition and Human Rights of the Child"*[90]:

> 56. This regulating principle regarding children's rights [best interests of the child] is based on the very dignity of the human being, on the characteristics of children themselves, and on the need to foster their development, making full use of their potential, as well as on the nature and scope of the Convention on the Rights of the Child.
> [...]
> 93. These fundamental values ['systems of values and principles distinctive of a democratic society'] include safeguarding children, both because they are human beings with their inherent dignity, and due to their special situation. Given their immaturity and vulnerability, they require protection to ensure exercise of their rights within the family, in society and with respect to the State.
> [...]
> 35. On the basis of all this notable development is found the principle of the respect for the dignity of the human person, independently of her existential condition. In virtue of this principle, every human being, irrespectively of the situation and the circumstances in which he finds himself, has the right to dignity. This fundamental principle is invoked in the preambles of the United Nations Convention on the Rights of the Child of 1989 as well as of the Declaration of the Rights of the Child of 1959.

The Criminal Court of Cassation of the Second Circuit Court of San José de Costa Rica said in *Judgment 011062, 02-002448-0369-PE, 20/10/2005*[91], a case concerning the corporal punishment by the father of a girl who had already attained her majority:

> In short, parents—even though vested with parental rights and duties—have no 'right' to hurt their children. Accepting otherwise would breach the principle of equality, established in article 33 of the Political Constitution, since aggression with weapons is not allowed among adults, let alone against persons who are vulnerable and/or within the family circle. Respect for physical integrity is part of respect for human dignity, and therefore, there is no legal standing to deteriorate the human rights of the victims in this case.

The High Court of Fiji at Lautoka said in *Naushad Ali v. State (Criminal Appeal N° HAA 0083 of 2001 (C. P. N° 0001 of 2001 L, Judgment on 21 March 2002)*[92], a case concerning an appeal against a judicial sentence of six strokes of corporal punishment:

> Children have rights no whit inferior to the rights of adults. Fiji has ratified the Convention on the Rights of the Child. Our Constitution also guarantees fundamental rights to every person. Government is required to adhere to principles respecting the rights of all individuals, communities and groups. By their status as children, children need special protection. Our educational institutions should be sanctuaries of peace and creative enrichment not places for fear, ill-treatment and tampering with the human dignity of students. It is clear that the Ministry of Education is aware of progressive educa-

[90] www.crin.org/docs/advisory-opinion17.pdf.

[91] http://200.91.68.20/SCIJ/busqueda/jurisprudencia/jur_ficha_sentencia.asp?nValor2=321746andnValor1=1andstrTipM=Tand1Resultado=, and: www.endcorporalpunishment.org/pages/hrlaw/judgments.html.

[92] www.endcorporalpunishment.org/pages/pdfs/Fiji-judgment.pdf.

tion policies. It itself admits: 'Excessive use of punishment is a general sign of teacher incompetence. If pupils are inattentive, noisy, frequently late or absent from the school, the teacher should try to establish the causes. The fault needs not always be that of the pupils, it could be the teacher's as well. The remedy is not to beat the pupils but to make school life and work attractive and interesting to ensure that pupils are happy and busily engaged all the time'.

In *Criminal Appeal 4596/98 Plonit v. A.G. 54(1) P.D. [2000]*[93]—a case concerning the parental corporal punishment—the Supreme Court of Israel said:

> … that corporal punishment of children, or humiliation and derogation from their dignity as a method of education by their parents, is entirely impermissible, and is a remnant of a societal-educational outlook that has lost its validity. The child is not the parent's property and cannot be used as a punching bag the parents can beat at their leisure, even when the parents honestly believe that they are fulfilling their duty and right to educate their child. The child depends upon the parents, is entitled to parental love, protection and the parents' gentle touch. The use of punishment which causes hurt and humiliation does not contribute to the child's personality or education, but instead damages his or her human rights. Such punishment injures his or her body, feelings, dignity and proper development. Such punishment distances us from our goal of a society free of violence. Accordingly, let it be known that in our society parents are now forbidden to make use of corporal punishments or methods that demean and humiliate the child as an educational system.

The Constitutional Court of South Africa said in *Christian Education South Africa v. Minister of Education (CCT4/00) [2000] ZACC 11; 2000 (4) SA 757; 2000 (10) BCLR 1051 (18 August 2000)*[94], a case concerning the claim that a law enacted by the Parliament to prohibit corporal punishment in schools violated the rights of parents of children in independent schools who, in line with their religious convictions, had consented to its use:

> [15] It is clear from the above that a multiplicity of intersecting constitutional values and interests are involved in the present matter—some overlapping, some competing. The parents have a general interest in living their lives in a community setting according to their religious beliefs, and a more specific interest in directing the education of their children. […] The overlap and tension between the different clusters of rights reflect themselves in contradictory assessments of how the central constitutional value of dignity is implicated. On the one hand, the dignity of the parents may be negatively affected when the state tells them how to bring up and discipline their children and limits the manner in which they may express their religious beliefs. The child who has grown up in the particular faith may regard the punishment, although hurtful, as designed to strengthen his character. On the other hand, the child is being subjected to what an outsider might regard as the indignity of suffering a painful and humiliating hiding deliberately inflicted on him in an institutional setting. Indeed, it would be unusual if the child did not have ambivalent emotions. It is in this complex factual and psychological setting that the matter must be decided.
>
> […]
>
> [50] … As part of its pedagogical mission, the Department [of Education] sought to introduce new principles of learning in terms of which problems were solved through reason rather than force. In order to put the child at the center of the school and to protect the

93 www.endcorporalpunishment.org/pages/pdfs/Israel_Judgment.pdf.

94 www.saflii.org/za/cases/ZACC/2000/11.pdf.

> learner from physical and emotional abuse, the legislature prescribed a blanket ban on corporal punishment. [...] The outlawing of physical punishment in the school accordingly represented more than a pragmatic attempt to deal with disciplinary problems in a new way. It had a principled and symbolic function, manifestly intended to promote respect for the dignity and physical and emotional integrity of all children.

The Supreme Court of Cassation in Rome (Italy's highest Court) said in *Republic of Italy v. Cambria* (1996)[95]—a case concerning the parental corporal punishment—that:

> ... the very expression 'correction of children', which expresses a view of child-rearing that is both culturally anachronistic and historically outdated, should in fact be re-defined, abolishing any connotation of hierarchy or authoritarianism and introducing the ideas of social and responsible commitment which should characterize the position of the educator *vis-à-vis* the learner. The term 'correction' should be understood as a synonym for education and refer to the conformative spirit which should be a part of any educational process. In any case, whichever meaning is to be reassigned to this term in family and pedagogic relationships, the use of violence for educational purposes can no longer be considered lawful. There are two reasons for this: the first is the overriding importance which the [Italian] legal system attributes to protecting the dignity of the individual. This includes 'minors' who now hold rights and are no longer simply objects to be protected by their parents or, worse still, objects at the disposal of their parents. The second reason is that, as an educational aim, the harmonious development of a child's personality, which ensures that he/she embraces the values of peace, tolerance and co-existence, cannot be achieved by using violent means which contradict these goals.

5.4.6 Dignity and the Treatment of Prisoners

The USA Supreme Court said in *Hope v. Pelzer et al.* (536 U.S. 730, 2002)[96], a case concerning the handcuffing of a prisoner to a hitching post for 7 h in the sun, as punishment for disruptive conduct:

> The obvious cruelty inherent in this practice should have provided respondents with some notice that their alleged conduct violated Hope's constitutional protection against cruel and unusual punishment. Hope was treated in a way antithetical to human dignity—he was hitched to a post for an extended period of time in a position that was painful, and under circumstances that were both degrading and dangerous.

The Court said in *Brown v. Plata* (563 US, 2011)[97], a case concerning persistent serious violations of constitutional rights in California's prison system:

> As a consequence of their own actions, prisoners may be deprived of rights that are fundamental to liberty. Yet the law and the Constitution demand recognition of certain other rights. Prisoners retain the essence of human dignity inherent in all persons. Respect for that dignity animates the Eighth Amendment prohibition against cruel and unusual punishment. 'The basic concept underlying the Eighth Amendment is nothing less than the dignity of

[95] www.endcorporalpunishment.org/pages/frame.html.

[96] http://supreme.justia.com/us/536/730/.

[97] http://supreme.justia.com/us/563/09-1233/opinion.html.

man.' *Atkins v. Virginia*, 536 U. S. 304, 311 (2002) (quoting *Trop v. Dulles*, 356 U. S. 86, 100 (1958) (plurality opinion)).
A prison that deprives prisoners of basic sustenance, including adequate medical care, is incompatible with the concept of human dignity and has no place in civilized society.

The Supreme Court of Israel said in *HCJ 2605/05 Academic Center of Law and Business v. Minister of Finance*[98], a case concerning an Amendment Law providing the possibility, for the first time, of a prison to be operated and managed by a private corporation rather than by the State:

> 35. Whatever the content of the constitutional right to human dignity may be, no one denies that the right to dignity applies with regard to preventing the denigration of a person and preventing any violation of his human image and his worth as a human being. The right to dignity is a right that every human being is entitled to enjoy as a human being. Admittedly, when a person enters a prison he loses his liberty and freedom of movement, as well as additional rights that are violated as a result of the imprisonment; but an inmate of a prison does not lose his constitutional right to human dignity. [...]
> 36. ...Imprisoning persons in a privately managed prison leads to a situation in which the clearly public purposes of the imprisonment are blurred and diluted by irrelevant considerations that arise from a private economic purpose, namely the desire of the private corporation operating the prison to make a financial profit. There is therefore an inherent and natural concern that imprisoning inmates in a privately managed prison that is run with a private economic purpose de facto turns the prisoners into a means whereby the corporation that manages and operates the prison makes a financial profit. It should be noted that the very existence of a prison that operates on a profit-making basis reflects a lack of respect for the status of the inmates as human beings, and this violation of the human dignity of the inmates does not depend on the extent of the violation of human rights that actually occurs behind the prison walls [...].
> 39. ... When the state transfers the power to imprison someone, with the invasive powers that go with it, to a private corporation that operates on a profit-making basis, this action—both in practice and on an ethical and symbolic level—expresses a divestment of a significant part of the state's responsibility for the fate of the inmates, by exposing them to a violation of their rights by a private profit-making enterprise. This conduct of the state violates the human dignity of the inmates of a privately managed prison, since the public purposes that underlie their imprisonment and give it legitimacy are undermined, and, as described above, their imprisonment becomes a means for a private corporation to make a profit.

Sitting in the same Court, Justice Barak said in *HCJ 355/79 Katlan v. Israel Prison Service*, as quoted in *HCJ 2605/05 Academic Center of Law and Business v. Minister of Finance*[99]:

> 35. ... The right to physical integrity and human dignity is also a right of persons under arrest and prison inmates. The walls of the prison are not a barrier between the inmate and human dignity. The regime in the prison naturally requires a violation of many liberties that free people enjoy [...] but the regime in the prison does not demand that the inmate is denied his right to physical integrity and to protection against a violation of his dignity as a human being. The inmate loses his freedom, but he is not deprived of his human image.

[98] http://elyon1.court.gov.il/files_eng/05/050/026/n39/05026050.n39.pdf.

[99] http://elyon1.court.gov.il/files_eng/05/050/026/n39/05026050.n39.pdf.

5.4.7 Dignity and the Death Penalty

In the USA Supreme Court Judgment of *Furman v. Georgia* (408 U.S. 238, 1972)[100]—in which the death penalty was at stake in sentencing—Justice Brennan said, concurring:

> In *Trop v. Dulles*, supra, at 356 U. S. 99 [... it] was said, finally, that: "The basic concept underlying the [Clause] is nothing less than the dignity of man. While the State has the power to punish, the [Clause] stands to assure that this power be exercised within the limits of civilized standards." Id. at 356 U. S. 100. At bottom, then, the Cruel and Unusual Punishments Clause prohibits the infliction of uncivilized and inhuman punishments. The State, even as it punishes, must treat its members with respect for their intrinsic worth as human beings. A punishment is 'cruel and unusual', therefore, if it does not comport with human dignity. [...]
> The primary principle is that a punishment must not be so severe as to be degrading to the dignity of human beings. [...]
> Indeed, a punishment may be degrading to human dignity solely because it is a punishment. A State may not punish a person for being 'mentally ill, or a leper, or... afflicted with a venereal disease', or for being addicted to narcotics. *Robinson v. California*, 370 U. S. 660, 370 U. S. 666 (1962). To inflict punishment for having a disease is to treat the individual as a diseased thing, rather than as a sick human being. [...]
> Death is truly an awesome punishment. The calculated killing of a human being by the State involves, by its very nature, a denial of the executed person's humanity. The contrast with the plight of a person punished by imprisonment is evident. An individual in prison does not lose 'the right to have rights'. A prisoner retains, for example, the constitutional rights to the free exercise of religion, to be free of cruel and unusual punishments, and to treatment as a 'person' for purposes of due process of law and the equal protection of the laws. A prisoner remains a member of the human family. Moreover, he retains the right of access to the courts. His punishment is not irrevocable. Apart from the common charge, grounded upon the recognition of human fallibility, that the punishment of death must inevitably be inflicted upon innocent men, we know that death has been the lot of men whose convictions were unconstitutionally secured in view of later, retroactively applied, holdings of this Court. [...] An executed person has indeed 'lost the right to have rights'.

The Court said in *Gregg v. Georgia* (428 U.S. 153, 1976)[101], a case concerning the death penalty for a petitioner charged with committing armed robbery and murder of two men:

> The Court, on a number of occasions, has both assumed and asserted the constitutionality of capital punishment. [...] But until *Furman v. Georgia*, 408 U. S. 238 (1972), the Court never confronted squarely the fundamental claim that the punishment of death always, regardless of the enormity of the offense or the procedure followed in imposing the sentence, is cruel and unusual punishment in violation of the Constitution. Although this issue was presented and addressed in Furman, it was not resolved by the Court. [...]
> As Mr. Chief Justice Warren said, in an oft-quoted phrase, '[t]he Amendment must draw its meaning from the evolving standards of decency that mark the progress of a maturing society'. *Trop v. Dulles*, supra at 356 U. S. 101. [...] Thus, an assessment of contemporary

[100] http://supreme.justia.com/search.py?query=Furman+v.+Georgia+andSearch=Search+Cases.

[101] http://caselaw.lp.findlaw.com/scripts/getcase.pl?navby=caseandcourt=usandvol=428andpage=153.

> values concerning the infliction of a challenged sanction is relevant to the application of the Eighth Amendment. [...]
> As we have seen, however, the Eighth Amendment demands more than that a challenged punishment be acceptable to contemporary society. The Court also must ask whether it comports with the basic concept of human dignity at the core of the Amendment. *Trop v. Dulles*, 356 U.S. at 356 U. S. 100 (plurality opinion).

The Court said in *Ford v. Wainwright* (477 U.S. 399, 1986)[102]—a case in Florida concerning the death penalty for a mentally ill petitioner convicted of murder—that:

> ... the natural abhorrence civilized societies feel at killing one who has no capacity to come to grips with his own conscience or deity is still vivid today. And the intuition that such an execution simply offends humanity is evidently shared across this Nation. Faced with such widespread evidence of a restriction upon sovereign power, this Court is compelled to conclude that the Eighth Amendment prohibits a State from carrying out a sentence of death upon a prisoner who is insane.

The Court said in *Roper v. Simmons* (543 U.S. 03-633, 2004)[103], a case concerning the death penalty for a murder committed by a juvenile at age 17, after he had turned 18:

> It is proper that we acknowledge the overwhelming weight of international opinion against the juvenile death penalty, resting in large part on the understanding that the instability and emotional imbalance of young people may often be a factor in the crime. [...] The opinion of the world community, while not controlling our outcome, does provide respected and significant confirmation for our own conclusions.
> Over time, from one generation to the next, the Constitution has come to earn the high respect and even, as Madison dared to hope, the veneration of the American people. [...] The document sets forth, and rests upon, innovative principles original to the American experience, such as federalism; a proven balance in political mechanisms through separation of powers; specific guarantees for the accused in criminal cases; and broad provisions to secure individual freedom and preserve human dignity. [...] It does not lessen our fidelity to the Constitution or our pride in its origins to acknowledge that the express affirmation of certain fundamental rights by other nations and peoples simply underscores the centrality of those same rights within our own heritage of freedom.
> The Eighth and Fourteenth Amendments forbid imposition of the death penalty on offenders who were under the age of 18 when their crimes were committed.

The same Court said in *Kennedy v. Louisiana* (554 U.S. 407, 420 2008)[104], a case concerning the death penalty for a Louisiana petitioner charged with the aggravated rape of his then 8-year-old stepdaughter: "Evolving standards of decency must embrace and express respect for the dignity of the person, and the punishment of criminals must conform to that rule".

The Constitutional Court of the Republic of South Africa said in the already quoted case of *The State v. T Makwanyane and M Mchunu (CCT3/94) [1995] ZACC 3; 1995 (6) BCLR 665; 1995 (3) SA 391; [1996] 2 CHRLD 164; 1995 (2) SACR 1 (6 June 1995)*[105]:

---

[102] http://supreme.justia.com/us/477/399/case.html.

[103] http://supreme.justia.com/us/543/03-633/case.html.

[104] http://supreme.justia.com/us/554/07-343/opinion.html.

[105] www.saflii.org/za/cases/ZACC/1995/3.pdf.

> [26] Death is the most extreme form of punishment to which a convicted criminal can be subjected. Its execution is final and irrevocable. It puts an end not only to the right to life itself, but to all other personal rights which had vested in the deceased under Chapter Three of the Constitution. [...] It is also an inhuman punishment for it '...involves, by its very nature, a denial of the executed person's humanity' [...].
> [...]
> [84] Section 8, the counterpart of sect. 33 of our Constitution, provides that laws shall not impose any limitations on the essential content of fundamental rights. According to the finding of the Court, capital punishment imposed a limitation on the essential content of the fundamental rights to life and human dignity, eliminating them irretrievably. As such it was unconstitutional. Two factors are stressed in the judgment of the Court. First, the relationship between the rights of life and dignity, and the importance of these rights taken together. Secondly, the absolute nature of these two rights taken together. Together they are the source of all other rights. Other rights may be limited, and may even be withdrawn and then granted again, but their ultimate limit is to be found in the preservation of the twin rights of life and dignity. These twin rights are the essential content of all rights under the Constitution. Take them away, and all other rights cease.

In the Canadian Supreme Court Judgment of *Kindler v. Canada (Minister of Justice), [1991] 2 S.C.R. 779*[106], three of the seven judges said, dissenting:

> If corporal punishment, lobotomy and castration are no longer acceptable [...] then the death penalty cannot be considered to be anything other than cruel and unusual punishment. It is the supreme indignity to the individual, the ultimate corporal punishment, the final and complete lobotomy and the absolute and irrevocable castration [...] the ultimate desecration of human dignity [...]. (VII.3)

5.4.8 Dignity of Life

As the CCPR said, in the GC 6[107], the right to life "should not be interpreted narrowly" (para. 1).

The Inter-American Court of Human Rights said in *'Street Children' (Villagran-Morales et al.) v. Guatemala* (1999)[108], a case concerning the abduction, torture and murder of five youths in Guatemala:

> 144 ... Owing to the fundamental nature of the right to life, restrictive approaches to it are inadmissible. In essence, the fundamental right to life includes not only the right of every human being not to be deprived of his life arbitrarily, but also the right that he will not be prevented from having access to the conditions that guarantee a dignified existence.

The USA Supreme Court said in *Goldberg v. Kelly* (397 U.S. 254, 1970)[109], a case concerning the termination of financial aid to New York City residents:

> From its founding, the Nation's basic commitment has been to foster the dignity and well-being of all persons within its borders. We have come to recognize that forces not within the control of the poor contribute to their poverty. This perception, against the background

---

106 http://scc.lexum.org/en/1991/1991scr2-779/1991scr2-779.pdf.

107 www.unhchr.ch/tbs/doc.nsf/0/84ab9690ccd81fc7c12563ed0046fae3.

108 www.unhcr.org/refworld/pdfid/4b17bc442.pdf.

109 http://caselaw.lp.findlaw.com/cgi-bin/getcase.pl?court=usandvol=397andinvol=254.

of our traditions, has significantly influenced the development of the contemporary public assistance system. Welfare, by meeting the basic demands of subsistence, can help bring within the reach of the poor the same opportunities that are available to others to participate meaningfully in the life of the community. At the same time, welfare guards against the societal malaise that may flow from a widespread sense of unjustified frustration and insecurity. Public assistance, then, is not mere charity, but a means to "promote the general Welfare, and secure the Blessings of Liberty to ourselves and our Posterity" [Preamble of the USA Constitution].

The German Federal Constitutional Court said in *BvL 1/09 (2010)*[110], a case concerning the constitutionality of some provisions of the Code of Social Law (*Sozialgesetzbuch Zweites Buch*—SGB II)[111] regarding the standard benefit for adults and children:

1. a) The fundamental right to guarantee a subsistence minimum that is in line with the human dignity, which follows from Article 1.1 GG in conjunction with the principle of the social state under Article 20.1 GG, ensures every needy person the material conditions that are indispensable for his or her physical existence and for a minimum participation in social, cultural and political life. Beside the right from Article 1.1 GG to respect the dignity of every individual, which has an absolute effect, this fundamental right from Article 1.1 GG has, in its connection with Article 20.1 GG, an autonomous significance as a guarantee right. This right is not subject to the legislature's disposal and must be honoured; it must, however be lent concrete shape, and be regularly updated, by the legislature. The legislature has to orient the benefits to be paid towards the respective stage of development of the polity and towards the existing conditions of life.

The Supreme Court of Israel said in *Commitment to Peace and Social Justice v. Minister of Finance (HCJ 366/03)* and *Bilhah Rubinova and Others v. Minister of Finance (HCJ 888/03)*[112], cases in which a governmental decision to reduce the amount of a complement to the income paid to individuals and families was at stake, as well as the cancellation of several subsidies:

12. It is now more than a decade that human dignity has enjoyed the status of a constitutional super-legislative right in our legal system. [...]
The duty of the state is two-fold: first, it has a duty not to violate human dignity. This is the negative aspect (the *status negativus*) of the right. It is enshrined in s. 2 of the Basic Law: Human Dignity and Liberty. Second, it has the duty to protect human dignity. This is the positive aspect (the *status positivus*) of the right. It is enshrined in s. 4 of the Basic Law: Human Dignity and Liberty. The two aspects, the negative (passive) aspect and the positive (active) aspect are different parts of the whole, which is the constitutional right to dignity. [...]
15. ... In such a situation it cannot be said that the existing Basic Laws give full and complete protection to social rights. The Basic Laws protect the right to dignity, which includes the physical existence aspect that is required in order to realize the right to dignity. [...] This is the outlook according to which the right to live with dignity is the right that a person should be guaranteed a minimum of material means, which will allow him to subsist in the society where he lives. This outlook has found its expression more than once in the case law of this court, in a variety of contexts. [...]
16. It can be assumed, therefore, for this case—without making a firm determination on the subject—that the duty of the state under the Basic Law: Human Dignity and Liberty

[110] www.bverfg.de/en/press/bvg10-005en.html.

[111] http://supreme.justia.com/search.py?query=Goldberg+v.+Kelly+andSearch=Search+Cases.

[112] http://elyon1.court.gov.il/files_eng/03/660/003/a39/03003660.a39.pdf.

> gives rise to the duty to maintain a system that will ensure a 'protective net' for persons in society with limited means, so that their physical position does not reduce them to a lack of subsistence. Within the framework, it must ensure that a person has enough food and drink in order to live; a place to live in which he can realize his privacy and his family life and be protected from the elements; tolerable sanitation and medical services, which will ensure him access to the facilities of modern medicine.

In India, although dignity is mentioned only in the Preamble to the Constitution, the Supreme Court said in *Francis Coralie Mullin v. The Administrator, Union Territory of Delhi (1981 AIR 746, 1981 SCR (2) 516)*[113]—a case concerning the right of a prisoner to be visited by members of his family and a lawyer—that:

> (5) The right to life enshrined in Article 21 cannot be restricted to mere animal existence. It means something much more than just physical survival.
> [...]
> (6) The right to life includes the right to live with human dignity and all that goes along with it, namely, the bare necessaries of life such as adequate nutrition, clothing and shelter and facilities for reading, writing and expressing oneself in diverse forms, freely moving about and mixing and commingling with fellow human beings.

This broad conception of the right to life is to be found in other cases in India such as *Tellis v. Bombay Municipal Corporation* (right to a livelihood); *Ahmedabad Municipal Corporation v. Nawab Khan Gulab Khan* (right to shelter); *Paschim Banga Khet Mazdoor Samity v. State of Bengal* (right to health); *Mohini Jain v. State of Karnataka* (right to education).

Also the Inter-American Court of Human Rights used the notion of *vida digna* (dignified life) to make economic, social and cultural rights justiciable in connection with the right to life.

5.4.9 *Dignity in Death*

The European Court of Human Rights said in *Pretty v. the United Kingdom (Application N°. 2346/02, Judgment on April 2002)*[114], a case concerning a woman suffering from an irreversible disease who had requested assisted suicide:

> 65. ...Without in any way negating the principle of sanctity of life protected under the Convention, the Court considers that it is under Article 8 that notions of the quality of life take on significance. In an era of growing medical sophistication combined with longer life expectancies, many people are concerned that they should not be forced to linger on in old age or in states of advanced physical or mental decrepitude which conflict with strongly held ideas of self and personal identity.

In the Supreme Court of the State of Montana (USA) Judgment of *Robert Maxter et al. v. State of Montana and Another* (2009 MT 449)[115]—a case concerning a

---

[113] http://indiankanoon.org/doc/78536/?type=print.

[114] http://cmiskp.echr.coe.int/tkp197/view.asp?item=1andportal=hbkmandaction=htmlandhighlight=Pretty%20-%7C%20v.%20-%7C%20The%20-%7C%20United%20-%7C%20Kingdomandsessionid=83346646andskin=hudoc-en.

[115] http://law.justia.com/cases/montana/supreme-court/2009/94adc027-086a-4b36-a80e-0aaf09a60127.html.

terminally ill patient wanting the option of ingesting a lethal dose of medication prescribed by his physician and self-administered—Justice James C. Nelson said in a concurring opinion worthy of being quoted at length:

> 58. I have lived a good and a long life, and have no wish to leave this world prematurely. As death approaches from my disease, however, if my suffering becomes unbearable I want the legal option of being able to die in a peaceful and dignified manner by consuming medication prescribed by my doctor for that purpose. Because it will be my suffering, my life, and my death that will be involved, I seek the right and responsibility to make that critical choice for myself if circumstances lead me to do so. I feel strongly that this intensely personal and private decision should be left to me and my conscience—based on my most deeply held values and beliefs, and after consulting with my family and doctor—and that the government should not have the right to prohibit this choice by criminalizing the aid in dying procedure.[116]
> [...]
> 66. First, let me be clear about one thing: This case is not about the 'right to die.' Indeed, the notion that there is such a 'right' is patently absurd, if not downright silly. No constitution, no statute, no legislature, and no court can grant an individual the "right to die." Nor can they take such a right away. [...] Within the context of this case, the only control that a person has over death is that if he expects its coming within a relatively short period of time due to an incurable disease, he can simply accept his fate and seek drug-induced comfort; or he can seek further treatment and fight to prolong death's advance; or, at some point in his illness, and with his physician's assistance, he can embrace his destiny at a time and place of his choosing. The only 'right' guaranteed to him in any of these decisions is the right to preserve his personal autonomy and his individual dignity, as he sees fit, in the face of an ultimate destiny that no power on earth can prevent.
> [...]
> 84. But what exactly is 'dignity'? It would be impractical here to attempt to provide an exhaustive definition. [...]
> 88. Experience teaches, and we understand innately, that once we strip an individual of dignity, the human being no longer exists. A subhuman is easy to abuse, torture, and kill, because the object of the abuse is simply that—an object without worth or value and devoid of the essential element of humanness: dignity. [...]
> [...]
> 90. Few of us would wish upon ourselves or upon others the prolonged dying that comes from an incurable illness. And it is for this reason that some of our fellow human beings demand—rightfully, in my view—that we respect their individual right to preserve their own human dignity at a time when they are mentally competent, incurably ill, and faced with death from their illness within a relatively short period of time.
> 91. The State asserts that it has compelling interests in preserving life and protecting vulnerable groups from potential abuses. This broad assertion, however, is entirely inadequate to sustain the State's position in opposition to physician aid in dying. We are dealing here with persons who are mentally competent, who are incurably ill, and who expect death within a relatively short period of time. [...]
> 92. Furthermore, it must be remembered that an individual's right of human dignity is inviolable; it is incapable of being violated. [...] The right of dignity is absolute, and it remains absolute even at the time of death. It may not be stripped from the individual by a well-meaning yet paternalistic government. Nor may it be stripped by third parties or institutions

[116] Aff. Robert Baxter ¶ 9 (June 28, 2008). Baxter (one of the plaintiffs-appellees in this case) died of leukemia on December 5, 2008– the same day the District Court issued its ruling in his favor, holding that under the Montana Constitution a mentally competent, incurably ill patient has the right to die with dignity by obtaining physician aid in dying.

driven by political ideology or religious beliefs. [...] Dignity defines what it means to be human. It defines the depth of individual autonomy throughout life and, most certainly, at death. Usurping a mentally competent, incurably ill individual's ability to make end-of-life decisions and forcing that person against his will to suffer a prolonged and excruciating deterioration is, at its core, a blatant and untenable violation of the person's fundamental right of human dignity. [...]
94. This right to physician aid in dying quintessentially involves the inviolable right to human dignity—our most fragile fundamental right. [...] Society does not have the right to strip a mentally competent, incurably ill individual of her inviolable human dignity when she seeks aid in dying from her physician. Dignity is a fundamental component of humanness; it is intrinsic to our species; it must be respected throughout life; and it must be honored when one's inevitable destiny is death from an incurable illness.[117]

5.5 Some Conclusions

An overview of the conceptual genealogy of HDP, of its place in IHRL and in Constitutional Law, as well as of its jurisprudential uses, and the points of view of juridical doctrine, has just been presented. There have been attempts to identify and categorize the multiple legal and jurisprudential uses of the term 'dignity'.

In fact, as Rao (2011) remarks: "Constitutional courts usually refer to dignity without elaborating its essential meaning and therefore overlook the very different meanings that dignity can have even within the context of particular legal disputes. In a single opinion a court may rely on multiple meanings of dignity, which sometimes will point in different directions or emphasize very different values" (p. 189).

Referring to USA Supreme Court jurisprudence, Henry (2011) notices "the conceptual chaos surrounding dignity", "a cacophony of uses so confusing that some critics argue the word ought to be abandoned altogether" (p. 1). As a consequence, some authors have suggested that dignity is at best useless, a *passe-partout* (catch-all) principle functioning as a placeholder for other concepts (see McCrudden 2008, p. 675); at worst, it is a 'two-edged sword' that may be used as a disguise for moralism and politically conservative stances[118]. So the Supreme Court of Canada, "per-

[117] As of the end of 2012, assisted suicide is legal in Oregon and Washington, but euthanasia is illegal throughout the USA. The difference is as follows: Assisted suicide means providing to a patient the means to end his or her own life, with knowledge of his or her intention (so it is the patient who performs the act); euthanasia means bringing about the death of a person at his or her request (so it is someone else who performs the act).

In the USA, there is a Death with Dignity National Center.

(www.deathwithdignity.org/advocates/national).

[118] An example of this, in Steven Pinker's opinion, Professor of Psychology at Harvard, is the Report *Human Dignity and Bioethics* prepared by the Council on Bioethics created in 2001 by the American President George W. Bush. The author says: "The problem is that 'dignity' is a squishy, subjective notion, hardly up to the heavyweight moral demands assigned to it". And further writes: "Although the Dignity report presents itself as a scholarly deliberation of universal moral concerns, it springs from a movement to impose a radical political agenda, fed by fervent religious impulses, onto American biomedicine. [...] The Judeo-Christian—in some cases, explicitly bibli-

suaded by some pedantic academic articles" (as wrote Waldron 2009b, p. 37), concluded that, "as critics have pointed out, human dignity is an abstract and subjective notion that [...becomes] confusing and difficult to apply" (*R. v. Kapp, 2 S.C.R. 483, 2008 SCC 41*, para. 22)[119].

Aiming to provide a synthesis and further clarification, some conclusions are now proposed, at times supported by further Case Law. Their headings are as follows:

- Dignity is a term with manifold uses
- Human dignity is a right and a principle
- Human dignity is multidimensional
- Human dignity is violable, vulnerable and variable

5.5.1 Dignity is a Term with Manifold Uses

The term 'dignity' is not applied only to human beings but also to institutions, offices, animals, vegetables, things, etc.

As Bostrom (2008) observes, dignity may mean "a quality, a kind of excellence admitting of degrees and applicable to entities both within and without the human realm". He explains: "While inanimate objects cannot possess Human Dignity, they can be endowed with a kind of Dignity as a Quality" (p. 173, 203). In this sense, entities such as States, some offices and symbols, professions, etc, may also be said to have dignity. Referring to the USA Supreme Court, Henry (2011) notices:

> Since deciding *The Schooner Exchange*, the Supreme Court consistently has invoked dignity to protect the institutional status of other nations in foreign sovereign immunity cases. The most noteworthy judicial function of institutional status as dignity, however, has been to dramatically expand the doctrine of *state* sovereign immunity. (p. 25)

'Dignitary' is a term applied to people who hold high-ranking positions. Francesco Mazzola painted, in the sixteenth century, a *Portrait of a Dignitary*, the German translation of which is *Bildnis eines Würdenträgers* (literally: portrait of a holder of dignity). The Constitution of Poland[120] states: "Judges shall be provided with appropriate conditions for work and granted remuneration consistent with the dignity of their office and the scope of their duties" (Article 178.2).

In *Ford v. Wainwright* (477 U.S. 399, 1986)[121]—a case concerning the death penalty for a mentally ill petitioner in Florida convicted of murder (aforementioned)—the USA Supreme Court referred also to the protection of "the dignity of society itself from the barbarity of exacting mindless vengeance".

---

cal—arguments found in essay after essay in this volume are quite extraordinary" ("The Stupidity of Dignity", published in *The New Republic*, May 28, 2008 (Retrieved July 2013 from: www.tnr.com/article/the-stupidity-dignity).

[119] http://scc.lexum.org/en/2008/2008scc41/2008scc41.html.

[120] www.sejm.gov.pl/prawo/konst/angielski/kon1.htm.

[121] http://supreme.justia.com/us/477/399/case.html.

The Constitution of the Islamic Republic of Iran (1979, amended)[122], in Article 2 (Foundational Principles), refers to "the exalted dignity and value of man, and his freedom coupled with responsibility before God" (6), but Article 22 (Human Dignity and Rights) states: "The dignity, life, property, rights, residence, and occupation of the individual are inviolate, except in cases sanctioned by law". Commenting on this provision, Alain Seriaux (1997) observed that it addresses "not the human dignity in itself but the honor of persons, their reputation". That is why it may be violated "in cases sanctioned by law" (p. 292). He points out: "Dignity is therefore what remains when one has lost all other dignities" (p. 293).

Animals are sometimes considered as having dignity, too. In the opinion of Martha Nussbaum (2008): "Animals other than human beings possess dignity for the very same reason that human beings possess dignity: they are complex living and sentient beings endowed with capacities for activity and striving. It seems to me morally unacceptable to harp on the importance of human dignity while denying this dignity to other animals" (p. 367). In *Let the Animals Live v. Hamat Gader Recreation Enterprises* (LCA 1648/96, 22.6.1997)[123]—a case concerning a claim that a show including a battle between a man and an alligator amounted to cruelty to animals—the Supreme Court of Israel went so far as to say:

> 28. Why do courts and legislatures see fit to set out rules for the protection of animals? [...]
> 29. The first and chief basis for these prohibitions is founded on our innermost feelings that abusing animals, treating them cruelly or torturing them is immoral and unfair. The empathy that we feel for abused animals derives from a place deep in our hearts, from our sense of morality, feelings imprinted in our hearts, elicited by the sight of the weak and helpless being harmed. From birth, we are taught to protect the weak—and animals are weak. Compared to humans, animals are like children, scared and helpless. The abuse of children disgusts us and so does the abuse of animals. Animals, like children, are innocent. They do not know the meaning of evil, or how to deal with it. Animals find it difficult to protect themselves from humans and the battle between man and beast is not one between peers. Man is therefore commanded to protect animals, as part of the moral imperative to protect the weak. The rule prohibiting cruelty to animals apparently comes to protect animals as creatures to which God gave a soul. [...]
> 41. ... An animal, like a child, is a defenseless creature. Neither are able to defend themselves, nor can either stand up for their rights, honor and dignity.

An old, majestic tree may also be said to have dignity.

Regarding human beings, Roberto Andorno (2009) notes "that an analysis of international human rights instruments and of the decisions of national and international courts shows indeed that human dignity does not play just one, but *several* roles". Although this notion has a primary meaning, which refers to the intrinsic value of human beings, it has multiple functions, which operate at different levels" (p. 9). Waldron (2009b) referrs to the distinction between restricted and universal meaning of dignity, made by Teresa Iglesias:

---

[122] http://web.parliament.go.th/parcy/sapa_db/cons_doc/constitutions/data/Iran/ICL%20-%20Iran%20-%20Constitution.htm.

[123] http://elyon1.court.gov.il/files_eng/96/840/016/g01/96016840.g01.pdf.

> Consulting the dictionary we can find that the term 'dignity' connotes 'superiority', and the 'decorum' relating to it, in two basic senses. One refers to superiority of role either in rank, office, excellence, power, etc., which can pertain only to some human beings. I will identify this as the 'restricted' meaning. The other refers to the superiority of intrinsic worth of every human being that is independent of external conditions of office, rank, etc. and that pertains to everyone. In this universal sense the word 'dignity' captures the mode of being specific to the human being as a human being. This latter meaning, then, has a universal and unconditional significance, in contrast with the former that is restrictive and role-determined. (Iglesias op. cit., p. 120) (p. 24, 25, note 84)

Henry (2011), considering that the primary judicial function of 'dignity' is to give weight to substantive interests that are implicated in specific contexts" (p. 20), proposed:

> … a new method of conceptualizing dignity that draws on philosopher Ludwig Wittgenstein's view that sharp definitions of words in natural languages often distort their meaning. Wittgenstein rejected the view that a word has an essential, core meaning that applies to all the ways in which that word is used. Instead, he claimed that 'the meaning of a word is its use in the language', not an abstract link between the word and what it signifies. (p. 17)

Ludwig Wittgenstein (1889–1951) called "family resemblance" the similarities between different meanings of a word[124]. Accordingly, Henry goes on, "dignity is [also] not a fixed category, but rather a series of meanings that share a Wittgensteinian family resemblance". So, it is not a concept, but many conceptions (p. 18). This is a "heterodox approach to conceptualizing dignity", but more flexible than the "the standard approaches" that, by reducing human dignity "to another concept, such as autonomy", or to "a core meaning that is applicable across all contexts" (p. 8), are "too narrowly or too broadly" understood (p. 15), are "too exclusive or too inclusive" (p. 16). Applying the Wittgensteinian approach to the jurisprudence of the USA Supreme Court when it uses the term dignity, she highlights five different conceptions, namely: "*institutional status as dignity*, *equality as dignity*, *liberty as dignity*, *personal integrity as dignity*, and *collective virtue as dignity*" (p. 19).

Bostrom (2008) proposes the following "taxonomy" of "the different uses that have been made of the idea of dignity in recent years":

> *Dignity as a Quality*: A kind of excellence; being worthy, noble, honorable. Persons vary in the degree to which they have this property.
> A form of Dignity as a Quality can also be ascribed to nonpersons. In humans, Dignity as a Quality may be thought of as a virtue or an ideal, which can be cultivated, fostered, respected, admired, promoted, etc. It need not, however, be identified with moral virtue or with excellence in general.
> *Human Dignity* (*Menschenwürde*): The ground upon which—according to some philosophers—rests the full moral status of human beings. It is often assumed that at least all normal human persons have the same level of human dignity. There is some disagreement about what precisely human dignity consists in, and this is reflected in disagreements about which individuals have human dignity: Only persons (as Kant maintained)? Or all human individuals with a developed nervous system who are not brain-dead? Or fetuses in the womb as well? Might some nonhuman primates also have this kind of dignity?

---

[124] Ludwig Wittgenstein, *Philosophical Investigations* (1953), para. 66, 67. (Retrieved July 2013 from: http://gormendizer.co.za/wp-content/uploads/2010/06/Ludwig.Wittgenstein.-.Philosophical.Investigations.pdf).

> Two other related ideas are:
> *Human Rights*: A set of inalienable rights possessed by all beings that have full moral status. One might hold that human dignity is the ground for full moral status. Human rights can be violated or respected. We might have a strict duty not to violate human rights, and an imperfect duty to promote respect for human rights.
> (*Dignity as*) *Social Status*: A relational property of individuals, admitting of gradation. Multiple status systems may exist in a given society. Dignity as Social Status is a widely desired prudential good.
> Each of these concepts is relevant to ethics, but in different ways. (p. 176, 177)

Donnelly (2009), after referring to the distinction between "thin" and "thick" conceptions of dignity, writes:

> My formulation, however, emphasizes the simultaneous presence of multiple converging thick accounts. The concept of human dignity, in other words, is inherently thin—at least as it functions in contemporary international human rights discourse. That concept, however, rests on a variety of thick conceptions that converge on the thin account.
> Still another way to make the point would be to consider human dignity an 'essentially contested concept' over which contestation concerning justificatory details does not prevent agreement on its quasi-foundational use in international human rights law. (p. 83)

That is why, "whilst there is a *concept* of human dignity with a minimum core, there are several different *conceptions* of human dignity" (p. 679).

The *minimum core*, according to Frédéric Mégret (2009):

> … can be taken to consist of three elements: the assumed intrinsic worth of all human beings, the consequent obligation on part of all to respect each other's dignity, and the concomitant commitment on part of organized political community, notably the state, to be instrumental to the realization of human dignity rather than to instrumentalize human beings for its purposes.
> These constitutive elements of dignity, therefore, articulate what, from this perspective, would be the 'minimum core' characteristics of 'being human', notably the singularity of each human being, the equality of all human beings, and the personal autonomy necessary to live a dignified life. (p. 3)

Clapham agrees, while adding something else:

> (1) the prohibition of all types of inhuman treatment, humiliation, or degradation by one person over another; (2) the assurance of the possibility for individual choice and the conditions for 'each individual's self-fulfillment', autonomy, or self-realization; (3) the recognition that the protection of group identity and culture may be essential for the protection of personal dignity; (4) the creation of the necessary conditions for each individual to have their essential needs satisfied. (as cit. in McCrudden 2008, p. 686)

5.5.2 *Human Dignity is a Right and a Principle*

As we saw above, in International and Constitutional Law human dignity is invoked in preambular texts or as a right in itself or in connection with particular human rights matters, or as the foundation of all human rights. When it is said to be a right, it is not put on an equal footing as other rights, however. The 'Text of the explanations relating to the complete text of the Charter [of Fundamental Rights of the

European Union] as set out in CHARTE 4487/00 CONVENT 50'[125] explains: "The dignity of the human person is not only a fundamental right in itself but constitutes the real basis of fundamental rights". Commenting on the legal force of its uses—"as an actual 'right' (subjective) in the technical legal sense, or as a fundamental (objective) legal principle ('value principle')"—a former President of the Constitutional Court of Portugal said:

> However, if, as a result, it is tempting to suggest that the principle of human dignity is somewhat less than a fundamental right, at the same time it can actually be said to be more than that, as it is the 'value principle' that constitutes the very foundation (and 'criterion') on which the fundamental rights listed in the Constitution are based, giving a 'unity of meaning' to the catalogue as a whole. (in European Commission for Democracy through Law 1998, l.c)

In other words, if said to be a right, human dignity is best understood as a *right to have rights* (see Enders 2010), that is, "a deeper and broader concept than a right", as the Union of South Africa representative (C. T. Te Water) said at the 95th meeting of the Third Committee of the UN General Assembly, on 7 October 1948 (A/C.3/SR.96). The Belgian representative (Count Henry Carton de Wiart) said that "it affirmed a principle which in some measure summed up the articles that followed". According to an European Report, human rights "constitute the legal way in which the principle of human dignity is given shape; they are the mode of its legal realization, the means whereby, in a particular field, human dignity exists" (Dominique Rousseau, Concluding Report, in European Commission for Democracy through Law 1998, point 2).

This is also Habermas's thesis. After noticing that "there is a striking temporal dislocation between the history of *human rights* dating back to the seventeenth century and the relatively recent currency of the concept of *human dignity* in codifications of national and international law, and in the administration of justice, over the past half century", Habermas (2012) asked: "Why does talk of 'human rights' feature so much earlier in the law than talk of 'human dignity'?" Another question is that "of whether 'human dignity' signifies a substantive normative concept from which human rights can be deduced by specifying the conditions under which human dignity is violated. Or does the expression merely provide an empty formula that summarizes a catalogue of individual, unrelated human rights?" Is it "merely a classificatory expression, an empty placeholder, as it were, that lumps a multiplicity of different phenomena together"? (p. 65).

His thesis is "that an intimate, if initially only implicit, *conceptual* connection has existed from the very beginning" (p. 64), between human dignity and rights. He argues "that changing historical conditions have merely made us aware of something that was inscribed in human rights implicitly from the outset—the normative substance of the equal dignity of every human being that human rights only spell out" (p. 66). Consequently, the HDP plays a role that "is far from that of a vague placeholder for a missing conceptualization of human rights. 'Human dignity' per-

[125] www.europarl.europa.eu/charter/pdf/04473_en.pdf.

forms the function of a seismograph that registers what is constitutive for a democratic legal order" (p. 67).

In Habermas' opinion, the HDP "forms the 'portal' through which the egalitarian and universalistic substance of morality is imported into law. The idea of human dignity is the conceptual hinge that connects the *morality* of equal respect for everyone with positive *law* and democratic lawmaking in such a way that their interplay could give rise to a political order founded upon human rights" (p. 68). Therefore, "this *internal* connection between human dignity and human rights gives rise to the explosive fusion of moral contents with coercive law as the medium in which the construction of just political orders must be performed" (p. 77). Habermas also refers to the "two genealogical aspects: (a) on the one hand, the mediating function of 'human dignity' in the shift of perspective from moral duties to legal claims, and (b) on the other hand, the paradoxical generalization of a concept of dignity that was originally geared not to any equal distribution of dignity but to *status differences*" (p. 72). This was a "process of unification of the content of moral reason with the form of positive law on the basis of the process of generalization of the notion of 'dignity' as originally indicating a social status, to that of 'human dignity'" that is "a highly moralized concept" (p. 73). As Andorno (2009) put it, the relationship between human dignity and rights "is that of a principle and the concrete legal norms that are needed to flesh out that principle in real life" (p. 9, 10).

Principles are the ethical soul of Law. The 37th Inter-Parliamentary Conference, held in Rome, 6–11 September 1948, adopted Principles of International Morality (A/C. 3/221), drawn in:

> ... the leading principles of international morality contained in the Declaration of the Four Freedoms, the Atlantic Charter, the Moscow, Teheran and Yalta Declarations, the United Nations Charter, the Potsdam Declaration, the Act of Chapultepec, the Nuremberg Charter, the Bogota Charter, and similar international documents, as also in the main international statements made during hostilities by the spokesmen of the great democracies.

The first one read: "Relations between states are governed by principles of morality as are relations between individuals". The ICJ Statute[126] mentions "the general principles of law recognized by civilized nations" (Article 38.1.c). The ICCPR refers to "the general principles of law recognized by the community of nations" (Article 15.2). The VCLT (1969)[127] refers to "the principles of international law embodied in the Charter of the United Nations" (Preamble and Article 52). The Court of Justice of the European Union resorts to "the general principles of Community Law" that include "the fundamental human rights", as the Court said for the first time in *Erich*

[126] http://treaties.un.org/doc/Publication/CTC/uncharter.pdf.

[127] http://untreaty.un.org/ilc/texts/instruments/english/conventions/1_1_1969.pdf.

Stauder v City of Ulm[128]. The EU Charter (2000)[129] refers to "the general principles common to the laws of the Member States" (Article 41.3), as well as to "the general principles recognized by the community of nations" (Article 49.2). It mentions, among others, "the principles of democracy and the rule of law" (Preamble). The German Federal Constitutional Court, in *BVerfGE 6, 32, 1957* (*Wilhelm E., Oberstadtdirektors i.R., gegen das Urteil des Bundesverwaltungsgerichts*)[130], abovementioned, referred "to unwritten fundamental constitutional principles" (para. 32).

Although the concept is controversial, General Principles of Law are principles common to most legal systems. Perelman (1980) observed: "More and more, jurists from all corners of the world have recourse to general principles of law, which one might liken to the ancient *jus gentium* and which would find their real and sufficient grounding in the consensus of civilized humanity" (p. 47). Following Trindade (2006), who was President of the Inter-American Court of Human Rights and is now Judge of the International Court of Justice:

> Principles of International Law are guiding principles of general content, and in that they differ from the norms or rules of positive International Law, and transcend them. As basic pillars of the international legal system (as of any legal system), those principles give expression to the *idée de droit* [idea of law] and furthermore to the *idée de justice* [idea of justice] reflecting the conscience of mankind. (p. 96, 97)

Moral and legal principles are abstract and general, by their very nature, resisting consensual definitions. They may have to resort to metalegal contents. Moreover, according to a Latin adage, *omnis definitio in iure periculosa est* (every legal definition is perilous), that is, rigid definitions may render applying legal rules more difficult. Being so, legal principles are to be interpreted on a case-by-case basis. An example is the principle of the primacy of the "best interests of the child", the backbone of the CRC (1989)[131], the most general formulation of which is articulated in its Article 3.1[132]. Referring to this principle, the Constitutional Court of South Africa said, in *M v The State Centre for Child Law (S v M (CCT 53/06)*

---

[128] http://eur-lex.europa.eu/LexUriServ/LexUriServ.do?uri=CELEX:61969CJ0029:EN:HTML. The Court of Justice reaffirmed in the Joined Cases C-402/05 P and C-415/05 P *Yassin Abdullah Kadi and Al Barakaat International Foundation v Council of the European Union and Commission of the European Communities:*

> Fundamental rights form an integral part of the general principles of law whose observance the Court ensures. For that purpose, the Court draws inspiration from the constitutional traditions common to the Member States and from the guidelines supplied by international instruments for the protection of human rights on which the Member States have collaborated or to which they are signatories. In that regard, the European Convention for the Protection of Human Rights and Fundamental Freedoms has special significance. Respect for human rights is therefore a condition of the lawfulness of Community acts, and measures incompatible with respect for human rights are not acceptable in the Community. (http://eur-lex.europa.eu/LexUriServ/LexUriServ.do?uri=CELEX:62005J0402:EN:HTML).

[129] www.europarl.europa.eu/charter/pdf/text_en.pdf.

[130] www.servat.unibe.ch/dfr/bv006032.html.

[131] www2.ohchr.org/english/law/crc.htm.

[132] Its inclusion in the conventional Law gave rise to controversy. For example, Geraldine Van Bueren (1995) observed:

[2007] ZACC 18; 2008 (3) SA 232 (CC) (26 September 2007)[133], that it is precisely its "contextual nature and inherent flexibility [...] that constitutes the source of its strength".

> Viewed in this light, indeterminacy of outcome is not a weakness. A truly principled child-centred approach requires a close and individualised examination of the precise real-life situation of the particular child involved. To apply a pre-determined formula for the sake of certainty, irrespective of the circumstances, would in fact be contrary to the best interests of the child concerned. (para. 24)

So is the HDP. For instance, the German Federal Constitutional Court said in *BvR 357/05 vom 15.2.2006 (Luftsicherheitsgesetz)*[134], referring to the State's duty to respect and protect human dignity:

> 119. What this obligation means in concrete terms for state action cannot be definitely determined once and for all (see BVerfGE 45, 187 (229); 96, 375 (399–400)). [...] What is thus absolutely prohibited is any treatment of a human being by public authority which fundamentally calls into question his or her quality of a subject, his or her status as a legal entity (see BVerfGE 30, 1 (26); 87, 209 (228); 96, 375 (399)) by its lack of the respect of the value which is due to every human being for his or her own sake, by virtue of his or her being a person (see BVerfGE 30, 1 (26); 109, 279 (312–313)). When it is that such a treatment occurs must be stated in concrete terms in the individual case in view of the specific situation in which a conflict can arise (see BVerfGE 30, 1 (25); 109, 279 (311)).

The Supreme Court of Israel said in the aforementioned cases of *Commitment to Peace and Social Justice v. Minister of Finance (HCJ 366/03)* and *Bilhah Rubinova and Others v. Minister of Finance (HCJ 888/03)*[135]:

> 13. In the petition before us, the petitioners request that we order the voidance of a law, which (in their opinion) unlawfully violates the 'positive' aspect of the right to dignity, in the context of the demand to live with dignity. What is the content of this 'positive' aspect? The answer to this question lies in the constitutional interpretation of the provisions of the Basic Law. In order to characterize the right [to dignity], the judge is required to consider the circumstances of time and place, the basic values of society and its way of life, the social and political consensus and the normative reality. All of these are tools that the judge has at his disposal for interpreting the legal concept of human dignity [...]. Thus, a state with the economic strength of a developed nation cannot be compared to a state with a weak economy. A state under a continual threat to its existence cannot be compared to a state that lives peacefully without any security concerns. A society that has chosen to enshrine human dignity as a constitutional right cannot be compared to a state that has not done so [...].

> There is, however, a danger that article 3(1) will become a fulcrum for regression rather than progress and that states will adopt an extreme culturally relativist position to defend their actions.
>
> [...]
>
> Hence although at first sight the inclusion of the bests interests of the child as found in the Convention is welcome, it does appear to prompt more questions than it answers. (p. 47, 48)

Notwithstanding, although it may serve as a Trojan horse of interests contrary to the very interests of a child, the principle of the primacy of the best interests of the child became a cornerstone of Child Law. It is a metalegal principle, that is, Tribunals have to determine its content in the concrete circumstances of each case, resorting to other professional knowledge. See GC 14 of the CoRC (CRC/C/GC/14).

[133] www.saflii.org/za/cases/ZACC/2007/18.pdf.

[134] www.servat.unibe.ch/dfr/bv115118.html, and: www.bverfg.de/en/decisions/rs20060215_1bvr035705en.html.

[135] http://elyon1.court.gov.il/files_eng/03/660/003/a39/03003660.a39.pdf.

Campbell (2006), after recalling that there are "no 'self-evident' intuitions beyond a degree of consensus as to the moral relevance of certain fundamental values, such as autonomy, altruism, happiness and wellbeing", observes too:

> Equal worth, human dignity, autonomy, wellbeing and interests, remain broad and indeterminate concepts that need to be developed and applied to concrete circumstances in ways that take into account the contexts of their application and the variety of values that feature in our moral discourse. Philosophy can clarify and explore these questions but philosophers have no more authority than anyone else to claim knowledge as to their correct interpretation and application. (p. 136)

As a consequence, Botha (2009) writes:

> ... dignity is a contested concept. Sometimes, the transnational consensus on the importance of dignity appears to be a function of the high level of generality at which it is formulated. Behind the agreement on abstract notions of the inviolability of the dignity and worth of the human person lurks disagreement over the scope and meaning of dignity, its philosophical foundations, and its capacity to guide the interpretation of human rights and to constrain judicial decision-making. Alongside the conviction that dignity places constitutional interpretation on a secure footing exists the opposite view—that a dignity-based jurisprudence is the antithesis of principled decision making, because it allows judges to resort to (subjective) values rather than (objective) rules, or because 'dignity' has such a wide range of meanings that it can be invoked in defense of multiple, often directly conflicting, outcomes and presuppositions. [...]
> Concerns about the instrumentalisation and objectification of human embryos or persons in the areas of assisted reproduction, pre-implantation diagnostics, research on superfluous embryos, stem cell research, genetic therapy and cloning are, admittedly, often real, and it is understandable that dignity is invoked in these contexts. There is nevertheless a danger that the—absolute and eternal—guarantee of human dignity could be used to forestall democratic debate on issues that are the subject of widespread and reasonable disagreement. (p. 171, 172, 183)

McCrudden (2008) concluded:

> By its very openness and non-specificity, by its manipulability, by its appearance of universality disguising the extent to which cultural context is determining its meaning, dignity has enabled East and West, capitalist and non-capitalist, religious and anti-religious to agree (at least superficially) on a common concept. But this success should not blind us to the fact that where dignity is used either as an interpretive principle or as the basis for specific norms, the appearance of commonality and universality dissolves on closer scrutiny, and significantly different conceptions of dignity emerge. (p. 710)

Nevertheless, the inherent indeterminacy of the HDP has two major advantages: cultural flexibility and openness to the recognition of new rights. They are highlighted by McCrudden:

- "Dignity allows each jurisdiction to develop its own practice of human rights", so accommodating cultural particularities.
- The HDP may function "as a source from which new rights may be derived, and existing rights extended". He mentions the Basic Law: Human Dignity and Liberty, in Israel, from which new human rights have been derived (p. 720, 721).

Also Habermas (2012) values this "heuristic function of human dignity" (p. 67), in spite of the possible "function of erecting a smokescreen for disguising more profound differences" (p. 66):

> Because of their abstract character, basic rights need to be spelled out in concrete terms in each particular case. In the process, lawmakers and judges often arrive at different results in different cultural contexts; today this is apparent, for example, in the regulation of controversial ethical issues, such as assisted suicide, abortion, and genetic enhancement. It is also uncontroversial that, because of this need for interpretation, universal legal concepts facilitate negotiated compromises. Thus, appealing to the concept of human dignity undoubtedly made it easier to reach an overlapping consensus, for example during the founding of the United Nations, and more generally when negotiating human rights agreements and international legal conventions, and when adjudicating international legal disputes between parties from different cultures. [...] So judges appeal to the protection of human dignity when, for instance, the unforeseen risks of new invasive technologies lead them to introduce a new right, such as a right to informational self-determination. [...]
> Thus, the experience of the violation of human dignity has performed, and can still perform, an inventive function in many cases [...]. In the light of such specific challenges, different aspects of the meaning of human dignity emerge from the plethora of experiences of what it means to be humiliated and be deeply hurt. The features of human dignity specified and actualized in this way can then lead both to a *more complete* exhaustion of existing civil rights and to the discovery and construction of new ones. (p. 65, 66)

An example of a broad and strategic use of the HDP is that of Hungary:

> The extreme circumstances in which the Hungarian court found itself in its early years of operation, and which saw the rapid transition from socialist law to the current system, have led to extremely intense use of the notion of human dignity [...]. Finally, and most importantly, it is through the notion of human dignity, this extraordinary instrument of interpretation, that the transition from one legal system to another has been achieved in such a short period of time (less than ten years). (Catherine Dupré, in European Commission for Democracy through Law 1998, II.B)

The USA Supreme Court wisely remembered in *Lawrence et al. v. Texas* (539 U.S. 558, 2003)[136], a case above-mentioned:

> Had those who drew and ratified the Due Process Clauses of the Fifth Amendment or the Fourteenth Amendment [[137]] known the components of liberty in its manifold possibilities, they might have been more specific. They did not presume to have this insight. They knew times can blind us to certain truths and later generations can see that laws once thought necessary and proper in fact serve only to oppress. As the Constitution endures, persons in every generation can invoke its principles in their own search for greater freedom.

5.5.3 Human Dignity is Multidimensional

Human dignity's multidimensionality is here understood in a triple sense: it is multisided, multifaceted and multileveled.

- Being multisided means the variety of its content.
- Being multifaceted means the diversity of its incarnations.
- Being multileveled means the plurality of its individual and collective expressions.

[136] http://supreme.justia.com/us/539/558/case.html.

[137] *Due Process Clauses* concern the protection of individual rights guaranteed by some Amendments to the USA Constitution, as the Supreme Court said in many cases.

- **Human Dignity as Multisided**

Human dignity has both an essential-absolute and existential-relative content.

- *Essential-absolute Dignity of Being Human*

Essential-absolute human dignity concerns its classical Western conception as the capacity for rationality, liberty and morality, which are attributes intrinsic and inherent in every person, constituting the basis of human equality. So understood, human dignity is often equated with personal autonomy (or self-determination) and negative liberties[138]. Autonomy originates from the Greek term *autonomia* whose etymological roots are the words *auto* (self) and *nomos* (law). Despite its ancient roots, the term only in modern times was applied to the individual. As quoted above, explaining why "the ideas of autonomy and equality, along with human rights, [...] only gained influence in the eighteenth century", Hunt (2008) writes: "Two related but distinct qualities were involved: the ability to reason and the independence to decide for oneself. Both had to be present if an individual was to be morally autonomous" (p. 27, 28).

Autonomy means, literally, to give the law to oneself that is a positive liberty as opposed to the negative liberty of mere absence of coercion. It commands respect for the human ability to make choices and respect for one's choices. This conception is epitomized by Kant, as we know. Moral autonomy makes the human being a person, that is, the "subject of ethico-active reason [...] invested with an internal dignity (an absolute worth)" (*Metaphysics of Morals*, Book I, Introduction, § 11). Later, Hegel wrote, as we saw above: "Human beings are all rational: the formula of this rationality is that the human being as such is free. Freedom is human nature; it belongs to the essence of humanity" (as cit. in Williams 1997, p. 355). This conception inspires the Supreme Court of Israel jurisprudence, for instance, when it said in *HCJ 6427/02 Movement for Quality Government in Israel v. Knesset*, quoted in *HCJ 2605/05 Academic Center of Law and Business v. Minister of Finance*[139], aforementioned:

> 34. ... What is human dignity according to the approach of the Supreme Court? [...] The right to human dignity is based on the recognition that man is a free creature, who develops his body and mind as he wishes in the society in which he lives; the essence of human dignity lies in the sanctity of his life and his liberty. Human dignity is based on the autonomy of the individual will, the freedom of choice and the freedom of action of a human being as a free agent. Human dignity relies on the recognition of the physical and spiritual integrity of a human being, his humanity, his worth as a human being, all of which irrespective of the degree of benefit that others derive from him (see Movement for Quality Government in Israel v. Knesset [19], at para. 35 of the judgment).

The Kantian concept of human dignity is reflected in the so-called *object-formula* applied by the German Federal Constitutional Court since the 1950s. It holds that respect for human dignity should consist, first and foremost, in not treating human

[138] In that sense, self-determination may be considered as "a summation of the very idea of human rights, with all other rights being either specific aspects of self-determination, as in the case of freedom of speech, or preconditions of self-determination, as is the case with the right to sustenance (Gewirth 1982)" (Campbell 2006, p. 171).

[139] http://elyon1.court.gov.il/files_eng/05/050/026/n39/05026050.n39.pdf.

beings as mere objects and means to other ends. For example, in *BVerfGE 45, 187 (Lebenslange Freiheitsstrafe 1977)*[140]—a case concerning the lifetime imprisonment—the Court said:

> 144. The sentence 'the human being must always remain an end in itself' [Kant] has unlimited validity in all areas of the law; for the dignity of man as person, which can never be taken, consists particularly therein, that he remains recognized as a person who bears responsibility for himself.
> 145. The command to respect human dignity means in particular that cruel, inhuman and degrading punishments are not permitted [...]. The offender may not be turned into a mere object of [the State's] fight against crime under violation of his constitutionally protected right to social worth and respect (BVerfGE 28, 389 [391]).

In *Akustische Wohnraumüberwachung* (Acoustic Surveillance)[141], the Court repeated: "This court has frequently expressed the view that it is inconsistent with the dignity of the individual for the state to treat him as an object" [116 (1)]. In *BvR 357/05, 15 February 2006 (Luftsicherheitsgesetz)*[142]—a case concerning legislation authorizing the armed forces to shoot down by the direct use of force an aircraft that is intended to be used against human lives (*Aviation Security Act*)[143]—the same Court said that:

> 119. ... the obligation to respect and protect human dignity generally precludes making a human being a mere object of the State (see BVerfGE 27, 1 (6)); 45, 187 (228); 96, 375 (399)).
> [...]
> 122. ... Such a treatment ignores the status of the persons affected as subjects endowed with dignity and inalienable rights. By their killing being used as a means to save others, they are treated as objects and at the same time deprived of their rights; with their lives being disposed of unilaterally by the state, the persons on board the aircraft, who, as victims, are themselves in need of protection, are denied the value which is due to a human being for his or her own sake.

Habermas (2012) comments: "The echo of Kant's categorical imperative is unmistakable in these words of the Court. The respect for the dignity of every person forbids the state to dispose of any individual merely as a means to another end, even if that end be to save the lives of many other people" (p. 64).

The European Court of Human Rights said in the case of *Tyrer v. The United Kingdom* (Application n° 5856/72, Judgment on 25 April 1978)[144], aforementioned, that:

> 33. ... although the applicant did not suffer any severe or long-lasting physical effects, his punishment—whereby he was treated as an object in the power of the authorities—constituted an assault on precisely that which it is one of the main purposes of Article 3 (art. 3) to

---

[140] www.servat.unibe.ch/dfr/bv045187.html, and www.hrcr.org/safrica/dignity/45bverfge187.html.

[141] www.utexas.edu/law/academics/centers/transnational/work_new/german/case.php?id=658.

[142] www.servat.unibe.ch/dfr/bv115118.html, and: www.bverfg.de/en/decisions/rs20060215_1bvr035705en.html.

[143] The background of the German Parliament legislative act were 11 September 2001 terrorist attacks on the Twin Towers of New York's World Trade Center and the Pentagon.

[144] http://cmiskp.echr.coe.int/tkp197/view.asp?action=htmlanddocumentId=695464andportal=hbkmandsource=externalbydocnumberandtable=F69A27FD8FB86142BF01C1166DEA398649.

> protect, namely a person's dignity and physical integrity. Neither can it be excluded that the punishment may have had adverse psychological effects.

In the USA Supreme Court Judgment of *Furman v. Georgia* (408 U.S. 238, 1972)[145], mentioned above, Justice Brennan said, concurring: "The true significance of these punishments is that they treat members of the human race as nonhumans, as objects to be toyed with and discarded".

The Constitutional Court of the Republic of South Africa said in the above mentioned case of *The State v. T Makwanyane and M Mchunu (CCT3/94) [1995] ZACC 3; 1995 (6) BCLR 665; 1995 (3) SA 391; [1996] 2 CHRLD 164; 1995 (2) SACR 1 (6 June 1995)*[146] that the death penalty treats the convicted person "as an object to be eliminated by the state" (para. 26). The State must respect human dignity even when "it punishes criminals. This is not achieved by objectifying murderers and putting them to death to serve as an example to others in the expectation that they might possibly be deterred thereby" (para. 144). Still in South Africa, Botha (2009) refers to *Coetzee v Comitis*, in which the Cape High Court found that the regulations of the National Soccer League not allowing a player to transfer to another club upon the termination of his contract unless a transfer fee is paid "strips the player of his human dignity" to the extent that the player was treated as an object (p. 202). He concludes:

> By far the most influential definition of dignity has been the so-called 'object formula'. This definition, which found its first systematic elaboration in the work of Günter Dürig, rests on Kant's categorical imperative in terms of which a human being is an end in itself and not simply a means to an end. According to Dürig, the dignity guarantee is rooted in the idea that man is distinct from impersonal nature by virtue of his mind, which enables him to become conscious of himself, to determine himself and to shape his own environment. To treat human beings as objects is to deny their capacity to shape themselves and their environment. [...]
> The influence of Kant's categorical imperative, in terms of which persons must always be treated as ends in themselves rather than as a means to an end, is evident from the courts' use of the object formulation and from judgments which stress the right of the individual freely to choose her own ends. Woolman reads the [South Africa] Constitutional Court's dignity jurisprudence as an elaboration on a few basic Kantian themes. He distils five definitions of dignity from the Court's jurisprudence, each of which corresponds to different strands of Kantian moral thought. First, the individual should always be treated as an end in herself which should not be objectified or instrumentalised. Secondly, all individuals are entitled to equal concern and equal respect. Thirdly, individuals have the right to a space for self-actualization. Fourthly, individuals are entitled to self-governance and have the right to participate in collective decision-making processes. And fifthly, dignity requires collective responsibility for the material conditions of individual agency. (p. 183, 207)

In this respect, we should also recall the ill treatment of children that became a world-wide concern especially since the adoption of the CRC (UN 1989). The CoRC said in the GC 8 (CRC/C/GC/8, 2007)[147]: "The Convention asserts the status

---

[145] http://supreme.justia.com/search.py?query=Furman+v.+Georgia+andSearch=Search+Cases.

[146] www.saflii.org/za/cases/ZACC/1995/3.pdf.

[147] www.unhchr.ch/tbs/doc.nsf/898586b1dc7b4043c1256a450044f331/6545c032cb57bff5c12571fc002e834d/$FILE/G0740771.pdf.

of the child as an individual person and holder of human rights. The child is not a possession of parents, nor of the State, nor simply an object of concern" (para. 47).

The Inter-American Court of Human Rights said in its Advisory Opinion OC-17/2002 of 28 August 2002 on the "Juridical Condition and Human Rights of the Child"[148]:

> 137. For the foregoing reasons, the Court [...] is of the opinion
> 1. That pursuant to contemporary provisions set forth in International Human Rights Law, including Article 19 of the American Convention on Human Rights, children are subjects entitled to rights, not only objects of protection.

The Supreme Court of Cassation in Rome recalled in *Republic of Italy v. Cambria* (1996)[149], as above quoted, that children "now hold rights and are no longer simply objects to be protected by their parents or, worse still, objects at the disposal of their parents".

However, human dignity is not an abstract category. Human beings are not disembodied and isolated entities. Certain conditions and means for a decent and meaningfull life, for living humanely, are required.

- *Existential-relative Dignity of Living Humanely*

According to Griffin's (2008) *personhood account*, what distinguishes human beings is their autonomy as normative agency that is the ontological foundation of human rights. "The word 'agency' is used more or less broadly within the spectrum from deliberation to choice to action to outcome. In the personhood account it is used broadly—to cover all of these stages" (p. 48). Indeed : "What we attach value to, what we regard as giving dignity to human life, is our capacity to choose and to pursue our conception of a worthwhile life" (p. 44). Human rights can "be seen as protections of our human standing" or personhood (p. 33). He distinguishes between liberty and autonomy and argues that the principal enemy of the first is indoctrination, and the principal enemy of the second is compulsion.

Human rights possess another ground, however: the "practicalities" that are the conditions for the existence of a right (p. 44).

> To be an agent, in the fullest sense of which we are capable, one must (first) choose one's own path through life—that is, not be dominated or controlled by someone or something else (call it 'autonomy'). And (second) one's choice must be real; one must have at least a certain minimum education and information. And having chosen, one must then be able to act; that is, one must have at least the minimum provision of resources and capabilities that it takes (call all of this 'minimum provision'). And none of this is any good if someone then blocks one; so (third) others must also not forcibly stop one from pursuing what one sees as a worthwhile life (call this 'liberty'). [...]
> My personhood account can be seen as trinist (if I may coin a word to come next in the sequence 'monist', 'dualist'). Human rights, I propose, have their ground in the three values of personhood: autonomy, liberty, and minimum provision. (p. 33, 51)

[148] www.crin.org/docs/advisory-opinion17.pdf.

[149] www.endcorporalpunishment.org/pages/frame.html.

Griffin does not include equality formally within the grounds for human rights, because he considers it implicated in personhood.

Consequently, we are normative agents because we deliberate, evaluate, choose and act in the light of a view of the good life. Human rights aim at enabling and protecting us as normative agents. They are autonomy rights, liberty rights and rights for a minimum of wellbeing.

Fagan (2005) observes that Alan Gewirth also "argues that the justification of our claims to the possession of basic human rights is grounded in what he presents as the distinguishing characteristic of human beings generally: the capacity for rationally purposive agency". Human rights "are the necessary means for rationally purposive action", notably "freedom and wellbeing"[150].

This is the substantive conception of human dignity taken on by the IHRL. The aforementioned *Complément à la Déclaration des Droits de l'Homme* (Complement to the Declaration of the Rights of Man and of the Citizen), adopted by the French League of Human Rights in 1936, stated in Article 2: "The right to life is the first human right". It implies economic, social and cultural rights detailed in Articles 3 and 4. Article 11 added: "The right to life implies the abolition of war".

Let us recall that President Roosevelt said in the 'Second Bill of Rights' (1944)[151]: 'Necessitous men are not free men'. The UDHR Article 22 states that everyone is entitled to the realization "of the economic, social and cultural rights indispensable for his dignity and the free development of his personality". Article 23.3 states that the right to work includes "the right to just remuneration ensuring for himself and his family an existence worthy of human dignity". According to the UN Millenium Declaration (2000)[152]: "Men and women have the right to live their lives and raise their children in dignity, free from hunger and from the fear of violence, oppression or injustice. Democratic and participatory governance based on the will of the people best assures these rights" (para. 6).

At the constitutional level, Bendor and Sachs (2011) note, referring to the Constitution of Weimar (1919), that "the economic dimension of human dignity has afterwards become part of the concept of human dignity in German Constitutional Law" (p. 4). According to the GG (1949)[153]: "The Federal Republic of Germany is a democratic and social Federal State" (Article 20.1). Article 28.1 states: "The constitutional order in the *Länder* [German States] must conform to the principles of republican, democratic, and social government based on the rule of law, within the meaning of this Basic Law". Following the jurisprudence of the German Federal Constitutional Court, these Articles, read with Article 1.1, impose an obligation on the State to provide at least minimal subsistence to every individual.

[150] Michael Ignatieff suggested "to link dignity to agency, on the assumption that cultures could then agree that what matters is the right of people to construe dignity as they wish, not the content they give to it. Dignity as agency is thus the most plural, the most open definition of the word I can think of" (as cit. in Rao 2011, p. 200, note 61).

[151] www.ushistory.org/documents/economic_bill_of_rights.htm.

[152] www.un.org/millennium/declaration/ares552e.htm.

[153] www.btg-bestellservice.de/pdf/80201000.pdf.

The Belgian Constitution expressly states (Article 23)[154]:

> Everyone has the right to lead a life worthy of human dignity.
> For this purpose, the law, the decree or the rule specified in Article 134 guarantees the conditions of their exercise, taking into account the corresponding obligations of economic, social and cultural rights.[155]

The Federal Constitution of the Swiss Confederation (1999)[156] states in Article 12 (Right to assistance when in need): "Whoever is in distress without the ability to take care of him- or herself has the right to help and assistance and to the means indispensable for a life led in human dignity". The Constitution of Finland (2000)[157] states in Action 19 (Right to social security): "Those who cannot obtain the means necessary for a life of dignity have the right to receive indispensable subsistence and care".

Turning to Case Law, the German Federal Constitutional Court said in the aforementioned case *BVerfGE 6, 32, 1957* (*Wilhelm E., Oberstadtdirektors i. R., gegen das Urteil des Bundesverwaltungsgerichts*)[158]: "Above all, laws must not violate a person's dignity which represents the highest value of the Basic Law, nor may they restrict the spiritual, political and economic freedom of the human being [*Menschen*] in a way that would erode his/her essence" (para. 32). In *BvL 1/09 (2010)*[159] it referred, as above quoted, to "a subsistence minimum that is in line with the human dignity" of every person, concerning "the material conditions that are indispensable for his or her physical existence and for a minimum participation in social, cultural and political life" (para. 1.a). Habermas (2012) points out this "groundbreaking decision" (p. 66)[160].

---

154 www.senate.be/doc/const_fr.html.

155 Delpérée commented:

> 2. The right to life may call for minimum means of subsistence. This is why social assistance is granted under the law of 8 July 1976. It is not simply a question of money; the law also provides for the granting of social, medical, psychological and other assistance. The aim, expressly stated in the law, is to enable the beneficiary to lead a life worthy of human dignity (in European Commission for Democracy through Law 1998, p. 1.2).

156 www.admin.ch/ch/f/rs/1/101.fr.pdf, and: www.admin.ch/ch/e/rs/1/101.en.pdf.

157 www.finlex.fi/fi/laki/kaannokset/1999/en19990731.pdf.

158 www.servat.unibe.ch/dfr/bv006032.html.

159 www.bverfg.de/en/press/bvg10-005en.html.

160 In this connection, Bryde (2005) observes:

> A very controversial question in German jurisprudence is to what extent a conceptualization of rights as principles must also lead to the recognition of social rights and claims for public services. [...]
> When fundamental rights are principles whose realization is important for people and society, the constitutional system cannot be neutral as to the question of whether people are able to enjoy such rights in practice. [...]
> An absolute exclusion of a social dimension of fundamental rights is no longer possible. While being reluctant to grant outright claims for public services based on fundamental rights, the Constitutional Court, along with other courts, has developed this social dimension. [...] Today it is generally recognized that the state is under a duty to provide for the

The extent of human rights demanded by a substantive conception of human dignity may vary. Examples of a broad interpretation are the jurisprudence of the Supreme Court of India and the Constitutional Court of South Africa, which stress the indivisibility of human rights.

USA Supreme Court jurisprudence is qualified as liberty-based for linking intrinsic human worth with negative freedoms that are freedoms from interference by the Government, in accordance with the Latin saying *de internis non judicat praetor*. Rao (2011) comments: "American courts are restrained, if not outright hostile, to inferring and imposing positive constitutional rights. But American constitutional law is exceptional in this regard" (p. 237)[161]. Bognetti (2003) writes:

> In a beautiful essay Professor Louis Henkin of Columbia University has rewritten the entire history of the rights in the American Constitution, from the time of the Framers to our times, in the light of the concept of the dignity of man [...]. In the name of human dignity he has asked that the death penalty be adjudicated unconstitutional and has stated that the Constitution should proclaim the right to work and to leisure, the right to food, housing, health care and education, and the right to an adequate standard of living: all rights not less "essential to human dignity" than the traditional liberties.

The Supreme Court of India said in *Francis Coralie Mullin v. The Administrator, Union Territory of Delhi and ORS, 1981, SCR (2) 516, 518*[162], a case already quoted, that "the magnitude and content of the components of [the right to life] would depend upon the extent of the economic development of the country, but it must, in any view of the matter, include the right to the basic necessities of life and also the right to carry on such functions and activities as constitute the bare minimum expression of the human-self" (para. 6).

The Constitutional Court of South Africa said in *Government of the Republic of South Africa and Others v Irene Grootboom and Others (Case CCT 11/10)*[163], a case concerning the eviction of people from their informal homes situated on private land earmarked for formal low-cost housing:

> [23] Our Constitution entrenches both civil and political rights and social and economic rights. All the rights in our Bill of Rights are inter-related and mutually supporting. There can be no doubt that human dignity, freedom and equality, the foundational values of our

---

minimal needs of existence to every inhabitant of Germany and that this claim is enforceable in court.

The Constitutional Court strengthened statutory welfare rights to pensions, unemployment benefits, and health insurance by giving them an interesting, perhaps even astonishing, constitutional basis. [...]

In sum, the traditional concept of basic rights as defensive rights has been replaced by a concept of basic rights as principles with many different functions. (p. 202, 203, 204)

[161] Frederick Schauer, quoted by Rao (2011), explains America's liberty-oriented exceptionalism in speech matters: "On a large number of other issues in which the preferences of individuals may be in tension with the needs of the collective, the United States, increasingly alone, stands as a symbol for a certain kind of preference for liberty even when it conflicts with values of equality and even when it conflicts with important community values" (p. 213).

[162] http://indiankanoon.org/doc/78536/?type=print.

[163] www.saflii.org/za/cases/ZACC/2000/19.pdf.

society, are denied those who have no food, clothing or shelter. Affording socio-economic rights to all people therefore enables them to enjoy the other rights enshrined in Chapter 2.

The Supreme Court of Israel refers to an intermediate interpretation. In *HCJ 2605/05 Academic Center of Law and Business v. Minister of Finance*[164], it said:

> In the judgment in HCJ 6427/02 Movement for Quality Government in *Israel v. Knesset*, it was held that the model adopted by the Supreme Court with regard to the scope of application of the constitutional right to human dignity is an 'intermediate model'; in other words, the right to human dignity does not only include those clear violations that relate to a person's humanity, such as physical and emotional injuries, humiliation and defamation, but it does not encompass all human rights.

In *Man, Nature and Law—Israel Environmental Protection Society v. Prime Minister of Israel*, according to a quotation in the above cited case of *Commitment to Peace and Social Justice v. Minister of Finance (HCJ 366/03)* and *Bilhah Rubinova and Others v. Minister of Finance (HCJ 888/03)*[165], the Court said:

> 15. [...] Constitutional interpretation of the right to dignity must determine its constitutional dimensions. It should not be restricted merely to torture and humiliation, since thereby we would fail to achieve the purpose underlying it; it should not be extended in such a way that every human right is included in it, since this would make all the other human rights provided in the Basic Laws redundant. The proper interpretation of the right to dignity should find its path between the two extremes. [...]

In any case, "the human right to dignity is also the right to conduct one's ordinary life as a human being, without being overcome by economic distress and being reduced to an intolerable poverty".

It should be noted that human dignity might also not be respected in the process of implementing human rights. For instance, in satisfying the right to social assistance, public or private bodies performing social welfare functions may not take into due account the right to privacy.

The right way to approach the absolute-relative nature of human dignity should avoid the Scylla of abstraction and the Charybdis of trivialization[166], let alone nullification. Avoiding abstraction means, as the Constitutional Court of South Africa Court said, in *National Coalition for Gay and Lesbian Equality and Another v Minister of Justice and Others (CCT11/98) [1998] ZACC 15; 1999 (1) SA 6; 1998 (12) BCLR 1517 (9 October 1998)*[167], not presupposing "that a holder of rights is as an isolated, lonely and abstract figure possessing a disembodied and socially disconnected self" (para. 117). An example of the trivialization of invoking human dignity occurred in Germany in a case regarding a telephone bill, electronically processed, in which the German 'ö' was transliterated into 'oe' (in *BVerwGE 31, 236, 1969*, cit. in Botha 2009, p. 183). An example of nullification would be to argue, for instance, as Botha notices, "that the right not to be tortured—always considered to be at the heart of the dignity guarantee—is not absolute, that there are circumstances

[164] http://elyon1.court.gov.il/files_eng/05/050/026/n39/05026050.n39.pdf.

[165] http://elyon1.court.gov.il/files_eng/03/660/003/a39/03003660.a39.pdf.

[166] Following mythology, Scylla and Charybdis were sea monsters whose names designate a rock and a vortex in the Strait of Messina (between Italy and Sicily). Seeking to avoid one of the two dangers, ships could be caught by the other one (Scylla devoured six of Ulysses' fellows).

[167] www.saflii.org/za/cases/ZACC/1998/15.pdf.

in which it is outweighed by the dignity of others, and that in such cases the state is under an obligation to torture a person in order to save the lives of innocent persons" (p. 195). A similar justification was that of the aforementioned German *Aviation Security Act.*

According to Mégret (2009):

> Two ideas, in particular, encapsulate this essence of dignity: justice and freedom. Justice here denotes the aspiration to organize society in way that every human is treated according to the fullness of his or her being, to not reduce him or her to abstract categories, and to do so equally with all. Freedom in relation to dignity refers to freedom from domination or freedom from instrumentalization. [...] Both justice and freedom, hence, give dignity its particular flavor: dignity is empowerment. (p. 3)

As Deputy Chief Justice Haim Cohn of the Israel Supreme Court said in *HCJ 355/79 Katalan v. Prison Services [1980] IsrSC 34(3) 294*: "A free and enlighted society is distinguished from a savage or oppressive society by the degree of dignity extended to any person as a human being" (as cit. in Bendor and Sachs 2011, p. 8). For example, the Constitutional Court of South Africa highlighted, in *August and Another v Electoral Commission and Others (CCT8/99) [1999] ZACC 3; 1999 (3) SA 1; 1999 (4) BCLR 363 (1 April 1999)*[168]: "The vote of each and every citizen is a badge of dignity and of personhood. Quite literally, it says that everybody counts" (para. 17). Furthermore, as Bryde (2005) observed:

> Increasingly, human rights are endangered not only by the state but also by other private actors. Therefore, a comprehensive protection of human rights must also protect them against private actors. This becomes even more important with an increased privatization of public services. Academic freedom must not only be protected against the state but also against sponsors and donors.
>
> Equally, the realization of human rights in modern societies often depends on conditions beyond the power of the individual.
>
> [...]
>
> Finally, human dignity requires that we are not mere objects of not only state control but also social conditions and market powers. For human beings to live their lives in dignity, the social dimension of human rights has to be recognized. In their positive function, human rights are an important impediment against a purely market- and profit oriented view of social organization. If one concentrates only on the negative function of human rights, one tends to protect established interests. [...] An adequate consideration of positive functions of human rights here strikes a necessary balance. That may be an unfashionable idea in the current ideological ascendancy of laissez-faire capitalism, which insists on repeating all the mistakes of the nineteenth century, but this does not make it any less important. (p. 207, 208)

- **Human Dignity as Multifaceted**

Dignity is an ethical quality of all human beings of whatever status that includes:

- not yet born human life and deceased human beings;
- people of genius as well as physically or mentally handicapped persons;
- virtuous people as well as criminals and torturers.

[168] www.saflii.org/za/cases/ZACC/1999/3.pdf.

- *There is dignity already in unborn human life*

This is a controversial matter, as we know.

The German Federal Constitutional Court said in *BVerfGE 39, 1, 1975 (Schwangerschaftsabbruch I)*[169], a case above quoted: "Where human life exists, human dignity is present to it. The potential faculties present in the human being from the beginning suffice to establish human dignity" (para. 147). This claim does not preclude us from distinguishing between human life and a human person, as the European Court of Human Rights did in *Case of Vo v. France* (Application 53924/00)[170], when it said that, while "there is no consensus on the nature and status of the embryo and/or foetus (see paragraphs 39–40 above)", it is recognized "that the embryo/foetus belongs to the human race. The potentiality of that being and its capacity to become a person [...] require protection in the name of human dignity, without making it a 'person' with the 'right to life' for the purposes of Article 2" (para. 84).

- *There is dignity still in a deceased human being*

The German Federal Constitutional Court said in the above mentioned case of *Mephisto*[171]: "It would be inconsistent with the constitutional mandate of the inviolability of human dignity, which underlies all basic rights, if a person could be belittled and denigrated after his death". Accordingly, the State bears the duty to protect a dead individual "from assaults on his human dignity" (para. 6). The Supreme Court of Israel said in *Women's Association for the Future of Israel v. The Broadcasting Authority (HCJ 6143/94, July 26, 1999)*[172], a case concerning a play on actual historical events in which, it was claimed, there was a scene containing falsehoods defaming a woman and survivors of the Holocaust:

> 12. ... The significance of preserving a person's reputation also derives from the values of the State of Israel as a democratic state. One who steals my property can compensate me monetarily, but he who robs me of my good name has stolen the very reason for my existence. One's good name determines the manner in which one perceives oneself and how one's peers and society relate to one. In effect, the only asset of many people, both public servants and those working in the private sector, is their reputation, which they cherish as life itself. This applies to both the living and the dead. We must protect the dignity of the deceased and their good name.

The dignity of deceased human beings survives physically in the genetic heritage they may have transmitted to their children, affectively in the memory of their most beloved, as well as symbolically in their names. Other aspects of moral survival are the authors' rights (copyright). Others are the online profiles and data (digital remains) whose legal statute is still generally in a limbo state[173]. Deceased human

---

[169] http://groups.csail.mit.edu/mac/users/rauch/germandecision/german_abortion_decision2.html.

[170] http://hudoc.echr.coe.int/sites/eng/pages/search.aspx?i=001-61887#{"itemid":["001-61887"]}.

[171] www.iuscomp.org/gla/judgments/tgcm/v710224.htm.

[172] www.concernedhistorians.org/content_files/file/le/131.pdf.

[173] The Programme of the 2012 Amsterdam Privacy Conference (7–10 October) included a Panel with the title "Death and Post-Mortem Privacy in the Digital Age". Presenting the topic, the Book

beings may also be immortalized by a country's people for the greateness of their creations or actions, to say nothing of faith in immortality.

- *Intrinsic human dignity is not increased by genius nor decreased by physical or mental handicaps*

The German Federal Constitutional Court said in *BVerfGE 87, 209 (Tanz der Teufel 1992)*[174], a case concerning a film where human dignity allegedly was not respected: "Everybody possesses it [human dignity], regardless of his characteristics, achievements, or social status. It is also possessed by those who cannot act in a meaningful way because of their physical or psychological condition" (para. 113).

- *Virtuous people as well as criminals and torturers are on an equal footing to the extent that they hold the same ontological dignity, without precluding them from differentiated judgments of dignified and undignified behaviors*

In the same case of *Tanz der Teufel*, the German Federal Constitutional Court said: "[Human dignity] is not lost even by means of 'undignified' behavior" (para. 113). In the USA Supreme Court Judgment of *Furman v. Georgia* (408 U.S. 238, 1972)[175], Justice Brennan stressed, concurring, that even "the vilest criminal remains a human being possessed of common human dignity". The same Court said in *Roper v. Simmons* (543 U.S. 03-633, 2004)[176], a case concerning the death penalty for a murder committed by a juvenile at age 17, after he had turned 18: "By protecting even those convicted of heinous crimes, the Eighth Amendment reaffirms the duty of the government to respect the dignity of all persons".

---

of Abstracts read:

> Dealing with the aftermath of someone's death is always a difficult and sensitive issue. In recognition of this, western society has developed rites, rituals and norms to aid the bereaved in dealing with the physical remains and redistribute the possessions of the deceased. This involves balancing an innate desire to respect the dignity and privacy of the deceased with the needs and interests of the bereaved and wider community.
> [...]
> Increasingly virtual lives are created online, but at death these digital lives are locked behind passwords; therefore without access these remains and their sentimental, economic, historical or educational value are lost.
> [...]
> Many of these puzzles revolve around privacy and raise interesting questions. Does a decedent have privacy interests that require recognition and/or protection? Who should control or exercise these interests on behalf of a decedent? How are these privacy interests reconciled with the interests of heirs or family members of the deceased, or with wider societal requirements? What role can and should Internet intermediaries and services providers play in protecting these competing privacy interests?
> (Retrieved July 2013 from: www.apc2012.org/sites/default/files/pdffiles/Book%20of%20Abstracts_1.pdf).

[174] www.servat.unibe.ch/dfr/bv087209.html.

[175] http://supreme.justia.com/search.py?query=Furman+v.+;Georgia+andSearch=Search+Cases.

[176] http://supreme.justia.com/us/543/03-633/case.html.

Reboul (1992) recalled: "Towards the end of the war, when Hitler was still alive, an Anglo-Saxon newspaper asked what one was going to make of him and proposed to put him inside a mobile cage to be exposed to the crowds worldwide, the amount paid for the spectacle serving to compensate his victims". He commented: "That would be to punish Hitler by putting oneself at the same level as Hitler, continuing his enterprise of profanation" (p. 91).

- **Human Dignity as Multileveled**

Human dignity is at stake at both individual and collective levels.

Human rights empowerment consists in protecting human beings' life and liberty without neglecting their basic needs and wellbeing by providing them with food, drink, shelter, health care, etc., as well as other rights that enable every human being to self-determination, to self-fulfillment, thus generating feelings of self-worth and self-esteem. However, self-esteem originates from feeling recognized and respected by others, individually and possibly collectively. In fact, self-esteem is mediated by the cultural and social environment within which a human being is born that forms a collective identity and models individual identities. The respect for individual dignity implies, therefore, respect for the collective dignity of the groups and the nation a person belongs to. The Canadian Supreme Court said in *R. v. Keegstra, [1990] 3 S. C. R. 697*[177], a case concerning a high school teacher charged with willfully promoting anti-Semitic hatred:

> A person's sense of human dignity and belonging to the community at large is closely linked to the concern and respect accorded the groups to which he or she belongs. [...] The derision, hostility and abuse encouraged by hate propaganda therefore have a severely negative impact on the individual's sense of self-worth and acceptance. [...] Such consequences bear heavily in a nation that prides itself on tolerance and the fostering of human dignity through, among other things, respect for the many racial, religious and cultural groups in our society.

The same Court said in *Law v. Canada (Minister of Employment and Immigration), [1999] 1 S. C. R. 497*, a case concerning a 30-year-old woman without dependent children or disability, who was denied survivor's benefits:

> 53. … Human dignity means that an individual or group feels self-respect and self-worth. It is concerned with physical and psychological integrity and empowerment. Human dignity is harmed by unfair treatment premised upon personal traits or circumstances which do not relate to individual needs, capacities, or merits. It is enhanced by laws which are sensitive to the needs, capacities, and merits of different individuals, taking into account the context underlying their differences. Human dignity is harmed when individuals and groups are marginalized, ignored, or devalued, and is enhanced when laws recognize the full place of all individuals and groups within Canadian society.

Referring to the jurisprudence of the South African Constitutional Court, in this respect, Botha (2009) comments, however:

> The Court has recognised the importance of the family to individual dignity and wellbeing, and acknowledged the centrality of religion and culture to the identity and dignity of the person. It has also tied dignity to the indigenous African concept of ubuntu, which refers

[177] http://scc.lexum.org/en/1990/1990scr3-697/1990scr3-697.pdf.

> to broad notions of human solidarity, respect and interdependence. These attempts to tie dignity to communitarian and solidaristic notions of interdependence and mutual respect have been controversial. The Court's reliance on Ubuntu has been criticised, inter alia, for romanticising traditional African values, uncritically conflating them with contemporary constitutional norms, and negating the conflict inherent in a pluralistic society. (p. 204, 205)

Moreover, the individuals and groups dignity is indissociable of the human species dignity, too.

In the above quoted case of *Tanz der Teufel*[178], the German Federal Constitutional Court said:

> With the human dignity concept [...] is tied the human being's social worth and entitlement to respect, which forbids [anyone] to make her/him a mere object of the State or to expose her/him to a treatment that calls into question essentially her/his subject quality. In this sense, human dignity is not only the individual dignity of every person, but also the dignity of the human being as a species. (para. 113)

In this connection, we should recall Kant's statement in the *Metaphysics of Morals* (Book II, § 38): "Humanity is itself a Dignity". The human being has a duty "to the humanity subsisting in his person".

As a consequence, the fact that human dignity is multileveled may give rise to *hard cases* (cases to which there is no clear legally written answer), regarding conflicts between human rights, between human rights and human dignity, between individual and collective levels of human dignity, as well as between two dignity positions, the solutions for which may be more or less controversial.

With regard to conflicts between the individual and the collective levels of human dignity, a group's dignity never can be invoked against an individual's dignity. The *honor killings* are cruel cases in point[179]. As the Universal Declaration on Cultural Diversity (UNESCO 2001)[180] remembers: "No one may invoke cultural diversity to infringe upon human rights guaranteed by international law, nor to limit their scope". Culture is a collective cradle, not an individual destiny. Personal identity is broadly a self-construction that should be open to horizons of possibilities without arbitrary frontiers. Should collective and personal identities be conflicting, the protection of individual human dignity must always prevail[181].

---

[178] www.servat.unibe.ch/dfr/bv087209.html.

[179] Honor killing is a kind of homicide of a family's or group's member, most frequently a girl or a woman, committed by other members (almost always the father, the husband and brothers), for behaviors allegedly dishonoring the family or group, such as having sex outside marriage or even having become the victim of rape. Honor killings occur throughout the world, but are typically associated with Muslim countries, although it is a practice predating Islam, rooted in ancient tribal customs. Following the Human Rights Commission of Pakistan, in 2011 almost 1,000 Pakistani women were murdered for allegedly dishonoring their families. 595 of the murdered women were accused of illicit sexual relations (premarital or extramarital), and 219 women married without family permission. On top of the killings, about 4,500 other women were victims of domestic violence last year.
(See: http://theweek.com/article/index/225998/pakistans-escalating-honor-killing-problem).

[180] www.un-documents.net/udcd.htm.

[181] The primacy of the individual is emphasized in the Universal Declaration on Bioethics and Human Rights (UNESCO 2005), whose Article 3.2 states: "The interests and welfare of the individual

Less undisputed are conflicts between human dignity and the protection of public interest[182]. The German Federal Constitutional Court said in the case of *Akustische Wohnraumüberwachung* (Acoustic Surveillance)[183], mentioned above, referring to the protection of human dignity:

> [121] (3) This protection must not be weakened by weighing it against the public interest in the prosecution of crime, even in the light of the principle of proportionality. It may well be that when there is cogent evidence that an extremely serious crime has been committed, many people would think the public interest in the effective repression of crime outweighs the dignity of the suspect. Nevertheless, the Constitution forbids the state to make any such evaluation (Art. 1(1), 79(3)).

A conflict between human rights and human dignity is possible and also very controversial. A paradigmatic case of decisions stating that the species' dignity should prevail over individual human rights is the banning of dwarf-throwing shows in France, which gave rise to appeals submitted to the *Conseil d'État* (Council of State), to the European Commission of Human Rights (Council of Europe) and to the CCPR (UN). Let us highlight their most relevant aspects, taking as main source the summary of the CCPR Decision.

Manuel Wackenheim, who suffers from dwarfism, began in July 1991 to appear in "dwarf tossing" shows organized by a company called *Société Fun-Productions*. The show consisted in clients of a discothèque grabbing him, with his consent, and trying to throw him, wearing suitable protective gear, onto an airbed, as far as possible. On 27 November 1991, the French Ministry of the Interior issued a circular on the policing of public events, in particular dwarf tossing, which should be banned, on the basis of Article 3 of the ECHR in particular. On 30 October 1991, Wackenheim applied to the Administrative Court in Versailles to annul an order dated 25 October 1991 by the Mayor of Morsang-sur-Orge banning a dwarf-tossing event. On 25 February 1992, the Court annulled the order. According to its decision, "even supposing, as the mayor maintains, that the event might have represented a degrading affront to human dignity, a ban could not be legally ordered in the absence of particular local circumstances". On 24 April 1992, Morsang-sur-Orge, represented by its Mayor, appealed against the ruling. On 20 March 1992, Wackenheim made another application against a similar order by the mayor of Aix-en-Provence. On 8 October 1992, the Administrative Court of Marseille annulled the order, jugding that dwarf tossing was not of a nature to affront human dignity. On 16 December 1992, Aix-en-Provence, represented by its Mayor, appealed against the ruling. On 27 October 1995, the *Conseil d'État* overturned both rulings on the

---

should have priority over the sole interest of science or society".

(http://portal.unesco.org/en/ev.php-URL_ID=31058andURL_DO=DO_TOPICandURL_SECTION=201.html).

[182] According to Campbell (2006), public interest is "the legitimate interests of all members of society as identified by criteria such as wellbeing, autonomy, justice and equality. The mechanisms whereby this is achieved are a combination of open elections for government office, ongoing debate and free political association and the promotion of an educated and informed population" (p. 96).

[183] www.utexas.edu/law/academics/centers/transnational/work_new/german/case.php?id=658.

grounds, among others, that dwarf tossing is, by its very nature, "an attraction that undermines the respect for the dignity of human person", and that "respect for human dignity is part of public order". Since then, the *Société Fun-Productions* has decided no longer to engage in activities of this kind, and Wackenheim has since been without a job. In the meantime, he had lodged a complaint with the European Commission of Human Rights against France, on 4 February 1994 (registered on 25 January 1996 under the N° 29961/96).

On 16 October 1996, the Commission declared the complaint inadmissible on the grounds that the author had not exhausted the domestic remedies available against some alleged violations of the ECHR, and that other complaints were inconsistent *ratione materiae* (because of their object). On November 1996, Wackenheim submitted a Communication to the CCPR (represented by Counsel Mr. Serge Pautot), registered under the N° 854/1999 (CCPR/C/75/D/854/1999). He claimed, in particular, that banning his activity represented an affront to his dignity; that he was the victim of a violation of his right to employment and of an act of discrimination and also that his job does not constitute an affront to human dignity since dignity consists in having a job. Commenting on the French Government observations dated 13 July 1999, the Counsel representing Wackenheim asked: "Are Mayors to become censors of public morality and defenders of human dignity?" And affirmed: "Depriving an individual of his employment is tantamount to diminishing his dignity".

The Committee decided on 26 July 2002. It found the Communication admissible and deliberated on the complaint's merits, but concluded that the ban on dwarf tossing "did not constitute an abusive measure but was necessary in order to protect public order, which brings into play considerations of human dignity that are compatible with the objectives of the Covenant"[184].

For a similar reason, the USA Supreme Court said in *Indiana v. Ahmad Edwards* (554 U.S. 164, 175, 2008)[185]—a case involving a mentally ill man who invoked his constitutional right to self-representation and was judged competent to stand trial—that the "right of self-representation at trial will not 'affirm the dignity' of a defendant who lacks the mental capacity to conduct his defense without the assistance of counsel. [...] To the contrary, given that defendant's uncertain mental state, the spectacle that could well result from his self-representation at trial is at least as likely to prove humiliating as ennobling".

Another example is the Constitutional Court of South Africa Judgment, in *State v Jordan and Others (Sex Workers Education and Advocacy Task Force and Others as Amici Curiae (CCT31/01) [2002] ZACC 22; 2002 (6) SA 642; 2002 (11) BCLR 1117 (9 October 2002)*[186], a case upholding a prohibition on prostitution. It referred to "the respect that the Constitution regards as inherent in the human body" and affirmed: "The very nature of prostitution is the commodification of one's body. Even though we accept that prostitutes may have few alternatives to prostitution,

184 www.unhchr.ch/tbs/doc.nsf/0/09d49050a9b34aaac1256c6e0031b919?Opendocument.

185 www.supremecourt.gov/opinions/07pdf/07-208.pdf.

186 www.saflii.org/za/cases/ZACC/2002/22.pdf.

the dignity of prostitutes is diminished [...] by their engaging in commercial sex work" (para. 74).

Botha (2009) cited a case in which a South African High Court affirmed that bestiality is "so repugnant to and in conflict with human dignity as to amount to perversion of the natural order", and that the State is under an obligation to "prevent any individual or group from descending to the level of the beast". He remarks, however, that the reliance on dignity "as the basis for the justification of the criminalization of bestiality risks reducing the scope of personal and sexual autonomy and conflating dignity with dignified behaviour". Linking dignity with 'natural order' "tends to naturalise dominant assumptions about what constitutes 'normal' sexual behavior" (p. 203). It was not the case when the Supreme Court of Israel, in *Station Film Co. v. Public Council for Film Censorship*, overturned a decision of the Film Censorship Board on the deletion of scenes it considered degrading to women, on the ground that the artistic value of the film had to be weighed against the need to protect human dignity (see McCrudden 2008, p. 702). Rao (2011) comments:

> These types of social policies reflect the idea that the law should prohibit immoral behavior for the benefit of the individual and society. This assumes that a choice of a degrading profession is either not a good choice or is not a true choice, in that the decision may be based on economic necessity or coercion by others. The regulations thus protect the individual from bad choices. The consent of individuals making pornography or engaging in prostitution is irrelevant because such persons misperceive the harms to their dignity or else are judged to be making such choices only under duress. Such reasoning is familiar and underlies a great part of the regulatory state.
> The issue here is not whether laws prohibiting prostitution or pornography may be desirable as social policy. Rather these examples demonstrate that the conception of dignity used to defend such policies is not that of human agency and freedom of choice, but rather represents a particular moral view of what dignity requires. (p. 229)

The official *Commentary* on the EU Charter remarks:

> A balancing of human dignity with another fundamental right therefore may not take place. A socalled fundamental right's collision, however, is not out of the question between two human dignity positions (for instance that of an embryo, if dignity is awarded to it, and that of its mother in questions of abortion). In such a case, careful consideration would have been attempted, aimed at finding a considerate balance. In a concrete case, however, this may result in one of the positions having to fully stand back. (EU Network of Independent Experts on Fundamental Rights 2006, p. 29)

The German Federal Constitutional Court concluded, in *BVerfGE 45, 187 (Lebenslange Freiheitsstrafe 1977)*[187], mentioned above: "Human dignity is something indisposable" (para. 146)[188]. Also, the German Federal Administrative Court stated in *BVerwGe 64, 274, 1981 (Sittenwidrigkeit von Peer-Shows)*[189], a case regarding sex work: "Human dignity is an objective, indisposable value [...], the respect of

---

[187] www.servat.unibe.ch/dfr/bv045187.html#Opinion.

[188] *Bei alledem darf nicht aus den Augen verloren werden: Die Würde des Menschen ist etwas Unverfügbares.*

[189] www.servat.unibe.ch/dfr/vw064274.html.

which the individual cannot give up validly". As Catherine Labrusse-Riou wrote, each human being is the "depository, but not proprietor" of human dignity (as cit. in Hennette-Vauchez 2008, p. 14)[190].

In any case, human dignity is violable, vulnerable and variable.

5.5.4 Human Dignity is Violable, Vulnerable and Variable

Human dignity is inviolable (*Die Menschenwüde ist unantastbar*)—as famously proclaimed German GG Article 1.1[191]. This emphatically echoed in the EU Charter Article 1. As observes its official *Commentary*: "The wording [of Article 1] follows the formulation of Article 1 § 1 of the German Constitution of 1949 almost word-to-word" (EU Network of Independent Experts on Fundamental Rights 2006, p. 23). It stressed:

> - The recognition of human dignity has not only taken place in the Preamble, but the Convention [the body that prepared the Charter] has placed it as a real provision of the Charter, as a guiding rule at the beginning.
> - In Article 1 human dignity stands alone. It is not bound with other rights (for instance the rights to freedom or to integrity),that might have weakened its absolute position.
> - Furthermore, in the provision of Article 1 the Convention did not include other fundamental rights (for instance the prohibition of torture or of death penalty); those rights can be found in the following provisions.
>
> In this way the recognition of human dignity is particularly pointed out in a central provision and this by an impressive and concise formulation. The words 'is inviolable' contain a statement which stresses the unrestricted recognition. 'Inviolable' means that human dignity cannot be taken away from any human being. It can be neither forfeited nor renounced. (p. 25)

The Constitutional Court of the Republic of South Africa said, in the already cited case of *The State v. T Makwanyane and M Mchunu (CCT3/94) [1995] ZACC 3; 1995 (6) BCLR 665; 1995 (3) SA 391; [1996] 2 CHRLD 164; 1995 (2) SACR 1 (6 June 1995)*[192], that the death penalty "strips the convicted person of all dignity and treats him or her as an object to be eliminated by the state" (para. 26), because "the death sentence destroys life" and "annihilates human dignity" (para. 95). Justice James C. Nelson of the Supreme Court of the State of Montana (USA) said in his already above quoted concurring opinion to *Robert Maxter et al. v. State of Montana and Another* (2009 MT 449)[193]: "Six million Jewish people, along with homosexuals, Gypsies, and persons with disabilities stand as mute testament to what happens when human beings are stripped of their dignity" (para. 88).

Is human dignity really inviolable or could it be annihilated and a human being be stripped of his or her dignity?

[190] Jean-Paul Sartre wrote: "Every man is all mankind" (as cit. ib. p. 20).

[191] https://www.btg-bestellservice.de/pdf/80201000.pdf.

[192] www.saflii.org/za/cases/ZACC/1995/3.pdf.

[193] http://law.justia.com/cases/montana/supreme-court/2009/94adc027-086a-4b36-a80e-0aaf09a60127.html.

Human dignity is violable to the extent that its biological basis—the human genome—can be endangered. As the Preamble to the 'Convention for the Protection of Human Rights and Dignity of the Human Being with Regard to the Application of Biology and Medicine: Convention on Human Rights and Biomedicine' (Council of Europe 1997)[194] reads, "the accelerating developments in biology and medicine" are a threat to "the dignity and identity of all human beings" (Article 1). Their misuse "may lead to acts *endangering human dignity* [italics added]". Therefore, Article 13 provides the statement: "An intervention seeking to modify the human genome may only be undertaken for preventive, diagnostic or therapeutic purposes and only if its aim is *not to introduce any modification in the genome of any descendants* [italics added]". The Universal Declaration on the Human Genome and Human Rights, adopted unanimously and by acclamation by UNESCO in 1997 and endorsed by the UN General Assembly in 1998[195], states (Article 11): "Practices which are contrary to human dignity, such as reproductive cloning of human beings, shall not be permitted". According to the Universal Declaration on Bioethics and Human Rights (UNESCO 2005)[196]: "In applying and advancing scientific knowledge, medical practice and associated technologies, *human vulnerability* [italics added] should be taken into account" (Article 8). It refers to "the interest of humanity" (Preamble) and warns: "The impact of life sciences on future generations, including on their *genetic constitution* [italics added] should be given due regard" (Article 16).

As a consequence, when human dignity is said to be inviolable, what is generally meant is that a human being born with an essentially intact human genome never loses his or her human dignity, whatever the ill-treatments he or she may suffer, and that it should not be attacked, even if it is nevertheless vulnerable.

Human dignity is vulnerable to the extent that it is consubstantial with human rights. In fact: "Recognition of the dignity of every human being and of his or her human rights are inseparable. They are not two acts that can be separated" (Menke 2007, p. 154). The respect for human dignity consists in protecting and fulfilling human rights, the foundation of which, in turn, is human dignity. Consequently, while human dignity "cannot be taken away from any human being [...], the entitlement to respect that results from it is vulnerable" (para. 113)[197], as the German Federal Constitutional Court said in *Tanz der Teufel*.

However, in spite of human rights being frequently qualified as 'inviolable', 'inalienable', 'imprescriptible', not all are equally fundamental, as not every human

[194] http://conventions.coe.int/Treaty/en/Treaties/html/164.htm.

[195] www.unesco.org/new/en/social-and-human-sciences/themes/bioethics/human-genome-and-human-rights/

[196] http://portal.unesco.org/en/ev.php-URL_ID=31058&URL_DO=DO_TOPIC&URL_SECTION=201.html.

[197] www.servat.unibe.ch/dfr/bv087209.html
Selbst durch "unwürdiges" Verhalten geht sie nicht verloren. Sie kann keinem Menschen genommen werden. Verletzbar ist aber der Achtungsanspruch, der sich aus ihr ergibt.

rights violation constitutes a direct attack on human dignity[198]; only a few human rights are considered non-derogeable, that is, never allowing suspension or restriction. They are the most inherent in human dignity.

Being the source of the whole of human rights, life is often considered as "the supreme right", as the CCPR said in the GC 6 (para. 1)[199]. The European Court of Human Rights also stated in *Streletz, Kessler and Krenz v. Germany* (2001)[200] that life is, "internationally, the supreme value in the hierarchy of human rights" (para. 72). The Supreme Court of India said in the aforementioned case of *Francis Coralie Mullin v. The Administrator, Union Territory of Delhi (1981 AIR 746, 1981 SCR (2) 516)*[201] that the right to life "is the most precious human right and which forms the ark of all other rights" (para. 4). Notwithstanding, intentional deprivations of life are admitted, such as killing in self-defence or in war, and a person may freely put at risk or even sacrifice her life to other ethical values in particular circumstances (a hunger strike being among the most dramatic).

A grave contradiction is the fact that the death penalty remains a punishment not formally in breach of the IHRL (see, for example: ICCPR, Article 6.2; ECHR, Article 2.1), tough Additional Protocols aiming at its abolition have been adopted[202]. In effect, it means a definitive deprivation of a human right, and is not compatible with the respect for human dignity. Worse still, the death penalty, in addition to be an objectifying and irrevocable punishment, puts an end not only to the right to life, but to all rights. Recall what Justice Brennan said, concurring in *Furman v. Georgia* (408 U.S. 238, 1972): "An executed person has indeed 'lost the right to have rights'". Further, lifetime imprisonment is a punishment that, depriving a human being definitively of the right to liberty, infringes human dignity.

Torture and slavery are considered two extreme kinds of human rights violation, as they are, besides deprivation of life, the gravest contempts of personal physical, psychological and moral integrity, with intensity possibly higher than death penalty itself. Nowak (2009a) wrote: "Torture and enforced disappearance are among the most brutal and horrendous human rights violations, constituting a direct attack on

---

[198] The European Court of Human Rights, in Albert et Le Compte (1983), admitted that "the nature of some of the rights safeguarded by the Convention is such as to exclude a waiver of the entitlement to exercise them [...] but the same cannot be said of certain other rights" (para. 35).

(http://hudoc.echr.coe.int/sites/eng/Pages/search.aspx#{"fulltext":["Albert and Le Compte"],"documentcollectionid":["COMMITTEE","DECISIONS","COMMUNICATEDCASES","CLIN","ADVISORYOPINIONS","REPORTS","RESOLUTIONS"],"itemid":["001-57422"]}).

[199] www.unhchr.ch/tbs/doc.nsf/0/84ab9690ccd81fc7c12563ed0046fae3.

[200] http://cmiskp.echr.coe.int/tkp197/view.asp?item=1andportal=hbkmandaction=htmlandhighlight=Streletz%2C%20-%7C%20Kessler%20-%7C%20Krenz%20-%7C%20v.%20-%7C%20Germanyandsessionid=82299373andskin=hudoc-en.

[201] http://indiankanoon.org/doc/78536/?type=print.

[202] Protocol No. 6 to the Convention for the Protection of Human Rights and Fundamental Freedoms concerning the Abolition of the Death Penalty (1983); Second Optional Protocol to the International Covenant on Civil and Political Rights, aiming at the Abolition of the Death Penalty (1989); Protocol to the American Convention on Human Rights to Abolish the Death Penalty (1990).

the core of human dignity. Like slavery, they are absolutely prohibited under international law" (p. 151). He further remarks elsewhere (2009b):

> It follows from a combined reading of various international and regional human rights instruments that, although human dignity serves as a moral and philosophical justification for all human rights, only certain human rights are directly linked to the concept of human dignity. Typical examples of threats to human dignity are poverty and starvation, genocide and ethnic cleansing, slavery, trafficking in human beings, torture, enforced disappearance and other forms of arbitrary detention, racism and similar forms of discrimination, colonialism and foreign occupation and domination. (para. 10)

As not all human rights are equally fundamental, the implementation of some of them is progressive, some others may be restricted, and still other suspended. Indeed:

- The enforcement and implementation of some human rights have a 'progressive' character because they depend on economic ressources. The ICESCR aims "to achieving progressively the full realization of the rights recognized in the present Covenant" (Article 2.1).
- Some human rights may be lawfully limited or restricted. For example, the right to freedom of expression may be limited by the right to privacy of others, and lawful punishments may imply restrictions of human rights, such as the right to freedom of movement.
- The exercise of some human rights may be temporarily suspended under certain circunstances and conditions. For example, according to the ICCPR Article 4.1:

> In time of public emergency which threatens the life of the nation and the existence of which is officially proclaimed, the States Parties to the present Covenant may take measures derogating from their obligations under the present Covenant to the extent strictly required by the exigencies of the situation, provided that such measures are not inconsistent with their other obligations under international law and do not involve discrimination solely on the ground of race, colour, sex, language, religion or social origin.

– In addition, a State may formulate valid reservations to, or declarations of interpretation of, a treaty, in conformity with the VCLT

In any case, the 'Text of the explanations relating to the complete text of the Charter [of Fundamental Rights of the European Union] as set out in CHARTE 4487/00 CONVENT 50'[203] highlights: "The dignity of the human person [...] is part of the substance of the rights laid down in this Charter. It must therefore be respected, even where a right is restricted". The Supreme Court of India said in *Francis Coralie Mullin v. The Administrator, Union Territory of Delhi (1981 AIR 746, 1981 SCR (2) 516)*[204]: "Section 8, the counterpart of sect. 33 of our Constitution, provides that laws shall not impose any limitations on the essential content of fundamental rights" (para. 84).

In addition to being violable and vulnerable, human dignity is variable.

---

[203] www.europarl.europa.eu/charter/pdf/04473_en.pdf.

[204] http://indiankanoon.org/doc/78536/?type=print.

Human dignity is variable to the extent that the expressions of its common essential content reflect individual differences. As the Universal Declaration on the Human Genome and Human Rights (UNESCO 1997)[205] affirms, it is "imperative not to reduce individuals to their genetic characteristics and to respect their uniqueness and diversity" (Article 2.b). The Universal Declaration on Bioethics and Human Rights (UNESCO 2005)[206] recalls "that a person's identity includes biological, psychological, social, cultural and spiritual dimensions" (Preamble).

To begin with, human dignity, in its essential conception, does not have a fully apparent and self-sufficient content *ab initio* (from the beginning). To the extent that it is equated with reason, conscience and autonomy, it is capacity-driven. Being so, little children and adults mentally disabled, for example, are diminished in their aptitude for expressing their human dignity.

In addition, a human being's life may be more or less dignified, depending on their behaviors and efforts regarding their moral and intellectual development, on their virtue and merit, as well on their human rights' empowerment. According to Kant's (1803) teaching: "Man's duty is to improve himself; to cultivate his mind; and, when he finds himself going astray, to bring the moral law to bear upon problem himself" (p. 11). Recall also his distinction between *inner worth* (the intrinsic human worth, related to the absolute dignity of being member of Humankind) and *moral worth* (depending on one's actions, which may violate "the dignity of humanity in his own person"). The latter refers to human beings' choices and behavior that may degrade the ethical dignity based on their inner worth, impair the social respect of one's dignity, and arouse social disapproval or even legal sanction. For instance, when "treating ourselves merely as a tool (such as by groveling to others, or selling ourselves into slavery)" or "acting in ways that would undermine our rational agency (such as by using intoxicants, or committing suicide)" (Bostrom 2008, p. 174, 175). In addition, those who offend against others' dignity do not respect the human dignity they share with all human beings.

In sum, human dignity demands, but nevertheless transcends human rights:

- Human dignity precedes the entitlement to human rights and remains after the definitive loss of the capacity to exercise them. It is inherent in human beings not yet or no more able to rational free agency.
- Human dignity is more than the sum of the human rights recognized at a given moment. It does not let itself be exhausted in a historically closed conception of human rights. As Justice Brennan said in a 1985 speech on constitutional interpretation, delivered at the Georgetown University Law Center, "a comprehensive definition" of the ideal of human dignity is "an eternal quest" whose demands "will never cease to evolve" (as cit. in Wermeil 1998, p. 239).

[205] www.unesco.org/new/en/social-and-human-sciences/themes/bioethics/human-genome-and-human-rights/.

[206] http://portal.unesco.org/en/ev.php-URL_ID-=-31058&URL_DO-=-DO_TOPIC&URL_SECTION=201.html.

McCrudden (2008) concluded that, from the legal and judicial uses of the HDP what may be considered a core content emerges that consists in agreeing:

> … that each human being possesses an intrinsic worth that should be respected, that some forms of conduct are inconsistent with respect for this intrinsic worth, and that the state exists for the individual not vice versa. The fault lines lie in disagreement on what that intrinsic worth consists in, what forms of treatment are inconsistent with that worth, and what the implications are for the role of the state. (p. 723)

Indeed, the human being's intrinsic worth remains largely obscure. An account is proposed below.

5.6 An Account of Human Worth

To explain the differences in rank and roles in his *Republic*, Plato (1997) tells "one of the useful falsehoods" (414b) to get people to believe it—the myth of the metals:

> 'All of you in the city are brothers', we'll say to them in telling our story, 'but the god who made you mixed some gold into those who are adequately equipped to rule, because they are most valuable. He put silver in those who are auxiliaries and iron and bronze in the farmers and other craftsmen'. (415a)

All human beings have in common an invaluable metal that requires protection and care. It is the dignity inherent in us. However, there is no agreed legal definition of 'human dignity' at either the international or national levels.

The HDP pervades IHRL and the international and constitutional jurisprudence on human rights. Besides 'human dignity', the most frequently used expression is probably 'dignity and worth of the human person'. If dignity and worth are not entirely redundant terms, however, human 'worth' should mean the source of human 'dignity'. As Kant wrote in the *Metaphysics of Morals* (Book II, § 37)[207]: "The respect that I have for others or that another can require from me (*observantia aliis praestanda*) is therefore recognition of a dignity (*dignitas*) in other human beings, that is, of a worth that has no price, no equivalent for which the object evaluated (*aestimii*) could be exchanged". That is why Charles Malik said in a speech on 'The Basic Issues of the International Bill of Human Rights', delivered before a conference of American educators in Lake Success, on 26 February 1948, that the CHR should begin by seeking "to give content and meaning to the pregnant phrase in the preamble of the Charter [of the United Nations], 'the worth and dignity of man'. What is the worth of man? What constitutes his proper dignity? These are the basic initial challenges which the Commission on Human Rights must try to meet" (as cit. in Facing History and Ourselves Foundation 2010, p. 148).

[207] *Achtung, die ich für andere trage, oder die ein anderer von mir fordern kann (*observantia aliis praestanda*), ist also die Anerkennung einer Würde (*dignitas*) an anderen Menschen, d.i. eines Werts, der keinen Preis hat, kein Äquivalent, wogegen das Objekt der Wertschätzung (*aestimii*) ausgetauscht werden könnte.*

In other words, to understanding human dignity we must answer the following question: What does it mean to be human?

As we saw, the CHR could agree on "the essential attributes of man": reason and conscience. In the opinion of Morsink (1999):

> This is an essentialist view of human nature because it looks upon reason and conscience as the essence of what it means to be human. If we accept as criterion that to be members of the human family people need to have these characteristics only potentially and not (necessarily) actually, then this is a defensible position. (p. 296)

The recognition of human dignity does not depend upon the actual capacity to act as rational and conscious beings, as the foregoing has shown, but every member of the human species is endowed with the faculties of reason and conscience, constitutive of human worth. This idea is restated by the Universal Declaration on Bioethics and Human Rights (UNESCO 2005)[208] that refers to "the unique capacity of human beings to reflect upon their own existence and on their environment, to perceive injustice, to avoid danger, to assume responsibility, to seek cooperation and to exhibit the moral sense that gives expression to ethical principles" (Preamble). However, the UDHR drafters could not and did not consider it to be essential to agree on "the origin of man's reason and conscience" (Hernan Santa Cruz) (A/C.3/SR.99).

There are religious, philosophical and scientific answers.

Following the traditional religious account, the human species is the most perfect creature of a Divinity[209]. Darwin's theory of evolution challenged this belief, as we know. Copernicus (1473–1543) and Freud (1856–1939), among others, also greatly contributed to the *narcissistic injury* caused to Humankind's self-image by scientific advancements, which increasingly reveal that the frontiers between animality and humanity are porous. Notwithstanding, a complex bio-cultural gap subsists whose explanation requires a broad approach.

The Universal Declaration on the Human Genome and Human Rights (UNESCO 1997)[210] begins by stating: "The human genome underlies the fundamental unity of all members of the human family, as well as the recognition of their inherent dignity and diversity" (Article 1). The following interdisciplinary account searches for the anthropological underpinnings of human worth, dignity and diversity. It will be argued that:

- Human worth consists in the perfectibility of the human species that demands the perfecting of human beings.
- The perfectibility of the human species is rooted in its semiotic nature that is the source of human beings' aptitude to the liberty of rationality.

---

[208] http://portal.unesco.org/en/ev.php-URL_ID=31058&URL_DO=DO_TOPIC&URL_SECTION=201.html.

[209] "The meaning of human life is to strive for perfection of love" (*Le sens de la vie humaine est de tendre à la perfection de la charité*) (as cit. in Blum 2003, p. 7).

[210] www.unesco.org/new/en/social-and-human-sciences/themes/bioethics/human-genome-and-human-rights/.

- The perfecting of human beings should consist in the cultivation of their semiotic seeds that require human rights' protection and provisions.
- The right to education is key for the human perfecting.

Some neurobiological insights are also added.

5.6.1 Human Worth Consists in the Perfectibility of the Human Species that Demands the Perfecting of Human Beings

In 2003, the European Commission's PATHFINDER Initiative launched the project *What it means to be human—Origins and Evolution of Human Higher Cognitive Faculties*. Following calls for proposals, 17 projects were selected. In 2005, a High Level Expert Group was established and published a report[211] that recommended a Human Mind Project falling within five broad thematic areas:

> § The genetics of human cognition […]
> § The developing mind […]
> § The process of thinking […]
> § Motivation and decision making […]
> § Cultural context […]
> (p. 11–12)

According to the Report:

> Our ancestors may have started out as just another ape, but along the way, we evolved an extraordinary mind, capable of self-awareness, of producing tools and language, of worshiping gods, feeling complex emotions such as gratitude, guilt and remorse, appreciating art, proving theorems and creating a marvelous variety of cultures. This mind is the core of our species' uniqueness and the essence of what it means to be human. (p. 8)

That is why:

> A central objective of the Human Mind Project will be to increase our understanding of characteristics of the human mind that are either unique or qualitatively different from those found in any other animal. The most striking of these are:
>
> § Learning and memory […]
> § Symbolism […]
> § Language […]
> § Consciousness and self-awareness […]
> § Innovation and creativity […]
> § Mind reading […]
> § Morality and spirituality […]
> § Trust and deception […]
> § Reciprocity, altruism and cooperation […]
> (p. 28–29)

[211] Retrieved July 2013 from: ftp://ftp.cordis.europa.eu/pub/nest/docs/whatitmeanstobehuman_b5_eur21795_en.pdf.

The Report pointed out: "Many of the problems, and opportunities, humanity will face in the coming years will not be met simply with technological fixes. We will also need to change our thinking and our behaviour if we want to survive and thrive in the overcrowded, polluted and bustling global village we now inhabit" (p. 5).

In January 2012, the French magazine *Sciences et Avenir* (Sciences and Future) published a special issue with the title "Qu'est-ce que l'Homme?—100 scientifiques répondent" (What is Man?—Answers by 100 scientists). While the answers are varied, most of them converge in some distinctively human features. They are subsequently summarized.

Following Axel Kahn:

> From an evolutionary point of view, *Homo sapiens* is an animal, vertebrate, mammal, primate of the *Homo* gender and of the *sapiens* species. At the DNA level coding his genetic characteristics, he possesses more than 98% of similarities to another primate hominid, the chimpanzee, and a little less than the gorilla. Following these criteria, it is evident that the banality of man is extreme. It is then rather from the side of the behaviorial traits and of the particular aptitudes made possible by his genome that it is advisable to capture human singularity.
> Even so, it is difficult to designate a 'peculiarity of man' totally specific to him. (in AAVV 2012, p. 72)

In fact, human beings have neither more genes than some other animals and vegetables (not the supposed 100,000, but 30,000 or fewer), nor the largest brain. What are then the sources, features and expressions of human specificity?

"Human specificity is, to a great extent, the fruit of a history that is not inscribed in the genes" (Michel Morange, ib. p. 46). It is a very long history from which emerged the creature *Homo Sapiens* only about 200,000 years ago. *Emergence* is "a concept that takes charge of the continuity animal-Man without denying the qualitative leaps [between species]", according to Élisabeth de Fontenay. "Man's historical advent would have been punctuated by the successive emergence of the abilities differentiating him from the animal" (ib. p. 57). The brain was the stage of the most decisive humanizing processes. "Man's peculiarity is due to the fact that his brain is shapped, structured so as to carry out operations peculiar to the human being" (Michael Gazzaniga, ib. p. 55). It is thus "the organ that best epitomizes the unique character of Man" (Yehezkel Ben-Ari, ib. p. 50).

The basis of the human brain's uniqueness is the "neuroplasticity" that is the "fourth dimension" of the neuron. A neuron is a special cell that "renders the brain a structure in perpetual construction, in which the plasticity of the neural connections inscribes continually the results of the interactions between the individual and his environment". This finding amounts to "a deep neurobiological conceptual revolution" (Marc Peschanski, ib. p. 52). In addition, brain complexity "expresses itself morphologicaly by the existence of the circumvolutions of the cerebral cortex, which increase enormously the surface and, therefore, the density and amplitude of the neurons' network" (Nicole Le Douarin, ib. p. 51). The condition and price of such humanizing potentialities is the human being's *premature birth* or *ontogenetic delay* (also called *neoteny*), compared with other mammals. "At birth, only 10% of our 100 bilions neurons are interconnected. The other 90% of the connexions are progressively constructed, following the influences of family, education, culture, society" (id. ib.). This means, following Axel Kahn, that "the condition for a primate endowed with a human genome really to humanize itself, that is, for developing its mental specific abilities, is to be educated in a family in touch with its relatives". He adds that this dependence implies that each human being recognizes the worth of the others, so acceding to what seals "its irreducible humanity, the notion of its responsibility" (ib. p. 72). This leads Arild Utaker to the following definition: "Man is a relational animal". Such openness "is what characterizes our species" (ib. p. 68). In Jean Guilaine's opinion: "Man is a social animal self-domesticated after the neolitic" (ib. p. 31). That is why it may be said, as Heinz Wismann does:

> Unlike other beings, Man has not a nature. His genetic programmation, which he shares with the whole living realm, does not entirely determine his existence. He has to become what he is. The Ancient Greeks had clearly distinguished between two kinds of life: natural life, *zoé*, and historical life, *bios*. [...] And this distinction is essential, because it shows that Man is himself only to the extent that he still is not what he will be. He is an historical being. [...] Man is then the artist of himself. (ib. p. 96)

The development of the human brain is then closely related to the human species' social nature. Evelyne Heyer notices: "The research of the British Robin Dunbar, biologist of the evolution, shows that, in primates, the size of the neo-cortex—the 'intelligent' part of brain—is correlated to that of the group" (ib. p. 22). Karl Marx is quoted by Marc Peschanski in this regard: "Man is not only a social animal, but an animal that only in society can individualize itself". Peschanski observes that this overcomes "terms for a long time opposed, individuation and socialization, innate and acquired, now reconciled in a dialectic that grounds the specification of the humankind" (ib. p. 52).

Humans' need for living in groups increasingly numerous is closely linked to the emergence of language that is a powerful kind of communication—a key to human uniqueness[212]. There are several kinds of animal communication, but none is comparable to the human language. Claude Hagège concluded: "Language is then to be considered as defining the human species. [...] Man is, therefore, first and foremost, a *Homo loquens*" (ib. p. 64).

According to Maurice Godelier, the great difference between the human species and the primates closest to it (chimpanzees and bonobos) is the "ability to invent worlds that do not exist" (ib. p. 59). In Jonah Lehrer's opinion:

> If I should have to choose a trait defining human nature, it would be creativity. [...] What no other species is able to do, making our singularity, is that: We can see the world as it is and imagine it as it would be if it were better. This particular talent does not exist anywhere in the animal realm. We can invent our own reality. [...]
> Imagination is a breaking point in Evolution, a turning point. (ib. p. 58)

Imagination is "specifically human", making us "without doubt the sole species that designs a vision of future" (Yves Quéré, ib. p. 60). The human being is "the sole animal able to live its life as a project" (Nayla Farouki, ib. p. 77).

---

[212] Language appeared probably about 2 millions years ago, with the *Homo Habilis*, but verbal language could have appeared only about 100 thousand years ago, with the modern *Homo Sapiens* or, following another hypothesis, about 35 thousand years ago.

The human brain's evolution, in evolving groups, and the emergence of language, imagination and creativity paved the way "to a new type of evolution, the cultural evolution, at least six times faster than the genetic evolution" (Richard Dawkins, ib. p. 11). Boris Cyrulnik stresses: "We have survived thanks to our invention of the world of the artifact: Tool and word. We became the sole animals able to escape from the animal condition" (ib. p. 71).

The human genome being, therefore, a "catalogue of possibles" (Marc Peschanski, ib. p. 52), which can be more or less realized, it may be argued that human worth is rooted in the perfectibility of the human species and in the perfecting of human beings. Culture and civilization are evolutionary outcomes of the human species' perfectibility.

An account by John Passmore (1970) covering 3,000 years, from Homer to our times, identified two main historical visions of human perfectibility, somewhat parallel with the two historical visions of human dignity described above.

- Elitist perfectibilism—Greek and Christian—following which only a very few are "endowed with exceptional talents or granted an extraordinary degree of divine grace".
- Universalist perfectibilism that "ascribes it to all men" (p. 27, 28).

The second is the modern notion of perfectibilism that, since the European *Renaissance*, equates human perfectibility with human dignity.

Pico della Mirandola, characterizing man "as the free and proud shaper" of its own being, in *De hominis dignitate oratio* (1486)[213], redefined humanity as perfectibility, noted Alain Renaut (2002). Such an antinaturalistic perspective was "for the first time so clearly affirmed in the history of humanity: What man is, is a becoming, not by nature but by a cultural process" (p. 157). Ernst Bloch (1972), in his *Vorlesungen zur Philosophie der Renaissance* (Lessons on the Philosophy of the Renaissance), affirmed: "Here is man's dignity: He is not born finished, his existence evolves!" (p. 15).

In the eighteenth century, perfectibility is a concept that takes "a flooding sense" (Crampe-Casnabet 1985, p. 36). *Esquisse d'un tableau historique des progrès de l'esprit humain* (Outlines of an historical view of the progress of the human mind) by Condorcet (Marie Jean Antoine Nicolas de Caritat, Marquis de) Jean Antoine Nicolas de Caritat, Marquis de) (1743-1794) is "a hymn to humankind" (p. 6). One reads in the Introduction (1793):

> Such is the object of the work I have undertaken; the result of which will be to show, from reasoning and from facts, that no bounds have been fixed to the improvement of the human faculties; that the pefectibility of man is absolutely indefinite; that the progress of this perfectibility, henceforth above the controul of every power that would impede it, has no other limit than the duration of the globe upon which nature has placed us. (p. 10)

Ch.-M. Talleyrand-Périgord, presenting his *Report on the public instruction* to the French National Assembly, in September 1791, affirmed: "One of the most

[213] www.cscs.umich.edu/~crshalizi/Mirandola.

impressive characteristics in man is *perfectibility*; and this characteristic, perceptible in the individual, is even more in the species" (in Muller 1999, p. 14). Michel Soëtard and Renaud Hétier (2003) remarks: "Rousseau inscribes the distinction between man and animal into two qualities: perfectibility and liberty" (p. 62).

In the ninteenth century, Alexis de Tocqueville (1805–1859) wrote in *Democracy in America* (1835–1840), Book I, Chaper VIII ('How equality suggests to the Americans the idea of the indefinite perfectibility of man')[214]:

> Although man has many points of resemblance with the brutes, one trait is peculiar to himself: he improves; they are incapable of improvement. Mankind could not fail to discover this difference from the beginning. The idea of perfectibility is therefore as old as the world; equality did not give birth to it, but has imparted to it a new character.[215]

Human life, perfectibility and human dignity were equated by the German Federal Constitutional Court when it said in *BVerfGE 39, 1, 1975 (Schwangerschaftsabbruch I)*[216], quoted above: "Where human life exists, human dignity is present to it [...]. The potential faculties present in the human being from the beginning suffice to establish human dignity" (para. 147).

The human species possesses, therefore, a bio-cultural nature emerging from a doubly dialectical evolutionary process that developed its perfectibility. A question remains, however: In what does human perfectibility consist?

5.6.2 The Perfectibility of the Human Species is Rooted in its Semiotic Nature that is the Source of Human Beings' Aptitude to the Liberty of Rationality

To capture the semiotic nature of the human species, an elementary and general approach to the study of Semiotics is useful.

According to Henry van Lier (1980), in the history of universe, the 'signal' first appeared, that is, information in the broad sense of the term, produced by physical events, before the emergence of life. These interactions in a world of only physical phenomena—"a theatre without spectator" (p. 2)—may be described as 'quasi-semiotic'. Billions of years later, the emergence of life caused "a first revolution", that of the 'stimulus-signal', because signals stimulate reactions from the vegetable and animal kingdoms. Several millions of years ago, the "appearance of the sign, contemporary of the appearance of man" (p. 3), gave rise to culture and civilization.

---

[214] http://seas3.elte.hu/coursematerial/LojkoMiklos/Alexis-de-Tocqueville-Democracy-in-America.pdf.

[215] In his speech at the Nobel Banquet in Stockholm, on 10 December 1962, John Steinbeck said: "I hold that a writer who does not passionately believe in the perfectibility of man has no dedication nor any membership in literature".

(www.nobelprize.org/nobel_prizes/literature/laureates/1962/steinbeck-speech_en.html).

[216] http://groups.csail.mit.edu/mac/users/rauch/germandecision/german_abortion_decision2.html.

Following Paul Burgess[217], Thomas A. Sebeok (1921–2001) distinguished three major strands in the development of semiotics, designated as the biological, the philosophical, and the linguistic traditions:

> The first tradition is rooted in medical practice and diagnostic methodology; Baltic biologist Jacob von Uexküll brought this approach to explicitly semiotic form in his study of animal behavior and perception between the two world wars. The second tradition leads from Plato and Aristotle through Augustine and the medieval scholastics via Leibniz, Locke, and others to thinkers such as Peirce, 'the real founder and first systematic investigator of modern semiotic'. The third tradition in its overtly semiotic form leads from Ferdinand de Saussure to writers such as Louis Hjelmslev, Roman Jakobson, and Roland Barthes. Although there has been creative borrowing among these traditions, Sebeok notes a continuing tension between more linguistically oriented and more philosophically oriented semiotic approaches.
> Among those who have dealt with questions of signs and symbols from a philosophical perspective, two whom it is especially fruitful to compare to Peirce are Ernst Cassirer (1874–1946) and Charles Morris (1901–1979). Cassirer's philosophy of symbolic forms and Morris' general theory of signs both have interesting points of convergence with Peirce's semiotic, while their divergences from Peirce's approach lie roughly in opposite directions.

Charles S. Peirce (1839–1914), whose main writings were gathered and published posthumously as the *Collected Papers* (six volumes in 1931–1935 and two in 1957–1958), proposed the term *Semiotics* to designate the general science of signs[218]. He defined sign as "everything which stands to somebody for something else in some respect or capacity", a definition that corresponds to the Latin *aliquid stat pro aliquot* (something standing for something).

Ferdinand de Saussure (1857–1913) belived in the possibility of conceiving of a science of signs called Sémiologie[219]. His main work is *Cours de linguistique générale* (Course in General Linguistics 1916), posthumously published, that is a synthesis realized by two colleagues (C. Bally and A. Séchehaye) based on records of his courses of 1907, 1908–1909 and 1910–1911. He moved away from the historic and descriptive approach to languages and became the founder of modern linguistics as part of Semiology.

Morris (1964), whose main work *Signs, Language and Behaviour* (1946) is a commentary of Peirce's Semiotics, gave the following definition: "Semiotic has for its goal a general theory of signs in all their forms and manifestations, whether

---

[217] Retrieved July 2013 from: www.paulburgess.org/flux.html.

[218] Morris (1964) observed: "The term 'semiotic' was adapted by John Locke from the Greek Stoics, who in turn were influenced by the Greek medical tradition that interpreted diagnosis and prognosis as sign processes. Charles S. Peirce (1839–1914), who followed John Locke's usage, is responsible for the present widespread employment of the term 'semiotic'" (p. 1).

[219] Jean Caune (1997) comments:

> The terms *semiology* and *semiotics* are very frequently used indistinctively. In the saussurian tradition, taken up by Barthes, one uses *semiology*. Peirce, on his turn, uses *semiotics* and examines phenomena not examined by Saussure. [...] Let us accept, as Humberto Eco and many other authors, to adopt the term *semiotics* as being that that covers both the considerations on the sign and the meaning's relations. (p. 83)

in animals or men, whether normal or pathological, whether linguistic or nonlinguistic, whether personal or social. Semiotic is thus an interdisciplinary enterprise" (p. 1). Linguistics is part of Semiotics[220].

Semiotics or Semiology is, therefore, the study of signs and of semiosis, that is, the process of 'meaning-making'. The fundamental difference between Saussure and Peirce is that, following Daniel Chandler (2002):

> In Saussure's model, the sign consisted of two elements: a signifier and a signified (though he insisted that these were inseparable other than for analytical purposes). This dyadic model makes no direct reference to a referent in the world, and can be seen as supporting the notion that language does not 'reflect' reality but rather constructs it.
> Peirce's model of the sign had three elements—the representamen, an interpretant and an object. It is thus a triadic model.

There is no well-established difference between sign and symbol (Peirce and Saussure, for example, used the term 'symbol' differently from each other). Both sign and symbol have an arbitrary nature, that is, their meanings are conventional[221], but a symbol may not be wholly arbitrary. While a sign simply denotes, a symbol is a sign connoted, that is, with a second cultural meaning. That is the difference, for instance, between a beach flag warning about potential safety risks (according to the respective colour) and a country flag, with its deep collective identity signification. It could be said that signs have meanings, and symbols make us feel something[222].

In line with the idea that Semiotics is "an interdisciplinary enterprise" (Morris 1964, p. 1), Sebeok developed "a wide-ranging vision of semiotics that coincides with the study of the evolution of life. After Sebeok's work our conception of the semiotic field and of the history of semiotics has changed significantly" (Petrilli and Ponzio 2007, p. 75). In the light of Sebok's global Semiotics, classical Semiotics appears as anthropocentric and reductive of the semiosphere, incurring a *pars pro toto* (taking a part for the whole) error in many ways that includes: reducing the complex

---

[220] In his text 'Foundations of the Theory of Signs' (1938) published in the *Encyclopaedia of Unified Science*, he distinguished three dimensions in language whose historical origins can be traced back to the medieval *artes dicendi* (Grammar, Rhetoric, Dialectic), namely: Sintax, Semantics and Pragmatics. Sintax is concerned with the relation between signs and the rules of their combinations. Semantics is concerned with the relation of signs with things. Pragmatics is concerned with the relation of signs with their users. The language dimensions are indissociable, however.

[221] The words' conventional character is highlighted by Juliet in this passage of Shakespeare's drama:

> "What's in a name? That which we call a rose.
> By any other word would smell as sweet.
> So Romeo would, were he not Romeo called.
> (*Romeo and Juliet*, II, ii, 1–2)
> (www.gutenberg.org/cache/epub/1112/pg1112.html).

[222] For further explanations and details see Chandler (2002).

(www.aber.ac.uk/media/Documents/S4B/semiotic.html).

life of signs to the human sphere; addressing only voluntary and conventional signs; letting itself be enclosed in the transmitter-receiver paradigm[223].

Global Semiotics addresses the signs of life and life of signs, as even a microorganism has to interpret signals to survive. Its object is the signs network of the semiosphere that includes the whole biosphere (a term coined by the Russian Vladimir Vernadsky in 1926), thus becoming a semiobiosphere or biosemiosphere. Anthroposemiotics is then only a part of the zoosemiotics (a term coined by Sebeok in 1976), which also includes an endosemiotics (another term coined by Sebeok in 1972) concerning especially the neural processes underlying mental activity. In sum: Sebeok's axiom is that semiosis and life coincide. Where there is life, there is semiosis.

Sebeok's fundamental concept is *modeling*, borrowed from the so-called Moscow-Tartu School of semioticians in the early 1960s, which he extended beyond the domain of anthroposemiotics. It means that each animal species is endowed with a species-specific modeling system that is the sensory system with which it forms and interprets the model of its own *Umwelt* (the surrounding world), a term proposed by Jacob von Uexküll (*Umwelt und Innenwelt der Tiere* 1909). "A frog survives with nothing we would call a brain, but we can infer from its behavior that to it the world is divided into wet and dry, small things that fly by and are edible, and large things such as herons that it had better avoid" (Stokoe 2000, p. 10).

As far as the human animal is concerned, its modeling device is language, understood in a broad sense that includes a pre-verbal dimension. "Sebeok argues that *Homo habilis,* the first member of genus *Homo,* 'must have had a mute verbal modeling system lodged in its brain, but it could not encode it in articulate, linear speech'. He proposed (his italics) that *'language evolved as an adaptation, whereas speech developed out of language as a derivative 'exaption'* (1994, 124)" (ib.). Verbal language consists in the ability to create an infinite variety of compositions of a finite number of elements—called 'syntax'—which is a distinctive feature of humans. It makes human beings capable of constructing other languages, that is, other communication systems, verbal and non-verbal, and of producing their specific cultural *Lebenswelt* (lifeworld), differently from other animals' genetically circumscribed *Umwelt.* Sebeok thus made a tripartite distinction concerning human modeling:

- Language, in its broadest sense, is the primary modeling device of the human species, before "the percept becomes concept" (p. 11). This earlier stage was probably analogous to that of a child under 1 year or so: "Like other creatures, from birth onward human infants model their world, and like many others, they make overt signs that represent pieces of their models—the things and events they perceive and react to" (p. 12).

[223] See Augusto Ponzio (1990). *Man as a Sign: Essays on the Philosophy of Language* (Trans. by Susan Petrilli). Berlin. Mouton de Gruyter; Susan Petrilli, & Augusto Ponzio (2005). *Semiotics Unbounded: Interpretive Routes through the Open Network of Signs*. Toronto, University of Toronto Press; Susan Petrilli, Augusto Ponzio, & John Deely (2005). *The Semiotic Animal*. Ottawa, Legas.

- Speech or verbal language ability—the most complex form of communication—is a secondary modeling system. The "infant perception-action begins everywhere by representing things and events gesturally and in due time replaces many of the gestures with words (or signs) of the adult language" (p. 15)[224].
- Human cultural systems.

Because of its unique semiotic aptitude, the human being has been characterized as a semiotic animal. This distinguishing characterization goes back to Peirce who said that "man is a sign" (as cit. in Lane 2009, p. 1) in a universe of signs. A person's mental life is a continuous flow of thought-signs, which are not limited to the logical ones, but includes all that may serve as sign.

Cassirer (1944) called man an *animal symbolicum*, as he is endowed with the ability to use *symbolic forms*, a concept central to his Philosophy that includes all cultural creations: language, political thought, arts, science, religion, etc.

> Man has, as it were, discovered a new method of adapting himself to his environment. Between the receptor system and the effector system, which are to be found in all animal species, we find in man a third link which we may describe as the symbolic system. This new acquisition transforms the whole of human life. As compared with the other animals, man lives not merely in a broader reality; he lives, so to speak, in a new dimension of reality. (p. 29)

Morris (1964) commented: "Ernst Cassirer called man 'the symbolic animal' ('*animal symbolicum*'), instead of 'the rational animal' ('*animal rationale*'), and much contemporary work has shown the aptness of this conception" (p. 1). Commenting on Cassirer too, Umberto Eco (1984) asked: "Who is not, then, a semiotic animal?" (p. 6). He wrote (1973): "humankind is instituted when society is instituted, but society is instituted when there is exchange of signs. With sign, man comes out the raw perception, the *hic et nunc* experience, and abstracts. Without *abstraction*, the concept does not exist, althought without it the sign does not exist either" (p. 127). In his opinion, "the whole culture is a system of systems of signs, where the signified of a signifier becomes, on its turn, the signifier of another signified, or even the signifier of the signified itself—irrespective of these being words, objects, goods, ideas, values, feelings, gestures and behaviors. Semiotics becomes so the scientific form of the cultural anthropology" (p. 222).

What is more, according to Hans Lenk (2008), commenting on Cassirer as well, while higher animals like primates (such as chimpanzees, gorillas and bonodos) are, within limits, symbolic beings, too (and are also capable of using elementary tools and of transmitting elementary skills), "*they certainly do not symbolically understand their functioning symbols as objects for a further symbolic analysis working on a higher ('meta-') level*".

> So it *does* seem to be a characteristic, unique trait of human beings that they are able to apply symbols at meta-levels—to designate and to interpret the use and function of symbols in a higher-level analysis. [...] The human being is therefore not merely an *animal symbo-*

[224] "Born somehow prematurely, incapable of feeding and moving, for many months, but benefiting of increased cerebral dispositions, the human being is led to search form and consistency in doubles, physical or mental images" (Lier and Laroche 1982).

> *licum*, but is uniquely the *animal metasymbolicum*: the being who not only interprets, but who also interprets its interpretations and interpretation processes, with the respective symbolizations and representations functioning as abstract 'objects' [...]. This creature called 'human' is the only being capable of creating and using symbols and meta-symbols, as well as interpretations and meta-interpretations. [...] Thus, the human being is uniquely the *metasymbolic being* and the *superinterpreting being*.

Van Lier (1980) wrote in his book titled *L'Animal Signé* (The Signed Animal): "So the human being is rigourously defined as the semiotic animal, that is, the animal in which the sign is constructed in constructing the man. The sign is the distinctive feature of man. Or better, the sign is the man himself. In the history of universe, sign and man came together" (p. 17). That is why, Tzvetan Todorov (2013) remarks: "Human beings aspire to symbolic recognition infinitely more than they search to satisfy their senses, and they are ready to sacrifice their lives, as A. Smith already pointed out, for so a derisory thing as a flag" (p. 63). In a paper published by Van Lier and Jean-Louis Laroche (1982), they wrote: "Maybe our species reached a moment when to have at its disposal a definition of itself that be the least wrong possible is not any more only a speculative satisfaction, but a request of this species as such".

Petrilli and Ponzio (2007) conclude:

> Therefore the expression 'semiotics' indicates: 1) the study of semiosis, or the general science of signs; and 2) from a specifically human perspective, the capacity that only human beings have to reflect on signs (i.e. to make signs the object of reflection), that is, metasemiosis. Semiotics in this second sense refers specifically to *human* semiosis, or anthroposemiosis. It follows that *Homo* can be described as a 'semiotic animal' [...]. (p. 33)

As a consequence, semiosis is what distinguishes the animate world from the inanimate one, but "the passage of the interaction mediated by gestures to interaction mediated by symbol marks the threshold of hominization" (Caune 1997, p. 58). Aristotle (2000) had written that "man is the only animal whom she [nature] has endowed with the gift of speech" (ζωον λογον εχων) (1253a). According to Émile Benveniste (1902–1976), "the language lies at the very foundation of the whole of culture" (as cit. in Herfray 2000, p. 55).

This aptitude for verbal language led to the definition of man as a *rational animal* by Porphyry (3th BC), even though it is not yet possible to affirm that language and thought are indissociable. In fact, language made human beings able to abstract from sensible reality to create 'mental representations', thus transcending their immediate world. "Through the gesture that shapes the things and the word that designates them, Man accedes to a breathtaking liberty: That of inscribing in the world what he imagined, of liberating himself from the heaviness of things by endowing them with a meaning" (Alain Supiot, in AAVV 2012, p. 62). As Condorcet wrote, "the arbitrariness of signs liberates the soul from its dependence of the object, it allows the consciousness to dedouble itself, to reflect on itself" (in Crampe-Casnabet 1985, p. 22). Thus, language may be considered to be "the support of rationality" (Auroux 2000, p. 20).

Human rationality must be conceived up to the fullness of its underlying semiotic liberty, however, contrary to a one-sided, intellectualist, positivist, hemiplegic concept of reason[225]. This is what Patrick Lee and Robert P. George (2008) mean, for instance, when they say:

> ... that what distinguishes human beings from other animals, what makes human beings *persons* rather than *things*, is their rational nature. Human beings are rational creatures by virtue of possessing natural capacities for conceptual thought, deliberation, and free choice, that is, the natural capacity to shape their own lives. These basic, natural capacities to reason and make free choices are possessed by every human being, even those who cannot immediately exercise them. (p. 410)

In this light, the acquisition of the symbolic function is a decisive moment in the child development, as pointed out by Jean Piaget (1975), one of the greatest psychologists of the twentieth century:

> The most decisive turn, no doubt, in the mental evolution of the child, is that which announces the beginings of representation [...] a capital event for the human thought [... that] implies certainly the constitution of a symbolic function, that is, of a differenciation between signified and signifiers, given that it consists in evoking signifieds not present and only then can we evoke them by means of differentiated signifiers. (p. 169, 170)

That is why, as Morris (1964) observed:

> ... under normal circumstances, man is the only symbolically sick animal. The signs that mark his power are also major sources of his distress.
> [...]
> Disturbances requiring the psychotherapist are seen as disturbances of communication, and the task of psychotherapist is seen as the restoration of communication. The analysis supporting this position does justice to the place of signs, values, and personality differences in communication and its disorders. (p. 82, 83)

Dolto (1985) remarked too: "Autism only exists because of the importance of the symbolic function in the human being. Autism does not exist in animals. It is a disease specific to the human being" (p. 391).

Human beings are so thoroughly semiotic animals that they may commit murder or risk and sacrifice their lives for valued symbols and signs. Morris (1964) highlighted: "Individual persons and social groups are human because of their symbol systems, and yet these symbols impose in turn heavy burdens on individual and social action. Man lives in his symbols, but he often maims himself, and even dies, because of them" (p. 87). *The Survivors' Manifesto—Message from the Holocaust Survivors for Posterity*, included in *To Bear Witness—Holocaust Remembrance at Yad Vashem*, an edition by the Jewish Holocaust Museum of Jerusalem, reads: "Why and for what purpose was the horror perpetrated? [...] How is it possible that amongst the German nation, a people of such apparent intellect and

[225] Damásio (1994) observes in the first note of this *Descartes' Error—Emotion, Reason, and the Human Brain*:

> A contemporary dictionary of philosophy has this to say about reason: 'In English the word 'reason' has long had, and still has, a large number and a wide variety of senses and uses, related to one another in ways that are often complicated and often not clear...' (*Encyclopedia of Philosophy*, P. Edwards, ed., 1967, New York: Macmillan Publishing Company and the Free Press). (p. 269).

modern culture who produced great artists, thinkers and teachers of ethics, could arise murderers who fashioned and operated this unprecedented killing machine?" (Gutterman and Shalev 2005, p. 315). The answer lies in the anthropological and ontological openness of the human species, as explained above. Human beings are born not bad or good, but they *become* either bad or good. They become compassionate or cruel, saints or monsters, depending on collective and personal values and symbols. In Pico Della Mirandola's *Oratio de Hominis Dignitate*, God spoke to man: "It will be in your power to descend to the lower, brutish forms of life; you will be able, through your own decision, to rise again to the superior orders whose life is divine". According to Van Lier (1980), the human drives—which correspond to the animal instincts, but are not predetermined, resulting from "interlacements of an anatomo-physiological body and images and symbols which configure this body"—explain:

> ... the opposition between aggressiveness and cruelty. Aggressiveness is a response to stimuli-signals; cruelty is moved by the stiffnesses and caprices of the signs. The animal, instinctive, is not cruel but aggressive. Man, full of drives, is aggressive and all his history is mostly the series of his cruelties, monstrous or trivial. (p. 50, 52)

Given that the human species displays both an animal and a human face, it might be said that the human being is a *de-natured animal*[226], that is, an animal with a second nonbiological nature, constructed over the biological one. Such a double identity is somewhat reflected in the two etymological origins of the word 'man' in European languages, as Odon Vallet notes: one originated in Latin, in which *homo* comes from *humus* that means earth (also the hebrew 'Adam' means "of the same coulour as earth"); the other relates the English *man* and the German *Mensch* to thought, according to the Indo-European root *men* (in AAVV 2012, p. 82).

If the semiotic perfectibility renders the human being a *de-natured animal*, not perfecting our natures makes us *de-natured human beings*. Lack of cultural *transfiguration* causes human *defiguration*. At the end of the day, what human beings *become* depends on the means and the ethical sense conditioning their perfecting.

5.6.3 The Perfecting of Human Beings Should Consist in the Cultivation of Their Semiotic Seeds that Require Human Rights' Protection and Provisions

The perfecting of human beings is concerned with the broad scope of their perfectibility.

Passmore (1970) noticed that, following the Latin etymology of the English word 'perfect'—*perficere*, the roots of which are *facere*, 'to make', and the prefix

[226] *Les animaux dénaturés* (The Denatured Animals) is the title of a novel by Vercors, variously translated into English.

per suggesting 'thoroughly'—the perfect is the 'thoroughly made', the 'completed' (p. 15). A multi-sided conception of human perfection was formulated by Sir William Hamilton, in the ninteenth century, who defined it as "the full and harmonious development of all our faculties, corporeal and mental, intellectual and moral", a definition that "came to be, for a time, the standard dictionary definition" (as cit. ib. p. 24).

Human perfectibility includes possibilities for two main kinds of perfection: moral (concerned with behavior) and technical (concerned with performance). It is generally agreed, however, that the most humanizing dimension of human beings' perfectibility is that which takes into due account the paramountcy of moral values for their living, surviving and flourishing. "Beginning with the Renaissance, but with increasing confidence in the seventeenth century", perfection "came gradually to be further particularised as 'doing the maximum of good'" (p. 260).

The close relation between Semiotics and Axiology, the studies of signs and values, was highlighted by Peirce, Morris and other authors, such as Victoria Welby and Mikhail Bakhtin.

According to Peirce, the relation between the interpretant and the interpreted is dialogic, understood as the *logic* of semiosis. Such a dialogue presupposes the capacity for interpretation that does not exist in the inorganic world. The sign has a dialogic nature to the extent that it "has its meaning in another sign which responds to it and which in turn is a sign if there is another sign to respond to it and interpret it, and so forth ad infinitum" (Petrilli and Ponzio 2007, p. 37): That is the Peircean principle of unlimited semiosis[227]. "The problem of otherness, dialogism and ethical responsibility is pivotal in Peirce's conception of the human subject, contrary to reductive interpretations of his semiotics" (p. 95).

Morris (1964) distinguished three dimensions in language: designative, appraisive and prescriptive.

> Language and the postlinguistic symbols made possible by language are distinctive features of human action. In their designative dimension they embody man's knowledge of the world and of himself; in their appraisive dimension they reflect the conceived values which serve as man's goals; in their prescriptive dimension they direct the specific course of human action toward envisaged goals. Language and post linguistic symbols are the power and the glory of human life. (p. 81)[228]

[227] Chandler (2002) informs us: "Umberto Eco coined the term 'unlimited semiosis' to refer to the way in which, for Peirce (via the 'interpretant'), for Barthes (via connotation), for Derrida (via 'free play') and for Lacan (via 'the sliding signified'), the signified is endlessly commutable—functioning in its turn as a signifier for a further signified".

[228] Prelinguistic, linguistic and postlinguistic signs are thus defined by Morris (1964):

> *Prelinguistic signs* are those which occur in the child's behavior before it speaks, or which later, even in the adult, are independent of language signs. *Linguistic signs* are those which occur in a language considered as a system of interpersonal signs restricted in their possibility of combination. *Postlinguistic signs* are signs which owe their signification to language but which are not themselves elements of language. The carved bear on a totem pole, the flag of a nation, the perception of a star as a large distant flaming object, and the policeman's badge are examples of postlinguistic signs. (p. 58).

Morris had the deep conviction that understanding the functioning of signs and values in human life is key to understanding the emerging "new and important outlook on the nature of man" (p. viii). He began the Preface to his *Signification and Significance—A Study of the Relations of Signs and Values* by affirming:

> For several decades my work has centered around two problems: the development of a general theory of signs and the development of a general theory of value. *Signs, Language and Behavior* was a product of the first concern, and *Varieties of Human Value* was a product of the second. Both problems were approached in terms of the theory of action or behavior developed in its essentials by George H. Mead.
> The present study is an attempt to bring together these two lines of development. [...]
> That there are close relations between the terms 'signification' and 'significance' is evident. In many languages there is a term like the English term 'meaning' which has two poles: that which something signifies and the value or significance of what is signified. [...] The fact that such terms as 'meaning' are so widespread in many languages (with the polarity mentioned) suggests that there is a basic relation between what we shall distinguish as *signification* and *significance*. The nature of signification and significance, as well as their relations within human behavior, is the subject matter of this book. (p. vii)

In Morris' opinion: "The difficulties with the term 'meaning' in semiotic are paralleled by those with the term 'value' in axiology. Both terms have such a variety of significations and uses that they serve only to indicate in a vague way an area of investigation" (p. 16). Defining values as conceptions of the desirable, he suggested "one possible view of the relation of semiotic and axiology, conceived as the studies of sign behavior and preferential behavior" (p. 43).

The semiotic virtualities or seeds—rational and moral—inherent in every human being require the protection and provisions afforded by human rights, tackling oppression, poverty, exclusion, passivity, self-undervaluing, etc.

As already above quoted, the Supreme Court of Israel reaffirmed in *HCJ 6427/02 Movement for Quality Government in Israel v. Knesset*, cited in *HCJ 2605/05 Academic Center of Law and Business v. Minister of Finance*[229], that the essence of the dignity of a human being "lies in the sanctity of his life and his liberty" and "relies on the recognition of the physical and spiritual integrity of a human being, his humanity, his worth as a human being" (para. 34). That is why the rights aimed at protecting human integrity deserve the highest level of legal protection, being qualified as *non-derogable*. They include, first and foremost, protection against genocide, torture and slavery. The same Court warned, however, in *Commitment to Peace and Social Justice v. Minister of Finance (HCJ 366/03)* and *Bilhah Rubinova and Others v. Minister of Finance (HCJ 888/03)*[230]:

> 14. ... The right to human dignity, in the substantive sense, constitutes a collection of rights that need to be protected in order that dignity may exist. These are those rights without which there is no significance to a person being a free entity, since his power to develop his body and spirit in accordance with his will, within the society in which he lives, has been taken away.

[229] http://elyon1.court.gov.il/files_eng/05/050/026/n39/05026050.n39.pdf.

[230] http://elyon1.court.gov.il/files_eng/03/660/003/a39/03003660.a39.pdf.

This jurisprudence is shared by other similar Courts, as we saw above. John Steinbeck said in concluding his speech at the Nobel Banquet in 1962[231]:

> We have usurped many of the powers we once ascribed to God. Fearful and unprepared, we have assumed lordship over the life or death of the whole world—of all living things. The danger and the glory and the choice rest finally in man. The test of his perfectibility is at hand.
> Having taken Godlike power, we must seek in ourselves for the responsibility and the wisdom we once prayed some deity might have. Man himself has become our greatest hazard and our only hope. So that today St. John the apostle may well be paraphrased: In the end is the Word, and the Word is Man—and the Word is with Men.

In this respect, let us recall Apel (1988) who considered as necessary an "*ethics of communication as an ethics of responsibility*", because it is "the first time in history of mankind that the conservation of life arouses a problem concerning the whole human species that should be solved by it" (p. 152). The Universal Declaration on Bioethics and Human Rights (UNESCO 2005)[232] also declares "that human beings are an integral part of the biosphere, with an important role in protecting one another and other forms of life, in particular animals" (Preamble). In syntony with this conscience, Petrilli and Ponzio (2007) wrote:

> Properly understood, the 'semiotic animal' is a responsible agent with a capacity for signs of signs, that is, for mediation, reflection, and awareness in relation to semiosis over the entire planet. In this sense global semiotics must be adequately founded in cognitive semiotics, but it must also be open to a third dimension beyond the quantitative and the theoretical, that is, the ethical which concerns the goals toward which we strive. We propose to designate this dimension with the expression 'semioethics' (see Petrilli and Ponzio 2003b, 2005). (p. 106)

In their opinion: "Semioethics proposes a new form of humanism", inspired in the "humanism of alterity" of Levinas. "Semiotics contributes to the humanism of alterity by bringing to light the extension and consistency of the sign network interconnecting each and every one of us to every other" (p. 107). The new humanism consists in a re-centering on otherness, a concept that includes not only human beings, neighbor or distant, but also nonhuman others. It implies "a radical operation of decentralization, nothing less than a Copernican revolution" (p. 108).

The authors recalls that semiotics originates from *semeiotics*, classified by Galen as one of the principal branches of medicine. "Besides auscultation and other ways of analyzing symptoms, diagnosis and anamnesis, following Galen, include listening to the patient describe his/her ailments" (p. 104). Moreover: "If semiotics is interested in life over the whole planet, given that life and semiosis converge, and if one of the original reasons for studying signs was 'health', a nonnegligible task of semiotics today in the era of globalization is to call attention to the need to care for life in its globality" (p. 105).

---

[231] www.nobelprize.org/nobel_prizes/literature/laureates/1962/steinbeck-speech_en.html.

[232] http://portal.unesco.org/en/ev.php-URL_ID=31058&URL_DO=DO_TOPIC&URL_SECTION=201.html.

A globalized world calls, therefore, for a globalized citizenship.

"Citizen" and "citizenship" are terms not present in the principal international instruments on human rights (whereas 'national' and 'nationality' are used). Nevertheless, the relationship between human rights and citizenship goes without saying.

Citizenship is a concept originating in classical Greece, as other concepts in Political Philosophy. The Greeks invented the city (*polis*, in Latin *civitas*) and the public space as the field where public power is exerted for the benefit of the common good or general interest or "public thing" (*res publica* in Latin). A citizen is, according to the most common definition, a member of the political community where he or she is born or of which he or she became member by naturalization. In modern times, citizenship became a principle of political legitimacy. The Declaration of the Rights of Man and of the Citizen (France 1789)[233] proclaimed this revolutionary principle (Article 3): "The principle of all Sovereignty resides essentially in the Nation. Nobody, no individual can exercise authority that does not proceed from it in plain terms". The nation is formed by free and equal citizens, each one holding a parcel of sovereignty, regardless of their differences. Since the late 1980s or so, two phenomena began to challenge the traditional State-centric approach to citizenship: the multiculturalism of societies and the world's globalization.

There were always restrictions to its attribution to non-nationals. The traditional correlation between citizenship and nationality continues to prevail, but in a world crossed by trends of migrants and refugees the concept of citizenship should be deepened and expanded. A legal statute of citizenship whose center of gravity is a difference-blind integration has the potential for discrimination and exclusion. While differences—of gender, ethnic, cultural, etc.—have to be recognized, a balance is needed between their right to recognition, possibly justifying special treatment, and the recognition of common values and principles of cohesion, to harmonizing the different with the common. Furthermore, the attachment of citizenship to a territorial sovereign State became controversial in a world so globalized and interdependent. The nature of sovereignty is changing, and citizenship's levels multiplied: Besides national citizenship, there are infra-national citizenships (at local level) and supra-national citizenships (at international regional level).

On 23 May 1979, the year of the 30th anniversary of the German GG, Dolf Sternberger published in the *Frankfurter Allgemeinen Zeitung* (a German influential newspaper), an article with the title 'Constitutional Patriotism' (*Verfassungspatriotism*)[234]. He wrote: "The national sentiment remains wounded; we do not live in a full Germany. But we live in a full constitution, a fully constitutional State, and that itself is a kind of fatherland". In the mid-1980s, the concept was popularized by Habermas. Opposed to *Nationalpatriotism*, based on blood[235], on particularities that separate and exclude—such as ethnic group, culture, lan-

233 www.historyguide.org/intellect/declaration.html.

234 http://germanhistorydocs.ghi-dc.org/sub_document.cfm?document_id=1154.

235 *Reich Citizenship Law*, 15 September 1935: "A citizen of the Reich is only that subject who is of German or kindred blood and who, through his conduct, shows that he is both willing and able to faithfully serve the German people and Reich".
(Retrieved July 2013 from: http://germanhistorydocs.ghi-dc.org/pdf/eng/English32.pdf).

guage, religion, traditions—the *Verfassungspatriotism* is about founding the collective identity in values of a common political culture that unite and include the members of a society, such as Rule of Law, human rights, democracy, pluralism, tolerance. "Habermas thus added a much stronger universalist element to the original conception of constitutional patriotism" (Müller 2006, p. 288).

According to the Draft Outline of an International Bill of Human Rights prepared by the Division of Human Rights of the UN Secretariat in 1947 (E/CN.4/AC.1/3), one of the four principles its Preamble shoud enuntiate was: "That man is a citizen both of his State and of the world". There is now a *global* citizenship, for three main reasons:

- Everyone's and every country's life is today more or less influenced by problems, decisions and politics of other Governments and international entities.
- Given the web of communication connecting the world, it is increasingly easier to know and to act at a distance against violations of human rights in regions of the world more or less remote.
- Every human being is a world-citizen to the extent that they carry their human rights everywhere they may go.

Everyone living within the frontiers of the Roman Empire could allege: *Civis romanus sum!* (I'm a Roman citizen!). Nowadays, every human being can allege everywhere: *Civis humanus sum!* (I'm a human citizen!).

A global understanding of the human being and human perfectibility reveals then education as a key human right.

5.6.4 Right to Education: Key for the Human Perfecting

Following Dolto (1985), the acquisition of the symbolic function means a *second birth.* The first birth is a mammal one; the second is a birth for language, "a birth for the spirit, for the consciousness of the symbolic life. It was perhaps this mutation that would have transformed this superior mammal into a human being" (p. 208). *Tout est langage* (All is language)—is the title of a book Dolto published in 1987.

Arendt also referred to a second birth as a "linguistic birth" (as cit. in Birmingham 2006, p. 17). She wrote in *The Human Condition* (1958): "With word and deed we insert ourselves into the human world, and this insertion is like a second birth, in which we confirm and take upon ourselves the nacked fact of our original physical appearance" (cit. ib. p. 23). The name a newborn is given means the entry into language that requires a political space, which is primarily "constituted in the realm of representation and the process of signification" (cit. ib. p. 26).

The second birth is the birth of a *second nature* that is to be learned as a culturally specific way of being and living (see Lenk 2008)[236], through a *principled* education, according to Kant (1803, p. 9). Also Hegel wrote:

[236] 'Second nature' is an expression probably first used by Poseidonius (2nd–1st centuries BC) and later used by Johann G. von Herder (1744–1803), for example, to characterize the human incompletenesses that explains the development of language and culture.

> Education [*Pädagogik*] is the art of making human beings ethical: it considers them as natural beings and shows them how they can be reborn, and how their original nature can be transformed into a second, spiritual nature so that this spirituality becomes habitual to them. (as cit. in Williams 1997, p. 203)

As Wilhelm von Humboldt said, "the mere individual has to be upgraded in all its capacities to become human" (*das bloße Individuum soll in allen seinen Kräften zum Menschen emporgeläutert werden*) (as cit. in Blum 2003, p. 2). In connection with the ancient ideal of *paideia* (education), the German philologist Werner Jäger (1888–1961) referred to "the education of the human being to its true form, that is, to be specifically human" (*die Erziehung des Menschen zu seiner wahren Form, dem eigentlichen Menschsein*) (ib. p. 3).

In fact, as François Jacob (1981), Nobel Prize winner in medicine in 1965 (shared with Jacques Monod and André Lwoff) remarked: "Almost everything that characterizes humankind is summarized in the word culture" (p. 123). The so-called *wolf children* (52, between 1344 and 1963) are historical dramatic experiments proving how the deprivation of the birth to a second, cultural nature handicaps a human being. "Deprived of the society of others, man becomes a monster. He cannot regress to his pre-cultural state, because such a state never existed" (Malson 1972, p. 35).

The importance of education and the primacy of early and moral education are leitmotifs in the history of the pedagogical thought. Referring to the new modern perfectibilism, Passmore (1970) wrote:

> Suppose we then go on to ask how this perfecting is to be brought about. The obvious candidate—obvious since the time of Plato—is education, and it is in education, or in education supplemented, as in Plato's *Republic*, by such other forms of social control as legislation, that eighteenth century perfectibilists placed their trust. But it had first to be shown that education, as distinct from divine grace, was capable, even, of leading men to virtue. The great turning point, in this respect, is Locke's *Some Thoughts Concerning Education*, first published in 1693.
> 'Of all the men we meet with', Locke there writes, 'nine parts of ten are what they are, good or evil, useful or not, by their education. It is that which makes the great difference in mankind'. Notice that Locke is talking about men's moral character; education, he is saying, makes men 'good or evil, useful or not'. For Locke, indeed, education is essentially moral education. 'It is virtue then', he maintains, 'direct virtue, which is the hard and valuable part to be aimed at in education'. (p. 242)

This implied the rejection of the doctrine of original sin that, following the Augustinian tradition dominating European thinking for over a thousand years, was too deep-seated in every human being to be corrigible. Locke did not think, however, that human beings are born with an inclination towards goodness. "Men have a natural tendency", he wrote, "to what delights and from what pains them. This, universal observation has established past doubt. But that the soul has such a tendency to what is morally good and from evil has not fallen under my observation, and therefore I cannot grant it" (as cit. ib. p. 245)[237]. Locke thus "laid the founda-

[237] In this regard, Passmore notes that the eighteenth century was "fascinated by Chinese civilization" and the Confucianism that "came to be committed to the view that man is naturally good". According to Mencius: "Man's nature is naturally good just as water naturally flows downward"

tions of what was to be one of the most influential forms of eighteenth- and nineteenth-century perfectibilism, according to which men can be morally improved to an unlimited degree by education and other forms of social action" (p. 250).[238] As Erasmus (1466–1536) wrote in *The education of children* (1529), "men (trust me) be not born, but fashioned"[239].

Human perfectibility means, therefore, human educability. For, being a semiotic animal, the human being is a *pedagogic animal*. This is why childhood stands out "as the quintessence of the perfectibility or process of enhancement of the naturality by means of which the humankind constitutes itself infinitely in us", notes Renaut (2002, p. 281). The eighteenth century—the "Great Century", as it was qualified by the historian Jules Michelet (1798–1874)—was the "century of pedagogy", in Bernard Bourgeois' opinion (in Hegel 1978, p. 7), because of the widespread belief in the ethical and political potential of the diffusion of knowledge.

Rousseau and Kant were two great thinkers of human educability. Rousseau (1762) wrote in the first lines of his *Émile*: "We are born weak, we need strength; helpless, we need aid; foolish, we need reason. All that we lack at birth, all that we need when we come to man's estate, is the gift of education" (p. 6). For Kant (1803), Rousseau's reader and admirer, the secret of human perfection lies in education:

> Man is the only being who needs education. [...]
> Man can only become man by education. He is merely what education makes of him. [...] It may be that education will be constantly improved, and that each succeeding generation will advance one step towards the *perfecting* [italics added] of mankind; for with education is involved the great secret of the perfection of human nature. [...] It is delightful to realise that through education human nature will be continually improved, and brought to such a condition as is worthy of the nature of man. This opens out to us the prospect of a happier human race in the future. (p. 1, 6, 7, 8)

Some centuries before (1657), Jan Amos Komensky (Comenius, in Latin) (1592–1670) had written in his *Didactica Magna* (The Great Didactic 1967, Chapter VI)[240]:

(Book of Mencius, 6A:2) (p. 244). Kant (1803), for example, said: "Evil is only the result of nature not being brought under control. In man there are only germs of good" (p. 15).

[238] Passmore informs us:

> Locke's *Some Thoughts Concerning Education* was an immensely popular book. By the end of the eighteenth century it had been reprinted at least twenty-one times: almost immediately translated into French, it was reprinted in that language at least sixteen times. At first, however, it was read, for the most part, as a manual for mothers rather than as incorporating, or suggesting, a revolutionary theory of human nature and the formation of moral character. It is interesting to observe the tenour of the protests which, even so, were raised against it. In general, they were protests that Locke had underestimated the importance of men's innate tendencies and, in consequence, had exaggerated the influence of education. Thus began that controversy between the proponents of 'nature' and the proponents of 'nurture' which was to prove as persistent and as obdurate as the controversy between Pelagians and Augustinians, of which, in important respects, it is the secular echo. (p. 250).

[239] www.manybooks.net/titles/erasmusd2833828338-8.html.

[240] http://core.roehampton.ac.uk/digital/froarc/comgre.

> 1. The seeds [italiscs added] of knowledge, of virtue, and of piety are, as we have seen, naturally implanted in us; but the actual knowledge, virtue, and piety are not so given. These must be acquired by prayer, by education, and by action. He gave no bad definition who said that man was a 'teachable animal'. And indeed it is only by a proper education that he can become a man.
> [...]
> 3. Let none believe, therefore, that any can really be a man, unless we have learned to act like one, that is, have been trained in those elements which constitute a man. [...]
> 6. Examples show that those who in their infancy have been seized by wild animals, and have been brought up among them, have not risen above the level of brutes in intellect, and would not have been able to make more use of their tongues, their hands, and their feet than beasts can, had they not once more come into the society of men.

Comenius alluded to the *wolf children*, which illustrate that, "without education, there is scarcely the possibility of man, let alone the promise" (Malson 1972, p. 80).

Given the consubstantiality between perfectibility and educability, we confront the *aporia* (literally: 'without passage') of Humankind having to educate itself. This Gordian knot was highlighted by Karl Marx in one of his *Theses on Feuerbach* first published as an appendix to *Ludwig Feuerbach and the End of Classical German Philosophy* (1888)[241]. Thesis III reads: "The materialist doctrine concerning the changing of circumstances and upbringing forgets that circumstances are changed by men and that it is essential to educate the educator himself". In the history of pedagogical thought, we hardly find a better approach than that of Kant.

In Kant's (1803) opinion, it is through education that "man must be made" (p. 18), by learning his proper second nature. "Under the present educational system man does not fully attain to the object of his adequate being; for in what various ways men live! Uniformity can only result when all men act according to the same principles, which principles would have to become with them a second nature" (p. 9). However: "It is noticeable that man is only educated by man—that is, by men who have themselves been educated. [...] Were some being of higher nature than man to undertake our education, we should then be able to see what man might become" (p. 6). This not being the case, educating itself is, no doubt, the most challenging art and the highest responsibility of Humankind.

> Education is an *art* which can only become perfect through the practice of many generations. Each generation, provided with the knowledge of the foregoing one, is able more and more to bring about an education which shall develop man's natural gifts in their due proportion and in relation to their end, and thus advance the whole human race towards its destiny. [...]
> Hence the greatest and most difficult problem to which man can devote himself is the problem of education. For insight depends on education, and education in its turn depends on insight. (p. 10, 11)

How is it possible to solve the Gordian knot of insight depending on education, and education depending on insight? How to think of, and practice, the "good education" through which "all the good in the world arises" (p. 15)? Kant's answer may be summarized as follows: The best education is that which is illuminated by the

[241] www.marxists.org/archive/marx/works/1845/theses/theses.htm.

best idea of human perfection, guided by the best knowledge of human and individual nature, and entrusted to the best human beings.

- The vision of education should be inspired by the "principle" according to which "children ought to be educated, not for the present, but for a possibly improved condition of man in the future; that is, in a manner which is adapted to the idea of humanity and the whole destiny of man" (p. 14).
- Furthermore:

> If education is to develop human nature so that it may attain the object of its being, it must involve the exercise of judgment. Educated parents are examples which children use for their guidance. If, however, the children are to progress beyond their parents, education must become a study, otherwise we can hope for nothing from it, and one man whose education has been spoilt will only repeat his own mistakes in trying to educate others. The mechanism of education must be changed into a science, and one generation may have to pull down what another had built up. (p. 13, 14)

- In addition, an education fit to bringing "our nature one step nearer to perfection" (p. 7) should be entrusted by each generation to "people of broader views, who take an interest in the universal good, and who are capable of entertaining the idea of a better condition of things in the future, that the gradual progress of human nature towards its goal is possible" (p. 17). Such people are likely the best of its members. Indeed, the secret of overcoming the aporia of Humankind educating itself through its children is, borrowing a luminous insight from Plato's *Republic* (1997), "fostering their best part with our own" (590d).

Reflecting the traditional cultural and political primacy of early and moral education, Kant envisages *good education* as one that, while being a matter of making human beings both "clever" and "good" (p. 18), should aim, first and foremost, at making good human beings. Indeed: "It is not enough that a man shall be fitted for any end, but his disposition must be so trained that he shall choose none but good ends, good ends being those which are necessarily approved by everyone, and which may at the same time be the aim of every one" (p. 20). This should be achieved early, by means of *discipline*.

> Discipline changes animal nature into human nature. Animals are by their instinct all that they ever can be; some other reason has provided everything for them at the outset. But man needs a reason of his own. Having no instinct, he has to work out a plan of conduct for himself. Since, however, he is not able to do this all at once, but comes into the world undeveloped, others have to do it for him. (p. 2)
>
> Unruliness consists in independence of law. By discipline men are placed in subjection to the laws of mankind, and brought to feel their constraint. This, however, must be accomplished early. Children, for instance, are first sent to school, not so much with the object of their learning something, but rather that they may become used to sitting still and doing exactly as they are told. And this to the end that in later life they should not wish to put actually and instantly into practice anything that strikes them. (p. 3, 4)
>
> Neglect of discipline is a greater evil than neglect of culture, for this last can be remedied later in life, but unruliness cannot be done away with, and a mistake in discipline can never be repaired. (p. 7)

These words echo this passage of Plato's (1997) *Protagoras*:

> Starting when they are little children and continuing as long as they live, they [good men] teach them and correct them. As soon as a child understands what is said to him, the nurse, mother, tutor, and the father himself fight for him to be as good as he possibly can, seizing on every action and word to teach him and show him that this is just, that is unjust, this is noble, that is ugly, this is pious, that is impious, he should do this, he should not do that. If he obeys willingly, fine; if not, they straighten him out with threats and blows as if he were a twisted, bent piece of wood. After this they send him to school and tell his teachers to pay more attention to his good conduct than to his grammar or music lessons. (325 d-e)

In *Laws* Book VI, Plato highlighted the importance of moral education and of it being entrusted to the best human beings:

> Here too there should be one official in charge under the law. He must be not younger than fifty years old, and the father of legitimate children—preferably both sons and daughters, though either alone will do. The chosen candidate himself and those who choose him should appreciate that this is by far the most important of all the supreme offices in the state. Any living creature that flourishes in its first stages of growth gets a tremendous impetus towards its natural perfection and the final development appropriate to it, and this is true of both plants and animals (tame and wild), and men too. Man is a 'tame' animal, as we put it, and of course if he enjoys a good education and happens to have the right natural disposition, he's apt to be a most heavenly and gentle creature; but his upbringing has only to be inadequate or misguided and he'll become the wildest animal on the face of the earth. That's why the legislator should not treat the education of children cursorily or as a secondary matter; he should regard the right choice of the man who is going to be in charge of the children as something of crucial importance, and appoint as their Minister the best all-round citizen in the state. (765e-766a)

Part of this passage was echoed in a quotation above from Aristotle's (2000, 1253a, 12, 15–16)[242].

Johann F. Herbart (1776–1841), Kant's disciple and successor in the teaching of Pedagogy at the University of Königsberg (Germany), summarized (1835): Educability is "the central concept of Pedagogy" and is principally "educability of the will for the morality". Indeed: "Virtue is the name of the whole purpose of education"

---

[242] Aristotle also wrote in the same work (Book VIII):

> No one will doubt that the legislator should direct his attention above all to the education of youth, or that the neglect of education does harm to states. [...] And since the whole city has one end, it is manifest that education should be one and the same for all, and that it should be public, and not private—not as at present, when every one looks after his own children separately, and gives them separate instruction of the sort which he thinks best; the training in things which are of common interest should be the same for all. [...]
> That education should be regulated by law and should be an affair of state is not to be denied, but what should be the character of this public education, and how young persons should be educated, are questions which remain to be considered. (1337a).

(§ 1, § 8)[243]. Although some animals are 'educable' to a certain extent, only the human being is educable for morality[244].

Moral education is fundamentally a matter of managing 'pleasure and pain', as Plato (1997) put it, with lasting influence, at the beginning of *Laws* Book II:

> I maintain that the earliest sensations that a child feels in infancy are of pleasure and pain, and this is the route by which virtue and vice enter the soul. [...] I call 'education' the initial acquisition of virtue by the child, when the feelings of pleasure and affection, pain and hatred, that well up in his soul are channeled in the right courses before he can understand the reason why. Then when he does understand, his reason and his emotions agree in telling him that he has been properly trained by inculcation of appropriate habits. Virtue is this general concord of reason and emotion. But there is one element you could isolate in any account you give, and this is the correct formation of our feelings of pleasure and pain, which makes us hate what we ought to hate from first to last, and love what we ought to love. Call this 'education', and I, at any rate, think you would be giving it its proper name. [...] Education, then, is a matter of correctly disciplined feelings of pleasure and pain. (653a-c)

As a consequence, the right to education may be said to be, on the one side, the most complex human right and, on the other, the first priority.

Mustapha Mehedi, who was member of the former UN Sub-Commission on Prevention of Discrimination and Protection of Minorities (E/CN.4/Sub.2/1999/10)[245], wrote:

> 51. It is generally accepted in the literature that the right to education, on account of its dual nature, belongs to both the first and the second generations of human rights. However, some authors even maintain that, on historical grounds and for reasons linked to the formulation of international and regional instruments, the right to education is a specific and possibly unique case of a right that belongs not only to the first two generations of rights but also to what is termed the third generation of human rights, namely collective rights and solidarity rights.

In Nowak's (2001) opinion, "the right to education is one of the most complex human rights under present international law" (p. 268). It "is a complex right", especially when children are concerned, Kiss (1975) noted, because "children are really its holders and beneficiaries but its realization is in charge of the State, and the parents have the choice of the modes of its practice" (p. 432).

Because of the human primacy of education, it was often evoked during the *travaux préparatoires* (preparation) of the main international norms on the right to education. For example, when the draft ICESCR Article 14 was examined by the Third Commission of the UN General Assembly, at its 12th session, in 1957

---

[243] *Der Grundbegriff der Pädagogik ist die Bildsamkeit des Zöglings. [...] Von der Bildsamkeit des Willens zeigen sich Spuren in den Seelen der edlern Thiere. Aber Bildsamkeit des Willens zur Sittlichkeit kennen wir nur beim Menschen. [...] Tugend is der Name für das Ganze des pädagogischen Zwecks.*

[244] The Constitutional Court of South Africa underlined in *M v The State Centre for Child Law (S v M (CCT 53/06) [2007] ZACC 18; 2008 (3) SA 232 (CC) (26 September 2007)*: "Children have a need and a right to learn from their primary caregivers that individuals make moral choices for which they can be held accountable" (para. 34) (www.saflii.org/za/cases/ZACC/2007/18.pdf).

[245] www.unhchr.ch/Huridocda/Huridoca.nsf/TestFrame/58e5842871e93edb802567cb0037fe9c?Opendocument.

(A/C.3/SR.790), UNESCO's Director-General (René Maheu) affirmed, in response to some questions arisen about the exceptional character of such a provision, that without education "the other rights hardly can be exercised; it should deserve, therefore, absolute priority"[246]. According to the *United Nations Yearbook 1957*[247]: "Most representatives agreed that the fundamental character of the right to primary education justified the inclusion of a special implementation clause, even though similar provisions were not made with regard to other rights".

The relative priority of the right to education has been rediscovered since the beginning of the last decade of the twentieth century by the International Community; and it has been put on the international agenda, especially education for human rights and citizenship, as testified by numerous Conferences, Declarations, Programs of Action and other initiatives. For example:

- In 1998, the CHR, following a Resolution concerning the implementation of the economic, social and cultural rights (Resolution 1998/33, of 17 April), decided to designate a Special Rapporteur on the Right to Education.
- In 1999, the CESCR consecrated to the ICESCR Articles 13 and 14, concerning the right to education, the GC 13 (E/C.12/1999/10) and the GC 11 (E/C.12/1999/4) respectively. The GC 13 begins by stating[248]:

> 1. Education is both a human right in itself and an indispensable means of realizing other human rights. As an empowerment right, education is the primary vehicle by which economically and socially marginalized adults and children can lift themselves out of poverty and obtain the means to participate fully in their communities. Education has a vital role in empowering women, safeguarding children from exploitative and hazardous labour and sexual exploitation, promoting human rights and democracy, protecting the environment, and controlling population growth. Increasingly, education is recognized as one of the best financial investments States can make. But the importance of education is not just practical: a welleducated, enlightened and active mind, able to wander freely and widely, is one of the joys and rewards of human existence.

- In 2001, the CoRC consecrated its first GC to the right to education (CRC/GC/2001/1, 17/04/2001, The aims of education, Article 29.1). It was a choice significant of the centrality of the right to education for the child's development and for the enjoyment of the whole human rights. The Committee states[249]:

[246] Article 14 provides:

> Each State Party to the present Covenant which, at the time of becoming a Party, has not been able to secure in its metropolitan territory or other territories under its jurisdiction compulsory primary education, free of charge, undertakes, within two years, to work out and adopt a detailed plan of action for the progressive implementation, within a reasonable number of years, to be fixed in the plan, of the principle of compulsory education free of charge for all.

[247] http://unyearbook.un.org/unyearbook.html?name-=-isysadvsearch.html.

[248] www.unhchr.ch/tbs/doc.nsf/0/ae1a0b126d068e868025683c003c8b3b?Opendocument.

[249] www.unhchr.ch/tbs/doc.nsf/(symbol)/CRC.GC.2001.1.En?OpenDocument.

> 2. … The education to which every child has a right is one designed to provide the child with life skills, to strengthen the child's capacity to enjoy the full range of human rights and to promote a culture which is infused by appropriate human rights values. The goal is to empower the child by developing his or her skills, learning and other capacities, human dignity, self-esteem and self-confidence. 'Education' in this context goes far beyond formal schooling to embrace the broad range of life experiences and learning processes which enable children, individually and collectively, to develop their personalities, talents and abilities and to live a full and satisfying life within society.

That is why *key* is a word often used in the texts of the UN organs and high representatives to mean the paramount role of the right to education. Sometimes it is qualified as *a* key, sometimes as *the* key. For example, the first Special Rapporteur on the Right to Education (Katarina Tomaševski 1998–2004) stressed in one of her annual reports to the CHR: "Education is increasingly defined as the key to development and the right to education as the key to the enjoyment of many other human rights" (E/CN.4/2001/52, para. 79)[250]. In another report, she observed that the consequences of denying the right to education "cannot be retroactively remedied" (E/CN.4/2004/45, para. 8)[251].

Let us recall that the 'Second Bill of Rights'[252] proposed by President Roosevelt (1944) included "The right to a good education". Indeed, being a human right, education is not whatever right to whatever education. The right to education is, by definition, right to an education quality that requires human rights based approach to education. As reads the Article I.1.b of the UNESCO's Constitution[253], it is a matter of the education "best suited to prepare the children of the world for the responsibilities of freedom".

In sum: The right to education may be considered as the most empowering and humanizing right (see Donnelly & Howard, 1988), as the following neurobiological insights suggest.

5.6.5 Neurobiological Insights

Global Semiotics "takes very seriously current scientific research as the basis for semiotic theory"[254]. In this regard, Lévi-Strauss stressed the "more than encyclopedic knowledge" of Sebeok, ranging from the natural sciences to the human sciences:

---

[250] www.unhchr.ch/Huridocda/Huridoca.nsf/e06a5300f90fa0238025668700518ca4/8774217173a3fde0c1256a10002ecb42/$FILE/G0110177.pdf.

[251] www.unhchr.ch/Huridocda/Huridoca.nsf/e06a5300f90fa0238025668700518ca4/05af86414ce903c9c1256e3000357284/$FILE/G0410332.pdf.

[252] www.ushistory.org/documents/economic_bill_of_rights.htm.

[253] http://portal.unesco.org/en/ev.php-URL_ID=15244&URL_DO=DO_TOPIC&URL_SECTION=201.html.

[254] Petrilli and Ponzio, in 'On the Semiotic Basis of Knowledge and Ethics: An interview with Susan Petrilli and August Ponzio about their book Semiotics Unbound' by Daniel Punday, Genders, 2008, 47 (Retrieved July 2013 from: www.genders.org/g47/g47_punday.html).

biology, zoology, ethology, medicine, cultural anthropology, philosophy, psychology, literature, linguistics, mathematics, etc.[255]

Some scientific insights have been already presented, highlighting the human species' biological distinctiveness. The following summarizes the findings of one of the most important neuroscientists at work today, as well as other contributions in the same field of research, which shed light on the biological underpinnings of the human species' semiotic nature, and the role of education in particular.

António Damásio (1994) brought to the fore how much human beings are bio-mental-cultural entities driven by their emotions, even at high-level reasoning. In *Descartes' Error—Emotion, Reason, and the Human Brain*—that is about an error that consisted in "the abyssal separation between body and mind" (p. 249)—he begins by remarking:

> Although I cannot tell for certain what sparked my interest in the neural underpinnings of reason, I do know when I became convinced that the traditional views on the nature of rationality could not be correct. I had been advised early in life that sound decisions came from a cool head, that emotions and reason did not mix any more than oil and water. [...]
> I began writing this book to propose that reason may not be as pure as most of us think it is or wish it were, that emotions and feelings may not be intruders in the bastion of reason at all: they may be enmeshed in its networks, for worse and for better. The strategies of human reason probably did not develop, in either evolution or any single individual, without the guiding force of the mechanisms of biological regulation, of which emotion and feeling are notable expressions. [...]
> Emotion, feeling, and biological regulation all play a role in human reason. The lowly orders of our organism are in the loop of high reason. (p. xi, xii, xiii)

In other words: "The human brain and the rest of the body constitute an indissociable organism [...] mental phenomena can be fully understood only in the context of an organism's interacting in an environment [...] mental activity, from its simplest aspects to its most sublime, requires both brain and body" (p. xvi, xvii). In a word: "The mind is embodied, in the full sense of the term" (p. 118). That fact should not be felt as a "downgrading" of the human, however, as "understanding neurobiological mechanisms behind some aspects of cognition and behavior does not diminish the value, beauty, or dignity of that cognition or behavior" (p. 176). On the contrary: "Perhaps the most indispensable thing we can do as human beings, every day of our lives, is remind ourselves and others of our complexity, fragility, finiteness, and uniqueness" (p. 252).

Approaching "rationality at work" (p. 170) in decision-making, Damásio affirms:

> There are at least two distinct possibilities: the first is drawn from a traditional 'high-reason' view of decision making; the second from the 'somatic-marker hypothesis'.
> The 'high-reason' view, which is none other than the commonsense view, assumes that when we are at our decision-making best, we are the pride and joy of Plato, Descartes and Kant. [...] Rational processing must be unencumbered by passion. (p. 171)

[255] Cit. by Petrilli, and Ponzio, in 'A Tribute to Thomas Sebeok' (Retrieved July 2013 from: www.augustoponzio.com/files/A_Tribute_to_Thomas_Sebeok.pdf).

Regarding the 'somatic-marker hypothesis', he explains that we are born with a neural machinery of primary emotions, which is encountered in other mammals and in birds.

> In the quest to understand human behavior, many have tried to overlook emotion, but to no avail. Behavior and mind, conscious and not, and the brain that generates them, refuse to yield their secrets unless emotion (and the many phenomena that hide under its name) is factored in and given its due.
> [...]
> Emotions are complex, largely automated programs of *actions* concocted by evolution. The actions are complemented by a *cognitive* program that includes certain ideas and modes of cognition, but the world of emotions is largely one of actions carried out in our bodies, from facial expressions and postures to changes in viscera and internal milieu.
> Feelings of emotion, on the other hand, are composite *perceptions* of what happens in our body and mind when we are emoting. As far as the body is concerned, feelings are images of actions rather than actions themselves; the world of feelings is one of perceptios executed in brain maps. (p. 108, 109, 110)

As for the somatic-markers, they are (in his italics):

> ... *a special instance of feelings generated from secondary emotions.* Those emotions and feelings *have been connected, by learning, to predicted future outcomes of certain scenarios.* When a negative somatic marker is juxtaposed to a particular future outcome the combination functions as an alarm bell. When a positive somatic marker is juxtaposed instead, it becomes a beacon of incentive (p. 174)

Most somatic-markers "probably were created in our brains during the process of education and socialization, by connecting specific classes of stimuli with specific classes of somatic state" (p. 177). It is by education and socialization that "the cultural instruments with which we can make the world better: ethics, law, art, science, technology" (p. 246) are transmitted.

> Culture and civilization could not have arisen from single individuals and thus cannot be reduced to biological mechanisms and, even less, can they be reduced to a subset of genetic specifications. [...]
> In human societies there are social conventions and ethical rules over and above those that biology already provides. [...]
> Realizing that there are biological mechanisms behind the most sublime human behavior does not imply a simplistic reduction to the nuts and bolts of neurobiology. In any case, the partial explanation of complexity by something less complex does not signify debasement. The picture I am drawing for humans is that of an organism that comes to life designed with automatic survival mechanisms, and to which education and acculturation add a set of socially permissible and desirable decision-making strategies that, in turn, enhance survival, remarkably improve the quality of that survival, and serve as the basis for constructing a *person.* [...] Moreover, out of that dual constraint, suprainstinctual survival strategies generate something probably unique to humans: a moral point of view that, on occasion, can transcend the interests of the immediate group and even the species. (124, 125, 126)

Emotion and reason are, therefore, 'two sides of the same coin'. In spite of their present complexity, "our brains still bear evidence of their original purpose: to manage our bodies and minds in the service of living, and living happily, in the world with other people" (Immordino-Yang and Damásio 2007, p. 4). In so doing, "emotions are not just messy toddlers in a china shop, running around breaking and obscuring delicate cognitive glassware. Instead, they are more like the shelves underlying the glassware; without them cognition has less support" (p. 5)[256]. *Emotional thought* is a term used "to refer to the large overlap between cognition and emotion":

> Emotional thought encompasses processes of learning, memory, and decision making, in both social and nonsocial contexts. It is within the domain of emotional thought that creativity plays out, through increasingly nuanced recognition of complex dilemmas and situations and through the invention of correspondingly flexible and innovative responses. [...] Rational thought can inform emotional thought. This is the pathway of high-level social and moral emotions, ethics, and of motivated reasoning. Creativity can also be informed by high reason.

Ethical thought and morality are a "specialized branch of decision making" concerned with "high-level social and moral emotions", to which "high reason and rational thought also contribute" (p. 8). The bio-mental-cultural unity of the human and humanizing rationality is epitomized in Damásio's (1994) statement: "The immune system, the hypothalamus, the ventromedial frontal cortices, and the Bill of Rights have the same root cause" (p. 262).

Another Damásio's groundbreaking essay *Self Comes to Mind—Constructing the Conscious Brain* (2010) is "dedicated to addressing two questions. First: how does the brain construct a mind? Second: how does the brain make the mind conscious?" (p. 6). An outline of his argument follows.

The brain, whose primary function is life regulation, is the main component of the central nervous system. The peripheral nervous system is formed of the sum of all nerves connecting the central nervous system to the whole body. It includes the autonomic nervous system, "so called because its operation is largely outside our volitional control. [...] The system plays a critical role in life regulation and in emotions and feelings. The brain and the body are also interconnected by chemical molecules such as hormones, which travel in the blood-stream" (p. 307).

The most distinctive feature of the human brain, however, is its "uncanny ability to create maps. Mapping is essential for sophisticated management, mapping and life management going hand in hand" (p. 63). That ability comes with the appearance of "a radical, game-changing actor": the neuron. Neurons are the creators of cerebral maps, volatiles, reflecting at every moment the alterations transmitted by neurons, originated both from the body itself and from the external world. They are special cells. "The essential functional difference has to do with the neuron's ability to produce electrochemical signals capable of changing the state of other cells" (p. 37). There are billions of neurons (about 10^{11}) that make trillions of connections or synapses among themselves (about 10^{15}) (p. 299).

> Changing the state of other cells is the very source of the activity that constitutes and regulates behavior, to begin with, and that eventually also contributes to making a mind. Neurons are capable of this feat because they produce and propagate an electrical current along the tubelike section known as the axon. [...] When the electrical current arrives at the tip of the neuron, the synapse, it causes the release of a chemical molecule, a transmitter, which in turn acts on the subsequent cell in the chain. [...] They end up *representing* the

[256] Emotion is understood "as a set of cognitive and physiological processes that constitute a person's automatic evaluative reaction to a perceived, remembered, or imagined circumstance" (Immordino-Yang 2009, p. 17).

> state of the body, literally mapping the body for which they work and constituting a sort of virtual surrogate of it, a neural double. (p. 37, 38)

The notion of a map is an abstraction. Neural pattern, map and image are practically almost interchangeable. Maps and images are the basis of mind, so that "mental states and brain states are essentially equivalent" (p. 314).

> A spectacular consequence of the brain's incessant and dynamic mapping is the mind. The mapped patterns constitute what we, conscious creatures, have come to know as sights, sounds, touches, smells, tastes, pains, pleasures, and the like—in brief, images. The images in our minds are the brain's momentary maps of everything and of anything, inside our body and around it, concrete as well as abstract, actual or previously recorded in memory. (p. 70)

However: "Brains begin building conscious minds not at the level of the cerebral cortex [especially the neocortex, its evolutionarily modern part] but rather at the level of the brain stem" (p. 22) that is "an old part of the brain shared with many other species" (p. 21).

Consciousness is the central problem of the research on brain and mind. It "is *a state of mind in which there is knowledge of one's own existence and of the existence of surroundings*" (p. 157), but it remains largely a mysterious phenomenon. A key for its understanding is brain's map-making dynamism. "The entire fabric of a conscious mind is created from the same cloth—*images generated by the brain's map-making abilities*" (p. 188).

> Ultimately, consciousness allows us to experience maps as images, to manipulate those images, and to apply reasoning to them.
> [...]
> Images represent physical properties of entities and their spatial and temporal relationships, as well as their actions. Some images, which probably result from the brain's making maps of itself making maps, are actually quite abstract. (p. 63, 70)

Consciousness is a mind endowed with subjectivity. "When the brain manages to introduce a knower in the mind, subjectivity follows" (p. 11). The *self* is the "single voice" of "a conscious brain" (p. 36). It is not a thing, but a process. "The self in each conscious mind is the first representative of individual life-regulation mechanisms, the guardian and curator of biological value" (p. 183). There is a "protoself" formed of "*an integrated collection of separate neural patterns that map, moment by moment, the most stable aspects of the organism's physical structure*" (p. 190).

One of the principal goals of the Neurobiology of consciousness is to understand when the self "came to mind" and "how the brain produces that something extra, the protagonist we carry around and call self, or me, or I" (p. 17), that generated "the biological revolution called culture" (p. 288) and "new devices of regulation".

> The conscious mind of humans, armed with such complex selves and supported by even greater capabilities of memory, reasoning, and language, engender the instruments of culture and open the way into new means of homeostasis at the level of societies and culture. In an extraordinary leap, homeostasis acquires an extension into the sociocultural space. Justice systems, economic and political organizations, the arts, medicine, and technology are examples of the new devices of regulation. (p. 26)

Moreover:

> Biology and culture are thoroughly interactive. Sociocultural homeostasis is shaped by the working of many minds whose brains have first been constructed in a certain way under the guidance of specific genomes. Intriguingly, there is growing evidence that cultural developments can lead to profound modifications in the human genome. (p. 20, 294)

For example: "The dramatic reduction of violence along with the increase in tolerance that has become so apparent in recent centuries would not have occurred without sociocultural homeostasis. Neither would the gradual transition from coercive power to the power of persuasion that hallmarks advanced social and political systems, their failures nothwithstanding" (p. 26, 27).

Van Lier (1980) recalled that the somato-semiotic interactions were called drives (*Triebe*) by Freud. They are "the key discovery of psychoanalysis" (p. 51), corresponding to the animal instincts, but are not predetermined. "The human being is neither an anatomo-physiological body, nor a soul, but the interlacements of an anatomo-physiological body and images and symbols which configure this body. [...] Weaved by signs, drive is built through an individual history" (p. 50, 51). In his opinion: "Sexuality remains the central theme of psychoanalysis because it is the most radical and the most initial experience of the reciprocal compenetration of flesh and sign" (p. 51, 52).

All in all:

> The brain is a dynamic, plastic, experience-dependent, social, and affective organ. Because of this, the centuries-long debate over nature versus nurture is an unproductive and overly dichotomous approach to understanding the complexities of the dynamic interdependencies between biology and culture in development. New evidence highlights how humans are fundamentally social and symbolic beings (Herrmann, Call, Hernandez-Lloreda, Hare, and Tomasello 2007), and just as certain aspects of our biology, including our genetics and our brains, shape our social, emotional and cognitive propensities, many aspects of our biology, including processes as fundamental as body growth, depend on adequate social, emotional and cognitive nurturance. Learning is social, emotional, and shaped by culture! (Immordino-Yang and Fischer 2010, p. 6)

Damásio and the other authors quoted above highlighted how much the politics of education and the school are called into question by neurobiological findings. *Mind, Brain and Education* (MBE) is a new research field emerging over the last few years that "encompasses educational neuroscience (a branch of neuroscience that deals with educationally relevant capacities in the brain), philosophy, linguistics, pedagogy, developmental psychology, and others" (p. 2, 3). In 2004, an International Mind, Brain, and Education Society (IMBES)[257] was created that launched the journal *Mind, Brain, and Education* in 2007 "to promote the integration of the diverse disciplines that investigate human learning and development—to bring together education, biology, and cognitive science to form the new field of mind, brain, and education"[258]. Without overlooking that "decisions about how to educate require not only scientific information about what is effective but also decisions about what is valuable", the promoters of the new approach share the conviction that it "can simultaneously inform effective practice and build fundamental knowl-

[257] www.imbes.org.

[258] In the same year, OECD published *Understanding the Brain: The Birth of a Learning Science.*

edge about the ways that children and adults learn and develop". It should be a reciprocal process: "Biology and cognitive science have as much to learn from education as education has to learn from them" (Fischer et al. 2007).

According to Immordino-Yang and Damásio (2007):

> Modern biology reveals humans to be fundamentally emotional and social creatures. And yet those of us in the field of education often fail to consider that the high-level cognitive skills taught in schools, including reasoning, decision making, and processes related to language, reading, and mathematics, do not function as rational, disembodied systems, somehow influenced by but detached from emotion and the body. [...] Any competent teacher recognizes that emotions and feelings affect students' performance and learning, as does the state of the body, such as how well students have slept and eaten or whether they are feeling sick or well. We contend, however, that the relationship between learning, emotion and body state runs much deeper than many educators realize and is interwoven with the notion of learning itself. It is not that emotions rule our cognition, nor that rational thought does not exist. It is, rather, that the original purpose for which our brains evolved was to manage our physiology, to optimize our survival, and to allow us to flourish. (p. 3, 4)

Referring creativity, they wrote:

> Neurobiologically and evolutionarily speaking, creativity is a means to survive and flourish in a social and cultural context, a statement that appears to apply from the relatively banal circumstances of daily living to the complex arena of ethical thought and behavior. In beginning to elucidate the neurobiological interdependencies between high reasoning, ethics, and creativity, all of which are fundamentally tied to emotion and critically relevant to education, we hope to provide a new vantage point from which to investigate the development and nurturance of these processes in schools. (p. 7)

Indeed, it may be asked:

> Why does a high school student solve a math problem, for example? The reasons range from the intrinsic reward of having found the solution, to getting a good grade, to avoiding punishment, to helping tutor a friend, to getting into a good college, to pleasing his/her parents or the teacher. All of these reasons have a powerful emotional component and relate both to pleasurable sensations and to survival within our culture. (p. 3, 4)

Consequently, Immordino-Yang (2011) writes elsewhere:

> ... even the driest, most logical academic learning cannot be processed in a purely rational way. Instead, the student's body, brain and mind come together to produce cognition and emotion, which are subjectively intertwined as the student constructs culturally relevant knowledge and makes decisions about how to act and think.
> Taken together, the neuroscientific evidence linking emotion, social processing, and self, suggests a new approach to understanding how children engage in academic skills, like reading and math. While skills like reading and math certainly have cognitive aspects, the reason why we engage in them, the importance we assign to them, the anxiety we feel around them, and the learning that we do about them, are driven by the neurological systems for emotion, social processing and self. (p. 101)

The current rationalist approach to learning arouses, then, two main problems, following Immordino-Yang and Damásio (2007):

> First, neither learning nor recall happen in a purely rational domain, divorced from emotion, even though some of our knowledge will eventually distill into a moderately rational, unemotional form. Second, in teaching students to minimize the emotional aspects of their

> academic curriculum and function as much as possible in the rational domain, educators may be encouraging students to develop the sorts of knowledge that inherently do not transfer well to real-world situations. [...] Simply having the knowledge does not imply that a student will be able to use it advantageously outside of school. (p. 9)

Their findings led them:

> ...to formulate two important hypotheses. First, because these findings underscore the critical role of emotion in bringing previously acquired knowledge to inform real-world decision making in social contexts, they suggest the intriguing possibility that emotional processes are required for the skills and knowledge acquired in school to transfer to novel situations and to real life. That is, emotion may play a vital role in helping children decide when and how to apply what they have learned in school to the rest of their lives. Second, [...] it may be via an emotional route that the social influences of culture come to shape learning, thought, and behavior. (p. 5)

They conclude:

> The more people develop and educate themselves, the more they refine their behavioral and cognitive options. In fact, one could argue that the chief purpose of education is to cultivate children's building of repertoires of cognitive and behavioral strategies and options, helping them to recognize the complexity of situations and to respond in increasingly flexible, sophisticated, and creative ways. In our view, out of these processes of recognizing and responding, the very processes that form the interface between cognition and emotion, emerge the origins of creativity—the artistic, scientific, and technological innovations that are unique to our species. Further, out of these same kinds of processing emerges a special kind of human innovation: the social creativity that we call morality and ethical thought. (p. 7)

In Immordino-Yang (2011) opinion:

> In conclusion, there is a revolution imminent in education. The past decade has seen unprecedented advances in scientists' understanding of the brain and mind, and new information about the brain is expanding the influence of cognitive neuroscience into the classroom. The neuroscientific findings from affective and social neuroscience in particular could have profound implications for education, eventually leading to innovations in practice and policy. To discover these, we must lay the findings on the table for theoretical and philosophical debate. Irrespective of their scientific value, the individual brain findings are powerful for education only insofar as they suggest changes to our general knowledge of how learning and development happen. This is the next frontier for educational neuroscience. (p. 102)

Let us summarize with some further highlights:

- After all, we humans cannot divorce ourselves from our biology, nor can we ignore the high-level sociocultural and cognitive forces that make us special within the animal kingdom. When we educators fail to appreciate the importance of students' emotions, we fail to appreciate a critical force in students' learning. One could argue, in fact, that we fail to appreciate the very reason that students learn at all. (p. 9)
- In essence, emotion can be seen as the rudder for learning, as it guides thought and behavior in order to foster the development of effective skills for acting in the social and physical world. (Immordino-Yang 2009, p. 19)
- Instead of one brain area, learning involves actively constructing neural networks that functionally connect many brain areas. (Immordino-Yang and Fischer 2010, p. 5)
- [E]ducators have long known that thinking and learning, as simultaneously cognitive and emotional processes, are not carried out in a vacuum, but in social and cultural contexts (Fischer and Bidell 2006). (Immordino-Yang 2011, p. 99)

- [T]he social exchanges of learning are paramount before the sharing of knowledge can take place. Therefore, teachers should strive to learn about the culture, mindset, mores, and values of their students to forge a strong social connection that can then lay the foundation for a successful learning experience. (Immordino-Yang 2009, p. 21)
- Neuroscientific evidence suggests that we can no longer justify learning theories that dissociate the mind from the body, the self from social context. (Immordino-Yang 2011, p. 101)
- These are all topics of eminent importance to educators as they work to prepare skilled, informed, and ethical students who can navigate the world's social, moral, and cognitive challenges as citizens. (Immordino-Yang and Damásio 2007, p. 3)

5.7 Synthesis: Human Worth, Dignity and Rights

This synthesis outlines the main arguments developed in the preceding account of human worth, without repeating quotations' complete references (some new are added, however). It evolves by descending layers until grasping the core content of human dignity. According to Plato (1997), he is dialectical "who is able to give an account of the being of each thing [...], who can achieve a unified vision" (534b, 537c). However, "the power of dialectic could reveal it only to someone experienced in the subjects we've described" (533a)[259].

The recognition of human dignity began to be universalized only when it became equated with the perfectibility of everyone, and no longer with the perfecting and superiority of a few. Alexis de Tocqueville showed, in *Democracy in America*, "how the ideas of progression and of the indefinite perfectibility of the human race belong to democratic ages" (Book I, Chapter XVII), and concluded: "It can hardly be believed how many facts naturally flow from the philosophical theory of the indefinite perfectibility of man" (Chapter VIII).

Human dignity "is a complex principle" that "extends to a broad range of human characteristics", as the Supreme Court of Israel said in *Commitment to Peace and Social Justice v. Minister of Finance (HCJ 366/03)* and *Bilhah Rubinova and Others v. Minister of Finance (HCJ 888/03)* (para. 14). It is multisided, multifaceted and multileveled, with broad *enjeux* (stakes)[260]. An account of human dignity adequate to its high value and comprehensiveness should avoid the Scylla of abstraction and the Charybdis of trivialization. Considering that human dignity is tied to human worth, an account of human dignity is a matter of answering the

[259] As said a contemporary Chinese performance artist, "when you use sameness and repetition as an element, you continue to develop in a spiral dialectic, you realize the artworks deepening as objective reality" (www.douban.com/note/132036963).

[260] http://elyon1.court.gov.il/files_eng/03/660/003/a39/03003660.a39.pdf.
In this connection, Francis Fukuyama refers to human dignity as a kind of an unknown variable, something hard to determine, to circumscribe, a je ne sais quoi... that "cannot be reduced to the possession of moral choice, or reason, language, or sociability, or sentience, or emotions, or consciousness, or any other quality that has been put forth as a ground for human dignity. It is all of these qualities coming together in a human whole that make up Factor X" (as cit. in Rao 2011, p. 199).

following main question: What is the meaning of human worth, in the sense used by Morris, according to whom 'meaning' is a term with "two poles: that which something signifies and the value or significance of what is signified"? In other words, what is the substance of human worth as the foundation of human beings' dignity and rights?

It was submitted above that the human worth consists in the human species' perfectibility and the human beings' perfecting. The faith in human dignity means "faith in the supreme value and self-perfectibility of human personality" (Charles Francis Potter, as quoted in Blum 2003, p. 5). Culture and civilization are manifestations of humans' evolutionary progress that presuppose anthropological perfectibility. The perfectibility of the human species is rooted in its semiotic nature that is the source of human beings' aptitude to the liberty of rationality. Its understanding requires a interdisciplinary approach, due to "characteristics of the human mind that are either unique or qualitatively different from those found in any other animal" (Report of the EU High Level Expert Group). Human perfectibility emerged from the evolution of the brain, in interaction with the environment, in increasingly larger groups.

The brain is the organ of the mind that "is the core of our species' uniqueness and the essence of what it means to be human" (Report of the EU High Level Expert Group). Its primary function is life regulation, but its most distinctive feature is the "uncanny ability to create maps" through the dynamism of neurons (Damásio). The "neuroplasticity" generated a "fourth dimension" of the neuron (Peschanski). There are billions of neurons (about 10^{11}) that make trillions of connections or synapses among themselves (about 10^{15}). Neural maps are the basis of images that are "sights, sounds, touches, smells, tastes, pains, pleasures, and the like", which represent "the brain's momentary maps of everything and of anything, inside our body and around it, concrete as well as abstract, actual or previously recorded in memory". Maps and images are practically almost interchangeable, constituting the basis of mind, so that "mental states and brain states are essentially equivalent" (Damásio).

The brain's map-making may be a key for the understanding of the phenomenon of consciousness as a state of mind regarding one's own existence and that of our surroundings. Consciousness is "a mind endowed with subjectivity"—a *self*—that "allows us to experience maps as images, to manipulate those images, and to apply reasoning to them". To understand it is to know when the self "came to mind" and "how the brain produces that something extra, the protagonist we carry around and call self, or me, or I" (Damásio). In addition, the brain's complexity "expresses itself morphologicaly by the existence of the circunvolutions of the cerebral cortex, which increase enormously the surface and, therefore, the density and amplitude of the neurons network" (Le Douarin).

The brain's complexity, neuroplasticity and map-making dynamism explains the openness that "characterizes our species" (Utaker). Human openness results from the semiotic nature that "marks the threshold of hominization" (Caune). Indeed, where there is life, there is semiosis (even endosemiosis, as even a microorganism has to interpret signals to survive). However, the human being is the sole animal that knows that there are signs and is able to know what signs are, thus being able to create and to use signs. There is metasemiosis, which is "the capacity that only human beings have to reflect on signs (i.e. to make signs the object of reflection)" (Petrilli and Ponzio). Some abstract images "probably result from the brain's making maps of itself making maps" (Damásio). That is why "what is original in human being is that it is a *semiotic animal*, at the same time creator of signs and intimately created by them in all areas of its existence: food, territory, job, sexuality, etc. Such is the best definition that can be given today and from which follows its whole structure" (Van Lier and Laroche).

Signs are abstractions of things that introduce a distance between the human being and the world and allow for the creation of "mental representations". This ability to transcend the immediacy of reality—"the raw perception, the *hic et nunc* experience" (Eco)—amounts to a liberation from the boundaries of the animal *Umwelt* (environment) by transforming it into a human *Lebenswelt* (lifeworld). In Ricoeur's (1990) opinion: "Liberty put us as the other of nature" (p. 62).

Language—the main tool of such a semiotic liberty—is "the power and the glory of human life" (Morris). It is more powerful than other kinds of animal communication, for its double articulation, syntax and intentionality. Double articulation "draws the frontier between animality and humanity" (Condorcet, in Crampe-Casnabet 1985, p. 12)[261]. Syntax is the ability to create an infinite variety of compositions of a finite number of elements. Intentionality is the "ability to speak of absent things, of past or future situations" (Journet 2000, p. 17). Language thus becomes "the support of rationality" (Auroux).

Rationality should be holistically understood, not in a positivist, hemiplegic fashion. This means, first, that brain does not function isolated from the body and emotions: "there are biological mechanisms behind the most sublime human be-

---

[261] As Chandler (2002) explains:

> A semiotic code which has 'double articulation' (as in the case of verbal language) can be analysed into two abstract structural levels: a higher level called 'the level of first articulation' and a lower level—'the level of second articulation' [...]. At the level of first articulation the system consists of the smallest meaningful units available (e.g. morphemes or words in a language). In language this level of articulation is called the grammatical level. [...] In systems with double articulation, these signs are made up of elements from the lower (second) level of articulation.
>
> At the level of second articulation, a semiotic code is divisible into minimal functional units which lack meaning in themselves (e.g. phonemes in speech or graphemes in writing) [...]. Semiotic codes have either single articulation, double articulation or no articulation. Double articulation enables a semiotic code to form an infinite number of meaningful combinations using a small number of low-level units (offering economy and power). [...] Traditional definitions ascribe double articulation only to human language, for which this is regarded as a key 'design feature' [...].
>
> Double articulation does not seem to occur in the natural communication systems of animals other than humans. [...]
>
> The notion of articulation is, in short, a way of dividing a semiotic system into basic levels: in the case of verbal language the levels can be termed those of sound and meaning.

havior" (Damásio). Emotional thought is a term used "to refer to the large overlap between cognition and emotion" (Immordino-Yang and Damásio). For the better or worse, emotion and reason are two sides of the same coin. "The immune system, the hypothalamus, the ventromedial frontal cortices, and the Bill of Rights have the same root cause" (Damásio).

Understood in the light of its emotional roots and of the human species' semiotic nature, human rationality is concerned with all dimensions of human life, but it regards mostly both the operation of theoretical, cognitive reason, concerned with facts and knowledge—that is, with the human aptitude for abstraction, representation, thought, imagination, creativity—and with the operation of practical, moral reason, concerned with values and behavior—that is, related to the human aptitude for deliberating and choosing as well as for autonomy and responsibility.

Moreover, while human perfectibility includes possibilities for both ethical and technical perfection, it is generally agreed that its most humanizing dimension is that which takes into due account the paramountcy of moral values for human living, surviving and flourishing. Human beings are moral animals because they are "able to distance themselves from situations they are confronted to" (Besnier 2004, p. 307) and to "say the morals" (Picq 2004). Morality and ethical thought are (Wood 1999, p. 307) "a special kind of human innovation", but there are "neurobiological interdependencies between high reasoning, ethics, and creativity, all of which are fundamentally tied to emotion" (Immordino-Yang and Damásio).

Indeed, signs are indissociable from values. Global Ethics contains a "semioethics" that implies "a radical operation of decentralization, nothing less than a Copernican revolution" (Petrilli and Ponzio). It calls for a new humanism that consists in a re-centering in otherness, a concept that includes not only human beings—neighbor or distant—but also nonhuman others. In this light, the human species' "irreducible humanity" lies in "its responsibility" (Kahn) for everything it is enabled to do by its semiotic power. At present, in times of increasing Globalization, it has to be a global responsibility that calls for a globalized citizenship.

As a consequence, the liberty of rationality allows human beings to open themselves to a temporality overflowing the present, made up of memory and projects. The human being became the sole animal able to imagine other possible better worlds according to values, able "to live its life as a project" (Farouki), with "a vision of future" (Quéré). Such "crowning evolutionary achievements" (Immordino-Yang and Damásio) endowed the human species with a unique creativity that is "a matter of a global talent requiring allying our different competences. Such as consciousness, it is a property stemming from billions of synaptic connexions accommodated in our cranial box" (Lehrer). It operated "the biological revolution called culture" and created "new devices of regulation" (Damásio).

In sum, scientific research sheds light on the human species' biological distinctiveness and, in particular, on the underpinnings of its semiotic nature, allowing human beings to live "in a new dimension of reality" (Cassirer). Brain, society, language, rationality, creativity, culture, civilization, responsibility—this is likely the chain of Humankind's anthropological becoming.

Human semiotic perfectibility implies that human beings' perfecting should consist in the cultivation of their semiotic seeds. If the human species holds a biocultural nature, with an animal and a human face, the human being is a *de-natured animal*, that is, an animal open to a second nonbiological nature. Therefore, without being perfected he or she becomes a *de-natured human being*, as the cases of *wolf children* prove. Lacking cultural *transfiguration* causes human *defiguration*. As the South African Constitutional Court said in *Ferreira v Levin NO and Others; Vryenhoek and Others v Powell NO and Others (CCT5/95) [1995] ZACC 13; 1996 (1) SA 984 (CC); 1996 (1) BCLR 1 (6 December 1995)*[262], two cases relating to the examination of persons in winding-up proceedings:

> [49] Human dignity cannot be fully valued or respected unless individuals are able to develop their humanity, their "humanness" to the full extent of its potential. Each human being is uniquely talented. Part of the dignity of every human being is the fact and awareness of this uniqueness. An individual's human dignity cannot be fully respected or valued unless the individual is permitted to develop his or her unique talents optimally.

Consequently:

- As perfectibility, human worth is concerned with what every human being can be and do, regardless of how his or her genotype (genetic potentials) becomes translated into the phenotype (what he or she actually is). The common inherent perfectibility of the human species is the core of human worth.
- As perfecting, human worth is concerned with what each human being really is and does. The varying perfection of human beings explains differences of individual images, luminous or fading. The differences are objective or subjective, and may be positive or negative.
  - Objective differences are those due to not imputable limitations.
  - Subjective differences are those concerning individual uniqueness and liberty.
  - Positive differences are those regarding personal virtues and talents.
  - Negative differences are those resulting from need and discrimination.

The human species' perfectibility requires the protection and provisions afforded by human rights. The Canadian Supreme Court summarized in *Law v. Canada (Minister of Employment and Immigration)*[263]: "What is human dignity? [...] It is concerned with physical and psychological integrity and empowerment" (para. 53). Nowak's (2003) wrote: "Empowerment of the individual is the very essence of human rights" (p. 25). Human rights' empowerment is concerned with human essence and existence, tackling oppression, exclusion, poverty, passivity, self-undervaluing, etc. The Supreme Court of Israel said in *Commitment to Peace and Social Justice v. Minister of Finance (HCJ 366/03)* and *Bilhah Rubinova and Others v. Minister of Finance (HCJ 888/03)*[264]:

---

[262] www.saflii.org/za/cases/ZACC/1995/13.pdf.

[263] http://scc.lexum.org/en/1999/1999scr1-497/1999scr1-497.html.

[264] http://elyon1.court.gov.il/files_eng/03/660/003/a39/03003660.a39.pdf.

> 13. … These rights are likely to be included within the framework of 'civil' (or 'political') rights, and even within the framework of 'social' (or 'economic') rights. Thus, for example, among the civil rights it is possible to hold that the right to equality is derived from the right to dignity, since discrimination denies the dignity of a human being as a human being, and leads to humiliation and rejection [...] At the same time, the variety of aspects of human endeavour to which human dignity extends also includes the 'social' aspect, which concerns the standard of living to which the human being is entitled. Indeed, the human right to dignity is also the right to have living conditions that allow an existence in which he will realize his liberty as a human being.

Empowering human dignity is to treat every human being as equal and different, as a being who feels and thinks, loves liberty and dreams of happiness, and to act in order that all human beings be what they can be, have what they need to have, and behave as they should behave.

As a consequence, human dignity and rights are two faces of the same coin. Human dignity amounts to a general *right to have rights* (Hegel, Arendt, Brennan). Their best ethical, legal and political shelter is the Rule of Law rightly understood.

The right to education is key for human perfecting. Each human being is born premature, that is, without his or her most specific nature. He or she "has to become" (Wismann). As the neurobiological revolution teaches us: "The brain is a dynamic, plastic, experience-dependent, social, and affective organ" (Immordino-Yang and Fischer). In fact: "At birth, only 10% of our 100 billion neurons are interconnected. The other 90% connexions are progressively constructed, following the influences of family, education, culture, society" (Le Douarin). The EU Report *What it means to be human—Origins and Evolution of Human Higher Cognitive Faculties* reads:

> Our genome does not dictate who we are or how we will think and behave, because the function of genes is intrinsically bound up with the environmental context in which they are turned on and off.
>
> [...]
>
> In addition, because human babies are born unusually immature and helpless, and because we continue to develop and learn throughout our lives, our physical and social environment is particularly influential. This feedback between our internal and external worlds is central to the human condition. On the one hand, our species has evolved like any other animal through a process of natural selection that favours individuals who are best suited to their environment. On the other, we have evolved an extraordinary mind that allows us to continually create and change our environment. As a consequence, you cannot understand the human mind without considering the environment that it shapes and that, in turn, shapes it. (p. 9)

Catherine Vidal adds:

> The brain plastic properties bring a new lighting on the processes contributing to form our identities. [...] It is the interaction with the familial, social, cultural environment that directs the development of certain aptitudes and contributes to forming the personality traits. In this dynamic, the structuration of the cerebral material is the close reflexion of the lived experience. The classic dilemma of an opposition between nature and culture is overcome.
>
> [...]
>
> That is a very revolution for the understanding of the human. (in AAVV 2012, p. 53)

Nature and culture, the innate and the acquired, form, therefore, "a dialectic that grounds the humankind specification" (Peschanski). In other words, human perfectibility means human educability.

Indeed, for being a semiotic animal, the human being is a *pedagogic animal*. Education amounts to a *second birth* for a *second nature* (Kant, Hegel, Arendt, Dolto) that is to be learned as a culturally specific way of being and living. That is why in education lies "the great secret of the perfection of human nature". It is through a "good education" that "all the good in the world arises". But while education is a matter of making human beings both "clever" and "good", good education should aim, first and foremost, at making good human beings (Kant). The anthropological role of education as well as the human primacy of early and moral education are leitmotifs in the history of pedagogical thought. It is by education and socialization that "the cultural instruments with which we can make the world better: ethics, law, art, science, technology" (Damásio) are transmitted and improved.

As a consequence, "the greatest and most difficult problem to which man can devote himself is the problem of education. For insight depends on education, and education in its turn depends on insight" (Kant). How to overcome such a Gordian knot? There is probably no better answer than the following: Children should be educated in light of the best idea of human perfection, in accordance with the best knowledge of human and individual nature, and by the best human beings. The secret of overcoming the *aporia* of Humankind educating itself through its children is, borrowing a luminous insight from Plato's *Republic*, "fostering their best part with our own".

That is why the right to education is said to be, on the one side, the most complex human right and, on the other, a high priority, because of the multiplicity of interests involved in it and because of humans' ontological educability.

Being a human right, education is not whatever right to whatever education. It is, by definition, the right to an education quality that requires a human rights (or human rights based) approach, taking advantage of the available scientific knowledge.

Educational neuroscience—defined as "a branch of neuroscience that deals with educationally relevant capacities in the brain" (Immordino-Yang and Fischer)—concluded that:

- Thinking and learning are cultural, social, emotional, moral and intellectual processes that consist in constructing neural networks connecting several areas of brain.
- Emotion is "the rudder for learning" (Immordino-Yang) and may play a vital role in the cultural and social influences that shape learning, thought and behavior, as well as in transferring and applying knowledge learned in school to life's situations.
- A great education's purpose should be to cultivate human creativity, that is, the ability to recognize the complexity of situations and to respond in increasingly refined and innovative ways.
- Consequently, "we can no longer justify learning theories that dissociate the mind from the body, the self from social context" (Immordino-Yang).

The findings of educational neuroscience support classical insights of the great authors of the history of education and confirm what the most competent, conscious and caring educators know from experience, while making evident how wrong, sterile and even harmful still prevailing education politics and schools are. One has to keep realistic, however. As Condorcet warned, "men retain the errors of their infancy, their country, and the age in which they live, long after the truths necessary to the removal of those errors are acknowledged" (in Crampe-Casnabet 1985, p. 14).

The conception of human worth as perfectibility and perfecting explains why human dignity is violable, vulnerable and variable:

- Human dignity is violable to the extent that the human species' perfectibility is founded on the human genome that may be endangered, but is inviolable in the sense that it should not be violated, especially by attacks to human beings' physical and moral integrity.
- Human dignity is vulnerable to the extent that the perfecting of each human being may be hindered by numerous obstacles, especially by genetic anomalies, and cultural, social and economic barriers.
- Human dignity is variable to the extent that, in addition to depending on collective conditions and means, it takes different expressions according to individual virtue, merit and identities.

Summarizing further[265]:

- According to IHRL, the source and foundation of human rights is human dignity.
- The notion of dignity evolved from a socially differentiating status to *a highly moralized concept.*
- There was always a historical and conceptual connection, at least implicit, between human dignity and rights.
- Human dignity became the *supreme value*. More than a right, it is a *right to have rights*, i.e. a *collection of rights.*

What human rights does human dignity demand? There are two main conceptions:

- An essential, negative, absolute conception, focused on the rights to life, physical integrity and liberty.

This is the classical Western conception of human dignity, whose most influential jurisprudential expression is the German *object-formula*. It is deeply inspired by the Kantian *categorical imperative* that commands us never to treat a human being as simply a means to an end but always as an end in itself. In accordance with this principle, *the essence of human dignity lies in the sanctity of his life and his liberty.* Life is the biological source of all human rights, and liberty lies at the core of being human. That is why torture and inhuman or degrading treatment or punishment, as well as slavery and servitude, are absolutely banned. Here the reciprocity principle of the Golden Rule applies unconditionally: All human beings are equally dignified and should be treated accordingly, regardless of their behaviors, merits and conditions.

[265] Terms in italics reproduce previous quotations.

- An existential, positive, relative conception, calling for other rights needed for a life with dignity.

According to this conception, human dignity also demands rights assuring more than an *animal existence*, rights empowering a *dignified existence*, worthy of human dignity, including *a minimum participation in social, cultural and political life*. This conception *grounds the indivisibility of all categories of human rights*.

The dignity of human beings is actually relative still in another regard: its individual expression and social respect depend upon individuals' physical and mental integrity, behavior and merit, as well as on their cultural, social and economic contexts and conditions. That is why it may be captured by collective representations not compatible with human worth, or undermined by individual behaviors that may legitimize public punitive measures.

- We have human rights because we are human. In what does being human consist? What are the biological underpinnings of the human species' uniqueness?

  – *Neuroplasticity*

  The *brain* is *the organ that best epitomizes the unique character of Man*, particularly because of its *neuroplasticity*. Neuroplasticity is a *fourth dimension* of the neuron, the discovery of which amounted to a *conceptual revolution*. It explains the most distinctive feature of the human brain, which is its *uncanny ability to create maps*. The neural maps are the objective basis of *sights, sounds, touches, smells, tastes, pains, pleasures, and the like—in brief, images*.

  – *Symbolic systems*

  Human beings *are human because of their symbolic systems*, that is, the aptitude to create and to use symbols and signs. Its highest expression is *language* that is *the power and the glory of human life* and *the very foundation of the whole culture*. It is so *definitive of the human species* that the human being may be considered, *first and foremost, a 'homo loquens'*.
  What is more, the human being may be *rigorously defined as the semiotic animal*, that is, *at the same time creator of signs and intimately created by them*. Semiotic power equipped the human species with a *new method* of adaptation to the environment, allowing for life *in a new dimension of reality*.

  – *Mind, consciousness, self*

  The mind *is the core of our species' uniqueness and the essence of what it means to be human*. It is formed by neural maps and images so that *mental states and brain states are essentially equivalent*. Whence emerged *consciousness* that is *a state of mind in which there is knowledge of one's own existence and of the existence of one's surroundings*. The *self* is the *single voice* of a *conscious brain*.

  – *Liberty, rationality and morality*

  The symbolic system endowed the human species with the liberty of rationality, that is, liberty of abstracting and transcending the sensible, *immediate world*. In fact, *the arbitrariness of signs liberates the soul from its dependence of the ob-*

ject. That is why language is said to be *the support of rationality*, which is *the true nature of man*, enabling the human species *to escape from the animal condition*. The human being is best defined, however, as *fundamentally a moral being*, that is, endowed with *moral freedom* or autonomy of the will, understood as *obedience to a law which we prescribe to ourselves*. Indeed, *considered as a person, i.e. as the subject of ethico-active reason*, the human being *is exalted beyond all price*, because it *is invested with an internal dignity (an absolute worth)*.

– *Cultural revolution*

The dialectical complexification of the human brain, closely related to the human species' social nature, paved the way *to a new type of evolution*—driven by *imagination* and *creativity*, traits *defining the human nature*—that amounted to a *biological revolution called culture*. The human being became *a social animal self-domesticated after the neolitic*, that is, *the artist of himself*. It is *the sole animal able to live its life as a project*, and Humankind *the sole species that designs a vision of future*.
The cultural revolution has been operated by *new devices of regulation*, which *are unique to our species*, such as *justice systems, economic and political organizations, the arts, medicine,* etc. but in particular by *a special kind of human innovation: the social creativity that we call morality and ethical thought*. This is *something probably unique to humans: a moral point of view that, on occasion, can transcend the interests of the immediate group and even the species*.
Close to morality is Law that was defined as *the dialectic by means of which man forces himself to a best he invents*. The idea of human rights, in particular, is *the principle of an indefinite surpassing of man by man*.

– *Born to rebirth*

The consequence of escaping from a mere *zoé* (natural life) and of inventing a *bios* (historical life) was the openness that *characterizes our species* and the *premature birth* of the human being who *is not born finished* but becomes. This is the natural human perfectibility that implies the cultural perfecting of human beings. Perfectibility and perfecting mean educability and education. Education amounts to a second birth for a second nature—the very *human* nature. The semiotic animal is a pedagogical animal.

- In sum
  - Following the most common, centuries-long philosophical definition, what distinguishes human beings from other animals, i.e. what makes them *humans* are the higher faculties of intellect, freedom, and will. The human being is a rational and moral animal, capable of autonomous agency. This idea should be understood in the light of the contemporary ethical-juridical conscience and scientific findings.
  - The concept of human dignity consecrates both the neurobiological and ethical worth of every member of the human species. It should be inclusive of both those human beings not yet or no more *capable for reason and moral agency*, as well of the conditions and means necessary to the realization of human perfectibility and perfecting.

  - Neuroplasticity, symbolic systems, mind, consciousness, self—together form the complex of the main features of the brain peculiar to the human species, constituting the infrastructure of its aptitude for liberty, rationality and morality. Such aptitude is the substance of the human worth underlying human dignity and needing the protection and provisions of human rights.
  - The human brain is a dynamic, plastic, experience-dependent, social, and affective organ, and the mind is embodied, in the full sense of the term. In this light:
    - Rationality should be holistically understood as a human power concerned with values and concepts, knowledge and behaviors, creativity and responsibility, present and future.
    - Nature-culture, innate-acquired, socialization-individuation, reason-emotion, are superseded dichotomies, now reconciled in a dialectic that grounds the specification of Humankind.
    - Education is driven by emotion and reason, in cultural, social and familial contexts, and should aim at cultivating moral and cognitive creativity and responsibility.

- The conception of human worth as consisting both in the perfectibility of the human species and the perfecting of individual human beings is epitomized in Article 3 of the Universal Declaration on the Human Genome and Human Rights (UNESCO 1997)[266]:

> The human genome, which by its nature evolves, is subject to mutations. It contains potentialities that are expressed differently according to each individual's natural and social environment, including the individual's state of health, living conditions, nutrition and education.

- The complex and dialectical profile of the human biological peculiarity and ethical dignity may be so drawn:

Human Duties
Human Rights
Human Dignity
Human Worth
Perfectibility-Perfecting
Creativity-Responsibility
Rationality-Morality
Signs-Liberty
Emotion-Brain

- Each human being becomes *human* insofar as his or her basic needs are satisfied and the *symbolic system*—created *between the receptor system and the effector system*—is fed by feelings of happiness, goodness, openness, otherness, responsiveness.

[266] www.unesco.org/new/en/social-and-human-sciences/themes/bioethics/human-genome-and-human-rights/.

- Dignity is the *sacré-mot* [sacred word] chosen by Humankind to vest human beings' animal distinctiveness with an ethical worthiness. Human dignity is the most brilliant star in the skies of human rights. It is the highest and most luminous lighthouse in the ocean of the human species' indefinite destiny.
- Human dignity is a principle open to the *Possible* as the utopian ethical and ontological place of the human species' perfectibility and perfecting…

References

AAVV. 2008. *Human dignity and bioethics—Essays commissioned by the president's council on bioethics*. Washington, D. C.

AAVV. 2012. Qu'est-ce que l'Homme?—100 scientifiques répondent. *Sciences et Avenir*, January.

Andorno, R. 2009. Human dignity and human rights as a common ground for a global bioethics. *Journal of Medicine and Philosophy* 34 (3): 223–240. www.unesco.org.uy/mab/fileadmin/shs/redbioetica/dignidad_Andorno.pdf. Accessed July 2013.

Apel, K.-O. 1988. *Discussion et responsabilité—1. L'Éthique après Kant* ('Diskurs und Verantwortung. Das Problem des Übergangs zur postkonventionnellen Moral', trad. par Christian Bouchindhomme, Marianne Charrière et Rainer Rochlitz). Paris: Les Éditions du Cerf (1996).

Aristotle. 1925. *The Nicomachean Ethics* (David Ross, Trans. and Introd., Revised by J. L. Ackrill and J. O. Urmson). Oxford: University Press (1928).

Aristotle. 2000. Politics (B. Jowett, Trans., with Introduction, Analysis and Index by H. Davis). Mineola. New York: Dover Publications, Incl.

Auroux, S. 2000. Entretien. *Sciences Humaines—Hors-série* (27 Décembre 1999/Janvier 2000): 20–22.

Balibar, É. 1989. Citoyen sujet—Réponse à la question de Jean-Luc Nancy: Qui vient après le sujet? *Cahiers Confrontation—20 (Après le sujet Qui vient)*, 23–47. Paris: Aubier.

Bendor, A., and M. Sachs 2011. Human dignity as a constitutional concept in Germany and in Israel. Israel Law Review, Vol. 44. http://ssrn.com/abstract=1743439. Accessed July 2013.

Besnier, J.-M. 2004. La brute et l'imbécile. *Sciences et Avenir—Hors-Série* (139 Juin/Juillet) 2004.

Birmingham, P. 2006. *Hannah Arendt and human rights—The predicament of common responsibility*. Bloomington: Indiana University Press.

Bloch, E. 1972. *La Philosophie de la Renaissance* ('Vorlesungen zur Philosophie der Renaissance', traduit de l'allemand par Pierre Kamnitzer). Paris: Petite Bibliothèque Payot/201 (1994).

Blum, P. 2003. Jacques Maritain Against Modern Pseudo-Humanism. *Atti del Congresso Tomista Internazionale su l'Umanesimo Cristiano nel III Millennio: La Prospettiva di Tommaso d'Aquino*, 21–25 Settembre 2003, 780–791, Vatican City (Pontificia Academia Sancti Thomae Aquinatis). http://e-aquinas.net/pdf/blum.pdf. Accessed Sept 2013.

Bognetti, G. 2003. The concept of human dignity in European and U. S. Constitutionalism. In *European commission for democracy through law (Venice Commission), European and U. S. Constitutionalism*. Proceedings of the UniDem Seminar organised in Göttingen on 23–24 May 2003 in co-operation with the Institute of International Law, University of Göttingen, and Yale Law School.

Bognetti, G. 2005. The concept of human dignity in European and US constitutionalism. In *European and US Constitutionalism*, 85–107. Cambridge: Cambridge University Press. (Now in print)

Bostrom, N. 2008. Dignity and enhancement. In *Human dignity and bioethics—Essays commissioned by the president's council on bioethics*, ed. AAVV, 173–206. Washington, D. C.

Botha, H. 2009. Human dignity in comparative perspective. *Stellenbosch Law Review* 20 (2): 171–220.

Bryde, B.-O. 2005. Fundamental rights as guidelines and inspiration: German constitutionalism in international perspective. *Wisconsin International Law Journal* 25 (2): 189–208. http://hosted.law.wisc.edu/wordpress/wilj/files/2012/02/bryde.pdf. Accessed July 2013.

Campbell, T. 2006. *Rights—A critical introduction*. London: Routledge.

Cassirer, E. 1944. *An essay on man—An introduction to a philosophy of human culture*. Hamburg: Felix Meiner Verlag, Gesammelte Werke, Hamburger Ausgabe Band 23 (2006).

Caune, J. 1997. *Esthétique de la communication*. Paris: Presses Universitaires de France, 'Que sais-je?'-3259.

Chandler, D. 2002. Semiotics for beginners. www.aber.ac.uk/media/Documents/S4B/semiotic.html. Accessed July 2013.

Comenius, J. 1967. *The great didactic* (M. W. Keatinge, Trans.). New York: Russell and Russell. http://core.roehampton.ac.uk/digital/froarc/comgre. Accessed July 2013.

Commission on Global Governance. 1995. *Our global neighborhood—Report of the commission on gobal governance*. Oxford University Press.

Condorcet, M. 1793. *Outlines of an historical view of the progress of the human mind* ('Esquisse d'un tableau historique des progrès de l'esprit humain'). Indianapolis: Liberty Fund, Inc. (1796). (http://files.libertyfund.org/files/1669/Condorcet_0878_EBk_v6.0.pdf).

Crampe-Casnabet, M. 1985. *Condorcet, lecteur des Lumières*. Paris: PUF.

Damásio, A. 1994. *Descartes' error—Emotion, reason, and the human brain*. York: Pantheon Books.

Damásio, A. 2010. *Self comes to mind: Constructing the conscious brain*. New York: Pantheon Books.

Dolto, F. 1985. *La cause des enfants*. Paris: Éditions Robert Laffont.

Donnelly, J., and Howard, R. 1988. Assessing national human rights performance: A theoretical framework. *Human Rights Quarterly* 10(2): 214–248.

Donnelly, J. 2009. Human dignity and human rights. Swiss initiative to commemorate the 60th anniversary of the UDHR—Protecting dignity: An agenda for human rights—Research project on human dignity. www.udhr60.ch/report/donnelly-HumanDignity_0609.pdf. Accessed July 2013.

Eco, U. 1973. *O signo* ('Segno', trad. Maria de Fátima Marinho, rev. de Wanda Ramos). Lisboa: Editorial Presença (1977).

Eco, U. 1984. *Conceito de texto* (Trad. de Carla de Queiroz, Apresentação de Cidmar Teodoro Pais). São Paulo: Editora Portuguesa de Livros Técnicos e Científicos.

Encyclopedia Britannica. 2012. *Encyclopedia Britannica ultimate reference suite. [DVD]*. Chicago: Encyclopedia Britannica.

Enders, Ch. 2010. A right to have rights—The German constitutional concept of human dignity. *NUJS Law Review* 3:253–264.

EU Network of Independent Experts on Fundamental Rights. 2006. Commentary of the Charter of fundamental rights of the European Union. http://ec.europa.eu/justice/fundamental-rights/files/networkcommentaryfinal_en.pdf. Accessed July 2013.

European Commission for Democracy through Law. (Venice Commission). 1998. The principle of respect for human dignity. Proceedings of the UniDem Seminar organised in Montpellier from 2 to 6 July 1998 in co-operation with the "Pôle Universitaire Européen de Montpellier et du Languedoc-Roussillon" and the Faculty of Law—C.E.R.C.O.P. University of Montpellier I. www.venice.coe.int/webforms/documents/CDL-STD (1998) 026-e.aspx. Accessed July 2013.

Facing History, and Foundation Ourselves. 2010. *Fundamental freedoms—Eleanor Roosevelt and the universal declaration of human rights*. Brookline: The Making History Series.

Fagan, A. 2005. Human rights. In *Internet Encyclopedia of Philosophy*. www.iep.utm.edu/hum-rts. Accessed July 2013.

Fischer, K., D. Daniel, M. Immordino-Yang, E. Stern, A. Battro, and H. Koizumi 2007. Why mind, brain, and education? Why now? *Mind, brain, and education* 1 (1): 1–2. www-bcf.usc.edu/~immordin/papers/Immordino-Yang_2007_WhyMBEWhyNow.pdf. Accessed July 2013.

Glendon, M. 2001. *A world made new—Eleanor Roosevelt and the universal declaration of human rights*. New York: Random House, Trade Paperbacks.

Griffin, J. 2008. *On human rights*. New York: Oxford University Press.
Gutterman, B., and A. Shalev 2005. *To bear witness—Holocaust Remembrance at Yad Vashem*. Jerusalem: Yad Vashem (2008).
Habermas, J. 2012. Chapter 4—The concept of human dignity and the realistic Utopia of human rights. In *Philosophical dimensions of human rights—Some contemporary views*, ed. C. Corradetti, 63–79. Dordrecht: Springer Science+Business Media B. V.
Hegel, G. 1978. *Textes pédagogiques* (Traduction et Présentation: La pédagogie de Hegel—par Bernard Bourgeois). Paris: Librairie Philosophique J. Vrin.
Hennette-Vauchez, S. 2008. A human dignitas? The contemporary principle of human dignity as a mere reappraisal of an ancient legal concept. European University Institute, Department of Law, EUI Working Papers, LAW 2008/18. http://cadmus.eui.eu/bitstream/handle/1814/9009/LAW_2008_18.pdf?sequence=1. Accessed July 2013.
Henry, L. 2011. The jurisprudence of dignity. University of Pennsylvania Law Review, Vol. 160, University of Maryland Legal Studies Research Paper No. 2011-42. http://ssrn.com/abstract=1928768. Accessed July 2013.
Herbart, J. 1835. *Umriss pädagogischer Vorlesungen*. Göttingen: Dieterichshen Buchhandlung.
Herfray, Ch. 2000. Richesses et indigences symboliques à l'École. In *Éducation et Sémiotique—Hommage à Michel Tardy*, ed. A. Jaillet (Textes réunis par), 51–69. Strasbourg: Presses Universitaires de Strasbourg.
Humphrey, J. 1984. *Human rights and the United Nations—A great adventure*. New York: Transnational Publishers.
Hunt, L. 2008. *Inventing human rights—A history*. New York: W. W. Norton and Company Ltd.
Immordino-Yang, M. 2009. Social neuroscience and its application to education. In *Emotional disorders: A neuropsychological, psychopharmacological, and educational perspective*, eds. S. Feifer and G. Rattan, 15–22. Middletown, MD: School Neuropsychology Press. www-bcf.usc.edu/~immordin/papers/Immordino-Yang_2009_SocialNeuroscienceEdApplications.pdf. Accessed July 2013.
Immordino-Yang, M. 2011. Implications of affective and social neuroscience for educational theory. Educational Philosophy and Theory 43 (1): 98–103. www-bcf.usc.edu/~immordin/papers/Immordino-Yang_EPAT_2011.pdf. Accessed July 2013.
Immordino-Yang, M., and A. Damásio 2007. We feel, therefore we learn: The relevance of affective and social neuroscience to education. *Mind, Brain and Education* 1:1:3–10. www-bcf.usc.edu/~immordin/papers/Immordino-Yang+Damasio_2007_RelevanceofNeurotoEdu.pdf. Accessed July 2013.
Immordino-Yang, M., and K. Fischer. 2010. Neuroscience bases of learning. In *International encyclopedia of education* (3th edn.), ed.V. G. Aukrust, 310–316. Oxford: Elsevier. www-bcfuscedu/~immordin/papers/Immordino-Yang+Fischer_2009_NeuroscienceBasesofLearningpdf. Accessed July 2013.
Jacob, F. 1981. *O jogo dos possíveis—Ensaio sobre a diversidade do mundo vivo*. ('The Possible and the Actual', trad. de Norberto Simão de Almeida, José d'Encarnação, Margarida Sérvulo Correia, Rev. de Luís J. Archer e de Manuel Joaquim Vieira). Lisboa: Publicações Gradiva (1982).
Journet, N. 2000. Le langage est-il naturel? *Sciences Humaines—Hors-série* (27): 16–19..
Kant, I. 1803. On education (A. Churton, Transl., with an Introduction by C. A. Foley Rhys Davids, M. A.). Boston, U.S.A.: D. C. Heath and Co., Publishers (1906). http://archive.org/details/kantoneducationu00kantuoft. Accessed July 2013.
Kiss, A.-Ch. 1975. La protection du droit à l'éducation dans le cadre de la protection internationale des droits de l'homme depuis 1948. In *Recueil de la Société Jean Bodin pour l'histoire comparative des institutions, XXXIX—L'enfant—Cinquième partie: Le droit à l'éducation*, 417–439. Bruxelles: Éditions de la Librairie Encyclopédique.
Lane, R. 2009. Persons, signs, animals: A peircean account of personhood. *Transactions of the Charles S. Peirce Society: A quartely journal in American Philosophy* 45 (1): 1–26. http://files.bloodedbythought.org/texts/On%20Peirce/Lane-45.1-Peircean%20Model%20of%20Personhood.pdf. Accessed July 2013.

Lebech, M. 2006. What is human dignity? In *Maynooth Philosophical Papers*, eds. M. Lebech, Maynooth, 59–69. http://eprints.nuim.ie/392/1/Human_Dignity.pdf. Accessed July 2013.
Lee, P., and R. George 2008. The nature and basis of human dignity. In *Human dignity and bioethics—Essays commissioned by the president's council on bioethics*, ed. AAVV, 409–433. Washington, D.C.
Lenk, H. 2008. What makes human beings unique? *Philosophy Now* 69.
Malson, L. 1972. *Wolf children and the problem of human nature*. New York: Monthly Review Press.
McCrudden, Ch. 2008. Human dignity and Judicial interpretation of human rights. *The European Journal of International Law* 19 (4): 655–724.
Mégret, F. 2009. Dignity: A special focus on vulnerable groups. Swiss initiative to commemorate the 60th anniversary of the UDHR—Protecting dignity: An agenda for human rights—Research project on human dignity. www.udhr60.ch/report/HumanDignity_Megret0609.pdf. Accessed July 2013.
Menke, Ch., and A. Pollmann 2007. *Philosophie der Menschenrechte—Zur Einfürung*. Hamburg: Junius Verlag (2008).
Morris, Ch. 1964. *Signification and significance—A study of the relations of signs and values*. Cambridge: The M.I.T Press.
Müller, J.-W. 2006. On the origins of constitutional Patriotism. *Contemporary political theory* 5:278–296. www.princeton.edu/~jmueller/CPT-CP-Origins-JWMueller.pdf. Accessed July 2013.
Muller, Ph. (Anthologie présentée par). 1999. *Vive l'École républicaine—Textes et discours fondateurs*. Paris: Librio.
Nowak, M. 2001. The right to education. In *Economic, social and cultural rights—A textbook*, eds. A. Eide, C. Krause, and A. Rosas, 245–271. The Hague: Kluwer Law International.
Nowak, M. 2003. *Introduction to international human rights regime*. Leiden: Martinus Nijhoff Publishers.
Nowak, M. 2009a. Torture and enforced disappearance. In *International protection of human rights: A textbook*, eds. C. Krause and M. Scheinin, 151–182. Turku/Åbo: Åbo Akademi University, Institute for Human Rights.
Nowak, M. 2009b. Progress report of the eminent persons panel. Swiss initiative to commemorate the 60th anniversary of the UDHR—Protecting dignity: An agenda for human rights—Research project on human dignity. www.udhr60.ch/agenda/ENG-Agenda.pdf. Accessed July 2013.
Nussbaum, M. 2008. Human dignity and political entitlements. In *Human dignity and bioethics—Essays commissioned by the president's council on bioethics*, ed. AAVV, 351–380. Washington, D.C.
Passmore, J. 1970. The perfectibility of man (3th ed.). Indianapolis: Liberty Fund (2000). http://files.libertyfund.org/files/670/0092_LFeBk.pdf. Accessed July 2013.
Pelé, A. 2006. Filosofía e Historia en el Fundamento de la Dignidad Humana—Tesis Doctoral, Universidad Carlos III de Madrid. Instituto de Derechos Humanos Bartolomé de las Casas. http://e-archivo.uc3m.es/bitstream/10016/3052/7/Tesis_Pele.pdf. Accessed July 2013.
Perelman, Ch. 1980. Can the rights of man be founded? In *The philosophy of human rights—International perspectives*, ed. A. S. Rosenbaum, 45–51. Westport: Greenwood Press.
Petrilli, S., and A. Ponzio 2007. Semiotics today—From global semiotics to semioethics: A dialogic response. *Signs* 1:29–127. www9.georgetown.edu/faculty/irvinem/theory/Petrilli-Ponzio-Semiotics-Today-Signs-2007.pdf. Accessed July 2013.
Piaget, J. 1975. Le rôle de l'imitation dans la formation de la représentation (Postface). In *Psychologie et marxisme—La vie et l'œuvre d'Henri Wallon*, ed. R. Zazzo, 169–181. Paris: Denoël/Gonthier.
Picq, P. 2004. Une innovation évolutive. *Sciences et Avenir—Hors-Série* (139): 26–30.
Plato (Ed. by J. Cooper and D. Hutchinson). 1997. Plato—Complete works. Indianapolis: Hackeht Publishing Company.
Puledda, S. 1997. On being human—Interpretations of humanism from the renaissance to the present (Andrew Hurley, Transl., with a Forward by Mikhail Gorbachev). Cardiff: Latitude Press, New Humanism Series. www.leonalado.org/en/node/4018. Accessed Sept 2013.
Rao, N. 2011. Three concepts of dignity in constitutional law. *Notre Dame Law Review* 86 (1): 183–271, George Mason Law and Economics Research Paper No. 11–20.
Reboul, O. 1992. *Les valeurs de l'éducation*. Paris: PUF.

Renaut, A. 2002. *La libération des enfants—Contribution philosophique à une histoire de l'enfance*. Paris: Calmann-Lévy.
Ricœur, P. 1990. Avant la loi morale: l'éthique. In *Encyclopaedia Universalis—Symposium: Les enjeux*, 62–66.
Ricœur, P. 1991. *Lectures I—Autour du politique*. Paris: Seuil.
Rousseau, J.-J. 1762. *Émile* (Barbara Foxley, Trans., Introdution by P. D. Jimack). J. M. Dent, London, Charles E. Tuttle, Vermont: Everyman Library (2004).
Sepúlveda, M., Th. Van Banning, G. Gudmundsdottir, Ch. Chamoun, and W. Van Genugten 2004. *Human rights reference hanbook* (Third, revised edition). Costa Rica: University for Peace. (www.hrc.upeace.org/files/human%20rights%20reference%20handbook.pdf)
Seriaux, A. 1997. La dignité humaine, principe universel du droit? *Acta Philosophica* 6 (2): 289–301.
Soëtard, M., and R. Hétier 2003. L'éducation entre fin, finalité et finalisme. Le sens de la pédagogie: repères philosophiques, résonances pédagogiques. *Revue Française de Pédagogie* (143 avril-mai-juin): 61–68.
Steiner, H., Alston, Ph., and Goodman, R. 2008. *International human rights in context—Law, politics, morals* (3th edn.). New York: Oxford University Press.
Stokoe, W. 2000. Models, signs, and universal rules. *Sign Language Studies* 1:10–16. http://muse.jhu.edu/journals/sign_language_studies/v001/1.1stokoe.pdf. Accessed July 2013.
Todorov, T. 2013. Sous le regard des autres. *Sciences Humaines—Les Grands Dossiers—L'amour: un besoin vital* (32): 56–63.
Trindade, A. 2006. International law for humankind: Towards a new Jus Gentium—General course on public international law. In *Recueil des Cours/Collected Courses of The Hague Academy of International Law—2005—Tome 316 de la Collection*, ed. Académie de Droit International. Leiden: Martinus Nijhoff Publishers.
Van Bueren, G. 1995. *The international law on the rights of the child*, vol. 35. Dordrecht: Martinus Nijhoff Publishers, International Studies in Human Rights.
Van Lier, H. 1980. L'Animal Signé. Rodhe-St-Genese: De Visscher. www.anthropogenie.com/anthropogenie_locale/semiotique/animal_signe.pdf. Accessed July 2013.
Van Lier, H., and Laroche, J.-L. 1982. Théorie sémiotique de la crise. *Revue québécoise de psychologie* 3 (2).
Verdoodt, A. 1964. *Naissance et signification de la Déclaration universelle des droits de l'homme* (Préface de René Cassin). Louvain-Paris: Éditions Nauwelaerts.
Waldron, J. 2009b. Dignity, rank and rights: The 2009 Tanner Lectures at UC Berkeley, NYU School of Law, Public Law Research Paper No. 09–50. http://ssrn.com/abstract=1461220. Accessed July 2013.
Weil, É. 1989. Morale. *Encyclopaedia Universalis—Corpus* 15:743–751.
Wermeil, S. 1998. Law and human dignity: The Judicial Soul of Justice Brennan. *William and Mary Bill of Rights Journal* 7 (1): 223–239. http://scholarship.law.wm.edu/cgi/viewcontent.cgi?article=1430&context=wmborj. Accessed July 2013.
Wetz, F. 1998. *Die Würde der Menschen is antastbar—Eine Provokation*. Stuttgart: Klett-Cotta.
Whitman, J. 2003. 'Human Dignity' in Europe and the United States: The social foundations. In European Commission for Democracy through Law (Venice Commission), European and U. S. Constitutionalism. Proceedings of the UniDem Seminar organised in Göttingen on 23–24 May 2003 in co-operation with the Institute of International Law, University of Göttingen, and Yale Law School.
Whitman, J. 2005. *'Human dignity' in Europe and the United States: The social foundations. In European and US Constitutionalism,* 108–124. Cambridge: Cambridge University Press. Cambridge Books Online. Web. 24 June 2013: http://dx.doi.org/10.1017/CBO9780511493904.008.
Williams, R. 1997. *Hegel's ethics of recognition*. Berkeley: University of California Press.
Wood, A. 1999. *Kant's ethical thought*. Cambridge: University Press.
Zaruk, D. 2001. The dignity of humanity in one's person—An analysis of Kant's concept of dignity. Katholieke Universiteit Leuven, Institute of Philosophy (Louvain, Belgium), Dissertation presented to fulfill the requirements for the degree of Doctor in Philosophy. http://users.telenet.be/zaruk/David/PhD/Dissertation.pdf. Accessed July 2013.

Chapter 6
Other Principles

Abstract The Human Dignity Principle is not the entirety of the Ethics of Human Rights. This chapter presents other values and rights, with their legal and doctrinal bases, possessing the normative strength of ethical principles from which other rights and duties derive.

In light of International Human Rights Law and other international normative documents, the following principles may be highlighted that, together with the Human Dignity Principle, may be considered as constituting the general framework of the Ethics of Human Rights: life, liberty, equality, diversity, non-discrimination, tolerance, solidarity, democracy, development and peace.

The Ethics of Human Rights—and some dimensions of it in particular—are a Common Responsibility of Humankind.

6.1 Life and Liberty

In *BVerfGE 39, 1, 1975 (Schwangerschaftsabbruch I)*[1], aforementioned, the German Federal Constitutional Court referred to the right to life "as the most fundamental and most original human right" (para. 78). It said: "Human life [...] is the living foundation of human dignity and the prerequisite for all other fundamental rights" (para. 149). And in *1 BvR 357/05, 2006*[2]: "Human life is the vital basis of human dignity as the essential constitutive principle, and as the supreme value, of the constitution (see *BVerfGE 39, 1 (42); 72, 105 (115); 109, 279 (311)*)" (para. 117). The same Court had stressed the indirect horizontal application (*mittelbare Drittwirkung*) of the State's duty to protect life:

> 118. In view of this relation between the right to life and human dignity, the state is prohibited, on the one hand, from encroaching upon the fundamental right to life by measures of its own, thereby violating the ban on the disregard of human dignity. On the other hand, the state is also obliged to protect every human life. This duty of protection demands of the state and its bodies to shield and to promote the life of every individual, which means above all to also protect it from unlawful attacks, and interference, by third parties (see BVerfGE 39, 1 (42); 46, 160 (164); 56, 54 (73)).

[1] www.servat.unibe.ch/dfr/bv039001.html.

[2] www.bundesverfassungsgericht.de/entscheidungen/rs20060215_1bvr035705en.html.

A. Reis Monteiro, *Ethics of Human Rights*, DOI 10.1007/978-3-319-03566-6_6,

The Constitutional Court of the Republic of South Africa, in *The State v. T Makwanyane and M Mchunu (CCT3/94) [1995] ZACC 3; 1995 (6) BCLR 665; 1995 (3) SA 391; [1996] 2 CHRLD 164; 1995 (2) SACR 1 (6 June 1995)*[3], also referred, as we saw above, to the rights to life and dignity as "twin rights", and stressed their "absolute nature", taken together, because "they are the source of all other rights" (para. 84) and, therefore, they "are the most important of all human rights" (para. 144).

A human life is a life in liberty. Liberty or freedom is the sign-value flying most closely to human dignity in IHRL[4]. According to Bossuyt (1975):

> Two rights are recognized as really absolute in all conventional texts regarding human rights: the ban on slavery and servitude, and the ban on torture and inhuman or degrading treatment or punishment. Indeed, torture and slavery are addressed by the most absolute ban, and the international law does not accept any exception, any derogation, any restriction. If torture appears as a breach of the right to life, slavery and servitude breach the right to liberty. [...] Life and freedom are undoubtedly the most precious interests of the human being. (p. 800, 801)

Indeed, as the Constitutional Court of the Republic of South Africa said in *Ferreira v Levin NO and Others; Vryenhoek and Others v Powell NO and Others (CCT5/95) [1995] ZACC 13; 1996 (1) SA 984 (CC); 1996 (1) BCLR 1 (6 December 1995)*[5]: "Human dignity has little value without freedom; for without freedom personal development and fulfilment are not possible. Without freedom, human dignity is little more than an abstraction. Freedom and dignity are inseparably linked" (para. 49). In Siegfried König's (1994) opinion, liberty is "the transcendental principle of all human rights" (p. 313).

For the Roman jurisconsults, "liberty is a priceless good" (*libertas inestimabilis est*). It was thus defined in the *Iustiniani Institutiones*[6]: "Freedom, from which men are said to be free, is the natural power of doing what we each please, unless prevented by force or by law"[7].

Montesquieu remarked in *De l'esprit des lois* (The Spirit of the Laws, Book XI): "No word has received more different meanings, and impressed the minds in so many ways, as the word liberty did". It is "the first human good, the most sacred natural right", Robespierre said (in Monchablon 1989, p. 86). It was the "treasure" of the French Revolution, as Jules Michelet wrote (ib. p. 177). The right to subjective freedom is, for Hegel, the watershed between ancient and modern times. In his opinion, "the essence of human being is freedom" (as cit. in Williams 1997, p. 356). According to Seriaux (1997): "The central paramount idea of the legal universe itself, for Hegel, is not dignity but rather liberty, but it is clear that this liberty is

[3] www.saflii.org/za/cases/ZACC/1995/3.pdf.

[4] The earliest-known written appearance of the word 'liberty' or 'freedom' was found in a document written about 2300 BC in Lagash, Summeria (*amagi*) (see first pages of Passmore 1970).

[5] www.saflii.org/za/cases/ZACC/1995/13.pdf.

[6] For Latin text: http://web.upmf-grenoble.fr/Haiti/Cours/Ak/.For English translation: http://classes.maxwell.syr.edu/His381/InstitutesofJustinian.htm#Book I.

[7] *Et libertas quidem est, ex qua etiam liberi vocantur, naturalis facultas eius quod cuique facere libet, nisi si quid aut vi aut iure prohibetur.*

human dignity *par excellence*" (p. 297). In Badinter's (1990) opinion, liberty not only "is the absolute in the human being, constituting its inalienable dignity", but "if we look at the history of humankind, it was from the liberty of thought and the liberty of expression of human beings that came out the progress of science, of the human condition and the great works of our culture" (p 186). Following Weil (1989), it might be said "that the modern world is born with the affirmation of liberty as the true nature of man" (p. 746). It is essentially moral liberty, according to Rousseau (1751), "which alone makes him truly master of himself; for the mere impulse of appetite is slavery, while obedience to a law which we prescribe to ourselves is liberty" (p. 195). According to John Stuart Mill: "The only freedom which deserves the name is that of pursuing our own good in our own way, so long as we do not attempt to deprive others of theirs or impede their efforts to obtain it" (as cit. in Rao 2011, p. 203).

Consequently, life and liberty are perhaps the principles that best consubstantiate the sense and coherence of the human rights idea and ideal. Nevertheless, as Chaskalson pointed out[8]:

> … total liberty for wolves is death to the lambs, total liberty of the powerful, the gifted, is not compatible with the rights to a decent existence of the weak and the less gifted… Equality may demand the restraint of the liberty of those who wish to dominate; liberty—without some modicum of which there is no choice and therefore no possibility of remaining human as we understand the word—may have to be curtailed in order to make room for social welfare, to feed the hungry, to clothe the naked, to shelter the homeless.

6.2 Equality and Diversity

Equality is the twin sister of liberty and elder child of human dignity. The Supreme Court of Israel said in *Adalah Legal Centre for Arab Minority Rights in Israel and others v Minister of Interior (HCJ 7052/03)*[9] a case related to a law allowing Palestinians from the occupied territories to apply to live in Israel within the framework of family reunifications: "The right to equality is an integral part of the right to human dignity. Recognition of the constitutional aspect of equality derives from the constitutional interpretation of the right to human dignity".

According to Rousseau, if we seek to know what is "the greatest good, which should be the purpose of every legislation system, we shall conclude that it is reducible to two main objects: *liberty and equality*" (in Monchablon 1989, p. 21). They were the "two main passions" of France in the eighteenthth century, Tocqueville said (ib. p. 189). Following Victor Hugo, "if liberty is the peak, the basis is equality" (ib. p. 211). Renouvier explained in his *Manuel Républicain des Droits de l'Homme et du Citoyen* (Republican Handbook of the Rights of Man and Citizen 1848):

[8] www.lrc.org.za/papers/419-the-third-bram-fischer-memorial-lecture-human-dignity-as-a-foundational-value-of-our-constitutional-order.

[9] http://elyon1.court.gov.il/files_eng/03/520/070/a47/03070520.a47.pdf.

> Powers men do not will or cannot ever give up entirely, as they are too inherent in their persons, are called natural rights. [...] They are reducible to two: liberty and equality [...] A republic consecrates this natural status under the empire of law [...] without depriving citizen of her/his natural rights, without making her/him slave of the community. (ib. p. 203...205)

However, Humankind is not a Palace of Mirrors, indefinitely reflecting each other, but rather a Symphony of Differences. Diversity is the very reality of the human species, both at individual and cultural levels. That is why there is a right to difference recognized, for the first time in a legal instrument, by the Declaration on Race and Racial Prejudice (UNESCO 1978)[10], Article 1.2:

> All individuals and groups have the right to be different, to consider themselves as different and to be regarded as such. However, the diversity of life styles and the right to be different may not, in any circumstances, serve as a pretext for racial prejudice; they may not justify either in law or in fact any discriminatory practice whatsoever, nor provide a ground for the policy of apartheid, which is the extreme form of racism.

In 2001, UNESCO adopted the Universal Declaration on Cultural Diversity, with Main Lines of an Action Plan for the Implementation[11]. It reaffirms, in Preamble, "that culture should be regarded as the set of distinctive spiritual, material, intellectual and emotional features of society or a social group, and that it encompasses, in addition to art and literature, lifestyles, ways of living together, value systems, traditions and beliefs". Article 1 (Cultural diversity: the common heritage of humanity) states:

> Culture takes diverse forms across time and space. This diversity is embodied in the uniqueness and plurality of the identities of the groups and societies making up humankind. As a source of exchange, innovation and creativity, cultural diversity is as necessary for humankind as biodiversity is for nature. In this sense, it is the common heritage of humanity and should be recognized and affirmed for the benefit of present and future generations.

According to Article 4 (Human rights as guarantees of cultural diversity): "The defence of cultural diversity is an ethical imperative, inseparable from respect for human dignity".

When this Declaration was adopted, the UNESCO Director-General (Koïchiro Matsuura, at the time) stressed its novelty and the fact that it aims "to prevent segregation and fundamentalism which, in the name of cultural differences, would sanctify those differences and so counter the message of the Universal Declaration of Human Rights". The new Declaration "can be an outstanding tool for development, capable of humanizing globalization". The Director-General concluded:

> This Declaration, which sets against inward-looking fundamentalism the prospect of a more open, creative and democratic world, is now one of the founding texts of the new ethics promoted by UNESCO in the early twenty-first century. My hope is that one day it may acquire the same force as the Universal Declaration of Human Rights.[12]

---

[10] www.unesco.org/education/information/nfsunesco/pdf/RACE_E.PDF.

[11] www.un-documents.net/udcd.htm.

[12] Ib.

In 2005, UNESCO adopted the Convention on the Protection and Promotion of the Diversity of Cultural Expressions. It reaffirms, in Preamble, "that cultural activities, goods and services have both an economic and a cultural nature, because they convey identities, values and meanings, and must therefore not be treated as solely having commercial value"; and recalls that "the processes of globalization [...] also represent a challenge for cultural diversity". Thereafter, Article 2 states eight 'Guiding principles', the first of them (Principle of respect for human rights and fundamental freedoms) reads as follows:

> Cultural diversity can be protected and promoted only if human rights and fundamental freedoms, such as freedom of expression, information and communication, as well as the ability of individuals to choose cultural expressions, are guaranteed. No one may invoke the provisions of this Convention in order to infringe human rights and fundamental freedoms as enshrined in the Universal Declaration of Human Rights or guaranteed by international law, or to limit the scope thereof.

Interculturality is so defined (Article 4.8): 'Interculturality' refers to the existence and equitable interaction of diverse cultures and the possibility of generating shared cultural expressions through dialogue and mutual respect". Article 10 addresses "Education and public awareness".

Regarding the respect for individual and cultural diversity, other international provisions deserve to be mentioned:

- Convention on the Rights of the Child (UN 1989)[13]

  > Article 30
  > In those States in which ethnic, religious or linguistic minorities or persons of indigenous origin exist, a child belonging to such a minority or who is indigenous shall not be denied the right, in community with other members of his or her group, to enjoy his or her own culture, to profess and practise his or her own religion, or to use his or her own language.

- Declaration on the Rights of Persons Belonging to National or Ethnic, Religious and Linguistic Minorities (UN 1992)[14]

  > Article 1
  > 1. States shall protect the existence and the national or ethnic, cultural, religious and linguistic identity of minorities within their respective territories and shall encourage conditions for the promotion of that identity.

- Convention on the Rights of Persons with Disabilities (UN 2006)[15]

  > Article 3—General principles
  > The principles of the present Convention shall be:
  > [...]
  > d. Respect for difference and acceptance of persons with disabilities as part of human diversity and humanity;
  > [...]

[13] www2.ohchr.org/english/law/crc.htm.

[14] www2.ohchr.org/english/law/minorities.htm.

[15] www.un.org/disabilities/convention/conventionfull.shtml.

h. Respect for the evolving capacities of children with disabilities and respect for the right of children with disabilities to preserve their identities.

- Declaration on the Rights of Indigenous Peoples (UN 2007)[16]

Article 15
1. Indigenous peoples have the right to the dignity and diversity of their cultures, traditions, histories and aspirations which shall be appropriately reflected in education and public information.

Georges Vedel (1991), after remarking that the right to difference is "coextensive to the right to liberty", wrote:

> Among human rights, there is the right each person is entitled to, not to be similar to others in all that one is, does or believes. And this right is undeniable because it is based on the most solid scientific data, which assure that nobody can, by its nature, be a duplicate or a copy of another. At the level of the national or cultural collectivity, the right to difference is also undisputable. [...] The right to difference is nothing more than a corollary of the liberty consisting in 'to do all that does not harm anybody'. It is a very human right.
> However, the right to difference does not imply the right to get out of the respect for this or that human right, universal in principle. [...] The right to difference is the affirmation, at the human rights level, of the right to behave differently, except when the matter is precisely human rights.

So understood, the right to difference—the author goes on—opens "the perspective of a true re-creation of the human being by human beings" (p. 355, 356, 360).

In sum, values are, by their very nature, relative and plural. Differences among human beings are physical and biological, but are mainly differences of worlds (of roots, of needs, of desires, of possibilities, of dreams, etc). The visible and frequently conflicting multiculturality of the contemporary world makes us more and more cultural harlequins. We are more, however. The reduction of the human essence to ethnic or cultural differences opens to the liquidation of the ethical by the ethnic and to a new form of racism—i.e. culturalism (see Béji, in Bindé 2004, p. 55...64). If the common human rights language may be spoken in cultural dialects, it must be universally comprehensible, that is, ethically acceptable.

6.3 Non-discrimination

Discrimination consists in putting some human beings unjustly and unlawfully at disadvantage for reasons such as age, gender, ethnicity, poverty, analphabetism, etc. Discrimination may be multidimensional and cumulative, as often occurs with children and women, for instance.

Non-discrimination is the corollary of the principles of liberty, equality and diversity. It is a cornerstone of human rights' normative architecture, starting from the UN Charter (especially Articles 1.3 and 55.c). It relates to acts or omissions concerning the enjoyment of all human rights, but is a self-standing principle, too. In this respect, Morsink (1999) wrote:

[16] www.un.org/esa/socdev/unpfii/documents/DRIPS_en.pdf.

> We have seen (1.1) that the United Nations Charter contains seven human rights references. But the drafters of that Charter never speak of these rights as being inalienable or inherent in the human beings that have them. Instead they unpack the notion of human rights negatively and in terms of the principle of non-discrimination. Thus the only way the UN Charter writers tell us what they mean by their recurring phrase 'human rights and fundamental freedoms' is to prohibit discrimination among people on the basis of 'race, sex, language, or religion.' This short list of non-discrimination items is the only explicit way the UN Charter gives content to the idea of human rights. (p. 92)

According to the record of the first session of the UDHR Drafting Committee (E/CN.4/AC.1/SR.5), the USSR representative (Pavlov) affirmed the question of discrimination "was the most important one to be included in a Bill of Eights". Morsink comments: "More than any other voting bloc the Communists pushed from the very start for the inclusion of clear antidiscrimination language in the Declaration. This nondiscrimination stamp is their mark on the document" (p. 93).

Cassin (1967, p. 11) pointed out that UDHR Article 1 must be interpreted in the light of its Articles 2 and 7 that state:

> Article 2
> Everyone is entitled to all the rights and freedoms set forth in this Declaration, without distinction of any kind, such as race, colour, sex, language, religion, political or other opinion, national or social origin, property, birth or other status. Furthermore, no distinction shall be made on the basis of the political, jurisdictional or international status of the country or territory to which a person belongs, whether it be independent, trust, non-self-governing or under any other limitation of sovereignty.
> Article 7
> All are equal before the law and are entitled without any discrimination to equal protection of the law. All are entitled to equal protection against any discrimination in violation of this Declaration and against any incitement to such discrimination.

The principle of non-discrimination is reaffirmed using the words "all", "everyone" and "no one" in Preamble and all Articles but the last of the UDHR. "This litany of universal terms reflects the drafters' conviction that there are no exceptions to the possession of human rights. All members of the human family possess them simply by virtue of that membership" (Morsink 1999, p. 129).

ICCPR and ICESCR Articles 2 and 3 address discrimination, but ICCPR Article 26 has a broader scope. It recognizes the right "without any discrimination to the equal protection of the law", which "shall prohibit any discrimination and guarantee to all persons equal and effective protection against discrimination on any ground such as race, colour, sex, language, religion, political or other opinion, national or social origin, property, birth or other status". According to the CCPR (GC 18)[17]:

> 12. While article 2 limits the scope of the rights to be protected against discrimination to those provided for in the Covenant, article 26 does not specify such limitations. That is to say, article 26 provides that all persons are equal before the law and are entitled to equal protection of the law without discrimination, and that the law shall guarantee to all persons equal and effective protection against discrimination on any of the enumerated grounds. In the view of the Committee, article 26 does not merely duplicate the guarantee already provided for in article 2 but provides in itself an autonomous right. It prohibits discrimination

[17] www.unhchr.ch/tbs/doc.nsf/0/3888b0541f8501c9c12563ed004b8d0e?Opendocument.

> in law or in fact in any field regulated and protected by public authorities. [...] In other words, the application of the principle of non-discrimination contained in article 26 is not limited to those rights which are provided for in the Covenant.

The non-discrimination principle is to be found in virtually every IHRL instrument, under more or less expanded wording. It may be addressed by a general clause, without specifications, by an exhaustive provision or by wording with detailed forbidden grounds of discrimination but open to others not included (as in UDHR Article 2). It is also addressed by a number of specific international human rights instruments. The Convention on the Prevention and Punishment of the Crime of Genocide may be considered the first one. It was adopted by the UN General Assembly on 9 December 1948, before the Universal Declaration itself. Other more specific instruments include:

- Convention concerning Equal Remuneration for Men and Women Workers for Work of Equal Value (C100) (OIT 1951)
- Convention concerning Discrimination in Respect of Employment and Occupation Convention (C111) (OIT 1958)
- Convention against Discrimination in Education (UNESCO 1960)
- International Convention on the Elimination of All Forms of Racial Discrimination (UN 1965)
- Declaration on Race and Racial Prejudice (UNESCO 1978)
- Convention on the Elimination of All Forms of Discrimination against Women (UN 1979)
- Declaration on the Rights of Persons Belonging to National or Ethnic, Religious and Linguistic Minorities (UN 1992)
- International Convention on the Rights of Persons with Disabilities (UN 2006)
- Declaration on the Rights of Indigenous Peoples (UN 2007)

The Declaration on Race and Racial Prejudice[18] states, in the Preamble, "that the essential unity of the human race and consequently the fundamental equality of all human beings and all peoples, recognized in the loftiest expressions of philosophy, morality and religion, reflect an ideal towards which ethics and science are converging today".

The non-discrimination principle became part of International Customary Law. The Inter-American Court of Human Rights qualified it as norm of *jus cogens* (see Moeckli 2010, p. 194).

IHRL instruments use the terms "discrimination" and/or "distinction", but the most rigourous is the first, as the realization of equality may legitimate some distinctions. If discrimination is always illegitimate, the adoption of special measures may be necessary to suppress conditions that perpetuate discrimination, until substantive equality has been achieved. As the former Permanent Court of International Justice said in 1935, in its Advisory Opinion on the *Minority Schools in Albania* (*Greece v. Albania*)[19]: "Equality in law precludes discrimination of any kind; whereas equality in fact may involve the necessity of different treatment in order to attain a result

---

[18] www.unesco.org/education/information/nfsunesco/pdf/RACE_E.PDF.

[19] www.macalester.edu/courses/intl245/docs/1935.04.06_albania.pdf.

which establishes an equilibrium between different situations". The European Court of Human Rights has also recognized the legitimacy of positive discrimination, for instance in *Thlimmenos v. Greece* (*Application nº 34369/97*)[20], a case relating to an applicant who, because of being a Jehovah's Witness, refused to enlist in the army for religious reasons. The Court said: "The right not to be discriminated against in the enjoyment of the rights guaranteed under the Convention is also violated when States without an objective and reasonable justification fail to treat differently persons whose situations are significantly different" (para. 44). The Court recalled "that Article 14 of the [European] Convention has no independent existence, since it has effect solely in relation to the rights and freedoms safeguarded by the other substantive provisions of the Convention and its Protocols" (para. 40). However:

> With Protocol Nº 12 [to the ECHR[21]] non-discrimination has become a right in itself, and no longer an accessory right. This has important and far-reaching implications as legal protection has been extended to a number of social and economic rights, which were previously not fully covered. (AAVV 2006, p. 7)

Emmanuel Decaux observed: "The principle is already broadly enshrined within the various countries and at international level. What is new is merely—though it is no doubt a great deal, not to say too much, for many states—the extension of the Strasbourg Court's jurisdiction" (ib. p. 105).

René-Jean Dupuy (1986) wrote: "Equality, a philosophical, moral and legal principle, only has a sense because human beings are not identical. So, the fundamental, first norm is that which prohibits discrimination, because it assumes, at the same time, equality and difference" (p. 176). Thus, legally, the right to equality amounts to the right not to be discriminated against. Not discriminating is to recognize the 'other' both in his/her equal human dignity and in his/her legitimate difference. In short, the non-discrimination principle means, as Morten Kjœrum (2009) concluded, "to acknowledge that individuals have multiple identities and should also be respected as such" (p. 203). As the Universal Declaration on Bioethics and Human Rights (UNESCO 2005) declares, "a person's identity includes biological, psychological, social, cultural and spiritual dimensions" (Preamble)[22].

Consequently, non-discrimination justifies measures of *positive discrimination* or *affirmative action*, if needed to establish conditions of equality (see Glossary).

6.4 Tolerance and Solidarity

Tolerance is mentioned in the UN Charter (Preamble), UDHR (Article 26.2), ICESCR (Article 13.1), CRC (Preamble and Article 29.2.d) and many other international human rights instruments. The Vienna Declaration and Program of Action

[20] http://cmiskp.echr.coe.int/tkp197/view.asp?item=1andportal=hbkmandaction=htmlandhighlight=Thlimmenos%20%7C%20v.%20%7C%20Greeceandsessionid=85527528andskin=hudoc-en

[21] http://conventions.coe.int/Treaty/en/Treaties/html/177.htm.

[22] http://portal.unesco.org/en/ev.php-URL_ID=31058&URL_DO=DO_TOPIC&URL_SECTION=201.html.

(1993)[23] mention tolerance and intolerance several times. Section II.B is entitled "Equality, dignity and tolerance".

In 1995, UNESCO adopted the Declaration of Principles on Tolerance[24], which is so defined in Article 1:

> 1.1 Tolerance is respect, acceptance and appreciation of the rich diversity of our world's cultures, our forms of expression and ways of being human. It is fostered by knowledge, openness, communication, and freedom of thought, conscience and belief. Tolerance is harmony in difference. It is not only a moral duty, it is also a political and legal requirement. Tolerance, the virtue that makes peace possible, contributes to the replacement of the culture of war by a culture of peace.
> 1.2 Tolerance is not concession, condescension or indulgence. Tolerance is, above all, an active attitude prompted by recognition of the universal human rights and fundamental freedoms of others. In no circumstance can it be used to justify infringements of these fundamental values. Tolerance is to be exercised by individuals, groups and States.
> 1.3 Tolerance is the responsibility that upholds human rights, pluralism (including cultural pluralism), democracy and the rule of law. It involves the rejection of dogmatism and absolutism and affirms the standards set out in international human rights instruments.
> 1.4 Consistent with respect for human rights, the practice of tolerance does not mean toleration of social injustice or the abandonment or weakening of one's convictions. It means that one is free to adhere to one's own convictions and accepts that others adhere to theirs. It means accepting the fact that human beings, naturally diverse in their appearance, situation, speech, behaviour and values, have the right to live in peace and to be as they are. It also means that one's views are not to be imposed on others.

The Declaration proclaimed 16 November the International Day for Tolerance (Article 6).

Solidarity is the term that progressively replaced the third element of the trilogy of the "immortal motto: Liberty, Equality, Fraternity" of the French Revolution, referred to in the Scholcher Commission Report on the definitive abolition of slavery, in 1848 (in Monchablon 1989, p. 201). The trilogy first appeared in the 1848 Constitution, whose Article IV stated: "[The French Republic] holds as principle liberty, equality and fraternity". Derivations of the word fraternity were used in Articles VII and VIII (see Antoine 1981, p. 134). For Victor Hugo, here is "the holy democratic formula: *liberty, equality, fraternity*" (as cit. in Maury 1999, p. 45).

The term 'solidarity' began to be associated to fraternity in expressions such as *solidarité fraternelle* (Michelet) and *fraternité solidaire* (Clemenceau). As Renouvier explained in his *Manuel Républicain des Droits de l'Homme et du Citoyen* (Republican Handbook of the Rights of Man and Citizen 1848):

> But liberty and equality together shall form a perfect Republic thanks to brotherhood. It is brotherhood that shall lead citizens, gathered in Assembly of representatives, to reconciling all their rights, so that they remain free men and become equal as far as possible. (in Monchablon 1989, p. 205)

---

[23] www.unhchr.ch/huridocda/huridoca.nsf/(symbol)/a.conf.157.23.en.

[24] http://portal.unesco.org/en/ev.php-URL_ID=13175andURL_DO=DO_TOPICandURL_SECTION=201.html.

The UDHR still mentions 'brotherhood' in Article 1, but the term virtually disappeared from the IHRL that favored 'solidarity' for not having the religious connotation of the first one.

During the UDHR drafting, the Chilean representative (Santa Cruz) proposed, in the Third Committee of the UN General Assembly, to include the term 'solidarity' in Article 29 (then Article 27), but it was considered that this idea was already implied in other provisions (A/C.3/304/Rev.1/Add.1).

As we know, the 'third generation' of 'new human rights' that emerged since the late 1960s is also called 'solidarity rights'. Moreover, a right to solidarity is being worked out. On 7 June 2013, the HRC adopted the Resolution A/HRC/23/L.23 on 'Human rights and international solidarity'[25]. The HRC:

> *Asserting* the necessity of establishing new, equitable and global links of partnership and intra-generational solidarity for the perpetuation of humankind,
> [...]
> *Resolved* to strive to ensure that present generations are fully aware of their responsibilities towards future ones, and that a better world is possible for both present and future generations,
> [...]
> 9. *Also recognizes* that the so-called 'third-generation rights' closely interrelated with the fundamental value of solidarity need further progressive development within the United Nations human rights machinery in order to be able to respond to the increasing challenges of international cooperation in this field;
> [...]
> 14. *Reiterates its request* to the Independent Expert, according to her work plan, to continue to work in the preparation of a draft declaration on the right of peoples and individuals to international solidarity and in further developing guidelines, standards, norms and principles with a view to promoting and protecting this right by addressing, inter alia, existing and emerging obstacles to its realization;

6.5 Democracy, Development and Peace

Democracy, development and peace form a triple context indispensable for respecting and implementing human rights in their interdependence. They are 'new human rights', collective rights, *metarights*[26].

---

[25] http://daccess-dds-ny.un.org/doc/UNDOC/LTD/G13/145/29/PDF/G1314529.pdf?OpenElement.

[26] The term 'metarights' was used by Amartya Sen, Nobel Prize winner in Economics (1998), and taken up by Arjun Sengupta, Independent Expert on the Right to Development, in note 4 of the *Fifth report of the independent expert on the right to development—Frameworks for development cooperation and the right to development*, presented to the CHR (E/CN.4/2002/WG.18/6, 8 September 2002). According to the UN Independent Expert:

> A metaright to something x can be defined as the right to have policies p (x), that genuinely pursues the objective of making the right to x realizable. [...] The outcomes of the process of development are human rights while the process of development that leads to these outcomes are also human rights. [...] Therefore, the right to the process of development can be regarded as a metaright.
> [...]

'Democracy' is a Greek term composed of the words *demos* (people) and *kraiten* or *kratos* (to rule). So the word means 'rule by (the) people'. The Greek *demokratia*, in Athens of the fourth century BC, was a very limited one, however: Citizens were only about six thousand out of about thirty thousand inhabitants, to the exclusion of women and slaves. USA President Abraham Lincoln (1809–1865) famously defined 'democracy', on 19 November 1863, by finishing his short speech at the dedication of the Gettysburg Civil War Cemetery (Pennsylvania), when he said that the "government of the people, by the people, for the people, shall not perish from the earth"[27]. The term became widespread in the nineteenth century. The Statement of Essential Human Rights[28] sponsored by the ALI, in the 1940s, stated in its Preamble: "To express those freedoms to which every human being is entitled and to assure that all shall live under a government of the people, by the people and for the people, this declaration is made". In the second half of the twentieth century, democracy became the *golden standard* of a political regime.

As Sen (1999) wrote, although the idea originated in ancient Greece, "democracy, as we know it, took a long time to emerge [...] and it is quintessentially a product of the twentieh century". It became "the preeminently acceptable form of government", a fact that means "a major revolution in thinking, and one of the main contributions of the twentieth century" (p. 1, 3). The right of all people to take part in the government of one's own country, either directly or indirectly, "has been described as 'a revolution within a revolution'" (Lauren 1998, p. 236).

Is there a right to democracy? There is no mention of democracy in the UN Charter[29], and its membership is not subject to democratic requirements, in line with the traditional International Law that did not concern itself with States' political form[30].

> It is probably much better to describe the right to development, as the right to a process of development, as a 'basic right' in the sense in which Henry Shue used this term (See Shue 1980). A basic right is one the enjoyment of which is essential to the enjoyment of all other rights.
> [...]
> The right to a process of development can in that sense effectively be described as basic relative to all the other rights, civil, political, economic, social and cultural. Without the realization of the basic right, none of the other rights can be enjoyed effectively and in a sustained manner. (See Sen 1984).

[27] http://rmc.library.cornell.edu/gettysburg/never_forget.htm.

[28] www.jstor.org/discover/10.2307/1025050?uid=3738880anduid=2129anduid=2anduid=70anduid=4andsid=47698954934967.

[29] The UNESCO Constitution, adopted the same year, mentions "democractic principles" in the Preamble.

[30] The Charter Article 4 provides the statement:

> 1. Membership in the United Nations is open to all other peace-loving states which accept the obligations contained in the present Charter and, in the judgment of the Organization, are able and willing to carry out these obligations.
> 2. The admission of any such state to membership in the United Nations will be effected by a decision of the General Assembly upon the recommendation of the Security Council.

During the 180th plenary meeting of the UN General Assembly, on 9 December 1948 (A/PV.180), the Chilean representative (Hernan Santa Cruz) said that the UDHR proposed "a conception of society which excluded all non-democratic regimes, and provided a criterion for distinguishing between true and false forms of democracy". Cassin (1951) asked: "Why do we not define as democratic only regimes that secure the respect for human rights?" (p. 243).

Although the UDHR avoids the term 'democracy' (only Article 29.2 refers to "a democratic society"), Tomuschat (2008) remarks that Article 21 "contains everything that is conceivable in terms of political rights of the citizen in a democratic polity" (p. 60). Moreover, Article 28 is often considered as containing an implicit right to democracy, as it proclaims: "Everyone is entitled to a social and international order in which the rights and freedoms set forth in this Declaration can be fully realized". ICCPR Article 25 takes up UDHR Article 21. According to it, "every citizen" has the right:

> a) To take part in the conduct of public affairs, directly or through freely chosen representatives;
> b) To vote and to be elected at genuine periodic elections which shall be by universal and equal suffrage and shall be held by secret ballot, guaranteeing the free expression of the will of the electors;

The CCPR said in the GC 25 (1996)[31]: "Article 25 lies at the core of democratic government based on the consent of the people and in conformity with the principles of the Covenant" (para. 1).

The 1993 Vienna Declaration and Programme of Action proclaimed: "Democracy, development and respect for human rights and fundamental freedoms are interdependent and mutually reinforcing" (I.8). In his address at the opening of the Conference[32], the UN Secretary-General (Boutros-Ghali, at the time) said:

> Only democracy, within States and within the community of States, can truly guarantee human rights. It is through democracy that individual rights and collective rights, the rights of peoples and the rights of persons, are reconciled. It is through democracy that the rights of States and the rights of the community of States are reconciled.

According to Article 1 of the Montevideo Convention on Rights and Duties of States (1933), adopted in the Seventh International Conference of American States:

The state as a person of international law should possess the following qualifications:

a. a permanent population;
b. a defined territory;
c. government; and
d. capacity to enter into relations with the other states.

Same Varayudej (2006) observes: "There are some who suggest that these criteria have been supplemented by the requirements that statehood must be achieved in accordance with the principle of self-determination and the fundamental human rights norms outlawing apartheid or racist policies" (p. 4, note 11).

[31] www.unhchr.ch/tbs/doc.nsf/8e9c603f486cdf83802566f8003870e7/d0b7f023e8d6d9898025651e004bc0eb?OpenDocument#2%2F%20The%20number.

[32] www.ohchr.org/EN/NewsEvents/Pages/DisplayNews.aspx?NewsID=7906andLangID=E.

The former CHR adopted a Resolution on "The promotion of the right to democracy"[33], in 1999, that reads:

> *Resolved*, on the eve of a new century and millennium, to take all measures within its power to secure for all people the fundamental democratic rights and freedoms to which they are entitled,
>
> 1. *Affirms* that democracy fosters the full realization of all human rights, and vice versa;
> 2. *Also affirms* that the rights of democratic governance include, *inter alia*, the following:
>
> (a) The rights to freedom of opinion and expression, of thought, conscience and religion, and of peaceful association and assembly;
> (b) The right to freedom to seek, receive and impart information and ideas through any media;
> (c) The rule of law, including legal protection of citizens' rights, interests and personal security, and fairness in the administration of justice and independence of the judiciary;
> (d) The right of universal and equal suffrage, as well as free voting procedures and periodic and free elections;
> (e) The right of political participation, including equal opportunity for all citizens to become candidates;
> (f) Transparent and accountable government institutions;
> (g) The right of citizens to choose their governmental system through constitutional or other democratic means;
> (h) The right to equal access to public service in one's own country;

The OHCHR stresses on its website[34]:

> Democracy is one of the *universal core values and principles of the United Nations*. Respect for human rights and fundamental freedoms and the principle of holding periodic and genuine elections by universal suffrage are essential elements of democracy. These values are embodied in the Universal Declaration of Human Rights and further developed in the International Covenant on Civil and Political Rights which enshrines a host of political rights and civil liberties underpinning meaningful democracies.

There is "The Rule of Law and Democracy Unit" within the OHCHR. On 8 November 2007, the General Assembly proclaimed 15 September as the International Day of Democracy (A/RES/62/7)[35].

The OAS adopted the Inter-American Democratic Charter in 2001[36]. It proclaims a broad conception of democracy, the core of which is human dignity. It begins by stating in Article 1: "The peoples of the Americas have a right to democracy and their governments have an obligation to promote and defend it". Article 3 affirms:

> Essential elements of representative democracy include, inter alia, respect for human rights and fundamental freedoms, access to and the exercise of power in accordance with the rule of law, the holding of periodic, free, and fair elections based on secret balloting and universal suffrage as an expression of the sovereignty of the people, the pluralistic system of political parties and organizations, and the separation of powers and independence of the branches of government.

---

[33] www.unhchr.ch/huridocda/huridoca.nsf/(symbol)/e.cn.4.res.1999.57.en?opendocument.

[34] www2.ohchr.org/english/issues/rule_of_law/democracy.htm.

[35] www.un.org/en/ga/search/view_doc.asp?symbol=A/RES/62/7.

[36] www.oas.org/charter/docs/resolution1_en_p4.htm.

Following Article 6: "It is the right and responsibility of all citizens to participate in decisions relating to their own development". Article 7 affirms: "Democracy is indispensable for the effective exercise of fundamental freedoms and human rights in their universality, indivisibility and interdependence, embodied in the respective constitutions of states and in inter-American and international human rights instruments".

The Inter-Parliamentary Union adopted, in 1997, a Universal Declaration on Democracy[37], according to which:

> 1. Democracy is a universally recognised ideal as well as a goal, which is based on common values shared by peoples throughout the world community irrespective of cultural, political, social and economic differences. It is thus a basic right of citizenship to be exercised under conditions of freedom, equality, transparency and responsibility, with due respect for the plurality of views, and in the interest of the polity.
> [...]
> 3. As an ideal, democracy aims essentially to preserve and promote the dignity and fundamental rights of the individual, to achieve social justice, foster the economic and social development of the community, strengthen the cohesion of society and enhance national tranquillity, as well as to create a climate that is favourable for international peace. As a form of government, democracy is the best way of achieving these objectives; it is also the only political system that has the capacity for self-correction.

While it is not risky to conclude that "the right to democratic governance has crystallized in the international legal order" (Ramcharan 2008, p. 6), the existence of a very right to democracy remains controversial. For example, Lawrence E. Modeme (2010) concluded "that international treaties and instruments, and state practice have not created a right to democracy or political participation in international law". In fact, while the 1999 CHR Resolution on "The promotion of the right to democracy" was adopted unanimously, its title was highly contested. Varayudej (2006) notes:

> International law has traditionally been neutral towards the concept of an entitlement to democracy. As a result of ideological tensions during the Cold War, the international legal engagement with such a concept remained elusive and uncertain. In this period, the relationship between international law and the concept of democracy attracted very little attention among international legal scholars. The demise of communism at the end of the Cold War has, however, placed liberal democracy—as the sole legitimate system of government—back on the international agenda. (p. 1)

The author further writes:

> While international law appears to have embraced the idea of democracy, it has not yet articulated a detailed normative framework or an extensive body of practical rules defining the meaning of democracy. A major problem with the notion of democratic governance is that no legal definition of 'democracy' has been generally agreed upon in State practice or in any international document. (p. 14)

In spite of that, many scholars consider that UDHR Article 21 and ICCPR Article 25 are undisputable international legal bases of a human right to democracy or democratic governance. At least, it is argued that the right to democracy has become Customary International Law. According to Tomuschat (2008): "Democracy is now explicitly acknowledged as the only legitimate form of governance" (p. 60). How-

---

[37] www.ipu.org/cnl-e/161-dem.htm.

ever, democracy rests too often confined to procedural forms, falling short of the whole of human rights' requirements.

Rousseau (1751) wrote in Chapter IV of Book III of *Du Contrat Social* (The Social Contract): "If we take the term in the strict sense, there never has been a real democracy, and there never will be. [...] Were there a people of gods, their government would be democratic. So perfect government is not for men" (p. 239, 240). Nevertheless, we may keep dreaming of a democracy such as that characterized by Pericles, the leader of democratic Athens, two and a half millennia ago (in 490 BC), in his official funeral oration for the soldiers who died at one of the opening battles of the Peloponnesian War (according to the *History of the Peloponnesian War* by Thucydides)[38]:

> Let me say that our system of government does not copy the institutions of our neighbours. It is more the case of our being a model to others, than of our imitating anyone else. Our constitution is called a democracy because power is in the hands not of a minority but of the whole people. When it is a question of settling private disputes, everyone is equal before the law; when it is a question of putting one person before another in positions of public responsibility, what counts is not membership of a particular class, but the actual ability which the man possess. No one, so long as he has it in him to be of service to the state, is kept in political obscurity because of poverty. [...]
> We give our obedience to those whom we put in positions of authority, and we obey the laws themselves, especially those which are for the protection of the oppressed, and those unwritten laws which it is an acknowledged shame to break.
> And here is another point. When our work is over, we are in a position to enjoy all kinds of recreation for our spirits. [...]
> Our love of what is beautiful does not lead to extravagance; our love of the things of the mind does not make us soft. [...]
> Taking everything together then, I declare that our city is an education to Greece [...].

As far as the right to development is concerned, UDHR Articles 22, 25, 26 and 28 seem to recognize it implicitly. The first international legal instrument mentioning it was the Declaration on Race and Racial Prejudice adopted by UNESCO in 1978[39]. Its Article 3 states:

> Any distinction, exclusion, restriction or preference based on race, colour, ethnic or national origin or religious intolerance motivated by racist considerations, which destroys or compromises the sovereign equality of States and the right of peoples to self-determination, or which limits in an arbitrary or discriminatory manner the right of every human being and group to full development is incompatible with the requirements of an international order which is just and guarantees respect for human rights;

The first treaty to include the right to development was the ACHPR (1981)[40], in Article 22.1: "All peoples shall have the right to their economic, social and cultural development with due regard to their freedom and identity and in the equal enjoyment of the common heritage of mankind".

---

[38] www.historywiz.com/primarysources/funeraloration.htm.

[39] www.unesco.org/education/information/nfsunesco/pdf/RACE_E.PDF.

[40] www.africa-union.org/official_documents/treaties_%20conventions_%20protocols/banjul%20charter.pdf

In 1986, the UN General Assembly proclaimed the Declaration on the Right to Development[41]. It states:

> Article 1
> 1. The right to development is an inalienable human right by virtue of which every human person and all peoples are entitled to participate in, contribute to, and enjoy economic, social, cultural and political development, in which all human rights and fundamental freedoms can be fully realized.
> [...]
> Article 2
> 1. The human person is the central subject of development and should be the active participant and beneficiary of the right to development.
> [...]

In the Vienna Declaration and Programme of Action: "The World Conference on Human Rights reaffirms the right to development, as established in the Declaration on the Right to Development, as a universal and inalienable right and an integral part of fundamental human rights" (I-10). In the opinion of Moahmmed Bedjaoui, the right to development is "the alpha and omega of human rights, the first and last human right, the beginning and the end, the means and the goal of human rights, in short it is the *core right* from which all the other stem [...] and its natural foundation is as a corollary of the right to life". All in all, it is a right that is "by its nature, so incontrovertible that it *should* be regarded as belonging to *jus cogens*" (in Steiner and Alston 2000, p. 1317, 1321, 1322, 1323).

The right to development may be defined as an individual and collective right to a process of development—economic, social, cultural, etc.—respecting and favoring the realization of all human rights for everyone. "If the democracy idea means that the will of the people must decide, the right to development means that the mission of government must be to realize the basic economic, social, cultural, civil, and political rights of people" (Ramcharan 2008, p. 158).

Peace is a flower of justice. *Iustitia Regnorum Fundamentum* (Justice is the Foundation of Kingdoms)—is written in a frontispiece beside the Austrian National Library in Vienna. A right to peace might also be thought implied in UDHR Article 28. In 1978, the UN General Assembly adopted the Declaration on the Preparation of Societies for Life in Peace[42]. It was the first time that the right to peace was recognized in International Law as an individual and collective right. In the Preamble, it is reaffirmed that "the right of individuals, States and all mankind to life in peace". Its first principle states:

> Every nation and every human being, regardless of race, conscience, language or sex, has the inherent right to life in peace. Respect for that right, as well as for the other human rights, is in the common interest of all mankind and an indispensable condition of advancement of all nations, large and small, in all fields,

[41] www.un.org/documents/ga/res/41/a41r128.htm.

[42] www.un-documents.net/a33r73.htm.

In 1984, in the Declaration on the Right of Peoples to Peace[43], the General Assembly:

> Recognizing that the maintenance of a peaceful life for peoples is the sacred duty of each State,
> 1. Solemnly proclaims that the peoples of our planet have a sacred right to peace;
> 2. Solemnly declares that the preservation of the right of peoples to peace and the promotion of its implementation constitute a fundamental obligation of each State;

The ACHPR[44] states: "All peoples shall have the right to national and international peace and security". The UNESCO Declaration of Principles on Tolerance also reaffirmed "the right to live in peace".

By a Resolution of 23 June 2010 (A/HRC/RES/14/3)[45], the HRC requested its Advisory Committee, "in consultation with Member States, civil society, academia and all relevant stakeholders, to prepare a draft declaration on the right of peoples to peace, and to report on the progress thereon to the Council at its seventeenth session" (para. 15). The HRC recalls the UN Declaration of the Right of Peoples to Peace and the Millennium Declaration; recognizes "that peace and security, development and human rights are mutually interlinked and reinforcing"; notes that "human rights include social, economic and cultural rights and the right to peace, a healthy environment and development, and that development is, in fact, the realization of these rights"; affirms "that life without war is the primary international prerequisite for the material well-being, development and progress of countries and for the full implementation of the rights and fundamental human freedoms proclaimed by the United Nations"; and stresses "that peace and security, development and human rights are the pillars of the United Nations system and the foundations for collective security and well-being".

The Advisory Committee concluded and presented a "Draft declaration on the right to peace" in 2012 (A/HRC/20/31, 16 April 2012)[46] with 14 Articles, so entitled: *Right to peace: principles; Human security; Disarmament; Peace education and training; Right to conscientious objection to military service; Private military and security companies; Resistance and opposition to oppression; Peacekeeping; Right to development; Environment; Rights of victims and vulnerable groups; Refugees and migrants; Obligations and implementation; Final provisions.* Article 1 states:

> 1. Individuals and peoples have a right to peace. [...]
> 2. States, severally and jointly, or as part of multilateral organizations, are the principal duty-holders of the right to peace.

According to Article 2:

> 1. Everyone has the right to human security, which includes freedom from fear and from want, all constituting elements of positive peace, and also includes freedom of thought,

---

[43] www2.ohchr.org/english/law/peace.htm.

[44] www.africa-union.org/official_documents/treaties_%20conventions_%20protocols/banjul%20charter.pdf.

[45] http://daccess-dds-ny.un.org/doc/UNDOC/GEN/G10/145/48/PDF/G1014548.pdf?OpenElement.

[46] http://daccess-dds-ny.un.org/doc/UNDOC/GEN/G12/130/76/PDF/G1213076.pdf?OpenElement

conscience, opinion, expression, belief and religion, in conformity with international human rights law. Freedom from want implies the enjoyment of the right to sustainable development and of economic, social and cultural rights. The right to peace is related to all human rights, including civil, political, economical, social and cultural rights.

Article 4 states: "All peoples and individuals have a right to a comprehensive peace and human rights education" (1). In effect: "Education and socialization for peace is a condition sine qua non for unlearning war and building identities disentangled from violence" (2).

By a Resolution of 17 July 2012 (A/HRC/RES/20/12)[47], the HRC decided "to establish an open-ended intergovernmental working group with the mandate of progressively negotiating a draft United Nations declaration on the right to peace, on the basis of the draft submitted by the Advisory Committee, and without prejudging relevant past, present and future views and proposals". The first session of the Open-ended Working Group took place from 18 to 21 February 2013.

The interplay between political democracy, economic, social and cultural development, and social and international peace, as well as their relation with the implementation of human rights, have been repeatedly proclaimed in international texts and addressed by several initiatives of UNESCO in particular. For instance, the Vienna Declaration and Programme of Action states (I.8):

> Democracy, development and respect for human rights and fundamental freedoms are interdependent and mutually reinforcing. Democracy is based on the freely expressed will of the people to determine their own political, economic, social and cultural systems and their full participation in all aspects of their lives. In the context of the above, the promotion and protection of human rights and fundamental freedoms at the national and international levels should be universal and conducted without conditions attached. The international community should support the strengthening and promoting of democracy, development and respect for human rights and fundamental freedoms in the entire world.

The aforementioned CHR Resolution on "Promotion of the right to democracy" affirmed:

> Recognizing that democracy, development and respect for all human rights and fundamental freedoms are interdependent and mutually reinforcing, and that democracy is based on the freely expressed will of the people to determine their own political, economic, social and cultural systems and their full participation in all aspects of their lives.
> [...]
> Recalling the large body of international law and instruments, including its resolutions and those of the General Assembly, which confirm the right to full participation and the other fundamental democratic rights and freedoms inherent in any democratic society.
> [...]
> 3. Notes that the realization of all human rights—civil, cultural, economic, political and social, including the right to development—are indispensable to human dignity and the full development of human potential and are also integral to democratic society;

[47] http://daccess-dds-ny.un.org/doc/RESOLUTION/GEN/G12/161/63/PDF/G1216163.pdf?OpenElement.

The 2005 World Summit Outcome[48] states:

> 9. We acknowledge that peace and security, development and human rights are the pillars of the United Nations system and the foundations for collective security and well-being. We recognize that development, peace and security and human rights are interlinked and mutually reinforcing.
> [...]
> 119. We recommit ourselves to actively protecting and promoting all human rights, the rule of law and democracy and recognize that they are interlinked and mutually reinforcing and that they belong to the universal and indivisible core values and principles of the United Nations, and call upon all parts of the United Nations to promote human rights and fundamental freedoms in accordance with their mandates.
> [...]
> 135. We reaffirm that democracy is a universal value based on the freely expressed will of people to determine their own political, economic, social and cultural systems and their full participation in all aspects of their lives. We also reaffirm that while democracies share common features, there is no single model of democracy, that it does not belong to any country or region, and reaffirm the necessity of due respect for sovereignty and the right of selfdetermination. We stress that democracy, development and respect for all human rights and fundamental freedoms are interdependent and mutually reinforcing.

6.6 Common Responsibility of Humankind

Some of the foregoing rights-principles are highlighted in two important international texts, adopted significantly at dawn of the new millennium.

- UN Millenium Declaration

Adopted by Heads of State and Government gathered at UN Headquarters in New York from 6 to 8 September 2000, the UN Millenium Declaration[49] begins by proclaiming "Values and principles".

> 3. We reaffirm our commitment to the purposes and principles of the Charter of the United Nations, which have proved timeless and universal. [...]
> 6. We consider certain fundamental values to be essential to international relations in the twenty-first century. These include:
>
> – *Freedom*
> [...]
> – *Equality*
> [...]
> – *Solidarity*
> [...]
> – *Tolerance*
> [...]
> – *Respect for nature*
> [...]
> – *Shared responsibility*

[48] http://unesdoc.unesco.org/images/0014/001408/140844e.pdf.

[49] http://daccess-dds-ny.un.org/doc/UNDOC/GEN/N00/559/51/PDF/N0055951.pdf?OpenElement.

- EU Charter

The EU Charter[50] states in Preamble:

> Conscious of its spiritual and moral heritage, the Union is founded on the indivisible, universal values of human dignity, freedom, equality and solidarity; it is based on the principles of democracy and the rule of law. [...]
> Enjoyment of these rights entails responsibilities and duties with regard to other persons, to the human community and to future generations.

According to the 1999 UNDP *Human Development Report*:

> Global governance with a human face requires shared values, standards and attitudes—wide acceptance of human responsibilities and obligations. Those values include respect—for life, liberty, justice and equality. And they include tolerance and mutual caring.
> Such values underlie the UN Charter and the Universal Declaration of Human Rights. They now need to be translated into the principles and practices of global governance. (p. 98)

The principles highlighted point to five ethical dimensions:

- A vertical dimension, concerning the relation between public powers and citizens.
- A horizontal dimension, concerning the private relations.
- A self-referential relation, concerning everyone's relation with oneself.
- An environmental dimension, concerning the relation between human beings and their environment.
- An intergenerational dimension, concerning the relation between present and future generations.

The Ethics of Human Rights—and some dimensions of it in particular—are a Common Responsibility of Humankind. It is the responsibility for all the conditions of its survival and potential for improvement, especially for safeguarding its genetic, natural and cultural inheritance.

In 1997, UNESCO adopted the Declaration on the Responsibilities of the Present Generations towards Future Generations[51]. In the Preamble, the UNESCO General Conference affirms to be: "*Conscious* that, at this point in history, the very existence of humankind and its environment are threatened"; asserts "the necessity for establishing new, equitable and global links of partnership and intra-generational solidarity, and for promoting intergenerational solidarity for the perpetuation of humankind"; recalls "that the responsibilities of the present generations towards future generations have already been referred to in various instruments"; recognizes "that the task of protecting the needs and interests of future generations, particularly through education, is fundamental to the ethical mission of UNESCO"; and expresses the conviction "that there is a moral obligation to formulate behavioural guidelines for the present generations within a broad, future-oriented perspective". The guidelines are articulated in 11 Articles with telling titles, namely:

---

[50] http://eur-lex.europa.eu/LexUriServ/LexUriServ.do?uri=OJ:C:2010:083:0389:0403:en:PDF.

[51] www.unesco.org/cpp/uk/declarations/generations.pdf.

Article 1—Needs and interests of future generations
[...]
Article 2—Freedom of choice
[...]
Article 3—Maintenance and perpetuation of humankind
[...]
Article 4—Preservation of life on Earth
[...]
Article 5—Protection of the environment
[...]
Article 6—Human genome and biodiversity
[...]
Article 7—Cultural diversity and cultural heritage
[...]
Article 8—Common heritage of humankind
[...]
Article 9—Peace
[...]
Article 10—Development and education
[...]
Article 11—Non-discrimination
[...]

There is a final Article 12 concerning implementation.

According to the Universal Declaration on Bioethics and Human Rights (UNESCO 2005)[52], one of its aims is "to safeguard and promote the interests of the present and future generations" (2.g). The EU Charter states in the Preamble: "Enjoyment of these rights entails responsibilities and duties with regard to other persons, to the human community and to future generations". The 2005 World Summit Outcome[53] reads, significantly (para. 12): "We are committed to creating a world fit for future generations, which takes into account the best interests of the child". The German GG provides: "Mindful also of its responsibility toward future generations, the state shall protect the natural foundations of life and animals by legislation and, in accordance with law and justice, by executive and judicial action, all within the framework of the constitutional order" (Article 20a)[54].

Shared responsibility also should mean that non-State actors can be held accountable for actions that violate human rights, especially new and powerful actors which, because of the world's Globalization, entered the international scene, arousing new concerns for the protection of human rights, as Krause and Scheinin observe:

> Firstly, globalization, with the emergence of other actors besides states as world-level agents that affect the lives of individuals in ways that traditionally were thought to be a monopoly of states, through trade, services, investments and other means, has put into question the very concept of human rights as a body of vertical norms between the state and the individual. If human rights are rights of the individual, should it not be for anyone who

---

[52] http://portal.unesco.org/en/ev.php-URL_ID=31058&URL_DO=DO_TOPIC&URL_SECTION=201.html.

[53] http://unesdoc.unesco.org/images/0014/001408/140844e.pdf.

[54] www.bundestag.de/dokumente/rechtsgrundlagen/grundgesetz/gg_02.html.

> has the power to affect the enjoyment of those rights to be obliged to respect them? (Krause and Scheinin 2009, p. ix)

Following Arendt:

> Mankind, whether a religious or humanistic ideal, implies a common sharing of responsibility. [...T]he idea of humanity, purged of all sentimentality, has the very serious consequence that in one form or another men must assume responsibility for all crimes committed by all men, and that eventually all nations will be forced to answer for the evil committed by all others. Tribalism and racism are the very realistic, if very destructive, ways of escaping this predicament of common responsibility. (as cit. in Birmingham 2006, p. 4)[55]

Summing up: The principles of the Ethics of Human Rights may be expressed in concentric circles:

- Human dignity is at the centre as the source and sense of human rights as a Common Ethics of Humankind.
- The first circle includes life and liberty as the substance of individual human dignity.
- The second circle includes equality, diversity, tolerance and solidarity as expressions and conditions of social harmony.
- The third circle includes non-discrimination as the broadest umbrella of the protection of common human dignity.
- The fourth circle includes democracy, development, and peace as the environment for the improvement and flourishing of human dignity and rights.

The Ethics of Human Rights may also be represented as a centenary tree:

- The root is human worth.
- The trunk is the human dignity principle.
- The main branches are other rights-principles.
- Other branches are the matured and growing human rights.

The Ethics of Human Rights may still be configured as a Palace of Values:

- Life, human dignity and liberty are the foundations.
- Equality and diversity are the portico's columns.
- Non-discrimination is the dome.
- Human rights are the intercommunicating salons.
- Tolerance and solidarity are the gardens.
- Democracy, development and peace are the oxygen, the bread and the music of the existence and survival of the species living in it.

The Ethics of Human Rights "is both radical and revolutionary" (Mégret 2010, p. 125), as we are going to see.

---

[55] See: Koen De Feyter (Ed.), *Globalization and Common Responsibilities of States*, 2013, Ashgate, p. 576.

References

AAVV. 2006. *Non-discrimination: A human right—seminar to mark the entry into force of Protocol N° 12*. Strasbourg: Council of Europe Publishing.

Antoine, G. 1981. *Liberté, Égalité, Fraternité—ou les fluctuations d'une devise*. Paris: UNESCO.

Badinter, R. 1990. Rapport final. In *Universalité des droits de l'homme dans un monde pluraliste—Actes du Colloque organisé par le Conseil de l'Europe en collaboration avec l'Institut international des droits de l'homme, Strasbourg, 17–19 avril 1989*, 181–188. Strasbourg: Conseil de l'Europe/Éditions N. P. Engel, p. 193.

Bindé, J., ed. 2004. *Où vont les valeurs—Entretiens du XXIe siècle II*. Paris: UNESCO/Albin Michel.

Birmingham, P. 2006. *Hannah Arendt and human rights—the predicament of common responsibility*. Bloomington: Indiana Univ. Press.

Bossuyt, M. 1975. La distinction juridique entre les droits civils et politiques et les droits économiques, sociaux et culturels. *Revue des droits de l'homme/Human rights journal—Droit international et Droit comparé/International and Comparative Law, Vol. VIII-4*, 783–820.

Cassin, R. 1951. La Déclaration universelle et la mise en œuvre des droits de l'homme. In Académie de droit international, *Recueil des Cours—1951, II, Tome 79 de la Collection*, 237–367. Paris: Librairie du Recueil Sirey.

Cassin, R. 1967. Vingt ans après la Déclaration universelle—'Liberté et égalité'. *Revue de la Commission Internationale des Juristes (Numéro spécial: 1968—Année internationale des droits de l'homme, Première partie), Tome VIII, N°2*, 1–17.

Dupuy, R.-J. 1986. *La communauté internationale entre le mythe et l'histoire*. Paris: Economica/UNESCO.

Shue, H. 1980. *Basic rights*. Princeton.

Kjœrum, M. (2009). Combating racial and related discrimination. In *International protection of human rights: a Textbook, ed.* C. Krause and M. Scheinin, 183–203. Turku/Åbo: Åbo Akademi University, Institute for Human Rights.

König, S. 1994. *Zur Begründung der Menschenrechte: Hobbes—Locke—Kant*. Freiburg: Verlag Karl Alber GmbH.

Krause, C., and M. Scheinin. (2009). Preface. In *International protection of human rights: a Textbook* (p. ix-x).C. Krause and M. Scheinin Turku/Åbo: Åbo Akademi University, Institute for Human Rights.

Lauren, P. 1998. *The Evolution of International Human Rights—Visions Seen*. Philadelphia: University of Pennsylvania Press.

Maury, L. 1999. *L'enseignement de la morale*. Paris: PUF.Que sais-je ?-3497

Mégret, F. 2010. Nature of obligations. In *International Human Rights Law,* Ed. D. Moeckli, S. Shah, and S. Sivakumaran, 124–149. Oxford: Oxford Univ. Press.

Modeme, L. (2010). Democratic entitlement in International Law? Still far from the promised land. Institute for Cultural Diplomacy, The Berlin Human Rights Congress, September. www.culturaldiplomacy.org/academy/content/pdf/participant-papers/2010biec/Democratic_Entitlement_In_International_Law_-_Still_far_from_the_Promised_Land.pdf. Accessed July 2013.

Moeckli, D. 2010. Equality and non-discrimination. In *International Human Rights Law,* Ed. D. Moeckli, S. Shah & S. Sivakumaran, 189–208. Oxford: Oxford Univ. Press.

Monchablon A (Coord. de). 1989. *L'esprit de 1789 et des droits de l'homme—Textes et documents (1725–1986)—Préface de Claude Nicolet*. Paris: Coédition CNDP/Larousse.

Morsink, J. 1999. *The universal declaration of human rights: origins, drafting, and intent*. Philadelphia: University of Pennsylvania Press.

Passmore, J. (1970). *The perfectibility of man*. 3th ed. Indianapolis: Liberty Fund (2000). http://files.libertyfund.org/files/670/0092_LFeBk.pdf. Accessed July 2013.

Ramcharan, B. 2008. *Contemporary human rights ideas*. London: Routledge.

Rao, N. 2011. Three concepts of dignity in constitutional law. *Notre Dame Law Review* 86 (1): 183–271, George Mason Law and Economics Research Paper No. 11–20.

Rousseau, J.-J. (1751). *The social contract and the discourses* (G. D. H. Cole, Trans., revised and augmented by J. H. Brumfitt, & J. C. Hall, with an Introduction by A. Ryan). New York: Everyman Library (1993).
Sen, A. 1984. 'The right not to be hungry'. In *The right to food*, ed. Alston and Tomaševski. Netherlands: SIM.
Sen, A. 1999. Democracy as a universal value. *Journal of Democracy* 10 (3): 3–17.
Seriaux, A. (1997). La dignité humaine, principe universel du droit? *Acta Philosophica* 6 (2): 289–301.
Steiner, H., and Ph Alston. 2000. *International human rights in context—law, politics, morals*. 2nd ed. New York: Oxford Univ. Press.
Tomuschat, Ch. 2008. *Human rights—between idealism and realism*. Oxford: Oxford Univ. Press. Collected Courses of the Academy of European Law XIII/1.
Varayudej, S. 2006. A right to democracy in international law: Its implications for Asia. *Annual Survey of International and Comparative Law* 12 (1) Article 2. http://digitalcommons.law.ggu.edu/cgi/viewcontent.cgi?article=1099 & context=annlsurvey. Accessed July 2013.
Vedel, G. 1991. Les droits de l'homme: Quels droits ? Quel homme?. In AAVV. *Humanité et Droit International—Mélanges René-Jean Dupuy*, 349–362. Paris: Éditions A. Pedone.
Weil, É. 1989. Morale. In *Encyclopaedia Universalis—Corpus*, *15*, p. 743–751.
Williams, R. 1997. *Hegel's ethics of recognition*. Berkeley: University of California Press.

Part III
Human Rights Revolution

Chapter 7
A Changed and Changing Legal Landscape

Abstract The recognition of human rights has had a revolutionary influence on the international and national legal fields that is outlined in this chapter.

Revolution is a term frequent in human rights literature. The Human Rights Revolution was a triple one:

- The human being has been recognized as the ethical-legal supreme universal value and gained international personality.
- Human rights have been internationally proclaimed, and mechanisms, including Courts, have been established for their protection.
- International Human Rights Law principles became the Law of Law, prompting ongoing changes of the international and national legal landscapes.

There has been a Copernican revolution in classic International Law. A New Constitutionalism has arisen too. The new International and Constitutional Law led to a refounding of the concept of Rule of Law, implying the rethinking of democracy.

Humanity is a notion polarizing core principles of morality. The notion of 'crimes against humanity' consecrates Humanity as rights-holder, embracing both the dignity of the whole human species and the uniqueness of each human being.

7.1 Revolution

Revolution is a frequent term in human rights literature[1]. Indeed, the proclamation of *human rights* meant, as Luc Ferry wrote, "a radical revolution that made the human being the first value that reverses the order of priorities between man and all that, until then, had primacy over him—nature, religion, community". What counts from now on is "membership to the human species, to humanity"[2].

According to Bertrand Russell (1938): "The Western world, from the Reformation until 1848, was undergoing a continuous upheaval which may be called the

[1] For instance: Drinan, R. (1987). *Cry of the Oppressed: The History and Hope of the Human Rights Revolution*. San Francisco, CA: Harper and Row; Schuster, E. (1981). *Human Rights Today: Evolution or Revolution*. New York: Philosophical Library; Iriye, A., Goedde, P., and Hitchcock, W. (Ed.) (2012). *The Human Rights Revolution—An International History*. Oxford University Press, USA.

[2] "Entretien", *Le Courrier de l'UNESCO, 1993, 4–8*, 49–50.

A. Reis Monteiro, *Ethics of Human Rights*, DOI 10.1007/978-3-319-03566-6_7,

Rights-of-Man Revolution" (p. 89). One may highlight three main moments and documents in the modern history of the Human Rights Revolution:

- The first moment was the proclamation of the *Déclaration des droits de l'homme et du citoyen* (Declaration of the Rights of Man and of the Citizen) on 26 August 1789.
  The 1789 French Declaration is a document that "marks a moment in the history of the world", Giorgio Del Vecchio (1878–1970) said, quoted by Jean Morange (1988), who concluded: "The Declaration enacts, therefore, a legal revolution" (p. 42, 46).
- The second moment was the proclamation of the Universal Declaration of Human Rights on 10 December 1948. It is a document that, as Janos Tóth (1972) stressed, "implies an ethical revolution in the life of mankind. [... The] revolution consists in the fact that the Universal Declaration is the first one that, taking human dignity as the basis, was elaborated and adopted by all mankind, with a universal scope and validity" (p. 76, 77). It gave rise to a "silent revolution" (Eckart Klein, as cit. in Menke and Pollmann 2007, p. 26).
  The revolutionary significance of human rights was clearly captured in the words of Charles Malik during the CHR first session (E/CN.4/SR.14, 5 February 1947):

  > In conclusion, he laid down the principle that the human person had not been created for the sake of the State, but that the State existed rather for the sake of the human person. The Bill of Rights ought, therefore, to subordinate everything to the interest of the human person, even the State.

  John Humphrey (1984), the first Director of the Division of Human Rights established by the UN Secretariat in 1946, and the author of the first UDHR draft, wrote in his autobiography: "There has never been a more revolutionary development in the theory and practice of international law and organization than the recognition that human rights are matters of international concern" (p. 46).
  In his course on 'The Universal Declaration and the realization of human rights', at The Hague Academy of International Law, René Cassin (1951) said that the Declaration gave rise to a "double legal revolution" (p. 342): the internationalization of human rights and the establishment of international bodies to protect them. Cassin referred to the revolutionary significance of human rights on several occasions. For instance, referring to the two 1966 International Covenants, he wrote (1967): "The entering into force of these Covenants shall represent a world event and will be the signal of a veritable legal revolution, irrefutably consecrating the individual's place amongst the effective subjects of the Law of Peoples" (p. 5). In his discourse when he was awarded the Nobel Peace Prize, in 1968, he repeated that they mean "a veritable legal revolution" (in Agi 1980, p. 341, 345).
- The third moment was the adoption of the Convention on the Rights of the Child by the UN General Assembly on 20 November 1989[3]. This Convention is a legal

[3] www.ohchr.org/Documents/ProfessionalInterest/crc.pdf.

instrument deepening the human rights juridical logic and ethical ideal. It is a visionary text, the beginning of a slow and long cultural revolution. Its revolutionary scope is recognized both by its defenders and detractors[4]. However, the Revolution of the Rights of the Child[5] is the most pacific one: As the CoRC stated in its GC 5 (CRC/GC/2003/5)[6], this is "the key message of the Convention – that children alongside adults are holders of human rights" (para. 21). The Constitutional Court of South Africa stressed in *M v The State Centre for Child Law (S v M (CCT 53/06) [2007] ZACC 18; 2008 (3) SA 232 (CC) (26 September 2007)*[7]:

> [18] Every child has his or her own dignity. If a child is to be constitutionally imagined as an individual with a distinctive personality, and not merely as a miniature adult waiting to reach full size, he or she cannot be treated as a mere extension of his or her parents, umbilically destined to sink or swim with them. [...]

All this meant the "recognition of the individual as subject of both domestic and International Law" that, according to Trindade (2006), "represents a true juridical revolution, conferring an ethical content upon the norms of both domestic public law and International Law" (p. 267). Sohn (1982) wrote too:

> The modern rules of international law concerning human rights are the result of a silent revolution of the 1940's, a revolution that was almost unnoticed at the time. Its effects have now spread around the world, destroying idols to which humanity paid obeisance for centuries. Just as the French Revolution ended the divine rights of kings, the human rights revolution that began at the 1945 San Francisco Conference of the United Nations has deprived the sovereign states of the lordly privilege of being the sole possessors of rights under international law. States have had to concede to ordinary human beings the status of subjects of international law, to concede that individuals are no longer mere objects, mere pawns in the hands of states. (p. 1)

Alexis de Tocqueville used the expression 'law of laws' in the beginning of Chap. IV, Book I, of *Democracy in America*[8]:

> The American revolution broke out, and the doctrine of the sovereignty of the people, which had been nurtured in the townships and municipalities, took possession of the State: every class was enlisted in its cause; battles were fought, and victories obtained for it, until it became the law of laws.

The French Revolution went further and made human rights the very Law of Laws. The Declaration of the Rights of Man and of the Citizen (1789) states in Article XVI: "Any society in which the guarantee of the rights is not secured, or the separation of powers not determined, has no constitution at all". VCLT Article 53 (1969)[9] recog-

---

[4] For example, Alain Finkielkraut, a French philosopher very critical of the Convention, wrote: "... a veritable mental revolution took place on 20 November 1989, in the UN" (La nouvelle statue de Pavel Morozov, *Le Monde*, 1990, January 9).

[5] See: Monteiro, A. 2008. *La Revolución de los Derechos del Niño*. Madrid: Editorial Popular.

[6] http://daccess-dds-ny.un.org/doc/UNDOC/GEN/G03/455/14/PDF/G0345514.pdf?OpenElement.

[7] www.saflii.org/za/cases/ZACC/2007/18.pdf.

[8] www.seas3.elte.hu/coursematerial/LojkoMiklos/Alexis-de-Tocqueville-Democracy-in-America.pdf.

[9] www.ilsa.org/jessup/jessup11/basicmats/VCLT.pdf.

nizes the existence of peremptory norms of general International Law (*jus cogens*). A norm so qualified is "a norm accepted and recognized by the international community of States as a whole as a norm from which no derogation is permitted" (see below, and Glossary).

At least some of human rights norms qualify as *jus cogens*. They became the Law of Law, an *indisposable Law* that limits the freedom of agreement between States and legitimizes the intervention of the International Community in extreme situations. As said the Appeals Chamber of the International Criminal Tribunal for the Former Yugoslavia, in 1995, "gradually the maxim of Roman law *hominum causa omne jus constitutum est* (all law is created for the benefit of human beings) has gained a firm foothold in the international community" (as cit. in Buquicchio 2006, p. 7).

As a consequence, the Human Rights Revolution was a triple one:

- The human being has been recognized as the ethical-legal supreme universal value and gained international personality.
- Human rights have been internationally proclaimed, and mechanisms, including Courts, have been established for their protection.
- International Human Rights Law principles became the Law of Law, prompting ongoing changes of the international and national legal landscapes.

7.2 Rebirth of International and Constitutional Law

The Human Rights Revolution gave rise to a Copernican revolution in traditional International Law. It was characterized by Humphrey (1987) as follows:

> A hundred years from now, jurists may well be saying that the most important, most radical indeed, development in international law in the twentieth century was the growth of an international law of human rights. Traditional international law had been a law that governed the relations of states and of states exclusively. Only states possessed international legal personality, which is to say that only states had the capacity under the order to possess rights and to woe duties. After the Second World War new actors appeared on the scene. War criminals were held to be personally responsible under international law for their crimes. [...] It was however the rapid development after the War of an international law of human rights, which confers rights on individual men and women, that most clearly demonstrated the radical change that is occurring not only in the content but in the very nature of international law. What traditionally had been a horizontal phenomenon is becoming vertical. International law is no longer a law applying simply to and between states as its traditional name implies. World law would be a better designation.
>
> The catalyst that was responsible for this radical new development, that brought into being this international law of human rights, was the gross violations of the most basic human rights during and immediately before the War. (p. XV)

Until modern times, *Jus Gentium* (literally Law of Peoples, of Nations)—the ancestor of the modern and contemporary International Law—was believed to have its source in universal natural reason, as we know. It originally applied to the relations between citizens, and to their relations with foreigners, as common principles governing legal relations in general. With Cicero, it became the Law common to all peoples, to all Humankind, a 'common reason of all nations'. According to Francisco de Vitoria: *quod naturalis ratio inter omnes gentes constituit, vocatur jus gentium* (what natural reason constitutes among all peoples is called *jus gentium*) (as cit. in Trindade 2006, p. 37).

Classical International Law, originating from the Treaties of Westphalia (1648), concerned only States. It was dominated by the principle of sovereignty and consent, and recognized war as a means to resolve international disputes, as well as conquest as a means of territorial expansion. The obligations accepted by States were contractual, relational and reciprocal in nature.

Alejandro Álvarez (1947)—pioneer since the beginning of the twentieth century, as we saw, of a *new* International Law and judge in the International Court of Justice from 1946 to 1955—noticed, after the Second World War, that International Law was undergoing "a grave crisis that amounts to some discredit" (p. 38). He called for "a renovated International Law, a new International Law" (p. 44), a reconstruction of the *Jus Gentium*. In his opinion, peoples felt two great needs: "a declaration of the rights and duties of States and a declaration of the rights and duties of the individuals" (p. 54). A decade later (Álvarez 1959), he spoke "of a *new age*, a *new Order* and, as a consequence, of a *new International Law*" (p. 7). Its subjects should be no more only the States, but also "the individual, the peoples, the continents, the international organizations with international personality" (p. 67). Human rights had become "a new field" of International Law and a new basis of social life (p. 77).

In fact, the atrocities committed during the Second World War imposed, as Cassin said and Humphrey recalled in the quotation above, "the recognition of the human being as a direct subject of the law of peoples towards a State that, in the name of its sovereignty, intends to further interpose itself as an opaque curtain between the individual and the human community" (in Verdoodt 1964, p. XII). The emergence of the human in international relations "constitutes a veritable legal revolution", as Jean-Marie Becet and Daniel Colard (1982) emphasized, especially as it denies the "theory of the two spheres", that is, the "radical separation between the internal and external politics", taken over by Article 15.8 of the Covenant of the League of Nations (1919) and by Article 2.7 of the UN Charter (p. 88). Frédéric Sudre (1990) also remarked that "the introduction of the protection of human rights into the legal international order puts an end to the radical distinction between the domestic order and the international order on which the classical international law is based" (p. 10).

The specificity of the IHRL lies, first and foremost, in the *special character* of the obligations it implies for States, as Mégret (2010) underlined: "The fundamental idea is that international human rights obligations differ from normal international law obligations in that they deal with the obligations of states towards individuals rather between states" (p. 127). Scheinin (2009a) also wrote:

> Traditional (interstate) international law is to a high degree characterized by symmetry and reciprocity in addressing the content and effect of human rights norms: it is all about mutual obligations and entitlements between presumably equal sovereign states. Human rights law, in contrast, is about states having obligations in respect of third-party beneficiaries who are

> not parties to a treaty and perhaps not even recognized as 'subjects' of public international law. (p. 19)

As a consequence, human rights treaties have a normative character, that is, "an 'objective' character in that they are not reducible to bilateral exchanges of advantages between the contracting states". This "produces a series of consequences in various areas related to the application of such treaties" (p. 53, 54). The specificity of the IHRL is recognized in VCLT (1969) Article 60.5 and was evoked by the ICJ, for the first time, in its Advisory Opinion on the Convention on the Prevention and Punishment of the Crime of Genocide (UN 1948), requested by the UN General Assembly (see below).

The UN Charter is the sole legal text universally compelling, and its General Assembly represents a Parliament of Humankind. Sohn (1982), who was a USA delegate to the Conference of San Francisco (where the Charter was adopted, in 1945), called the UN Charter the "constitution of the world, the highest instrument in the intertwined hierarchy of international and domestic documents". It contains great ideas "which revolutionized the world", the most influential of them being "that human rights are of international concern" (pp. 12–14).

The recognition of universal human rights "for the first time in history transformed individuals from mere objects of international compassion into actual subjects of international law" (Lauren 1998, p. 206). Such a refoundation of International Law began with the establishment of the UN and the internationalization of the principle of the protection of human rights. It meant an historical rupture that was recalled time and again during the drafting process of the UDHR. For example, at the CHR first session, in February 1947, the Indian representative (Hansa Mehta) presented a draft resolution (E/CN.4/11) reading that "the United Nations has been established for the specific purpose of enthroning the natural rights of man to freedom and equality before the law, and for upholding the worth and dignity of human personality". During the CHR second session, in December, in Geneva, when the draft Universal Declaration was being discussed (E/600): "The representative of France requested that the following comment be inserted in the report: [...] the fact that it contributes something new: the individual becomes a subject of international law in respect of his life and liberty".

According to the Report of the ECOSOC's 215th meeting, on 25 August 1948 (E/SR.215), the Brazilian representative (Ramiro Saraiva Guerreiro) said that: "The United Nations Charter had laid down, three years previously, specific legal obligations in respect of human rights and fundamental freedoms which Members were obliged to respect; hence such rights had been removed from the purely domestic jurisdiction of States, and had become of international concern". Therefore, "the adoption of a Declaration on Human Rights might lead to considerable changes in present concepts of international law".

Following the record of the 90th meeting of the General Assembly Third Committee, on 1 October (A/C.3/SR.90), the Bolivian representative (Eduardo Anze Matienzo) stated that:

> He regarded the draft Declaration as a new international constitution, whereby the rights of States were limited in the interests of the rights of individuals and he hoped that it would become an integral part of international law.
> [...]
> He wished to object to the oft-repeated sophistry that the United Nations was helpless to prevent violation of human rights because under Article 2, paragraph 7 of the Charter it could not interfere in matters which were within the domestic jurisdiction of States. The Charter also included provisions concerning human rights. Article 2, paragraph 7 dealt only with questions which fell exclusively within domestic jurisdiction, and could not apply to matters covered under international law. Consequently, it could not be invoked in the case under discussion.

During the same meeting, the Costa Rican representative (Alberto F. Cañas) affirmed that:

> It was a matter for pride that, at a time when individual rights seemed fated to bow before the tyranny of State rights, an international meeting had produced a draft Declaration of human rights. [...]
> In the struggle between man and the State, the Costa Rica delegation was proud to embrace the cause of man.

At the 92th meeting (2 October) (A/C.3/SR.90), the Brazilian representative (Belarmino Austregésilo de Athayde) stated that: "By making human rights international, the United Nations Charter had placed upon States positive legal obligations; it was the greatest of the victories achieved at the cost of the sacrifices made during the Second World War".

At the 181th plenary meeting of the General Assembly, on 10 December (A/PV.181), when the draft UDHR began to be discussed, the Uruguayan representative (Enrique C. Armand Ugon) said: "The human being must be the *raison d'être* and the ultimate aim of the international community and of international law". During the same debate, the Icelandic representative (Thor Thors) said that the Declaration was "regarded as a preamble to a future world constitution".

At the 182th plenary meeting, on the same day (A/PV.182), the Bolivian representative (Eduardo Anze Matienzo) said that the adoption of the Universal Declaration shall mean the beginning of "a new phase which should lead to the establishment of a true international constitution, founded on the limitation of the sovereignty of States for the benefit of the individual". Indeed: "The majority of the drafters believed that by proffering the notion of human rights [the UN Charter] had opened the door that gave the individual a status in international law and affairs" (Morsink 1999, p. 252), so abandoning part of their sovereignty[10].

Trindade (2006), in his General Course on Public International Law at The Hague Academy of Internationl Law, under the title 'International Law for Humankind: Towards a New *Jus Gentium*', recalled the recognition of the necessity

[10] Nevertheless, Tomuschat (2008) remarks: "If and to what extent individuals are subjects of international law is still highly controversial. One can interpret in different ways the legal status which human beings enjoy under the treaties for the protection of human rights" (p. 370).

"of the reconstruction of International Law" in the mid-twentieth century (p. 198), motivated by the "*expansion* of international legal personality [...] with the advent of international organizations and of the human person, individually or in groups, and of mankind as a whole, also as subjects of the law of nations" (p. 203)[11]. Here is his thesis:

> It is my basic contention, in the present General Course, that the purely inter-State dimension of International Law has surely been overcome and belongs to the past; that international legal personality has expanded, so as to encompass nowadays, besides States and international organizations, also individuals – the human person – as true subjects (and not only 'actors') of International Law; that the conditions are met for us to move towards the construction of a new *jus gentium*, at this beginning of the twenty-first century, to the extent that account is taken of the social needs and aspirations of the international community (*civitas maxima gentium*) of humankind as a whole, so as to provide responses to attempt to fulfill them. (p. 34)

Trindade's argument goes back to "the founding fathers of International Law (F. Vitoria, F. Suárez, H. Grotius, among others)", when "*Jus Gentium* was endowed with ethical foundations by the *recta ratio*, emanating, ultimately, from the universal juridical conscience (its material source *par excellence*); found inspiration in the legacy of the ancient Greeks, followed by those of Cicero and Aquinas, in identifying *recta ratio* in the very foundations of jus gentium itself" (p. 41).

---

[11] In this regard, Trindade said in his concurring Opinion to the Inter-American Court of Human Rights *Advisory Opinion OC-17/2002 of 28 August 2002 on the 'Juridical Condition and Human Rights of the Child'*:

> 45. There is no way to dissociate the recognition of the international juridical personality of the individual from the dignity itself of the human person. In a wider dimension, the human person appears as the being who brings within himself his supreme end, and who achieves it throughout his life, under his own responsibility. In fact, it is the human person, essentially endowed with dignity, who articulates, expresses and introduces the 'ought to be' ('*deber ser*') of the values in the world of the reality in which he lives, and only is he capable of this, as bearer of such ethical values. The juridical personality, in its turn, manifests itself as a juridical category in the world of Law, as a unitary expression of the aptitude of the human person to be *titulaire* [holder] of rights and duties at the level of the regulated behaviour and human relations.
> 46. It may be recalled, in the present context, that the conception of individual *subjective right* already has a wide historical projection, originated in particular in the jusnaturalist thinking in the XVIIth and XVIIIth centuries, and systematized in the juridical doctrine along the XIXth century. Nevertheless, in the XIXth century and the beginning of the XXth century, that conception remained in the framework of domestic public law, emanated from public power, and under the influence of legal positivism. The subjective right was conceived as the prerrogative of the individual such as defined by the legal order at issue (the objective law).
> 47. Notwithstanding, there is no way to deny that the crystallization of the concept of individual subjective right, and its systematization, achieved at least an advance towards a better understanding of the individual as a *titulaire* of rights. And they rendered possible, with the emergence of human rights at international level, the gradual overcoming of positive law. In the mid-XXth century, the impossibility became clear of the evolution of Law itself without the individual subjective right, expression of a true 'human right'. (www.crin.org/docs/advisory-opinion17.pdf).

The "illuminating thoughts" were gradually surpassed "mainly by the emergence of legal positivism" (p. 256), which became predominant in the late nineteenth century. According to it, the "State is superior to any legal principle" (G. Jellinek) (p. 45).

Trindade's case is for "the humanization of contemporary International Law", for a reconstructed or new *Jus Gentium* as an International Law of Humankind, whose main feature is that it "can no longer be regarded as an international legal order which exhausts itself in the domain of strictly inter-States relations" (p. 35), and must fully recognize "the international juridical subjectivity of human beings" (p. 282), which is already a fact.

> In the ambit of the International Law of Human Rights, [...] the recognition of the direct access of individuals to international justice reveals, at this beginning of the twenty-first century, the new primacy of the *raison de l'humanité* over the *raison d'État*, inspiring the historical process of *humanization* of International Law. [...] The international legal subjectivity of individuals is nowadays an irreversible reality, and the human being emerges, at last, even in the most adverse conditions, as the ultimate subject of Law, both domestic and international, endowed with full juridico-procedural capacity. (p. 282, 283)

These advances are due to the growing of the "universal juridical conscience":

> Over a decade of experience so far, serving as Judge of an international tribunal of human rights, has reinforced my feelings that the universal juridical conscience is the material source *par excellence* of International Law. [...] International Law cannot at all be reduced to an instrument at the service of power. (p. 201)

In his opinion:

> The consolidation of the legal personality and capacity of the individual as subject of International Law constitutes the most precious legacy of the international legal thinking of the second half of the twentieth century. [...T]he same can be said of the recognition of his condition as bearer of duties emanating from International Law (passive subjectivity). Individuals appear nowadays as true subjects – rather than simply 'actors' – of International Law. (p. 252)

The fact of individuals becoming "also bearers of duties under International Law [...] reflects the consolidation of their international legal personality" (p. 278), bringing to an end "the old dogma that the individual is not a 'subject' of international politics and law" (p. 94). And "there being nothing inherent to International Law impeding the individual to become subject of the International Law and to become a party in proceedings before international tribunals" (p. 269), Trindade concluded that "the right of individual petition is undoubtedly the most luminous star in the universe of human rights" (p. 279). It means the possibility for a citizen to stand before an international body against his or her own State for alleged violations of human rights it should respect, protect and implement.

Such recognition of the international legal subjectivity of the individual reached its full achievement, for the first time, in the ECHR. Endowing everyone under the jurisdiction of every State Party with a right of international action, it gave "its most revolutionary contribution" (Conseil de l'Europe 1991, p. 2) to the mutation of International Law. Establishing also a right and duty of interference in the domestic affairs of States, concerning human rights, though freely consented, the European Convention instituted a kind of public action. Polys Modinos (1975) asked: "How to deny the importance of this innovation that abstracts from nationality and is only concerned with the human being?" (p. 689). Jacques Velu and Rusen Ergec (1990) commented:

> The European Convention on Human Rights does not only constitutes the most achieved expression of International Human Rights Law specificity. It does not suffer from much of its weaknesses either.
> The Convention institutes, firstly, a *sui generis* legal order, in the turning-point between the international legal order and the domestic legal order. [...] The central role it recognizes to the individual reflects a 'revolutionary advancement in the legal position of the individual' (Friedmann, W.). (p. 35)

Scheinin (2006) remarks:

> The European Court of Human Rights often refers to the constitutional nature of the ECHR, and on the universal level one could speak of human rights treaties as an embryonic form of a global constitution. [...]
> This kind of an approach of human rights law as a constitutional dimension of public international law may build its articulation partly with reference to the category of *jus cogens*, also recognized in the VCLT itself. [...] In a more general sense, the constitutional nature of human rights norms rests on their close substantive link to fundamental moral values and to their structure with third parties as beneficiaries. [...] Rather than speaking of a formal hierarchy of sources that would claim supremacy to human rights *treaties* with respect to other treaties, the constitutional dimension of human rights norms is based in their substantive content and, hence, represents a constitution in the substantive, rather than formal sense. (p. 48, 49)

In accordance with a maxim of Roman Law, *Hominum causa jus constitutum est* (Law is established for the benefit of man). The IHRL consecrated "the sanctity of human personality", in Lauterpacht's words (1948, p. 10), who affirmed: the "State is not itself an end. [...T]he individual is the final subject of all law" (p. 9). Also Héctor Gros Espiell (1985) reaffirmed "that the human being is the ultimate addressee, the *raison d'être*, the objective and purpose of every legal order. The International Community and States exist by and for the Human Being" (p. 164). In Antonio Cassese's (1991) view, "human rights constitute the modern attempt to introduce reason into world history" (p. 67).

The IHRL breached, therefore, the positivist vicious circle of legality-legitimacy and increasingly dilutes the distinction between International Law and domestic legal orders. Such a Copernician revolution gave rise to the "rebirth of international legality and of constitutional democracy" since 1945 (Antonio La Pergola, in Conseil de l'Europe 1993, p. 4).

Indeed, a New Constitutionalism has arisen, characterized by the inclusion in constitutional texts of the fundamental values of a society, which are first and foremost human rights. It is "a new constitutional law of freedoms" (Velu and Ergec 1990, p. 36), born "from the confrontation and, why not, the complementarity between constitutional law and international law in the field of human rights" (Delpérée 1987, p. 5). In effect, Constitutions adopted or revised after the UDHR proclamation engaged, in general, with the principle of respect for human rights. The German GG (1949) is the symbol of the New Constitutionalism, as we know.

The New Constitutional Law renovated the concept of Rule of Law and the conception of democracy.

7.3 Refounding the Rule of Law and Rethinking Democracy

It may be said that the history of the Rule of Law began with the history of Law itself, but its development took centuries to reach its present conception (Chesterman 2008).

Within European culture, Aristotle is the clearest starting point (Peerenboom 2005). In his *Politics* (2000), "inquiring whether it is more advantageous to be ruled by the best man or by the best laws" (III.15, 1286a)—that he called the "vexed question" (III.16, 1287b) of knowing "what kind of government would be best and most in accordance with our aspirations" (IV.1, 1288b)—he concluded that "the rule of the law is preferable to that of any individual". And observed: "He who bids the law rule, may be deemed to bid God and Reason alone rule, but he who bids man rule adds an element of the beast; for desire is a wild beast, and passion perverts the minds of rulers, even when they are the best of men. The law is reason unaffected by desire" (III.16, 1287a). That is why "laws, when good, should be supreme" (III.11, 1282a). Without the authority of the laws, "there is no constitution" (IV.30-31, 1292a).

The modern conception of the Rule of Law in the European continent originated in Germany. It evolved with Robert von Mohl in the 1820s, very probably under the influence of Kant, opposing it to the Absolutist State. The German term *Rechtsstaat* was probably first used by Johann W. Peterson (1758–1815). In France, its equivalent *État de Droit* is a term probably first used by Maurice Hauriou (1856–1935). It was, however, especially Pierre M. N. L. Duguit (1859–1928) who has made its use common. Equivalents, in other languages, are *Stato di Diritto* (Italia), *Estado de Derecho* (Spanish), *Estado de Direito* (Portuguese), for instance.

The concept of Rule of Law arouses the following crucial question: Does Rule of Law mean simply a State ruled by Law, whatever Law, or a State submitted to a superior Law? Which Law?

Until the Second World War, a minimalist conception of Rule of Law was prevalent. It meant merely a Law-based State[12], stressing "the formal or instrumental aspects of rule of law—those features that any legal system must possess to function effectively as a system of laws, regardless of whether the legal system is part of a democratic or non-democratic society, capitalist or socialist, liberal or theocratic" (Peerenboom 2005, p. 20). It was a positivist drift of the juridical thought:

[12] *Primauté du droit* is the translation of Rule of Law in the Canadian Charter of Rights and Freedoms.

the *Rechtsstaat* reduced to a *Geseztstaat* (State of laws), that is, meaning purely to govern according to the Law, so admitting whatever ruling. In that sense, Nazi Germany was a Rule of Law. Early in 1933, only a few days after the Nazis had come to power, a decree was issued that affirmed: *Recht ist was dem Führer dient* (The law is what suits the Führer)[13]. This was the denial of the democratic principle in favor of the personality principle. The members of the SS (*Schutzstaffel*: Protective Squadron), the armed wing of the Nazi Party, took an oath that read: "I swear to you, Adolph Hitler—as the Führer and Chancellor of the Reich—loyalty and bravery. I Pledge to you and to my superiors, appointed by you, obedience unto death, so help me God" (as cit in Morsink 1999, p. 42).

After the Second World War, the "revolution of fundamental righs"—Olivier Dord (2008) wrote—caused the refounding of Rule of Law. Respect for human rights henceforth became the principle of Governments' legitimacy, that is, "at the same time the limit and the purpose of the State power" (p. 333, 334). This conception was already meant in the Declaration of the Rights of Man and of the Citizen (1789)[14], especially in Articles II and XVI:

> Article II
> The aim of every political association is the preservation of the natural and imprescriptible rights of man. These rights are liberty, property, security, and resistance to oppression.
> [...]
> Article XVI
> Any society in which the guarantee of rights is not secured, or the separation of powers not determined, has no constitution at all.

The UDHR states, in Preamble, that "it is essential, if man is not to be compelled to have recourse, as a last resort, to rebellion against tyranny and oppression, that human rights should be protected by the *rule of law*" (italics added)[15]. The 1966 International Covenants do not mention the Rule of Law, but it is implicit there.

The 1993 World Conference on Human Rights included in its Declaration and Programme of Action[16] several references to the Rule of Law, among them the following one:

---

[13] After reading such a statement, Ernst Cassirer, who had been elected Rector of the University of Hamburg in 1929 (the first Jew to gain such a position in German Universities), but who was dismissed after a law made it impossible for Jews to hold official positions, declared: "Law is what suits the Führer", he declared: "If not tomorrow all legal scholars of Germany rise up as one and object to these phrases, Germany is lost" (*Wenn morgen nicht alle Rechtsgelehrten Deutschlands sich wie ein Mann erheben und gegen diesen Paragraphen protestieren, ist Deutschland verloren*). Not one single voice was heard, however, and he decided to leave Germany (as cit. in Coskun, 2007, p. 5).

[14] www.historyguide.org/intellect/declaration.html.

[15] According to UNESCO Constitution Article 1:

> 1. The purpose of the Organization is to contribute to peace and security by promoting collaboration among the nations through education, science and culture in order to further universal respect for justice, for the *rule of law* [italics added] and for the human rights and fundamental freedoms which are affirmed for the peoples of the world, without distinction of race, sex, language or religion, by the Charter of the United Nations.

[16] www.unhchr.ch/huridocda/huridoca.nsf/(symbol)/a.conf.157.23.en.

> 79. States should strive to eradicate illiteracy and should direct education towards the full development of the human personality and to the strengthening of respect for human rights and fundamental freedoms. The World Conference on Human Rights calls on all States and institutions to include human rights, humanitarian law, democracy and *rule of law* [italics added] as subjects in the curricula of all learning institutions in formal and non-formal settings.

The 2005 World Summit Outcome[17] acknowledged "that good governance and the *rule of law* [italics added] at the national and international levels are essential for sustained economic growth, sustainable development and the eradication of poverty and hunger" (para. 11).

At the European level, in the Statute of the Council of Europe (1949)[18], the signing governments reaffirmed "their devotion to the spiritual and moral values which are the common heritage of their peoples and the true source of individual freedom, political liberty and the *rule of law* [italics added], principles which form the basis of all genuine democracy" (Preamble). The Preamble to the ECHR (1950)[19] also refers to "a common heritage of political traditions, ideals, freedom and the *rule of law* [italics added]". The European Court of Human Rights considers the Rule of Law as a principle inherent in the Convention and uses the term *État de Droit* (not only *prééminence du droit*) in substantive (not merely formal) sense.

The Treaty on European Union[20] uses the term Rule of Law several times. For example:

> Article 2
> The Union is founded on the values of respect for human dignity, freedom, democracy, equality, the *rule of law* [italics added] and respect for human rights, including the rights of persons belonging to minorities. These values are common to the Member States in a society in which pluralism, non-discrimination, tolerance, justice, solidarity and equality between women and men prevail.
> Article 21
> 1. The Union's action on the international scene shall be guided by the principles which have inspired its own creation, development and enlargement, and which it seeks to advance in the wider world: democracy, the *rule of law* [italics added], the universality and indivisibility of human rights and fundamental freedoms, respect for human dignity, the principles of equality and solidarity, and respect for the principles of the United Nations Charter and international law.

Also the EU Charter[21] refers to the Rule of Law (Preamble):

> Conscious of its spiritual and moral heritage, the Union is founded on the indivisible, universal values of human dignity, freedom, equality and solidarity; it is based on the principles of democracy and the *rule of law* [italics added]. It places the individual at the heart

---

[17] http://daccess-dds-ny.un.org/doc/UNDOC/GEN/N05/487/60/PDF/N0548760.pdf?OpenElement.

[18] http://conventions.coe.int/Treaty/en/Treaties/html/001.htm.

[19] http://conventions.coe.int/treaty/en/Treaties/Html/005.htm.

French versions of the Convention and of the Statute translate 'rule of law' as 'prééminence du droit'.

[20] http://bookshop.europa.eu/is-bin/INTERSHOP.enfinity/WFS/EU-Bookshop-Site/en_GB/-/EUR/ViewPublication-Start?PublicationKey=QC3209190.

[21] http://eur-lex.europa.eu/LexUriServ/LexUriServ.do?uri=OJ:C:2010:083:0389:0403:en:PDF.

> of its activities, by establishing the citizenship of the Union and by creating an area of freedom, security and justice.

At the national level, the idea of Rule of Law appears as a main feature of the State in a number of old and new Constitutions. A landmark in refounding the Rule of Law was the German GG (1949)[22], in which the *Rechtsstaat* is formally tied to "fundamental rights". Article 28 provides:

> 1. The constitutional order in the *Länder* [Federation's States] must conform to the principles of a republican, democratic and social state governed by the *rule of law* [italics added], within the meaning of this Basic Law. [...]
> 3. The Federation shall guarantee that the constitutional order of the *Länder* conforms to the basic rights and to the provisions of paragraphs (1) and (2) of this Article.

Most Constitutions of former socialist countries of Central and Eastern Europe refer to the Rule of Law (see European Commission for Democracy through Law, 2011, para. 32).

Rule of Law is also one of the Worldwide Governance Indicators of the World Bank[23].

Governance and 'good governance' are terms entered into use since the 1990s. According to Simon Chesterman (2008):

> The term 'governance' itself had emerged within the development discourse in the 1990s as a means of expanding the prescriptions of donors to embrace not merely projects and structural adjustment but government policies. Though intergovernmental organizations like the World Bank and the International Monetary Fund are technically constrained from referring to political processes as such, 'governance' provides a convenient euphemism for precisely that. (p. 21)

Following the World Bank[24]:

> What is governance? Conceptually, governance (as opposed to 'good' governance) can be defined as the rule of the rulers, typically within a given set of rules. One might conclude that governance is the *process* – by which authority is conferred on rulers, by which they make the rules, and by which those rules are enforced and modified. Thus, understanding governance requires an identification of both the rulers and the rules, as well as the various processes by which they are selected, defined, and linked together and with the society generally.
> Nonetheless, within this concept of governance, the obvious second question is: What is good governance? Again, the debate on the quality of governance has been clouded by a slew of slightly differing definitions and understandings of what is actually meant by the term. Typically, it is defined in terms of the *mechanisms* thought to be needed to promote it. For example, in various places, good governance has been associated with democracy and good civil rights, with transparency, with the rule of law, and with efficient public services.

---

[22] www.bundestag.de/dokumente/rechtsgrundlagen/grundgesetz/index.html

[23] http://info.worldbank.org/governance/wgi/resources.htm, and *A Decade of Measuring the Quality of Governance—Governance Matters—2006—Worldwide Governance Indicators* (http://siteresources.worldbank.org/INTWBIGOVANTCOR/Resources/1740479-1150402582357/2661829-1158008871017/booklet_decade_of_measuring_governance.pdf.

[24] http://web.worldbank.org/WBSITE/EXTERNAL/COUNTRIES/MENAEXT/EXTMNAREGTOPGOVERNANCE/0,print:Y~isCURL:Y~contentMDK:20513159~pagePK:34004173~piPK:34003707~theSitePK:497024,00.html.

The UN Millennium Declaration[25] states in its Sect. 'III. Development and poverty eradication':

> 13. Success in meeting these objectives depends, *inter alia*, on good governance within each country. It also depends on good governance at the international level and on transparency in the financial, monetary and trading systems. We are committed to an open, equitable, rule-based, predictable and non-discriminatory multilateral trading and financial system.

Section V bears the title 'Human rights, democracy and good governance'.

The idea of International Rule of Law has emerged too. The draft International Bill of Rights proposed by the UK in 1947 (E/600) referred, in Article 5, "to the United Nations as the community of states organized under the rule of law". The concept underlies the UN Charter. The Declaration of Principles of International Law Concerning Friendly Relations and Co-operation Among States in Accordance with the Charter of the United Nations (1970)[26] refers, in its Preamble, to "the paramount importance of the Charter of the United Nations in the promotion of the rule of law among nations". In the UN Millennium Declaration (2000)[27], the Member States resolved (para. 9): "To strengthen respect for the rule of law in international as in national affairs". The 2005 World Summit Outcome[28] affirms the need for "universal adherence to and implementation of the *rule of law at both the national and international levels* [italics added]" (para. 134). Chesterman (2008) asked, however: "What, then, might the rule of law mean at the international level?" He concluded "that there is presently no such thing as the international rule of law, or at least that international law has yet to achieve a certain normative or institutional threshold to justify use of the term" (p. 33, 36).

Rule of Law became, therefore, according to Jacques Chevallier (1994), "a *value in itself*", bearing "*legitimization effects*", and "a very axiological imperative in international life: now it is hoped that every State presents itself under the flag of Rule of Law" (p. 134, 143). It is, however, a political label as universal as it is ambiguous. We agree, in general, that the Rule of Law is desirable and necessary for economic growth, the enjoyment of human rights, the global stability and peace, highest levels of wellbeing, but the concept remains debated.

The UN General-Secretary, in the *Report of the Secretary-General: The rule of law and transitional justice in conflict and post-conflict societies* (2004)[29], described the Rule of Law as follows:

> 6. … It refers to a principle of governance in which all persons, institutions and entities, public and private, including the State itself, are accountable to laws that are publicly promulgated, equally enforced and independently adjudicated, and which are consistent with international human rights norms and standards. It requires, as well, measures to ensure adherence to the principles of supremacy of law, equality before the law, accountabil-

[25] www.un.org/millennium/declaration/ares552e.htm.

[26] http://daccess-dds-ny.un.org/doc/RESOLUTION/GEN/NR0/348/90/IMG/NR034890.pdf?OpenElement.

[27] http://daccess-dds-ny.un.org/doc/UNDOC/GEN/N00/559/51/PDF/N0055951.pdf?OpenElement.

[28] http://unesdoc.unesco.org/images/0014/001408/140844e.pdf.

[29] www.unrol.org/files/2004%20report.pdf.

> ity to the law, fairness in the application of the law, separation of powers, participation in decision-making, legal certainty, avoidance of arbitrariness and procedural and legal transparency.

According to the World Bank: "*Rule of law* captures perceptions of the extent to which agents have confidence in and abide by the rules of society, and in particular the quality of contract enforcement, property rights, the police, and the courts, as well as the likelihood of crime and violence"[30]. Nevertheless, according to the World Bank's Rule of Law Index, non-democracies may have strong Rule of Law, and democracies may have weak Rule of Law[31].

The participants in the Conference on the Human Dimension of the OSCE that took place in Copenhagen in 1990[32] affirmed, in its final document that:

> 2. ... They consider that the rule of law does not mean merely a formal legality which assures regularity and consistency in the achievement and enforcement of democratic order, but justice based on the recognition and full acceptance of the supreme value of the human personality and guaranteed by institutions providing a framework for its fullest expression.

The following definition/description is found in an OSCE publication in 2005[33]:

> There is no internationally agreed definition of rule of law, but the concept first and foremost seeks to emphasize the necessity of establishing a rule-based society in the interests of legal certainty and predictability. The rule of law also operates so as to prevent any abuse of the state's monopoly on legitimate use of force. The basic rule is that public authorities can interfere with citizens' rights only if duly and legitimately authorized to do so. The minimum quality of the contents of those rules may be found in international human rights conventions, national constitutions, etc.
> The rule of law is composed of the following separate fundamental elements, which must advance together:
>
> - The existence of basic rules and values that a people share and by which they agree to be bound (constitutionalism). This can apply as much to an unwritten as to a written constitution.
> - The law must govern the government.
> - An independent and impartial judiciary interprets the law.
> - Those who administer the law act consistently, without unfair discrimination.
> - The law is transparent and accessible to all, especially the vulnerable in most need of its protection.
> - Application of the law is efficient and timely.
> - The law protects rights, especially human rights.
> - The law can be changed by an established process that is itself transparent, accountable and democratic.[34]

---

[30] http://info.worldbank.org/governance/wgi/pdf/rl.pdf.

[31] *A Decade of Measuring the Quality of Governance—Governance Matters—2006—Worldwide Governance Indicators* (http://siteresources.worldbank.org/INTWBIGOVANTCOR/Resources/1740479-1150402582357/2661829-1158008871017/booklet_decade_of_measuring_governance.pdf.

[32] www.osce.org/odihr/elections/14304.

[33] Development Assistance Committee (DAC), *Preventing Conflict and Building Peace—A Manual of Issues and Entry Points, Equal Access to Justice and the Rule of Law* (www.oecd.org/dataoecd/26/3/35785584.pdf).

[34] *The World Justice Project Rule of Law Index—2011* includes data on nine dimensions of the Rule of Law:

A Report of the European Commission for Democracy through Law (2011) concludes: "Looking at the legal instruments, national and international, and the writings of scholars, judges and others, it seems as if there is now a consensus on the core meaning of the rule of law and the elements contained within it" (para. 35). They are (para. 41):

1. Legality, including a transparent, accountable and democratic process for enacting law.
2. Legal certainty.
3. Prohibition of arbitrariness.
4. Access to justice before independent and impartial courts, including judicial review of administrative acts.
5. Respect for human rights.
6. Non-discrimination and equality before the law.

- Limited government powers
- Absence of corruption
- Order and security
- Fundamental rights
- Open government
- Effective regulatory enforcement
- Access to civil justice
- Effective criminal justice
- Informal justice

These nine factors are further disaggregated into 52 sub-factors. The scores of these sub-factors are built from over 400 variables drawn from assessments of the general public (1,000 respondents per country) and local legal experts. The outcome of this exercise is one of the world's most comprehensive data sets measuring the extent to which countries adhere to the rule of law—not in theory but in practice.

[...]

As used by the World Justice Project, the rule of law refers to a rules-based system in which the following four universal principles are upheld:

- The government and its officials and agents are accountable under the law.
- The laws are clear, publicized, stable, and fair, and protect fundamental rights, including the security of persons and property.
- The process by which the laws are enacted, administered, and enforced is accessible, fair, and efficient.
- Access to justice is provided by competent, independent, and ethical adjudicators, attorneys or representatives, and judicial officers who are of sufficient number, have adequate resources, and reflect the makeup of the communities they serve.

These principles are derived from international sources that enjoy broad acceptance across countries with differing social, cultural, economic, and political systems, and incorporate both substantive and procedural elements. (www.worldjusticeproject.org/sites/default/files/wjproli2011_0.pdf)

The World Justice Project (WJP) presents itself as a multinational and multidisciplinary effort to strengthen the rule of law throughout the world.

According to the Report:

> 66. … The rule of law must be tailored in a way that freedom for all will be ensured even in areas where hybrid (state-private) actors or private entities are responsible for tasks, which formerly have been the domain of state authorities. The substance of the rule of law as a guiding principle for the future has to be extended not only to the area of cooperation between state and private actors but also to activities of private actors whose power to infringe individual rights has a weight comparable to state power. Governmental actors at the national, transnational and international level all have to act as guarantors of the fundamental principles and elements of the traditional rule of law in these areas.

Concluding, we may distinguish two principal meanings of Rule of Law: one formal, qualified as *thin*, another one substantial, qualified as *thick*.

- Under its formal or *thin* meaning, Rule of Law includes the rejection of 'rule of man' in favor of controlling Government powers by Law; its application to everybody and equality before the laws; and the existence of specific institutions, such as the judiciary, to apply the laws.
- Under its substantial or *thick* meaning, Rule of Law incorporates an idea of justice as its political purpose, consubstantiated in the ideal of human rights. Its main elements are the protection of citizens' fundamental rights, the separation of powers, the legality of administrative acts and the independence of judicial power.

The International Community professes and promotes a substantial conception of Rule of Law. In 2007, the Parliamentary Assembly of the Council of Europe adopted a Resolution (1594) on 'The principle of the rule of law'[35]. Drawing attention to the fact that in some recent democracies in Eastern Europe the main trends in legal thinking foster an understanding of the "rule of law" as "supremacy of statute law", in line with "certain traditions of the totalitarian state", the Assembly observes: "Such a formalistic interpretation of the terms 'rule of law' and *État de droit* (as well as of *Rechtsstaat*) runs contrary to the essence of both 'rule of law' and *prééminence du droit*" (para. 4). That is why the Assembly:

> 6.1. stresses that the terms 'rule of law' and *prééminence du droit* are substantive legal concepts which are synonymous, and which should be considered as such in all English and French language versions of documents issued by the Assembly as well as in the member states in their official translations;

From the preceding emerges this fundamental idea: The Rule of Law lies in the consubstantiality between human rights and democracy. However, there is a tension between them: it is the tension between the ethical principle (human rights) and the majority principle (democracy).

As Campbell (2006) pointed out: "The eternal problem of political philosophy is how we can guard the guardians" (p. 100). Indeed, "power can be misused and has a tendency to be abused" (p. 95). Democracy, "the supreme expression of autonomy" (p. 79), is a solution, but only the less bad one, because "democracies can be manipulated by powerful minorities or abused by self-interested majorities"

[35] http://assembly.coe.int/main.asp?Link=/documents/adoptedtext/ta07/eres1594. htm.

(p. 96). Jean-Marie Denquin (2008) remarks: "Ancient Greece invented democracy, but never conceived of the idea of subjective rights opposable to State". And "a democratic rhetoric may coexist with a totalitarian practice" (p. 263, 266). In addition, Langlois (2003) observes:

> As a State does not have to be democratic in order to be member of the United Nations and to be part in its human rights instruments, and democracy is not needed to implement many human rights (mostly the economic and social rights), it has been suggested 'that one way to promote an international human rights regime [...] is to separate respect for human rights from the Western-centric notion of democratization'. (p. 994)

There is another surprising criticism addressed to International Law in general but regarding human rights in particular: IHRL lacks democratic legitimacy, especially for absence of popular participation in the process of its drafting. The controversy became particularly topical in the USA, within the context of the debate on the abuses committed in the *Global War on Terror* (Mayerfeld 2009).

Randall Peerenboom (2005) points out:

> The relationship between rule of law, democracy and human rights is difficult to sort out conceptually because of the contested meanings and interpretations of each and is difficult to test empirically because of problems in operationalizing and measuring them. (p. 59).

The American Declaration of Independence (1776) and the *Déclaration des droits de l'homme et du citoyen* (Declaration of the Rights of Man and of the Citizen, 1789) made a direct link between them, by making the respect for human rights a principle of limitation of popular sovereignty, constituent of political legitimacy.

- American Declaration of Independence (Preamble):

> We hold these truths to be self-evident – that all men are created equal; that they are endowed by their creator with certain inalienable rights; that among these are life, liberty, and the pursuit of happiness. That, to secure these rights, governments are instituted among men deriving their just powers from the consent of the governed.

- *Déclaration des droits de l'homme et du citoyen* (Article II):

> The aim of every political association is the preservation of the natural and imprescriptible rights of man. These rights are liberty, property, security, and resistance to oppression.

Consequently, the principle of respect of human rights and the principle of the popular sovereignty are historically, conceptually and politically indissociable. Evelyne Maes (2008) notes that "political and private autonomy, i.e. popular sovereignty and human rights, are co-original [...] mutually presuppose each other in such a way that neither human rights nor popular sovereignty can claim primacy over its counterpart" (p. 76, 77). A democracy based on these two principles is a constitutional democracy, as Habermas thinks of it, according to whom, Maes wrote, "there are two sources of political legitimacy: procedural legitimacy, reflecting the general will of the citizens, and substantial or content-based legitimacy, by respecting the rights of the citizens. The former is guaranteed by the form of government (democracy), and the latter by the constitutionalism" (p. 78). This dimension of Constitutionalism is, therefore, a way of limiting the majority principle. Others include the separation of powers and the control of the constitutionality of laws, in particular (Elster 1993). David Beetham and Kevin Boyle (1995) underline that democracy "entails the twin principles of *popular control* over collective decision-making and *equality of rights* in the exercise of that control" (p. 1). Simply put, democracy is a political regime that takes human rights seriously. That is why: "The international human rights movement is also aiming at a global revolution in the way people are governed" (Ramcharan 2008, p. 157).

The consubstantiality of human rights and democracy has been reaffirmed by international and national Courts. For example, in *Gündüz v. Turkey* (Application n° 35071/97, Judgment on 4 December 2003)[36], the European Court of Human Rights said:

> 40. The present case is characterized, in particular, by the fact that the applicant was punished for statements classified by the domestic courts as "hate speech". Having regard to the relevant international instruments (see paragraphs 22–24 above) and to its own case-law, the Court would emphasize, in particular, that tolerance and respect for the equal dignity of all human beings constitute the foundations of a democratic, pluralistic society.

In *Movement for Quality Government in Israel v. The Prime Minister* (HCJ 1993/03)[37], the Israel Supreme Court said:

> 9. ... All of these principles – the rule of law, the separation of powers, the checks and balances that accompany this separation, the power of judicial review, and the other mechanisms of democracy – form the central pillars of a democratic society. They constitute the essential conditions for the preservation of human rights. They form the nucleus of any democratic society that strives to promote human welfare. [...]
> 13. Judicial review thus requires striking a balance between respecting decisions of government authorities within their area of power and the need to preserve the rule of law and protect human rights. This is one of the axioms of democracy. This balance is not static, but changes according to the character of the power under discussion. [...]

In *August and Another v Electoral Commission and Others* (CCT8/99) [1999] ZACC 3; 1999 (3) SA 1; 1999 (4) BCLR 363 (1 April 1999)[38], the Constitutional Court of South Africa said:

> [17] Universal adult suffrage on a common voters roll is one of the foundational values of our entire constitutional order. The achievement of the franchise has historically been important both for the acquisition of the rights of full and effective citizenship by all South Africans regardless of race, and for the accomplishment of an all-embracing nationhood. The universality of the franchise is important not only for nationhood and democracy. The vote of each and every citizen is a badge of dignity and of personhood. Quite literally, it says that everybody counts.

The Constitution of the Republic of South Africa (1996)—one of the most human rights friendly Constitutions—is cited by Jamie Mayerfeld (2009) as an example of popular participation in drafting human rights. He concluded: "To say that international human rights law subverts democracy is to adopt an unworthy conception of

[36] http://cmiskp.echr.coe.int/tkp197/view.asp?item=2andportal=hbkmandaction=htmlandhighlight=M%FCsl%FCm%20%7C%20G%FCnd%FCz%20%7C%20v.%20%7C%20Turkeyandsessionid=82444978andskin=hudoc-en

[37] http://elyon1.court.gov.il/files_eng/03/930/019/P26/03019930.p26.pdf.

[38] www.saflii.org/za/cases/ZACC/1999/3.pdf.

democracy" (p. 88). As Sir Ernest Simon said in 1937: "The essence of democracy is the belief in the ultimate importance of every individual; that the state exists for man, not man for the state" (as cit. in Burgers 1992, p. 461). The concomitance of the expansion of human rights and of democracy testifies to their reciprocal implication as the main features of the contemporary Rule of Law. Understood as a political regime based on the recognition and protection of human rights, able to legitimate and to limit "the powers of governments, businesses and other social institutions" (Campbell 2006, p. 95), Rule of Law is the best political device to "protect both majorities and minorities" (p. 97).

7.4 New Law of Humanity?

The term 'humanity' is used in the Preamble to the UNESCO Constitution[39] that refers to "the education of humanity for justice and liberty and peace", a reference recalled in Preamble of the Universal Declaration on Cultural Diversity (UNESCO 2001)[40].

The 'principle of humanity' underlies the laws of war. It aims to establish "that, in contradistinction to the savage cruelty of former times, fairness of conduct and respect for human rights should be observed in the realization of the purpose of war" (United Nations War Crimes Commission 1948, p. 25). The IV Hague Convention—Convention Respecting the Laws and Customs of War on Land (1907)[41]—aimed at serving "the interests of humanity and the ever-progressive needs of civilization". It refers to "the principles of the law of nations, as they result from the usages established among civilized peoples, from the laws of humanity, and the dictates of the public conscience" (Preamble).

As the International Military Tribunal at Nuremberg said, "from the beginning of the war in 1939 war crimes were committed on a vast scale, which were also crimes against humanity" (as cit. in United Nations War Crimes Commission 1948, p. 194). For example: "Prisoners of war were ill-treated and tortured and murdered, not only in defiance of the well-established rules of international law, but in complete disregard of the elementary dictates of humanity" (p. 2).

'Crimes against humanity' is a phrase used, for the first time, in the Joint Declaration on 24 May 1915 by France, Great Britain and Russia[42], in connection with the massacres of the Armenian population in Turkey, denouncing them as "crimes of Turkey against humanity and civilization". However, "the Nuremberg Charter is the first legal enactment to formulate the definition of crimes against humanity" (id. p. 192). Article 6 of the Charter of the International Military Tribunal at Nuremberg

[39] http://portal.unesco.org/en/ev.php-URL_ID=15244&URL_DO=DO_TOPIC&URL_SECTION=201.html.

[40] http://unesdoc.unesco.org/images/0012/001271/127162e.pdf.

[41] http://avalon.law.yale.edu/20th_century/hague04.asp.

[42] www.armenian-genocide.org/Affirmation.160/current_category.7/affirmation_detail.html.

declared that the "crimes coming within the jurisdiction of the Tribunal for which there shall be individual responsibility" were *crimes against peace, war crimes* and *crimes against humanity*. The latter were so described:

> Namely, murder, extermination, enslavement, deportation, and other inhumane acts committed against any civilian population, before or during the war; or persecutions on political, racial or religious grounds in execution of or in connection with any crime within the jurisdiction of the Tribunal, whether or not in violation of the domestic law of the country where perpetrated.

The Control Council and Coordinating Committee of the Allied Control Authority in post-World War II-occupied Germany enacted on 20 December 1945 the 'Law N° 10—Punishment of Persons Guilty of War Crimes, Crimes Against Peace and Against Humanity'[43], generally known as 'Control Council Law N° 10'. The 'crimes against humanity' included (II.1.c):

> Atrocities and offenses, including but not limited to murder, extermination, enslavement, deportation, imprisonment, torture, rape, or other inhumane acts committed against any civilian population, or persecutions on political, racial or religious grounds whether or not in violation of the domestic laws of the country where perpetrated.

In the Charter of the International Military Tribunal for the Far East[44] they were described as follows (5.c):

> Namely, murder, extermination, enslavement, deportation, and other inhumane acts committed against any civilian population, before or during the war, or persecutions on political or racial grounds in execution of or in connection with any crime within the jurisdiction of the Tribunal, whether or not in violation of the domestic law of the country where perpetrated. Leaders, organizers, instigators and accomplices participating in the formulation or execution of a common plan or conspiracy to commit any of the foregoing crimes are responsible for all acts performed by any person in execution of such plan.

The Peace Treaties signed on 10 February 1947, in Paris, after the Peace Conference (1946), "were a further step in making the notion of 'crimes against humanity' part of the common law of nations" (United Nations War Crimes Commission 1948, p. 211). The Peace Treaty with Italy included the punishment of crimes against peace, war crimes and crimes against humanity committed during the Italo-Abyssinian War of 1935–1936.

In 1968, the UN General Assembly adopted the Convention on the Non-Applicability of Statutory Limitations to War Crimes and Crimes against Humanity[45]. Janusz Symonides and Vladimir Volodin (2003) underlined that this Convention "conveys the idea that certain norms are so basic to humanity and to the international community that grave infringements of these norms in no way lose their criminal character through the passage of time" (p. 88). The authors of such crimes are *hostes humanis generis* (enemies of the humankind).

---

[43] http://avalon.law.yale.edu/imt/imt10.asp.

[44] www.jus.uio.no/english/services/library/treaties/04/4-06/military-tribunal-far-east.xml.

[45] http://daccess-dds-ny.un.org/doc/RESOLUTION/GEN/NR0/243/51/IMG/NR024351.pdf?OpenElement.

In 1973, the General Assembly adopted Resolution 3074 (XXVIII) referring to "The principles of international cooperation as regards the detection, the arrest, the extradition and the punishment of the individuals guilty of war crimes and of the crimes against the humanity"[46]. In 1974, the Council of Europe adopted, in Strasbourg, the European Convention on the Non-Applicability of Statutory Limitation to Crimes against Humanity and War Crimes[47].

The jurisdiction of the ICC—"limited to the most serious crimes of concern to the international community as a whole"—includes "the following crimes: (a) The crime of genocide; (b) Crimes against humanity; (c) War crimes; (d) The crime of aggression" (Article 5.1 of the Statute)[48]. Crimes against humanity are so described (Article 7):

1. For the purpose of this Statute, 'crime against humanity' means any of the following acts when committed as part of a widespread or systematic attack directed against any civilian population, with knowledge of the attack:

   a. Murder;
   b. Extermination;
   c. Enslavement;
   d. Deportation or forcible transfer of population;
   e. Imprisonment or other severe deprivation of physical liberty in violation of fundamental rules of international law;
   f. Torture;
   g. Rape, sexual slavery, enforced prostitution, forced pregnancy, enforced sterilization, or any other form of sexual violence of comparable gravity;
   h. Persecution against any identifiable group or collectivity on political, racial, national, ethnic, cultural, religious, gender as defined in paragraph 3, or other grounds that are universally recognized as impermissible under international law, in connection with any act referred to in this paragraph or any crime within the jurisdiction of the Court;
   i. Enforced disappearance of persons;
   j. The crime of apartheid;
   k. Other inhumane acts of a similar character intentionally causing great suffering, or serious injury to body or to mental or physical health.

These terms are defined in paragraph 2.

Crimes against Humanity are imprescriptible because they are the most grave attempt against "the symbolic order that permits to build the humanity of the human being", stressed Mireille Delmas-Marty (1996, p. 76). Their particular gravity lies in annihilating somebody only because he or she exists. Trying to define 'humanity' starting "from the content already given to non-derogable rights and to crimes against humanity", Delmas-Marty concludes:

> The foundation of the non-derogable rights remains individual, that of 'human rights'. With the crime against 'humanity', we see the rising of a collective foundation, what is perhaps the greatest novelty. [...] What may we draw from that recurrent reference to the group, in terms of definition? Maybe the idea that the human being, even though

[46] http://daccess-dds-ny.un.org/doc/RESOLUTION/GEN/NR0/281/46/IMG/NR028146.pdf?OpenElement.

[47] http://conventions.coe.int/Treaty/Commun/QueVoulezVous.asp?NT=082&CM=1&CL=ENG.

[48] www.icc-cpi.int/NR/rdonlyres/ADD16852-AEE9-4757-ABE7-9CDC7CF02886/283503/RomeStatutEng1.pdf.

> profoundly inscribed in a familiar, cultural or religious group, never should lose its individuality and become a permutable element, and as such rejected, not by what it does, but by its membership in this or that group. In other words, what we try to protect is alterity, that is, both the singularity of each human being, recognized as a unique being, and its equal belonging to the human community. [...]
> Indeed, it seems that we may move forward towards a definition starting from these two pillars founding humanity as a plurality of unique beings. [...]
> These examples show that the crime against humanity, so defined, may consist both in destroying human life and in making living beings without respecting the principles of uniqueness and equal membership. That is essential, if we want to control not only the past but also the future. (p. 85...87)

She argues that the values and principles of human rights are the embryo of a "common law of humanity" whose foundation is human dignity, absolute and indivisible. It is absolute for being irreducible, and indivisible because it encompasses both the uniqueness of each human being and the universality of the human species. In her opinion:

> ... in addition to 'human' rights, from now on the question arises concerning the legal construction of the idea of humanity around notions such as the crime against humanity or even human dignity, for a long time circumscribed to person, now that biotechnologies concern humanity as a whole: genetic manipulations, for instance, may affect the integrity of the human species, from a point of view not only physical but, in some way, metaphysical. Michel Foucault showed that 'the human being is a recent invention', going back to the 19th century, with the rising of the human sciences. Having still more recently appeared, Humanity should, to a great extent, be invented. And Law could pave the way. (p. 72)

In sum, "affirming solemnly that human beings 'are born free and equal' is to protest against a purely biological approach to the human being" (p. 102). Levinas qualified human rights as "the God's sign in human being" and so the standard of Law, its Ethics, "ultra-Ethics", Lionel Ponton (1990, p. 188).

Although there are doubts on whether "humanity may be considered, in the present state of International Law, as a subject of Law" (Salmon 2011, p. 40), some authors argue that it has been so recognized, for the first time, in the Declaration on the Prohibition of the Use of Nuclear and Thermo-Nuclear Weapons (UN 1961)[49] that states: "The use of nuclear and thermo-nuclear weapons would exceed even the scope of war and cause indiscriminate suffering and destruction to mankind and civilization and, as such, is contrary to the rules of international law and to the laws of humanity" (1.b). And thereafter: "Any State using nuclear and thermo-nuclear weapons is to be considered as violating the Charter of the United Nations, as acting contrary to the laws of humanity and as committing a crime against mankind and civilization" (1.d).

In this connection, recall Trindade's (2006) case for "the humanization of contemporary International Law", for a reconstructed or new *Jus Gentium* as an International Law of Humankind (p. 35).

Following Arendt, the citizen being "by definition a citizen among citizens of a country among countries", the fundamental task of political theory is "to find a

[49] http://daccess-dds-ny.un.org/doc/RESOLUTION/GEN/NR0/167/06/IMG/NR016706.pdf?OpenElement.

political principle which would prevent nations from developing nationalism and would thereby lay the fundamentals of an international community capable of presenting and protecting the civilization of the modern world" (as cit. in Birmingham 2006, p. 135). In her opinion, the basis of human rights is "the idea of humanity which constitutes the sole regulating idea of international law" (cit. ib. p. 38). Indeed:

> Man of the twentieth century has become just as emancipated from nature as eighteenth-century man was from history. [...] This new situation in which "humanity" has in effect assumed the role formerly ascribed to nature or history would mean in this context that the right to have rights or the right of every individual to belong to humanity should be guaranteed by humanity itself. It is by no means certain whether it is possible. (cit. ib. p. 5, 6)

The ICJ said in the Advisory Opinion on the Reservations to the Convention on the Prevention and Punishment of the Crime of Genocide, in 1951, that this Convention "was manifestly adopted for a purely humanitarian and civilizing purpose", and "to confirm and endorse the most elementary principles of morality" (as cit. in Kiss 2006, p. 13). They are principles related to two legal concepts: *jus cogens* (peremptory norms) and obligations *erga omnes* (towards all).

Already in 1935, in his lectures delivered at The Hague Academy of International Law, Alfred Verdross invoked the "general principles of *jus cogens*" (as cit. in Trindade 2006 p. 92). However, they entered International Law only with the VCLT (1969)[50], whose Article 53, bearing the title "Treaties conflicting with a peremptory norm of general international law ('*jus cogens*')", reads:

> A treaty is void if, at the time of its conclusion, it conflicts with a peremptory norm of general international law. For the purposes of the present Convention, a peremptory norm of general international law is a norm accepted and recognized by the international community of States as a whole as a norm from which no derogation is permitted and which can be modified only by a subsequent norm of general international law having the same character.

According to Karl Zemanek (2009): "The most far-reaching development of the law was the introduction of the concept of *jus cogens* into positive international law in articles 53 and 64" (of the VCLT)[51]. In Trindade's (2006) opinion, the *jus cogens* ultimately emanate "from the universal juridical conscience" (p. 176) that becomes *opinio juris vel necessitatis* (conviction of juridical value) (see also Glossary)[52].

---

[50] http://treaties.un.org/doc/Publication/UNTS/Volume%201155/volume-1155-I-18232-English.pdf.

[51] The UN International Law Commission placed the codification of Customary International Law of Treaties on its agenda in its first session, in 1949. As Rapporteurs were appointed successively James Brierly, Sir Hersch Lauterpacht, Sir Gerald Fitzmaurice and Sir Humphrey Waldock. The last one prepared six reports that enabled the Commission to submit, in 1966, a draft Convention to the UN General Assembly with a recommendation to convene an international conference. The General Assembly endorsed the recommendation and decided that the conference would take place in 1968 and 1969, in Vienna.

[52] The concept of *opinio juris vel necessitatis* "emerged in the nineteenth century as a construction above all of the German historical school (Puchta, Savigny), in reaction precisely to the voluntarist conception; in this way, it succeeded in gradually discarding the 'will' of the States, and in moving

> There is a general awareness nowadays of the importance of the work of multiple multilateral forums for the expression of *opinio juris communis* and the development of general International Law. [...] *Opinio juris* is affirmed as a key factor in the *formation* itself of International Law [... giving expression] to the 'juridical conscience', not only of nations and peoples (as sustained in the past by the historical school), but of the international community as a whole. (p. 175)
> One acknowledges here a conceptual evolution which has moved, as from the sixties, from the international to the universal dimension (under the great influence of the development of the International Law of Human Rights itself). (p. 196)

The Vienna Convention Article 53 transformed, in part, International Law, which is horizontal in nature, into a vertical legal order. *Jus cogens* may be considered the equivalent, within the international public order, to the national 'public order'[53]. In this connection, the European Commission of Human Rights emphasized in *Austria v. Italy* (Application N°. 788/60)[54]:

> ... that the purpose of the High Contracting Parties in concluding the [European] Convention was not to concede to each other reciprocal rights and obligations in pursuance of their individual national interests but to realize the aims and ideals of the Council of Europe...

---

towards the 'common juridical conscience', of which the customary norms were an expression" (Trindade 2006, p. 174).

[53] Public order is a concept originating from Article 6 of the French Civil Code: *On ne peut déroger, par des conventions particulières, aux lois qui intéressent l'ordre public et les bonnes moeurs* (Statutes relating to public policy and morals may not be derogated from by private agreements). This concept encompasses principles concerning fundamental representations and values in a legal system, which should be protected specially by Tribunals.

In *Loizidou v. Turkey* (Application n° 15318/89, Judgment on 23 March 1995), the European Court of Human Rights referred to "the Convention as a constitutional instrument of European public order (*ordre public*)" (para. 35).

(http://cmiskp.echr.coe.int/tkp197/view.asp?item=1andportal=hbkmandaction=htmlandhighlight=Loizidou%20%7C%20v.%20%7C%20Turkeyandsessionid=93503969andskin=hudoc-en)

In *Cyprus v. Turkey* (Application n° 25781/94, 10 May 2001), the European Court said that the European Convention is "an instrument of European public order (*ordre public*) for the protection of individual human beings" (para. 78).

(http://cmiskp.echr.coe.int/tkp197/view.asp?item=1andportal=hbkmandaction=htmlandhighlight=Cyprus%20%7C%20v.%20%7C%20Turkeyandsessionid=93304673andskin=hudoc-en)

According to the Document quoted above prepared by the UN Secretary-General, regarding the draft International Covenants on Human Rights:

> The English expression 'public order' and the French expression *l'ordre public* gave rise to considerable discussion. It was observed that the English expression 'public order' was not equivalent to – and indeed was substantially different from – the French expression *l'ordre public* (or the Spanish expression *orden publico).* In civil law countries *l'ordre public* is a legal concept used principally as a basis for negating or restricting private agreements, the exercise of police power or the application of foreign law. In common law countries the expression 'public order' is ordinarily used to mean the absence of public disorder. The common law counterpart of *l'ordre public* is 'public policy' rather than 'public order'.

[54] Quoted by the Inter-American Court of Human Rights in its Advisory Opinion OC-2/82 of September 24, 1982, requested by the Inter-American Commission on Human Rights on "The Effect of Reservations on the Entry into Force of the American Convention on Human Rights (Arts. 74 and 75)".

(www1.umn.edu/humanrts/iachr/b_11_4b.htm)

> and to establish a common public order of the free democracies of Europe with the object of safeguarding their common heritage of political traditions, ideas, freedom and the rule of law.

Jus cogens "introduces a material hierarchy (established by virtue of the substantial content of norms) into the international legal order" (Dupuy 2008, p. 566, 567), in which there is no formal hierarchy. In classical International Law, founded on States' consent, no legal instrument is inherently superior to another one. There are few cases of precedence of some norms over other ones: when the principle *Lex posterior priori derogat* (primacy of the most recent norms) applies; when the norms apply only between some States; or when the precedence is commanded by a treaty, as is the case of the UN Charter[55], whose Article 103 provides: "In the event of a conflict between the obligations of the Members of the United Nations under the present Charter and their obligations under any other international agreement, their obligations under the present Charter shall prevail".

By beginning his Course at The Hague Academy of International Law on 'The international *jus cogens*', Antonio Robledo (1982) affirmed:

> Its reception in the Vienna Convention on the Law of Treaties meant, unquestionably, a deep innovation and a great step forward, as it constitutes, in the positive International Law, the incorporation of an institution that, until then, had not come out of the frameworks of the international doctrine and jurisprudence. (p. 17)

And by concluding:

> When all has been said and repeated, what remains, whatever philosophy one may adopt, is that *jus cogens* is no more than the juridical expression of the international community at the moment when it eventually becomes aware of itself and of the values on the recognition of which it is based and constituded. It is at present that, indeed, the international community became, as Gros Espiell said, 'a veritable subject of international law', and no more, as before, a conglomerate of disperse entities, without any link among them other than that of contracts and treaties, most of them bilateral, that their reciprocal interest may have led them to agree.
> The International Court of Justice echoed this new conception, that of the international community as a subject of international law, in the *Case Barcelona Traction*, although not in precise terms. (p. 204, 205)[56]

Indeed: "It has generally been assumed, to date, that the core rights which are directly related to human existence are to be classified as *jus cogens*, i.e. as rules from which no derogation is permitted" (Tomuschat 2008, p. 38). What human rights may be so qualified?

Christine Chinkin (2010) observes: "Since the 1990s, international, regional, and national courts have recognized certain norms as *jus cogens*, including the prohibitions against torture, genocide, and fundamental rules of humanitarian law" (p. 113). For instance, both the European Court of Human Rights and the International Criminal Tribunal for ex-Yugoslavia qualified prohibition against torture as

---

[55] http://treaties.un.org/doc/Publication/CTC/uncharter.pdf.

[56] However: "Only recently has the ICJ ventured to pronounce the word *jus cogens* which in earlier years some judges considered to be anathema" (Tomuschat 2008, p. 38).

a *jus cogens* norm (p. 166). According to the CCPR, some non-derogable rights included in ICCPR Article 4.2 possess *jus cogens* statute, such as the right to life and the prohibition of torture and of cruel, inhuman or degrading treatment or punition. In Dinah Shelton's (2006) view: "Taking into account the absence of permissible suspensions, reservations or denunciations in respect to the common non-derogable rights, at least at the global level, they come close to being absolute in nature and thus can be seen as the pinnacle of positive human rights law" (p. 185). She concludes:

> Other rights that have been recognized as simultaneously being *jus cogens* norms, core and non-derogable rights, and as obligations *erga omnes* are few in number: the right to life, the right to be free from slavery, and the right to be free from torture, together with fundamental judicial protections necessary to ensure the enjoyment of other rights. Among these, the right to life, as has been recognized by human rights tribunals, imposes both negative and positive obligations on states and encompasses some of the obligations corresponding to core economic, social and cultural rights, i.e. ensuring the right to food, shelter and health care. (p. 185, 186)

Cecilia M. Quiroga (2009) notes that the Inter-American Court of Human Rights considers that the prohibition of discrimination is both a right and "a principle underlying all human rights", being "the most fundamental principle of international human rights law", and belonging to the *jus cogens* (p. 498). The Inter-American Commission of Human Rights regarding the right to life said the same.

Olivier de Schutter (2009a) concluded that there does exist a consensus about the *jus cogens* nature of some IHRL norms, which "include at a minimum the prohibition of aggression, slavery and the slave trade, genocide, racial discrimination, apartheid and torture, as well as basic rules of international humanitarian law applicable in armed conflicts, and the right to self-determination" (p. 50).

According to Cesare Pinelli (2006), a progressive concept of *jus cogens* should include the following rights:

- the right to life,
- the right to a fair trial,
- the right to racial equality,
- the right to be free from torture,
- the right not to be arbitrarily deprived of liberty, and
- the right to the fundamental protections of humanitarian law during armed conflict (presumably the guarantees of common article 3 of the 1949 Geneva Conventions). (p. 174)

Recall that, according to the concept of the *Responsibility to Protect* (R2P) (A/RES/60/1): "Each individual State has the responsibility to protect its populations from genocide, war crimes, ethnic cleansing and crimes against humanity" (p. 138).

Jus cogens appears, therefore, as the hard core of the constitutional dimension of International Law. The UN Charter, IHRL and VCLT are cornerstones of an emerging Constitution of the International Community.

Jus cogens norms imply obligations *erga omnes*. This category of obligations was first identified by the ICJ in the above-quoted *Barcelona Traction, Light and Power, Limited* (1970)[57]. According to the Court:

> 33. … an essential distinction should be drawn between the obligations of a State towards the international community as a whole, and those arising vis-à-vis another State in the field of diplomatic protection. By their very nature the former are the concern of all States. In view of the importance of the rights involved, all States can be held to have a legal interest in their protection; they are obligations *erga omnes*.
> 34. Such obligations derive, for example, in contemporary international law, from the outlawing of acts of aggression, and of genocide, as also from the principles and rules concerning the basic rights of the human person, including protection from slavery and racial discrimination.

According to Teraya Koji (2001), the *Barcelona Traction* is "the first case which appears to recognize an emerging hierarchy in international human rights norms" as obligations *erga omnes* (p. 931).

The close relation existing between obligations *erga omnes* and norms *jus cogens* may cause confusion. All *jus cogens* norms generate obligations *erga omnes*, but these ones are not necessarily tied to *jus cogens* norms. Schutter (2009a) explains:

> They refer to different consequences: while the *jus cogens* character of a norm implies that it is hierarchically superior to any other norm of international law which does not possess the same character, the *erga omnes* nature of an obligation simply means that all states may be recognized a legal interest in the obligation being complied with. (p. 51, 52)

Obligations *erga omnes* are, therefore, obligations towards the whole International Community, insofar as all States are deemed to have an interest in their being complied with. They are distinct from obligations inherent to the bilateralism of International Law in general, as they are not subjected to the reciprocity rule. Most of them emerged within IHRL and IHL. Mégret (2010) remarks that "it could be said that international human rights obligations have become a typical example of *erga omnes* obligations" (p. 129). As the Inter-American Court of Human Rights highlighted, in the Advisory Opinion OC-2/82 of September 24, 1982, above referred to[58]:

> 29. The Court must emphasize, however, that modern human rights treaties in general, and the American Convention in particular, are not multilateral treaties of the traditional type concluded to accomplish the reciprocal exchange of rights for the mutual benefit of the contracting States. Their object and purpose is the protection of the basic rights of individual human beings irrespective of their nationality, both against the State of their nationality and all other contracting States. In concluding these human rights treaties, the States can be deemed to submit themselves to a legal order within which they, for the common good, assume various obligations, not in relation to other States, but towards all individuals within their jurisdiction.

In this regard, the Court quoted the European Commission of Human Rights, which declared:

---

[57] www.icj-cij.org/docket/files/50/5387.pdf.

[58] www1.umn.edu/humanrts/iachr/b_11_4b.htm.

> … that the obligations undertaken by the High Contracting Parties in the European Convention are essentially of an objective character, being designed rather to protect the fundamental rights of individual human beings from infringements by any of the High Contracting Parties than to create subjective and reciprocal rights for the High Contracting Parties themselves. [Austria vs Italy, Application No. 788/60, 4 European Yearbook of Human Rights 116, at 140 (1961)]

That is why, wrote Julio P. Vallejo (1990), who was member of the CCPR: "A State that persistently violates human rights acts against the community of nations and against the ethical and legal values that guide and condition the conscience of humanity" (p. 70). Kiss (2006) comments:

> The understanding that humankind has common values has given rise to a change in the very nature of a growing number of international treaties. Until the second half of the nineteenth century, most treaties were bilateral and contained equal and reciprocal benefits and burdens for each party. The new type of treaties proclaiming common values of humankind – peace, human rights, environment – and aiming at their protection do not grant reciprocal benefits to the parties, in the same way that trade or extradition treaties do, but instead impose obligations often referred to as 'unilateral' because the primary beneficiaries of the obligations are either the world community (including the global commons) or persons or groups within the States parties themselves. (p. 12)

Giuseppe Barile (1987) pointed out:

> The international rules on human rights […] tend to protect, in a primary and not in a subordinate manner, the interests of mankind as such. These are interests which are protected by international law for the purpose of directly safeguarding 'the inherent dignity of all members of the human family'. For this reason the international norms in question do not respond to the logic of reciprocity and, in particular, to the logic on the basis of which specific reprisals might be taken. (p. 4)

In José J. Ruiz' (1979) opinion, "the figure of *erga omnes* obligations constitutes an essential moment in the passage from the old great powers international law to the new international law of the whole humanity" (p. 233)[59], every State becoming, in some way, an "international ombudsman" of human rights (Sohn 1982, p. 23)[60].

Jus cogens norms and obligations *erga omnes* are notions with an open content, which develop through their concrete application.

As a consequence, Humanity is a concept transcending that of the International Community. This one is a laborious and slow construction, of which the UN is the symbol and the hope, in spite of its anachronisms and powerlessness. Humanity is an inter-spatial concept embracing the present and coming generations. It represents "a conscience jump", but there is still the need to give it "legal and institutional form", apart from the fact that "we are seeking a future and a humanity still to be discovered", wrote René-Jean Dupuy (1986, p. 159, 177). Postulating that the

[59] Mégret (2010) remarks: "Another way of putting it would be to say that becoming a party to a human rights treaty is declaratory of states' obligations rather than constitutive of them" (p. 129).

[60] Denmark, Norway, Sweden and Netherlands acted this way when, in 1967, each addressed a communication against Greece to the European Commission of Human Rights (*The Greek Case*).

human nature is not a given but rather a becoming, Humanity is an ethical-legal category moving towards the *Possible*...

References

Agi, M. 1980. *De l'idée d'universalité comme fondatrice du concept des Droits de l'Homme d'après la vie et l'œuvre de René Cassin*. Antibes: Éditions Alp'Azur.

Álvarez, A. 1947. *Méthodes de la codification du Droit international public (État actuel de ce droit). In Annuaire de l'Institut de Droit International—Session de Lausanne, Août*, 38–71. Bruxelles: Ad. Goemaere.

Álvarez, A. 1959. *Le droit international nouveau dans ses rapports avec la vie actuelle des peuples*. Paris: Éditions Pedone.

Barile, G. 1987. *The protection of human rights in article 60, paragraph 5 of the Vienna Convention of the law of treaties. In Le Droit international à l'heure de sa codification—Études en l'honneur de Roberto Ago/Il Diritto internazionale al tempo della sua codificazione—Studi in onore di Roberto Ago/International law at the time of its codification—Essays in honour of Roberto Ago, II*, 3–14. Milano: Dott. A. Giuffre Editore.

Becet, J.-M., and D. Colard. 1982. *Les droits de l'homme—I Dimensions nationales et internationales*. Paris: Economica.

Beetham, D., and K. Boyle. 1995. *Introducing democracy: 80 questions and answers*. Oxford: Polity Press/UNESCO.

Birmingham, P. 2006. *Hannah Arendt and human rights—The predicament of common responsibility*. Bloomington: Indiana University Press.

Buquicchio, G. 2006. Introductory address. In *The status of international treaties on human rights*, ed AAVV, 7–9. Strasbourg: Council of Europe Publishing, Venice Commission.

Burgers, J. 1992. The road to San Francisco: The revival of the human rights idea in the twentieth century. *Human Rights Quarterly* 14 (4): 447–477. http://humanrightsinitiative.ucdavis.edu/files/2012/10/burgerroadtosf.pdf. Accessed July 2013.

Campbell, T. 2006. *Rights—A critical introduction*. London: Routledge.

Cassese, A. 1991. La valeur actuelle des droits de l'homme. In *Humanité et Droit International—Mélanges René-Jean Dupuy*, ed. AAVV, 65–75. Paris: Éditions A. Pedone.

Cassin, R. 1951. La Déclaration universelle et la mise en œuvre des droits de l'homme. In *Recueil des Cours—1951, II, Tome 79 de la Collection*, ed. Académie de droit international, 237–367. Paris: Librairie du Recueil Sirey.

Cassin, R. 1967. Vingt ans après la Déclaration universelle—'Liberté et égalité'. Revue de la Commission Internationale des Juristes (*Numéro spécial: 1968—Année internationale des droits de l'homme, Première partie*), Tome VIII, N°2, décembre, 1–17.

Chesterman, S. 2008. An international rule of law? *American Journal of Comparative Law* 56 (2): 331–362. http://papers.ssrn.com/sol3/papers.cfm?abstract_id=1081738. Accessed July 2013.

Chevallier, J. 1994. *L'État de droit* (2e éd.). Paris: Montchrestien.

Chinkin, Ch. 2010. Sources. In *International human rights law*, ed D. Moeckli, S. Shah, and S. Sivakumaran, 103–124. Oxford: Oxford University Press.

Conseil de l'Europe. 1991. *Feuille d'information n° 27 (mai 1990-6 novembre 1990)*. Strasbourg: Droits de l'homme.

Conseil de l'Europe. 1993. *Les rapports entre le droit international et le droit interne—Actes du Séminaire UniDem organisé à Varsovie du 19 au 21 mai 1993 en coopération avec l'Université de Wroclaw et le Centre des droits de l'homme de Poznan et avec le soutien du Programme Phare des Communautés Européennes*. Strasbourg: Commission européenne pour la démocratie par le droit.
Now in print: Conseil de l'Europe. 1993. Les rapports entre le droit international et le droit interne (Actes, Varsovie, 19–21 mai 1993) (Science et technique de la démocratie n° 5).

Coskun, D. 2007. *Law as symbolic form—Ernst Cassirer and the anthropocentric view of law*. Vol 82. Dordrecht: Springer, Law and Philosophy Library. www.international-ul.com/pdf/ebook/ebooksclub.org__Law_as_Symbolic_Form__Ernst_Cassirer_and_the_anthropocentric_view_of_law__Law_and_Philosophy_Library_.pdf. Accessed July 2013.

Delmas-Marty, M. 1996. *Vers un droit commun de l'humanité—Entretien avec Philippe Petit*. Paris: Les Éditions Textuel.

Delpérée, F. 1987. Avant-Propos/Les formes de participation des citoyens au fonctionnement de l'État. In *Le nouveau Droit constitutionnel—apports belges au IIe Congrès mondial de droit constitutionnel, Paris—Aix-en-Provence, 31 août—5 septembre 1987*, ed. AAVV, 5–6 et 173–186. Louvain-la-Neuve/Bruxelles: Centre Interuniversitaire de Droit public, A.S.B.L., Academia, Édition et Diffusion/Bruylant.

Denquin, J.-M. 2008. Démocratie. In *Dictionnaire des Droits de l'Homme*, ed Joël Andriantsimbazovina et al. (Sous la direction de), 262–267. Paris: PUF.

Dord, O. 2008. Droits fondamentaux. In *Dictionnaire des Droits de l'Homme*, ed J. Andriantsimbazovina et al. (Sous la direction de), 332–336. Paris: PUF.

Dupuy, P.-M. 2008. Jus cogens. In *Dictionnaire des Droits de l'Homme*, ed Joël Andriantsimbazovina et al. (Sous la direction de), 566–570. Paris: PUF.

Dupuy, R.-J. 1986. *La communauté internationale entre le mythe et l'histoire*. Paris: Economica/UNESCO.

Elster, J. 1993. Mehrheitsprinzip und individualrechte. In *Die Idee der Menschenrechte* (Aus dem Englischen von Michael Bischoff), ed. S. Shute & S. Hurlery, 207–253. Frankfurt a. M.: Fischer Taschenbuch Verlag GmbH (1996).

Espiell, H. 1985. *Estudios sobre Derechos Humanos I. San José*. Costa Rica: Instituto Interamericano de Derechos Humanos/Caracas: Editorial Jurídica Venezolana.

European Commission for Democracy through Law (Venice Commission). 2011. *Report on the Rule of Law* (CDL-AD (2011) 003 rev).

Humphrey, J. 1984. *Human rights and the United Nations—A great adventure*. New York: Transnational Publishers.

Humphrey, J. 1987. Preface. In *Guide to the "Travaux Préparatoires" of the International Covenant on Civil and Political Rights*, ed. Marc J. Bossuyt, XV–XVI. Dordrecht: Martinus Nijhoff Publishers.

Kiss, A.-Ch. 2006. International human rights treaties: A special category of international treaty? In *The status of international treaties on human rights*, ed AAVV, 11–29. Strasbourg: Council of Europe Publishing, Venice Commission.

Koji, T. 2001. Emerging hierarchy in international human rights and beyond: From the perspective of non-derogable rights. EJIL. 12(5): 917–941. www.ejil.org/pdfs/12/5/1555.pdf. Accessed Sept 2013.

Langlois, A. 2003. Human rights without democracy? A critique of the separationist thesis. *Human Rights Quartely* 25:990–1019.

Lauren, P. 1998. *The evolution of international human rights—Visions seen*. Philadelphia: University of Pennsylvania Press.

Lauterpacht, H. 1948. The international protection of human rights. In *Recueil des Cours—1947, I—Tome 70 de la Collection*, ed. Académie de Droit International, 5–108. Paris: Recueil Sirey.

Maes, E. 2008. Constitutional democracy, constitutional interpretation and conflicting rights. In *Conflicts between fundamental rights*, ed. E. Brems, 69–89. Antwerp: Intersentia.

Mayerfeld, J. 2009. The democratic legitimacy of international human rights law. *Indiana International and Comparative Law Review* 19:49–88. http://faculty.washington.edu/jasonm/Mayerfeld_Democratic_Legitimacy_of_International_Human_Rights_Law.pdf. Accessed July 2013.

Mégret, F. 2010. Nature of obligations. In *International human rights law*, ed D. Moeckli, S. Shah, and S. Sivakumaran, 124–149. Oxford: Oxford University Press.

Menke, Ch. and Pollmann, A. 2007. *Philosophie der Menschenrechte—Zur Einfürung*. Hamburg: Junius (2008).

Modinos, P. 1975. Dialogue avec les droits de l'homme/Introduction à l'étude des droits de l'homme/La Convention européenne des droits de l'homme—Ses origines, ses objectifs, ses réalisations. *Revue des droits de l'homme/Human rights journal—Droit international et Droit comparé/International and Comparative Law—25e Anniversaire de la Convention Européenne des Droits de l'Homme (4 Novembre 1950–4 Novembre)* VIII (N° Spécial), 631–636, 648–658, 689–716.

Morange, J. 1988. *La Déclaration des droits de l'homme et du citoyen*. 2e éd. Paris: PUF, Que sais-je? (1989).

Morsink, J. 1999. *The universal declaration of human rights: Origins, drafting, and intent*. Philadelphia: University of Pennsylvania Press.

Peerenboom, R. 2005. human rights and rule of law: What's the relationship? University of California, Los Angeles School of Law, Public Law and Legal Theory Research Paper Series, 05-31. http://papers.ssrn.com/sol3/papers.cfm?abstract_id=816024. Accessed July 2013.

Pinelli, C. 2006. International treaties and agreements making trade and foreign aids conditional on respect for human rights. In *The status of international treaties on human rights*, ed AAVV, 151–158. Strasbourg: Council of Europe Publishing, Venice Commission.

Ponton, L. 1990. *Philosophie et droits de l'homme de Kant à Levinas*. Paris: J. Vrin.

Quiroga, C. 2009. The Inter-American system for the protection of human rights. In *International protection of human rights: A textbook*, ed. C. Krause, and M. Scheinin, 475–501. Turku/Åbo: Åbo Akademi University, Institute for Human Rights.

Ramcharan, B. 2008. Contemporary human rights ideas. London: Routledge.

Robledo, A. 1982. Le jus cogens international: sa genèse, sa nature, ses fonctions. In *Recueil des Cours/Collected Courses of The Hague Academy of International Law—1981, III—Tome 172 de la collection*, ed. Académie de Droit International, 9–217. The Hague: Martinus Nijhoff Publishers.

Ruiz, J. 1979. *Las obligaciones erga omnes en Derecho Internacional Público. In Estudios de Derecho Internacional—Homenaje al Profesor Miaja de la Muela—I*, 219–233. Madrid: Editorial Tecnos.

Russell, B. 1938. *Power—A new social analysis*. London: Routledge.

Salmon, J. 2011. Quelle place pour l'État dans le Droit International d'aujourd'hui?. In *Recueil des Cours/Collected Courses of The Hague Academy of International Law—2010—Tome 347 de la Collection*, ed. Académie de Droit International. Leiden: Martinus Nijhoff Publishers.

Scheinin, M. 2006. Human rights treaties and the Vienna Convention on the Law of treaties: Conflict or harmony? In The status of international treaties on human rights, ed AAVV, 43–54. Strasbourg: Council of Europe Publishing, Venice Commission.

Scheinin, M. 2009a. Characteristics of human rights norms. In *International protection of human rights: A textbook*, ed. C. Krause, and M. Scheinin, 19–37. Turku/Åbo: Åbo Akademi University, Institute for Human Rights.

Shelton, D. 2006. Are there differentiations among human rights? Jus cogens, core human rights, obligations erga omnes and non-derogability. In *The status of internacional treaties on human rights*, ed AAVV, 159–186. Strasbourg: Council of Europe Publishing, Venice Commission.

Schutter, O. 2009a. The status of human rights in international law. In International protection of human rights: A textbook, ed. C. Krause, and M. Scheinin, 39–58. Turku/Åbo: Åbo Akademi University, Institute for Human Rights.

Sohn, L. 1982. The new international law: Protection of the rights of individuals rather than states. *American University Law Review* 32 (1): 1–64. www.wcl.american.edu/journal/lawrev/32/sohn.pdf. Accessed July 2013.

Sudre, F. 1990. *La Convention européenne des droits de l'homme*. Paris: PUF, 'Que sais-je?' - 2513.

Symonides, J., and V. Volodin ed. 2003. *A guide to human rights—Institutions, standards, procedures*. Paris: UNESCO.

Tomuschat, Ch. 2008. *Human rights—Between idealism and realism*. Oxford: Oxford University Press, Collected Courses of the Academy of European Law, XIII/1.

Tóth, J. 1972. Les droits de l'homme et la théorie du droit. In *René Cassin Amicorum Discipulorumque Liber—IV. Méthodologie des Droits de l'Homme*, ed. AAVV, 69–90. Paris: Éditions Pedone, Institut International des Droits de l'Homme, 'Jura Hominis ac Civis'.

Trindade, A. 2006. International law for humankind: Towards a new Jus Gentium—General Course on Public International Law. In *Recueil des Cours/Collected Courses of The Hague Academy of International Law—2005—Tome 316 de la Collection*, ed. Académie de Droit International. Leiden: Martinus Nijhoff Publishers.

United Nations War Crimes Commission. 1948. *History of the united nations war crimes commission and the development of the laws of war*. London: His Majesty's Stationery Office. www.cisd.soas.ac.uk/documents/un-war-crimes-project-history-of-the-unwcc,52439517,p2. Accessed Sept 2013.

Vallejo, J. 1990. Force et développement des droits de l'homme. *Bulletin des Droits de l'Homme—Mise en œuvre des instruments internationaux des droits de l'homme* 89/1:70–76.

Velu, J., and R. Ergec. 1990. *La Convention européenne des droits de l'homme*. Bruxelles: Bruylant.

Verdoodt, A. 1964. *Naissance et signification de la Déclaration universelle des droits de l'homme* (Préface de René Cassin). Louvain-Paris: Éditions Nauwelaerts.

Zemanek, K. 2009. Vienna Convention on the law of treaties. United Nations Audiovisual Library of International Law. http://untreaty.un.org/cod/avl/pdf/ha/vclt/vclt-e.pdf. Accessed July 2013.

Chapter 8
Answering Some Questions

Abstract Human rights have always been and remain a controversial matter. This chapter addresses and answers what are likely the most general and lasting criticisms of human rights. The answers are summarized in the following sentences:

1. Human rights have Western origins but have become universal ethical values.
2. Human rights are individualistic, by their very nature, but do not overlook the sociability of human beings.
3. The ethical universality and cultural diversity of human rights form an undeconstructible unity.
4. Human rights are an ideal and a struggle.

We should be realistic without being pessimistic. The Human Rights Revolution is an individual, collective, everyday and endless struggle…

8.1 Are Human Rights Cultural Fruits Whose Colors and Flavors are Exclusively Western?

When the UDHR was drafted, many peoples in Africa, Asia, and the Pacific and Caribbean regions were still not independent countries. According to an estimate of Philippe De La Chapelle, the UN membership at the time of the adoption of the UDHR was as follows: "North and South America with 21 countries represented 36% of the total, Europe with 16 countries 27%, Asia with 14 countries 24%, Africa with 4 countries a mere 6%, and the South Sea Islands with three countries 5%" (as cit. in Morsink 1999, p. 96)[1]. Anyway, together they represented four-fifths of the world's population. It is also true that the modern concept of 'human right' is impregnated with Western philosophical, legal and political thought. Again following "Philippe De La Chapelle's calculations, 37 of the member nations stood in the Judeo-Christian tradition, 11 in the Islamic, six in the Marxist, and four in the Buddhist tradition" (p. 21).

Human rights have hardly been addressed by Chinese thinkers in terms similar to those of the Modern Western Philosophy (the Chinese language lacked even a term equivalent to 'rights'). Nevertheless, the human rights sentiment is deeply rooted in Chinese wisdom, where the people's right to rebellion has long been acknowledged.

[1] See: www.un.org/depts/dhl/unms/founders.shtml

A. Reis Monteiro, *Ethics of Human Rights*, DOI 10.1007/978-3-319-03566-6_8,

That is why the term 'revolution' holds a positive connotation in Chinese political tradition. It connotes ideals which justified removing rulers. The people's will was deemed to be Heaven's Will. Mencius, the second great Confucianist thinker, said: "People are of primary importance. The State is of less importance. Sovereignty even less" (Lo 1948, p. 186).

The report of a Seminar on 'Human Rights in Islam' that took place in Kuwait, in 1980, affirmed: "Islam was the first to recognize basic human rights and almost fourteen centuries ago it set up guarantees and safeguards that have only recently been incorporated in universal declarations of human rights", as cit. by Heiner Bielefeldt (2009), who adds: "It is assumed in the report of the Kuwait seminar that it was via the influence of Islamic philosophy in the Middle Ages that Europe finally adopted the concept of human rights whose 'roots' supposedly lie in Islam" (p. 13).

The record of human rights violations in Western world was no less negative than that of the rest of world, before the end of the eighteenth century. Only then the human rights liberating power began to transform for better the fate of individuals and societies, in European countries and worldwide. Remarking that there was no pre-existing cultural predisposition for the idea of human dignity and rights in the Western world, Donnelly (2009) writes: "Rather, it arose from the fact that the dangers and indignities of modern economic, political, and social life happened to be first experienced there" in modern times, and not before (p. 80). He argues "that human rights are tied to social structure not culture—and that standard 'the West versus the Rest' formulations are therefore fundamentally misguided" (p. 13). After noting that "the West not only lacks a long and deeply embedded historic culture of human dignity and human rights, but for most of the past 2,500 years has actually rejected these ideas" (p. 44), he rightly concludes that "traditional Western societies, when it comes to dignity and rights, had much more in common with traditional Hindu and Chinese societies than with modern Western societies" (p. 49). The author highlights some facts and episodes of cruelty in early European modern times. One of them is described as follows:

> Consider the case of Gyorgy Dozsa. In 1514 he was appointed military leader of a new Crusade that had been authorized by Pope Leo X against the Ottomans. Dozsa assembled a rag-tag army of 50,000 men or more, drawn largely from the lower ranks of society. This provoked considerable fear among the Hungarian authorities, who managed to get the papal bull authorizing the crusade rescinded. But when the army refused the call of the Hungarian king to disband, they were violently repressed. Dozsa was executed in a particularly gruesome fashion. He "was compelled to sit on a red-hot 'throne' and a burning 'crown' was place on his head. His closest followers, who had been starved for twelve days, were then forced under penalty of death to bite into his burning body and to drink his flowing blood. (p. 37)

Criminal Law continued to be as atrocious as illustrated by the *Affaire Calas* in France in the eighteenth century (see Sect. 3.2), and the popular sensibility followed. Hunt (2008) informs: "Reporting on a hanging in the winter of 1776, the *Morning Post* of London complained that the 'remorseless multitude behaved with the most inhuman indecency—shouting, laughing, throwing snowballs at each other, particularly at those few who had a proper compassion for the misfortunes of their fellow creatures" (p. 95).

Locke, the author of the famous *A Letter Concerning Toleration* (1689), did not challenge slavery, which throve with the colonial imperialism. Jefferson was a slave-owner. In France, slavery remained unchanged in spite of the Revolution. It was abolished only in 1848 as "an affront to human dignity" (Decree of April 27)[2], decades after the Vienna Peace Conference had adopted a Declaration on the Abolition of the Slave Trade, on 8 February 1815. In the USA, negro slaves were excluded from voting, and were counted a only three-fifths of a person for representational purposes. Even women conquered their right to vote, in several Western countries, very late in the twentieth century.

In sum: Europe was the ground of the modern idea of human rights as it was the continent of Crusades, Inquisition, Colonialism, Stalinism, Hitlerism. Krsysztof Drzewicki (2009) put it this way:

> Throughout history, Europe has demonstrated its Janus-faced identity. This may be safely suggested because Europe is known both for its great achievements and its tragic, man-made disasters. One face shows what Europe has contributed to world civilization as birthplace of Roman law, Christianity, industrial revolution, liberal democracy, the rule of law and human rights. Another face, however, reminds one of a Europe deeply infected with the syndromes of colonialism, Communism and Nazism, which have proved to be the greatest enemies of humanity as a whole. (p. 365)

Consequently: "The important division with respect to human rights and human dignity is 'modern' versus 'traditional' or 'pre-modern', not Western versus non-Western, societies. Social structure rather than culture is central to ideas and practices of human rights and human dignity largely irrespective of time, place, and culture" (Donnelly 2009, p. 44). Referring to the universality of human rights, Donnelly writes: "Common responses to common problems have indeed helped to foster what many people today refer to as an emerging global human rights culture". That is why "people across the globe have and continue to come to the idea of human dignity and the practice of human rights from a great variety of cultural traditions and philosophical and religious foundations" (p. 81). The wide support to the UDHR from the major religious traditions of the world was documented by Robert Traer *Faith in Human Rights* (1991) (see Morsink 1999, p. 374, note 8).

The following quotations from the drafting of the UDHR recall how debated it was, as well as its plural origins[3].

At the ECOSOC's 215th meeting, on 25 August 1948 (E/SR.215), the Turkish representative (Eren) affirmed that:

> The Declaration included all the principles which had ennobled man since the time of Plato, and for the first time brought them together on an international plane. It was encouraging to reflect that after two world wars men of all creeds and climes had been able to devise a common standard of rights for all mankind.

At the 90th meeting of the UN General Assembly Third Committee, on 1 October (A/C.3/SR.90), the Colombian representative (Augusto Ramírez Moreno) said that:

---

[2] http://abolitions.free.fr/spip.php?article50

[3] It is recalled that the Documents related to the history of the UDHR drafting quoted in this study are available at: www.un.org/depts/dhl/udhr.

"The Declaration expressed the same love of humankind that had moved all great political thinkers since Plato".

According to the record of the Third Committee 91st meeting, on 2 October (A/C.3/SR.91), the Saudi Arabian representative (Jamil M. Baroody):

> ...briefly called attention to the fact that the Declaration was based largely on Western patterns of culture, which were frequently at variance with the patterns of culture of Eastern States. That did not mean, however, that the Declaration went counter to the latter, even if it did not conform to them.

The Chinese representative (Peng-chun Chang) significantly remarked:

> In the eighteenth century, when progressive ideas with respect to human rights had been first put forward in Europe, translations of Chinese philosophers had been known to and had inspired such thinkers as Voltaire, Quesnay and Diderot in their humanistic revolt against feudalistic conceptions. Chinese ideas had been intermingled with European thought and sentiment on human rights at the time when that subject had been first speculated upon in modern Europe.

At the General Assembly 183th plenary meeting, on 10 December (A/PV.183), the Ecuadoran representative (Jorge Carrera Andrade) stated:

> From the ruins of the destruction brought by the Second World War, man had once again fanned the immortal flame of civilization, freedom, and law. The multiplicity of origins of human rights could be detected in reading the articles of the Declaration.

The Syrian representative (Abdul Rahman Kayaly) said that:

> ...civilization had progressed slowly, through centuries of persecution and tyranny, until, finally, the present Declaration had been drawn up. It was not the work of a few representatives in the Assembly or in the Economic and Social Council; it was the achievement of generations of human beings who worked towards that end.

In this respect, UNESCO's worldwide consultation, in 1947, should also be borne in mind.

The contribution of Latin America, in particular, to the internationalization and scope of human rights deserves to be highlighted. According to Carozza (2003):

> Latin American contributions to the formal birth of international human rights law in 1948 were the reflection of a long and deep tradition of the idea of human rights in the region, one that was as old as the turbulent encounter between Europe and the New World. [...] When this heritage met the economic and political transformations of the 20th century, the tradition aimed again at synthetizing the individualistic with the social and economic dimensions of human dignity. (p. 311, 312)

At the San Francisco Conference (1945), "Latin American countries represented the largest single regional group, accounting for twenty-one of the fifty nations" (p. 204). While several countries in the continent were not very democratic, at the time, they represented, in spite of the European influence, its cultural kaleidoscopic. They struggled to have a Declaration of Rights included in the UN Charter. Ricardo Alfaro had persuaded the Inter-American Conference on Problems of War and Peace, meeting in Mexico City in February-March 1945, to request the Inter-American Juridical Committee to prepare a draft Declaration of the International Rights and Duties of Man. The American Declaration of the Rights and Duties of

Man was adopted on 2 May 1948 by the Ninth International Conference of American States (Bogota, Colombia), about 7 months before the UDHR, having influenced its drafting.

The Latin American representatives in the drafting process of the UN Charter and of the UDHR were not mere useful echoes of the Western powers. "Latin American nations provided strong examples of constitutionalized individual rights long before the countries of Europe", such as the 1812 Constitution of the Republic of Colombia (p. 302). Article 123 of the 1917 Mexican Constitution included social and economic provisions that "were the first of their kind in any constitutional document" (p. 304). Another example of the Latin American humanist heritage and of its distinctive voice was that "several Latin American countries were the only non-Soviet-bloc delegations to support a failed proposal to include in the right to life a prohibition of capital punishment" (p. 287).

The UDHR was greatly influenced by the "great juridical tradition" of Latin America (Verdoodt 1964, p. 15). It links human dignity, liberty and equality, includes economic, social and cultural rights, recognizes the importance of the family and the protection of motherhood and childhood, recalls that rights imply duties, and admits legitimate restrictions to some rights. Glendon (2003) concluded:

> Indeed, Latin American diplomats, documents, and traditions had such a profound influence upon both the decision to include human rights protection among the purposes of the UN, and the content of the Universal Declaration, that it is fair to refer to Latin America as the forgotten crucible of the universal human rights idea.
> [...]
> In 1948, they helped to prevent the Universal Declaration from falling into the excesses of individualism or collectivism. Now that the UDHR has become the single most important point for discussion of human rights in international settings today, Latin America may once again help the human rights movement to realize the full promise of the Declaration's vision of human dignity. (p. 27, 39)

As a consequence of the plurality of the UDHR sources, the drafting process required numerous meetings, as well as the discussion and vote of lots of amendment proposals. According to Verdoodt, each Article of the Declaration was amended "on average ten times" (Verdoodt 1964, p. 10)[4].

At ECOSOC's 218th meeting on 26 August 1948 (E/SR.218), the Australian representative (Herbert V. Evatt) had observed that the CHR had taken into account twenty-four drafts and discussed approximately two hundred proposals. At the General Assembly's 180th plenary meeting, on 9 December (A/PV.180), the President of its Third Committee (Malik) recalled that it "had devoted 85 meetings to the discussion of the draft Declaration, in addition to 20 meetings held by various sub-committees", and that 1,000 speeches were made and 200 amendments submitted[5]. He further informed that 18 Articles of the draft Declaration "had been

[4] "Most articles in the declaration are like onions with layers of drafting around an original core" (Morsink 1999, p. 191).

[5] The *United Nations Yearbook* (1948) reports: "Altogether, the Third Committee spent eighty-one meetings in considering and discussing the draft Declaration prepared by the Commission on Human Rights. One hundred and sixty-eight formal draft resolutions containing amendments to

adopted without any opposition. Of a total of 1,233 individual votes, 88.08 % had been affirmative, 3.73 % negative and 8.19 % had been abstentions". Malik also recalled that the starting point of the drafting process was the Secretariat Outline of an International Bill of Human Rights (E/CN.4/AC.1/3). In his opinion:

> It could be said that the present Declaration had been drafted on a firm international basis, for the Secretariat's draft was a compilation not only of hundreds of proposals made by Governments and private persons, but also of the laws and legal findings of all the Member States of the United Nations.

Consequently: "Thousands of minds and hands have helped in its formation". Some of those which contributed a very significant input were not Western[6].

The price of the consensus achieved is reflected in the weaknesses of the text adopted: apart from the fact of what was not included, such as the rights of minorities[7] and the right to petition, some formulations are very generic, especially as the economic, social and cultural rights are concerned, using terms as vague as 'arbitrary', 'reasonable', and 'adequate'. The main division among the UN Member States regarding the conception of the UDHR was pointed out by the Bolivian representative (Eduardo Anze Matienzo) during the 182th plenary meeting of the General Assembly, on 10 December 1948 (A/PV.182) in these terms:

> Two opposing schools of thought had confronted each other in the discussion on that international moral code. There had been, on the one hand, the thesis upheld by the USSR, characterized by the desire to subordinate the individual to the State, and, on the other hand, the thesis supported by all the democratic countries, which was designed to make the individual capable of organizing a state, which, in turn, would respect the rights of the individual.

In effect, the criticism of the draft Declaration was voiced especially by the USSR Delegation and its allies, though other States also took issue with some aspects.

For example, according to the record of the ECOSOC's 215th meeting, on 25 August 1948 (E/SR.215), the USSR representative (Alexei P. Pavlov), after mentioning the "new rights related to work, leisure, education, social security, etc." as "the positive aspect of the Declaration", concluded that "the Declaration as a whole [...] was unsatisfactory". Its omissions and shortcomings included the following:

- The principle of non-discrimination should be reinforced.
- The implementation of rights should be guaranteed.
- Obligations should also be defined.
- The rights and sovereignty of States should be affirmed.
- Fascist and Nazi propaganda should be prohibited.

---

the various articles of the draft Declaration were submitted during the course of the Committee's debate" (p. 526).
(http://unyearbook.un.org/unyearbook.html?name=isysadvsearch.html).

[6] "Proponents of the cultural-imperialism critique sometimes say that the educational backgrounds or professional experiences of men like Chang and Malik 'westernized' them, but their performance in the Human Rights Commission suggest something rather different" (Glendon 2001, p. 225).

[7] Morsink (1999) pointed out "the greatest defect of the declaration, which is the omission of a separate article on the rights of members of minority religious, educational, and especially of ethnic or cultural minority groups" (p. 241).

- It was not sufficient to mention democracy only once.

In sum: "The Soviet Union delegation was certain that instead of the weak and, in many ways, absolutely unsatisfactory draft before the Council, a Declaration would eventually be drawn up which would effectively serve the cause of historical progress and democracy"[8].

During the same meeting, the Polish representative (Juliusz Katz-Suchy) affirmed:

> It was not sufficient to say that human rights had been violated during the war. It should be emphasized that violation of human rights and contempt of human dignity lay at the very roots of fascist ideology. The Declaration must condemn fascism first of all, and then make it impossible for fascism to rise again.
> In its present form, the Declaration made no reference to democracy; he felt that the Commission on Human Rights had purposely omitted that word. [...] His delegation could not understand, therefore, why the Declaration contained no reference to democracy and to the eradication of fascism.
> [...]
> The fact that human rights involved the duties of the individual towards his neighbor, his family, his nation and society was not clearly stated in the Declaration. [...] A Declaration of Human Rights should strike a balance between the rights and the duties of an individual, and he considered that the document before the Council was no more than a compilation of traditional human rights and freedoms of the old liberal school of thought.

At the Third Committee's 92th meeting in Paris, on 2 October (A/C.3/SR.92), Pavlov "drew the Committee's attention to the opinion of his delegation, expressed in the report of the Commission on Human Rights (E/800)", and said that: "The USSR delegation felt that the draft Declaration could not contribute to democratic progress, nor could it prevent the reappearance of fascism or help to strengthen world peace. His delegation therefore reserved the right to put forward numerous amendments".

At the General Assembly's 181th plenary meeting on 10 December (A/PV.181), the Czechoslovakian representative (Zdenek Augenthaler) "regretted to have to state that the proclamation of the Universal Declaration of Human Rights would not be the splendid event, acclaimed by the masses and immortalized by history, as might have been expected". It was not imbued with "revolutionary spirit", and "was neither bold nor modern".

At the 183th plenary meeting, on the same day (A/PV.183), the USSR representative (Andrei Y. Vyshinsky) resumed the main objection of his Government, namely: The draft Declaration did not take into due account "the sovereign rights of democratic Governments". In effect, "human rights could not be conceived outside the State; the very concept of right and law was connected with that of the State. Human rights meant nothing unless they were guaranteed and protected by the State; otherwise they became a mere abstraction, an empty illusion easily created but just

[8] Verdoodt (1964) observed that the USSR representative "wanted to be introduced into almost all the Articles of the Declaration a repeated amendment: 'in accordance with the national legislation'. For him, it was a guarantee of implementation. For his colleagues, however, it was a dangerous limitation" (p. 66).

as easily dispelled". Regarding "the problem of the State and the individual, in its historical sense", he affirmed that, in his country, the problem was already solved. "The State and the individual were in harmony with each other; their interests coincided". A USSR resolution proposing amendments that had been already submitted to the CHR and to the General Assembly Third Committee—especially in the 'Statement made by the Delegation of the Union of Soviet Socialist Republics, on 18 June 1948, in the Commission on Human Rights on the Results of the Commission's Work', annexed to the Report of its third session (E/800, 28 June 1948)—was rejected by 45 votes to 6 with 3 abstentions.

Anyway:

> The fact was that *all* of the major powers were fiercely protective of their sovereignty, and Britain of its colonial empire.
> Washington and London may not have seen entirely displeased at Soviet obstructionism in the Human Rights Commission. As historian Brian Simpson has demonstrated, the Foreign Office viewed human rights as basically for export and as a weapon to be used against the Soviet Union. (Glendon 2001, p. 87)[9]

In effect, no country could claim an entirely honorable record concerning human rights. If the USSR was exposed to charges regarding freedoms, the USA could be charged with racial discrimination and the UK with the colonial problem. Hence the *name-calling* between the great powers during the debates, in spite of the CHR's "unritten rule that delegates were not supposed to refer to 'violations' in various countries" (Morsink 1999, p. 32). For instance, at the ECOSOC's 218th meeting on 26 August 1948 (E/SR.218), the UK representative (H. M. Phillips) said that 'democracy' was a word that "had depreciated in value, [...] had become a catchphrase, [...and] was subject to many different interpretations"; and "the word 'fascism' had also lost its value. Indeed, a responsible representative at the General Assembly had called one of the UK Prime Ministers [Winston Churchill], whom he had just quoted, a fascist". It had been the USSR representative (Alexei P. Pavlov) who also compared the UK representative (Christopher Mayhew) to Goebbels. At the Third Committee's 93th meeting on 4 October (A/C.3/SR.93), the UK representative (Hector McNeil) added: "Everyone realized that by 'democracy' the communists meant 'people's democracy', which was nothing more than the communist oppression of the people". This prompted the Yugoslavian representative (Vlado Bakaric) to remark: "The representatives of certain countries had, however, taken advantage of the discussions on the draft declaration to give way to a propaganda campaign against another group of countries, and particularly against the USSR". At the 182st plenary meeting of the General Assembly, on 10 December (A/PV.182), the Canadian representative (L. B. Pearson) said that: "The term 'fascism',

[9] "The Soviet delegation could not accept any of the group's proposals [on implementation] since they constituted 'an attempted gross infringement' of the UN Charter's protection of every state's domestic jurisdiction. [...] The arguments made by the Soviet bloc concerning implementation were not too different from those that would be made by the United States when the balance of voting power shifted in the UN in the 1950s—and again in 1998, when the United States was one of the few dissenters from the vote to establish an International Criminal Court" (Glendon 2001, p. 95, 96).

which once had a definite and dreadful meaning in the dictionary of despotism, was now being blurred by the abuse of applying it to any person or idea which was not communist".

Further criticism of the draft UDHR came from other Delegations.

For example, at the ECOSOC's 215th meeting on 25 August (E/SR.215), the Danish representative (Max Soerensen) said that "it was unsatisfactory that a Declaration intended to be a guide for world public opinion should not expressly state the rights of minorities". This remark was repeated during the debates in the Third Committee. According to the record of the Third Committee's 90th meeting on 1 October (A/C.3/SR.90), the representative of the Union of South Africa (E. H. Louw) affirmed that its Delegation "could not possibly accept the thesis that human dignity would be impaired if a person were told he could not reside in a particular area. [...] It would be a tragedy if human rights became a *cliché* or developed into a political slogan". At the General Assembly 183th plenary meeting, on 10 December (A/PV.183), the Egyptian representative (Wahid Fikry Raafat) formulated reservations with regard to the provisions on freedom to contract marriage and on freedom of thought, conscience and religion. "His delegation feared that by proclaiming man's freedom to change his religion or belief the Declaration would be encouraging, even though it might not be intentional, the machinations of certain missions, well known in the Orient, which relentlessly pursued their efforts to convert to their own beliefs the masses of the population of the Orient".

Considering that the draft UDHR could be perfected, the Delegations from Czechoslovakia, Poland, Ukraine, and the USSR proposed the postponement of its adoption to the fourth session of the General Assembly (1949). Some other Delegations were of the same opinion. Conversely, in the General Assembly's 180th plenary meeting, on 10 December (A/PV.180), the Philippines representative (Carlos P. Rómulo) affirmed that: "The document certainly could make no claims to perfection since it had been the result of a compromise. At the same time, compromise was the essence of democracy and the very basis of the United Nations". In the General Assembly's 181th plenary meeting (A/PV.181), the Brazilian representative (Belarmino Austregésilo de Athayde) observed that:

> The draft Declaration did not reflect the particular point of view of any one people or of any one group of peoples. Neither was it the expression of any particular political doctrine or philosophical system. It was the result of the intellectual and moral cooperation of a large number of nations; that explained its value and interest and also conferred upon it great moral authority.

Another *a contrario sensu* (in the contrary or opposite sense) illustration of the universal character of the UDHR came from the President of the American Bar Association (Frank E. Holman), who in January 1949 said that the Declaration was a manifesto that would "promote state socialism, if not communism, throughout the world", noting that the CHR had included only three members from "English-speaking countries" (as cit. in Glendon 2001, p. 193). In the early months of 1950, the anti-communist crusade of the Republican Senator Joseph McCarthy rose to power. Furthermore:

> Shortly after Eisenhower's inauguration in January 1953, the new secretary of State, John Foster Dulles, announced a major shift in policy: the United States would no longer partici-

> pate actively in the Human Rights Commission's work on a binding Convention and would not become a party to any such Covenant. [...] With U.S. troops in Korea, the Soviet Union in possession of 'the Bomb', and McCarthyism aggravating a climate of fear, the country was in no mood to think internationally. [...]
> The Eisenhower administration took a dim view of economic and social rights and invoked the principle of national sovereignty to oppose binding Covenants, including the 1948 Genocide Convention [...]. The United States did not ratify that widely accepted treaty until 1988, when the Reagan State Department realized its value in the propaganda war against communism. (p. 205, 207)

In such an international political context, "the proclamation of the Declaration in 1948 was really something of a miracle"—Malik wrote in September 1952 in the *U.N. Weekly Bulletin* (p. 208). Humphrey (1984) observed too: "It was something of a miracle that the great General Assembly debate on the Declaration took place in 1948" (p. 66). Had the debate been delayed, it could have gone lost through the Cold War winds. In effect, on 5 March 1946, at Westminster College in the small town of Fulton, Missouri, Winston Churchill delivered the famous 'Iron Curtain' speech to a crowd of 40,000 people. He said: "From Stettin in the Baltic to Trieste in the Adriatic, an iron curtain has descended across the Continent"[10]. During the spring of 1948, "many expected war to break out between the two superpowers" (Glendon 2001, p. 99), so that "it was now or never for the Declaration" (p. 132). Anyway: "All through the cold war, the United States and the USSR traded charges of human rights violations while overlooking their own failures and those of their client states" (p. 214).

As the drafting of the 1948 UDHR documents, human rights could no long be considered merely Western creatures, nor was there a monolithic Western understanding of human rights. Cases in point are the death penalty (that remains a penal sanction in most USA States and other States) and abortion (that is object of diverging legal approaches worldwide). The Chilean representative (Hernan Santa Cruz) testified during the Third Committee 91th meeting, on 2 October (A/C.3/SR.91):

> Tremendous difficulties had been involved in preparing a Declaration of human rights which would meet the frequently divergent views of fifty-eight States. It had been necessary to reconcile the different ideologies of the Soviet Union and other Eastern European countries and of the other Members of the United Nations; the difference between the economic and social rights recognized by Christian Western civilization and those recognized by the Oriental civilization; the varying legal systems of Latin and Anglo-Saxon countries.

The UDHR is an alchemy of religious, philosophical and political values that became an ethical-legal lighthouse and a liberation flag. Its worldwide acceptance and influence have conferred to much of its content the statute of International Customary Law and the character of *jus cogens*. From it are born new and legal binding and non-binding instruments that today form the IHRL. The 1966 International Covenants were prepared and adopted by a UN General Assembly where developing countries, recently liberated from colonial powers, had already gained the majority. The core human rights treaties have been adhered to by an increasingly larger International Community. At present, all UN Member States have ratified one of them,

[10] www.history.com/this-day-in-history/churchill-delivers-iron-curtain-speech

and more than 80 % have ratified four or more. Two legal instruments are virtually universal: the UN Charter (1945) and the CRC (1989).

In any case, every UN State Member is bound by the principle of respect and protection of human rights, even States not parties in any human rights treaty. This was just reiterated by Cassin (1951) at The Hague Academy of International Law: "The San Francisco Charter constitutes the basis of the legal obligation of the Member States of the United Nations to the respect and progress of the fundamental human rights and freedoms" (p. 245). Moreover, as Åkermark (2009) stresses: "Customary law, general principles of international law and *jus cogens* apply to all subjects of the international community" (p. 347). The UN's universal system of human rights protection expanded and has been strengthened; regional systems of human rights protection were established in Europe, the Americas and Africa.

Summing up: Does the universality quarrel still hold any legitimacy? The IHRL is sufficiently flexible to be compatible with legitimate cultural diversities.

At the end of the day, as Bielefeldt (2009) rightly points out: "More important than the cultural 'territory' on which human rights were first publicly declared is the *common experience of injustice* to which human rights give a specifically post-traditional political response. From this perspective, human rights are relevant for people living in other cultural contexts, too, whenever they struggle for justice" (p. 15). In other words, at the end of the day, what should matter is not where the moral, artistic, scientific, technological or other advancements come from, but how good and beneficial they are to the whole of Humankind. "As Jacques Maritain put it, many different kinds of music could be played on the document's thirty strings", the UDHR's 30 Articles (Glendon 2001, p. 230).

8.2 Are Human Rights Individualistic, Neglecting the Corresponding Duties to Others and Community?

The individualism objection, also known as communitarian critique, focuses on the allegedly excessive liberalism of the individual freedoms.

> The first theme of the communitarian critique is that liberal individualism is based on an unreal abstraction: the idea of the autonomous individual with an existence independent of all social relationships. The second theme of the communitarian critique is that abstract individualism encourages the values of individual autonomy over those of community well-being, thus endorsing selfishness and anti-social behavior. (Campbell 2006, p. 12)

This kind of criticism arose already during the drafting of the UDHR. For instance, according to the record of the UN General Assembly 183th plenary meeting on 10 December 1948 (A/PV.183), the day of its proclamation, the Yugoslavian representative (Milivoje Radovanovic) said:

> The text before the Assembly was based on individualistic concepts which considered man as an isolated individual having rights only as an individual, independently of the social conditions in which he was living and of all the forces which acted upon his social status. [...]

> The Declaration was, in certain respects, not based on reality, because it described man as an isolated individual and overlooked the fact that he was also a member of a community.

Sociologically, *individualism* is the opposite of *holism*. These are two categories used by Louis Dumont to explain the emergence of the modern Western ideology.

In Dumont's (1983) opinion, the term *individual* means "two things at the same time: an object outside of ourselves and a value" (p. 37). That is, each human being is at the same time a concrete, situated *empirical subject*, and a *moral being*, possessing a value above his or her belongings and circumstances. "From this point of view, there are two types of societies. Where the Individual is the supreme value, that is *individualism*; in the opposite case, where value lies in society as a whole, that is *holism*" (p. 11). There are, therefore, "two kinds of sociologies, as their start point and global procedure" (p. 12) are concerned: If one starts from individuals to the society, that is named methodological individualism; when one starts from society to the individuals, that is named methodological holism. As a consequence, there are two main types of political theories too: those (ancient and some modern) where the Whole (social) prevails over all (individuals) and those (modern) where the Individual is the central value.

The most ancient model of organization of the human communities is holistic. It consecrates the primacy of the soil, blood and cultural ties over individual autonomy. Each one is no more than a fragment of the Whole—the We—the organic community. He or she does not exist otherwise than by belonging to the group. The individual is then *absent*, and *deviation* is intolerable. Exclusion or death is the extreme sanction. This was the sole social paradigm known until the fourth century BC, and the sole legitimate paradigm until the beginning of modern times.

Defining ideology as "a system of ideas and values common in a given social environment" (p. 20), Dumont saw the epistemological difference of modern ideology in the recognition of the Individual as supreme value. Modern individualism appears as "a phenomenon exceptional in the history of civilizations" (p. 35); its genesis and development are controversial, however. In his view, the problem:

> ...consists in knowing how, from the general type of holistic societies, a new type could develop that fundamentally contradicted the common conception. How could this transition have been possible, how can we conceive of a transition between these two opposite universes, these two irreconcilable ideologies? (p. 37)

The case of India suggested to him the following hypothesis:

> Since more than two thousand years, Indian society is characterized by two complementary traits: society imposes to each one a close interdependence that replaces the individual as we know it with constringent relations, but the institution of renunciation of the world allows the full independence of whoever chooses that way. [...]
> The renouncer is self-sufficient, cares only about himself. His thinking is similar to that of the modern individual, except for one essential difference: we live in the social world, he lives outside it. That is why I called the Indian renouncer "individual-outside-the-world". By comparison, we are 'individual-in-the-world' [...].
> What is precious for us, in all that, is that Indian development is easy to understand and seems indeed 'natural'. Starting from it, we may formulate the following hypothesis: if the individualism appears in a society of traditional, holistic type, it shall happen in opposition to society and as a kind of supplement in relation to it, that is, under the form of an

> individual-outside-the-world. May we think that the individualism began like that in the Western world? That is what I'm trying to show. (p. 37, 38, 39)

In Dumont's opinion, the emergence of individualism in the Western world begins with philosophical thinking. In effect:

> ... the philosophical activity, the constant exercise of rational endeavor by generations of thinkers, on itself, should have fed individualism, as reason, if it is universal in principle, works, in practice, through the particular person exercising it, and prevails over all things, at least implicitly. (p. 41)

The transition between Plato's and Aristotle's times, on the one hand, and the Epicurean, Cynic and Stoic schools, in the Hellenistic period, on the other hand, "shows a gap" caused by the sudden emergence of individualism" (p. 39, 40) in the proclamation of the self-sufficiency ideal of the individual and of the renunciation of the world as principle of the true wisdom. It is possible that this philosophical individualism has been "directly or indirectly influenced by the Indian type of renouncer" (p. 42). In addition, "we find in the founder of *Stoa*, three centuries before Christ, the principle of all later development. For Zenon of Citium—rather a prophet than a philosopher, following Edwyn Bevan—the Good is that which makes man independent from all external circumstances. The sole Good is inner in man" (p. 48).

According to Dumont, the Christian conception of the human being is not different from that of the Indian sociological type: "as Tröltsch said, *man is an individual-in-relation-to-God*, what means, for our ends, an individual essentially outside-the-world" (p. 45). This "extra-mundane encompasses recognition and obedience regarding this world's powers", as two concentric circles. In this configuration, "the primary reference, the fundamental definition, encompasses the mundane life as its antithesis, where the individualism-outside-the-world subordinates the normal holism of the social life", so that "the individual-outside-the-world became the modern individual-in-the-world" (p. 46). This means that "something of modern individualism is present in the first Christian people and their surrounding world, but is not the individualism familiar to us. In fact, the old and the new forms are separated by a so radical and so complex transformation that it nothing less than seventeen centuries of Christian history was needed to achieve it and it continues maybe even in our days" (p. 36).

To prove his hypothesis, Dumont studied "the Church of the first centuries, with an extrapolation over the Reform" (p. 27), especially Calvin's "revolution" (p. 80), in order to show how Christian people were increasingly involved in world's activities. In his opinion, the mundane element antagonistic to Christian individualism "completely disappears in Calvin's theocracy. The field is completely unified. *The individual is now in the world and the individualistic value reigns without restriction or limitation*. In front of us is the individual-in-the-world" (p. 73). He concluded that "individualism could not have developed otherwise, to appear another way, from the traditional holism" (p. 70). Consequently, "the *pedigree* of the modern individualism is, let us say, double: an origin or accession of a given kind, *and* a slow transformation into another one" (p. 36). The author traced this transformation following the emancipation of the *economic* category, since the seventeenth century, and the emancipation of the *political* category, since the eighteenth century.

Therefore, in the primitive social groups (clan, tribe, city, etc.), individuals were entirely absorbed by the group. Jean P. Resweber (1989) recalled that, "according to Benveniste, the Indo-European root of the term '*subject*' expresses the to-be-in-relation-to-relatives and so the being as institution. The Kardiner's notion of basic personality points to that determination, without doubt, which, in spite of its imprecision, covers the socio-cultural instituting of the subject" (p. 40). It is not then surprising that the first alphabetical languages are unaware of the words 'man', 'individual', 'person'.

Although the silhouette of the 'individual' already becomes philosophically identifiable in the history of the Greek-Latin culture, *individuum* is a term that appears only in the fourteenth century, during the European Renaissance, when an individualistic ideology asserts itself and expands, in opposition to the old holistic ideology. Bloch (1972) wrote an impressive fresco of the historical-cultural irruption of the modern individualism.

> It was in Italy that the economic constraints of the feudal epoch were, for the first time, pushed back; it was in Italy that the renaissance took its start. It introduced two new facts: the consciousness of the individual as it developed from the individual capitalist economy in face of the closed market of the corporations; and the impression of immensity that replaced the image of the artificial and closed world of the feudal and theological society. [...]
> For economic reasons, the principles of that evolution are located in Italy. In this country, the pagan Antiquity, which had been repressed by the medieval society, still remained present enough and was still sufficiently lively in memories so that it could be possible to resume the pagan world's tradition, an essentially earthly world [...].
> The world is a pagan world again, man recovered his Greek dignity, gave up the penitent posture, lives no more on one's knees [...]. Here is man's dignity: He is not born finished, his existence evolves! (p. 5...15)

In fact, the veil of the collective identity began to be removed in the Italian Renaissance. Individualism's ferment was the *rinascita* (rediscovering) of the Greek-Latin culture. In the opinion of Jacob Burckhardt (1818–1897), in the Italian peninsula, in the fourteenth century, "nobody fears to be remarked, to be and to look different from the common people". Great figures of the *uomo singolare* and *universale* (singular and universal man) make their appearance, such as Dante Alighieri, who wrote: "My homeland is the whole world". The rupture was favored by the political situation. The tyrant's individuality emerged first. Frederick II (1194–1250) "is, with crown, the first modern man" (1860, p. 112, 114, 10).

Michel de Montaigne (1533–1592) is "the first of the great individualists", according to Alain Laurent (1993), and Shakespeare the first to put on the stage characters saying 'I' instead of 'We'. Christopher Columbus (about 1451–1506) is an exemplar figure of the rising of the individual. In Jacques Attali's opinion, 1492—the year of America's 'discovering'—"is the birth of the individual". Laurent summarized:

> From the Reform and the Renaissance onwards, the individualist paradigm began to take form culturally [...]. With the classical epoch, Western Europe is going, within less than two centuries, to move from an old holistic world—where the individual began, unconsciously and inwardly, to live and even to pave the way—towards a new world of which it becomes the figure and the institutional vault. A kind of 'Copernican revolution' liberates it from its traditional status as dependent member of the whole community, to install it at the

> center of a society that revolves around it, that recomposes itself starting from its autonomy and independence. […]
> This alchemical process of the inner power of self-determination and of the desire of external sovereignty leads to the full recognition of the individual as the full and unique expression of mankind. It finds expression in a semantic innovation decisive in the 17th century trend: the word 'individual' begins to be used to designate the human being, understood in its peculiarity and universality. (p. 27, 25, 28, 29)

Hunt (2008) agrees: "Over the long term of several centuries, individuals had begun to pull themselves away from the webs of community and had become increasingly independent agents both legally and psychologically" (p. 29).

The ideological weapons invented to secularize and individualize the foundations of societies and to oppose the popular sovereignty as principle of political legitimacy to the arbitrary 'divine' power of the kings were, as we saw, *naturalism* and *contractualism*—critical and liberating fictions, anti-religious and anti-feudal. Philosophers used the concepts of 'state of nature' and 'social contract' to answer, Dumont (1983) wrote, "to the main problem of the natural law theory: to establish the society or the ideal State on the isolation of the 'natural' individual" (p. 100). It was a matter of reconciling individual and authority, natural equality and social differences. The three great figures of the Social Contract Philosophies, in the seventeenth and eighteenth centuries, were Hobbes, Locke and Rousseau, three fathers of modern juridical and political individualism.

The modern individualistic ideology underlies the UDHR, as we know. At the UN General Assembly Third Committee's 92th meeting, on 2 October 1948 (A/C.3/SR.91), answering to the Polish and the USSR Delegations, the Chilean representative (Hernan Santa Cruz) observed that:

> The draft Declaration rested on the assumption that the interests of the individual came before those of the State and that the State should not be allowed to deprive the individual of his dignity and his basic rights. The opposing conception was that the rights of the individual must give precedence to the interests of society.

At the following Third Committee meeting, on the same day (A/C.3/SR.92), the Brazilian representative (Belarmino Austregésilo de Athayde) stressed that: "The draft Declaration of human rights was based on the most ancient ideas of the great philosophers and on the concept that the power of the State must rest on the respect for the human person. It was a concrete expression of that trend of thought which now shaped the conscience of nations".

Human rights are thus, by definition, ethically individualistic, that is, concerned with personal worth, dignity, autonomy and self-development. It may be said "that a well-developed human individual is the highest product of evolution to date" (Huxley, 1946, 16). The individual is, by definition, at the core of the ideal of human rights. In this connection, Jean Piaget (1948) wrote an illuminating commentary on the Universal Declaration Article 26, in 1948, that deserves to be quoted at some length:

> The text of Article 26 gives no definition of "personality." However, it does state that its development is accompanied by a return to the respect for the rights and freedoms that belong to other personalities. Such precision seems almost tautological, but it is really important; an entire concept of personality could be defined by terming it a reciprocal 'rapport'. From a psychological point of view as well as from the sociological, it is essential

> to distinguish the individual and the personality. In the degree that the individual is self-centered, he creates an obstacle by his moral, or intellectual egocentrism to the inherent relations of reciprocity that all evolved social living contains. Whereas, on the contrary, the part of an individual that is a 'person' freely accepts some kind of discipline, or contributes to its creation, by voluntarily subjecting himself to a system of mutual 'norms' that subordinate his liberty in respect to that of others. Personality, therefore, means a certain form of intellectual and moral conscience, as removed from the autonomy that is part of egocentrism as from the heteronomy of outside pressure, since it attains its independence by regulating it through reciprocity. It can be expressed more simply by saying that the personality is opposite to anarchy at the same time that it is opposite to any restraints since it is autonomous, and two such 'autonomies' can only maintain reciprocal relations. To sum up, that 'education shall be directed to the full development of the human personality and to the strengthening of respect for human rights and fundamental freedoms' is really to create individuals capable of intellectual and moral autonomy and of respecting this autonomy in others by applying the rule of reciprocity that makes it legitimate for themselves.
> [...]
> We have stated that the two correlative aspects of the personality are independence and reciprocity. In contrast to the individual who has not yet reached the state of 'personality', and whose characteristics are to be oblivious of all rules and to center on himself whatever interrelations he has with his physical and social environments, the person is an individual who situates his ego in its true perspective in relation to the ego of others. He inserts it into a system of reciprocity which implies simultaneously an independent discipline, and a basic de-centering of his own activity. The two basic problems of ethical education are, therefore, to assure this de-centering and to build this discipline. (p. 90, 91, 111, 112)

The Preamble of the American Declaration of the Rights and Duties of Man (1948) affirms that "spiritual development is the supreme end of human existence and the highest expression thereof". Who stands against this?

The individualistic core of the idea of human rights does not at all mean conceiving of the individual as an entity abstracted and isolated from the groups he or she belongs to. Human rights do not exist in a cultural and social *vacuum*. Nevertheless, one of the most common criticisms of human rights discourse is that it neglects individual duties. This is a vexed issue going back to the 1789 French Declaration. It mentions 'duties' once in the Preamble, but the 1795 French Constitution was introduced by a Declaration of Rights and Duties of Man and Citizen[11], in which 22 rights and 9 duties were enunciated. The latter included the following:

> 2. All the duties of man and citizen spring from these two principles graven by nature in every heart:
>   Not to do to others that which you would not that they should do to you.
>   Do continually for others the good that you would wish to receive from them.
>
> [...]
> 4. No one is a good citizen unless he is a good son, good father, good brother, good friend, good husband.

The issue revived during the UDHR drafting process. Following the record of the 95th meeting of the UN General Assembly's Third Committee, in Paris, on 6 October 1948 (A/C.3/SR.95), the Argentinian representative (Enrique V. Corominas) "concluded by saying that the Committee would bear before the world the respon-

[11] http://chnm.gmu.edu/revolution/d/298/

sibility of not wishing, in the course of the discussion on human rights, also to examine the duties corresponding thereto".

At the General Assembly's 182th plenary meeting on 10 December (A/PV.182), the Polish representative (Juliusz Katz-Suchy) said that:

> ...the draft Declaration before the Assembly only went so far as to state traditional freedoms and rights of the old liberal school. It omitted to mention that the counterpart of those rights was the duties of the individual towards his neighbors, his family, his group and his nation. [...] For the Polish people, freedom and duty went together.

The Secretariat Outline of an International Bill of Rights (E/CN.4/AC.1/3) began by stating in Article 1: "Every one owes a duty of loyalty to his State and to the (international society) United Nations". And Article 2 affirmed: "In the exercise of his rights every one is limited by the rights of others and by the just requirements of the State and of the United Nations". This way of beginning a Bill of Rights dictated by the "barbarous acts which have outraged the conscience of mankind" (Preamble of the Universal Declaration) was felt as inappropriate. When the Drafting Committee began to discuss the text (E/CN.4/AC.1/SR.2), on 13 June 1947, Malik "expressed the opinion that it was odd that such limitations should be placed at the very beginning of a Bill and expressed the opinion that they were not of such a nature as to be included in the Committee's draft". That was also the feeling of other delegates.

The principle of the correlation of rights and duties was consensual, however. At the first session of the Drafting Committee (E/CN.4/AC.1/3/Add.1), the representative of Australia (Colonel William Roy Hodgson) observed: "Everyone of these rights has a corresponding duty". The Indian representative (Lakshmi N. Menon) pointed out, during the UN General Assembly's 182th meeting (A/PV.182): "From the very fact that it proclaimed rights, therefore, the Declaration was a Declaration of obligations". Glendon (2001) notes: "When read as it was meant to be, namely as a whole, the Declaration's vision of liberty is inseparable from its call to social responsibility". It "begins with an exhortation to act in 'a spirit of brotherhood' and ends with community, order, and society" (p. xviii, 227). Article 29.1 states: "Everyone has duties to the community in which alone the free and full development of his personality is possible". Cassin (1951) drew attention to the fact that they are "duties to the community", not "duties to the State" (p. 280). A UN publication (1995) observes that the three last Articles "express the conception of the Declaration of the relationships between the human person, the society and the State: each one should submit to the requirements of the common good defined by the organized society, whose *raison d'être* is, however, the promotion of human rights by democracy" (p. 26).

Morsink (1999) notes that Cassin "believed that the principle of the correlation of rights and duties is the backbone of any community, which is why he intertwined these ideas and why they are both present in Articles 1 and 29" (p. 296). He points out: "The word 'alone' [in Article 29.1] may well be the most important single word in the entire document, for it helps us answer the charge that the rights set forth in the declaration create egotistic individuals who are not closely tied to their respective communities" (p. 248).

Afterwards, the evocation of duties became frequent in the legal instruments on human rights, both at universal and regional levels[12].

Here are some examples at universal level:

- The Declaration on Race and Racial Prejudice (UNESCO 1978)[13] provides (Article 8.1):

> Individuals, being entitled to an economic, social, cultural and legal order, on the national and international planes, such as to allow them to exercise all their capabilities on a basis of entire equality of rights and opportunities, have corresponding duties towards their fellows, towards the society in which they live and towards the international community.

- The Recommendation concerning Education for International Understanding, Co-operation and Peace and Education relating to Human Rights and Fundamental Freedoms (UNESCO 1974)[14] declares that one of the "major guiding principles of educational policy" should be: "Awareness not only of the rights but also of the duties incumbent upon individuals, social groups and nations towards each other" (para. 4.e).
- The Declaration on the Right to Development (UN 1986)[15] refers to the dialectical relation between rights and duties in Article 2.2:

> All human beings have a responsibility for development, individually and collectively, taking into account the need for full respect for their human rights and fundamental freedoms as well as their duties to the community, which alone can ensure the free and complete fulfillment of the human being, and they should therefore promote and protect an appropriate political, social and economic order for development.

Here are some examples at regional level:

- Duties feature in the title of the American Declaration of the Rights and Duties of Man (1948)[16], whose Preamble begins by stating:

> All men are born free and equal, in dignity and in rights, and, being endowed by nature with reason and conscience, they should conduct themselves as brothers one to another.
> The fulfillment of duty by each individual is a prerequisite to the rights of all. Rights and duties are interrelated in every social and political activity of man. While rights exalt individual liberty, duties express the dignity of that liberty.
> Duties of a juridical nature presuppose others of a moral nature which support them in principle and constitute their basis.

- The ACHR (1969)[17] includes an Article entitled "Relationship between Duties and Rights" (Article 32) that states:

[12] See: International Council on Human Rights. (1999). *Taking Duties Seriously: Individual Duties in International Human Rights Law—A Commentary* (www.ichrp.org/files/reports/10/103_report_en.pdf).

[13] www.unesco.org/education/information/nfsunesco/pdf/RACE_E.PDF

[14] http://portal.unesco.org/en/ev.php-URL_ID=13088andURL_DO=DO_TOPICandURL_SECTION=201.html

[15] www2.ohchr.org/english/law/rtd.htm

[16] www.cidh.oas.org/Basicos/English/Basic2.American%20Declaration.htm

[17] www.oas.org/juridico/english/treaties/b-32.html

1. Every person has responsibilities to his family, his community, and mankind.
2. The rights of each person are limited by the rights of others, by the security of all, and by the just demands of the general welfare, in a democratic society.

- The ACHPR (1981)[18] dedicates Part I to "Rights and Duties". Its Chapter II, headed "Duties", includes three Articles, the first of which (Article 27) states:

1. Every individual shall have duties towards his family and society, the State and other legally recognized communities and the international community.
2. The rights and freedoms of each individual shall be exercised with due regard to the rights of others, collective security, morality and common interest.

- The EU Charter (2000)[19] states in its Preamble: "Enjoyment of these rights entails responsibilities and duties with regard to other persons, to the human community and to future generations".

That is why *InterAction—A United Voice for Global Change*[20] was not succeeded in proposing the adoption by the UN General Assembly of a Universal Declaration of Human Responsibilities in 1998, the year of the UDHR's 50th anniversary[21]. The idea was largely supported by Asian countries, but Western countries and many human rights activists, on the contrary, feared it could be instrumentalized by dictatorial regimes. Also the media feared it could weaken the freedom of information. Instead, the Declaration on the Right and Responsibility of Individuals, Groups and Organs of Society to Promote and Protect Universally Recognized Human Rights and Fundamental Freedoms was adopted (UN 1998)[22] that recalls in Article 18.1: "Everyone has duties towards and within the community, in which alone the free and full development of his or her personality is possible".

The value of duties is deeply rooted in oriental cultures shaped by Confucianism, Hinduism, as well as in Buddhism and Islam. They were stressed by many respondents to the above mentioned 'Memorandum and Questionnaire Circulated by UNESCO on the Theoretical Bases of Human Rights'. For example, Mahatma Gandhi, one of the personalities addressed, sent a brief letter to the UNESCO Director-General (written "in a moving train", as he informed), in which he said:

> I learnt from my illiterate but wise mother that all rights to be deserved and preserved came from duty well done. Thus the very right to live accrues to us only when we do the duty of citizenship of the world. From this one fundamental statement, perhaps it is easy to define the duties of Man and Woman and correlate every right to some corresponding duty to be first performed. (UNESCO 1948, p. 3)

Responding to the same 'Memorandum', Chung-shu Lo said:

> The basic ethical concept of Chinese social political relations is the fulfillment of the duty to one's neighbor, rather than the claiming of rights. The idea of mutual obligations is

[18] www.achpr.org/english/_info/charter_en.html

[19] http://eur-lex.europa.eu/LexUriServ/LexUriServ.do?uri=OJ:C:2010:083:0389:0403:en:PDF

[20] *InterAction* is an NGO created in 1983 by Takeo Fukuda, former Prime-Minister of Japan, and Helmut Schmidt, former Chancellor of the Federal Republic of Germany. It gathers former Chiefs of State or of Government and other personalities from different sectors to discuss world problems (www.interaction.org).

[21] www.global-ethic-now.de/gen-eng/0c_weltethos-und-politik/0c-pdf/decl_human_respons.pdf

[22] www.unhchr.ch/huridocda/huridoca.nsf/(Symbol)/A.RES.53.144.En

> regarded as the fundamental teaching of Confucianism. The five basic social relations described by Confucius and his followers are the relations between (1) ruler and subjects, (2) parents and children, (3) husband and wife, (4) elder and younger brother, and (5) friend and friend. (p. 186)

The principle of reciprocity is inherent to the concept of human rights. Even from a psychological point of view, "autonomy and reciprocity" are "the two correlative aspects of personality", as Piaget wrote (1948, p. 41). Being so, as Rivero (1988) outlined:

> ... the simple affirmation of the human rights carries a profound ethical demand
> [...]
> Thus, by the simple fact of recognizing human rights, a fundamental ethical demand is elevated to the juridical level, the respect for Other. Each right recognized to all imposes upon each one the obligation of not impeding its exercise. (p. 634, 635)

As a consequence, if everyone holds rights, everyone bears duties. Rights and duties are two sides of the same coin. "In other words, rights are characteristically correlative to duties. [...] The language of rights is also a language of duties". They "are equal constituent parts of the normative relationship involved" (Campbell 2006, p. 20, 90). Levinas (1989) went further: "That Human Rights are originally the rights of another human being [...] such is to me the sense of their novelty". Echoing Arthur Rimbaud, he (1972) said: "I is another" (*Je est un autre*) (p. 98). In Dostoevsky's *The Brothers Karamazov* (1879-80), one reads: "We are each responsible to all for all" (as cit. in Thiselton 2002, p. 89)[23]. Louis-Edmond Pettiti went so far to say: "The exercise of rights does not necessarily reveal dignity. *Dignity has more to do with respecting duties and obligations*" (as cit. in Hennette-Vauchez 2008, p. 14). In *BVerfGE 45, 187, 1977 (Lebenslange Freiheitsstrafe)*[24], the German Constitutional Court referred to:

---

[23] Much of the ethical sense of human rights is encapsulated in the word *Ubuntu* that originates from one of the Bantu dialects of Africa, spoken by a South African People called Xhosa. It means essentially: A person can only be a person through other people (*umuntu ngumuntu ngabantu*). It has been translated as 'Humaneness'. As explained by the South African Nobel Laureate Archbishop Desmond Tutu, of Xhosa descent himself, in a quotation from his book *God has a dream: a vision of hope for our time* (2004), Ubuntu:

> ...is the essence of being human. It speaks of the fact that my humanity is caught up and is inextricably bound up in yours. I am human because I belong. It speaks about wholeness, it speaks about compassion. A person with *ubuntu* is welcoming, hospitable, warm and generous, willing to share. Such people are open and available to others, willing to be vulnerable, affirming of others, do not feel threatened that others are able and good, for they have a proper self-assurance that comes from knowing that they belong in a greater whole. They know that they are diminished when others are humiliated, diminished when others are oppressed, diminished when others are treated as if they were less than who they are. The quality of *ubuntu* gives people resilience, enabling them to survive and emerge still human despite all efforts to dehumanize them.

That is why to say "Yu, u nobuntu" (He or she has Ubuntu) is the highest praise to someone (www.africafiles.org/article.asp?ID=20359).

[24] www.servat.unibe.ch/dfr/bv045187.html, and: www.hrcr.org/safrica/dignity/45bverfge187.html

> … the conception of man as a spiritual-moral being, that has the potential to determine himself in freedom and develop from within. This freedom, within the meaning of the Basic Law, is not the one of an isolated and self-regarding individual, but rather of an individual member of a community and bound by it […]. Given that membership, it cannot be 'in principle unlimited'. The individual must allow those limitations of his freedom to act that the legislator deems bearable in particular factual circumstances for the nourishment and support of the communal living with each other; however, the autonomy of the individual must be protected […]. (para. 144, 145)[25]

8.3 Is the Ethical Universality of Human Rights Compatible with the Cultural Diversity of the World?

Already Herodotus (fifth century BC) pointed out the diversity of customs among human societies. Singer wrote in the *Encyclopedia Britannica* (2012—Ethics):

> In *The Origin and Development of the Moral Ideas* (1906–08), the Finnish anthropologist Edward Westermarck (1862–1939) compared differences between societies in matters such as the wrongness of killing (including killing in warfare, euthanasia, suicide, infanticide, abortion, human sacrifice, and dueling); the duty to support children, the aged, or the poor; forms of permissible sexual relationship; the status of women; the right to property and what constitutes theft; the holding of slaves; the duty to tell the truth; dietary restrictions; concern for nonhuman animals; duties to the dead; and duties to the gods. Westermarck had no difficulty in demonstrating tremendous diversity in what different societies considered good conduct in all these areas.

In 1947, the American Anthropological Association (AAA), invited to give an opinion on the Universal Declaration project, addressed to the CHR a Statement on Human Rights[26] that read:

---

[25] Botha (2009) comments:

> The idea of the constitutional 'image of man' has thus helped the Federal Constitutional Court to avoid a strict dichotomy between individual autonomy and the public interest. It also constrains constitutional decision-making to the extent that it rules out certain interpretive options. However, it neither provides us with an account of the various ways in which human dignity and the public interest intersect, overlap and clash, nor tells us where to draw the boundary, in concrete cases, between individual autonomy and the public interest. What is needed is a better theoretical understanding of the concept of human dignity, its various meanings and manifestations, and its relationship to other constitutional values. (p. 188)

In this regard, Henry (2011) mentions the Good Samaritan commandment in the USA:

> As a matter of law, most states do not require individuals to engage in supererogatory behavior. For example, the vast majority of states do not compel bystanders to provide emergency aid to people in need, or even call […]. Exceptions to that general standard include Minnesota and Vermont, both of which have Good Samaritan laws that require any person at the scene of an emergency to provide reasonable assistance to another person in need. (note 204).

[26] http://direitosehumanos.files.wordpress.com/2008/03/satement-45.pdf

> How can the proposed Declaration be applicable to all human beings, and not be a statement of rights conceived only in terms of the values prevalent in the countries of Western Europe and America?
> [...]
> Yet if the essence of the Declaration is to be, as it must, a statement in which the right of the individual to develop his personality to the fullest is to be stressed, then this must be based on a recognition of the fact that the personality of the individual can develop only in terms of the culture of his society.

Based on "the study of human psychology and culture", it made three proposals "essential in drawing up a Bill of Human Rights in terms of existing knowledge", namely:

> 1. The individual realizes his personality through his culture, hence respect for individual differences entails a respect for cultural differences.
> [...]
> 2. Respect for differences between cultures is validated by the scientific fact that no technique of qualitatively evaluating cultures has been discovered.
> [...]
> 3. Standards and values are relative to the culture from which they derive so that any attempt to formulate postulates that grow out of the beliefs or moral codes of one culture must to that extent detract from the applicability of any Declaration of Human Rights to mankind as a whole.[27]

According to cultural relativism, human rights cannot be conceived of, let alone exercised, independently of the local cultural traditions. A recent version of it can be found in the 'Asian Values' argument, sometimes called the 'Lee thesis', referring to the former Prime Minister of Singapore Lee Kuan Yew (1959–1990). Following Xiaorong Li (2001)

> ... official statements by governments in the region typically make the following claims about the so-called 'Asian view' of human rights:
>
> *Claim I: Rights are 'culturally specific'.* Human rights emerge in the context of particular social, economic, cultural and political conditions. The circumstances that prompted the institutionalization of human rights in the West do not exist in Asia. [...]
> *Claim II: The community takes precedence over individuals.* The importance of the community in Asian culture is incompatible with the primacy of the individual, upon which the

[27] Such a cultural relativism is absent from the Declaration on Anthropology and Human Rights adopted by the AAA in 1999 that reads:

> The capacity for culture is tantamount to the capacity for humanity. [...]
> Anthropology as a profession is committed to the promotion and protection of the right of people and peoples everywhere to the full realization of their humanity, which is to say their capacity for culture. [...] This implies starting from the base line of the Universal Declaration of Human Rights and associated implementing international legislation, but also expanding the definition of human rights to include areas not necessarily addressed by international law. These areas include collective as well as individual rights, cultural, social, and economic development, and a clean and safe environment. (www.aaanet.org/stmts/humanrts.htm)

> Western notion of human rights rests. The relationship between individuals and communities constitutes the key difference between Asian and Western cultural 'values'. […]
> *Claim III: Social and economic rights take precedence over civil and political rights.* Asian societies rank social and economic rights and 'the right to economic development' over individuals' political and civil rights. […]
> *Claim IV: Rights are a matter of national sovereignty.* The right of a nation to self-determination includes a government's domestic jurisdiction over human rights. […]. (p. 399, 400)

These are claims voiced mainly by Asian Governments following which the concept of human rights is a product of Western philosophies unsuited to Asian cultures. The latter value community interests over individual autonomy, duties over rights, as well as order, authority and obedience over freedoms. Democracy is also dismissed as 'Western-centric'.

The Final Declaration of the Regional Meeting for Asia of the World Conference on Human Rights, which took place in Bangkok from 29 March to 2 April 1993, in the context of preparations for the World Conference on Human Rights (Vienna 1993)[28], while recognizing that "human rights are universal in nature" (para. 8), and not using the term 'Asian Values', reflects a somewhat relativist approach. The Asian Values argument was restated during the Vienna Conference, as Sen (1997) mentioned:

> Cultural and value differences between Asia and the West were stressed by several official delegations at the 1993 World Conference on Human Rights in Vienna. The foreign minister of Singapore warned that 'universal recognition of the ideal of human rights can be harmful if universality is used to deny or mask the reality of diversity'. The Chinese delegation played a leading role in emphasizing regional differences and in making sure that the prescriptive framework adopted in the declarations made room for regional diversity. The spokesman for China's foreign ministry even put on record the proposition, apparently applicable in China and elsewhere, that 'individuals must put the state's rights before their own'. (p. 9, 10)

Sen concluded:

> The so-called Asian values that are invoked to justify authoritarianism are not especially Asian in any significant sense. Nor is it easy to see how they could be made into an Asian cause against the West, by the mere force of rhetoric. […]
> I have disputed the usefulness of a grand contrast between Asian and European values. There is a lot we can learn from studies of values in Asia and Europe, but they do not support or sustain the thesis of a grand dichotomy. Contemporary ideas of political and personal liberty and rights have taken their present form relatively recently, and it is hard to see them as 'traditional' commitments of Western cultures. There are important antecedents of those commitments in the form of the advocacy of tolerance and individual freedom, but those antecedents can be found plentifully in Asian as well as Western cultures.
> […]
> Authoritarian readings of Asian values that are increasingly being championed in some quarters do not survive scrutiny. The thesis of a grand dichotomy between Asian values and European values adds little to our comprehension, and much to the confusion about the normative basis of freedom and democracy. (p. 30, 31)

[28] http://law.hku.hk/lawgovtsociety/Bangkok%20Declaration.htm

In Sen's (1999) opinion: "The monolithic interpretation of Asian values as hostile to democracy and political rights does not bear critical scrutiny" (p. 8). The argument has been easily dismissed from different sides.

- To begin with, Asia is not a culturally homogeneous region. As religions are concerned, there are four main creeds: Buddhism, Hinduism, Islam and Christianity. Singapore, for example, is a multi-racial, multi-cultural, multi-lingual and multi-religious State. There are 'Easts' and 'Wests'.
- Even though Confucian texts do not mention 'human rights', Confucianism is a humanism relying on reciprocity. Its influence in Japan, Taiwan and South Korea, for instance, does not preclude these countries from being democratic States, committed to human rights.
- Cultures are not monolithic ways of thinking and living, isolated and frozen in time. They evolve over time and interact, much more in a time of increasing Globalization of the world. Traditional practices may become unacceptable and be banned, because of their inhumanity. An example of that is the banning of *Sati* (widow burning) in India by the Prevention of Sati Act (1987)[29].
- A matter of fact is, as above mentioned, that the cultural particularity argument comes, in general, from oppressive or authoritarian leaders, more comfortable with economic, social and cultural rights than with civil and political rights, alleging that their people prefer rice over rights... This argument is usually encapsulated in slogans such as 'You can't eat the right to vote'. It is even claimed that Asia's economic success (until the 1997-98 crisis) was due to Asian Values.

As Bertrand Ramcharan (2008) points out:

> Oftentimes, this is simply opportunistic, as the representatives of repressive governments seek to counter criticism by asserting that human rights are alien values. [...]
> Can anyone say that a human being should not be free of enslavement, torture, and discrimination? That women should be subjected to violence, honor killings, and trafficking? And children should be sexually exploited? (p. 1, 2, 156)[30]
> This is the proper test to the universality of human rights values. Concerning women, in particular, the author further remarks:
> The elimination of gender and racial discrimination will require continuing global mobilization. Violence and injustice against women remains rampant. Pernicious practices such as honor killings and trafficking into slavery and prostitution are widespread. Education for girls is often disadvantaged. Women remain at the mercy of men. The world can never be content with this as a matter of simple justice for more than half of the global population. What is required is no less than a revolution as far as the human rights of women is concerned.
> One is dealing here with entrenched biases and discriminations rooted in millennia of societal approaches and mores. What else can drive the movement for change if not the universal human rights idea and its championship of the rights of women? International human

[29] http://wcd.nic.in/commissionofsatiprevention.htm

[30] Why are there 'Love Commandos' in India, "dedicated to helping India's lovebirds who want to marry for love", by providing "assistance in protecting couples, helping them fight harassment and giving them shelter so they can marry freely"? (http://lovecommandos.org)

rights norms battle against social and cultural practices that adherents of cultural relativism choose to overlook. Take the practice of female genital mutilation for example. When this problem was first brought up before the United Nations in the last quarter of the twentieth century, some governments raised arguments of cultural history and context. But they no longer do so. Nonetheless, the problem has not disappeared. Its final disappearance will come with global education of people in the values of human rights. But the practice is on the defensive, and the international human rights movement brought this about. The mission of human rights is to help change the world for the better. (p. 156)

- Authoritarian Governments do not necessarily represent their peoples' views, at least large parts of them, as illustrated by the Bangkok NGOs Declaration on Human Rights[31], approved by some 240 participants from 110 NGOs in the Asia-Pacific region, meeting in Bangkok on 24–28 March 1993. It states (italics are in the original text):

Universal human rights standards are rooted in many cultures. We affirm the basis of universality of human rights which afford protection to all of humanity […].
As human rights are of universal concern and are universal in value, the advocacy of human rights cannot be considered to be an encroachment upon national sovereignty.
[…]
There must be a holistic and integrated approach to human rights. One set of rights cannot be used to bargain for another.
[…]
Crimes against women are crimes against humanity, and the failure of governments to prosecute those responsible for such crimes implies complicity.
[…]
Democracy is a way of life; it pervades all aspects of human life—in the home, in the workplace, in the local community, and beyond. It must be fostered and guaranteed in all countries.

According to Neil Englehart (2000): the "Singaporean Confucian Ethics campaign [launched in the 1980s] provides the most well-articulated of the Asian values arguments" (p. 549)[32]. He notices: "The broader 'Asian values' movement is an example of a kind of rhetoric that is increasingly common in authoritarian countries since the end of the Cold War" (p. 567). Li (2001) observes that:

… the 'Asian view' creates confusions by collapsing 'community' into the state and the state into the (current) regime. […] What begins as an endorsement of the value of community and social harmony ends in an assertion of the supreme status of the regime and its leaders. (p. 402, 403)

As Campbell (2006) remarks:

Sometimes community oriented critiques are little more than an attempt to turn the clock back to a more hierarchical form of society governed by tradition, as with Burke. […] The fact that egotistical people are selfish about how they use their rights does not mean that having and asserting rights is necessarily a selfish activity. (p. 13, 14)

[31] http://graduateinstitute.ch/faculty/clapham/hrdoc/docs/bangkokNGO.pdf

[32] The campaign was launched by Lee Kuan Yew.

Another expression of resistance to the universality of human rights is the Islamic claim of the supremacy of *Shari'ah*. It was formalized in the Cairo Declaration on Human Rights in Islam (1990)[33], the two last Articles of which read:

> Article 24
> All the rights and freedoms stipulated in this Declaration are subject to the Islamic Shari'ah.
>
> Article 25
> The Islamic Shari'ah is the only source of reference for the explanation or clarification of any of the articles of this Declaration.

According to the Islamic perspective, human rights are not recognized by virtue of being human, but their base is the Islamic faith. All Muslim believers are equal, except for the religious distinction between men and women. As Katerina Dalacoura points out:

> A man is allowed to use physical violence against his wife; he can divorce her without explanation; he can be polygamous if he so chooses; he has exclusive rights of custody over the children in case of separation; and the testimony of one male witness is equal to that of two women. Attitude to women are shaped by the belief that their sexuality poses a threat to social order and must therefore be concealed and controlled. (as cit. in Hansungule 2010, p. 23)

This is not reconcilable with IHRL.

Human rights discourse is also sometimes reproached for being a tool of cultural imperialism and neo-colonialism. It is true that human rights have been often used as an enchanting or ideological device by political rhetoric. As Michael Freeman (2004) admits, for example, "US foreign policy often confuses American interests with universal values" (p. 304).

The universality of human rights is also challenged by postmodernism, a philosophical view rejecting all 'metanarratives', understood as foundational or universalistic accounts of the human condition. After noting that 'postmodernity' and 'postmodernism' are vague and ambiguous concepts, Zühtü Arslan (1999) pointed out that "the most important feature of the postmodern discourse, which makes impossible a friendly relationship with human rights, is its hostility to the concept of the autonomous subject and to the idea of universality" (p. 196). Postmodernists "argue that the liberal conception of the self as autonomous moral agent is merely an abstraction, even an illusion"; and they celebrate "the end of humanity" and of all "foundations", emphasizing cultural relativism and contextuality (p. 204). However, postmodernism may be refuted as turning out to be a new grand narrative too. Moreover, Arslan observes: "Difference and otherness, the magical terms of postmodern discourse, are in fact quite compatible with such conceptions as autonomy and universality" (p. 214).

In sum: IHRL is not 'culture-blind'. The ethical universality of human rights is sensitive to cultural diversity. The right to difference is recognized. Human rights are compatible with all cultural differences not incompatible with their ethical significance. Anyway, as Glendon (2001) rightly remarks: "A strong emphasis on racial and cultural difference was, after all, one of the worst evils of colonialism and Nazism" (p. 232).

---

[33] www.arabhumanrights.org/publications/regional/islamic/cairo-declaration-islam-93e.pdf

8.4 Today, What About the *Faith* in Human Rights Proclaimed in the United Nations Charter and the Universal Declaration of Human Rights?

This is a legitimate question, in light of the massive human rights violations worldwide and of the frequent political hypocrisy of human rights discourse. As a UN publication (2003b) reads:

> Humanity's yearning for respect, tolerance and equality goes a long way back in history, but the curious thing to note is that, although our societies have in many respects made great strides in the technological, political, social and economic fields, contemporary grievances remain very much the same as they were hundreds, even thousands of years ago. (p. 2)

Violations of human rights exist and shall remain the overwhelming picture of the world for an indefinitely long time[34]. They are a daily reality everywhere human beings are victims of grave deprivations or violence hurting their lives and dignity. Contemporary technological means not only may be used against human rights but also serve to give their contempt a worldwide resonance and visibility. Whence 'the so-much-that-is-still-to-be-done' discourse.

It is too well known that international politics and diplomacy often applies a double standard in condemning human rights violators and violations. On the one hand, the great political, economic and military powers tend to be condescending with collaborative dictatorships or authoritarian regimes. On the other hand, gross violations of some human rights may be condemned, while those of other human rights are silenced. The regional Bangkok Declaration (1993) rightly stressed "the need to avoid the application of double standards in the implementation of human rights and its politicization, and that no violation of human rights can be justified" (para. 7)[35]. Even more shocking is that:

> Recent empirical studies even seem to have proved that the general performance of states regarding their human rights obligations declines after the ratification of key human rights instruments. Through ratification of such instruments, governments show to the outside world that they belong to the group of 'good countries', a gesture which removes them for a while from the sharp focus of international attention. (Tomuschat 2008, p. 72)

The world being as it is, a more positive approach may ask: How would things be without the proclamation, some decades ago, of the UDHR? If it has been possible

[34] Even people engaged in human rights militancy are not always examples of coherence, and the International Organizations most devoted to human rights are not just sanctuaries for their cult. In this respect, Humphrey (1984) observed: "People do not become angels simply because they are working for an international organization. In terms of human rivalry and intrigue, the United Nations Secretariat was not unlike other bureaucracies, and personal struggle for power was often compounded by international politics" (p. 8).

[35] In this connection, Joshua Castellino (2010) observes:

> Thus there has to be consistency in criticizing the United States of America and focusing on it adhering to human rights values as much as there needs to be a focus on Sudan and its rights violations. After all, a Sudanese life is worth just as much as an American, Afghani or Iraqi life, with the same inherent dignity. (p. 48)

to advance so much during so few decades, at an increasing less slow speed, we may be hopeful. At the historical scale of Civilization, IHRL is a newborn…

Anyway, Law is no panacea. It only establishes a normative order. Unlike a physical law that tells what will happen, a juridical law tells what ought to happen. It is a rule of conduct whose ultimate source, in case of International Law, is a certain international legal consensus. Notwithstanding, even tough legal instruments do not change the realities, by themselves, they are 'weapons' States were forced to put at the hands of citizens for being used, if needed, against them.

The Swiss Government launched an initiative to commemorate the 60th anniversary of the UDHR, called 'Protecting Dignity: An Agenda for Human Rights', and appointed a Panel of Eminent Persons with the task of drafting an Agenda for Human Rights. Nowak, Panel's member and rapporteur, wrote[36]:

> 1. We know what human rights are, we know the obligations of states and other duty-bearers to respect, protect and fulfil these human rights, and we know that these human rights are systematically violated, disregarded and non-fulfilled in all regions of our planet. *Universal standard setting* by means of legally binding treaties and *universal monitoring* of states' compliance with their human rights obligations constitute important *achievements* from the last sixty years. *The gap between the high aspirations of human rights and its sobering realities on the ground, between human rights law and its implementation, between the lofty rhetoric of governments and their lack of political will to keep their promises is the major problem, and bridging this gap the major challenge of our time.* We know what needs to be done to empower the people of our globalized world to live in dignity, enjoying freedom from want and freedom from fear, and we have the global resources and powers to fulfil this dream.

Among what needs to be done, Nowak includes:

- To take a shared responsibility

This must include "not only accountability for actions that violate human rights, but also positive actions aimed at progressively fulfilling human rights". Their protection should "extend to all attacks on human dignity, and above all, to extreme poverty, consistent patterns of violations of economic, social and cultural rights and the negative effects of global climate change". Poverty, in particular, "is by far the most systematic and dramatic violation of essential human rights, both in the sphere of economic, social and cultural rights as well as in the sphere of civil and political rights"[37].

- To fight against terrorism in a holistic way

A security-dominated strategy against terrorism is insufficient. "Much more needs to be done in taking concerted efforts to address the root causes of global terrorism,

[36] www.udhr60.ch/docs/Panel-humanDignity_rapport2011.pdf

[37] In 2006, the OHCHR adopted Principles and Guidelines for a Human Rights Based Approach to Poverty Reduction Strategies (www.ohchr.org/Documents/Publications/PovertyStrategiesen.pdf).

Another aspect of the fight against the poverty concerns the phenomenon of Globalization. In 2004, the Report of the World Commission on the Social Dimension of Globalization, created by ILO, was published: *A Fair Globalization: Creating Opportunities for All.*

(www.ilo.org/public/english/wcsdg/docs/report.pdf).

As we saw, the Constitutional Court of South Africa and the Supreme Court of India are examples of jurisprudence developing a human rights based approach to poverty.

including poverty, global injustice and unresolved conflicts, as well as the reasons for increasing religious fundamentalism and intolerance".

- To address human rights abuses by non-State actors

"Policies of deregulation and privatization have led to an erosion of governmental power and responsibilities and the taking over the essential governmental functions by private business". This applies also to IGOs.

> In post-conflict situations, the United Nations and relevant regional inter-governmental organizations [...] exercise governmental functions without being directly accountable under international treaty law. The same holds true for the military, financial and economic power exercised respectively by NATO [North Atlantic Treaty Organization], the World Bank, the World Trade Organization and similar inter-governmental organizations. The international community must look for ways to make international institutions accountable under international human rights law standards.

This was already recognized by the Security Council by including, for the first time, human rights "as essential civilian components in newly designed peacekeeping and peace-building operations, as well as in UN transitional administrations, such as those established in Kosovo and East Timor".

- To establish a World Court of Human Rights

This is the last conclusion and recommendation (112) of the Report: "The United Nations Secretary-General is requested to commission an expert study on ways to advance towards the establishment of a World Court of Human Rights".

The need for, and the nature of, a World Court of Human Rights had previously been explained in the same Report:

> 75. ... The term 'human rights' with its corresponding obligations of duty-bearers implies accountability, i.e. the rights-holders should have the legal possibility in case of an alleged violation of such obligation to hold the duty-bearer accountable before an independent national, regional or international court. If the court finds a violation, it must have the power to order adequate reparation, including restitution, rehabilitation, compensation, satisfaction and guarantees of non-repetition. This is the general legal approach to civil wrongs. Why should it be different for violations of human rights? Needless to say, binding judgments of human rights courts need to be enforced by the competent law enforcement agencies.
> 76. Like the International Criminal Court, the World Court of Human Rights could be a permanent court with professional full time judges to be established by a multilateral treaty *under the auspices of the United Nations. It should be competent to decide in a final and binding manner on any complaints brought by individuals, groups or legal entities* alleging a violation of any human right found in an international human rights treaty binding on the duty-bearer. Such complaints could be lodged against states which have ratified the Statute of the Court and the respective human rights treaty. Taking into account the global responsibilities of inter-governmental organizations, such as the United Nations and its specialized agencies, the World Bank and NATO, such organizations should also be subject to the jurisdiction of the Court. The Court should also have jurisdiction over transnational corporations and other business enterprises, faith-based organizations and any other legal entities which have their seat or operate in the territory of a state party.
> 77. Individual complaints should only be admissible after exhaustion of all available domestic remedies. In order to avoid flooding of the court with thousands of complaints, as has happened with the European Court of Human Rights, states could be encouraged to

> establish or design domestic human rights courts competent to directly apply all human rights treaties subject to the jurisdiction of the World Court for the state concerned. If domestic remedies do not provide satisfactory relief to the victim, he or she should have the right to submit a complaint to an international human rights court, either at the regional or global level. [...]

The Panel of Eminent Persons appointed by the Swiss Government requested the Ludwig Boltzmann Institute of Human Rights, in Vienna (Manfred Nowak and Julia Kozma), as well as Martin Scheinin (Institute for Human Rights, Abo Akademi in Turku, Finland, and European University Institute in Florence), to draft Statutes for a World Court of Human Rights[38]. Scheinin (2012) explains:

> Human rights law has traditionally focused on vertical relationships, i.e. the obligations of the state in relation to the individual, or groups of individuals. This structural feature of human rights norms is reflected in the framework of international human rights treaties that proclaim rights to the individual and establish a range of monitoring mechanisms, such as periodic reporting or individual complaints, through which a regional human rights court or international expert body examines whether the states that have ratified the treaty in question are complying with their human rights obligations. Human rights law addresses relationships between two private parties only indirectly, through the prism of so-called positive obligations of the state to ensure people's enjoyment of human rights also in relation to attacks from third parties.
> In the age of globalization this exclusively vertical nature of human rights norms appears inadequate. Actors other than states, including international financial institutions, other international organizations and transnational corporations, exercise powers that affect the enjoyment of human rights by individuals, both within a given country and across borders.
> [...]
> Article 5 of the proposed statute lists 21 international human rights treaties as constituting the applicable law at the World Court. Each state or other actor that accepts the jurisdiction of the court will decide under which of the 21 treaties (or their particular articles) the court will be competent to receive complaints.
> Although the statute would be an international treaty drafted and adopted by states, it would allow also other actors to accept the jurisdiction of the court. These other actors are called 'entities' in the draft statute and defined in Article 4 as 'any inter-governmental organization or non-state actor, including any business corporation'.
> [...]
> This arrangement will result in a variable geometry of human rights obligations to be monitored by the court, so that the applicable law will differ from case to case, depending on the scope of treaties and their provisions that the entity in question has accepted.
> In order to counter the negative consequences of this variable geometry, the draft statute includes a clause (Article 6, paragraph 2) that declares that the court shall be guided by the principles of universality, interdependence and indivisibility of all human rights, by general international law, general principles of law and by the jurisprudence of other international and regional courts. This provision is intended as a cure against the dangers of fragmentation.
> [...]
> To facilitate an institutional culture of human rights awareness and compliance, the proposed statute applies also in relation to IOs [International Organizations] and TNCs [Transnational Corporations] the traditional international law rule of exhaustion of domestic remedies, i.e. that an international complaint is admissible only if the complainant has first sought internal recourse to stop or prevent the human rights violation.
> [...]

---

[38] www.udhr60.ch/docs/Panel-humanDignity_rapport2011.pdf

> Although the proposal may appear radical, experience tells us that once a proposal is carefully prepared, momentum for its adoption may emerge surprisingly fast. The rapid adoption of the Rome Statute for the International Criminal Court in 1998, after decades of debates on the subject that for a large part of the time appeared hopeless, is an illustrative precedent.

The three experts wrote in the Preface of their Draft Statutes:

> The idea of a World Court of Human Rights, together with an International Criminal Court and a High Commissioner for Human Rights, has been on the agenda of the United Nations since the late 1940s. [...]
> The absence of a United Nations Court of Human Rights is however difficult to explain. After all, human rights constitute one of the three major aims and objectives of the world organization, in addition to peace/security and development. [...] It seems that the United Nations is still caught in the spirit of the Cold War when any suggestions to create a World Court of Human Rights are belittled as utopian or revolutionary. (Kozma, Nowak, and Scheinin 2010)

In this connection, one of President Roosevelt's radio address titled 'We choose human freedom' (27 May 1941), announcing the Proclamation of an Unlimited National Emergency, deserves to be remembered[39]. He said:

> We will accept only a world consecrated to freedom of speech and expression—freedom of every person to worship God in his own way—freedom from want—and freedom from terrorism. Is such a world impossible of attainment? Magna Carta, the Declaration of Independence, the Constitution of the United States, the Emancipation Proclamation, and every other milestone in human progress—all were ideals which seemed impossible of attainment—yet they were attained.

Hunt (2008) asks: "What are we to conclude from the resurgence of torture and ethnic cleansing, the continuing use of rape as a weapon of war and enduring oppression of women, the growing sexual traffic in children and women, and the remaining practices of slavery?" (p. 209). In her opinion:

> The human rights framework, with its international bodies, international courts, and international conventions, might be exasperating in its slowness to respond or repeated inability to achieve its ultimate goals, but there is no better structure available for confronting these issues. (p. 213)

As Ramcharan (2008) rightly notes:

> The fact that many governments do not live up to those obligations does not diminish their legal force. The task, rather, is to work for faithful compliance. The fact that laws are violated does not negate their validity. The case is the same with international human rights law. (p. 5)

Consequently, "as a matter of principle and of policy, there can be no alternative to insisting that governments should be inspired by and should live up to their commitments to implement international human rights norms" (p. 155). Hunt (2008) recalls: "The human rights revolution is by definition ongoing" (p. 29). In Habermas' (2012) view:

[39] www.usmm.org/fdr/emergency.html

> Human rights constitute a *realistic* utopia insofar as they no longer paint deceptive images of a social utopia that guarantees collective happiness but anchor the ideal of a just society in the institutions of constitutional states themselves (Bloch 1987). [...]
> This investment of the law with a moral charge is a legacy of the constitutional revolutions of the eighteenth century. (p. 75, 77)

We should be realistic without being pessimistic. The Human Rights Revolution is an everyday, individual, collective, and endless struggle...

References

Åkermark, S. 2009. Human rights, globalization, trade and development. In *International protection of human rights: A textbook*, eds. C. Krause and M. Scheinin, 343–362. Turku/Åbo: Åbo Akademi University, Institute for Human Rights.

Arslan, Z. 1999. Taking rights less seriously: Postmodernism and human rights. *Res Publica* 5:195–215. www.philosophy.ru/library/pdf/234617.pdf. Accessed July 2013.

Bielefeldt, H. 2009. Philosophical and historical foundations of human rights. In *International protection of human rights: A textbook*, eds. C. Krause and M. Scheinin, 3–18.Turku/Åbo: Åbo Akademi University, Institute for Human Rights.

Bloch, E. 1972. *La Philosophie de la Renaissance* ('Vorlesungen zur Philosophie der Renaissance', traduit de l'allemand par Pierre Kamnitzer). Paris: Petite Bibliothèque Payot/201 (1994).

Botha, H. 2009. Human dignity in comparative perspective. *Stellenbosch Law Review* 20 (2): 171–220.

Burckhardt, J. 1860. *A Civilização do Renascimento em Itália* ('La Civilisation de la Renaissance en Italie', trad. de António Borges Coelho). Lisboa: Editorial Presença.

Campbell, T. 2006. *Rights—A critical introduction*. London and New York: Routledge.

Carozza, P. 2003. From conquest to constitutions: Retrieving a Latin American tradition of the idea of human rights. *Human Rights Quarterly* 25:281–313. http://ssrn.com/abstract=984953. Accessed July 2013.

Cassin, R. 1951. La Déclaration universelle et la mise en œuvre des droits de l'homme. In *Recueil des Cours—1951, II, Tome 79 de la Collection*, ed. Académie de droit international, 237–367. Paris: Librairie du Recueil Sirey.

Castellino, J. 2010. Civil and political rights. In *An introduction to international human rights law*, eds. A. Chowdhury and Md. Bhuiyan, 31–49. Leiden: Brill. http://therights.files.wordpress.com/2012/07/an_introduction_to_international.pdf. Accessed Sept 2013.

Donnelly, J. 2009. Human dignity and human rights. *Swiss Initiative to Commemorate the 60th Anniversary of the UDHR—Protecting Dignity: An Agenda for Human Rights—Research Project on Human Dignity*. www.udhr60.ch/report/donnelly-HumanDignity_0609.pdf. Accessed July 2013.

Drzewicki, K. 2009. European systems for the promotion and protection of human rights. In *International protection of human rights: A textbook*, eds. C. Krause and M. Scheinin, 365–388. Turku/Åbo: Åbo Akademi University, Institute for Human Rights.

Dumont, L. 1983. *Essais sur l'individualisme—Une perspective anthropologique sur l'idéologie moderne*. Paris: Éditions du Seuil (1991).

Encyclopædia Britannica. 2012. *Encyclopædia Britannica ultimate reference suite. [DVD]*. Chicago: Encyclopædia Britannica.

Englehart, N. 2000. Rights and culture in the Asian values argument: The rise and fall of confucian Ethics in Singapore. *Human Rights Quartely* 22:548–568.

Freeman, M. 2004. The problem of secularism in human rights theory. *Human Rights Quartely* 26:375–400.

Glendon, M. 2001. *A world made new—Eleanor Roosevelt and the universal declaration of human rights*. New York: Random House, Trade Paperbacks.
Glendon, M. 2003. The forgotten crucible: The Latin American influence on the universal human rights idea. *Harvard Human Rights Journal*. 16:27–39.
Habermas, J. 2012. Chapter 4—The concept of human dignity and the Realistic Utopia of human rights. In *Philosophical dimensions of human rights—Some contemporary views*, ed. C. Corradetti, 63–79. Dordrecht: Springer Science + Business Media B. V.
Hansungule, M. 2010. The historical development of international human rights law. In *An introduction to international human rights law*, eds. A. Chowdhury and Md. Bhuiyan, 1–30. Leiden: Brill. http://therights.files.wordpress.com/2012/07/an_introduction_to_international.pdf. Accessed Sept 2013.
Hennette-Vauchez, S. 2008. A human dignitas? The Contemporary Principle of human dignity as a mere reappraisal of an ancient legal concept. European University Institute, Department of Law, EUI Working Papers, LAW 2008/18. http://cadmus.eui.eu/bitstream/handle/1814/9009/LAW_2008_18.pdf?sequence=1. Accessed July 2013.
Henry, L. 2011. The Jurisprudence of dignity. *University of Pennsylvania Law Review, Vol. 160*, University of Maryland Legal Studies Research Paper No. 2011-42. http://ssrn.com/abstract=1928768. Accessed July 2013.
Humphrey, J. 1984. *Human rights and the United Nations—a Great adventure*. New York: Transnational Publishers.
Hunt, L. 2008. *Inventing human rights—A history*. New York: W. W. Norton and Company Ltd.
Huxley, J. 1946. *UNESCO—Its purpose and its philosophy*. Preparatory Commission of the United Nations Educational, Scientific and Cultural Organisation, 62 p. http://unesdoc.unesco.org/images/0006/000681/068197eo.pdf.
Kozma, J., Nowak, M., and Scheinin, M. 2010. *A World Court of Human Rights—Consolidated Statute and Commentary*. Wien/Graz: Neuer Wissenschaftlicher Verlag.
Laurent, A. 1993. *Histoire de l'individualisme*. Paris: PUF, Que sais-je?-2712.
Levinas, E. 1972. *Humanisme de l'autre homme*. Paris: Fata Morgana, Le Livre de Poche, Série Biblio-essais/4058.
Levinas, E. 1989. Les droits de l'autre homme. In Commission nationale consultative des droits de l'homme, *Les droits de l'homme en questions—Livre Blanc*, 43–45. Paris: La Documentation française.
Li, X. 2001. 'Asian Values' and the universality of human rights. In *The philosophy of human rights*, ed. P. Hayden, 397–408. St. Paul: Paragon House.
Lo, Ch.-Sh. 1948. Human Rights in the Chinese Tradition. In *Human Rights—Comments and interpretations—A symposium edited by UNESCO, with an Introduction by Jacques Maritain*, ed. UNESCO, 185–189. http://unesdoc.unesco.org/images/0015/001550/155042eb.pdf. Accessed July 2013.
Morsink, J. 1999. *The universal declaration of human rights: Origins, drafting, and intent*. Philadelphia: University of Pennsylvania Press.
Piaget, J. 1948. The Right to Education in the Present World. In *To Understand is to Invent—The Future of Education*, 41–142. (Le droit à l'éducation dans le monde actuel, English language translation by George-Anne Roberts). New York: Grossman Publishers (1973). unesdoc.unesco.org/images/0000/000061/006133Eo.pdf. Accessed July 2013.
Ramcharan, B. 2008. *Contemporary human rights ideas*. London: Routledge.
Resweber, J.-P. 1989. *L'institution—Métaphores, stratégies et méthodes d'analyse*. Strasbourg, C.E.F.E.A. (Cahiers Européens pour la Formation, l'Étude et l'Apprentissage).
Rivero, J. 1988. Une éthique des droits de l'homme. In *Mélanges en l'honneur Phédon Vegleris—La crise des institutions de l'État, Tome premier*, ed. P. J. Pararas (Responsable de l'Édition), 627–638. Athènes: Editions Ant. N. Sakkoulas.
Scheinin, M. 2012. International Organizations and Transnational Corporations at a World Court of Human Rights. *Global Policy, 3:4*, November, 488–491. http://onlinelibrary.wiley.com/doi/10.1111/j.1758-5899.2012.00204.x/pdf. Accessed July 2013.

Sen, A. 1997. Human rights and Asian VALUES. New York, Carnegie Council on Ethics and Foreign Policy, Sixteenth Morgenthau Memorial Lecture.
Sen, A. 1999. Democracy as a Universal Value. *Journal of Democracy 10*, 3:3–17.
Thiselton, A. 2002. *A concise encyclopedia of the philosophy of religion*. Oxford: Oneworld Publications, 344.
Tomuschat, Ch. 2008. *Human rights—Between idealism and realism*. Oxford: Oxford University Press, Collected Courses of the Academy of European Law XIII/1.
UNESCO. 1948. *Human rights—Comments and interpretations—A symposium edited by UNESCO, with an Introduction by Jacques Maritain*. http://unesdoc.unesco.org/images/0015/001550/155042eb.pdf. Accessed July 2013.
United Nations. 2003b. *Human rights in the administration of justice: A manual on human rights for judges, prosecutors and lawyers*. New York: OHCHR, in cooperation with the International Bar Association, Professional Training Series N° 9. www.ohchr.org/Documents/Publications/training9Titleen.pdf. Accessed July 2013.
Verdoodt, A. 1964. *Naissance et signification de la Déclaration universelle des droits de l'homme (Préface de René Cassin)*. Louvain-Paris: Éditions Nauwelaerts.

Chapter 9
Conclusion

Abstract This concluding chapter adds two reflections:

- The human rights ideal proclaimed in the Universal Declaration of Human Rights was ignited and has been kept lit by great human beings.
- As the advancement of the liberating power of human rights deeply depends on their being rooted in hearts, minds and everyday life, human rights education should be of paramount concern.

The 'mothers and fathers' of the 1948 Universal Declaration were aware that the promotion and protection of human rights should begin… at the beginning, i.e. with education. Human rights education especially concerns two professional fields: Law and Education.

Human beings are, under and above all, their values and sentiments. Human rights education—understood according to its contemporary comprehensive, holistic scope—is an ethical, civic and international education that is crucial for contemporary societies and the survival and perfecting of Humankind…

Bertrand Russell (1938) once wrote:

> The great ethical innovators have not been men who *knew* more than others: they have been men who *desired* more, or, to be more accurate, men whose desires were more impersonal and of larger scope than those of average men. Most men desire their own happiness; a considerable percentage desires the happiness of their children; not a few desire the happiness of their nation; some, genuinely and strongly, desire the happiness of all mankind. These men, seeing that many others have no such feeling, and that this is an obstacle to universal felicity, wish that others felt as they do; this wish can be expressed in the words 'happiness is good'. All great moralists, from Buddha and the Stoics down to recent times, treated the good as something to be, if possible, enjoyed by all men equally. They did not think of themselves as princes or Jews or Greeks; they thought of themselves merely as human beings. Their ethic had always a twofold source: on the one hand, they valued certain elements in their own lives; on the other hand, sympathy made them desire for others what they desired for themselves. (p. 202, 203)

The drafters of the UDHR were not such great moralists, but the majority among them were great human beings. Glendon (2001) rightly remarks:

> The story of the Declaration is, to a large extent, the story of a journey undertaken by an extraordinary group of men and women who rose to the challenge of a unique historical moment. [...] The members of the first Human Rights Commission were well aware that they were engaged in a race against time: around them, relations between Russia and

A. Reis Monteiro, *Ethics of Human Rights*, DOI 10.1007/978-3-319-03566-6_9,

the West were deteriorating, the Berlin blockade raised the spectre of another world war, the Palestine question divided world opinion, and conflict broke out in Greece, Korea, and China. Shortly after the Declaration's adoption, the window of opportunity closed, to remain shut for forty years.
[...]
The story of the parent document of the modern human rights movement is the story of a group of men and women who learned to cooperate effectively despite political differences, cultural barriers, and personal rivalries. It is an account of their attempt to bring forth from the ashes of unspeakable wrongs a new era in the history of rights. It is an unfinished story, whose course will be influenced, for better or worse, by actions and decisions being taken today. (p. xix, xxi)

Among the "extraordinary group of men and women" who drafted the UDHR, the *Big Five* of the inner core were Eleanor Roosevelt (1884–1962), René Cassin (1887–1976), Charles Malik (1906–1987), Peng-chun Chang (1892–1957), and John Humphrey (1905–1995). They were the right people at the right time.

Eleanor Roosevelt was named "the woman most admired by other American women" in January 1947 (p. 35). Someone said that "she is the personification of the American conscience" (p. 206). Her nightly prayer ended so: "[Our Father...] show us a vision of a world made new" (p. 202).

After Franklin Roosevelt died, in April 1945, the new President Harry S. Truman wanted to have Mrs. Roosevelt "on his political team [...] because of her influence with the Negro voter" (as cit. in Morsink 1999, p. 343, 344, note 64). He invited her to a governmental duty, but she refused. Then, she was invited to be member of the official American Delegation to the San Francisco Conference where the UN Charter would be adopted on 26 June 1945. "How could I be a delegate to help organize the United Nations when I have no background or experience in international meetings?" (Glendon 2001, p. 21)—she objected, but eventually accepted. However, the nomination aroused reservations within the Department of State.

As a political activist and popular journalist, she had developed a formidable reputation for her independence of mind and determination to champion progressive causes. [...] No wonder the foreign-policy establishment was nervous.
The decision, however, was the president's. And Harry Truman was less concerned with possible risks than with keeping the prestige of the Roosevelt name associated with his administration. [...]
Truman pressed Mrs. Roosevelt to accept the UN assignment. (p. 22)

Within the new Organization, her fellow members of the USA Delegation relegated her to the General Assembly Third Committee, deemed to be of minor importance. They could not foresee the role she would play, with her human qualities, working capacities, and parliamentary skills. The fact that she was fluent in French contributed too.

From the beginning, one of Mrs. Roosevelt's greatest contributions to the Human Rights Commission consisted of fostering and providing a setting for cross-cultural understanding. Her dinners and teas enabled delegates to get to know one another as human beings and to exchange views off the record. (p. 114)

When the draft UDHR was discussed in the General Assembly Third Committee, many States' representatives paid tribute to Eleanor Roosevelt. They included representatives of Argentina (Enrique V. Corominas), the Dominican Republic (Minerva Bernardino), Colombia (Augusto Ramirez Moreno), Peru (Luis Alvarado), Brazil (Belarmino Austregésilo de Athayde), Paraguay (Edgar Insfran), the UK (Christopher P. Mayhew), and even of Yugoslavia (Vlado Bakaric). When presenting the draft UDHR to the General Assembly's 180th plenary meeting, on 9 December 1948 (A/PV.180), the rapporteur of the Third Committee (Émile Saint-Lot) "paid a stirring tribute to Mrs. Roosevelt for her wholehearted collaboration, as well as for her tempered authority and the deep knowledge she had brought to the preparation of that historic document". At the 182th plenary meeting on 10 December (A/PV.182), the Paraguayan representative (Carlos A. Vasconcellos) "paid a grateful tribute to Mrs. Roosevelt", and evoked her husband, President Franklin Roosevelt: "In proclaiming the principles of the Atlantic Charter, he had both inspired and foreshadowed the Universal Declaration of Human Rights". In the same meeting, the representative of the Union of South Africa (Roland Andrews Egger) wished also "to pay tribute to the magnificent work accomplished by Mrs. Franklin Roosevelt". At the 183th plenary meeting, on the same day (A/PV.183), the UN General Assembly President (Herbert V. Evat) paid tribute to:

> ... the person who, with the assistance of many others, had played a leading role in that work, the person who had raised to even greater heights even so great a name: Mrs. Roosevelt, the representative of the United States of America.

After retiring from the United Nations, she became member of the American Association for the United Nations.

Eleanor Roosevelt had of herself a diminished image, when compared with her mother's beauty, who called her, sometimes, Granny… Eleanor wrote: "I used to tell my husband that, if he could make *me* understand something, it would be clear to all the other people in the country—and perhaps that will be my real value on this drafting commission!"[1]. There are in her life some particularly dramatic moments: the loss of her parents and a brother, in 2 years, when she was still a child, and the poliomyelitis of her husband. In spite of this, Franklin Roosevelt was elected USA President with 57% of the votes in 1932. In the speech accepting the Democratic Party's nomination he had promised a *New Deal* with the fight against the Great Depression caused by the Wall Street Crash in 1929. Eleanor's social ideas inspired much of the New Deal's politics that, as President Roosevelt said in the first speech after his second election, in 1937, demand to control "blind economic forces and blindly selfish men"[2].

Since 1936 until her death in 1962, Eleanor Roosevelt wrote, almost without interruption, a weekly column headed *My Day* that was carried by 75 to 90 newspapers. It was the opinion column of her militancy especially against racial non-discrimination (making her a target of the Ku Klux Klan). In reality, many decades after Abraham Lincoln's 1883 *Emancipation Proclamation*, black people were still lynched for not abiding by the racial segregation laws (Jim Crow Laws), in public

---

[1] www.gwu.edu/~erpapers/myday/displaydoc.cfm?_y=1947and_f=md000572

[2] http://avalon.law.yale.edu/20th_century/froos2.asp

spectacles reminiscent of the Inquisition's executions in medieval times. A little time after her death on 7 November 1962, at 78 years old, her book *Tomorrow is Now* was published (1963), a chapter of which bearing the title 'The Social Revolution'.

René Cassin was so described by Humphrey (1984): "A little man with a Van Dyke beard, he had a dynamic personality and a sharp and quick mind; he was one of the best public speakers I have ever heard" (p. 24). He was the Vice-Chair of the Nuclear Commission that made proposals for the establishment of the CHR. He was the chief delegate from France to the UDHR Drafting Committee and to all the Commission's sessions. He was "the legal genius of the Free French, who transformed what might have been a mere list or 'bill' of rights into a geodesic dome of interlocking principles", although his English was shaky (Glendon 2001, p. xx).

> Over the weekend of June 14–15 [1947], Cassin revised Humphrey's draft with the help of Émile Giraud, the French international lawyer who had assisted Humphrey. [...] Cassin preserved most of the substantive content of Humphrey's draft, but under his hand the document acquired an internal logic and achieved greater unity. (p. 63)

At the 98th meeting of the Third Committee of the UN General Assembly, on 9 October 1948 (A/C.3/SR.98), Chang "paid a particular tribute to the contribution to the work of preparing the draft Declaration made by Professor Cassin, the representative of France, who had so ably exposed French doctrines of the eighteenth century".

Cassin had been seriously injured in the First World War, and was a representative of France to the League of Nations and to the Geneva Disarmament Conferences from 1924 through 1938. From Jewish origin, he lost 29 members of his family in the Holocaust. When the Second World War started, he was among the first to join Charles de Gaulle, in the UK, to organize the Resistance. In May 1941, the Vichy Regime (proclaimed by Marshal Philippe Pétain, succeeding the Third Republic, which closely collaborated with Nazi Germany) deprived him of the French citizenship, and a Military Tribunal sentenced him to death in 1942[3].

Among other duties, Cassin was President of the French Constitutional Council; member of the Permanent Conference of Allied Ministers of Education (1942–1945); delegate to the UNESCO conferences between 1945 and 1960; Vice-Chairman (1948–1955, and in 1959), Chairman (1955–1957) and member of the CHR until 1971; French delegate to the UN General Assembly (1946, 1948, 1950, 1951, 1968); President of the Court of Arbitration at The Hague (1950–1960); and one of the first Judges of the European Court of Human Rights, in 1959, of which he was twice elected President. As mentioned above, he was awarded the Nobel Peace Prize in 1968. He "became the personification *par excellence* of the human rights idea" (Burgers 1992, p. 462).

Charles Malik was born in Lebanon, having graduated in Mathematics and Physics in the American University of Beyrut. He studied under Alfred N Whitehead at Harvard University (USA), where he arrived in 1932. In 1935, he won one of Havard's fellowships and went to study with Martin Heidegger, in Freiburg (Germany). He returned to the USA before the term of the fellowship, after being beaten

[3] In this regard, Humphrey (1984) wrote in his memoirs: "I visited him several times in his Boulevard St. Michel apartment where he had left on the door the black seal of the Gestapo the Nazis put there when they condemned him to death in absentia" (p. 24).

up on the streets of Freiburg "on account of his Semitic looks"[4]. In 1937, he came home to teach philosophy at the American University of Beyrut.

On 6 April 1945, he flew again to the USA to assume the duties of delegate of Lebanon at the Conference of San Francisco. His contribution to the drafting of the UDHR was considered brilliant and decisive. He was elected by secret ballot to key positions within the UN: Rapporteur of the CHR, President of the ECOSOC, President of the Third Committee, President of the CHR (when Eleanor Roosevelt retired in 1951), President of the 13th session of the UN General Assembly in 1958, and member of the Security Council. In this regard, Glendon remarks:

> In February [1948] Malik, the rapporteur of the Commission on Human Rights, was elected president of the Economic and Social Council, to which the Commission had to submit its draft Declaration. That fall he was elected chairman of the UN's third committee (the Social, Humanitarian, and Cultural Affairs Committee), which had to present the Declaration for approval by the General Assembly at its December meeting in Paris. Thus Malik found himself 'as Rapporteur submitting to myself, as President of the Economic and Social Council at its summer session in Geneva, the draft of the declaration prepared by the Commission, and then submitting, as President of ECOSOC, again to myself as Chairman of the Third Committee, the draft text as passed on by ECOSOC'. The delegate from tiny Lebanon was wearing three big hats as the Declaration moved through its crucial final stages in the fall of 1948. By the time he finally returned to his native Lebanon, he would also be elected president of the General Assembly (in 1958) and would serve on the powerful UN Security Council. (p. 124)

According to Humphrey (1984): "He was one of the most independent people ever to sit on the commission, and he was dedicated to human rights" (p. 23). Commenting on Maliks' presentation of the draft UDHR in the General Assembly, on 9 December 1948, Hernan Santa Cruz wrote:

> He gave a detailed account of the whole long process of elaboration of the instrument that was being discussed. No one was able to do it with such authority, not only because of the responsibilities he had assumed in the process, but also by virtue of his lucid intelligence and his extraordinary talent for explanation. (as cit. in Glendon 2001, p. 165)

Peng-chun Chang, representative of China, was a philosopher, writer, musician and educator. Expert in Confucianism, he received his doctorate at Columbia University's Teachers College (New York) in the 1920s, with an American fellowship, under John Dewey. He was China's Ambassador to Chile and Turkey, in the 1940s, and Vice-Chairman of the CHR, having remained in the UN until 1952. Glendon observes: "Chang's relations were tense with both the Soviets and the Americans, for Russia was supporting Mao Tse-tung's Communist insurgents and the Truman administration was cool toward the corrupt Kuomintang military regime" (p. 53). He was a diplomat whose qualities and pragmatic sense of compromise contributed to the success of the CHR's work. In Hernan Santa Cruz' opinion, he "combined his Mandarin learning with a broad understanding of Western culture" (as cit. ib. p. 44). He often raised "the level of the debate", as remarked the Cuban representative (Guy Pérez-Cisneros) at the General Assembly Third Committee's 95th meeting

[4] Glendon (2001) mentions the following Maliks' testimony: "The Professors at the University beginning their classes with the Nazi salute to which the students respond" (p. 126).

(A/C.3/SR.95). Malik, when he took the stage at the General Assembly's 180th plenary meeting, on 9 December 1948, to introduce the draft UDHR (A/PV.180), named, among others, Chang, who had "never failed to broaden our perspective by his frequent references to the wisdom and philosophy of the Orient and who, by a special drafting gift, was able happily to rectify many of our terms". Glendon writes:

> Chang played a mediating role time and again throughout the third committee debates in the fall of 1948. [...] As a poet and playwright he intuitively grasped the relations among the parts of the text and, like the good teacher he was, could explain them to many different sorts of listeners. (p. 147, 148)

Referring to Chang and Malik, she observes that "a serious personal and philosophical rivalry between these two intellectual giants of the Commission was one of the factors that got the human rights project off to a rocky start" (p. 33). Humphrey witnessed that they dominated the Commission intellectually, and their philosophical confrontation were between Thomism and Confucianism.

"From 1948 onward, P. C. Chang was the target of attacks by the Soviet bloc seeking to seat Mao Tse-tung's government in the UN (efforts that succeeded only much later, in 1971, when the UN under the Nixon administration dropped its opposition)" (p. 211). He resigned from the UN in 1952 and died in 1957. Humphrey wrote in his diary: "P. C. Chang is dead. [...] What a giant he seems in contrast with the time-servers" (as cit. ib. p. 212).

John P. Humphrey, a Canadian lawyer, authored the Secretariat Outline of an International Bill of Rights. He attached great value to the economic, social and cultural rights, very influenced by his "Latin American connection". It Morsink's (1999) opinion:

> ... a fortunate moment in history when Hegel's World Spirit made a hot-tempered Canadian law professor take a giant step forward in the dialectic of history. Someone else with a different background and of a different philosophical persuasion than Humphrey might well have prepared a first draft without including any of the social and economic provisions. He or she might have seen what the Latin American nations were offering and ignored it or fought it. Humphrey's borrowing was not of the blind kind. He was in fact the perfect person to make this connection. (p. 133)

Humphrey lived an unfortunate childhood: he lost his father as a little child and his mother when he was 11 years old (both from cancer). Meanwhile, being 6 years old, he suffered the amputation of an arm, as a consequence of an accident with fire. Moreover, he has endured 4 years of painful schooling in college. He was Professor at the McGill University, in Montreal, when he was called, in June 1946, by his friend Henri Laugier, Assistant Secretary-General of the United Nations in charge of social affairs, to become Director of the UN Division of Human Rights. He remained in this post for 20 years. After his retirement from the UN, in 1966, he helped to establish the Canadian Branch of Amnesty International.

Herman Santa Cruz, Chile's Permanent UN Representative, was a Chilean lawyer and Judge, an aristocratic member of the Chilean Popular Front and close friend from boyhood of the regretted President Salvador Allende. He was the principal spokesman for the Latin American bloc, and Humphrey's friend. "After Humphrey had put in most of the social, economic and cultural rights, no other delegate was more vigilant and more effective in keeping them in than Santa Cruz" (Morsink 1999, p. 90).

Morsink (1999) observes that, "until fairly recently, the human rights community believed that Cassin was 'the author', 'the father', and 'the architect' of the Universal Declaration" (p. 29), and "Cassin did not correct editors and interviewers in cases where it seems that he should have" (p. 343, note 58). In his memoirs, Humphrey (1984) regretted "the myth that Cassin was the father of the Declaration"[5], noting that "Cassin's new text reproduced my own in most of its essentials and style". In his opinion: "The Universal Declaration of Human Rights has no father in the sense that Jefferson was the father of the American Declaration of Independence. Very many people [...] contributed to the final result" (p. 43). Glendon (2001) puts the case this way:

> A regrettable dispute developed many years later over the question of who had written the 'first' draft of the Universal Declaration. It was not exactly a question of paternity, since neither Cassin nor Humphrey ever claimed to be the 'author' of the Declaration. But when Cassin was in his seventies, he claimed in a speech that he had had 'sole responsibility' for the 'first draft' and dismissed Humphrey's contribution as 'excellent basic documentary work'. This claiming, repeated in a 1968 article, was puzzling but not without historical precedent. [...]
>
> Cassin's more enthusiastic admirers began calling him the 'father' of the declaration. [...] That Humphrey wrote the first draft, and that Cassin's draft was a revision of Humphrey's, is clear from the official UN records. Some confusion resulted, perhaps, from the frequent use of the term *outline* to describe Humphrey's work. But the records leave no room for doubt. On June 17, 1947, the verbatim transcript finds Mrs. Roosevelt saying, 'Now we come to Mr. Cassin's draft, which has based itself on the Secretariat's comparative draft'. Cassin himself acknowledged in the drafting committee that 'it is always the Secretariat's draft which should be considered the basic source of the Committee's work'.
>
> Unfortunately a few careless authors created the impression not only that Cassin had written the first draft, but that he was the principal architect of the Universal Declaration of Human Rights. This error not only scanted the roles of other key individuals such as Humphrey, Malik, and Chang, but it detracted from the universality of the document. [...]
>
> To give each man his due, one might say that Humphrey's work was to Cassin's as Tycho Brahe' was to Johannes Kepler's. Just as Kepler could not have had his paradigm-breaking insight into the movements of the planets without Tycho's meticulous records, so Cassin could not have produced an integrated document of worldwide applicability without Humphrey's distillation of the material he had collected. But just as Tycho was unable to see in his own data what Kepler saw, Humphrey had simply compiled a list of rights, loosely grouped into categories. Cassin's draft illuminated their meaning and relations. [...] It was about this time that the committee began to use the term *declaration* more often than *bill*. [...]
>
> Cassin's synthesis yielded a whole that was greater than the sum of its parts. By fusing rights from an older tradition of political and civil liberty to those reflecting a more modern preoccupation with social and economic needs, by providing both sets of rights with an interpretive framework, and by declaring that all these rights belonged to everyone, everywhere, the Declaration was bringing something new into the world. (p. 65, 66, 69)

Likewise Morsink (1999) concluded "that Cassin did not really enter the room until after the baby was born" (p. 29). In fact: "Comparing the Humphrey and Cassin

[5] Example: Agi, M. (1998). *René Cassin, Prix Nobel de la Paix (1887–1976): Père de la Déclaration universelle des droits de l'homme*. Paris: Librairie Académique Perrin.

texts I found only three completely new articles [...]. By my rough calculation three-quarters of the Cassin draft was taken from Humphrey's first draft" (p. 8). Therefore:

> Humphrey's draft is both the first and the basic draft of the Universal Declaration, first in time and basic in that it became the basis for all further deletions and additions. This document, numbered E/CN.4/AC.1/3 of June 4, 1946, is the first draft of the Universal Declaration. (p. 6)

As a consequence, "there is no such thing as 'the author of the Declaration'. [...] The drafting structure was such that the entire United Nations membership was given a chance to participate and actually did so" (p. 28)[6]. Moreover, many NGOs were present at the meetings of the CHR and the Drafting Committee, such as: Inter-Parliamentary Union, World Federation of United Nations Associations, International Committee of the Red Cross, American Federation of Labor, International Federation of Christian Trade Unions, International Abolitionist Federation, International Council of Women, World Jewish Congress, etc.

Malik wrote in his memoirs:

> Those were great days twenty years ago when we were in the throes of elaborating for final submission to the General Assembly of the United Nations the draft Universal Declaration of Human Rights. Mrs. Roosevelt, M. Cassin, Mr. Chang, Mr. Santa Cruz and I, together with our respective advisers and assistants, soon achieved a fairly close identity of views on aims and objectives. We worked more or less as a team. (as cit. in Glendon 2001, p. 134)

These are the kind of people Cassin had probably in mind when he said that human rights need "men and women of thought, of reason, of science. People of heart, however, are also needed" (Cassin 1967, p. 331)[7]. That is also why members of the CCPR (and of other UN Committees) "shall be persons of high moral character and recognized competence in the field of human rights", as reads ICCPR Article 28.2.

According to Richard Rorty (1993), "the idea of founding human rights became anachronism" (p. 148). The last two centuries have been "a time characterized by a surprisingly fast progress of feelings" (p. 166). In his opinion, we should concentrate, not in the rational foundation of morality, but rather in "culture or education of feelings" (p. 155). Indeed, as warned President Truman at the Closing Session of the San Francisco Conference, on 26 June 1945: "It is easier to remove tyrants and destroy concentration camps than it is to kill the ideas which gave them birth and strength"[8]. That is why the first preambular paragraph of UNESCO's Constitution famously proclaimed:

> The Governments of the States Parties to this Constitution on behalf of their peoples declare: That since wars begin in the minds of men, it is in the minds of men that the defences of peace must be constructed;

[6] According to the record of the Third Committee 92nd meeting, on 2 October 1948 (A/C.3/SR.92), Cassin "wished to pay a tribute to the Secretariat's work, which had proved of great value to the Commission on Human Rights".

[7] As reads the History of the United Nations War Crimes Commission and the Development of the Laws of War, "law by itself is not enough, unless it voices, and is inspired by, a change of heart among the nations, an active sense of justice, charity and humanity" (United Nations War Crimes Commission 1948, p. vii).

[8] www.presidency.ucsb.edu/ws/?pid=12188.

Julian Huxley (1887–1975), UNESCO's first Director-General, drew attention (1946) to the fact that literacy does not lead necessarily:

> … either to democracy or, even if it does so, to a right development of society. Nazi Germany demonstrated all too clearly the way in which one of the most literate and most thoroughly educated peoples of the world could be led into false ways and anti-democratic developments; and in democratic countries the manipulation of the press and the debasement of literature and the cinema for financial or political ends is all too possible. (p. 31)

In fact, Nazi concentration camps were conceived and supervised by very educated people, as recalls *To Bear Witness—Holocaust Remembrance at Yad Vashem*, an edition by the Jewish Holocaust Museum of Jerusalem:

> The planners and perpetrators of the "Final Solution" were Germans and Austrians, abetted by members of the occupied peoples—foremost from the Baltic countries—who did their bidding. Most of the murderers belonged to the SS, an organization commanded mainly by men in their thirties. Two-thirds of them had attended university; about half held doctoral degrees in law, economics, political science or philosophy. By enlisting for service in the SS, they expressed their belief that they were the elite of the Arian race, driven by the sense of a historical mission to implement the ideology and shape the new world order in the Nazi image. (Gutterman and Shalev 2005, p. 129)

Adolf Eichmann invoked the Nazi education during his trial in Jerusalem.

The 'mothers and fathers' of the UDHR were aware of the need of human rights to be rooted in minds and hearts. That is why Santa Cruz "shared the opinion of various delegations that the Declaration should as far as possible be brief, so as to be easily understandable to the common man", as he observed during the CHR third session (E/CN.4/SR.50). According to the record of the first session of the Drafting Committee on an International Bill of Human Rights, from 9 to 25 June 1947 (E/CN.4/21): "The Drafting Committee considered that in addition to enforcement measures the United Nations should promote through education the widest possible respect for human rights" (para. 20). The CHR decided, during its second session (December 1947), in Geneva (E/600), to request the ECOSOC:

> To invite UNESCO to consider the creation of a committee of world leaders in educational theory and practice, which should make it its business to study and select the most common and basic principles of a democratic and universal education in order to combat any spirit of intolerance or hostility as between nations and groups. (para. 37.e)

At the 91th meeting of the General Assembly Third Committee, on 2 October 1948 (A/C.3/SR.91), Chang affirmed:

> Stress should be laid upon the human aspect of human rights. A human being had to be constantly conscious of other men, in whose society he lived. A lengthy process of education was required before men and women realized the full value and obligations of the rights granted to them in the Declaration: it was only when that stage had been achieved that those rights could be realized in practice. It was therefore necessary that the Declaration should be approved as soon as possible, to serve as a basis and a programme for the humanization of man.

The paramount role of education is acknowledged in the UDHR Preamble that mentions "teaching and education to promote respect for these rights and freedoms". Cassin drew attention to the following:

> The Preamble of the Declaration mentions 'the progressive measures of national and international order' only in second line. [...]
> In fact, the influence of education is previous to the 'measures' and conditions its respect. Furthermore, it is mainly up to it to prepare the spirits for the great national or international transformations necessary for human rights to be better respected, as the International Community consolidates itself morally and legally. (in Verdoodt 1964, p. 325, 327)[9]

The UDHR Article 26 states:

> 2. Education shall be directed to the full development of the human personality and to the strengthening of respect for human rights and fundamental freedoms. It shall promote understanding, tolerance and friendship among all nations, racial or religious groups, and shall further the activities of the United Nations for the maintenance of peace.

Morsink (1999) pointed out: "Article 26 (on education) is one of the articles most clearly shaped by the experience of the war" (p. 90). Its second paragraph resulted from a remark of Alexis Easterman, a British journalist representing the World Jewish Congress in the Working Group on the Declaration (E/CN.4/AC.2/SR.8):

> Mr Easterman (World Jewish Congress) said that his Organization felt very strongly on this subject. Article 31 as drafted provided a technical framework of education but contained nothing about the spirit governing education which was an essential element. Neglect of this principle in Germany had been the main cause of two catastrophic wars. He proposed the following wording: 'This education shall be directed to the full development of the human personality [and] to strengthening respect for human rights and fundamental freedoms, and shall combat the spirit of intolerance and hatred against other nations or racial or religious groups everywhere'.

The proposal was sponsored by the representative of Panama (Adamo) and supported by the representatives of the Philippines, the USSR and UNESCO. Adamo suggested the inclusion of the words "physical, spiritual and moral". After having been discussed and amended, the text submitted by the World Jewish Congress was adopted by the Working Group by five votes to none, with one abstention, reading as follows (Article 31.a):

> Education will be directed to the full physical, spiritual and moral development of the human personality, to the strengthening of respect for human rights and fundamental freedoms and to the combating of the spirit of intolerance and hatred against other nations or racial or religious groups everywhere.

This text was adopted by the full Commission at the end of its second session, with the addition of the word 'intellectual' after 'physical'. During the Commission's third session, the words 'physical, intellectual, spiritual and moral' were taken out, for the sake brevity. At the 67th meeting of the CHR same session, on 10 June 1948 (E/CN.4/SR.67):

> Mr. Bienenfeld (World Jewish Congress) recalled the circumstances in which the Commission had adopted article 28 [that would become Article 26.2] at its second session in Geneva. As the result of interventions on the part of the World Jewish Congress and certain

[9] Deeply convinced of the primacy of education in promoting the respect for human rights, Cassin applied the Nobel Peace Prize he was awarded in 1968 to creating the *Institut International des Droits de l'Homme*.

> other organizations, the Commission had recognized that a Declaration which failed to indicate the spirit in which everyone was to be educated would not fulfil its purpose, and had agreed to devote a separate article—article 28– to that question.
> As the representative of UNESCO had pointed out, education in Germany and other fascist countries had been carried out in compliance with the principle of the right of education for everyone; yet the doctrines on which that education had been founded had led to two world wars. If the Declaration failed to define the spirit in which future generations were to be educated, it would lose its value as a guide for humanity.
> The Declaration was not merely an appeal to the State; it was an appeal also to parents, teachers and educators. It was necessary to stress the importance of the article devoted to the spirit of education, which was possibly greater than that of all the other articles of the Declaration.

This statement was supported by Malik who said that:

> The human being was, by definition, a creature gifted with the power of reason, and the study of the ways in which that power could be developed was the Commission's concern. It was not enough to say that everyone had the right to education; it was necessary to specify the nature of such education. That was the only possible guarantee that future generations would not be educated in a spirit contrary to the aims of the United Nations as defined in the Preamble to the Charter.
> In connexion with the part played by the family in the education of children, Mr. Malik stressed the need to exclude the possibility of situations in which dictators had the power to prevent parents from educating their children as they wished. Control of education could not be left entirely to the discretion of the State; parents should be allowed the freedom to determine the spirit in which they wished their children to be brought up.

Indeeed, National Socialism had instituted the program envisaged by Hitler in *Mein Kampf*:

> The crown of the folkish state's entire work of education and training must be to turn the racial sense and racial feeling into the instinct and intellect, the heart and brain of the youth entrusted to it. No boy or girl must leave school without having been led to an ultimate realization of the necessity and essence of blood purity. (as cit. in Morsink 1999, p. 90)

In the General Assembly Third Committee, a Mexican amendment proposed the addition of a new paragraph immediately after the existing text of paragraph 2 as follows (A/C.3/266/Corr.1):

> Education shall promote, likewise, understanding and friendship among all peoples, as well as an effective support of the activities of the United Nations for the maintenance of peace.

Later a joint Mexico/USA amendment proposed that the wording of paragraph 2 of the article be as follows (A/C.3/356):

> 2. Education shall be directed to the full development of the human personality, to strengthening respect for human rights and fundamental freedoms and to the promotion of understanding, tolerance and friendship among all peoples, as well as the activities of the United Nations for the maintenance of peace

Just before the vote on this amendment, the representative of Lebanon suggested that the words "all peoples" should be replaced by words "all nations, and racial and religious groups" (as read the original draft of paragraph 2). The proposal was accepted and the joint amendment was adopted by 35 votes to none, with one abstention. The Subcommittee on style set up by the Third Committee replaced the words "as well as" with "and shall further".

In Morsink's (1999) opinion, the UDHR has "an open and explicit educational goal and a hidden legislative one" (p. 324).

> It is not just that the Declaration is an authoritative exposition of the principles enunciated in the Charter, and not just that Article 26 of the Declaration makes human rights an educational goal. Human rights education itself is the first and primary purpose of the Universal Declaration as a whole. (p. 326)

In other words: The promotion and protection of human rights should begin… just at the beginning, i.e. with education. Because "preventing a fire is always cheaper than having to extinguish one", Nowak (2003) pointed out: "Human rights should be imprinted on the hearts and minds of everyone in a process of life-long learning as well as being practiced in our day-to-day behavior towards our fellow human beings" (p. 23). Eleanor Roosevelt is often quoted for having said on 27 March 1958, at the presentation of *IN YOUR HANDS: A Guide for Community Action for the Tenth Anniversary of the Universal Declaration of Human Rights*, in the UN Headquarters (New York)[10]:

> Where, after all, do universal human rights begin? In small places, close to home—so close and so small that they cannot be seen on any maps of the world. Yet they are the world of the individual person; the neighborhood he lives in; the school or college he attends; the factory, farm or office where he works. Such are the places where every man, woman and child seeks equal justice, equal opportunity, equal dignity without discrimination. Unless these rights have meaning there, they have little meaning anywhere. Without concerned citizen action to uphold them close to home, we shall look in vain for progress in the larger world.

Gudmundur Alfredsson (2001) observed that "many of the major international human rights instruments actually establish a right to human rights education" (p. 273). It is recognized by IHRL since the UDHR as an element of the right to education understood as a normative complex of rights aiming at the full development of the human personality. ICESCR Article 13.1 provides: "The States Parties […] agree that education shall be directed to the full development of the human personality and the sense of its dignity, and shall strengthen the respect for human rights and fundamental freedoms".

As a consequence, Mayerfeld (2009) wrote: "Knowledge of human rights law and the values on which it rests should be a required element of everyone's education" (p. 80).

Indeed, as affirmed the 'Sexennial report on the progress achieved in the implementation of the Recommendation concerning Education for International Understanding, Cooperation and Peace and Education relating to Human Rights and Fundamental Freedoms (UNESCO 1974) (26 C/32)[11], "apart from the international legal validity of human rights, they may be considered as the basis of a universal ethics to be known and conformed to by everyone who receives a formal education" (para. 46).

[10] www.un.org/en/globalissues/briefingpapers/humanrights/quotes.shtml

[11] unesdoc.unesco.org/images/0008/000893/089326eo.pdf

The scope and content of the 1974 UNESCO Recommendation[12]—an extended document (45 paras.) that remains the principal international legal instrument in this field—are far reaching. It refers to "international education", "international dimension" of education, "international and inter-cultural understanding", "study of the major problems of mankind", "solving the world problems affecting the individuals' and communities' life", "ethical and civic aspects", "cultural aspects" of learning, training and action. The UNESCO General Conference, in its Resolution 27 C/5.7 (1993), refers to this Recommendation saying "or Recommendation on international education"[13].

In successive international Declarations, Recommendations, Programs, etc. States engaged with the promotion of human rights education. As a guiding UN document recalls:

> 5. With a view to encouraging human rights education initiatives, Member States have adopted various specific international frameworks for action, such as the World Public Information Campaign on Human Rights (1988-ongoing), focusing on the development and dissemination of human rights information materials, the United Nations Decade for Human Rights Education (1995–2004) and its plan of action, encouraging the elaboration and implementation of comprehensive, effective and sustainable strategies for human rights education at the national level, the International Decade for a Culture of Peace and Non-Violence for the Children of the World (2001–2010), the United Nations Decade of Education for Sustainable Development (2005–2014), the International Year for Human Rights Learning (2008–2009) as well as the International Year for the Rapprochement of Cultures (2010).

This document is the Plan of Action prepared by the OHCHR for the second phase (2010–2014) of the World Programme for Human Rights Education proclaimed in 2004 by the UN General Assembly[14], which offers the following definition, after recalling provisions on human rights education incorporated into many international instruments and documents:

> 3. In accordance with these instruments, which provide elements of a definition of human rights education as agreed upon by the international community, human rights education can be defined as any learning, education, training and information efforts aimed at building a universal culture of human rights, including:
> (a) The strengthening of respect for human rights and fundamental freedoms;
> (b) The full development of the human personality and the sense of its dignity;

---

[12] www.unesco.org/education/nfsunesco/pdf/Peace_e.pdf

[13] http://unesdoc.unesco.org/images/0009/000956/095621E.pdf

[14] www.ohchr.org/EN/Issues/Education/Training/WPHRE/SecondPhase/Pages/Secondphaseindex.aspx

On 24 September 2013, the HRC adopted the Resolution A/HRC/24/L.12/Rev.1 where it:

> 3. Decides to make media professionals and journalists the focus group of the third phase of the World Programme for Human Rights Education [2015–2019], with a special emphasis on education and training in equality and non-discrimination, with a view to combating stereotypes and violence, fostering respect for diversity, promoting tolerance, intercultural and interreligious dialogue and social inclusion, and raising awareness of the universality, indivisibility and interrelatedness of all human rights among the general public:
> (http://daccess-dds-ny.un.org/doc/UNDOC/LTD/G13/174/98/PDF/G1317498.pdf?OpenElement)

(c) The promotion of understanding, tolerance, gender equality and friendship among all nations, indigenous peoples and minorities;
(d) The enabling of all persons to participate effectively in a free and democratic society governed by the rule of law;
(e) The building and maintenance of peace;
(f) The promotion of people-centred sustainable development and social justice.
4. Human rights education encompasses:
(a) Knowledge and skills—learning about human rights and mechanisms, as well as acquiring skills to apply them in a practical way in daily life;
(b) Values, attitudes and behavior—developing values and reinforcing attitudes and behaviour which uphold human rights;
(c) Action—taking action to defend and promote human rights.

According to this present comprehensive conception, human rights education should be understood as an ethical education having civic and international dimensions:

- It is an ethical education for aiming at knowledge, adhesion to, and respect of, the Ethics of Human Rights as a Common Ethics of Humankind.
- It has a civic dimension because human rights are the most fundamental rights of citizens, in democracy, needing a national legal framework to be effectively protected.
- It has an international dimension because the respect for human rights constitute the foundation of peace among nations and of justice, as the founding texts of the contemporary international legal order (the UN Charter and the UDHR) state.

The United Nations Declaration on Human Rights Education and Training, adopted by the General Assembly on 19 December 2011 (A/RES/66/137)[15], begins by recalling (Article 1.1): "Everyone has the right to know, seek and receive information about all human rights and fundamental freedoms and should have access to human rights education and training". Its purpose is to provide persons with knowledge, skills and understanding, and to develop corresponding attitudes and behaviors, "to empower them to contribute to the building and promotion of a universal culture of human rights" (Article 2.1). According to Article 7.4:

> States, and where applicable relevant governmental authorities, should ensure adequate training in human rights and, where appropriate, international humanitarian law and international criminal law, of State officials, civil servants, judges, law enforcement officials and military personnel, as well as promote adequate training in human rights for teachers, trainers and other educators and private personnel acting on behalf of the State.[16]

[15] www.ohchr.org/EN/Issues/Education/Training/Pages/UNDHREducationTraining.aspx

[16] On 19 December 2013 – the second anniversary of the adoption of the Declaration on Human Rights Education and Training—Amnesty International, Arab Institute of Human Rights, Democracy and Human Rights Education in Europe (DARE Network), Human Rights Educators USA (HRE USA), Forum Asia, Informal Sector Service Centre (INSEC), Institute for Human Rights and Development in Africa (IHRDA), Human Rights Education Association (HREA), People's Watch, Peruvian Institute for Human Rights and Peace (IPEDEHP), Raoul Wallenberg Institute of Human Rights and Humanitarian Law, and Soka Gakkai launched Human Rights Education 2020. This global coalition aims to systematically monitor the existing international standards and commitments regarding the right to human rights education.

Two professional fields are especially concerned: Education and Law.

Human rights are still widely missing in the education and training of Law professionals. "Many lawyers across the globe still pass through law school without obtaining any education in human rights law" (Marks 2011, p. 55), particularly about their international dimension (see Boerefijn 2009, p. 591). Tomuschat remarks that, "as a rule, national judges are not very familiar with the guarantees laid down in international human rights instruments and are more often than not reluctant to accord them precedence over the applicable national laws and regulations"[17].

In the educational field, the matter remains a poor relative in school education, with a few exceptions. In Finland, for example, according to the Finnish National Core Curriculum for Basic Education 2004[18]:

> The underlying values of basic education are human rights, equality, democracy, natural diversity, preservation of environmental diversity, and the endorsement of multiculturalism. Basic education promotes responsibility, a sense of community, and respect for the rights and freedoms of the individual.

These values "are to be incorporated into the objectives and contents of basic education, and into everyday activity" (2.1). Human rights permeate, formally or implicitly, the whole basic education national curricular framework. One of the curricular subject-matters is Ethics (7.12) that should, among others, "further the pupils' efforts to [...] gain an introduction to the principles of human rights, tolerance, justice, and sustainable development, and learn to assume responsibility for themselves, other people, the community, and nature". Its content includes:

- foundations of living together, rules, agreements, promises, trust, honesty and fairness, the golden rule
- rights of children, right and obligation, human rights
- equality, peace, democracy, the world of the future
- foundations of ethics, moral justification of action, purpose and consequence of action, my own life's ethical problems and their solutions

At grades 6–9, its core contents formally include "ethics of human rights".

For Arendt, "our predicament" lies in our capacity for the best and the worst, "in the double face of humanity: our Janus-like humanity" (as cit. in Birmingham 2006, p. 112). This idea echoes in the words of the UN Secretary-General (Kofi Annan, at the time) during the ceremony commemorative of the UDHR's 50th anniversary, at *Palais de Chaillot*, Paris, on 10 December 1998: "The Declaration drew from the best of human imagination and the worst of human experience"[19].

[17] http://untreaty.un.org/cod/avl/ha/iccpr/iccpr.html
"Most major works on international law continue to ignore this growingly important subject [IHRL] largely because of traditional attitudes in which international law is limited to the classical terrain" (Hansungule 2010, p. 2).

[18] www.oph.fi/english/publications/2009/national_core_curricula_for_basic_education

[19] www.un.org/News/fr-press/docs/1998/19981210.sgsm6828.html
"Never again! This is one of the most decisive messages of the Universal Declaration of Human Rights" (Fritzsche 2004, p. 52).

At the center of Mexico City, not far from the old Palace of Inquisition, there is a Memory and Tolerance Museum[20] showing the twentieth century genocides, "the crime without a name", as Winston Churchill called genocide and Schabas (2000) recalled in his study on *Genocide in International Law—The Crimes of Crimes* (p. 14). *The Survivors' Manifesto* reads: "The Holocaust belongs to the universal legacy of all civilized people as the benchmark of absolute evil" (Gutterman and Shalev 2005, p. 316). It bears witness to the "eternal truth that barbarity is never behind us, but under us", as remembered Sir David Maxwell-Fyfe in the 1940s, during the drafting of the ECHR (as cit. in Modinos 1975, p. 699).

Human beings are, under and above all, their values and sentiments. Human rights education—understood according to its contemporary comprehensive, holistic scope—is an ethical, civic and international education that is crucial for the contemporary societies and the survival and perfecting of our Humanity…

References

Alfredsson, G. 2001. The right to human rights education. In *Economic, social and cultural rights—A textbook,* ed. A. Eide, C. Krause, and A. Rosas, 273–288. 2nd Revised ed. The Hague: Kluwer Law International.

Birmingham, P. 2006. *Hannah arendt and human rights—The predicament of common responsibility*. Bloomington: Indiana University Press.

Boerefijn, I. 2009. International human rights in national law. In *International protection of human rights: A textbook*, ed. C. Krause and M. Scheinin, 577–599. Turku/Åbo: Åbo Akademi University, Institute for Human Rights.

Burgers, J. 1992. The road to San Francisco: The revival of the human rights idea in the twentieth century. *Human rights quarterly* 14 (4): 447–477. http://humanrightsinitiative.ucdavis.edu/files/2012/10/burgerroadtosf.pdf. Accessed July 2013.

Cassin, R. 1967. Vingt ans après la Déclaration universelle—'Liberté et égalité'. *Revue de la Commission Internationale des Juristes (Numéro spécial: 1968– Année internationale des droits de l'homme, Première partie), Tome VIII, N°2*, décembre, 1–17.

Fritzsche, K. 2004. *Menschenrechte—Eine Einführung mit Dokumenten* (2. überarbeitete und aktualisierte Aufl.). Paderborn: Ferdinand Schöningh (2009).

Glendon, M. 2001. *A world made new—Eleanor Roosevelt and the Universal declaration of human rights*. New York: Random House, Trade Paperbacks.

Gutterman, B., and A. Shalev. 2005. *To bear witness—Holocaust remembrance at Yad Vashem*. Jerusalem: Yad Vashem (2008).

Hansungule, M. 2010. The historical development of international human rights law. In *An introduction to international human rights law*, ed. A. Chowdhury and Md. Bhuiyan, 1–30. Leiden: Brill. http://therights.files.wordpress.com/2012/07/an_introduction_to_international.pdf. Accessed Sept 2013.

Humphrey, J. 1984. *Human rights and the United Nations—A great adventure*. New York: Transnational Publishers.

Huxley, J. 1946. UNESCO – *Its purpose and its philosophy*. Preparatory Commission of the United Nations Educational, Scientific and Cultural Organisation, 62 p. http://unesdoc.unesco.org/images/0006/000681/068197eo.pdf.

[20] www.myt.org.mx

Marks, J. 2011. Toward a unified theory of professional ethics and human rights. *Michigan Journal of International Law*. http://papers.ssrn.com/sol3/papers.cfm?abstract_id=1818331##. Accessed July 2013.

Mayerfeld, J. 2009. The democratic legitimacy of international human rights law. *Indiana International and Comparative Law Review* 19:49–88. http://faculty.washington.edu/jasonm/Mayerfeld_Democratic_Legitimacy_of_International_Human_Rights_Law.pdf. July 2013.

Modinos, P. 1975. Dialogue avec les droits de l'homme/Introduction à l'étude des droits de l'homme/ La Convention européenne des droits de l'homme—Ses origines, ses objectifs, ses réalisations. *Revue des droits de l'homme/Human rights journal—Droit international et Droit comparé/ International and Comparative Law—25e Anniversaire de la Convention Européenne des Droits de l'Homme*. 4 Novembre 1950–4 Novembre, Vol. VIII, N° Spécial, 631–636, 648–658, 689–716.

Morsink, J. 1999. *The universal declaration of human rights: Origins, drafting, and intent*. Philadelphia: University of Pennsylvania Press.

Nowak, M. 2003. *Introduction to international human rights regime*. Leiden: Martinus Nijhoff Publishers.

Rorty, R. 1993. Menschenrechte, Rationalität und Gefühl. In *Die Idee der Menschenrechte* (Aus dem Englischen von Michael Bischoff), ed. S. Shute and S. Hurlery, 144–170. Frankfurt am Main: Fischer Taschenbuch Verlag GmbH (1996).

Russell, B. 1938. *Power—A new social analysis*. London: Routledge.

Schabas, W. 2000. *Genocide in international law—The crimes of crimes*. Cambridge: University Press.

United Nations War Crimes Commission. 1948. *History of the united nations war crimes commission and the development of the laws of war*. London: His Majesty's Stationery Office. www.cisd.soas.ac.uk/documents/un-war-crimes-project-history-of-the-unwcc,52439517,p2. Accessed Sept 2013.

Verdoodt, A. 1964. *Naissance et signification de la Déclaration universelle des droits de l'homme (Préface de René Cassin)*. Louvain-Paris: Éditions Nauwelaerts.

Appendices

A Glossary Relating to Human Rights

The following Glossary borrows fundamentally from two UN sources: *Treaty Handbook—Prepared by the Treaty Section of the Office of Legal Affairs*[1], and Treaties and Commission Branch, the branch of the Office of the United Nations High Commissioner for Human Rights (OHCHR), which provides secretariat support to most UN human rights bodies[2]. Additional definitions are drawn on other sources or taken up from the main text. For further information see:

- OHCHR. 2000. *Human rights: A basic handbook for UN staff*[3]
- OHCHR. 2012. *The United Nations human rights treaty system: An introduction to the core human rights treaties and the treaty bodies—Fact sheet N° 30 (Rev. 1)*[4]
- OHCHR. 2006. *The core international human rights treaties*[5]
- OHCHR. 2007. *The new core international human rights treaties*[6]
- OHCHR. 2008. *A handbook for civil society*[7]
- OHCHR. 2005. *Human rights: A handbook for parliamentarians*[8]
- Condé, H. 2004. *A handbook of international human rights terminology* (2th revised edition). University of Nebraska Press.
- Smith, R., and Anker, Ch. 2005. *Human rights*. London: Hodder Arnold.

---

[1] http://treaties.un.org/doc/source/publications/THB/English.pdf

[2] www2.ohchr.org/english/bodies/Treaty/glossary.htm

[3] www.ohchr.org/Documents/Publications/HRhandbooken.pdf

[4] www2.ohchr.org/english/bodies/docs/OHCHR-FactSheet30.pdf

[5] www.ohchr.org/Documents/Publications/CoreTreatiesen.pdf

[6] www.ohchr.org/Documents/Publications/newCoreTreatiesen.pdf

[7] www.ohchr.org/EN/AboutUs/CivilSociety/Documents/Handbook_en.pdf

[8] www.ohchr.org/Documents/Publications/training13en.pdf

A. Reis Monteiro, *Ethics of Human Rights*, DOI 10.1007/978-3-319-03566-6,

The electronic site of the American Society of International Law provides a broad and updated *Electronic Resource Guide* to research concerning the IHRL[9]. See also the selected bibliography below.

Some recursivity and redundancy is inherent in a Glossary of this kind. It uses the following abbreviations:

ACHR	American Convention on Human Rights
AU	African Union
CCPR	Human Rights Committee
CEDAW	Convention on the Elimination of All Forms of Discrimination against Women
CERD	Committee on the Elimination of Racial Discrimination
CESCR	Committee on Economic, Social and Cultural Rights
CHR	Commission on Human Rights
CoEDAW	Committee on the Elimination of All Forms of Discrimination against Women
CRC	Convention on the Rights of the Child
CRC-OP1	Optional Protocol to the CRC on the involvement of children in armed conflict
CPED	International Convention for the Protection of All Persons from Enforced Disappearance
ECHR	European Convention on Human Rights (Convention for the Protection of Human Rights and Fundamental Freedoms)
ECOSOC	Economic and Social Council (United Nations)
GC	General Comment
HRC	Human Rights Council
ICC	International Criminal Court
ICCPR	International Covenant on Civil and Political Rights
ICCPR-OP1	First Optional Protocol to the ICCPR
ICCPR-OP2	Second Optional Protocol to the ICCPR
ICERD	International Convention on the Elimination of All Forms of Racial Discrimination
ICESCR	International Covenant on Economic, Social and Cultural Rights
ICESCR-OP	Optional Protocol to the ICESCR
ICJ	International Court of Justice
IGO	Intergovernmental Organization
IHL	International Humanitarian Law
IHRL	International Human Rights Law
ILO	International Labor Organization
M.O.U.	Memorandum of Understanding
NATO	North Atlantic Treaty Organization
NGO	Non-Governmental Organization
NHRI	National Human Rights Institution
OAU	Organization of African Unity

[9] www.asil.org/erg/?page=ihr

OHCHR	Office of the High Commissioner for Human Rights
OP	Optional Protocol
SPT	Subcommittee on Prevention of Torture
TMB	Treaty Monitoring Body
UDHR	Universal Declaration of Human Rights
UN	United Nations
UNESCO	United Nations Educational, Scientific and Cultural Organization
UNHCHR	United Nations High Commissioner for Human Rights
USA	United States of America
VCLT	Vienna Convention on the Law of Treaties

Abuse of Rights Abuse of rights means to exercise one's rights in a way that violates the rights of others or to prevent them from exercising their rights. It is a general principle of the IHRL so worded in the ECHR (Article 17—Prohibition of abuse of rights)[10]:

> Nothing in this Convention may be interpreted as implying for any State, group or person any right to engage in any activity or perform any act aimed at the destruction of any of the rights and freedoms set forth herein or at their limitation to a greater extent than is provided for in the Convention.

Accession Accession is the act whereby a State that has not signed a treaty expresses its consent to become a party to that treaty by depositing an "instrument of accession" with the UN Secretary-General. Accession has the same legal effect as ratification, acceptance or approval. However, unlike ratification, which must be preceded by signature to create binding legal obligations under International Law, accession requires only one step, namely, the deposit of an instrument of accession. The Secretary-General, as depositary, has tended to treat instruments of ratification that have not been preceded by signature as instruments of accession, and the States concerned have been advised accordingly.

The conditions under which accession may occur and the procedure involved depend on the provisions of the relevant treaty. Accession is generally employed by States wishing to express their consent to be bound by a treaty where the deadline for signature has passed. However, many modern multilateral treaties provide for accession even during the period that the treaty is open for signature.

Accountability Accountability is an old English term whose etymology is 'count'. It entered the dictionaries and encyclopedias in the 1980s to mean the ability and obligation to be answerable. In the political field, Governments should be answerable to the people, and everyone holding public power is accountable for the way it is used. In the human rights field, nobody enjoys impunity for their violations. The principle of individual responsibility is now well-established in International Criminal Law.

[10] http://conventions.coe.int/Treaty/en/Treaties/Html/005.htm

Admissibility Requirements When a written complaint or communication is submitted to a competent international body (Committee, Commission, Court) alleging the violation of a human right by a State, it is first decided whether it may be accepted, following established criteria. In general, a petition under a human rights convention must meet the following requirements: the alleged violating State must have ratified the convention invoked; the right or rights allegedly violated must be protected by it; all domestic remedies must have been exhausted; the complaint should not be manifestly ill-founded or groundless.

Adoption of a Treaty Adoption is the formal act by which negotiating parties establish the form and content of a treaty. The treaty is adopted through a specific act expressing the will of the States and the international organizations participating in the negotiation of that treaty, e.g. by voting on the text, initialing, signing, etc. Adoption may also be the mechanism used to establish the form and content of amendments to a treaty, or regulations under a treaty.

Treaties that are negotiated within an international organization are usually adopted by resolution of the representative organ of that organization. For example, treaties negotiated under the UN auspices, or any of its bodies, are adopted by a resolution of the UN General Assembly.

Where an international conference is specifically convened for the purpose of adopting a treaty, the treaty can be adopted by a vote of two thirds of the States present and voting, unless they have decided by the same majority to apply a different rule.

Advisory Opinion Advisory Opinion is the opinion of a Court or Court-like body that provides an interpretation of a law or norm. Advisory Opinions differ from other forms of opinions in that the advisory opinion need not concern a concrete case (one presenting real parties claimed to be harmed and entitled to a remedy).

Amendment Amendment, in the context of Treaty Law, means the formal alteration of the provisions of a treaty by its parties. Such alterations must be effected with the same formalities that attended the original formation of the treaty. Multilateral treaties typically provide specifically for their amendment. In the absence of such provisions, the adoption and entry into force of amendments require the consent of all the parties.

Amicus Curiae *Amicus curiae* (Latin for 'friend of the court') is a person or organization that is not a party to a case, but is interested in it and offers to participate or is invited by the Court, furnishing information or advice on questions of Law or fact, generally in support of one party's position.

Authentication Authentication is the procedure whereby the text of a treaty is established as authentic and definitive. Once a treaty has been authenticated, its provisions cannot be modified except by formal amendment. If procedures for authentication have not been specifically agreed, the treaty will usually be authenticated by signature, or initialing, by the representatives of those States. It is this authenticated text that the depositary uses to establish the original text.

Authentic Language A treaty typically specifies its authentic languages—the languages in which the meaning of its provisions is to be determined.

Authentic or Authenticated text The authentic or authenticated text of a treaty is the version of the treaty that has been authenticated by the parties.

Backlog Some TMBs have found it difficult to keep up with the high number of reports that they have to consider each year. The resulting backlog means up to two years may go by between the submission of a report by a State Party and its examination by the TMB.

Civil Society Civil Society is a collective name for the whole range of voluntary associations that interpose between the individual and the State. It includes families, a variety of groups, political parties and even multinational corporations.

Codification Codification is the process of formalizing Law or rights into written instruments.

Common Core Document Common core document is a document submitted by a State Party to a human rights treaty to the Secretary-General containing information of a general nature about the country which is of relevance to all of the treaties, including information on land and people, the general political structure and the general legal framework within which human rights are protected in the State. The common core document constitutes the initial part of all reports to the TMBs. It was introduced in 1991 as a way of reducing some of the repetition of information found in States' reports to the various TMBs.

Concluding Observations Concluding Observations or Concluding Comments or Recommendations are the observations, comments or recommendations issued by a TMB after consideration of a State Party's report. They refer both to positive aspects of a State's implementation of the treaty and areas where the TMB recommends that further action needs to be taken by the State. The TMBs are committed to issuing concluding observations which are concrete, focused and implementable and are paying increasing attention to measures to ensure effective follow-up to their concluding observations.

Consent In order to become a party to a multilateral treaty, a State must demonstrate, through a concrete act, its willingness to undertake the legal rights and obligations contained in the treaty. In other words, it must express its consent to be bound by the treaty. A State can express its consent to be bound in several ways, in accordance with the final clauses of the relevant treaty. The most common ways are: definitive signature; ratification; acceptance or approval; and accession.

Constructive Dialogue All TMBs have developed the practice of inviting States Parties to send a delegation to attend the session at which their report is being considered by the TMB in order to allow them to respond to members' questions and provide additional information on their efforts to implement the provisions of the relevant treaty. This procedure is not supposed to be adversial and the TMB does not aim to pass judgment on the State Party in a judicial sense. Instead the aim is to engage with the State Party in a constructive dialogue with the aim of assisting the Government in its efforts to implement the treaty as fully and effectively as possible. The notion of constructive dialogue underpins the view that the TMBs are not judicial bodies (even if some of their functions are quasi-judicial) but rather are bodies created to monitor the implementation of the treaties.

Content, Core Content and Minimum Core Content Defining the normative content of a human right is to determine its right-holders, object and duty-bearers. While right-holders and duty-bearers are largely the same for all human rights, and some principles are also common (notably the principle of non-discrimination), each right entails specific norms to be implemented and enforced. They constitute its unique 'core content'. There is still the concept of 'minimum core content' that means a level below which a State may not descend concerning its immediate obligations, regardless of economic constraints or other circumstances.

Contracting State A Contracting State is a State that has expressed its consent to be bound by a treaty where the treaty has not yet entered into force or where it has not entered into force for that State.

Copy

Certified True Copy for Depositary Purposes A certified true copy for depositary purposes means an accurate duplication of an original treaty, prepared in all authentic languages, and certified as such by the depositary of the treaty. The UN Secretary-General circulates certified true copies of each treaty deposited with the Secretary-General to all States and entities that may become parties to the treaty. For reasons of economy, the Secretary-General, as depositary, normally provides only two certified true copies to each prospective participant in the treaty. States are expected to make any additional copies required to fulfill their domestic needs.

Certified True Copy for Registration Purposes A certified true copy for registration purposes means an accurate duplication of a treaty submitted to the UN Secretariat for registration. The registering party must certify that the text submitted is a true and complete copy of the treaty and that it includes all reservations made by the parties. The date and place of adoption, the date and the method whereby the treaty has come into force, and the authentic languages must be included.

Certifying Statement A certifying statement is the statement accompanying the certified true copy of a treaty or a treaty action for registration purposes, certifying that it is such a copy.

Core Human Rights Treaties The most general framework of the IHRL is composed of the International Bill of Human Rights, formed of the 1948 Universal Declaration and the 1966 International Covenants, with their Protocols, and some other treaties and protocols. Together, they are the 'core' human rights treaties, so-called because of their broad scope, the vulnerability of the groups they address or the gravity of human rights violations they target. That is why they are supervised by special monitoring bodies. The 'core' human rights treaties are nine treaties and nine protocols establishing complaints procedures or providing additional rights (see subsection 3.3.7).

Every State is party to at least one of the core human rights treaties, and about 80% have ratified four or more. The implementation of the treaties provisions by the States Parties is monitored by Committees of independent experts, known as Treaty Monitoring Bodies (TMBs).

Crimes against Humanity 'Crimes against humanity' is a phrase used for the first time in the Joint Declaration by France, Great Britain and Russia, on 24 May 1915, in connection to the massacres of the Armenian population in Turkey, denouncing them as "crimes of Turkey against humanity and civilization". Their first definition was formulated in the Charter of the International Military Tribunal at Nuremberg (1945). In 1998, the Rome Statute of the International Criminal Court (entered into force on 1 July 2002), recalling "that during this century millions of children, women and men have been victims of unimaginable atrocities that deeply shock the conscience of humanity", defined its jurisdiction as including "the following crimes: (a) The crime of genocide; (b) Crimes against humanity; (c) War crimes; (d) The crime of aggression" (Article 5.1). Crimes against humanity are defined as follows (Article 7):

1. For the purpose of this Statute, 'crime against humanity' means any of the following acts when committed as part of a widespread or systematic attack directed against any civilian population, with knowledge of the attack:

a. Murder;
b. Extermination;
c. Enslavement;
d. Deportation or forcible transfer of population;
e. Imprisonment or other severe deprivation of physical liberty in violation of fundamental rules of international law;
f. Torture;
g. Rape, sexual slavery, enforced prostitution, forced pregnancy, enforced sterilization, or any other form of sexual violence of comparable gravity;
h. Persecution against any identifiable group or collectivity on political, racial, national, ethnic, cultural, religious, gender as defined in paragraph 3, or other grounds that are universally recognized as impermissible under international law, in connection with any act referred to in this paragraph or any crime within the jurisdiction of the Court;
i. Enforced disappearance of persons;
j. The crime of apartheid;
k. Other inhumane acts of a similar character intentionally causing great suffering, or serious injury to body or to mental or physical health.

These terms are defined in paragraph 2 (see subsection 3.4.1).

Customary International Law Human rights having Customary International Law status are considered fundamental or basic rights. Many UDHR provisions became customary for having been included in treaties, national constitutions and States' practice. The Universal Periodic Review by the HRC includes compliance with the UDHR. At least the Article 3 common to the 1949 Geneva Conventions is considered Customary International Law. According to the *Restatement (Third) of Foreign Relations Law of the United States* (§701), certain human rights have Customary International Law status, namely: prohibition on genocide, slavery or slave trade; murder or causing the disappearance of individuals; torture or other cruel, inhumane, or degrading treatment or punishment; prolonged arbitrary detention; systematic racial discrimination; and consistent pattern of gross violations of internationally recognized human rights. This is quoted by *Operational Law Handbook* (2013)[11], according to which the Customary International Law also includes the prohibition of all violence to life or limb, hostages taking, punishment without fair trial, and failure to care for and collect the wounded and sick.

The VCLT is considered to codify Customary International Law.

De jure and De facto *De jure* means that something is commanded by Law. *De facto* means that something actually happens, even if it is unlawful. For example, corporal punishment of children is *de jure* prohibited in some tens of countries[12], but continues occur *de facto*.

Declaration A declaration, in legal terms, means a non-binding instrument stating agreed upon principles and standards, or another kind of legal statement. The former declarations are adopted by the UN General Assembly, IGOs, international conferences, etc. Although not legally binding, a declaration may be very influential, as was the UDHR. The latter may serve the following purposes:

Interpretative Declaration An interpretative declaration is a declaration by a State as to its understanding of some matter covered by a treaty or its interpretation of a particular provision. Unlike reservations, declarations merely clarify a State's position and do not purport to exclude or modify the legal effect of a treaty. The Secretary-General, as depositary, pays specific attention to declarations to ensure that they do not amount to reservations.

Usually, declarations are made at the time of signature or at the time of deposit of an instrument of ratification, acceptance, approval or accession. Political declarations usually do not fall into this category as they contain only political sentiments and do not seek to express a view on legal rights and obligations under a treaty.

Mandatory Declaration Treaties may provide for States to make optional and/or mandatory declarations. These declarations are legally binding on the declarants. A mandatory declaration is a declaration specifically required by the treaty itself. Unlike an interpretative declaration, a mandatory declaration is binding on the State making it.

See, for example, Article 41 of the ICCPR (1966) and Article 3(2) of the CRC-OP1 (2000).

Objections to Declarations States sometimes object to declarations relating to a treaty that is silent on reservations or where the declaration seems in fact to be a true

---

[11] See: www.loc.gov/rr/frd/Military_Law/pdf/operational-law-handbook_2013.pdf

[12] See: www.endcorporalpunishment.org/

reservation sufficient to modify the legal effects of the treaty. If the objecting State concludes that the declaration is a reservation and/or incompatible with the object and purpose of the treaty, the objecting State may prevent the treaty from entering into force between itself and the reserving State. However, if the objecting State intends this result, it should specify it in the objection.

An objecting State sometimes requests that the declarant "clarify" its intention. In such a situation, if the declarant agrees that it has formulated a reservation, it may either withdraw its reservation or confirm that its statement is only a declaration.

Democracy The consubstantiality of human rights and democracy, understood as a political regime based on the recognition and protection of human rights, has been reaffirmed by international and national Courts. The concomitance of the expansion of human rights and of democracy testifies to their reciprocal implication as the main features of the contemporary Rule of Law.

The existence of a very right to democracy remains controversial, but many scholars consider that UDHR Article 21 and ICCPR Article 25 are undisputable international legal bases of a human right to democracy or democratic governance. Moreover, UDHR Article 28 is often considered as containing an implicit right to democracy, as it proclaims: "Everyone is entitled to a social and international order in which the rights and freedoms set forth in this Declaration can be fully realized". At least, it is argued that the right to democracy has become Customary International Law (see sections 6.5 and 7.3).

Depositary The depositary of a treaty is the custodian of the treaty and is entrusted with the functions specified in Article 77 of the VCLT. The Secretary-General, as depositary, accepts notifications and documents related to treaties deposited with the Secretary-General, examines whether all formal requirements are met, deposits them, registers them subject to Article 102 of the UN Charter and notifies all relevant acts to the parties concerned. Some treaties describe depositary functions.

A depositary can be one or more States, an international organization, or the chief administrative officer of the organization, such as the UN Secretary-General. In certain areas, such as dealing with reservations, amendments and interpretation, the Secretary-General's depositary practice, which has developed since the UN establishment, has evolved further since the conclusion of the VCLT. The Secretary-General is not obliged to accept the role of depositary, especially for Treaties negotiated outside the UN auspices. It is the usual practice to consult the Treaty Section prior to designating the Secretary-General as depositary. The Secretary-General, at present, is the depositary for over 500 multilateral treaties.

Derogation Most human rights may be subject to reservations or declarations of interpretation, and lawfully restricted or even derogated from or suspended. In effect:

- A State may formulate valid reservations and declarations of interpretation to a treaty, if they are allowed. In particular, they should not be "incompatible with the object and purpose of the treaty" (VCLT Article 19. c)[13]. For instance, giving precedence to national laws or customs over International Law ('claw back clauses') is inconsistent with the IHRL. In its GC 24 [14], the CCPR states that provisions representing Customary International Law and peremptory norms (*jus cogens*) may not be subject to reservations.

- A treaty may allow for restrictions or limitations of human rights, following established criteria. Some rights contain specific limitation clauses. The ICCPR Article 19 provides an example:

  1. Everyone shall have the right to hold opinions without interference.
  2. Everyone shall have the right to freedom of expression; this right shall include freedom to seek, receive and impart information and ideas of all kinds, regardless of frontiers, either orally, in writing or in print, in the form of art, or through any other media of his choice.
  3. The exercise of the rights provided for in paragraph 2 of this article carries with it special duties and responsibilities. It may therefore be subject to certain restrictions, but these shall only be such as are provided by law and are necessary:

     (a) For respect of the rights or reputations of others;
     (b) For the protection of national security or of public order (*ordre public*), or of public health or morals.

  In addition, limitations are also implied in terms such as 'reasonable' or 'arbitrary'.

- Temporary suspension or derogations from States' obligations under IHRL are possible in exceptional circumstances and subject to certain conditions, essentially the following: existence of a "public emergency" and official proclamation of that emergency and informing other parties to the treaty. In this regard, the ICCPR Article 4.1 states:

  1. In time of public emergency which threatens the life of the nation and the existence of which is officially proclaimed, the States Parties to the present Covenant may take measures derogating from their obligations under the present Covenant to the extent strictly required by the exigencies of the situation, provided that such measures are not inconsistent with their other obligations under international law and do not involve discrimination solely on the ground of race, colour, sex, language, religion or social origin.

  Derogations are also permitted, for example, by the ECHR (Article 15) and the ACHR (Article 27). However, according to the ICCPR Article 4.2: "No derogation from articles 6, 7, 8 (paragraphs 1 and 2), 11, 15, 16 and 18 may be made under this provision". These Articles are concerned with:

  - Right to life (Article 6)
  - Prohibition of torture or cruel, inhuman or degrading treatment or punishment (Article 7)
  - Prohibition of slavery (Article 8)

[13] http://legal.un.org/ilc/texts/instruments/english/conventions/1_1_1969.pdf

[14] http://tbinternet.ohchr.org/_layouts/treatybodyexternal/Download.aspx?symbolno=CCPR%2fC%2f21%2fRev.1%2fAdd.6&Lang=en

- Prohibition of imprisonment because of an inability to fulfill contractual obligation (Article 11)
- Principle of legality in Criminal Law (Article 15)
- Recognition of everyone as a person before the law (Article 16)
- Freedom of thought, conscience and religion (Article 18)

Moreover, as the CCPR observes in its GC 29[15]:

> 6. The fact that some of the provisions of the Covenant have been listed in article 4 (paragraph 2), as not being subject to derogation does not mean that other articles in the Covenant may be subjected to derogations at will, even where a threat to the life of the nation exists. The legal obligation to narrow down all derogations to those strictly required by the exigencies of the situation establishes both for States parties and for the Committee a duty to conduct a careful analysis under each article of the Covenant based on an objective assessment of the actual situation.

As a consequence, the Committee expanded the interpretation on the scope of non-derogable rights. It has identified other non-derogable aspects of human rights:

- Peremptory norms, such as: prohibition of arbitrary deprivation of liberty, principles of fair trial, prohibition of collective punishments.
- Elements that cannot be subject to valid derogation, such as: right to respect for personal dignity and to be always treated with humanity; freedom of opinion, rights of persons belonging to minorities; prohibition of evidence obtained under torture; right to an effective remedy; prohibition of propaganda of war; etc.

Non-derogation clauses are also stipulated in the ECHR Article 15.2 and the ACHR Article 27.2. While their lists vary, the three human rights treaties have in common the following non-derogable rights: right to life, prohibition of torture or cruel, inhuman or degrading treatment or punishment, prohibition of slavery, and prohibition of retroactive penal measures. In any case, legitimate derogations should not involve any discrimination16.
The ICESCR, the CRC and the ACHPR do not include non-derogation clauses, but the CESCR identified in its GC 317 "minimum core obligations".
It should be noted that there is a distinction between non-derogable and absolute rights. An absolute right is, by definition, non-derogable, but a non-derogable right may not be absolute. For instance, the right to life is non-derogable because it cannot be suspended at any time, for any reason, but it is not absolute to the extent that it is allowed to kill for legitimate reasons, i.e. not "arbitrarily". For example, as we know, it is lawful to kill in legitimate defense.

---

[15] www.unhchr.ch/tbs/doc.nsf/898586b1dc7b4043c1256a450044f331/71eba4be3974b4f7c1256ae2005173361/$FILE/G0144470.pdf

[16] In this regard, see also: *Siracusa Principles on the Limitation and Derogation Provisions in the International Covenant on Civil and Political Rights* (1985) (E/CN.4/1985/4, Annex).(www.refworld.org/docid/4672bc122.html)

[17] http://tbinternet.ohchr.org/_layouts/treatybodyexternal/Download.aspx?symbolno=E%2f1991%2f23(SUPP)&Lang=en

Displaced Persons Displaced persons are persons who fly their homeland due to political persecution or war, but does not cross State borders. The term can be used to refer to people who may consider themselves to be refugees but who do not qualify for official refugee status under the Convention Relating to the Status of Refugees (UN, 1951).

Double Standard A double standard is applied regarding human rights violations and violators especially when the great political, economic and military powers are permissive with collaborative dictatorships or authoritarian regimes. Moreover, violations of some human rights may be condemned, while those of other human rights are silenced. The case may also be that a State condemns another State for violations that it commits itself.

Education The right to education is not merely right to an education. It is not whatever right to whatever education, but a new right to a new education. It is a human right to human rights based approach to education, that is, right to an education in accordance with the core content of the right to education. In other words, the right to education is right to a Rightful Education, understood as education respectful of the educational rights that demand a Politics, a Pedagogy and a School of the Right to Education.

Enforced Disappearances The International Convention for the Protection of All Persons from Enforced Disappearance (UN, 2006) defines 'enforced disappearance' as follows (Article 2):

> For the purposes of this Convention, 'enforced disappearance' is considered to be the arrest, detention, abduction or any other form of deprivation of liberty by agents of the State or by persons or groups of persons acting with the authorization, support or acquiescence of the State, followed by a refusal to acknowledge the deprivation of liberty or by concealment of the fate or whereabouts of the disappeared person, which place such a person outside the protection of the law.

Ensure/Implement/Enforce To ensure is a general term to mean the States' obligations regarding the full realization of human rights, including causing others to do so as well. To implement refers to all concrete steps and means—legal, administrative, political, economic and other measures—necessary to ensure or give full effect to human rights. To enforce has a rather stronger legal connotation, as it implies the threat or application of sanctions to address the respect of, or redress, the violations of human rights.

Entitlement, Enjoyment and Empowerment Holding human rights means to be entitled to their enjoyment, that is, to be empowered with the legal faculties of claiming their respect, protection and all means for their enforcement and realization. Indeed, empowering human beings is a multidimensional process that consists in ensuring their survival and integrity, as well as fostering their liberty. The empowerment of human beings requires, therefore, the realization of the human rights indispensable to their self-fulfillment and autonomy, thus generating feelings of self-worth and self-esteem.

Entry into Force

Definitive Entry into Force Entry into force of a treaty is the moment in time when a treaty becomes legally binding on the parties to the treaty. The provisions of the treaty determine the moment of its entry into force. This may be a date specified in the treaty or a date on which a specified number of ratifications, approvals, acceptances or accessions have been deposited with the depositary. The date when a treaty deposited with the Secretary-General enters into force is determined in accordance with the treaty provisions.

Entry into Force for a State A treaty that has already entered into force may enter into force in a manner specified in it for a State or international organization that expresses its consent to be bound by it after its entry into force.

Provisional Entry into Force Provisional entry into force may be allowed by the terms of a treaty, for example, in commodity agreements. Provisional entry into force of a treaty may also occur when a number of parties to a treaty that has not yet entered into force decide to apply the treaty as if it had entered into force. Once a treaty has entered into force provisionally, it creates obligations for the parties that agreed to bring it into force in that manner.

Erga Omnes *Erga omnes* is a Latin term literally meaning 'towards all'. In International Law, it means States' obligations towards the International Community as a whole, intended to protect and promote common basic values. This category of obligations was first identified by the ICJ in the famous *Case Barcelona Traction* (1970). The Court said: "Such obligations derive, for example, in contemporary international law, from the outlawing of acts of aggression, and of genocide, as also from the principles and rules concerning the basic rights of the human person, including protection from slavery and racial discrimination" (para. 34).

Ethics and Morals Morals and Ethics are terms etymologically synonymous, with Latin (*mos*) and Greek (*ethos*, *êthos*) etymologies, respectively. Both refer to 'right' or 'wrong' conduct, to custom or character. There is no common understanding about the difference between them. A number of authors use Morals to denote the *what* of values (which they are), that is, a set of values and norms concerning the right and wrong individual behaviors within a given human community, and Ethics or Moral Philosophy to designate e theory of morality, that is, the reflection on the *why* of moral values,clauses are provisions typically on the principles of good and evil, pointing to a universal horizon. One says, for instance, 'Ethics of Human Righs', and not 'Morals of Human Rights'.

Final Act A Final Act is a document summarizing the proceedings of a diplomatic conference. It is normally the formal act by which the negotiating parties bring the conference to a conclusion. It is usually part of the documentation arising from the conference, including the treaty, the resolutions and interpretative declarations made by participating States. There is no obligation to sign the Final Act, but signature may permit participation in subsequent mechanisms arising from the conference, such as preparatory committees. Signing the Final Act does not normally create legal obligations or bind the signatory State to sign or ratify the treaty attached to it.

Final Clauses Final clauses are provisions typically found at the end of a treaty, dealing with such topics as signature, ratification, acceptance, approval, accession, denunciation, amendment, reservation, entry into force, settlement of disputes, depositary matters and authentic texts.

In the case of multilateral treaties to be deposited with the Secretary-General, parties should submit for review draft final clauses to the Treaty Section well in advance of the adoption of the treaty.

Friendly Settlement A friendly settlement consists in a mutual accord to resolve a dispute. In cases of individual communications alleging violations of human rights by States, a friendly settlement procedure usually results in payment to the applicant by the respondent State of a specified sum of money.

Gender Gender is a term without a generally agreed definition. While traditionally 'gender' has been a grammatical category ('masculine', 'feminine' and 'neuter' gender), the term has become used to refer to sex-based categories. Its relationship with the term 'sex' is not clear, however. Sex refers to biological differences, gender relates to cultural and social perceptions and expectations concerning the roles and behaviors of men and women. It might be said that, while 'male' and 'female' are invariable sex categories, 'masculine' and 'feminine' are variable gender categories, underlying many kinds of discrimination.

General Comment (GC) General Comment is a TMB's interpretation of the content of human rights provisions, either related to a specific article or to a broader thematic issue. They often seek to clarify the reporting duties of States parties with respect to certain provisions and suggest approaches to implementing treaty provisions. This practice was initiated by the CCPR (based in Article 40.4 of the ICCPR). CERD and CEDAW use the term General Recommendation. In the Introduction of its GC 1 (E/1989/22), the CESCR explained "the purpose of general comments":

> At its second session, in 1988, the Committee decided (E/1988/14, paras. 366 and 367), pursuant to an invitation addressed to it by the Economic and Social Council (resolution 1987/5) and endorsed by the General Assembly (resolution 42/102), to begin, as from its third session, the preparation of general comments based on the various articles and provisions of the International Covenant on Economic, Social and Cultural Rights with a view to assisting the States parties in fulfilling their reporting obligations.

General Principles of Law General Principles of Law are principles that appear nearly universally in states' domestic Law and, thus, over time become binding on all nations. They are one of the main sources of International Law.

'Generations' of Human Rights The history of the juridification of human rights is frequently put in terms of 'generations', following the principles of *Liberté*, *Égalité* and *Fraternité* of the French Revolution.

- The civil and political rights are called 'first generation' rights or 'liberty rights'.

- The economic, social and cultural rights are called 'second generation' rights or 'equality rights'.
- Rights such as the right to development, the right to a healthy environment, the right to peace, the right to be different, are called 'third generation' rights or 'solidarity rights' or 'collective rights' or 'new human rights'.

The 'generations' nomenclature is often considered unfortunate—except for didactic or research purposes—because it is not historically accurate and may weaken the principle of the interdependence and unity of all human rights.

Genocide The term 'genocide' was devised by Raphael Lemkin, in 1944, from two words: *genos* that means race, nation or tribe in Greek, and *caedere* that means killing in Latin. In 1948, the UN General Assembly adopted the Convention on the Prevention and Punishment of the Crime of Genocide (UN, 1948), a day before the Universal Declaration. The Convention adopted the following definition (Article II):

> In the present Convention, genocide means any of the following acts committed with intent to destroy, in whole or in part, a national, ethnical, racial or religious group, as such:
>
> a. Killing members of the group;
> b. Causing serious bodily or mental harm to members of the group;
> c. Deliberately inflicting on the group conditions of life calculated to bring about its physical destruction in whole or in part;
> d. Imposing measures intended to prevent births within the group;
> e. Forcibly transferring children of the group to another group.

This definition is evolving.

Golden Rule Golden Rule is a principle of reciprocity and compassion, with both positive and negative formulations, namely: 'Do unto others as you would have them do unto you', and 'Do not do unto others what you would not have them do unto you'. The second one is sometimes named Silver Rule. Another formulation commands: 'Treat others in the way that they wish to be treated'.

While the term 'Golden Rule' is relatively recently (17th century), its command is millenary (dating from the 5th century BC) and is found in all cultural and religious traditions. There are Confucian, Buddhist, Hinduist, Jewish, Christian and Islamic versions of it.

Group/Collective Rights Although human rights are individual rights, by definition, some are collective, by their very nature. These are rights whose exercise is only possible with others, such as freedom of association and assembly, the freedom to form or join a trade union, and the 'third generation' human rights, or related to membership of a colletive entity (national, ethnic, cultural or other), such as typically the right to self-determination. However, it should not be loosed of sight that no colletive right may infringe on individual rights. The CoRC affirms in its 'General comment No. 14 (2013) on the right of the child to have his or her best interests taken as a primary consideration (art. 3, para. 1)' (CRC/C/GC/14)[18]:

[18] www2.ohchr.org/English/bodies/crc/docs/GC/CRC_C_GC_14_ENG.pdf

> 23. … The Committee underlines that the child's best interests is conceived both as a collective and individual right, and that the application of this right to indigenous children as a group requires consideration of how the right relates to collective cultural rights.

Notwithstanding, 'collective rights' derive from individual rights, i.e. their ultimate holders are always the members of protected groups. This is recalled, for instance, in the Declaration on the Rights of Persons Belonging to National or Ethnic, Religious and Linguistic Minorities (UN, 1992): "The exercise of the rights set forth in the present Declaration shall not prejudice the enjoyment by all persons of universally recognized human rights and fundamental freedoms" (Article 8.2)[19].

Habeas Corpus *Habeas corpus* is a writ (written command in the name of a Court) requiring that a person be brought before a judge or into Court, especially to investigate the lawfulness of their detention.

Hard Law and Soft Law *Hard* Law refers to the agreements between States creating legal obligations on States Parties to them (Treaty Law), in form of charter, covenant, convention, protocol, statute, etc. (this variety of denominations does not mean any legal difference), as well to Customary Law. *Soft* Law refers to rules neither formally legally binding in themselves nor completely lacking legal value. It takes different names too, such as declaration, recommendation, principles, minimum standards, guidelines, etc. While not directly enforceable, they express broad international consensus, having a more or less strong moral and political authority. Declarations are the most authoritative kind of Soft Law.

Human Life The right to life is not, obviously, the right to be born, nor just the right of not being arbitrarily deprived of life. It is right to a human life, a dignified existence, and not to a mere *animal existence.*

Life is the primordial right for being the natural condition of holding rights, but it is not absolute and the highest human value. To the extent that a human life is a life in liberty, a person may put at risk his or her life for living in freedom, or even sacrifice her life to other ethical values.

Human Right 'Human rights' is the most common term in International Law, but 'fundamental freedoms' is a term frequently associated with human rights. 'Fundamental rights' is the most used term in constitutional texts. There is no agreed conceptual distinction between human or fundamental rights and fundamental freedoms. Rights are freedoms and freedoms are rights. The American term 'civil rights' and the French term *libertés publiques* are restrictive terms that do not cover all human rights.

The IHRL does not provide any definition of 'human right' (nor do national laws). Following the most common definition, a 'human right' is a right one possesses simply for being human. It is a legal right recognized of every member of the human species, without discrimination, irrespective of ethnic, cultural, religious, political or other membership, of gender, age, handicap or of whatever circumstances. That is why human rights are universal and have been qualified as imprescriptible and inalienable:

[19] www.ohchr.org/Documents/Publications/GuideMinoritiesDeclarationen.pdf

- *Universal* because they are held by every human being everywhere in the world and in all situations.
- *Imprescriptible* because they are not subject to prescription, i.e., they are 'natural', inextinguishable, and not capable of being lost.
- *Inalienable* because they are inherent in human dignity, ethically indisposable, not capable of being transferred, renounced or expropriated.

'Imprescriptible' and 'inalienable' are terms of 18th century Declarations, but only the second subsists in IHRL, subsuming the idea of imprescriptibility. The metaphysical notion of 'human nature', as an innate and immutable essence, was replaced with the historical moral idea of 'human dignity', recognized and consecrated by universal or universalizable consensus. Human rights are the answer to the following question: What do human beings need to live a dignified life, free "from fear and want" (UDHR)?

Defining the normative content of a human right is to determine its right-holders, object and duty-bearers.

- *Right-holders* of human rights are, by definition, "every human being", "all persons", "everyone", "anyone", except when a legal instrument addresses a particular, more vulnerable category of persons (women or children, for example). 'Collective rights' are based on individual rights.
- The *object* of a human right is that to which the right-holder is entitled. It should be something "of fundamental character and derive from the inherent dignity and worth of the human person", as the UN General Assembly said (A/RES/41/120), [20]as well as being precise and obtainable, however difficult to enforce and to implement.
- *Duty-bearers* are mainly States, individually and collectively, but human rights have a horizontal dimension, too: they create (passive or active) duties between individuals and between them and other non-State actors. Moreover, each individual has duties towards his or her own human dignity and the species' dignity.

While right-holders and duty-bearers are largely the same for all human rights, and some principles also apply to every human right (notably the principle of non-discrimination), each right entails unique norms that constitute its specific 'core content'. There is still the concept of 'minimum core content' that means a level below which a State may not descend in complying with its obligations, regardless of economic constraints or other circumstances (see Young, 2008).

It should be noted, however, that a distinction must be made between entitlement and the ability to exercise human rights. A child, for example, is entitled to all human rights but only progressively becomes able to exercise them autonomously.

Human Rights Based Approach Human rights based approach means addressing a matter (poverty, for instance) or designing a course of action (a development policy, for example) taking into account their implications for the respect, protection and realization of human rights. It aims at reinforcing the ability of the

---

[20] http://daccess-dds-ny.un.org/doc/RESOLUTION/GEN/NR0/496/28/IMG/NR049628.pdf?OpenElement

rights-holders to enjoy their rights and the accountability of the duty-bearers. It is analogous to a human rights impact assessment.

Human Rights Council (HRC) The HRC is the principal UN human rights body, established in 2006 by the General Assembly to replace the Commission on Human Rights created in 1946. It is a subsidiary body of the General Assembly, entrusted with a broad mandate, reporting directly to it, composed of 47 representatives of the Member States. Its greatest novelty is the Universal Periodic Review (UPR). It is based in the UN headquarters in Geneva (*Palais des Nations*) and should meet in regular session three times a year, for at least ten weeks. Special sessions may be requested by one-third of its members. The sessions are almost always held in public (see subsection 3.4.1).

Human Rights Education Human rights education is an element of the core content of the right to education generally recognized as a priority one. It is increasingly recognized as a human right in itself. The United Nations Declaration on Human Rights Education and Training (2011)[21] begins by stating: "Everyone has the right to know, seek and receive information about all human rights and fundamental freedoms and should have access to human rights education and training" (Article 1.1). According to Article 2:

> 2. Human rights education and training encompasses:
> (a) Education about human rights, which includes providing knowledge and understanding of human rights norms and principles, the values that underpin them and the mechanisms for their protection;
> (b) Education through human rights, which includes learning and teaching in a way that respects the rights of both educators and learners;
> (c) Education for human rights, which includes empowering persons to enjoy and exercise their rights and to respect and uphold the rights of others.

In its present comprehensive and holistic concept, human rights education is an ethical education having civic and international dimensions.

Inclusion and Exclusion In the human rights field, inclusion means to consider and treat everyone both as an equal and different, without discrimination whatsoever. Exclusion, notably 'social exclusion', is a term probably first used by René Lenoir, in the 1970s, in France, in connection with poverty and disadvantage. Thereafter, it became increasingly a widespread catch-all term.

Incorporation To be effective in domestic or municipal Law, International Law has to be made part of it or 'incorporated'. This may be automatic or need a legal process of transformation, depending on the relationship between the two levels of Law: monist, if there is no difference between them, International Law being automatically valid and applicable within the national legal framework; or dualist, if they are considered distinct legal systems, so that International Law requires a 'transformation' into domestic norms, by means of implementing legislation, to be internally applicable.

[21] www.ohchr.org/EN/Issues/Education/Training/Pages/UNDHREducationTraining.aspx

Individual Responsibility After the Second World War, the defense of the war criminals, especially of the 'major' war criminals in the Nuremberg and Tokyo Tribunals, invoked both the doctrine of acts of State and that of immunity of State administrators. It was also objected that an International Tribunal is incapable of applying the international laws of war to individuals, because International Law is binding only on the States as such. However, according to the Charter of the International Military Tribunal at Nuremberg (Article 7): "The official position of defendants, whether as Heads of State or responsible officials in Government Departments, shall not be considered as freeing them from responsibility or mitigating punishment". Also the Rome Statute of the International Criminal Court (1998) affirms that the individual is no more only holder of international rights but is also internationally accountable of "the most serious crimes of concern to the international community as a whole" (Article 5). The Convention against Torture and Other Cruel, Inhuman or Degrading Treatment or Punishment provides (Article 2.3): "An order from a superior officer or a public authority may not be invoked as a justification of torture".

Indivisibility of Human Rights The principle of the indivisibility and interdependence of human rights is encapsulated in the second preambular paragraph of the UDHR, recalled in the Preambles of the 1996 International Covenants, and was restated again and again to counter the international tendency prevailing during the Cold War to give precedence to and focus either on *blue* civil and political rights (Western countries) or on *red* economic, social and cultural rights (Eastern and developing countries).

Nevertheless, the IHRL does not place all human rights on the same footing, they have not the same standing. A few are qualified as non-derogable, i.e. never allowing suspension or restriction. Non-derogation clauses are stipulated in the ICCPR Article 4.2, in the ECHR Article 15.2 and in the ACHR Article 27.2. The ICESCR and other human rights treaties (the CRC and the ACHPR, for example) do not include non-derogation clauses, but the CESCR affirmed in its GC 3[22] that it is incumbent upon every State Party "a minimum core obligation to ensure the satisfaction of, at the very least, minimum essential levels of each of the rights", such as the provision "of essential foodstuffs, of essential primary health care, of basic shelter and housing, or of the most basic forms of education" (para. 10). And in GC 14 on 'The right to the highest attainable standard of health (article 12 of the International Covenant on Economic, Social and Cultural Rights)' (E/C.12/2000/4)[23] it said:

> 47. ... If resource constraints render it impossible for a State to comply fully with its Covenant obligations, it has the burden of justifying that every effort has nevertheless been made to use all available resources at its disposal in order to satisfy, as a matter of priority, the obligations outlined above. It should be stressed, however, that a State party cannot, under any circumstances whatsoever, justify its non-compliance with the core obligations set out in paragraph 43 above, which are *non-derogable* [italics added].

[22] http://tbinternet.ohchr.org/_layouts/treatybodyexternal/Download.aspx?symbolno=E%2f1991%2f23(SUPP)&Lang=en

[23] www.unhchr.ch/tbs/doc.nsf/(symbol)/E.C.12.2000.4.En

Paragraph 43 refers to "the core obligations arising from article 12".

'Non-derogable rights' is a floating notion, however. The ICCPR Article 4.2, the ECHR Article 15.2 and the ACHR Article 27.2 do not list the same non-derogable rights; only four are common to the three treaties. They are often equated with *jus cogens,* a norm from which "no derogation is permitted", according to the VCLT Article 53, and with obligations *erga omnes* (towards all), or Customary International Law, but these are not well defined concepts, either. Neither is there an uncontested concept of "minimum essential levels".

In any case, a fact seems to be indisputable: The recognition of *jus cogens* norms and of obligations *erga omnes* have introduced a hierarchy in International Law, just as *non-derogable rights* introduce a hierarchy in IHRL. This raises a major question: How to reconcile such a hierachy with the principle of the indivisibility and interdependence of human rights?

A possible way to escape this *prima facie* contradiction is to try distinguishing between the ethical and legal dimensions of human rights, and between their indivisibility and interdependence:

- Human rights are as ethically indivisible as human dignity is, insofar as they are all valuable for a secured and dignified life, a decent and meaningful human existence. They all require protection and appropriate remedies, because every human right is more or less affected by the realization or deprivation of the others.
- Notwithstanding this fact, the legal protection of some human rights and of the rights of some persons may justify differentiation or priorities, notably for these main reasons:
  - Some rights call for stronger protection because their violations constitute a more direct attack on the most inherent attributes of human dignity–life, physical integrity and moral autonomy. That is why the UDHR begins by proclaiming the rights to life, liberty, and security (Article 3), and the freedoms of slavery, servitude (Article 4), torture or cruel, inhuman or degrading treatment or punisihment (Article 5).
  - The ability to enjoy most human rights is more conditional upon the enforcement and implementation of some rights. In *Barcelona Traction, Light and Power, Limited* (1970)[24], the ICJ referred to "the basic rights of the human person" (para. 34).
  - There are situations of scarcity or emergency when choices should be made and priorities must be established.

It should be further noted that, as the European Court of Human Rights said in *Streletz, Kessler and Krenz v. Germany* (2001)[25], life is "the supreme value in the hierarchy of human rights" (para. 72), but the right to life is not absolute, as the ECHR itself admits (Article 2). Nevertheless, broadly understood, the right to life epitomizes the human rights indivisibility and interdependence.

---

[24] www.icj-cij.org/docket/files/50/5387.pdf

[25] http://hudoc.echr.coe.int/sites/eng/pages/search.aspx?i=001-59353#{"itemid":["001-59353"]}

Interest Interest is a term holding mainly financial and moral meanings. Under the financial meaning, it may be used to indicate the price paid for the use of credit. It may also indicate the income derived from contractual promises. According to the Interest Theory of rights, human beings have interests that imply obligations on the part of the correlative duty-bearers. There is still the Common Good or 'general interest' or 'general welfare'. These are open categories that include 'public policy' as the Common Law counterpart of the French *ordre public* that encompasses principles concerning fundamental representations and values in a legal system, which should be protected specially by tribunals. Referring to the general welfare in the light of the ACHR, the Inter-American Court of Human Rights said in its Advisory Opinion OC-5/85, November 13, 1985[26]:

> 66. Within the framework of the Convention, it is possible to understand the concept of general welfare as referring to the conditions of social life that allow members of society to reach the highest level of personal development and the optimum achievement of democratic values. In that sense, it is possible to conceive of the organization of society in a manner that strengthens the functioning of democratic institutions and preserves and promotes the full realization of the rights of the individual as an imperative of the general welfare. [...]
>
> 67. The Court must recognize, nevertheless, the difficulty inherent in the attempt of defining with precision the concepts of "public order" and "general welfare." It also recognizes that both concepts can be used as much to affirm the rights of the individual against the exercise of governmental power as to justify the imposition of limitations on the exercise of those rights in the name of collective interests. In this respect, the Court wishes to emphasize that "public order" or "general welfare" may under no circumstances be invoked as a means of denying a right guaranteed by the Convention or to impair or deprive it of its true content. [...]

Intergovernmental Organization (IGO) IGOs are organizations of States for some determined purpose. They may be universal (such as UNESCO) or regional (such as the OAU or the NATO).

International Bill of Human Rights The International Bill of Human Rights should not be confused with the UDHR.

The former Commission on Human Rights decided at its second session, held in Geneva from 2 to 17 December 1947: "To apply the term 'International Bill of Human Rights', or, for brevity, 'Bill of Rights', to the entirety of documents in preparation: the Declaration, the Convention and the Measures of Implementation". The International Bill of Human Rights is thus composed of the Universal Declaration of Human Rights adopted in 1948, and the International Covenants adopted in 1966, with their Protocols, namely:

- International Covenant on Economic, Social and Cultural Rights (ICESCR)
- International Covenant on Civil and Political Rights (ICCPR)
- Optional Protocol to the ICCPR (ICCPR-OP1)

[26] www.oas.org/en/iachr/expression/showarticle.asp?artID=149&lID=1

- Optional Protocol to the ICCPR aiming at the abolition of the death penalty (ICCPR-OP2)
- Optional Protocol to the ICESCR enabling the Committee on Economic, Social and Cultural Rights to receive and consider individual communications (ICESCR-OP)

International Human Rights Law (IHRL) The UDHR laid the groundwork for a new branch of International Law–the IHRL. It may be narrowly or broadly defined:

– Narrowly defined, it is the body of International Law focused on the human dignity and rights: their normative *corpus,* protection mechanisms, jurisprudence, content, doctrine. Its most general framework is the International Bill of Human Rights, reinforced by the core treaties and developed by dozens of other legal instruments.
– Broadly defined, it is a field of inter-disciplinary research on human rights, to which contribute several juridical disciplines of domestic and international Law, as well as other multi-disciplinary approaches: historical, philosophical, political, sociological, etc. (see: AAVV, 1972)[27].

To IHRL applies the classification of sources as formulated in Article 38 of the Statute of the International Court of Justice[28], namely:

a. international conventions, whether general or particular, establishing rules expressly recognized by the contesting states;
b. international custom, as evidence of a general practice accepted as law;
c. the general principles of law recognized by civilized nations ;
d. subject to the provisions of Article 59, judicial decisions and the teachings of the most highly qualified publicists of the various nations, as subsidiary means for the determination of rules of law.

International conventions and international custom thus come first. Conventions are contracts between States that must conform to and be interpretated in accordance with the VCLT. The specificity of the IHRL consists in the fact that the obligations contracted therein do not have a reciprocal nature but concern the treatment of all individuals within a State's jurisdiction. This was highlighted by the International Court of Justice that stated in its Advisory Opinion on Reservations to the Convention on the Prevention and Punishment of the Crime of Genocide (1951)[29]:

> What is the character of the reservations which may be made and the objections which may be raised thereto? The solution must be found in the special characteristics of the Convention on Genocide. The principles underlying the Convention are recognised by civilised nations as binding on States even without any conventional obligation. It was intended

[27] "The concept of 'international human rights norm' is broad, and it overlaps with rights protected under other areas of international and domestic law, including international humanitarian law, international criminal law, international environmental law, development law, labor law, refugee and asylum law, constitutional law, domestic criminal law and procedure, and even the law of the sea" (Edwards 2010, p. 152).

[28] http://treaties.un.org/doc/Publication/CTC/uncharter.pdf

[29] www.icj-cij.org/docket/index.php?sum=276&code=ppcg&p1=3&p2=4&case=12&k=90&p3=5

> that the Convention would be universal in scope. Its purpose is purely humanitarian and civilising. The contracting States do not have any individual advantages or disadvantages nor interests of their own, but merely a common interest.

The Inter-American Court of Human Rights said in its Advisory Opinion on 'The effect of reservations on the entry into force of the American Convention on Human Rights (Arts. 74 and 75)' (OC-2/82, 24 September 1982)[30]:

> 29. The Court must emphasize, however, that modern human rights treaties in general, and the American Convention in particular, are not multilateral treaties of the traditional type concluded to accomplish the reciprocal exchange of rights for the mutual benefit of the contracting States. Their object and purpose is the protection of the basic rights of individual human beings irrespective of their nationality, both against the State of their nationality and all other contracting States. In concluding these human rights treaties, the States can be deemed to submit themselves to a legal order within which they, for the common good, assume various obligations, not in relation to other States, but towards all individuals within their jurisdiction.

The Inter-American Court quoted the International Court of Justice, as well as the former European Commission on Human Rights that also declared in its Decision on the admissibility of the Application N°. 788/60 (*Austria v. Italy,* 1961)[31]:

> ... that the obligations undertaken by the High Contracting Parties in the European Convention are essentially of an objective character, being designed rather to protect the fundamental rights of individual human beings from infringements by any of the High Contracting Parties than to create subjective and reciprocal rights for the High Contracting Parties themselves.

International human rights instruments may address human rights in general or a specific right or the rights of more vulnerable categories of persons, such as children and women. Today, there are more than 100 international human rights instruments (treaties, declarations, recommendations, principles, guidelines, etc.), more than 50 of which are major international conventions. This number includes instruments adopted by the UNESCO and the ILO, but not all of them (the ILO adopted around two hundred Conventions and about as many Recommendations on different aspects of the right to work).

The drafting and entering into force of an international human rights instrument may be a long process. For example, it took about fifteen years to draft the ICCPR and the ICESCR, which entered into force only ten years after their adoption. The CRC took ten years to be drafted, but entered into force nine months after its adoption. The Convention on the Rights of Persons with Disabilities was drafted by an *Ad Hoc* Committee established by the UN General Assembly in 2001, was adopted (with its Optional Protocol) in 2006, and entered into force in May 2008.

Usually, States sign a treaty, submit it to their legislature for approval and then ratify it. The gap between signing and ratifying may be long as well, however. For instance, the USA signed the CRC in 1995 but has not yet ratified it.

---

[30] www.corteidh.or.cr/docs/opiniones/seriea_02_ing.pdf

[31] http://hudoc.echr.coe.int/sites/eng/pages/search.aspx?i=001-115598#{"itemid":["001-115598"]}

International Humanitarian Law (IHL) The IHL is sometimes referred to as 'the law of armed conflict' and 'the law of war' (*jus in bello*). It can be defined as that part of International Law comprising conventional and customary Law that seeks to protect persons who are not, or are no longer, taking part in the hostilities (sick, wounded or shipwrecked combatants, prisoners of war and civilians), and to restrict the means of warfare between parties to a conflict.

In 1863, was created the International Committee of the Red Cross. The following year, were laid down the foundations for the IHL by the 1864 Geneva Convention for the Amelioration of the Condition of the Wounded in the Field of Battle (first Geneva Convention). Other milestones were the 1874 Diplomatic Conference and the Hague Peace Conferences of 1899 and 1907. The Hague Conference of 1907 adopted 13 conventions and one declaration.

The contemporary IHL is mainly embodied in the four 1949 Geneva Conventions and the two 1977 Additional Protocols to those Conventions, namely:

- Geneva Convention (I) for the Amelioration of the Condition of the Wounded and Sick in Armed Forces in the Field (Diplomatic Conference, 1949)
- Geneva Convention (II) for the Amelioration of the Condition of Wounded, Sick and Shipwrecked Members of Armed Forces at Sea (Diplomatic Conference, 1949)
- Geneva Convention (III) Relative to the Treatment of Prisoners of War (Diplomatic Conference, 1949)
- Geneva Convention (IV) Relative to the Protection of Civilian Persons in Time of War (Diplomatic Conference, 1949)
- Additional Protocol I Relative to the Protection of Victims of International Armed Conflicts (Diplomatic Conference, 1977)
- Additional Protocol II Relative to the Protection of Victims of Non-international Armed Conflicts (Diplomatic Conference, 1977)

In 2005, it was adopted an Additional Protocol (III) to the Geneva Conventions relating to the adoption of an additional distinctive emblem (Diplomatic Conference).

All the Geneva Conventions have a common Article 3 establishing minimum rules to be observed by each party to an internal armed conflict.

Other IHL instruments deal with the protection of cultural property in the event of armed conflicts, the prohibition of biological and chemical weapons and of certain conventional weapons which may be deemed to be excessively injurious or to have indiscriminate effects. Examples are the 1995 Protocol on Blinding Laser Weapons and the 1997 Convention on the Prohibition of the Use, Stockpiling, Production and Transfer of Anti-Personnel Mines and On Their Destruction (Ottawa Treaty).

Following the classic view, the IHRL and the IHL were two separate branches of International Law, the latter being considered as *lex specialis* (specific rule) applying in situations of armed conflict. At present, they are mostly viewed as complementary and overlapping: the former addresses the respect, protection and realization of human rights and applies to all situations at all times; the latter is a legal regime that does not set out particular rights but only deals with aspects of the respect and protection of human rights in armed conflicts, international and national as well. The IHL is based on two major principles:

- A principle of humanity aiming at limiting the means of war for relieving human suffering and preventing atrocities.
- A principle of distinction between military and civilian persons and objects.

The International Convention for the Protection of All Persons from Enforced Disappearance (2006) is unique in that it brings together general human rights provisions with international humanitarian and criminal law provisions.

International Law Regulation of relationships between nations has since long existed. The modern international system of State relations was founded with the Treaty of Westphalia, signed in 1648. It is based upon the principle of State sovereignty. The contemporary International Law emerged after the First World War when was established the League of Nations, in 1919. UN, its successor established in 1945, became the main stage for making of the International Law. According to the UN Charter (Article 13.1.a), the General Assembly should encourage "the progressive development of international law and its codification". Its sources are those famously set down in Article 38 of the ICJ Statute, established by the UN Charter as one of its principal organs, namely:

1. The Court, whose function is to decide in accordance with international law such disputes as are submitted to it, shall apply:

a. international conventions, whether general or particular, establishing rules expressly recognized by the contesting states;
b. international custom, as evidence of a general practice accepted as law;
c. the general principles of law recognized by civilized nations;
d. subject to the provisions of Article 59, judicial decisions and the teachings of the most highly qualified publicists of the various nations, as subsidiary means for the determination of rules of law.

2. This provision shall not prejudice the power of the Court to decide a case *ex aequo et bono*, if the parties agree thereto.

The two principal types of international sources are, therefore, Treaty Law, i.e. agreements between States, and International Customary International Law. Following the ICJ, "the international custom" includes two elements: a continuous practice of States (objective element) and the belief in its legal necessity (subjective element or *opinio juris*). While the former binds only States Parties to the relevant treaty, the latter is binding on all States. The treaties' rules are more precise than the customary ones, because they are found in written texts (not in States' practice), i.e. on how States use to act (custom) because they consider themselves obliged to do so. The jurisprudence of international Courts plays a decisive role in defining customary principles. Furthermore, Customary International Law is progressively entering into the Treaty Law, especially through the statutes of international criminal courts.

Jurisdiction Jurisdiction is the authority of Courts or Court-like bodies to hear and decide claims. It can refer to the Court's ability to hear particular subjects and/or to review cases brought by certain types of claimants. Jurisdiction can also refer to a geographic area of authority.

Jus cogens *Jus cogens* is a Latin term literally meaning 'cogent/compelling law'. It refers to principles of International Law based on values taken to be so fundamental to the International Community that no derogation from them is permitted.

The concept of *jus cogens* entered International Law with the VCLT (Article 53). However, there is no consensus about the content of *jus cogens*. Human rights figure prominently in the debate, of course. While some scholars go so far as to argue that all human rights have *jus cogens* status, others limit it to a few that include the prohibitions of genocide, torture, slavery, racial discrimination, war crimes, and crimes against humanity.

Justiciability Justiciability means the possibility for an issue to be brought before a judicial instance competent to adjudicate it. In the human rights field, the justiciability of economic, social and cultural rights has traditionally been questioned. It is alleged that they are not enforceable because of their vague formulation, and that their realization must be progressive because it depends on economic resources. However, there is significant Case Law on economic, social and cultural rights at both international and national levels. The full justiciability of economic, social and cultural rights has been finally recognized by way of the Optional Protocol to the ICESCR enabling the CESCR to receive and examine individual communications. It was, significantly, adopted on 10 December 2008 – the 60th anniversary of the UDHR.

Lex lata and Lex ferenda *Lex lata* and *lex ferenda* are Latin terms that mean, respectively, the Law 'as it exists', and the Law 'as it should be'.

Limburg Principles The Limburg Principles on the Implementation of the International Covenant on Economic, Social and Cultural Rights were adopted by a group of 29 experts in International Law, coming from several countries, and meeting in Maastricht (Netherlands), from 2 to 6 June 1986[32]. They were invited by the International Commission of Jurists (Geneva, Switzerland), the Faculty of Law of the University of Limburg (Netherlands), and the Urban Morgan Institute on Human Rights, University of Cincinnati (Ohio, USA):

> … to consider the nature and scope of the obligations of States Parties to the International Covenant on Economic, Social and Cultural Rights, the consideration of States Parties reports by the newly constituted ECOSOC Committee on Economic, Social and Cultural Rights, and international co-operation under Part IV of the Covenant.

They agreed unanimously upon a number of principles "which they believed reflect the present state of international law", and formulated certain recommendations.

Maastricht Guidelines The Maastricht Guidelines on Violations of Economic, Social and Cultural Rights were adopted by more than 30 experts on International Law, meeting in Maastricht from 22 to 26 January 1997, on the occasion of the 10th anniversary of the Limburg Principles. They were invitated by the International Commission of Jurists, the Urban Morgan Institute on Human Rights, and

---

[32] www.uu.nl/faculty/leg/NL/organisatie/departementen/departementrechtsgeleerdheid/organisatie/onderdelen/studieeninformatiecentrummensenrechten/publicaties/simspecials/20/Documents/20–10.pdf.

the Centre for Human Rights of the Faculty of Law of Maastricht University, "to elaborate on the Limburg Principles as regards the nature and scope of violations of economic, social and cultural rights and appropriate responses and remedies". They unanimously agreed on guidelines "which they understand to reflect the evolution of international law since 1986"[33].

Margin of Appreciation/Discretion As every international regime of human rights protection (norms, mechanisms and procedures) is subsidiary to the national legal orders, when a complaint is submitted to international instances they recognize to domestic tribunals a margin of appreciation and discretion in dealing with each case and situation, because of their more direct and concrete knowledge of what is at stake.

Member States Member States are States that are members of an IGO, such as the UN or the AU.

Memorandum of Understanding (M.O.U.) M.O.U. is a term often used to denote a less formal international instrument than a typical treaty or international agreement. It often sets out operational arrangements under a framework international agreement. It is also used for the regulation of technical or detailed matters. An M.O.U. typically consists of a single instrument and is entered into among States and/or international organizations. The UN usually concludes M.O.U.s with Member States in order to organize its peacekeeping operations or to arrange UN conferences. The UN also concludes M.O.U.s regarding cooperation with other international organizations. It considers M.O.U.s to be binding and registers them if submitted by a party or if the UN is a party.

Minorities and Indigenous Peoples Minority refers to groups with (1) fewer members, that is, not the majority of a population, or (2) less power in society.

Erika- Irene Daes and Asbjørn Eide are the authors of a 'Working paper on the relationship and distinction between the rightsof persons belonging to minorities and those of indigenous peoples' prepared for the former Sub-Commission on the Promotion and Protection of Human Rights (E/CN.4/Sub.2/2000/10)[34]. Following Eide, the difference between both categories of rights "can probably best be formulated as follows": While the "instruments concerning persons belonging to minorities aim at ensuring a space for pluralism in togetherness, the instruments concerning indigenous peoples are intended to allow for a high degree of autonomous development" (para. 8).

> 23. … Persons belonging to minorities often have several identities and participate actively in the common domain. Indigenous rights, on the other hand, tend to consolidate and strengthen the separateness of these peoples from other groups in society. The underlying assumption is that persons belonging to indigenous peoples have a predominantly indigenous identity and participate less in the common domain.

---

[33] www.uu.nl/faculty/leg/NL/organisatie/departementen/departementrechtsgeleerdheid/organisatie/onderdelen/studieeninformatiecentrummensenrechten/publicaties/simspecials/20/Documents/20–01.pdf

[34] http://daccess-dds-ny.un.org/doc/UNDOC/GEN/G00/142/37/PDF/G0014237.pdf?OpenElement

According to Daes:

> 43. Classification as a "minority" or as "indigenous" has very different implications in international law. Both categories of groups possess the right to perpetuate their distinctive cultural characteristics and to be free from adverse discrimination on the basis of those cultural characteristics. Both kinds of groups enjoy the right to participate meaningfully in the social, economic and political life of the State as a whole—as groups if they choose, and in any case without adverse discrimination. *In my opinion, the principal legal distinction between the rights of minorities and indigenous peoples in contemporary international law is with respect to internal self-determination: the right of a group to govern itself within a recognized geographical area, without State interference (albeit in some cooperative relationship with State authorities, as in any federal system of national government).*

In 1992, the UN adopted the Declaration on the Rights of Persons Belonging to National or Ethnic, Religious and Linguistic Minorities that affirms:

> States shall protect the existence and the national or ethnic, cultural, religious and linguistic identity of minorities within their respective territories and shall encourage conditions for the promotion of that identity. (Article 1.1)
> Persons belonging to national or ethnic, religious and linguistic minorities (hereinafter referred to as persons belonging to minorities) have the right to enjoy their own culture, to profess and practise their own religion, and to use their own language, in private and in public, freely and without interference or any form of discrimination. (Article 2.1)

In 2007, the UN adopted the United Nations Declaration on the Rights of Indigenous Peoples that recognizes and reaffirms "that indigenous individuals are entitled without discrimination to all human rights recognized in international law, and that indigenous peoples possess collective rights which are indispensable for their existence, well-being and integral development as peoples".

Most Favorable Protection As IHRL aims at ensuring a minimum level of protection of the individual, many human rights' international instruments include a clause preventing States Parties from invoking a treaty to downgrade an otherwise more favorable domestic protection of human rights. It is known as 'Savings Clause'.

National Human Rights Institution (NHRI) NHRIs exist since late 1970s. In 1991, their first international meeting, in Paris, adopted the 'Principles relating to the Status of National Institutions' (Paris Principles) that were endorsed by the UN General Assembly in 1993. They have varying denominations and powers. They may be named Commission, Ombudsman (a masculine name now often replaced with the neutral *Ombudsperson*), Mediator, *Defensor del Pueblo*, *Provedor de Justiça*, etc. They may even have the rank of a Ministry or a Secretary of State. There are more than one hundred such institutions, half of them corresponding to the Paris Principles.

Natural Law Natural Law or 'Law of Nature' (*jus natural* or *lex naturalis*, in Latin) is the theory or belief following which there is a higher Law inherent to the whole Universe or *Cosmos*.

The feeling and belief in the correspondence between what is 'natural' and what is 'right' go back to the most ancient of times. However, as the meaning of nature is variable in the course of time, the history of the idea of Natural Law presents a variety of theories. There are religious and secular versions of it. In Western world, the idea originated in classical Greece of the 5th century BC, with the first philosophers, but its most influential philosophical elaboration happened in the Middle Ages with St. Thomas Aquinas.

Towards the end of the 18th century, the attractiveness of Natural Law theory was declining, for many reasons, in particular because of the rise of the legal positivism which became dominant during the 19th through the mid-20th centuries. According to it, Law is only the one created or *posited* by the State. The idea of Natural Law and natural rights revived after the horrors of the Second World War.

According to its present Christian version, since God is the Creator of the world, the whole creation—the world and the human beings—were created following a divine idea. It constitutes the eternal or Natural Law imprinted in the world, including seeds or principles of morality, i.e. of good and evil, right and wrong, which apply to human conduct and to which every human written Law must conform. They are naturally knowable and, therefore, universally binding for human beings endowed with the faculty of reason.

However, Natural Law entails levels of precepts. Only the first principles of morality are immutable and within everyone's reach. Other precepts are not evident in all eras for everybody. Their knowledge depends upon cultural circumstances and the evolving of moral conscience. Therefore, Natural Law is, at the same time, eternal-immutable and historical-relative. Its historicity and relativity explain mistakes and wrongdoings, such as social divisions and discriminations, including slavery. Principles and norms recognized by the universal moral conscience eventually merge with 'human nature' and qualify as 'Natural Law', though their conquest may have implied great suffering.

Consequently, laws can be divided into divine, natural or human types:

- *Divine laws* are those written in the Bible and the teachings of the Catholic Church doctrine.
- *Natural laws* are those which are inscribed in physical and human nature, permanent and universal, being discoverable through the use of reason common to all peoples.
- *Positive laws* are human-made laws, created by a State, varying from society to society and changing over time.

The Natural Law idea was the most influential in birth of the human rights idea and ideal. Whether there is a natural, unwritten higher Law to which all written positive Law should conform in order to be legitimate and obeyed—this remains a central problem of the Legal Philosophy. Maybe the tension between Natural Law and Positive Law is insoluble.

Non bis in idem *Non bis in idem* (not twice in the same thing) is a general legal principle (principle of double jeopardy, as it is known in the USA) meaning that no person shall be tried or punished twice for the same offence. Another formulation is *Nemo bis vexari pro una et eadam causa* ('a man shall not be twice vexed or tried for the same cause').

Non-binding A non-binding legal instrument, like a declaration, carries no formal legal obligations. It may, however, carry moral and political obligations or attain the force of Law.

Non-Governmental Organization (NGO) Strictly speaking, a human rights NGO is a private, non-profit and independent entity, i.e. not founded or controlled by a Government, in particular, to promote and protect internationally recognized human rights at local, national, sub-regional, regional or global levels, if needed by *naming, blaming and shaming*. Some are large and international, others may be small and local. They are the *watchdogs* of the human rights that fall within their mandate, forming a dense, worldwide network. Thousand NGOs have consultative status with the main IGOs, especially with the UN. They contributed greatly to the strengthening of the human rights profile in the UN Charter, to the drafting of the UDHR and to virtually all, if not to all of, the UN's major international human rights instruments. Several NGOs and preeminent human rights activists were awarded Nobel Peace Prizes.

There is a Conference of Non-Governmental Organizations in consultative relationship with the UN (CoNGO), founded in 1948, as well as a World Association of Non-Governmental Organizations (WANGO) founded in 2000. In the same year, the CHR appointed a UN Special Representative on the Situation of Human Rights Defenders. In 2001, Front Line Defenders was founded, which is an International Foundation for the Protection of Human Rights Defenders (see subsection 3.4.5).

Non-State Actors Under IHRL, States are the only agents directly responsible for compliance with treaties, thus excluding non-State actors, which are manifold: NGOs, national and international; indigenous and minority groups; multinational enterprises; paramilitary groups; terrorists; etc. While the question of attribution is a complex area of International Law, the acts of non-State actors may be attributed to the State if it is proved that it failed to prevent, prohibit and remedy human rights violations committed by people under its jurisdiction. In any case, one of the most significant changes in the human rights debate is the increased recognition of the link between business and human rights. In the era of the world's globalization and of the privatisation of public services, private entities are taking on roles previously held by the State. Moreover, for-profit powerful transnational corporations play a determinant role in the international scene, arousing new concerns for the protection of human rights. That is why there are attempts to get them also legally accountable for human rights violations.

Obligations of States States are the authors and first addressees of the IHRL they adopt and undertake to comply with. Consequently, they are the main human rights duty-bearers. When a State becomes party to a human rights treaty, it assumes a legal obligation to respect and protect the human rights of all people within their territory and jurisdiction.

A distinction is often made between the protection of 'civil liberties' and of 'social rights'. While the former are said to require the State's non-interference (an immediate obligation, consisting principally in legal guarantees), the latter are deemed to require, rather, the State's intervention (a progressive obligation, conditional on the necessary resources). On this ground, civil and political rights have been considered precise and justiciable, that is, able to be adjudicated by a judicial or similar body, while economic, social and cultural rights have been depreciated as vague and non-justiciable. This is a simplistic distinction. All human rights are expensive and justiciable.

Using the terminology of the UN International Law Commission, States have 'obligations of conduct' (to undertake a specific step, act or omission) and 'obligations of result' (to attain a particular outcome). Within the UN framework, States' generic obligations regarding human rights are commonly summarized as follows:

• *Obligation to respect*
The obligation to protect requires the State's organs and officials to refrain from committing human rights violations themselves against individuals under their jurisdiction. This is called the 'vertical effect' of States' obligations.

• *Obligation to protect*
The obligation to protect requires States to prevent human rights violations by third parties, individuals or other non-State actors, as well as to provide remedies when they occur. This is called the 'horizontal effect' of States' obligations.

• *Obligation to fulfill*
The obligation to fulfill requires States to ensure enjoyment of human rights by taking legislative, administrative, judicial, economic, educational and other measures.

This triple obligation applies both to civil and political rights, as well as economic, social and cultural rights. Retrogressive measures are hardly compatible with States' obligations and, in any case, there are 'non-derogable rights' and 'minimum core obligations'. While States do not necessarily have to fulfill human rights directly by themselves, they are ultimately responsible for ensuring their implementation, as providers of last resort.

The European Court of Human Rights distinguishes two categories of States' obligations: negative and positive. The former require it to refrain from interference; the latter require intervention. They correspond to negative and positive rights. A negative human right is a right not to do something or not to be interfered with in enjoying one's rights (examples are the right not to have any religious belief and the right to privacy). A positive human right is a right to do something or to a State's action (examples are the right to practice a religion or to the goods and services necessary to the enjoyment of economic, social and cultural rights).

The distinction between negative and positive rights and obligations does not actually counter the UN typology, however.

- *Obligation to respect*, sometimes called negative obligation, because States are obliged to abstain from certain actions.
- *Obligation to protect*, which is a positive one, because States are obliged to take action in order to prevent third parties from attacking human rights.
- *Obligation to fulfill*, that is, to take appropriate measures to implement human rights standards.

While States do not necessarily have to fulfill human rights directly by themselves, they are the ultimately responsible for ensuring their implementation, as providers of last resort.

Opinio Juris Communis As said the Inter-American Court of Human Rights (*Baena-Ricardo et al. v. Panama*, 2003, para. 102)[35]: "The *opinio juris communis* means the expression of the universal juridical conscience through the observance, by most of the members of the international community, of a determined practice because it is obligatory".

Pacta sunt servanda *Pacta sunt servanda* is a classic principle of the International Law, in particular, commanding that agreements must be kept by the parties, unless the clause *rebus sic stantibus* (as things stand, i.e. if no fundamental change of circumstances occurs) or peremptory norms (*jus cogens*) come into play. It relies upon the *bona fides* (good faith) principle.

Petition Petition (or 'complaint' or 'communication' or 'application') is a collective term embracing the various procedures for bringing complaints before a judicial or quasi-judicial body. Petitions may consist of complaints from individuals alleging violations of a treaty by a State Party or from a State Party alleging violations of a treaty by another State Party (inter-State complaints). For submitting a communication to an international judicial body, several conditions should be met. They include:

- the defendant State should have ratified the relevant treaty;
- the treaty should already have entered into force for the said State;
- the relevant right(s) should be protected by that treaty;
- possible restrictions, reservations and derogations should be taken into account;
- the plaintiff should have standing to do so and must first have exhausted all effective domestic remedies;
- and the State must have recognized the competence of the international judicial body to deal with the complaint.

Plenipotentiary A Plenipotentiary is the person authorized by an instrument of full powers to undertake a specific treaty action.

Positive Discrimination/Affirmative Action The concept of positive discrimination or affirmative action was introduced in the mid-1960s, especially following passage of the Civil Rights Act of 1964 in the USA. This is why North American Case Law is particularly developed on this issue. The famous case *Plessy v. Ferguson,* 163 US 537 (1896) had upheld racial segregation of public services. The landmark case *Brown v. Board of Education,* 347 US 483 (1954), followed by other cases, overturned the *Plessy v. Fergusson* jurisprudence.
Positive discrimination or reverse discrimination or affirmative action refer to policies and programs, in areas such education and employment, designed to redress past discrimination because of race, sex, etc., for the most vulnerable or disadvantaged

[35] www.corteidh.or.cr/docs/casos/articulos/seriec_104_ing.pdf.

people to have the opportunity to become equal within society. Those policies and programs function as an elevator mechanism. However, it should be noted that affirmative action is of a temporary nature; it should not continue after its objectives have been achieved.

Affirmative action was defined by the CCPR in its GC 18 (A/45/40(VOL.I) (SUPP) as follows[36]:

10. The Committee also wishes to point out that the principle of equality sometimes requires States parties to take affirmative action in order to diminish or eliminate conditions which cause or help to perpetuate discrimination prohibited by the Covenant. For example, in a State where the general conditions of a certain part of the population prevent or impair their enjoyment of human rights, the state should take specific action to correct those conditions. Such action may involve granting for a time to the part of the population concerned certain preferential treatment in specific matters as compared with the rest of the population. However, as long as such action is needed to correct discrimination in fact, it is a case of legitimate differentiation under the Covenant.

Prima facie *Prima facie* is a Latin term that means literally 'at first sight/look/ appearance', before closer examination. A *prima facie* human rights violation is one that at first glance is evident.

Pro Homine *Pro Homine* is a general legal principle meaning that *Hominum causa jus constitutum est* (Law is established for the benefit of man). It means, therefore, that every Law must be interpreted and applied in the way most protective of human beings.

Proportionality Proportionality is a legal principle regulating the exercise of the State's power, especially prohibiting the use of excessive force, applying a disproportionate punishment or taking unnecessary measures.

Protection and Promotion While protecting human rights contributes to their promotion, and promoting human rights contributes to their protection, protecting human rights is mostly a matter of standard-setting and legal enforcement and remedies; promoting them is mostly a matter of information and education.

Protocol A protocol, in the context of Treaty Law and practice, has the same legal characteristics as a treaty. The term protocol is often used to describe agreements of a less formal nature than those entitled treaty or convention. Generally, a protocol amends, supplements or clarifies a multilateral treaty. It is normally open to participation by the parties to the parent agreement. It may be called 'optional' because a Government that has ratified the original treaty can choose whether or not to ratify the changes made in the protocol.

In recent times, States have negotiated a number of protocols that do not follow this principle. The advantage of a protocol is that, while it is linked to the parent agreement, it can focus on a specific aspect of that agreement in greater detail.

[36] http://tbinternet.ohchr.org/_layouts/treatybodyexternal/TBSearch.aspx?Lang=en&TreatyID=8&DocTypeID=11

Ratification Ratification, acceptance, approval and accession—all refer to the act undertaken on the international plane, whereby a State establishes its consent to be bound by a treaty. Most multilateral treaties expressly provide for States to express their consent to be bound by signature subject to ratification, acceptance or approval. Ratification, acceptance and approval all require two steps:

- The execution of an instrument of ratification, acceptance or approval by the Head of State, Head of Government or Minister for Foreign Affairs, expressing the intent of the State to be bound by the relevant treaty; and
- For multilateral treaties, the deposit of the instrument with the depositary; and for bilateral treaties, the exchange of the instruments between parties.

The instrument of ratification, acceptance or approval must comply with certain international legal requirements. This should not be confused with the act of ratification at the national level, which a State may be required to undertake in accordance with its own constitutional provisions, before it consents to be bound internationally. Ratification at the national level is inadequate to establish the State's consent to be bound at the international level.

Providing for signature subject to ratification allows States time to seek approval for the treaty at the domestic level and to enact any legislation necessary to implement the treaty domestically, prior to undertaking the legal obligations under the treaty at the international level. Once a State has ratified a treaty at the international level, it must give effect to the treaty domestically. Generally, there is no time limit within which a State is requested to ratify a treaty which it has signed. Upon ratification, the State becomes legally bound under the treaty.

Refugee The term 'refugee' is so defined by the Convention Relating to the Status of Refugees (UN, 1951), Article 1:

> A. For the purposes of the present Convention, the term "refugee" shall apply to any person who:
> [...]
> 2) As a result of events occurring before 1 January 1951 and owing to well-founded fear of being persecuted for reasons of race, religion, nationality, membership of a particular social group or political opinion, is outside the country of his nationality and is unable or, owing to such fear, is unwilling to avail himself of the protection of that country; or who, not having a nationality and being outside the country of his former habitual residence as a result of such events, is unable or, owing to such fear, is unwilling to return to it.

Registration Registration, in the context of Treaty Law and practice, refers to the function of the UN Secretariat in effecting the registration of treaties and international agreements under Article 102 of the UN Charter.

Remedy Remedy, in legal terms, is the means by which the violation of a right is redressed or compensated.

Reporting Guidelines for States Parties Each TMB has produced written guidelines for States Parties giving advice on the form and content of the reports which States are obliged to submit under the relevant treaty. These guidelines vary in approach to some degree: Some Committees have provided detailed guidance on an Article-by-Article basis, whereas others have given more general guidance (see Compilation of Reporting Guidelines, HRI/GEN/2/Rev.6, 2009).

Reservation A reservation is a unilateral statement, however phrased or named, made by a State, by which it purports to exclude or alter the legal effect of certain provisions of a treaty in their application to that State. A reservation may enable a State to participate in a multilateral treaty that it would otherwise be unable or unwilling to participate in. States can make reservations to a treaty when they sign, ratify, accept, approve or accede to it. When a State makes a reservation upon signing, it must confirm the reservation upon ratification, acceptance or approval.

However, this right is not unlimited either. Article 19.c of the VCLT excludes reservations "incompatible with the object and purpose of the treaty".

Reservations to human rights conventional instruments is a very controversial question (see GC 24 of the CCPR).

Reservations after Deposit Where the Secretary-General, as depositary, receives a reservation after the deposit of the instrument of ratification, acceptance, approval or accession that meets all the necessary requirements, the Secretary-General circulates the reservation to all the States concerned. The Secretary-General accepts the reservation in deposit only if no such State informs him that it does not wish him to consider it to have accepted that reservation.

Objections to Reservations Where a State concerned lodges an objection to a treaty with the Secretary-General, the Secretary-General circulates it as a 'communication'.

Effect of Objection on Entry into Force of Reservations An objection to a reservation "does not preclude the entry into force of the treaty as between the objecting and reserving States unless a contrary intention is definitely expressed by the objecting State" (Article 20.4.b of the VCLT). Normally, to avoid uncertainty, an objecting State specifies whether its objection to the reservation precludes the entry into force of the treaty between itself and the reserving State. The Secretary-General circulates such objections. If a State does not object to a reservation made by another State, the first State is deemed to have tacitly accepted the reservation.

Withdrawal of Reservations A State may, unless the treaty provides otherwise, withdraw its reservation or objection to a reservation completely or partially at any time. The Vienna Declaration and Programme of Action (1993) read (II.5):

> The World Conference on Human Rights encourages States to consider limiting the extent of any reservations they lodge to international human rights instruments, formulate any reservations as precisely and narrowly as possible, ensure that none is incompatible with the object and purpose of the relevant treaty and regularly review any reservations with a view to withdrawing them.

Modifications to Reservations An existing reservation may be modified so as to result in a partial withdrawal or to create new exemptions from, or modifications of, the legal effects of certain provisions of a treaty. A modification of the latter kind has the nature of a new reservation. The Secretary-General, as depositary, circulates such modifications and grants the States concerned a specific period within which to object to them. In the absence of objections, the Secretary-General accepts the modification in deposit.

Responsibility to Protect The concept of *Responsibility to Protect* (R2P) was adopted by the 2005 United Nations World Summit (A/RES/60/1). It is worded thus:

> 138. Each individual State has the responsibility to protect its populations from genocide, war crimes, ethnic cleansing and crimes against humanity. This responsibility entails the prevention of such crimes, including their incitement, through appropriate and necessary means. We accept that responsibility and will act in accordance with it. [...]
> 139. The international community, through the United Nations, also has the responsibility to use appropriate diplomatic, humanitarian and other peaceful means, in accordance with Chapters VI and VIII of the Charter, to help to protect populations from genocide, war crimes, ethnic cleansing and crimes against humanity. [...]

Review Review or revision basically means amendment. However, some treaties provide for revisions/reviews separately from amendments (see, e.g. Article 109 of the UN Charter). In that case, revision/review typically refers to an overriding adaptation of a treaty to changed circumstances, whereas the term amendment refers to changes to specific provisions.

Review Procedure Review Procedure is the procedure by which a TMB will consider the situation in a country at one of its sessions in the absence of a report from the State Party. The procedure is used in cases where the report has been overdue for an excessive period and the State Party has not responded to the TMB's requests for a report. In many cases, States Parties choose to submit a report to avoid the review procedure; in other cases, States choose to send a delegation to the TMB's session and answer questions from its experts even though they have been able to submit a report.

Rights and Duties One one of the most common criticisms of human rights discourse is that it neglects individual duties.

The individual being, by definition, at the core of the idea and ideal of human rights, they are ethically individualistic, that is, concerned with personal worth, dignity, autonomy and self-development. This does not at all mean conceiving of the individual as an entity abstracted and isolated from the groups he or she belongs to. Human rights do not exist in a cultural and social *vacuum*. If everyone holds rights, everyone bears duties. Rights and duties are two sides of the same coin. The principle of reciprocity is inherent to the concept of human rights. It is frequently recalled in the legal instruments on human rights, both at universal and regional levels.

Rights-Holder and Duties-Bearer If a person has a right, someone else has a correspondent duty. The former is the right-holder, the latter is the duty-bearer. Regarding human rights, every person is inherently a right-holder, and States are the principal legally and politically duty-bearers.

Rule of Law *Rule of Law, Rechtsstaat* (German), *État de Droit* (French), *Stato di Diritto* (Italian), *Estado de Derecho* (Spanish), *Estado de Direito* (Portuguese) – are equivalent terms.

It may be said that the history of the Rule of Law began with the history of Law itself, but its development took centuries. We agree, in general, that the Rule of Law is desirable and necessary for economic growth, the enjoyment of human rights, the global stability and peace, highest levels of wellbeing, but the concept remains debated. It arouses the following crucial question: Does Rule of Law mean simply a State ruled by Law, whatever Law, or a State submitted to a superior Law? Which Law?

Until the Second World War, a minimalist conception of Rule of Law was prevalent. The Second World War caused a refounding of Rule of Law, respect for human rights becoming the principle of Governments' legitimacy. Therefore, we may distinguish two principal meanings of Rule of Law: one formal, qualified as *thin*, another one substantial, qualified as *thick*.

- Under its formal or *thin* meaning, Rule of Law includes the rejection of 'rule of man' in favor of controlling Government powers by Law; its application to everybody and equality before the laws; and the existence of specific institutions, such as the judiciary, to apply the laws.
- Under its substantial or *thick* meaning, Rule of Law incorporates an idea of justice as the State's political purpose, consubstantiated in the ideal of human rights. Its main elements are the protection of citizens' fundamental rights, the separation of powers, the legality of administrative acts and the independence of judicial power.

In sum, at present, Rule of Law does not mean the mere existence of, and conformity with, whatever formal legal framework, but a conception of political legitimacy and social justice based upon the supreme worth and dignity of the human person and inherent rights. So understood, human rights and democracy are inherent elements of the Rule of Law. The UDHR warns that "it is essential, if man is not to be compelled to have recourse, as a last resort, to rebellion against tyranny and oppression, that human rights should be protected by the rule of law" (third preambular paragraph). The European Court of Human Rights reaffirmed in *Sirmanov v. Bulgaria* (Application 67353/01, Judgment in 10 August 2007)[37]: "The rule of law, one of the fundamental principles of a democratic society, is inherent in all Articles of the Convention" (para. 31).

The International Community professes and promotes a substantial conception of Rule of Law. The idea of International Rule of Law has emerged too.

While there is a tension between human rights (the ethical principle) and democracy (the majority principle), the principle of respect of human rights and the principle of the popular sovereignty are historically, conceptually and politically indissociable. At present, the Rule of Law is generally understood as lying in the consubstantiality between human rights and democracy. The UN General Assembly adopted on 24 September 2012 a 'Declaration of the high-level meeting of the

[37] http://hudoc.echr.coe.int/sites/eng/pages/search.aspx?i=001-80492#{"itemid":["001-80492"]}

General Assembly on the rule of law at the national and international levels' (A/RES/67/1)[38] that reads:

> 5. We reaffirm that human rights, the rule of law and democracy are interlinked and mutually reinforcing and that they belong to the universal and indivisible core values and principles of the United Nations.

The same Declaration, after considering (in its introduction) that the Rule of Law "is the foundation of friendly and equitable relations between States and the basis on which just and fair societies are built", affirms:

> 2. We recognize that the rule of law applies to all States equally, and to international organizations, including the United Nations and its principal organs, and that respect for and promotion of the rule of law and justice should guide all of their activities and accord predictability and legitimacy to their actions. [...]

Rules of Procedure Rules of Procedure are the formal rules adopted by a TMB to govern the way in which it undertakes its business. Each Committee is empowered by the relevant treaty to adopt its own Rules of Procedure. They usually cover such matters as election of officers and procedures for adopting decisions especially where no consensus can be reached. Rules of Procedure are related to, but distinct from, working methods.

Self-executing Self-executing are international norms capable of becoming automatically part of domestic Law, upon ratification, being so directly applicable by national tribunals. If they are not self-executing, further implementing legislation is required to incorporate them into the domestic legal order and make them enforceable.

Shadow Report Shadow Report (or 'parallel' or 'alternative' report) is an unofficial report prepared by institutions or individuals representing civil society submitted to a TMB. Such reports usually add to, or may contradict, the official report on treaty compliance and implementation submitted by a Government as part of its treaty obligations.

Signature

Definitive Signature (Signature not Subject to Ratification) Definitive signature occurs where a State expresses its consent to be bound by a treaty by signing the treaty without the need for ratification, acceptance or approval. A State may definitively sign a treaty only when the treaty so permits. A number of treaties deposited with the Secretary-General permit definitive signature.

Simple Signature (Signature Subject to Ratification) Simple signature applies to most multilateral treaties. This means that when a State signs the treaty, the signature is subject to ratification, acceptance or approval. The State has not expressed its consent to be bound by the treaty until it ratifies, accepts or approves it. In that

[38] www.un.org/en/ga/search/view_doc.asp?symbol=A/RES/67/1
The UN Secretary-General published a report entitled 'Delivering justice: programme of action to strengthen the rule of law at the national and international levels' (A/66/749).
(www.unrol.org/doc.aspx?d=3141)

case, a State that signs a treaty is obliged to refrain, in good faith, from acts that would defeat the object and purpose of the treaty. Good faith is a general principle of international law (see UN Charter Article 2.2 and the Preamble and Articles 26 and 31.1 of the VCLT). Signature alone does not impose on the State obligations under the treaty. It is a preparatory step on the way to ratification of the treaty by the State. Signatory States are so the States that have signed a treaty.

Sovereignty of States The traditional principle of national sovereignty – the bedrock of the International Law enshrined in Article 15.8 of the Covenant of the League of Nations and in Article 2.7 of the UN Charter – implies the noninterference in the domestic affairs of any State. One exception was provided by the 18th doctrine of humanitarian intervention in case of systematic and shocking human rights violations. The Second World War moral tragedy has prompted "a truly revolutionary" change in International Law, as reads an USA official publication[39]:

> Prior to modern IHRL, how States treated their own citizens was regarded as a purely domestic matter. International law regulated State conduct vis-à-vis other States, and chiefly protected individuals as representatives of their parent States (e.g., diplomatic immunity). As sovereigns in the international system, States could expect other States not to interfere in their internal affairs. IHRL, however, pierced the veil of sovereignty by seeking directly to *regulate how States treated their own people within their own borders.*

The principle of national sovereignty is still often invoked by States accused of gross violations of human rights. However, as the UN Charter refers to nonintervention "in matters which are essentially within the domestic jurisdiction of any state", but made the respect of human rights one of its principles, human rights have become an international concern, as restated the 1993 Vienna Declaration and Programme of Action (I.4)[40]:

> The promotion and protection of all human rights and fundamental freedoms must be considered as a priority objective of the United Nations in accordance with its purposes and principles, in particular the purpose of international cooperation. In the framework of these purposes and principles, the promotion and protection of all human rights is a legitimate concern of the international community.

The last major international development of this principle is the concept of *Responsibility to Protect* (R2P) adopted by the 2005 UN World Summit (A/RES/60/1)[41], according to which:

> 139. The international community, through the United Nations, also has the responsibility to use appropriate diplomatic, humanitarian and other peaceful means, in accordance with Chapters VI and VIII of the Charter, to help to protect populations from genocide, war crimes, ethnic cleansing and crimes against humanity. In this context, we are prepared to take collective action, in a timely and decisive manner, through the Security Council, in accordance with the Charter, including Chapter VII, on a case-by-case basis and in cooperation with relevant regional organizations as appropriate, should peaceful means be inadequate and national authorities are manifestly failing to protect their populations from genocide, war crimes, ethnic cleansing and crimes against humanity.

[39] See: www.loc.gov/rr/frd/Military_Law/pdf/operational-law-handbook_2013.pdf

[40] www.unhchr.ch/huridocda/huridoca.nsf/(symbol)/a.conf.157.23.en

[41] http://mdgs.un.org/unsd/mdg/Resources/Attach/Indicators/ares60_1_2005summit_eng.pdf

As a consequence, there is an international right and duty to interfere or intervene in the domestic affairs of a State committing grave and shocking human rights violations. In addition, the principle of State sovereignty has been significantly eroded by many international changes demanding international cooperation, as well as by the world's globalization.

Special Procedures The Special Procedures, created by the former Commission on Human Rights, consist in independent human rights experts being appointed to undertake specific mandates that may be a 'thematic mandate', i.e. to deal with a specific human rights issue, or a 'country mandate', i.e. to deal with the human rights situation in a specific country. Thematic mandates are usually created for a period of three years and can be renewed for the same period. Country mandates are usually created and renewed on an annual basis. They number about 50 at present.

Mandate holders can be individuals or groups of five members, one from each of the five UN geographical regions (African Group, Asian Group, Latin American and Caribbean Group, Western European and Others Group, Eastern European Group). So far, the independent experts were named Special Rapporteur, Independent Expert or Special Representative, but now they are generally called Special Rapporteur. The groups are called Working Groups. The mandates' working methods include undertaking studies, conducting country visits, receiving and investigating complaints from alleged victims of human rights violations, issuing urgent action requests, and annually reporting on their activities.

Being Charter-based mechanisms, the action of the Special Procedures is not dependent upon a State being party in any relevant human rights instrument (see section 3.4.1).

State Party A State Party to a treaty is a State that has expressed its consent to be bound by that treaty by an act of ratification, acceptance, approval or accession, etc., where that treaty has entered into force for that particular State. This means that the State is bound by the treaty under International Law.

Some treaties are only open to States whereas others are also open to other entities with treaty-making capacity. The two 1966 Covenants and ICERD are open to signature and ratification by "any State Member of the United Nations or member of any of its specialized agencies, by any State Party to the Statute of the International Court of Justice, and by any other State which has been invited by the General Assembly of the United Nations". The other core human rights treaties are open to all States. The optional protocols are all restricted to States Parties to the parent treaty except the CRC-OP1 to which any State may accede.

State Party Report State Party Report is the report that each State Party to a human rights treaty is required, under the provisions of that treaty, to submit regularly to the respective TMB, indicating the measures it has adopted to implement the treaty and the difficulties it has encountered. All treaties require a comprehensive initial report within a fixed time after ratification and, with the exception of the CPED, also subsequent periodic reports at regular intervals. The report to each TMB consists of a common core document, which is the same for all, and a treaty-specific document for each specific TMB.

Subsidiarity Subsidiarity is a typical principle of the IHRL. Indeed, the primary responsibilities in the field of human rights remain with States, which cannot relieve themselves of their human rights obligations by 'delegating' them to non-State entities or IGOs. International protection is complementary of national legal systems, so that, in case of human rights violations, the domestic remedies must be exhausted before having recourse to an international body.

Succession Succession takes place only if a State, which is a party to a treaty, has undergone a major constitutional transformation which raises some doubt as to whether the original expression of consent to be bound is still valid. Such circumstances may include independence (for example, through decolonization), dissolution of a Federation or Union, and secession of a State or entity from a State or Federation.

Travaux préparatoires *Travaux préparatoires* is a French term that literally means 'preparatory works'. It is frequently used to refer to the official documents of the legislative history of a legal instrument, based on the records of its negotiations, debates and drafting. According to the VCLT (Article 32 – Supplementary means of interpretation)[42]: "Recourse may be had to supplementary means of interpretation, including the preparatory work of the treaty and the circumstances of its conclusion".

Treaty The VCLT defines a treaty as "an international agreement concluded between States in written form and governed by international Law, whether embodied in a single instrument or in two or more related instruments and whatever its particular designation" (Article 2.1.a). Accordingly, conventions, agreements, protocols, and exchange of letters or notes may all constitute treaties. Although the VCLT does not apply to non-written agreements, its definition of a treaty states that the absence of writing does not affect the legal force of international agreements. No international rules exist as to when an international instrument should be entitled a treaty. However, usually the term treaty is employed for instruments of some gravity and solemnity.

Whereas in the last century the term 'convention' was regularly employed for bilateral agreements, it is now generally used for formal multilateral treaties with a broad number of parties. Conventions are normally open for participation by the International Community as a whole, or by a large number of States. Usually instruments negotiated under the auspices of an international organization are entitled conventions. The same holds true for instruments adopted by an organ of an international organization.

Each treaty provides for its entry into force, usually by indicating the number of ratifications ore accessions needed to that effect, which varies from treaty to treaty. While a State is allowed to enter reservations or declarations when accepting to be bound by a treaty, they must not be contrary to the purpose and scope of the relevant treaty and their validity may be objected by other States Parties.

The adoption of a human rights treaty is often preceded by the adoption of a declaration, a recommendation or other text. These instruments are approved by the

[42] http://legal.un.org/ilc/texts/instruments/english/conventions/1_1_1969.pdf

UN General Assembly typically by consensus. They serve also to give substance to general principles and norms.

Bilateral Treaty A bilateral treaty is a treaty between two parties.

Multilateral Treaty A multilateral treaty is a treaty between more than two parties.

Treaty Monitoring Body (TMB) Each State Party to human rights treaties is under an obligation to submit regular reports to Committees of experts that supervise how the rights are being implemented. They originated in a resolution of the ECOSOC in 1956. The idea was first incorporated into the 1965 International Convention on the Elimination of All Forms of Racial Discrimination. After a comprehensive initial report within one or two years of the treaty entering into force for it, each State must continue to report periodically, usually every four or five years (with the exception of the CPED).

The Committees are widely known as 'Treaty Bodies' or 'Treaty Monitoring Bodies' (TMBs), because they are created in accordance with the provisions of the respective treaty (except for the CESCR that was not established directly under the terms of the ICESCR but was created by ECOSOC Resolution 1985/17). Their membership varies from 10 to 23 members. They meet in Geneva for two or three sessions each year, each session being of two or three weeks. The CCPR and the CoEDAW usually hold one of their annual sessions in New York. Their mandate includes:

- Considering the periodic reports the States Parties undertake to send, in accordance with the treaties' provisions (all but the SPT). This is the primary mandate of all the Committees and the softest and most common international procedure to monitoring States' compliance with their human rights obligations.
- Receiving and examining complaints or 'communications' (as they are generally referred to in the international human rights system) from individuals on alleged violations by States Parties of the human rights whose respect they supervise (all but the SPT). Five treaties established an inter-State complaints procedure. States concerned must have expressly recognized the competence of the Committee in this regard. While the complaints procedures of the HRC and the Special Procedures are universal, as they apply to all UN Member States, the TMBs procedure applies only to States Parties to the relevant treaty.
- Conducting country inquiries and/or visits, if they receive reliable information on serious, grave or systematic violations of the particular treaty. Inquiries may only be undertaken with respect to States Parties who have made a declaration accepting the competence of the Committee in this regard.

Each Committee can also take urgent action.

In addition, the TMBs play an interpreting role accomplished by issuing General Comments or General Recommendations that seek to define the States Parties' obligations.

The Chairpersons of the TMBs have met regularly, since 1984, to discuss matters of mutual concern and to coordinate their activities. Since 1995, the meetings have been annual and have taken place in Geneva, normally in May.

UN Charter-based Mechanisms UN Charter-based or non-conventional mechanisms are those created under the UN Charter and therefore apply to all Member States. At present, the principal UN human rights body is the Human Rights Council that replaced the Commission on Human Rights in 2006. Its main mechanism is the Universal Periodic Review. Others include the '1503 Procedure' and the 'Special Procedures' (see subsection 3.4.1).

UN High Commissioner for Human Rights (UNHCHR) The UNHCHR was established by the UN General Assembly in 1993, following a recommendation of the World Conference on Human Rights held in Vienna in the same year. She or he is the principal UN official as far as human rights are concerned, under the authority of the Secretary-General.

The Office of the United Nations High Commissioner for Human Rights (OHCHR) is seated in Geneva, having a little branch in New York and being present in over 50 countries. It absorbed the Centre for Human Rights and provides secretariat services for all UN activities in the field of human rights. Its Human Rights Treaties Division supports the TMBs in particular. A complaint may be sent to the OHCHR that refers it to the most appropriate mechanism.

UN Treaty-based Mechanisms UN Treaty-based or conventional mechanisms are those based on human rights treaties and thus apply only to the States Parties to the relevant treaties. They are concerned with States' commitments and obligations under the core human rights treaties to which they are parties. Each one is supervised by a Committee of independent experts, known as TMBs, created by the treaty itself (except for ICESCR). In spite of being elected by the States Parties to the particular treaty, their members are independent human rights experts, not States' representatives, serving in their personal capacities. Consequently, in contrast with the HRC, these are legal, not political, bodies.

As all States are parties to at least one of the core human rights treaties, the Treaty-based system applies universally too (see subsection 3.4.1).

Universal/World Court of Human Rights The establishment of a Universal or World Court of Human Rights is an aspiration as old as the UDHR (see subsect. 3.4.4). The idea was revived within the Swiss Government initiative to commemorate the 60th anniversary of the UDHR, called 'Protecting Dignity: An Agenda for Human Rights'. Statutes for a World Court of Human Rights were drafted (see sect. 8.4). Let us recall that, many years before the adoption of the ICC Rome Statute, the International Association for Penal Law and the International Law Association had been working on draft Statutes for it.

Universal Jurisdiction The jurisdiction of the International Criminal Court (1998)[43] includes "the following crimes: (a) The crime of genocide; (b) Crimes against humanity; (c) War crimes; (d) The crime of aggression" (Article 5.1). However, every State has the right and the duty to prosecute or extradite alleged perpetrators of international crimes, regardless of their nationality or of where the alleged

[43] www.icc-cpi.int/NR/rdonlyres/ADD16852-AEE9-4757-ABE7-9CDC7CF02886/283503/RomeStatutEng1.pdf

crimes were committed, if they are formally criminalized by domestic Law. This is the principle of universal jurisdiction. For instance, the Convention against Torture and Other Cruel, Inhuman or Degrading Treatment or Punishment (UN, 1984) establishes the principle of universal jurisdiction (Articles 5 to 8). An example of its application was the arrest of the former Chilean dictator Augusto Pinochet in 1998 in London.
See: *Universal Jurisdiction: A Preliminary Survey of Legislation around the World* (Amnesty International Publications, 2011)[44].

Universality of Human Rights The universality of human rights is still sometimes resisted and challenged, alleging the cultural diversity of the world.

When the UDHR was drafted, many peoples in Africa, Asia, and the Pacific and Caribbean regions were still not independent countries. Notwithstanding, the UN was in no way a culturally and ideologically homogenous organization, as it emerges from the documentation related to the UDHR drafting process: It took into account 24 drafts and discussed approximately two hundred proposals; 85 meetings were devoted to the discussion of the draft Declaration, in addition to 20 meetings held by various sub-committees; 88.08 % of a total of 1233 individual votes were affirmative, 3.73 % negative and 8.19 % were abstentions; 1000 speeches were made and 200 amendments submitted; each Article was amended on average ten times; 18 Articles were adopted without any opposition.

The resulting Universal Declaration is an alchemy of religious, philosophical and political values that has become an ethical-legal lighthouse and a liberation flag. During the 1950s and 1960s, tens of countries that became independent joined the UN and thus endorsed the values and principles laid down in the UDHR, as testifies the Proclamation of Tehran of 1968, adopted by 85 states, of which more than 60 countries did not belong to the Western Group. The Proclamation affirmed (para. 2)[45]: "The Universal Declaration of Human Rights states a common understanding of the peoples of the world concerning the inalienable and inviolable rights of all members of the human family and constitutes an obligation for the members of the international community". This was restated by the Vienna Declaration and Programme of Action (1993), attended by 171 States.

In any case, every UN State Member is bound by the principle of respect and protection of human rights. Moreover, the UN's universal system of human rights protection expanded and has been strengthened, andregional systems of human rights protection were also established in Europe, the Americas and Africa.

In sum, what should matter is not where the moral, scientific, technological or other advancements come from, but how good and beneficial they are to the whole of Humankind. In any case, the IHRL is sufficiently flexible to be compatible with legitimate cultural diversities. As of 28 September 2013, of the 193 United Nations Member States, 160 are parties to the ICESCR, 167 are parties to the ICCPR, and 193 are parties to the CRC.

---

[44] www.amnesty.org/en/library/asset/IOR53/004/2011/en/d997366e-65bf-4d80-9022-fcb8fe284c9d/ior530042011en.pdf

[45] http://untreaty.un.org/cod/avl/pdf/ha/fatchr/Final_Act_of_TehranConf.pdf

Vertical and Horizontal Human Rights Obligations Human rights being inherent in human dignity, they must be protected not only against breaches by States, but also by third parties. These are the so-called 'vertical effect' of human rights' protection (individual-State relationship) and the 'horizontal effect' (individual-individual, and individuals-other non-State actors) or *Drittwirkung* (the German term). States are responsible for human rights violations committed between individuals when they have been legally or materially unable to prevent them and failed to punish their perpetrators.

Xenophobia Xenophobia According to an OHCHR text[46]:

> Xenophobia is a broad notion, associated with a variety of meanings. The term 'xenophobia' comes from the Greek words ξένος (*xenos*), meaning 'foreigner', 'stranger', and φόβος (*phobos*), meaning 'fear'. Manifestations of xenophobia are usually triggered by intense dislike or hatred against people that are perceived as outsiders, strangers or foreigners to a group, community or nation, based on their presumed or real descent, national, ethnic or social origin, race, colour, religion, gender, sexual orientation or other grounds.
> [...]
> Migrants, refugees and asylum seekers, indigenous peoples, persons belonging to national or ethnic, religious and linguistic minorities are among the hardest hit by xenophobic acts. People with different sexual orientation or gender identities are also victims of hate crimes. Abuse of persons with disabilities is also widely unaddressed. Women and children who belong to these groups are often at greater risk and suffer from multiple forms of discrimination.
> [...]
> It has been noted that manifestations of xenophobia often increase during periods of economic hardship, election campaigns, political instability and conflict.

A Chronology of Human Rights[47]

18th BC	Code of Hammurabi (Babylon)
13th BC	Biblical Decalogue
6th BC	Cyrus Charter (Persian)
1215	Magna Carta or The Great Charter of Liberties of England
1628	Petition of Rights
1679	Habeas Corpus Act (England)
1689	Bill of Rights (England)
1776	Virginia Declaration of Rights (USA) American Declaration of Independence
1789	*Déclaration des droits de l'homme et du citoyen* (France)
1791	First Ten Amendments to the United States Constitution (Bill of Rights)

[46] https://docs.google.com/file/d/0B6XUJ0SW4C68TlpMb1JWUDJ2LWc/edit?usp=sharing&pli=1

[47] For a thorough Human Rights Timeline see, for instance, the Eleanor Roosevelt Papers Project: www.gwu.edu/~erpapers/humanrights/timeline. For an almost complete list of human rights international instruments, see *Human Rights: A Compilation of International Instruments–Universal Instruments* (United Nations, 2003).

1792	A Vindication of the Rights of Woman (Mary Wollstonecraft)
1809	Ombudsman institution in Sweden
1833	Abolition Act, ending slavery in the British Empire
1863	International Committee of the Red Cross (ICRC)
	Emancipation Proclamation by President Abraham Lincoln, abolishing slavery in the USA
1864	First Geneva Convention for the Amelioration of the Condition of the Wounded in Armies in the Field
1865	Abolition of slavery in the USA by the Thirteenth Amendment
1885	Antislavery Act (Berlin Conference on Africa)
1890	Antislavery Act (Brussels Conference)
1898	League of Human Rights (France), following the *Dreyfus Affaire*
1899/1907	The Hague Conventions on the laws of war
1914–1918	World War I
1917	Russian Revolution
	Constitution of the Mexican United States
1918	Declaration of Rights of the Working and Exploited People (USSR)
1919	League of Nations (Versailles, France)
	International Labour Organisation (ILO), within the framework of the Covenant of the League of Nations
	Constitution of Weimar (Germany)
1922	Permanent Court of International Justice
1924	Declaration of the Rights of the Child (Geneva Declaration)
1926	Slavery Convention (Convention to Suppress the Slave Trade and Slavery, League of Nations)
1929	Geneva Convention relative to the Treatment of Prisoners of War (Diplomatic Conference)
1939–1945	World War II
1941	'Four Freedoms Speech' by President Franklin D. Roosevelt
1943	United Nations War Crimes Commission
1944	Declaration of Philadelphia (ILO)
1945	Organisation of the United Nations (UN)
	United Nations Educational, Scientific and Cultural Organization (UNESCO)
	International Court of Justice
	International Military Tribunal at Nuremberg
1946	United Nations Commission on Human Rights
	International Military Tribunal at Tokyo
1948	Universal Declaration of Human Rights (UN)
	Convention on the Prevention and Punishment of the Crime of Genocide (UN)
	Organisation of American States (OAS, Bogota)
	American Declaration of the Rights and Duties of Man (OAS)
1949	Convention for the Suppression of the Traffic in Persons and of the Exploitation of the Prostitution of Others (UN)
	Geneva Conventions (International Humanitarian Law)

Council of Europe
Grundgesetz (Basic Law/Constitution) of the Federal Republic of Germany
Chinese Revolution

1950 Geneva Convention (I) for the Amelioration of the Condition of the Wounded and Sick in Armed Forces in the Field (Diplomatic Conference)
Geneva Convention (II) for the Amelioration of the Condition of Wounded, Sick and Shipwrecked Members of Armed Forces at Sea (Diplomatic Conference)
Geneva Convention (III) Relative to the Treatment of Prisoners of War (Diplomatic Conference)
Geneva Convention (IV) Relative to the Protection of Civilian Persons in Time of War (Diplomatic Conference)
European Convention for the Protection of Human Rights and Fundamental Freedoms (European Convention on Human Rights, Council of Europe)
United Nations High Commissioner for Refugees
10 December adopted as Human Rights Day by the United Nations General Assembly

1951 Convention Relating to the Status of Refugees (UN)

1952 Convention on the Political Rights of Women (UN)

1953 Protocol amending the Slavery Convention (UN)
European Commission and European Court of Human Rights (Council of Europe)

1954 Convention Relating to Status of Stateless Persons (UN)
European Cultural Convention (Council of Europe)

1955 Political and Civil Rights Movement in USA

1956 Supplementary Convention on the Abolition of Slavery, the Slave Trade, and Institutions and Practices of Slavery (Geneva Conference of Plenipotentiaries convened by the UN Economic and Social Council)

1957 Convention on the Nationality of Married Women (UN)
Standard Rules for the Minimum Treatment of Prisoners (UN)
Abolition of Forced Labour Convention (ILO)

1958 Convention concerning Discrimination in Respect of Employment and Occupation (ILO)

1959 Declaration of the Rights of the Child (UN)

1960 Convention relating to the Status of Stateless Persons (UN)
Convention against Discrimination in Education (UNESCO)
Declaration on the Granting of Independence to Colonial Countries and Peoples (UN)
Inter-American Commission on Human Rights (OAS)

1961 Convention on the Reduction of Statelessness (UN)
Declaration on the Prohibition of the Use of Nuclear and Thermo-Nuclear Weapons (UN)
European Social Charter (Council of Europe, revised in 1996)
Amnesty International

1962 Convention on Consent to Marriage, Minimum Age for Marriage and Registration of Marriages (UN)

1963 Declaration on the Elimination of all Forms of Racial Discrimination (UN)
Organisation of African Unity (OAU)
1965 Recommendation on Consent to Marriage, Minimum Age for Marriage and Registration of Marriages (UN)
Declaration on the Promotion among Youth of the Ideals of Peace, Mutual Respect and Understanding between Peoples (UN)
1966 International Covenant on Civil and Political Rights, with an Optional Protocol (UN)
International Covenant on Economic, Social and Cultural Rights (UN)
International Convention on the Elimination of all Forms of Racial Discrimination (UN)
1967 Declaration on the Elimination of Discrimination against Women (UN)
1968 Convention on the Non-Applicability of Statutory Limitations to War Crimes and Crimes against Humanity (UN)
Proclamation of Tehran (First World Conference on Human Rights)
1969 Vienna Convention on the Law of Treaties (UN)
Declaration on Social Progress and Development (UN)
American Convention on Human Rights (OAS)
Convention Governing the Specific Aspects of Refugee Problems in Africa (OUA)
1970 Declaration of Principles of International Law Concerning Friendly Relations and Co-operation Among States in Accordance with the Charter of the United Nations (UN)
1971 Declaration of the Rights of Mentally Retarded Persons (UN)
1972 Convention Concerning the Protection of the World Cultural and Natural Heritage (UNESCO)
Stockholm Declaration (UN Conference on the Environment)
1973 International Convention on the Suppression and Punishment of the Crime of Apartheid (UN)
Principles of international co-operation in the detection, arrest, extradition and punishment of persons guilty of war crimes and crimes against humanity (UN)
1974 Declaration on the Establishment of a New International Economic Order (UN)
Charter of Economic Rights and Duties of States (UN)
Declaration on the Protection of Women and Children in Emergency and Armed Conflict (UN)
Recommendation concerning Education for International Understanding, Co-operation and Peace and Education relating to Human Rights and Fundamental Freedoms (UNESCO)
1975 Declaration on the Rights of Disabled Persons (UN)
Declaration on the Protection of All Persons from Being Subjected to Torture and Other Cruel, Inhuman or Degrading Treatment or Punishment (UN)
Declaration on the Use of Scientific and Technological Progress in the Interests of Peace and for the Benefit of Mankind (UN)

Declaration on the Use of Scientific and Technological Progress in the Interests of Peace and for the Benefit of Mankind (UN)
International Declaration against Apartheid in Sports (UN)
Final Act of the Helsinki Conference on Security and Cooperation in Europe (CSCE)

1977 Additional Protocol I to the Geneva Conventions Relative to the Protection of Victims of International Armed Conflicts (Diplomatic Conference)
Additional Protocol II to the Geneva Conventions Relative to the Protection of Victims of Non-international Armed Conflicts (Diplomatic Conference)

1978 Declaration on the Preparation of Societies for Life in Peace (UN)
Declaration on Race and Racial Prejudice (UNESCO)
Human Rights Watch

1979 Convention on the Elimination of All Forms of Discrimination against Women (UN)
Code of Conduct for Law Enforcement Officials (UN)
Inter-American Court of Human Rights (OAS)

1980 Working Group on Enforced or Involuntary Disappearances (the first Special Procedure of the UN Commission on Human Rights)
International Agreement for the Establishment of the University for Peace and Charter of the University for Peace (UN)

1981 Declaration on the Elimination of all Forms of Intolerance and of Discrimination Based on Religion or Belief (UN)
African Charter on Human and People's Rights (OAU)

1982 Principles of Medical Ethics relevant to the Role of Health Personnel, particularly Physicians, in the Protection of Prisoners and Detainees against Torture and Other Cruel, Inhuman or Degrading Treatment or Punishment (UN)
World Charter for Nature (UN)
Protocol N° 6 to the Convention for the Protection of Human Rights and Fundamental Freedoms concerning the Abolition of the Death Penalty (Council of Europe)

1983 Protocol N° 6 to the Convention for the Protection of Human Rights and Fundamental Freedoms concerning the Abolition of the Death Penalty (Council of Europe) Charter on the Rights of the Arab Child (League of Arab States)

1984 Convention against Torture and Other Cruel, Inhuman or Degrading Treatment or Punishment (UN)
Declaration on the Right of Peoples to Peace (UN)

1985 International Convention against Apartheid in Sports (UN)
Declaration on the Human Rights of Individuals Who are not Nationals of the Country in Which They Live (UN)
Declaration of Basic Principles of Justice for Victims of Crime and Abuse of Power (UN)
Basic Principles on the Independence of the Judiciary (UN Congress on the Prevention of Crime and the Treatment of Offenders)

United Nations Standard Minimum Rules for the Administration of Juvenile Justice (The Beijing Rules)
Committee on Economic, Social and Cultural Rights (UN)
Inter-American Convention to Prevent and Punish Torture (OAS)

1986 Declaration on the Right to Development (UN)
Declaration on Social and Legal Principles relating to the Protection and Welfare of Children, with Special Reference to Foster Placement and Adoption Nationally and Internationally (UN)
Limburg Principles on the Implementation of the International Covenant on Economic, Social and Cultural Rights (Group of International Experts in International Law)

1987 European Convention for the Prevention of Torture and Inhuman or Degrading Treatment or Punishment (Council of Europe)

1988 Body of Principles for the Protection of All Persons under Any Form of Detention or Imprisonment (UN)
Additional Protocol to the American Convention on Human Rights in the area of Economic, Social, and Cultural Rights (known as the "Protocol of San Salvador") (OAS)
African Commission on Human and Peoples' Rights (OAU)

1989 Convention on the Rights of the Child (UN)
(Second) Optional Protocol to the International Covenant on Civil and Political Rights Aiming at the Abolition of the Death Penalty (UN)
Principles on the Effective Prevention and Investigation of Extra-legal, Arbitrary and Summary Executions (United Nations Economic and Social Council)
Convention on Technical and Vocational Education (UNESCO)
Recommendation on the Safeguarding of Traditional Culture and Folklore (UNESCO)
Indigenous and Tribal Peoples Convention (ILO)
Fall of the Berlin Wall
Tiananmen Square Protests

1990 International Convention on the Protection of the Rights of All Migrant Workers and Members of Their Families (UN)
United Nations Guidelines for the Prevention of Juvenile Delinquency (The Riyadh Guidelines)
United Nations Rules for the Protection of Juveniles Deprived of Their Liberty
Basic Principles on the Role of Lawyers (UN Congress on the Prevention of Crime and the Treatment of Offenders)
Guidelines on the Role of Prosecutors (UN Congress on the Prevention of Crime and the Treatment of Offenders)
Basic Principles for the Treatment of Prisoners (UN)
Guidelines for the Regulation of Computerized Personal Data Files (UN)
African Charter on the Rights and Welfare of the Child (OAU)
Protocol to the American Convention on Human Rights to Abolish the Death Penalty (OAS)

Cairo Declaration on Human Rights in Islam (Islamic Conference)Charter of Paris for a New Europe (CSCE)
Nelson Mandela released from prison after 27 years

1991 United Nations Principles for Older Persons
Principles for the Protection of Persons with Mental Illness and for the Improvement of Mental Health Care (UN)

1992 Declaration on the Rights of Persons Belonging to National or Ethnic, Religious and Linguistic Minorities (UN)
Declaration on the Protection of all Persons from Enforced Disappearance (UN)
European Charter for Regional or Minority Languages (Council of Europe)
Treaty on European Union

1993 Vienna Declaration and Programme of Action (World Conference on Human Rights)
Declaration on the Elimination of Violence against Women (UN)
Standard Rules on the Equalization of Opportunities for Persons with Disabilities (UN)
Principles relating to the Status of National Institutions for the Promotion and Protection of Human Rights ('Paris Principles') (UN)
Final Declaration of the Regional Meeting for Asia of the World Conference on Human Rights (Bangkok Declaration)
Bangkok NGOs Declaration on Human Rights (Non-Governmental Organisations)
International Criminal Tribunal for the Former Yugoslavia (UN Security Council)
United Nations High Commissioner for Human Rights (UNHCHR)

1994 Inter-American Convention on the Prevention, Punishment and Eradication of Violence Against Women "Convention of Belém do Pará" (OAS)Arab Charter on Human Rights (League of Arab States)
International Criminal Tribunal for Rwanda (UN Security Council)

1995 World Summit for Social Development (Copenhagen)
World Conference on Women (Beijing)
Declaration of Principles on Tolerance (UNESCO)Additional Protocol to the European Social Charter Providing for a System of Collective Complaints (Council of Europe)
Framework Convention for the Protection of National Minorities (Council of Europe)
Organization for Security and Co-operation in Europe (OSCE), replacing CSCE

1996 International Code of Conduct for Public Officials (UN)
Safeguards guaranteeing protection of the rights of those facing the death penalty (UN Economic and Social Council)
European Social Charter (Revised) (Council of Europe)

1997 Guidelines for Action on Children in the Criminal Justice System (UN Economic and Social Council)

Universal Declaration on the Human Genome and Human Rights (UNESCO)
Declaration on the Responsibilities of the Present Generations Towards Future Generations (UNESCO)
Convention for the Protection of Human Rights and Dignity of the Human Being with regard to the Application of Biology and Medicine: Convention on Human Rights and Biomedicine (Council of Europe)
Universal Declaration on Democracy (Inter-Parliamentary Council, 1997)
Maastricht Guidelines on Violations of Economic, Social and Cultural Rights (Group of International Experts in International Law)

1998 Declaration on the Right and Responsibility of Individuals, Groups and Organs of Society to Promote and Protect Universally Recognized Human Rights and Fundamental Freedoms (UN)
Rome Statute of the International Criminal Court (Diplomatic Conference)
Convention on Access to Information, Public Participation in Decision and Access to Justice in Environmental Matters (Aaharus Convention) (UN Economic Commission for Europe)
Declaration on Fundamental Principles and Rights at Work (ILO)Our Common Humanity—Asian Human Rights Charter—A Peoples' Charter (Asian Human Rights Commission)

1999 Optional Protocol to the Convention on the Elimination of All Forms of Discrimination against Women (UN)
Declaration and Programme of Action on a Culture of Peace (UN)
Worst Forms of Child Labour Convention (ILO)
Inter-American Convention on the Elimination of all Forms of Discrimination against Persons with Disabilities (OAS)

2000 United Nations Convention against Transnational Organized Crime Optional Protocol to the Convention on the Rights of the Child on the Involvement of Children in Armed Conflict (UN)
Optional Protocol to the Convention on the Rights of the Child on the sale of children, child prostitution and child pornography (UN)
Protocol to Prevent, Suppress and Punish Trafficking in Persons, Especially Women and Children, supplementing the United Nations Convention against Transnational Organized Crime (UN)
Principles on the Effective Investigation and Documentation of Torture and Other Cruel, Inhuman or Degrading Treatment or Punishment (UN)
United Nations Millenium Declaration and Millennium Development Goals
Charter of Fundamental Rights of the European Union
Human Rights Defenders: Support for the Individuals, Groups and Organizations of Civil Society Working to Promote and Protect Human Rights in the Americas (OAS)

2001 World Conference against Racism, Xenophobia and all Forms of Discrimination (Durban, South Africa)
Universal Declaration on Cultural Diversity (UNESCO)
Inter-American Democratic Charter (OAS)

	Macchu Picchu Declaration on Democracy, the Rights of Indigenous Peoples and the War against Poverty (OAS)
	African Union (AU, replacing OAU)
	Attacks on the World Trade Center and the Pentagon (September 11)
2002	Optional Protocol to the Convention against Torture and other Cruel, Inhuman or Degrading Treatment or Punishment (UN)
	Special Session on Children of the UN General Assembly
2003	United Nations Convention against Corruption
	Convention for the Safeguarding of Intangible Cultural Heritage (UNESCO)
	Charter on the Preservation of Digital Heritage (UNESCO)
	International Declaration on Human Genetic Data (UNESCO)
	African Union Convention on Preventing and Combating Corruption
	Protocol to the African Charter on Human and Peoples' Rights on the Rights of Women in Africa (AU)
2004	World Programme for Human Rights Education (UN)
	African Court on Human and Peoples' Rights (AU)
	Covenant of the Rights of the Child in Islam
2005	United Nations Declaration on Human Cloning
	Basic Principles and Guidelines on the Right to a Remedy and Reparation for Victims of Gross Violations of International Human Rights and Serious Violations of International Humanitarian Law (UN)
	Convention on the Protection and Promotion of the Diversity of Cultural Expressions (UNESCO)
	Universal Declaration on Bioethics and Human Rights (UNESCO)
	Additional Protocol (III) to the Geneva Conventions (Diplomatic Conference)
	Council of Europe Convention on Action against Trafficking in Human Beings
	World Summit (UN)
2006	International Convention on the Rights of Persons with Disabilities, with an Optional Protocol (UN)
	International Convention for the Protection of All Persons from Enforced Disappearance (UN)
	United Nations Declaration on the Rights of Indigenous Peoples
	United Nations Human Rights Council, replacing the Commission on Human Rights
	African Youth Charter (AU)
2007	Declaration on the Rights of Indigenous Peoples (UN)
	Treaty of Lisbon (European Union)
	African Charter on Democracy, Elections and Governance (AU)
2008	Optional Protocol to the International Covenant on Economic, Social and Cultural Rights (UN)
	Declaration of Medellín: Youth and Democratic Values (OAS)
2009	Asian Intergovernmental Commission on Human Rights

2011 Optional Protocol to the Convention on the Rights of the Child on a Communications Procedure (UN)
Guiding Principles on Business and Human Rights: Implementing the United Nations 'Protect, Respect and Remedy' Framework
United Nations Declaration on Human Rights Education and Training
Maastricht Principles on Extraterritorial Obligations of States in the area of Economic, Social and Cultural Rights (Group of International Experts in International Law)
2012 African Court of Justice and Human Rights the jurisdiction (AU)
ASEAN Human Rights Declaration (Association of Southeast Asian Nations)Draft Declaration on the Right to Peace (UN)

Summary

1. **Introduction** This introduction justifies the relevance of the study and presents its purpose, structure, content and methodology.

During the last decades, international initiatives were launched with the purpose of identifying universal values. The Universal Declaration of Human Rights was an unprecedented proclamation of common moral values. Human rights are likely the most universal idea in the contemporary world.

This study is a long journey focused on the ethical significance of human rights. It aims at contributing to a universal culture of human rights, one with deep roots and wide horizons. Its purpose, scope and rationale are reflected in its three-part structure, namely:

- Part I (Ethics and Human Rights), after a general introduction, presents an overview of ethical thought, including its specific epistemology, and a historical and theoretical introduction to the human rights idea, as well as to International Human Rights Law, including a brief look at the drafting of the International Bill of Human Rights.
- Part II (Human Rights: Common Ethics of Humankind) argues fundamentally the following:
  - The Ethics of Human Rights is best understood as an Ethics of Recognition of human worth, dignity and rights.
  - The human worth consists in the perfectibility of the human species, rooted in its semiotic nature, to be accomplished through the perfecting of human beings.
  - The Human Dignity Principle is the bedrock of the International Human Rights Law architecture designed to protecting and enhancing the human worth.
- Part III (Human Rights Revolution) highlights the main legal and political revolutionary influences of International Human Rights Law on International and

Constitutional Law, on the conceptions of Rule of Law and democracy, on the vision of the whole Humanity as a global rights-holder in space and time, and includes answers to most common criticisms of human rights. The conclusion highlights the human stature of the Big Five drafters of the Universal Declaration of Human Rights, as well as the priority that should be recognized to human rights education for promoting the Ethics of Human Rights. Some appendices add to this volume purpose, scope and usefulness.

While not discussing every viewpoint quoted for the sake of a comprehensive culture of human rights, nor elaborating on too specific matters, the study touches on much of the typical syllabus of a human rights course, and explores emerging issues. It consists principally of normative research, drawing on International Human Rights Law as it is and functions, combines different approaches, but takes a predominantly juridical one. Its extended legal and jurisprudential content, as well as the communicative and argumentative rationality peculiar to the normative field, require broad quotations from a variety of sources. Indeed, while making a case for the ethical high value and liberating power of the human rights idea and ideal, objections, controversies and uncertainties are not at all overlooked.

2. **Overview of Ethical Thought** This overview of ethical thought has a merely introductory character. It does not enter into discussions of philosophical views.

Axiology or Theory of Value is the discipline addressing values in general; it comprises the study of what makes things desirable. Morals and Ethics are terms etymologically synonymous, with Latin and Greek etymologies, respectively, but they are frequently distinguished as follows: Morals denotes the *what* of moral values, that is, a set of individual or collective standards/norms concerning right and wrong behaviors; Ethics or Moral Philosophy is reflection on the *why* of moral values, on the principles of good and evil, of a good life, pointing to a worldwide horizon.

Metaethics, Normative Ethics, Applied Ethics—constitute the current main partitions of studies in ethical field. Metaethics addresses the most general of moral questions, such as: Is there a specific human moral sense? Is there a fundamental universal moral principle? In what does the distinctiveness of an Ethical Epistemology consist? Normative Ethics is concerned with setting moral principles/standards/norms on right and wrong, which are necessary to guiding human conducts. Applied Ethics examines specific and controversial moral issues.

There is no reason to exclude the moral phenomenon from the evolutionist account, but human morality seems to possess a specificity irreducible to any biological roots. So far, no other animal species has been able to reason, debate and agree about good and evil, right and wrong. The most ancient and universal moral commandment is the Golden Rule that is a principle of reciprocity and compassion.

In the history of Western Philosophy there are three main Normative Ethics theories: Virtue Ethics, Consequentialist Ethics, and Deontological Ethics. None is complete. There is no moral algorithm. Human morality is a matter of being and doing. Around the middle of the 20th century, Virtue Ethics reflourished, focusing on the complex mindset demanded by the practical wisdom of the virtuous person. It emphasizes the importance of moral education, understood as character education.

Rationality is traditionally equated with experimental or mathematical scientificity, and epistemology is currently often defined as the study of knowledge as justified true belief. Ethical or Moral Epistemology is concerned with moral beliefs. If human beings are rational and moral animals, it is not rational to exclude from rationality aspects of their lives as fundamental and far-reaching as their moral values, sentiments and behaviors. The scope of rationality are whatever beliefs (not only the true ones) and their justifications by convincing reasons (not only experimental or mathematical).

Reason being theoretical and practical, unique and multiple, valid belief is a broader epistemological category and seemingly more accurate than true belief, as it encompasses all kinds of beliefs and agreed reasons for justifying them.

3. **Historical and Theoretical Rising of Human Rights and their International Codification and Protection** This chapter offers a synthesis of the history of the advent and elaboration of the idea of human rights, as well as of their international juridification and protection.

If the term 'human rights' appeared only in modern times, the corresponding sentiment and ideal are likely as ancient and cross-cultural as human suffering itself. In Western Philosophy, the idea of human rights has its roots in the theories of Natural Law that go back to the Judeo-Christian scriptures, Greek-Roman Philosophy, notably Stoicism, and Roman juridical thought. An offspring of Natural Law theories of the Middle Ages is the conception of natural rights that was further elaborated in the 16th, 17th and 18th centuries. Natural Law and natural rights were major groundbreaking insights in the genealogy of human rights, whose modern era began with the American and French Revolutions and Declarations of Rights.

The attractiveness of Natural Law declined during the 19th through to the mid-20th centuries, for many reasons, in particular because of the rising of legal positivism, according to which the only Law is that which is created by State. Likewise the term natural/human rights eclipsed, to a great extent, in spite of steps toward their constitutionalization. After the Second World War, the discourses of Natural Law and natural rights revived. The new era of international recognition and protection of human rights began with the establishment of the Organization of the United Nations, in 1945, and the proclamation of the Universal Declaration of Human Rights in 1948. It was the first piece of the so-called International Bill of Human Rights, completed in 1966 with the adoption of two human rights International Covenants. The taboo of States' omnipotent sovereignty was definitely challenged.

The history of the juridification of human rights is frequently put in terms of 'generations'. While human rights are an open-ended concept, this terminology is controversial. The principle of the indivisibility and interdependence of all human rights is a cornerstone of International Human Rights Law.

The protection of human rights has two faces, like the god Janus: one turned to the outside, to International Law, the other one turned to the inside, to domestic legal orders. Within the United Nations framework, it is addressed by Charter-based and Treaty-based mechanisms. The establishment of a Universal Court of Human Rights is an aspiration as old as the Universal Declaration of Human Rights. At the regional level, there are the mechanisms of the European, American and African systems that include human rights courts. However, States—the authors and the first addressees of the International Law that they have engaged to comply with—are legally and politically the main entities responsible for all human rights. Moreover, human rights are also a general responsibility, epitomized by the Non-Governmental Organizations movement. An educated world public opinion may be considered their ultimate protection.

4. Ethics of Recognition This chapter, after some terminological and conceptual clarifications, highlights the ethical essence of human rights, summarizes the philosophical debate on their foundation/justification, and argues that they are best understood as an Ethics of Recognition.

The need to avoid sexism in human rights language was debated during the *travaux préparatoires* (elaboration) of the International Bill of Human Rights. Although 'human rights' is the most usual term in International Law, the most used in constitutional texts is 'fundamental rights'. There is also the term 'fundamental freedoms'. The main rights theories are the 'Will Theory' and the 'Interest Theory'. International Human Rights Law does not provide any definition of 'human right' (nor do national Laws). According to the most common definition, a human right is a right every person possesses simply by virtue of being human.

Human rights are then rights with deep ethical significance. They became a Common Ethics of Humankind. It might be said that the history of human rights is the history of the invention of the Human Being by human beings.

The theoretical question of the foundation or justification of human rights was debated by the Commission on Human Rights at the beginning of the drafting of the Universal Declaration of Human Rights. The disagreement was pragmatically overcome. The philosophical question of foundationalism remains, however. There are three main accounts of human dignity and rights foundation/justification: Naturalism, Self-evidence and Consensus. I submit that human rights originate from a double Historical Consensus:

- Consensus of religious traditions and philosophical wisdom, condensed in the Golden Rule that is a principle of reciprocity and compassion, which epitomizes a moral heritage so culturally deeply shared that it seems to be natural, i.e. innate.
- Consensus laid down in the legal human rights instruments adopted by the International Community, with the increasing influence of public opinion, giving rise to an expanding protection network.

The Historical Consensus founding human rights means their recognition—a topical and multi-purpose concept, with anthropological, political, juridical, psychological, etc, stakes. Human rights may be said to be the highest expression of a general need for, desire of, and right to recognition. The Ethics of Human Rights is probably best understood as an Ethics of Recognition of the worth, dignity and rights of every and each human being.

5. **Human Dignity Principle** This chapter presents an historical, philosophical, and jurisprudential approach to the Human Dignity Principle, as well as an interdisciplinary account of the human worth underlying human dignity and rights.

'Human dignity' is the core of Human Rights Philosophy and the bedrock of International Human Rights Law. Nothwithstanding, there is no generally agreed legal definition of human dignity, any more than of human rights. In the Western world, the idea of human dignity has both religious and philosophical roots. In the Roman Republic, *dignitas* was an attribute of he who commanded respect because of his social standing, office or achievements. Until the 17th and 18th centuries, there are very few examples of dignity being referred to as an attribute, not of the few, but of every human being. Immanuel Kant represents the climax of such an historical moral conquest in the history of Western Philosophy.

The term 'dignity', referring to every human being, does not yet feature in the American and French Declarations of the 18th century. Its humanistic meaning began entering legal texts only during the first half of the 20th century, when it was incorporated into several European and American Constitutions. After the Second World War, it became the foundational idea on which the different visions of human rights could agree, when the United Nations Charter and the Universal Declaration of Human Rights were drafted. Human dignity is a leitmotif of International Human Rights Law. All European Constitutions refer to it. It is incorporated in many Constitutions on other continents as well. There is also a significant international and constitutional Case Law applying the Human Dignity Principle.

In International Human Rights Law, besides 'human dignity', the most frequently used expression is probably 'dignity and worth of the human person'. Considering that human dignity is consubstantial to human worth, an account of human dignity should be a matter of answering to the following principal question: In what does human worth consist? An interdisciplinary account of human worth is submitted, whose main operative categories are the human species' perfectibility, rooted in its semiotic nature, and human beings' perfecting, for which the right to education is key. Indeed, human perfectibility is equivalent to human educability for, being a semiotic animal, the human being is a pedagogic animal.

In sum: The history of the concept of human dignity is one of transubstantiation from an elitist social distinction into a universal moral quality that served as a principle-interface between human worth and human rights. The Human Dignity Principle is the most brilliant star in the skies of human rights, the alpha and omega of Constitutional Law and a powerful device for the international and constitutional courts to protect human rights.

6. **Other Principles** The Human Dignity Principle is not the entirety of the Ethics of Human Rights in a nutshell. This chapter presents other values and rights, with their legal and doctrinal bases, possessing the normative strength of ethical principles from which other rights and duties derive.

In light of International Human Rights Law and other international normative documents, the following principles may be highlighted that, together with the Human

Dignity Principle, may be considered as constituting the general framework of the Ethics of Human Rights:

- *Life and liberty*. Life may be considered as the supreme right to the extent that it provides the biological basis and condition for holding rights. A human life is a life in liberty. Life and liberty are perhaps the principles that best consubstantiate the sense and coherence of the idea and ideal of human rights.
- *Equality and diversity*. Equality is the twin-sister of liberty and elder child of human dignity. However, Humankind is not a Palace of Mirrors, indefinitely reflecting each other, but rather a Symphony of Differences. In any case, if the common human rights language may be spoken in cultural dialects, it must be universally comprehensible, that is, ethically acceptable.
- *Non-discrimination*. Non-discrimination is the corollary of the principles of liberty, equality and diversity. It is a cornerstone of International Human Rights Law, under more or less expanded wording. It relates to acts or omissions concerning the enjoyment of all human rights, but is a self-standing right-principle too.
- *Tolerance and solidarity*. Tolerance is mentioned in many international human rights instruments. It should be understood in a positive way, as appreciation of individuals' and cultures' enriching diversity. Solidarity is a term that progressively replaced 'brotherhood', a term with a rather religious connotation.
- *Democracy, development and peace*. Democracy, development and peace form a triple context indispensable for respecting, protecting and implementing human rights in their interdependence. Their interplay, as well as their relation with the implementation of human rights, in general, has been repeatedly affirmed in various international texts.

The Ethics of Human Rights—and some dimensions of it in particular—are a Common Responsibility of Humankind.

7. **A Changed and Changing Legal Landscape** The recognition of human rights has had a revolutionary influence on the international and national legal field that is outlined in this chapter.

Revolution is a term frequent in human rights literature. The Human Rights Revolution was a triple one:

- The human being has been recognized as the ethical-legal supreme universal value and gained international personality.
- Human rights have been internationally proclaimed, and mechanisms, including courts, have been established for their protection.
- International Human Rights Law principles became the Law of Law, prompting ongoing changes of the international and national legal landscape.

The individual was endowed with international legal subjectivity, notably through the right to petition. This gave rise to a Copernican revolution in classic International Law. A New Constitutionalism has arisen too, characterized by the inclusion in constitutional texts of human rights as the social fundamental values. Its symbol is the 1949 German *Grundgesetz* (Basic Law).

The new International and Constitutional Law led to a refounding of the concept of Rule of Law, implying the rethinking of democracy. Human rights became the core link between Rule of Law and democracy, thus overcoming the tension between the ethical principle (human rights) and the majority principle (popular sovereignty), which are historically, conceptually and politically indissociable. So understood, the Rule of Law epitomizes the consubstantiality between human rights protection and democratic legitimacy.

Humanity is a notion polarizing core principles of morality, addressed by two legal concepts: *jus cogens* (peremptory norms) and obligations *erga omnes* (towards everyone). *Jus cogens* norms are those from which no derogation is permitted. *Erga omnes* are States' obligations towards the whole International Community, insofar as each State is deemed to have an interest in their being complied with. The notion of 'crimes against humanity' consecrates the Humanity statute as rights-holder, embracing both the dignity of the whole human species and the uniqueness of each human being.

8. Answering Some Questions Human rights have always been and remain a controversial matter. We must now address and answer what are likely the most general and lasting criticisms of human rights.

1. Human rights have Western origins, but became universal ethical values.
   The modern concept of human rights is impregnated with Western philosophical, legal and political thought, but their sentiment and ideal are probably as old as human suffering itself. Furthermore, as its drafting process testifies, the Universal Declaration of Human Rights was not a merely Western creature and there was not a monolithic understanding of human rights either. It is an alchemy of cross-cultural moral values that became an ethical-legal lighthouse and a liberation flag. International Human Rights Law is sufficiently flexible to be compatible with legitimate cultural diversities. In any case, at the end of the day, what should matter is not where the moral, artistic, scientific, technological or other advancements come from, but how good and beneficial they are to the whole Humankind.
2. Human rights are individualistic, by their very nature, but do not overlook the sociability of human beings.
   Human rights are, by definition, ethically individualistic, that is, concerned with personal worth, dignity, autonomy and self-development. Nevertheless, the individualistic core of the idea of human rights does not at all mean conceiving of the individual as an entity abstracted and isolated from the groups to which he or she belongs. The principle of reciprocity is inherent to the concept of human rights. If everyone holds rights, everyone bears duties. Rights and duties are two sides of the same coin.
3. The ethical universality and cultural diversity of human rights form an undeconstructible unity.

International Human Rights Law is not 'culture-blind'. The ethical universality of human rights is sensitive to cultural diversity, the right to difference being recognized. They are compatible with all cultural differences, which are not incompatible with their universal ethical significance.

4. Human rights are an ideal and a struggle.
   Violations of human rights shall remain for an indefinitely long time the overwhelming picture of the world. We may ask, however: How would the world be without the proclamation, some decades ago, of the Universal Declaration of Human Rights? We should be realistic without being pessimistic. The Human Rights Revolution is an individual, collective, endless and everyday struggle...

9. Conclusion This concluding chapter adds two reflections:

- The human rights ideal proclaimed in the Universal Declaration of Human Rights was ignited and has been kept lit by great human beings.
- As the advancement of the liberating power of human rights deeply depends on their being rooted in hearts, minds and everyday life, human rights education should be of paramount concern.

The principal drafters of the Universal Declaration of Human Rights were great human beings, in particular the *Big Five*: Eleanor Roosevelt, René Cassin, Charles Malik, Peng-chun Chang and John Humphrey. They were the right people at the right time. Since then, the ideal of human rights has been advanced by women and men of the same stature, people of great vision and sentiments.

The 'mothers and fathers' of the 1948 Universal Declaration were aware that the promotion and protection of human rights should begin... at the beginning, i.e. with education. That is why human rights education is an element of the right to education as a normative complex of rights aiming at the full development of human personality. The right to human rights education has been recognized by International Human Rights Law since the Universal Declaration, and was restated by the United Nations Declaration on Human Rights Education and Training (2011). Its purpose is to provide each person with knowledge and understanding, and to develop corresponding attitudes and behaviors, in order to contribute to a universal culture of human rights.

Human rights education especially concerns two professional fields: Law and Education. Human rights are still widely missing in the education and training of Law professionals. In the educational field, in spite of successive international Declarations, Recommendations, Programs, etc., since long ago, the subject remains, in general, a poor relative in school education.

Human beings are, under and above all, their values and sentiments. Human rights education—understood according to its contemporary comprehensive, holistic scope—is an ethical, civic and international education that is crucial for contemporary societies and the survival and perfecting of Humankind.

Internet Resources

IGOs at universal level	
United Nations	www.un.org
United Nations Treaty Collection	http://untreaty.un.org
The United Nations Human Rights Treaties	www.bayefsky.com
UN Documentation: Human Rights	http://research.un.org/en/docs/humanrights
UDHR Drafting Process	www.un.org/depts/dhl/udhr
OHCHR	www.ohchr.org
Universal Human Rights Index	http://uhri.ohchr.org
UNESCO	www.unesco.org/
UNICEF	www.unicef.org
UNHCR	www.unhcr.org/cgi-bin/texis/vtx/home
ILO	www.ilo.org
ILOLEX (Database on International Labour Standards)	www.ilo.org/ilolex/english
International Committee of the Red Cross (ICRC)	www.cicr.org/eng
IGOs at regional level	
Council of Europe	www.coe.org
European Court of Human Rights	www.echr.coe.int
European Union (EU)	http://europa.eu.int
OSCE	www.osce.org
Organization of American States (OAS)	www.oas.org
Inter-American Court of Human Rights	www.corteidh.or.cr
Inter-American Commission on Human Rights (IACHR)	www.cidh.oas.org
Africa Union (AU)	www.au.int
African Commission on Human and Peoples' Rights	www.achpr.org/english/_info/news_en.html
Academic institutions	
University of Minnesota Human Rights Library	www1.umn.edu/humanrts
Icelandic Human Rights Centre	www.humanrights.is/english
Institute for Human Rights (Abo Akademi University, Finland)	www.abo.fi/instut/imr
Inter-American Institute of Human Rights	www.iidh.ed.cr
NGOs and other networking organizations	
Amnesty International	www.amnesty.org
Human Rights Watch	www.hrw.org
Asian Human Rights Commission	www.humanrights.asia
Human Rights Internet	www.hri.ca
Human Rights Network International	www.hrni.org/
INTERIGHTS: The International Center for the Legal Protection of Human Rights	www.interights.org
International Council on Human Rights	www.ichrp.org
Equipo Nizkor	www.derechos.org/nizkor/eng.html
The International Network for Economic, Social and Cultural Rights (ESCR-NET)	www.escr-net.org
Thesaurus of Economic, Social, and Cultural Rights	http://shr.aaas.org/escr/thesaurus.htm
International Service for Human Rights	www.ishr.ch.
Human Rights First	www.humanrightsfirst.org
Human Rights Education Associates (HREA)	www.hrea.org

Selected Bibliography

AAVV. 2006. *Non-discrimination: A human right—Seminar to mark the entry into force of Protocol N° 12*. Strasbourg: Council of Europe Publishing.

Andriantsimbazovina J., et al. (Sous la direction de). 2008. *Dictionnaire des Droits de l'Homme*. Paris: PUF.

APF (Asia Pacific Forum of National Human Rights Institutions). 2012. *International human rights and the international human rights system—A manual for national human rights institutions*. Sidney. www.asiapacificforum.net/support/resources/training/int-hr-systems/downloads/resources/international-human-rights-and-the-international-human-rights-system-a-manual-for-nhris-2012. Accessed Sept 2013.

Botha, H. 2009. Human dignity in comparative perspective. *Stellenbosch Law Review* 20 (2): 171–220.

Cassin, R. 1976. Les droits de l'homme. In Académie de Droit International, *Recueil des Cours/Collected Courses of the Hague Academy of Internationl Law—1974—Tome 140 de la collection*, 221–231. Boston: Martinus Nijhoff Publishers.

Donnelly, J. 2009. Human dignity and human rights. *Swiss initiative to commemorate the 60th anniversary of the UDHR—protecting dignity: an agenda for human rights—research project on human dignity*. www.udhr60.ch/report/donnelly-HumanDignity_0609.pdf. Accessed July 2013.

Espiell, H. 1985. *Estudios sobre Derechos HumanosI*. San José, Costa Rica: Instituto Interamericano de Derechos Humanos/Caracas: Editorial Jurídica Venezolana.

European Commission for Democracy through Law (Venice Commission). 1998. *The principle of respect for human dignity. Proceedings of the UniDem Seminar organised in Montpellier from 2 to 6 July 1998 in co-operation with the "Pôle Universitaire Européen de Montpellier et du Languedoc-Roussillon" and the Faculty of Law—C.E.R.C.O.P. University of Montpellier I*. www.venice.coe.int/webforms/documents/CDL-STD(1998)026-e.aspx. Accessed July 2013.

European Commission for Democracy Through Law (Venice Commission). 2011. *Report on the Rule of Law* (CDL-AD (2011) 003 rev).

Glendon, M. 2001. *A world made new—eleanor roosevelt and the universal declaration of human rights*. New York: Random House, Trade Paperbacks.

Habermas, J. 2012. Chapter 4—the concept of human dignity and the realistic utopia of human rights. In *Philosophical Dimensions of Human Rights—Some Contemporary Views*, ed. C. Corradetti, 63–79. New York: Springer Science+Business Media B. V.

Hayden, P. 2001. *The philosophy of human rights*. St. Paul: Paragon House.

Hersch, J. (A selection of texts prepared under the direction of). 1969. *Birthright of man*. New York: UNESCO/UNIPUB Inc.

Humphrey, J. 1984. *Human rights and the united nations—a great adventure*. New York: Transnational Publishers.

Humphrey, J. 1989. *No distant millennium: the international law of human rights*. Paris: UNESCO.

Hunt, L. 2008. *Inventing human rights—a history*. New York: W. W. Norton and Company Ltd.

Kozma, J., M. Nowak, und Scheinin, M. 2010. *A World court of human rights—consolidated statute and commentary*. Wien: Neuer Wissenschaftlicher Verlag.

Krause, C., und Scheinin, M., Ed. 2009. *International protection of human rights: a Textbook*. Turku/Åbo: Åbo Akademi University: Institute for Human Rights.

Lawson, E., und Bertucci, M. 1996. *Encyclopedia of human rights*. Washington: Taylor & Francis.

McCrudden, Ch. 2008. Human dignity and judicial interpretation of human rights. *The European Journal of International Law* 19 (4): 655–724.

Menke, Ch., und Pollmann, A. 2007. *Philosophie der Menschenrechte—Zur Einfürung* (2008). Hamburg: Junius Verlag.

Moeckli, D., S. Shah, und Sivakumaran, S., Ed. 2010. *International human rights law*. Oxford: Oxford University Press.

Morsink, J. 1999. *The universal declaration of human rights: origins, drafting, and intent*. Philadelphia: University of Pennsylvania Press.

OAS. 2012. *Basic documents pertaining to human rights in the inter-american system*. www.corteidh.or.cr/docs/libros/docsbas2012_eng.pdf.
Peerenboom, R. 2005. Human rights and rule of law: What's the relationship? University of California, Los Angeles School of Law, public law and legal theory research paper series 05–31. http://papers.ssrn.com/sol3/papers.cfm?abstract_id=816024. Accessed July 2013.
Pelé, A. 2006. Filosofía e historia en el fundamento de la dignidad humana—Tesis Doctoral, Universidad Carlos III de Madrid. Instituto de Derechos Humanos Bartolomé de las Casas. http://e-archivo.uc3m.es/bitstream/10016/3052/7/Tesis_Pele.pdf. Accessed July 2013
Ramcharan, B. 2008. *Contemporary Human Rights Ideas*. New York: Routledge.
Ricœur, P. 2004. *Parcours de la reconnaissance*. Paris: Gallimard, Folio Essais-459.
Russ, J. 1994. *La pensée éthique contemporaine*. Paris: PUF, Que-sais-je?-2834.
Smith, R., und Anker, Ch. 2005. *The Essentials of Human Rights*. London: Hodder Arnold.
Sohn, L. 1982. The new international law: Protection of the rights of individuals rather than states. *American University Law Review* 32 (1): 1–64. www.wcl.american.edu/journal/lawrev/32/sohn.pdf. Accessed July 2003.
Steiner, H., Alston, Ph., und Goodman, R. 2008. *International Human Rights in Context—Law, Politics, Morals* 3rd ed. New York: Oxford University Press.
The Limburg Principles on the Implementation of the International Covenant on Economic, Social and Cultural Rights. 1987. *Human Rights Quarterly* 9 (2): 122–146. www.uu.nl/faculty/leg/NL/organisatie/departementen/departementrechtsgeleerdheid/organisatie/onderdelen/studieeninformatiecentrummensenrechten/publicaties/simspecials/20/Documents/20–10.pdf.
Tierney, B. 2004. The idea of natural rights—origins and persistence. *Nordwestern Journal of International Human Rights* 2: http://scholarlycommons.law.northwestern.edu/cgi/viewcontent.cgi?article=1005&context=njihr. Accessed July 2013 .
Tomuschat, Ch. 2008. *Human Rights—Between Idealism and Realism* (Collected Courses of the Academy of European Law, XIII/1). Oxford: Oxford University Press.
Trindade, A. 2006. *International law for humankind: Towards a new jus gentium—general course on public international law. Académie de Droit international, recueil des cours/ collected courses of the Hague Academy of International Law—2005—Tome 316 de la Collection.* Leiden: Martinus Nijhoff Publishers.
United Nations. 2003a. *Human rights: A compilation of international instruments—universal instruments.*
United Nations. 2003b. Human rights in the administration of justice: A manual on human rights for judges, prosecutors and lawyers. New York and Geneva: OHCHR, in cooperation with the International Bar Association, Professional Training Series N° 9. www.ohchr.org/Documents/Publications/training9Titleen.pdf. Accessed July 2013
United Nations. 2005. The United Nations human rights treaty system: An introduction to the core human rights treaties and the treaty bodies. New York, Geneva: Office of the united nations high commissioner for human rights, Fact Sheet N° 30 from UNOHCHR. www.ohchr.org/Documents/Publications/FactSheet30en.pdf. Accessed July 2013.
Verdoodt, A. 1964. *Naissance et signification de la Déclaration universelle des droits de l'homme (Préface de René Cassin)*. Louvain-Paris: Éditions Nauwelaerts.
Waldron, J. 2009b. Dignity, rank and rights: The 2009 tanner lectures at UC berkeley, NYU school of law, public law research paper No, 09–50. http://ssrn.com/abstract=1461220. Accessed July 2013.
Whitman, J. 2003. 'Human Dignity' in Europe and the United States: The social foundations. European Commission for Democracy through Law (Venice Commission), *European and U. S. Constitutionalism. Proceedings of the UniDem Seminar organised in Göttingen on 23–24 May 2003 in co-operation with the Institute of International Law, University of Göttingen, and Yale Law School.*
Whitman, J. 2005. *'Human dignity' in Europe and the United States: The social foundations. European and US Constitutionalism*, 108–124. Cambridge: Cambridge University Press. Cambridge Books Online. Web. 2013 http://dx.doi.org/10.1017/CBO9780511493904.008. Accessed 24 June 2013.

Additional Bibliography Not Quoted in the Present Study

Alfredsson, G., und A. Eide, eds. 1999. *The universal declaration of human rights*. The Hague: Martinus Nijhoff Publishers.

Bair, J. 2005. *The international covenant on civil and political rights and its (First) optional protocol: A short commentary*. Frankfurt am Main: Peter Lang.

Beco, G., ed. 2012. *Human rights monitoring mechanisms of the council of Europe*. New York: Routledge.

Bond, M. 2010. *The council of Europe and human rights: An introduction to the European convention on human rights*. Strasbourg: Council of Europe Publishing.

Bossuyt, M. 1987. *Guide to the "Travaux Preparatoires" of the international covenant on civil and political rights*. Dordrecht: Martinus Nijhoff Publishers.

Burgorgue-Larsen, L. 2011. *The inter-American court of human rights: Case law and commentary*. Oxford: Oxford University Press.

Bürgenthal, Th., D. Shelton, und Stewart, D. 2009. *International human rights in a Nutshell* 4th ed. USA: West Publishing.

Clayton, R., und H. Tomlinson. 2009. *The law of human rights*. Oxford: Oxford University Press.

Condé, H. 2004. *A handbook of international human rights terminology* 2nd ed. University of Nebraska Press.

Donnely, J. 2003. *Universal Human Rights in Theory and Practice* 2nd ed. Ithaca: Cornell University Press.

Evans, M., und R. Murray, ed. 2002. *The African charter on human and peoples' rights*. Cambridge: Cambridge University Press.

Forsythe, D. ed. 2009. *Encyclopedia of human rights*. 5 Vols. Oxford: Oxford University Press.

Frans, V. 2012. *International human rights law in Africa*. Oxford: Oxford University Press.

Ghandhi, S. 2012. *Blackstone's International Human Rights Documents* 8th ed. Oxford: Oxford University Press.

Harris, D., und S. Livingstone, eds. 1998. *The Inter-American System of Human Rights*. Oxford: Clarendon Press.

Jacob Burns Law Library. 2012. *Conducting research in international human rights law—legal research guide series—specialized research guide # 8*, George Washington University, Law School.

Menon, G., ed. 2009. *Genesis and role of NGOs in protecting human rights*. New Delhi: Dominant Publishers and Distributors.

Meron, Th. 2006. *The humanization of international law* (The Hague Academy of International Law). Leiden: Martinus Nijhoff Publishers.

Merrilis, J., und A. Robertson. 2001. *Human rights in Europe* 4 ed. Manchester: Manchester University Press.

Mertus, J. 2009. *The United Nations and human rights: A guide for a New Era* 2nd ed. London: Routledge.

Normand, R. 2008. *Human Rights at the UN: The political history of universal justice* (United Nations Intellectual History Project Series). Bloomington and Indianapolis: Indiana University Press.

Ovey, C., und R. White. 2002. *European convention on human rights* 3rd ed. Oxford: Oxford University Press.

Provost, R. 2002. *International human rights and humanitarian law*. Cambridge: Cambridge University Press.

Ramcharan, B. 2011. *The fundamentals of international human rights treaty law*. Leiden: Martinus Nijhoff Publishers.

Reid, K. 2012. *A practitioner's guide to the European convention on human rights* 4 ed. Thomson/Sweet & Maxwell.

Robertson, D. 2004. *A dictionary of human rights* 2nd ed. London: Europa Publications.

Roca, J., und P. Santolaya, ed. 2012. *Europe of rights: A compendium on the european convention of human rights*. Leiden: Martinus Nijhoff Publishers.

Schabas, W. 2001. *An introduction to the international criminal court.* Cambridge: Cambridge University Press.

Shue, H. 1996. *Basic rights: subsistence, affluence and U.S. foreign policy* 2nd Ed. New Jersey: Princeton University Press.

Skogly, S. 2001. *The human rights obligations of the world bank and the international monetary Fund.* London: Cavendish Publishing Limited.

Ssenyonjo, M., ed. 2012. *The African regional human rights system: 30 years after the african charter on human and peoples' rights.* Leiden: Martinus Nijhoff Publishers.

Index

Names/Authors

A
Abbott, Th., 204
Acton, L., 64
Adam, S.A., 29, 187
Agamben, G., 186
Agi, M., 356
Åkermark, S., 7, 146, 399
Albuquerque, C., 108
Alcock, J., 23
Alfaro, R., 83, 89
Alfredsson, G., 434
Allen, W., 189
Allende, S., 149, 428
Al-Samman, S., 70
Alston, Ph., 343
Alvarado, L., 425
Álvarez, A., 72, 73, 359
Andorno, R., 247, 251
Andrade, J., 96, 167, 185, 392
Andrews, R., 100, 425
Angell, N., 75
Anker, Ch., 132
Annan, K., 437
Anscombe, G., 31
Antigone, 46
Antoine, G., 336
Apel, K.-O., 25, 36, 37, 293
Aquinas, Th., 49, 53, 201, 469
Aranguren, J.-L., 22
Aréchaga, J., 174, 176
Arendt, H., 193
Aristotle, 20, 22, 30, 33, 36, 46, 188, 201, 288, 300, 365
Arslan, Z., 62, 414
Assoun, P.-L., 188
Athayde, B., 176, 361, 397, 403, 425
Attali, J., 402
Augenthaler, Z., 395
Augustine, St., 20, 47, 284
Aulard, A., 88
Auroux, S., 288, 313
Austin, J., 52
Azkoul, K., 175

B
Bachelard, G., 188
Badinter, R., 58, 145, 329
Badiou, A., 6
Bakaric, V., 396, 425
Bakhtin, M., 291
Balibar, É., 208
Ballantyne, M., 26
Barak (Justice), 238
Barbeyrac, J., 50
Barile, G., 384
Baroody, J., 392
Barret-Kriegel, B., 53
Barthes, R., 188, 284
Bates, E., 58, 67
Batiffol, H., 53
Battegay, A., 185
Baumard, N., 24
Beccaria, C., 61
Becet, J.-M., 359
Beck, L., 208
Bedjaoui, M., 343
Beetham, D., 374
Begtrup, G., 162
Béji, H., 332
Ben-Ari, Y., 280

A. Reis Monteiro, *Ethics of Human Rights*, DOI 10.1007/978-3-319-03566-6,

Bendor, A., 219, 221, 260, 264
Benedict XIV (Pope), 20
Bentham, J., 31, 52, 65, 164
Benveniste, É., 288, 402
Bergson, H., 75
Berlin, I., 164
Bernardino, M., 425
Bernheim, F., 71
Bertram, G., 185
Besnier, J.-M., 24, 314
Bessis, S., 151
Bevan, E., 401
Bielefeldt, H., 390, 399
Bienenfeld, F., 432
Bindé, J., 20, 332
Birmingham, P., 193, 295, 349, 379, 437
Birnbacher, D., 180
Bloch, E., 282, 402, 420
Blum, P., 278, 296, 312
Bobbio, N., 7, 177–179, 181, 184
Bodil, H., 162
Boerefijn, I., 136, 437
Bognetti, G., 68, 203, 262
Bogomolov, A., 96
Bolivar, S., 55
Bond, M., (Not cited)
Bordum, A., 38
Bossuyt, M., 163, 328
Bostrom, N., 212, 246, 248, 276
Botha, H., 203, 220, 222, 223, 226, 232, 254, 258, 263, 267, 271, 409
Boudon, R., 36
Bouelles, Ch., 202
Bourgeois, B., 219, 297
Boutmy, É., 64
Boutros-Ghali, B., 169, 339
Boyle, J., 53
Boyle, K., 374
Brahe, T., 429
Brennan (Justice), 239, 258, 266, 274, 276, 316
Brierly, J., 379
Broch, H., 193
Brunet, R., 77
Brunsvick, Y., 8
Bryde, B.-O., 220, 224, 226, 261, 264
Buquicchio, G., 358
Burckhardt, J., 402
Burgers, J., 70, 72, 74, 75, 77, 375, 426
Burgess, P., 284
Burlamaqui, J., 56
Burke, E., 65
Bush, G.W., 245
Byrnes, A., 143

C

Caillé, A., 189
Calvin, 401
Campbell, T., 7, 11, 31, 45, 53, 56, 152, 163–165, 182, 204, 254, 269, 372, 375, 399, 408, 413
Cañas, A., 361
Canto-Sperber, M., 23, 180
Carozza, P., 55, 392
Carter, J., 149
Cassese, A., 364
Cassin, R., 7, 71, 77, 93, 96, 98, 99, 169, 174, 333, 339, 356, 399, 405, 424, 426, 429, 430
Cassirer, E., 284, 287
Castellino, J., 132, 149, 415
Caune, J., 284, 288, 312
Cazeneuve, J., 186
Cecil, R., 70
Cézilly, F., 23
Chan, J., 28
Chandler, D., 285, 291, 313
Chang, P., 424
Chardin, T., 91
Chaskalson, A., 199, 220, 222, 329
Chebel, M., 188
Chesterman, S., 365, 368, 369
Chevallier, J., 7, 369
Chinkin, Ch., 381
Christ, 30, 55, 401
Christopher, E., 100, 143, 396, 402, 425
Churchill, W., 78, 79, 118, 396, 398, 438
Cianciardo, J., 38
Cicero, 21, 47, 201, 203, 204, 210, 359, 362
Clapham, A., 122, 249
Clemenceau, 336
Cobo, M. (Silo), 3
Cohen-Jonathan, G., 147
Cohn, H. (Justice), 264
Coke (Justice), 119
Colard, D., 359
Columbus, Ch., 402
Comenius, 297, 298
Comte, A., 65
Condorcet, 63, 282, 288, 313, 318
Confucius/Confucianism, 27
Connally Resolution, 78
Coomans, F., 12
Cooper, J., 33
Copernicus, 278
Corominas, E., 57, 95, 176, 404, 425
Corradetti, C., 7
Coskun, D., 366
Courtis, Ch., 108

Crampe-Casnabet, M., 282, 288, 313, 318
Creon, K., 46
Croce, B., 75, 91
Cyrulnik, B., 282

D
Dalacoura, K., 414
Damásio, A., 25, 289, 304–306, 309, 311–313
Daniel, D., 285
Dante, 402
Danzin, A., 8
Darwin, Ch., 23, 26
Davies, E., 168
Dawkins, R., 382
Decaux, E., 335
Deely, J., 286
De Gaulle, C., 426
Dehousse, F., 91
Delmas-Marty, M., 377
Delpérée, F., 222, 261, 364
Del Vecchio, G., 356
Dembour, M.-B, 179, 180
Denquin, J.-M., 373
Derrida, J., 39, 291
Descartes, R., 22
Dewey, J., 4, 75, 427
Diderot, 392
Dolto, F., 188, 289, 295
Domínguez-Redondo, E., 124
Donnelly, J., 57, 180, 202, 249, 303, 390, 391
Dord, O., 366
Dostoevsky, 408
Douarin, N., 280, 312, 316
Dozsa, G., 390
Drinan, R., 355
Drzewicki, K., 391
Duguit, P., 365
Dukeston, C., 6
Dulles, J., 397
Dumas, J., 73
Dumont, L., 400, 401, 403
Dunbar, R., 281
Dupréel, E., 38
Dupuy, P.-M., 381
Dupuy, R.-J., 335, 384
Dürig, G., 258

E
Easterman, A., 432
Ebadi, Sh., 151
Eco, U., 287, 291
Edwards, G., 6, 148, 149, 289
Egger, R., 100, 425
Eichelberger, C., 84
Eichmann, A., 431
Eide, A., 114
Eigeldinger, F., 28
Einstein, A., 4, 75
Eisenhower (General), 398
Elchardus, M., 20
Elias, T., 183
Ellington, J., 204
Elster, J., 374
Éluard, P., 190
Enders, Ch., 250
Engels, F., 8
Englehart, N., 413
Erasmus, 297
Eren, 391
Ergec, R., 130, 364
Espiell, H., 364, 381
Etzioni, A., 180
Evans, M., 231
Evatt, H., 84, 144, 393

F
Fabre-Magnan, M., 181
Fagan, A., 11, 53, 56, 260
Farouki, N., 281, 314
Fauchille, P., 73
Feldman, R., 35
Ferrarese, E., 185
Ferri, L., 8
Feuerbach, L., 56, 298
Feyter, K., 349
Fieser, J., 32
Finkielkraut, A., 357
Finnis, J., 53
Fischer, K., 308, 309, 310
Fischl, J., 22
Fitzmaurice, G., 379
Fontenay, É., 280
Foucault, M., 378
Fournier, M., 190
Fox, J., 9
Frangulis, A., 72, 74
Frans, V., 23
Fraser, N., 186
Frederick II, 402
Freeman, M., 6, 201, 414
Freud, S., 69, 278, 308
Freund, J., 194
Friedmann, W., 130, 364
Fritzsche, K., 437
Fukuda, T., 407
Fukuyama, F., 311
Fuller, S., 35

G
Gaius, 48
Galen, 293
Gallie, W., 10
Gandhi, M., 30, 76, 91, 407
Gardner, H., 36
Gazzaniga, M., 280
George, R., 53, 289
Gerson, J., 54
Gewirth, A., 256, 260
Giraud, É., 89, 426
Glendon, M., 6, 81, 84, 85, 88, 89, 91–96, 99, 144, 175, 184, 193, 194, 213, 393, 394, 396–399, 405, 414, 423, 424, 426, 427, 429, 430
Godelier, M., 281
Goebbels, J., 71, 120, 396
Goedde, P., 355
Goldin, W., 26
Goldman, A., 34, 35
Goodman, J., 27
Gouges, O., 67
Goyard-Fabre, S., 53
Gramain, P., 72
Gratian, 48
Greco, J., 35
Greer, S., 144
Gregory XVI (Pope), 20
Griffin, J., 11, 31, 53, 165, 194, 259
Grisez, G., 53
Grotius, H., 50, 55, 61
Grumbach, S., 176
Grunberg, I., 171
Grünfeld, F., 12
Guerreiro, R., 214, 360
Guilaine, J., 281
Gurvitch, G., 213
Gutierrez, G., 89
Gutterman, B., 290, 431, 438

H
Habermas, J., 12, 36–38, 68, 115, 147, 165, 168, 194, 201, 203, 250, 254, 257, 261, 419
Hagège, C., 281
Haldane, J., 75
Hamilton, W., 291
Hansungule, M., 56, 58, 69, 414, 437
Harris, D., 180
Harry, R., 162
Hart, H., 52, 164, 192
Hartmann, E., 19
Hauriou, M., 365
Hayden, P., 50, 56
Hegel, F., 21, 297
Heidegger, M., 4, 426
Henkin, L., 6, 7, 53, 64, 66, 101, 111, 171, 262
Hennette-Vauchez, S., 180, 222, 272, 408
Henrich, D., 190
Henry, L., 203, 222, 225, 245, 246, 248, 409
Herbart, J., 390
Herder, J., 295
Herfray, Ch., 288
Herodotus, 409
Hersch, J., 58, 76
Hess, R., 184
Hétier, R., 283
Heyer, E., 281
Heyman, S., 194
Higgins, R., 147, 229
Himmelfarb, G., 29
Hitchcock, W., 355
Hitler, A., 70, 71, 184, 266, 267, 366
Hjelmslev, L., 284
Hobbes, Th., 50, 53
Hodgson, W.R., 144, 405
Holman, F., 397
Holmes, O., 182
Honneth, A., 38, 185, 194
Hugo, V., 64, 329, 336
Humboldt, W., 296
Hume, D., 23, 52
Humphrey, J., 87, 96, 97, 107, 356, 358, 398, 415, 424, 426, 427, 429
Hunt, L., 29, 32, 56, 59, 61, 63, 69, 70, 181, 256, 390, 403, 419
Huxley, A., 26
Huxley, J., 4, 22, 36, 403, 431

I
Iglesias, T., 247, 248
Ignatieff, M., 260
Ikramullah, Sh., 167
Immordino-Yang, M., 305, 306, 310, 311
Innocent III (Pope), 202
Insfran, E., 425
Iriye, A., 355
Isaacs, I., 76

J
Jackson, R., 119
Jacob, F., 296
Jacquin, A.-P., 60
Jäger, W., 296
Jakobson, R., 4, 284
Jaurès, J., 64
Jefferson, Th., 56, 63, 89, 391
Jellineck, G., 64

Jhering, C.R., 164
John XXIII (Pope), 94
Jones, H., 4
Journet, N., 23, 24, 313
Justinian (Emperor), 48

K
Kabir, H., 144
Kahn, A., 280, 281, 314
Kai-shek, C., 79
Kamminga, M., 12
Kant, I., 38, 295, 297, 298
Katz-Suchy, J., 395, 405
Kaul, I., 171
Kayaly, A., 175, 392
Kelsen, H., 52, 192
Kepler, J., 429
Kim, Y., 2
King, A., 1
King, M., 119
Kiss, A.-Ch., 6, 301, 379, 384
Kissangoula, J., 53
Kjœrum, M., 335
Klein, E., 356
König, S., 328
Koretsky, V., 161
Kotzee, B., 35
Kovak, E., 39
Kozma, J., 418, 419
Krause, C., 146, 348
Kummer, H., 25
Kuomintang, 427
Kyi, A.S., 151

L
La Pergola, A., 364
Labrusse-Riou, C., 271
Lacan, J., 188
Lafayette, M., 63
Lamont, C., 4
Lane, R., 287
Langlois, A., 373
Laozi, 27
Laroche, J.-L., 287, 288, 313
Las Casas, B., 55
Lauren, P., 338, 360
Laurent, A., 402
Lauterpacht, H., 76, 101, 111, 379
Lawson, R., 144
Lebech, M., 200, 201, 203
Lee, P., 229, 289
Lehrer, J., 314
Leibniz, 284
Lemkin, R., 455
Lenin, 67
Lenk, H., 287, 295
Leo X (Pope), 390
Leo XIII (Pope), 49, 208
Letherby, G., 34
Lev, D., 194
Lévi-Strauss, C., 4, 28, 303
Levinas, E., 39, 408
Li, X., 410, 413
Lincoln, A., 338
Lindsay, R., 162
Listing, J., 24
Lo, Ch.-Sh., 390
Locke, J., 51
Louis XVI, 63
Louw, E., 397
Lovejoy, W., 201
Lutz, D., 62
Lwoff, A., 296

M
MacBride, S., 145
MacIver, R., 27
Madison, J., 56, 62
Maes, E., 373
Maheu, R., 167, 302
Maistre, C., 65
Mäkinen, V., 55
Makino, B., 70
Malik, Ch., 87, 174, 277, 356, 424, 426, 501
Malson, L., 296, 298
Mandela, N., 30
Mandele, V., 94, 176
Mandelstam, A., 72
Manetti, G., 202
Mann, Th., 75
Marie, J.-B., 58, 59, 65
Maritain, J., 49, 75, 76, 91, 176, 180, 182
Marks, J., 437
Marshall, G., 94
Martenson, J., 130
Marx, K., 8, 281, 298
Matienzo, A., 169, 176, 360, 361, 394
Matsuura, K., 8, 330
Maury, L., 336
Maxwell-Fyfe, D., 438
Mayerfeld, J., 373, 374, 434
Mayhew, C., 100, 396, 425
Mayor, F., 169
Mazzola, F., 246
McArthur, D., 118
McBride, C., 186
McBride, S., 145

McCarthy, J., 38, 397
McCrudden, Ch., 143, 208, 212, 213, 223, 245, 249, 254, 271, 277
McNeil, H., 396
McNitt, R., 76
Mead, G., 292
Mégret, F., 249, 264, 349, 359, 383, 384
Mehedi, M., 301
Mencius, 27, 296, 297, 390
Mendel, G., 9
Menke, Ch., 273, 356
Menon, L., 405
Metha, H., 87, 162
Meyer, M., 38
Michelet, J., 64, 297, 328, 336
Mill, J.S., 31, 182, 329
Mirabella, D., 53
Mirandola, G., 202, 203, 282, 290
Mirkine-Guetzdvitch, B., 88
Möbius, A., 24
Modeme, L., 341
Modinos, P., 364, 438
Moeckli, D., 334
Monchablon, A., 64, 328, 329, 336
Monod, J., 296
Montaigne, 402
Monteiro, A., 357
Montesquieu, 51, 52, 62, 65, 328
Moore, G., 52
Morange, J., 356
Morange, M., 280
Moreno, A., 5, 168, 391, 425
Morris, Ch., 19, 284, 285, 287, 289, 291, 292, 312, 313
Morsink, J., 90, 173, 175, 177, 184, 193, 278, 332, 333, 361, 366, 391, 393, 394, 396, 405, 424, 429, 432, 433
Mortera, S., 187
Müller, J.-W., 283, 295
Muller, Ph., 283
Murray, G., 167

N
Napoleon, 64
Nehru, J., 76
Nelson, J., 244, 272
Néraudau, J.-P., 186
Newlands, A., 95
Newton, I., 31
Niethammer, F., 3
Nietzsche, F., 208
Nixon (President), 428
Nolde, F., 83
Nowak, M., 6, 66, 68, 114, 274, 416, 418, 419, 434
Nunge, O., 187
Nussbaum, M., 247

O
Ockham, W., 54
Ogien, R., 23, 180
Orr, J., 75
Ortega y Gasset, J., 179

P
Paine, Th., 56, 59, 66, 161
Parsons, W., 76
Partsch, J., 120
Passmore, J., 282, 290, 296, 297, 328
Paton, H., 204
Paul, St., 47
Pavlov, A., 93, 333, 394–396
Payet, J.-P., 185
Pearson, L., 168, 396
Peccei, A., 1
Peerenboom, R., 365, 373
Peirce, Ch., 33, 284, 285, 291
Pelé, A., 210, 211, 419
Perelman, Ch., 38, 53, 252
Pérez-Cisneros, G., 174, 176, 427
Pericles, 342
Peschanski, M., 280–282, 312, 317
Pétain, M., 426
Peterson, J., 365
Petrilli, S., 285, 286, 288, 291, 293, 303, 304, 313
Pettiti, L.-Ed., 408
Phillips, H., 396
Piaget, J., 289, 403, 408
Picq, P., 24, 314
Pierrot, A., 36
Pillay, N., 128, 168
Pinelli, C., 382
Pinker, S., 245
Pius IX, Pope, 20
Plantinga, A., 181
Plato, 14, 20, 21, 32, 33, 46, 57, 210, 277, 284, 296, 300, 301, 304, 311, 391, 392
Pogge, W., 12, 59
Pojman, L., 22, 25–27
Pollmann, A., 356
Polybe, 8, 47
Ponton, L., 58, 278
Ponzio, A., 285, 286, 288, 291, 293, 303, 313, 314
Porphyry, 288

Poseidonius, 295
Potter, C., 4, 312
Pradelle, A., 73
Proskauer (Judge), 83
Protagoras, 299
Pufendorf, S., 32, 50, 55, 56
Puledda, S., 3, 4, 202
Punday, D., 303
Pythagoras, 21

Q
Quéré, Y., 281, 314
Quesnay, 392
Quiniou, Y., 24
Quiroga, C., 382

R
Raafat, W., 397
Rabouin, D., 188
Radovanovic, M., 399
Ramcharan, B., 57, 115, 129, 182, 183, 341, 343, 374, 412, 419
Rao, N., 32, 194, 195, 199, 225, 245, 260, 262, 271, 329
Rawls, J., 182
Reagan, R., 398
Reboul, O., 194, 266
Renaut, A., 8, 282, 297
Renault, E., 186
Renouvier, Ch., 212, 329, 336
Renshaw, C., 143
Resweber, J.-P., 3402
Ricœur, P., 21, 36, 39, 58, 185, 187, 206, 313
Riedel, E., 146
Rimbaud, A., 408
Rishmawi, M., 113
Rivero, J., 112, 168, 408
Robledo, A., 381
Rockefeller, J., Jr., 81
Rodley, N., 127
Roijen, J., 168, 177
Rolin, H., 73
Rolston III, H., 25, 179
Rómulo, C.P., 397
Roncalli (Cardinal), 94
Roosevelt, E., 76, 86, 87, 98, 162, 167, 424, 425, 434
Roosevelt, F., 80, 86, 181, 424, 425
Rorty, R., 430
Rosas, A., 7, 114
Rosenbaum, A., 47, 51, 59
Rousseau, J.-J., 28, 52, 56, 59, 99, 187, 297, 329, 342
Rousseau, D., 250
Roy, O., 27, 177, 183, 190
Rozakis, 174
Ruggie, J., 147
Ruiz, J., 384
Rusen, J., 56, 364
Russ, J., 21
Russell, B., 29, 75, 355, 423
Ryle, G., 33

S
Sachs, M., 219, 221, 260, 264
Saint-Just, L., 64
Saint-Lot, É., 168, 425
Salmon, J., 378
Salomon, M., 138, 176
Samnøy, Å., 83
Sankey, V., 75
Santa Cruz, H., 98, 145, 167, 176, 184, 278, 337, 339, 398, 403, 427, 428–431
Sartre, J.-P., 272
Saussure, F., 284, 285
Scelle, G., 73
Schabas, W., 68, 120, 127, 143, 438
Schauer, F., 262
Scheinin, M., 137, 146, 348, 349, 359, 364, 418, 419
Schiller, F., 208
Schulman, A., 211
Schutter, O., 102, 116, 130, 138, 147, 382, 383
Scott, Ja., 72
Scott, Jo., 34
Sebeok, Th., 284–286, 303
Seglow, J., 186
Segni, L., 202
Seiderman, I., 138
Semple, J., 204
Sen, A., 167, 182, 337, 338, 411
Seneca, 47, 206, 210
Sengupta, A., 337
Sepúlveda, J., 54, 55, 112, 203
Seriaux, A., 247, 328
Shaftesbury (3rd Earl), 23
Shakespeare, W., 64, 402
Shalev, A., 290, 431, 438
Shapiro, S., 192
Shotwell, J., 83
Shue, H., 338
Siep, L., 187
Simma, B., 78, 79, 100
Simon, E., 55, 74, 368
Simpson, B., 396
Singer, P., 31, 409

Smith, A., 19, 29, 187, 288
Smith, R., 132
Smuts, J., 76, 213
Socrates, 21, 30, 39, 46, 57, 187, 190
Soerensen, M., 397
Soëtard, M., 283
Sohn, L., 116, 357, 360, 384
Sophocles, 46, 189
Spaak, T., 192
Spector, H., 164
Spinoza, B., 179, 188
Spring, J., 8
Stalin, J., 70, 79, 93
Steinbeck, J., 283, 293
Steiner, H., 146, 223, 343
Stern, M., 171
Sternberger, D., 294
Stettinius, E., 80, 84
Stiglitz, J., 9
Stokoe, W., 286
Styron, W., 26
Suárez, F., 55, 362
Sudre, F., 359
Sulmasy, D., 202
Supiot, A., 288
Symonides, J., 376

T
Talleyrand-Périgord, Ch.-M., 282
Taylor, Ch., 182, 185
Teresa (Mother), 1979, 151
This, B., 188
Thiselton, A., 408
Thomas, A., 201, 284
Thorn, J., 94
Thorp, W., 167
Thors, T., 361
Thucydides, 342
Tierney, B., 48, 54, 55
Tigani, J., 142
Tocqueville, A., 283, 311, 329, 357
Todorov, T., 187, 288
Tomaševski, K., 303
Tomuschat, Ch., 67, 68, 73, 99, 147, 165, 339, 341, 361, 381, 415, 431
Tort, P., 24
Tóth, J., 53, 356
Touraine, A., 63
Trechsel, S., 145
Trindade, A., 50, 53, 110, 151, 179, 183, 252, 357, 359, 361–363, 378–380
Trousson, R., 28
Truman, H., 80, 424
Truncellito, D., 34
Tse-tung, M., 427, 428
Tum, R., 151
Turgot, A., 64
Turri, J., 35
Tutu, D., 408

U
Ugon, E., 361
Ulpian, 208
Utaker, A., 281, 312

V
Vallejo, J., 384
Vallet, O., 290
Van Bueren, G., 252
Van Dyke, 426
Van Lier, H., 283, 288, 308, 313
Varayudej, S., 339, 341
Vasak, K., 69, 112
Vasconcellos, C., 168, 425
Vedel, G., 332
Védrine, H., 9
Velu, J., 130, 364
Vercors, 290
Verdoodt, A., 71, 214, 359, 393, 395, 432
Verdross, A., 379
Vernadsky, V., 286
Vidal, C., 316
Villey, M., 54
Vincent, L., 190
Vincent, S., 74, 190
Viola, F., 49
Vitoria, F., 54, 359, 362
Volodin, V., 376
Voltaire, 20, 60
Von Mohl, R., 365
Von Uexküll, J., 284, 286
Vyshinsky, A., 395

W
Waal, F., 24
Wackenheim, M., 269, 270
Waldock, H., 379
Waldron, J., 56, 66, 208, 246, 247
Warren (Justice), 239
Water, C., 250
Weber, M., 69
Weil, É., 25, 329
Weizmann, Ch., 76
Welby, V., 291
Wells, H., 75, 76
Wenders, W., 190
Wermeil, S., 276

Westermarck, E., 409
Wetz, F., 220
White, L., 204
Whitehead, A.N., 75, 211, 426
Whitman, J., 209, 222
Wiart, C., 95, 168, 176, 177, 214, 250
Wilberforce, W., 149
Williams, F., 75
Williams, M., 34
Williams, R., 51, 75, 188–190, 193, 256, 296
Williams, Th., 53
Williamson, J., 8
Wilson, E., 23
Wilson, G., 174
Wilson, W., 70, 81
Wiseberg, L., 148, 149
Wismann, H., 281, 316
Wittgenstein, L., 33, 248
Wood, A., 204, 314

Y

Yew, L., 410, 413

Z

Zambrano, P., 36
Zaruk, D., 208
Zemanek, K., 379
Zenon, 401
Zuckert, M., 51, 62

Terms/Concepts

A

Abortion, 22, 226, 231–233, 255, 271, 398, 409
Abu Ghraib Prison, 181
Académie Diplomatique Internationale, 72
Affaire Calas, 60, 61, 390
Africa, 57, 132, 389, 399, 408, 484
African Group, 120, 122
Agreement for the Prosecution and Punishment of the Major War Criminals of the European Axis, 118
Allied Powers, 77, 118
All-Russia Congress of Soviets, 67
American Association for the United Nations, 83, 89, 84, 425
American Bar Association, 397
American Civil Liberties Union, 163
American Federation of Labor, 89, 90, 213, 430
American Indians, 54
American Institute of International Law, 72
American revolution, 56, 193, 357
American Society of International Law, 141, 442
American University of Beyrut, 426, 427
American War of Independence, 63
Amsterdam Privacy Conference, 265
Animals' rights, 22
Anthropology, 28, 287, 304, 410
Apartheid, 6, 221, 225, 330, 339, 377, 382, 447
Applied ethics, 21, 495
Argumentation, 37–40
Asia, 57, 132–134, 142, 389, 410–413
Asian group, 120, 122, 480
Asian values, 134, 410–413
Asia Pacific Forum of National Human Rights Institutions, 115, 122
Assisted suicide, 243, 245, 255
Atlantic conference, 78
Austrian National Library, 343
Autonomy, 33, 47, 55, 61, 68, 164, 165, 182, 203–205, 207, 208, 211, 228–230, 232, 244, 245, 248, 249, 254, 256, 259, 260, 269, 271, 276, 314, 320, 372, 373, 399, 400, 403, 404, 408, 409, 411, 414
Axis powers, 78

B

Bandung conference, 107
Bastille, 63
Behavioral ethology, 24
Benefit theory, 164
Bergen-Belsen Lager, 84
Berlin blockade, 424
Berlin wall, 8, 219
Bible, 49, 66, 469
Big Five, 12, 424, 495, 501
Bill of Rights, 58, 66, 67, 76, 82, 83, 85, 86, 88, 89, 92, 115, 116, 144, 181, 213, 214, 260, 262, 306, 314, 356, 369, 405, 426, 428
Bioethics, 217, 268, 273, 278, 293, 348
Biological revolution, 307, 314, 320
Biology, 32, 34, 184, 190, 191, 217, 273, 304, 305, 308–310
Biomedicine, 130
Brain, 23, 26, 32, 191, 280, 281, 286, 304–310, 312–314, 316, 317, 319–321, 433
British Commonwealth Conference, 80
British Empire, 69
Buchenwald Lager, 84
Buddhism/Buddha, 407, 412

C

Catechism, 201
Categorical imperative, 32, 38, 206, 207, 209, 257, 258, 318
Catholic Church/Catholicism, 49, 178, 201, 208, 469
Central Park, 27
Century of pedagogy, 297
Charter-based mechanisms, 122, 124, 480, 483
Charter of an International Military Tribunal, 118
Christian/Christianism/Christianity, 55, 203, 212, 391, 412
Citizenship, 74, 193, 294, 295, 302, 314, 341, 368, 374, 407, 426
Civil law, 50, 52, 62, 191, 193, 227, 380
Civil rights, 76, 105, 114, 163, 168, 255, 316, 368, 411, 456, 472
Civil society, 66, 147, 148, 150–152, 171, 187, 344
Civilization, 4, 5, 8, 24, 48, 57, 125, 183, 186, 211, 213, 282, 283, 305, 312, 314, 375, 378, 379, 391, 392, 400
Cloning, 5, 22254, 273
Cognition, 35, 36, 59, 193, 259, 304–306, 309, 310, 314
Cold war, 6, 8, 131, 150, 341, 398, 413, 419
Collective rights, 116, 166, 301, 337, 339
Colonialism, 222, 226, 275, 391, 414
Columbia University, 262
Committee on the Theoretical Bases of Human Rights, 91, 182
Common Core Document/Expanded Core Document, 126, 445, 480
Common Ethics of Humankind/Humanity, 12, 152, 436, 494, 497
Common law, 223, 376, 378, 380, 461
Common responsibility, 195, 346, 347, 349, 499
Commons, 169–171, 384
Communism/Communist block, 6, 214, 341, 391, 397, 398
Communitarianism, 267, 399
Community law, 223, 251
Compassion/Empathy/Pity/Sympathy, 20, 23, 26–29, 32, 61, 183, 190, 191, 290, 360, 390, 408
Complaints/Communications, 81, 107, 108, 123, 126, 127, 131, 144, 146, 454, 462, 466, 482
Concentration camps, 84, 181, 430, 431
Concluding Observations/Concluding Comments, 126, 233, 445
Conditionality, 7
Conference of Allied Ministers of Education, 79, 426
Conference on the Human Dimension of the OSCE, 370
Conference of San Francisco, 78, 360, 427
Congress of Dijon, 74
Connally resolution, 78
Consciousness, 26, 149, 174, 178, 190, 288, 295, 307, 311, 312, 314, 319, 321, 402
Conseil d'État, 269
Conseil de l'Europe, 363, 364
Consensus, 13, 24, 25, 35, 37, 38, 40, 91, 98, 166, 177, 179–185, 192, 220, 225, 226, 232, 252–255, 265, 371, 382, 394, 416, 456, 457, 466, 478
Consequentialism/Consequentialist ethics, 31, 32
Constitutional council, 221, 426
Constitutional law, 12, 112, 218, 219, 222–225, 245, 249, 260, 262, 358, 364, 365
Constitutional patriotism/Verfassungspatriotism, 294, 295
Constitutionalism, 62, 66, 68, 222, 364, 365, 370, 373, 500
Control council, 376
Conventional mechanisms, 483
Copernican revolution, 208, 293, 314, 358, 402, 499
Core human rights treaties, 109, 124, 125, 446
Cosmos, 45, 47, 201, 468
Creativity, 202, 279, 281, 282, 306, 309, 310, 314, 317, 320, 321, 330
Crimes against humanity, 129, 140, 375–377, 382, 413, 447, 466, 476
Crusades, 391
Cultural diversity, 2, 9, 12, 168, 173, 268, 330, 331, 348, 409, 414
Cultural relativism, 410, 413, 414
Cultural revolution, 320, 357
Culture, 5, 11, 13, 21, 35, 38, 46, 58, 68, 111, 173, 191, 209, 211, 213, 249, 267, 268, 282, 283, 287, 294–296, 303, 305, 307–312, 314, 316, 317, 319–321, 329–331, 336, 365, 366, 390–392
Culture of human rights, 11, 13, 418, 435, 436, 494, 501

D

De-natured animal, 290, 315
De-natured human being, 290, 315
Death penalty, 22, 69, 108, 131, 133, 209, 210, 215, 226, 239–241, 246, 258, 262, 266, 272, 274, 398

Democracy, 6, 8, 12, 74, 93, 144, 222, 250, 252, 261, 302, 311 *passim*
Deontologism/Deontological Ethics, 32, 495
Derechos del hombre, 162, 163
Deregulation, 8, 417
Desire, 20, 25, 28, 49, 61, 187–191, 193, 205, 238, 266, 365, 394, 403, 423
Development, 3, 4, 5, 9, 10, 23, 53, 56, 57, 60, 66, 79, 99, 109 *passim*
Dignitas, 200–202, 206, 208, 210–212, 277, 498
Dignity, 5, 7, 11, 64, 68, 84, 100, 113, 115, 129, 130, 134, 138 *passim*
Diplomatic protection, 69, 383
Disabilities, 217, 272, 331, 332
Diversity, 2, 3, 5, 6, 9, 12, 132, 134, 168, 172, 173, 187, 195, 255, 268, 276, 278, 329–332, 336, 349, 409, 411, 414, 437, 484
Divine Law, 48, 49
Documented outline, 88, 90
Double articulation, 313
Drafting committee, 75, 76, 88–92, 96, 97, 145, 161, 174, 175, 333, 405, 426, 429
Droits naturels/Droits de l'homme/Libertés publiques, 51, 65, 161
Due Process Clauses, 255
Dumbarton Oaks conversations, 79, 83
Duty, 31–33, 39, 47, 111, 113, 115, 135, 137, 139, 140 *passim*
Duty-bearers, 112, 113, 166, 417
Dwarf-throwing, 269

E

Eastern Bloc, 67, 131
Eastern Europe, 93, 368, 372
Eastern European Group, 121, 122, 480
Educability, 297, 298, 300, 317, 320
Educational Neuroscience, 308, 310, 317, 318
Emotion, 28, 29, 289, 301, 304–306, 309, 310, 314, 317, 321
Emotional thought, 306, 314
Encyclical, 20, 49, 208
Encyclopedia Britannica, 31, 32, 47, 49, 70, 409
Endosemiosis/Endosemiotics, 312
Enlightenment, 47, 60, 74, 152, 173, 182, 185, 203
Episteme, 33, 35, 36
Epistemology, 11, 14, 33–35, 39, 40, 180, 182
Epistolary novels, 60
Equality, 5, 47, 61, 67, 70, 73, 78, 82, 98, 99, 112, 138 *passim*
Erga omnes, 139, 379, 382–384, 453, 460
Ethical/Moral epistemology, 35, 180
Ethics, 3, 6, 21, 22, 27–29, 31, 37–39, 50, 120, 164, 168, 169, 177, 178, 182, 185, 189, 249, 293, 305, 306, 309, 314, 317, 330, 334, 434, 437
Ethics of communication, 293
Ethics of Human Rights, 6, 12, 168, 195, 347, 349, 436, 437
Ethics of Recognition, 12, 161, 185, 193, 195
Ethics of responsibility, 293
EU Network of Independent Experts on Fundamental Rights, 200, 223, 271, 272
European Commission for Democracy through Law, 222, 250, 255, 261, 371
European Movement, 77
European University Institute, 418
Euthanasia, 22, 245, 409
Extraterritorial obligations of States, 138

F

Facing History and Ourselves Foundation, 84, 277
Family, 82, 98, 134, 141, 169, 170, 172, 174–176, 187, 189, 191–193 *passim*
Family law, 193
Fascism, 93, 209, 222, 395, 396
Final solution, 431
Foundationalism, 497
Fraternity, 67, 98, 99, 112, 174, 336
Freedom, 2, 6, 8, 20, 26, 33, 50, 51, 68, 69, 70, 73, 75, 77, 81, 82, 86, 87, 89, 97, 101 *passim*
Freedom of speech/expression, 81, 115, 182, 225, 226, 419
French Civil Code, 193
French National Assembly, 282
French National Commission of UNESCO, 182
French resistance, 75
French revolution, 63, 64, 66, 210, 328, 336, 357, 454
Friendship, 187, 190, 191, 432, 433, 436
Fundamentalism, 9, 135, 330, 417
Future generations, 134, 169, 273, 330, 337, 347, 348, 407, 433
Führer, 366

G

Garden of Eden, 47, 51
General Comment (GC), 454, 455
General Discussion Day, 128
General Principles of Law, 101, 140, 183, 251, 252, 418, 454
General recommendation, 143, 454

Genesis, 201, 400
Genocide, 68, 99, 116, 117, 129, 140, 275, 292, 334, 377, 379, 381–383, 398, 438
Genome, 26, 172, 217, 273, 276, 278, 280–282, 308, 316, 318, 321, 348
Georgetown University, 276
German Parliament, 257
German Reich, 67
Gestapo, 426
Gettysburg Civil War cemetery, 338
Global compact, 146
Global Public Goods (GPGs), 9, 171
Global semiotics, 285, 286, 293, 303
Globalization, 3, 7–10, 47, 133, 134, 138, 141, 146, 149, 171, 293, 294, 314, 330, 331, 348, 412, 416, 418
God/Creator/Supreme Being, 21, 39, 49, 63, 175, 176, 201, 212, 313, 319, 373
Golden mean, 29
Golden rule, 27–29, 183, 190, 191, 206, 318, 437, 455, 495, 497
Good education, 82, 298–300, 303, 317
Good governance, 367–369
Goodness, 31, 32, 60, 296, 321
Good samaritan laws, 409
Good will, 205
Gordian knot, 298, 316
Governance, 31, 260, 340, 341, 347, 367–370
Grand Chamber, 231, 232
Great October Socialist revolution, 67
Greek-Latin culture, 402
Guinness Book of Records, 97

H

Happiness, 5, 20, 26, 30, 31, 63, 64, 82, 116, 166, 212, 254, 316, 321, 373, 420, 423
Hard law, 456
Hindu/Hinduism, 21, 407, 412
Hitlerism, 391
Holism, 401
Holocaust, 26, 184, 191, 265, 289, 426, 431, 438
Holy Grail, 214
Homeostasis, 25, 26, 307, 308
Hominization, 288, 312
Homo, 280, 286, 288
Homo Habilis, 281
Homo Loquens, 281, 319
Homo Sapiens, 25, 280, 281
Homosexual/Homosexuality, 22, 229, 230
Honor killings, 268, 412
Human dignity, 11, 12, 68, 85, 97, 113, 115, 134, 138, 166, 174, 180, 185, 199, 200–204, 208, 228, 234, 235, 237, 248, 267, 269, 311, 312, 315, 316, 318, 319, 327, 340, 347
Human Dignity Principle (HDP), 12, 195, 214, 349, 494
Humanism, 3–5, 202, 293, 314, 412
Humanist movement, 3, 4
Humanist society, 4
Humanitarian intervention, 69, 77, 479
Humanity/Humankind, 2, 12, 21, 29, 37, 57, 58, 64, 152, 168, 170, 183, 195, 202, 276, 281, 282, 287, 296–299, 317, 320, 321, 322, 329, 330, 337, 347, 349, 359, 360–363, 376, 378, 384, 392, 299, 436
Human Mind Project, 279
Human rights day, 102, 103
Human rights education, 12, 345, 434–436, 438, 458
Human rights movement, 11, 83, 149, 150, 152, 374, 393, 413, 424
Human rights philosophy, 200, 498
Human rights revolution, 12, 396, 357, 358, 419, 420, 495, 499
Human worth, 11, 12, 207, 208, 276–279, 282, 311, 312, 315, 318, 319, 321, 349
Hunter college, 86, 97

I

Ideology of human rights, 6
Imprescriptible, 63–65, 74, 166, 173, 273, 366, 373, 377
Inalienable, 5, 63, 67, 74, 82, 99, 166, 173, 176, 193, 215, 249, 257, 273, 329, 333, 343, 373
Independent Experts, 116, 123, 124, 200, 223, 271, 272
Index of Forbidden Books, 60, 61
Individualism, 12, 63, 64, 214, 393, 399–402
Indivisibility, 115, 116, 144, 262, 319, 341, 367, 418
Inner worth, 207, 276
Inquisition, 20, 391, 438
Intentionality, 313
Inter-American Conference, 79, 83, 392
Inter-American Conference on Problems of War and Peace, 83, 392
Inter-American Juridical Committee, 83, 89, 392
InterAction—A United Voice for Global Change, 407
Interculturality, 331
Interdependence and indivisibility of all human rights, 107, 115, 418, 459
Interest Theory, 164, 461, 497

Intergovernmental Organization (IGO), 130, 146, 368, 442, 461
International Bill of Human Rights, 11, 88, 89, 92, 94, 95, 103, 109, 111, 215, 216, 277, 295, 394, 431, 446, 461, 462, 494
International Community, 3, 6, 9, 68, 71, 73, 102, 110, 111, 115, 118, 120, 129, 133, 134, 139, 140, 144, 146, 149, 169, 183, 302, 358, 361, 362, 364, 372, 376, 379, 381, 383, 384, 398, 399, 406, 407, 417, 432
International Conference on Human Rights, 110, 169
International Customary Law, 100, 123, 183, 334, 398
International Day of Democracy, 340
International Human Rights Law (IHRL), 5, 11–13, 109, 110, 115, 117, 133, 135, 137, 140, 165, 166, 177, 183, 191, 193–195, 214, 217, 245, 260, 274, 277, 318, 328, 334, 337, 359, 360, 364, 373, 382, 398, 399, 414, 416, 434, 437
International Humanitarian Law (IHL), 69, 110, 129, 382, 436
International Labor office, 71
International Law, 11, 50, 55, 72, 73, 101, 102, 110, 111, 113, 114, 117, 119, 135, 136, 138, 139, 141, 144, 147, 148, 151, 152, 163, 169, 179, 183, 192, 252, 338, 343, 356–364, 369, 378, 381, 383, 399, 416, 438
International Law of Humankind, 363, 378
International legal personality, 358, 362, 363
International Mind, Brain, and Education Society (IMBES), 308
International Red Cross, 69
International Theological commission, 27, 50, 167, 169, 177
International Union of Associations for the League of Nations, 73
International/Universal/World/Court of Human Rights, 93, 144, 145, 146, 417, 418, 483, 497
Internet, 8, 170, 172, 266
Inter-State complaints, 127, 472, 482
Iron Curtain, 93, 398
Islam/Islamism, 133, 268, 390, 407, 412, 414
Italo-Abyssinian War, 376

J

Jim Crow laws, 425
Judaism, 208, 209
Juridical conscience, 72, 73, 168, 183, 320, 362, 363, 379, 380
Jus civile, 48
Jus cogens, 102, 140, 334, 343, 358, 364, 379, 398, 399
Jus gentium, 48, 252, 358, 359, 362, 363, 378
Jus naturale, 48, 54
Justinian code, 48
Jus vitae necisque, 186

K

Kellogg-Briand pact, 118
Kingdom of ends, 206, 207
Knesset, 225
Ku Klux Klan, 425

L

Language, 50, 161, 173, 279, 281, 286, 291, 292, 313, 408
La Revue Diplomatique, 74
Latin America, 72, 74, 83, 99, 100, 120, 122, 149, 392, 393, 428
Latin American and Caribbean Group, 120, 122, 480
Law of Law, 357, 358, 499
Law of the Twelve Tables 186
League of Nations, 70–74, 77, 78, 81, 91, 97, 100, 102, 359, 426
Learning, 36, 115, 236, 279, 298, 299, 303, 305, 306, 308–311, 317, 345, 367, 427, 434, 435
Lebenswelt, 286, 313
Legal Philosophy, 45, 53, 192, 469
Legal rights, 11, 65, 105, 163–165, 182
Lex ferenda, 13, 466
Lege lata, 48
Liberation theology, 149
Liberty, 2, 5, 20, 29, 37, 39, 51 *passim*
Life, 2, 5, 19, 25 33, 46, 48, 49 *passim*
Linguistic, 39, 69, 70, 284, 285, 291, 295, 331
Linguistic birth, 295
Love, 23, 28, 49, 166, 187–191, 201, 233, 236, 278, 301, 342, 412
Love commandos, 412
Lovingness, 75

M

Maastricht University, 12, 138, 467
Mandate system, 70
Mapping, 306, 307
Market, 3, 8, 9, 133, 170, 171, 182, 207, 264, 402
McGill University, 428
Mein Kampf, 184, 433
Metaethics, 21, 22, 35, 39, 495

Metarights, 337
Middle Ages, 4, 20, 49, 53, 54, 202, 203, 210, 390
Minority/Minorities Treaties, 71, 72
Möbius strip, 24
Modernism, 20
Moral conscience, 6, 25, 40, 49, 184, 404
Moral education, 30, 32, 296, 299–301, 317
Moral philosophy, 21, 29, 32, 164, 185, 208, 211
Moral rights, 33, 163, 173
Moral sense, 22–24, 278, 495
Moral worth, 31, 205, 207, 276
Morality, 5, 7, 21–27, 29, 31, 32, 37, 38, 49, 60, 165, 168, 180, 185, 192, 204, 205, 207, 22, 225, 247, 251, 270, 279, 314, 319, 320, 379
Morals, 20, 21, 24, 25, 31, 38, 52, 190, 204, 256, 314
Morning post, 390
Multinational corporations, 8, 146
My Day, 425

N
Napoleonic empire, 66
National Human Rights Institutions (NHRIs), 142, 143, 152
National Socialism, 184, 220, 433
Naturalized Epistemology, 35
Natural law/Naturalism, 46–56, 60, 68, 178, 183, 184, 192, 214, 220, 403
Natural rights, 12, 45–56, 58, 61, 63, 65, 66, 68, 152, 161, 184, 330, 360
Nazi/Nazism, 84, 93, 209, 391
Neo-liberalism, 8, 9
Neo-Scholasticism, 55
Neurobiology, 190, 305, 307
Neuron, 280, 306, 312, 319
Neuroplasticity, 280, 312, 319, 321
Neuroscience, 308, 310, 317, 318
New Constitutional law, 364, 365
New Constitutionalism, 364, 365, 500
New Deal, 425
New human rights/Solidarity rights, 112, 114, 301, 337
New Humanism, 3, 4, 293, 314
New Rhetoric, 38
Ninth International Conference of American States, 83, 393
Nobel Prize, 9, 26, 75, 149, 151, 170, 292, 296, 356, 408, 426
Non-Aligned movement, 107
Non-derogable, 292, 377, 382
Non-discrimination, 70, 73, 98, 109, 136, 144, 195, 332–335, 348, 349, 367, 371, 394
Non-Governmental Organization (NGO), 80, 103, 146, 148, 150, 151
Non-State actors, 137, 139, 147, 348, 417
Normative ethics, 21, 22, 27, 30, 32
Nuclear commission, 85–87, 97, 184, 426
Nuremberg principles, 99
Nuremberg trials, 52, 77

O
Object-formula, 256, 318
Ombudsman/Defensor del Pueblo/Provedor de Justiça, 143, 468
Ordre public, 380, 461
Original sin, 47, 203, 296
Otherness, 291, 293, 314, 321, 414
Overlapping consensus, 182, 255

P
Paideia, 3, 296
Palace of Values, 349
Palais des Nations, 94, 122, 458
Pan-American/Inter-American Conference, 79, 83, 392
Pan-American Union, 55
Paris Peace Conference, 144
Parlamentarischer Rat, 219
Parliament of the World's Religions, 2
Patria potestas, 186
Peace, 65, 77, 82, 85, 129 *passim*
Peace of Westphalia, 68
Pedagogic animal, 297, 317
Pentagon, 257
Perfectibilism, 282, 296, 297
Perfectibility, 12, 278, 279, 282, 283, 290, 291, 293, 295, 297, 298, 311, 315, 318, 320, 321
Perfecting, 12, 278, 279, 282, 290, 295, 296, 311, 312, 315, 316, 318, 320, 321, 438
Permanent Conference of Allied Ministers of Education, 426
Philosophy of Law, 191
Phronesis, 30, 36
Portrait of a Dignitary, 246
Positive discrimination/Affirmative action, 144, 335, 472
Positive law, 45, 49, 52, 53, 69, 165, 184, 251, 362
Positivism, 52, 53, 69, 192, 194, 362, 363
Postmodernism, 152, 414
Poverty, 9, 10, 54, 134, 146, 172, 217, 226, 241, 263, 292, 302, 315, 342, 367, 416, 417

Practical reason, 27, 40, 50, 178, 205
Privacy, 33, 114, 226, 228–230, 243, 263, 275
Privatisation, 8, 470
Proclamation of an Unlimited National Emergency, 419
Psychoanalysis, 188, 308
Public Goods (PGs), 9, 170, 171
Public Reason, 182

Q
Quarantine speech, 78
Quasi-jurisprudence, 144

R
Rational animal, 22, 28, 39, 287, 288
Rationality, 13, 34, 36–40, 50, 51, 173, 180, 182, 212, 256, 278, 283, 288, 304, 306, 312–314, 319, 320, 321, 495
Rechtsstaat, 365, 366, 368, 372
Recognition, 7, 12, 26, 35, 37, 38, 40, 54, 69 *passim*
Recta ratio, 47, 362
Regulation, 8, 25, 26, 48, 112, 171, 192, 230, 232, 255, 258, 271, 304, 306, 307, 312, 314, 320, 417, 437
Reich, 67, 71, 219, 227, 294, 366
Religion, 4, 60, 67, 70, 73, 74, 85, 86, 97, 138, 172, 189, 225, 239, 267, 275, 295, 331, 333, 334, 340, 345, 397
Renaissance, 3, 4, 48, 53, 202, 210, 282, 291, 402
Resistance, 12, 20, 51, 64, 75, 219, 344, 366, 373, 414, 426
Responsibility, 2, 37, 83, 118, 119, 121, 128, 129, 134 *passim*
Responsibility to Protect, 129, 382, 476
Responsiveness, 149
Revolution, 8, 12, 56, 61–66, 72, 149, 185, 193, 208, 210 *passim*
Rhetoric, 7, 38, 56, 85, 185, 285, 373, 411, 413, 414, 416
Right-holders, 166, 446, 457
Rights of man, 53, 56, 59–61, 63, 65, 66, 72–76, 88, 152, 161, 176, 177, 182, 260, 294, 360, 366, 373
Right to a fair trial, 382
Right to (a healthy) environment, 113, 455
Right to be free from torture, 382
Right to citizenship, 193
Right to communication, 113
Right to democracy, 338–341, 345
Right to development, 10, 113, 114, 122, 337, 338, 342–345, 406
Right to die, 244
Right to difference (be different), 330, 332, 414
Right to due process, 33
Right to education, 112, 115, 225, 243, 279, 295, 301–303, 317, 433, 434, 452
Right to employment, 270
Right to equality, 225, 316, 329, 335
Right to food, 137, 234, 262, 382
Right to freedom/liberty, 115, 163, 175, 179, 225, 275, 340
Right to freedom of thought, 163
Right to have rights, 193, 239, 250, 274, 316, 318
Right to health, 114, 148, 225, 243
Right to (human) dignity, 223, 238, 245, 256, 263, 292, 329
Right to human rights education, 434, 436, 501
Right to human security, 344
Right to information, 113, 255
Right to international cooperation, 139
Right to just remuneration, 260
Right to life, 113, 114, 116, 163, 173, 213, 214, 231, 232, 233, 241, 243, 260–261, 274, 328, 343, 382, 393
Right to marriage, 97
Right to peace, 113, 114, 343, 344, 345, 455
Right to petition, 144, 394, 499
Right to physical integrity, 234, 238
Right to privacy, 114, 229, 263, 275, 471
Right to property, 67, 98, 107, 114, 409
Right to rebellion, 389
Right to recognition, 193, 194, 294, 498
Right to resistance, 51
Right to self-determination, 106, 114, 382
Right to social security, 215, 261
Right to speech, 419
Right to strike, 115
Right to the common heritage of the mankind/ humankind/humanity, 113, 114
Right to vote, 115, 391, 412
Right to work, 110, 112, 115, 147, 260, 262
Roman Empire, 7, 295
Roman law, 48, 186, 358, 364, 391
Rule of Law, 12, 130, 144, 224, 295, 316, 340, 365, 366–372, 375
Russian revolution, 72

S
San Francisco Opera house, 80
Scholcher commission, 336
School of Salamanca/Second Scholastic, 55
Scylla and Charybdis, 263
Second birth, 295, 317, 320

Second nature, 295, 298, 317, 320
Secretariat Outline of an International Bill of Rights, 214, 405, 428
Self, 26, 28, 60, 226, 243, 256, 263, 307, 309, 312, 319, 414
Self-evidence, 177, 181
Semiology, 284, 285
Semioethics, 293, 314
Semiotic animal/Animal symbolicum, 287–289, 293, 297, 313, 317, 319, 320
Sex/Sexuality, 226, 228–230, 308, 313, 414
Shari'ah, 414
Sign/Semiosis/Semiotics/Sémiologie, 283–288, 291, 293, 303
Silver Rule, 27, 455
Slave/Slavery, 20, 50, 55, 58, 66, 67, 69, 71, 77, 134, 149, 193, 203, 211, 217, 221, 274, 275, 276, 318, 328, 329, 336, 338, 377, 382, 383, 391, 409, 412, 419
Social Contract/Contractualism, 24, 51, 52, 54, 56, 59, 65, 173, 180, 342, 403
Social Epistemology, 35
Sociobiology, 23
Soft law, 456
Solidarity, 37, 68, 72, 99, 112, 114, 116, 134, 150, 195, 226, 267, 301, 335–337, 346, 347, 349, 367
Somatic-marker, 304, 305
Sophist, 361
Southwestern University, 76
Sovereignty, 62, 68, 71, 77, 85, 100, 119, 129, 134, 140, 149, 294, 333, 340, 346, 357, 359, 361, 373, 390, 394, 396, 398, 403, 411, 413
Specialized agency, 78, 145, 150
Special procedures, 123, 124, 127, 480
Special Rapporteurs, 113, 124, 137, 138, 141, 302, 303, 480
Special Rapporteur on the Right to Education, 302, 303
Special Representatives/Special Envoys, 124, 147, 148, 151, 470
Stalinism, 80, 385
State of nature, 50, 51, 55, 56, 403
State of the Union, 81, 82, 181
Statement on Atrocities, 118
Stoa/Stoic/Stoicism, 47, 58, 208, 496
Strait of Messina, 263
Structuralism, 4
Subjectivity, 5, 34, 50, 144, 312, 363, 499
Sumeria, 57
Survivors' Manifesto, 289, 438
Syllabus, 1, 12, 495
Symbolic system, 287, 319, 321
Synaptic connexions, 314
Syntax, 286, 313

T
Terrorism, 171, 416, 419
The Club of Rome, 1
Theorized subjectivity, 34
Third Reich, 71, 227
Tolerance, 60, 64, 134, 135, 195, 237, 267, 295, 335, 336, 344, 347, 349, 367, 374, 411, 415, 432, 435–438
Torture, 60, 61, 68, 109, 120, 125, 128, 130, 140, 152, 181, 217, 218, 223, 244, 263, 272, 292, 328, 376, 381, 382, 419
Totalitarian, 70, 75, 77, 193, 220, 222, 226, 372
Treaties of Westphalia, 359
Treaty-based Bodies/Treaty Monitoring Bodies (TMB), 121, 124, 125, 183, 483
Twentieth Century association, 76

U
Ubuntu, 267, 408
Umwelt, 286, 313
United Nations Conference on International Organization, 80
United Nations geographical regions, 122, 124
United Nations Human Rights Day, 102
United Nations Special Rapporteur on Human Rights and the Environment, 113
Universal Court of Human Rights, 144, 145
Universal values, 1, 11, 37, 168, 347, 367, 414
University of Cambridge, 76
University of Hamburg, 366
University of Königsberg, 300
University of Paris, 72
Utilitarianism, 31

V
Vatican, 5, 149
Vedas, 21, 46
Veterans War Memorial Building, 80
Vichy regime, 426
Vienna Peace conference, 66, 391
Vietnam war, 149
Virtue Epistemology, 35
Virtue ethics, 30–32

W
War crimes, 53, 77, 118, 119, 129, 140, 375, 376, 377, 382, 430
Washington consensus, 8
Westminster college, 398

Western constitutionalism, 68
Western European group and other states, 121, 122, 480
Western German zone, 219
Western Philosophy, 30, 57, 203, 389, 495
Westphalia treaty, 68, 359, 465
Will theory, 164, 497
Wolf children, 296, 298, 315
World Commission on the Social Dimension of Globalization, 416
World Conference on Human Rights (Vienna), 10, 109, 111, 128, 150, 151, 169, 171, 172, 343, 366, 367, 411
World Government association, 89
World Heritage, 171
World Jewish Congress, 430, 432
World Justice project, 371
World Summit, 129, 345, 348, 367, 369
World Trade center, 257, 493
World war, 5, 11, 68–70, 73, 75, 77, 78, 149, 165, 185, 194, 212, 213, 218, 222, 358, 359, 361, 365, 366, 376, 392, 426
Worldwide governance, 368

X
Xhosa, 408

Z
Zionism, 133
Zoosemiotics, 286

United Nations organs, agencies, bodies and related organizations

A
Advisory Committee, 71, 122–124, 344, 345

C
Centre for Human Rights, 12, 117, 128
Committee against Torture (CoAT), 125, 127, 128
Commission on Human Rights (CHR), 6, 76, 84–88, 90, 94, 95, 102, 103, 106, 131–133, 141, 277, 380, 395, 396, 427, 430
Committee on Non-Governmental Organizations, 150
Committee on Economic, Social and Cultural Rights (CESCR), 108, 125, 127, 128, 136, 138, 142, 147, 148, 200, 234, 302
Committee on the Elimination of Discrimination against Women (CEDAW), 109, 110, 115, 125, 127
Committee on the Elimination of Racial Discrimination (CERD), 109, 125, 126
Committee on Enforced Disappearances (CED), 125
Committee on Migrant Workers (CMW), 125
Committee on the Rights of the Child (CoRC), 125, 234
Committee on the Rights of Persons with Disabilities (CoRPD), 125

D
Division of Human Rights, 87, 89, 117, 295, 428

E
Economic and Social Council (ECOSOC), 84–88, 93, 94, 97, 99, 103–106, 108, 116, 117, 120, 121, 124, 125, 150, 167, 175, 213, 214, 360, 391, 393, 394, 396, 397
Expert Mechanism on the Rights of Indigenous Peoples, 124

F
Food and Agriculture Organization (FAO), 75, 79
Forum on Minority Issues, 124

G
General Assembly, 5, 6, 57, 81, 83, 85, 86, 88, 89, 92–117, 120, 121, 128, 133, 162, 167, 169, 185, 250, 273

H
Human Rights Committee (CCPR), 104, 125, 234
Human Rights Council (HRC), 121, 458
Human Rights Treaties Division, 128, 483

I
International Labor Organization (ILO), 71, 104, 110, 127, 129, 147, 213
International Law Commission, 117, 136, 379
International Monetary Fund (IMF), 7, 79, 368

O
Office of United Nations High Commissioner for Human Rights (OHCHR), 97, 111, 128, 129, 143, 340, 416

S
Secretary-General, 72, 87, 92, 103, 105, 108, 121, 128, 129, 147, 148, 150, 169, 339, 369, 417, 428, 437
Security Council, 79, 80, 117, 120, 121, 129, 141, 417, 427
Sub-commission on Freedom of Information and the Press, 87
Sub-commission on Prevention of Discrimination and Protection of Minorities/Sub-commission on the Promotion and Protection of Human Rights, 113, 116, 301
Subcommittee on Prevention of Torture (SPT), 125

T
Third Committee, 5, 57, 94–96, 99–107, 121, 162, 163, 167–169, 174–177, 214, 250, 337, 360, 391–393, 395–398, 403, 404, 424–428, 430, 431, 433, 434
Trusteeship Council, 120, 121

U
United Nations Children's Fund (UNICEF), 502
United Nations Development Program (UNDP), 9, 171, 347
United Nations Educational, Scientific and Cultural Organization (UNESCO), 1–3, 6, 58, 79, 91, 104, 110, 113, 128, 144, 173, 180, 182, 185, 213, 217, 268, 273, 276, 278, 293, 321, 330, 331, 334, 336, 338, 342, 344, 345, 347, 348, 375, 406, 407, 426, 431, 432, 435
United Nations High Commissioner for Human Rights (UNHCHR), 128, 132
United Nations High Commissioner for Refugees (UNHCR), 502
United Nations Non-Governmental Liaison Service (NGLS), 151
United Nations War Crimes Commission, 53, 77, 118, 119, 375, 376

W
World Bank/International Bank for Reconstruction and Development (IBRD), 79
World Health Organization (WHO), 104, 129
World Trade Organization (WTO), 8
Working Group of Experts on People of African Descent, 124

Regional intergovernmental organizations and institutions/bodies

A
African Commission of Human and Peoples' Rights, 132
African Union (AU), 132, 467, 493, 494
Arab Commission for Human Rights, 133
ASEAN Human Rights Commission, 132
Asian Intergovernmental Commission on Human Rights (AICHR), 132
Association of Southeast Asian Nations (ASEAN), 132, 494

C
Commonwealth of Independent States (CIS), 131
Conference on Security and Cooperation in Europe (CSCE), 131
Council of Europe/Conseil de l'Europe, 111, 130, 143, 217, 231, 269, 273, 363, 364, 367, 372, 377

E
European Commission for Democracy through Law, 219, 222, 250, 255, 261, 371
European Commission of Human Rights, 130, 145, 269, 270, 380, 383
European Commissioner on Human Rights, 130
European Committee of Social Rights, 125
European Parliament, 223
European Union (EU), 7, 115, 130, 131, 250–252, 275, 367

I
Inter-American Commission on Human Rights, 131, 380

L
League of Arab States, 133

O
Organization of African Unity (OAU), 111, 488, 489
Organization of American States (OAS), 83, 89, 131, 132, 340
Organization for Economic Cooperation and Development (OECD), 308
Organization for Security and Cooperation in Europe (OSCE), 130, 131, 370

P
Parliamentary Assembly of the Council of Europe, 372

Other international and national institutions/ entities concerned with human rights

A
Abo Akademi, in Turku (Finland), 418
Académie Diplomatique Internationale, 72
Agency for Fundamental Rights, 131
American Anthropological Association (AAA), 409
American Jewish Committee, 83, 149
American Jewish Congress, 89
American Law Institute (ALI), 76, 89, 89
Amnesty International, 142, 148, 149, 151, 428, 436, 484
Anti-Slavery International, 149
Association for Education in Citizenship, 74

C
Catholic Association for International Peace, 76
Coalition for the International Criminal Court, 150
Conference of Non-Governmental Organizations in consultative relationship with the UN (CoNGO), 151

D
Death with Dignity National Center, 245
Defense for Children International (DCI), 149

F
Federal Council of Churches, 149
Front Line Defenders, 151

H
Human Rights Internet (HRI), 148
Human Rights Watch, 148, 194

I
Institut de Droit International, 72
Institut des Hautes Études Internationales, 73
Institut International des Droits de l'Homme (Strasbourg), 112
Inter-American Institute for Human Rights, 148
Inter-Parliamentary Conference, 251
Inter-Parliamentary Union, 341, 430
International Commission of Jurists, 138
International Committee of the Red Cross (ICRC), 149, 151, 430, 464
International Coordination Committee of National Institutions for the Promotion and Protection of Human Rights, 143
International Federation of Leagues for the Defense of the Rights of Man and of the Citizen, 73
International Peace Bureau, 149
International Worker's Association, 149

J
Jewish Holocaust Museum of Jerusalem, 289, 431

L
Ligue des Droits de l'Homme, 74
Ludwig Boltzmann Institute of Human Rights, 418

M
Médecins Sans Frontières, 151
Memory and Tolerance Museum, 438
Minority Rights Group (MRG), 149

N
North Atlantic Treaty Organization (NATO), 417

S
South Asia Forum for Human Rights (SAFHR), (Not cited in the text)

T
The Hague Academy of International Law, 73, 101, 111, 151, 169, 356, 379, 381, 399
Tomales Bay Institute, 169
Transnational Corporations (TNCs), 111, 146, 147, 417, 418, 470

U
Union for Civil Liberties (PUCL), 148
Union of International Associations, 149
Urban Morgan Institute on Human Rights, 466

W
World Association of Non-Governmental Organizations (WANGO), 151, 470

Human rights legal instruments and other related instruments at universal level

A
Abolition of Forced Labour Convention (1957), 487
Additional Protocol I to the Geneva Conventions Relative to the Protection of Victims of International Armed Conflicts (Diplomatic Conference) (1977), 489
Additional Protocol II to the Geneva Conventions Relative to the Protection of Victims of Non-international Armed Conflicts (Diplomatic Conference) (1977), 489
Additional Protocol (III) to the Geneva Conventions (Diplomatic Conference) (2005), 464

B
Basic Principles and Guidelines on the Right to a Remedy and Reparation for Victims of Gross Violations of International Human Rights Law and Serious Violations of International Humanitarian Law (2005), 129
Basic Principles for the Treatment of Prisoners (1990), 490
Basic Principles on the Independence of the Judiciary (UN Congress on the Prevention of Crime and the Treatment of Offenders) (1985), 490
Basic Principles on the Role of Lawyers (UN Congress on the Prevention of Crime and the Treatment of Offenders) (1990), 490
Body of Principles for the Protection of All Persons under Any Form of Detention or Imprisonment (1988), 490

C
Charter of Economic Rights and Duties of States (1974), 488
Charter on the Preservation of Digital Heritage (2003), 493
Code of Conduct for Law Enforcement Officials (1979), 489
Convention against Discrimination in Education (1960), 334
Convention against Torture and Other Cruel, Inhuman or Degrading Treatment or Punishment (CAT) (1984), 109, 120, 125, 459, 484, 489, 493
Convention concerning Discrimination in Respect of Employment and Occupation (1958), 334, 487
Convention concerning Equal Remuneration for Men and Women Workers for Work of Equal Value (1951), 334
Convention Concerning the Protection of the World Cultural and Natural Heritage (1972), 173
Convention for the Safeguarding of Intangible Cultural Heritage (2003), 173, 493
Convention on Access to Information, Public Participation in Decision and Access to Justice in Environmental Matters (Aaharus Convention) (1998), 492
Convention on Consent to Marriage, Minimum Age for Marriage and Registration of Marriages (1962), 488
Convention on Technical and Vocational Education (1989), 490
Convention on the Elimination of All Forms of Discrimination against Women (CEDAW, 1979), 109, 216, 334, 442, 489, 492
Convention on the Nationality of Married Women (1957), 487
Convention on the Non-Applicability of Statutory Limitations to War Crimes and Crimes against Humanity (1968), 376, 488
Convention on the Political Rights of Women (1952), 487
Convention on the Prevention and Punishment of the Crime of Genocide (1948), 116, 334, 360, 379, 455

Convention on the Protection and Promotion of the Diversity of Cultural Expressions (2005), 173, 331
Convention on the Protection of the Underwater Cultural Heritage (2001), 173
Convention on the Reduction of Statelessness (1961), 487
Convention on the Rights of the Child (CRC, 1989), 109, 152, 216, 234, 235, 331, 356, 442, 490, 492
Convention for the Suppression of the Traffic in Persons and of the Exploitation of the Prostitution of Others (1949), 486
Convention Relating to the Status of Refugees (1951), 452, 474
Convention Relating to the Status of Stateless Persons (1954), 487
Convention Relating to the Status of Stateless Persons (1960), 487

D

Declaration and Programme of Action on a Culture of Peace (1999), 492
Declaration of Basic Principles of Justice for Victims of Crime and Abuse of Power (1985), 489
Declaration of Principles of International Law Concerning Friendly Relations and Co-operation Among States in Accordance with the Charter of the United Nations (1970), 369
Declaration of Principles on Tolerance (1995), 336, 344, 491
Declaration of the Rights of Mentally Retarded Persons (1971), 488
Declaration of the Rights of the Child (1959), 235, 486, 487
Declaration on Fundamental Principles and Rights at Work (1998), 492
Declaration on Race and Racial Prejudice (1978), 113, 330, 334, 342, 406, 489
Declaration on Social and Legal Principles relating to the Protection and Welfare of Children, with Special Reference to Foster Placement and Adoption Nationally and Internationally (1986), 490
Declaration on Social Progress and Development (1969), 488
Declaration on the Elimination of all Forms of Intolerance and of Discrimination Based on Religion or Belief (1981), 488, 489, 491
Declaration on the Elimination of all Forms of Racial Discrimination (1963), 488
Declaration on the Elimination of Discrimination against Women (1967), 488
Declaration on the Elimination of Violence against Women (1993), 491
Declaration on the Establishment of a New International Economic Order (1974), 488
Declaration on the Granting of Independence to Colonial Countries and Peoples (1960), 487
Declaration on the Human Rights of Individuals Who are not Nationals of the Country in Which They Live (1985), 489
Declaration on the Preparation of Societies for Life in Peace (1978), 343, 489
Declaration on the Prohibition of the Use of Nuclear and Thermo-Nuclear Weapons (1961), 378, 487
Declaration on the Promotion among Youth of the Ideals of Peace, Mutual Respect and Understanding between Peoples (1965), 488
Declaration on the Protection of All Persons from Being Subjected to Torture and Other Cruel, Inhuman or Degrading Treatment or Punishment (1975), 488
Declaration on the Protection of all Persons from Enforced Disappearance (1992), 491
Declaration on the Responsibilities of the Present Generations Towards Future Generations (1997), 347, 492
Declaration on the Right of Peoples to Peace (1984), 344, 489
Declaration on the Rights of Disabled Persons (1975), 488
Declaration on the Rights of Indigenous Peoples (2007), 123, 332, 334, 468, 493
Declaration on the Rights of Persons Belonging to National or Ethnic, Religious and Linguistic Minorities (1992), 331, 334, 456, 468, 491
Declaration on the Right to Development (1986), 10, 343, 406, 490
Declaration on the Use of Scientific and Technological Progress in the Interests of Peace and for the Benefit of Mankind (1975), 489

F
First Geneva Convention for the Amelioration of the Condition of the Wounded in Armies in the Field (1864), 486

G
Geneva Conventions (1949), 217, 382, 447, 464, 486, 489, 493
Geneva Convention relative to the Treatment of Prisoners of War (Diplomatic Conference) (1929), 486
Guidelines for Action on Children in the Criminal Justice System (1997), 492
Guidelines for the Regulation of Computerized Personal Data Files (1990), 490
Guidelines on the Role of Prosecutors (UN Congress on the Prevention of Crime and the Treatment of Offenders) (1990), 490
Guiding Principles on Business and Human Rights: Implementing the United Nations 'Protect, Respect and Remedy' Framework (2011), 147, 494

I
Indigenous and Tribal Peoples Convention (1989), 490
International Code of Conduct for Public Officials (1996), 491
International Covenant on Civil and Political Rights (ICCPR, 1966), 91, 107, 274, 340, 442, 461, 488, 490
International Covenant on Economic, Social and Cultural Rights (ICESCR, 1966), 107, 108, 139442, 454, 459, 461, 466, 490, 493
International Convention against Apartheid in Sports (1985), 489
International Convention on the Elimination of All Forms of Racial Discrimination (ICERD, 1965), 109, 216, 334, 442, 482
International Convention for the Protection of All Persons from Enforced Disappearance (CPED, 2006), 109, 123, 442, 452, 465, 493
International Convention on the Protection of the Rights of All Migrant Workers and Members of Their Families (ICPRMW, 1990), 109, 490
International Convention on the Rights of Persons with Disabilities, with an Optional Protocol (CRPD, 2006), 334, 493
International Convention on the Suppression and Punishment of the Crime of Apartheid (1973), 488
International Declaration against Apartheid in Sports (1975), 489
International Declaration on Human Genetic Data (2003), 217

O
Optional Protocol to the CAT (2002), 110
Optional Protocol to the CEDAW (1999), 110, 127
Optional Protocol to the CRC (2011), 110, 127, 442
Optional Protocol to the ICCPR (1966), 108, 442, 461, 462
Optional Protocol to the ICESCR (2008), 108, 127, 442, 462
Optional(s) Protocol(s) to the CRC (2000), 110, 127, 442

P
Principles for the Protection of Persons with Mental Illness and for the Improvement of Mental Health Care (1991), 491
Principles of international co-operation in the detection, arrest, extradition and punishment of persons guilty of war crimes and crimes against humanity (1973), 488
Principles of Medical Ethics relevant to the Role of Health Personnel, particularly Physicians, in the Protection of Prisoners and Detainees against Torture and Other Cruel, Inhuman or Degrading Treatment or Punishment (1982), 489
Principles on the Effective Investigation and Documentation of Torture and Other Cruel, Inhuman or Degrading Treatment or Punishment (2000), 492
Principles on the Effective Prevention and Investigation of Extra-legal, Arbitrary and Summary Executions (1989), 490
Proclamation of Tehran (1968), 484, 488
Principles relating to the Status of National Institutions for the Promotion and Protection of Human Rights ('Paris Principles') (1993), 142, 468
Protocol to Prevent, Suppress and Punish Trafficking in Persons, Especially Women and Children, supplementing

the United Nations Convention against Transnational Organized Crime (2000), 492

R

Recommendation concerning Education for International Understanding, Co-operation and Peace and Education relating to Human Rights and Fundamental Freedoms (1974), 6, 406, 488
Recommendation on Consent to Marriage, Minimum Age for Marriage and Registration of Marriages (1965), 488
Recommendation on the Safeguarding of Traditional Culture and Folklore (1989), 173, 490
Resolution on 'Education of youth in the respect for human rights and fundamental freedoms' (1968), 169
Rome Statute of the International Criminal Court (Diplomatic Conference) (1998), 117, 146, 447, 459, 492

S

Safeguards guaranteeing protection of the rights of those facing the death penalty (1996), 491
Second Optional Protocol to the International Covenant on Civil and Political Rights Aiming at the Abolition of the Death Penalty (1989), 274
Slavery Convention (1926), 71
Standard Rules on the Equalization of Opportunities for Persons with Disabilities (1993), 491
Standard Rules for the Minimum Treatment of Prisoners (1957), 487
Stockholm Declaration (UN Conference on the Environment) (1972), 488
Supplementary Convention on the Abolition of Slavery (1953), 77
Supplementary Convention on the Abolition of Slavery, the Slave Trade, and Institutions and Practices of Slavery (1956), 77

U

UNESCO Constitution (1945), 338, 366, 375
United Nations Convention against Corruption (2003), 493
United Nations Convention against Transnational Organized Crime (2000), 492
United Nations Declaration on Human Rights Education and Training (2011), 436, 458, 494, 501
United Nations Declaration on Human Cloning (2005), 493
United Nations Standard Minimum Rules for the Administration of Juvenile Justice (The Beijing Rules) (1985), 490
United Nations Guidelines for the Prevention of Juvenile Delinquency (The Riyadh Guidelines) (1990), 490
United Nations Principles for Older Persons (1991), 491
United Nations Rules for the Protection of Juveniles Deprived of Their Liberty (1990), 490
United Nations (UN) Charter (1945), 81, 101, 162, 199, 251, 333, 360, 361, 367, 415, 498
United Nations (UN) Millennium Declaration (2000), 10, 138, 172, 344, 369
United Nations (UN) Summit Outcome (2005), 345348, 367, 369
Universal Declaration on Bioethics and Human Rights (2005), 217, 268, 273, 276, 278, 293, 335, 348
Universal Declaration of Human Rights (UDHR, 1948), 5, 87, 89, 96, 97, 99, 100, 103, 108, 133, 163, 169, 173, 179, 200, 234, 330, 331, 340, 347, 356, 395, 415, 425, 429, 430, 434, 461, 484, 486, 495
Universal Declaration on Cultural Diversity (2001), 173, 268, 330, 375
Universal Declaration on the Human Genome and Human Rights (1997), 172, 217, 273, 276, 278, 321

V

Vienna Convention on the Law of Treaties (VCLT, 1969), 137, 144, 381
Vienna Declaration and Programme of Action (1993), 10, 120, 135, 172, 339, 343, 345, 475, 479, 484

W

World Charter for Nature (1982), 489
Worst Forms of Child Labour Convention (1999), 492

Other documents at universal level

C
Convention Respecting the Laws and Customs of War on Land (IV Hague Convention, 1907), 375

D
Declaration of Philadelphia (1944), 213
Draft Declaration of Principles on Human Rights and the Environment (1994), 113
Draft Declaration on the Right to Peace (2012), 344

M
Montevideo Convention on Rights and Duties of States (1933), 339

Human rights legal instruments and other related instruments at regional level

A
Additional Protocol to the American Convention on Human Rights in the area of Economic, Social, and Cultural Rights (known as the "Protocol of San Salvador") (1988), 131, 490
Additional Protocol to the European Social Charter Providing for a System of Collective Complaints (1995), 491
African Charter on Democracy, Elections and Governance (2007), 493
African Charter on Human and Peoples' Rights (ACHPR, 1981), 111, 132, 493
African Charter on the Rights and Welfare of the Child (OAU, 1990), 132, 490
African Union Convention on Preventing and Combating Corruption (2003), 493
African Youth Charter (2006), 493
American Convention on Human Rights (ACHR, 1969), 111, 231, 259, 274, 380, 442, 463, 488
American Declaration of the Rights and Duties of Man (1948), 83, 92, 217, 404, 406
Arab Charter on Human Rights (1994), 218, 491
ASEAN Human Rights Declaration (2012), 494

C
Cairo Declaration on Human Rights in Islam (Islamic Conference) (1990), 133, 414, 491
Charter of Fundamental Rights of the European Union (EU Charter, 2000), 115, 492
Charter of the Organization of American States (OAS, 1948), 83
Convention for the Protection of Human Rights and Dignity of the Human Being with regard to the Application of Biology and Medicine: Convention on Human Rights and Biomedicine (1997), 130, 217, 273
Convention Governing the Specific Aspects of Refugee Problems in Africa (1969), 132, 488
Council of Europe Convention on Action against Trafficking in Human Beings (2005), 130, 493

D
Declaration of Medellín: Youth and Democratic Values (2008), 493

E
European Charter for Regional or Minority Languages (1992), 491
European Convention for the Prevention of Torture and Inhuman or Degrading Treatment or Punishment (1987), 130, 490
European Convention on Human Rights (ECHR, 1950), 91, 111, 140, 364
European Convention on the Non-Applicability of Statutory Limitation to Crimes against Humanity and War Crimes (1974), 377
European Convention on the Recognition of the Legal Personality of International Non-Governmental Organisations (1986), 150
European Cultural Convention (1954), 487
European Social Charter (ESC, 1961, 1996), 130, 218, 491
European Social Charter (Revised) (1996), 130, 218, 487, 491

F
Final Act of Helsinki (1975), 131, 149
Final Declaration of the Regional Meeting for Asia of the World Conference on Human Rights (Bangkok Declaration) (1993), 411, 491
Framework Convention for the Protection of National Minorities (council of Europe) (1995), 491

I
Inter-American Convention on the Elimination of all Forms of Discrimination against Persons with Disabilities (1999), 492
Inter-American Convention on the Prevention, Punishment and Eradication of Violence Against Women "Convention of Belém do Pará" (1994), 491
Inter-American Convention to Prevent and Punish Torture (OAS, 1985), 490
Inter-American Democratic Charter (2001), 340, 493

M
Macchu Picchu Declaration on Democracy, the Rights of Indigenous Peoples and the War against Poverty (2001), 493

P
Protocol No. 6 to the Convention for the Protection of Human Rights and Fundamental Freedoms concerning the Abolition of the Death Penalty (1982), 274
Protocol No. 6 to the Convention for the Protection of Human Rights and Fundamental Freedoms concerning the Abolition of the Death Penalty (1983), 274
Protocol to the African Charter on Human and Peoples' Rights on the Rights of Women in Africa (2003), 493
Protocol to the American Convention on Human Rights to Abolish the Death Penalty (1990), 274, 491

T
Treaty on European Union (1992), 131, 367, 491
Treaty of Lisbon (2007), 131, 493

Other documents at regional level

B
Bangkok NGOs Declaration on Human Rights (1993), 413

C
Cairo Declaration on Human Rights in Islam (1990), 133, 414

F
Final Declaration of the Regional Meeting for Asia of the World Conference on Human Rights (1993), 411

O
Our Common Humanity—Asian Human Rights Charter—A Peoples' Charter (1998), 133

R
Recommendation N° R(97)14 on the establishment of independent national institutions for the promotion and protection of human rights (1997), 143

Human rights legal instruments and other related instruments at national level

A
American Declaration of Independence (1776), 61, 63, 175, 373, 429, 485

B
Basic Law: Freedom of Occupation (1994), 221
Bill of Rights (1689), 58, 66, 67, 82, 83, 85, 86, 88, 92, 144, 181, 213, 214, 260, 262, 303, 306, 314, 369

D
Déclaration des droits de l'homme et du citoyen (1789), 29, 356, 373

Declaration of the Establishment of the State of Israel (1948), 221

E
Eighth Amendment, 237, 240, 266
Emancipation Proclamation (1863), 67, 419, 425

F
Fifth Amendment, 255
Fourteenth Amendment, 232, 240, 255

H
Habeas Corpus Act (1679), 58

I
Israel Basic Law: Human Dignity and Liberty (1992), 221, 225, 242, 254

M
Magna Carta (1215), 57–59, 75, 98, 419

P
Petition of Rights (1628), 58

T
Ten Amendments (1791), 63

V
Virginia Declaration of Rights (1776), 62, 63

Other documents/sources

A
A Common Framework for the Ethics of the 21th Century, 2
Act of Chapultepec, 251
Antigone, 46, 189
Atlantic Charter, 78, 82, 251, 425

B
Biblical Decalogue, 57

C
Code of Hammurabi, 57, 58
Complément à la Déclaration des Droits de l'Homme, 213, 260
Constitution of Medina, 58
Corpus Iuris Civilis, 48
Cyrus Charter, 58

D
Daily Herald, 75, 76
Declaration by the United Nations, 78, 82, 83
Déclaration des droits de la femme et de la citoyenne, 67
Déclaration des droits internationaux de l'homme, 72, 73
Declaration of Four Nations on General Security, 78
Declaration on Anthropology and Human Rights, 410
Declaration on the Abolition of the Slave Trade, 391
Declaration toward a Global Ethic, 2, 29
Decretum, 48, 49, 54
De l'esprit des lois, 51, 328
Doctrine of the Mean, 30

E
Émile, 28, 59, 64, 89, 168, 288, 297, 425, 426

F
Four Freedoms Speech, 486

H
Human Development Report (UNDP), 9, 171, 347

I
Index of Forbidden Books, 60, 61
In search of a wisdom for the world, 1
Institutes, 48, 148, 328, 364
Iustiniani Institutiones, 48, 328

L
Limburg Principles, 466, 467

M
Maastricht guidelines, 466
Maastricht Principles on Extraterritorial Obligations of States in the area of Economic, Social and Cultural Rights, 138
Memorandum and Questionnaire Circulated by UNESCO on the Theoretical Bases of Human Rights, 91, 144, 407
Moscow declaration, 79

P
Paris principles, 142, 143
Phaedrus, 190
Prevention of Sati Act, 412
Proposals for the Establishment of a General International Organization, 79, 83
Protecting Dignity: An Agenda for Human Rights, 416, 483

R
Reich Citizenship Law, 294
Republic, 46, 67, 82, 131, 212
S
Second Bill of Rights, 82, 115, 116, 181, 260, 303
Seconde Lettre sur la Tolérance, 64
Slavery Convention, 71
Statement of Essential Human Rights, 76, 88
Summa Theologiae, 49, 178, 202
Symposium, 1, 187, 190

T
Ten Commandments, 32, 176
The Analects, 28
The Grounds of an International Declaration of Human Rights, 182
The Search for Universal Ethics: A New Look at Natural Law, 5, 29
The Times, 75
Traité sur la tolérance à l'occasion de la mort de Jean Calas, 60
Treaty of Nimègue, 69
Treaty of Oliva, 69
Treaty of Passarowitz, 69

V
Vedas, 21, 46

W
What it means to be human—Origins and Evolution of Human Higher Cognitive Faculties, 279, 316

Y
Yalta Agreement, 79

National Constitutions

A
American Constitution (1787), 62, 66, 262

C
Constitution of Belgium (1831), 221
Constitution of Cuba (1940), 218
Constitution of Finland (2000), 261
Constitution of Germany (GG) (1949), 219, 224, 228, 242, 260, 272, 294, 348, 365, 368
Constitution of Greece (1975), 218
Constitution of Ireland (1937), 218
Constitution of Italy (1947), 218
Constitution of Japan (1947), 218
Constitution of Poland (1997), 246
Constitution of Portugal (1933), 218
Constitution of Portugal (1976), 218
Constitution of Spain (1978), 218
Constitution of the Islamic Republic of Iran (1979), 247
Constitution of the Mexican United States (1917), 67
Constitution of the Republic of Colombia (1812), 393
Constitution of the Republic of South Africa (1996), 221, 374
Constitution of the Russia Soviet Federative Socialist Republic (1918), 67

F
French Constitution (1793), 29
French Constitution (1795), 65, 404
French Constitution (1848), 69
French Constitution (1946), 67
Federal Constitution of the Swiss Confederation (1999), 261

P
Prussia Constitution (1850), 67

S
Soviet Constitution (1936), 112

W
Weimar Constitution (1919), 67, 219, 220

International Courts and Case Law

B
Barcelona Traction, Light and Power, Limited, 383

C
Court of Arbitration at The Hague, 426

G
Greece v. Albania (Minority Schools in Albania), 334

I
International Criminal Court (ICC), 117, 120, 150, 223, 377
International Court of Justice (ICJ), 102, 110, 120, 121, 127, 143, 147, 148, 223, 229, 251, 360, 379, 383
International Criminal Tribunal for Former Yugoslavia, 117
International Criminal Tribunal for Rwanda, 117
International Military Tribunal at Nuremberg, 77, 118, 375, 447, 459
International Military Tribunal for the Far East, 118, 119

P
Permanent Court of International Justice, 71, 102, 334

Regional Courts and Case Law

A
Advisory Opinion OC-17/2002 of 28 August 2002 on the 'Juridical Condition and Human Rights of the Child, 235, 259, 362
African Court on Human and Peoples' Rights, 132
African Court of Justice and Human Rights, 132
Albert et Le Compte (1983), 274
Austria v. Italy (1960), 380

B
Baena-Ricardo et al. v. Panama, 472

C
Court of Justice of the European Union, 251
Cyprus v. Turkey (2001), 380

E
Erich Stauder v City of Ulm (1969), 252
European Court of Human Rights, 73, 130, 135, 140, 144, 145, 218, 223, 229, 231, 233, 243, 257, 265, 274, 335, 364, 367, 374, 380, 381, 417, 426, 460
Evans v. the United Kingdom (2007), 231

G
Gündüz v. Turkey (2003), 374

I
Inter-American Court of Human Rights, 131, 223, 235, 241, 243, 259, 334, 362, 380, 382, 383

L
Loizidou v. Turkey (1995), 380

N
Netherlands v. European Parliament and Council (2001), 223

P
Pretty v. The United Kingdom (2002), 218, 243

S
Street Children (Villagran-Morales et al.) v. Guatemala (1999), 241
Streletz, Kessler and Krenz v. Germany (2001), 274

T
Tyrer v. The United Kingdom (1978), 223, 233, 257
Thlimmenos v. Greece (1997), 335

V
Vo v. France (2004), 231, 265

National Courts and Case Law

A
Abrams v. United States (1919), 182
Academic Center of Law and Business v. Minister of Finance (HCJ 2605/05), 238, 256, 263, 292

Adalah Legal Centre for Arab Minority Rights in Israel and others v Minister of Interior (HCJ 7052/03), 329
Ahmedabad Municipal Corporation v. Nawab Khan Gulab Khan, 243
August and Another v Electoral Commission and Others (CCT8/99) [1999] ZACC 3; 1999 (3) SA 1; 1999 (4) BCLR 363 (1 April 1999), 264, 374

B
Belgium Constitutional Council, 221
Bilhah Rubinova and Others v. Minister of Finance (HCJ 888/03), 242, 253, 263, 292, 311, 315
Brown v. Plata (563 US, 2011), 237
BVerfGE 6, 32 (1957), 224, 252, 261
BVerfGE 7, 198 (1958), 224, 226
BVerfGE 30, 173 (1971), 224
BVerfGE 33, 367 (1972), 228
BVerfGE 39, 1 (1975), 232, 265, 283, 327
BVerfGE 45, 187 (1977), 225, 253, 257, 271, 408
BVerfGE 54, 148 (1980), 228
BVerwGE 31, 236 (1969), 263
BVerwGE 64, 274 (1981), 271
BVerfGE 65, 1 (1983), 228
BVerfGE 87, 209 (1992), 266
BVerfGE 109, 279 (2004), 253, 327
1 BvR 2378/98 (2004), 228
1 BvR 1084/99 (2004), 228
1 BvR 357/05 (2006), 327
1 BvL 1/09 (2010), 242, 261

C
Canadian Supreme Court, 241, 267, 315
Cape High Court (South Africa), 258
Christian Education South Africa v Minister of Education (CCT4/00) [2000] ZACC 11; 2000 (4) SA 757; 2000 (10) BCLR 1051 (18 August 2000), 236
Coetzee v Comitis (2001), 258
Cohen v. California (403 U.S. 15, 1971), 227
Commitment to Peace and Social Justice v. Minister of Finance (HCJ 366/03), 242, 253, 263, 292, 311, 315
Conseil d'État (France), 269
Constitutional Court of Portugal, 250
Constitutional Court of the Republic of South Africa, 240, 258, 272, 328
Criminal Appeal 4596/98 Plonit v. A.G. 54(1) P.D. [2000], 236
Criminal Court of Cassation of the Second Circuit Court of San José de Costa Rica, 235

D
Dred Scott v Sandford (1857), 67

F
Ferreira v Levin NO and Others; Vryenhoek and Others v Powell NO and Others (CCT5/95) [1995] ZACC 13; 1996 (1) SA 984 (CC); 1996 (1) BCLR 1 (6 December 1995), 315, 328
Ford v. Wainwright (477 U.S. 399, 1986), 240, 246
Francis Coralie Mullin v. The Administrator, Union Territory of Delhi and ORS, 1981, SCR (2) 516, 243, 262, 274, 275
Furman v. Georgia (408 U.S. 238, 1972), 239, 258, 266, 274

G
German Federal Constitutional Court, 220, 223, 224, 226, 228, 232, 242, 252, 253, 256, 260, 261, 265, 266, 268, 269, 271
Goldberg v. Kelly (397 U.S. 254, 1970), 241
Government of the Republic of South Africa and Others v Grootboom and Others (CCT11/00) [2000] ZACC 19; 2001 (1) SA 46; 2000 (11) BCLR 1169 (4 October 2000), 262
Gonzales v. Carhart et al. (550 U.S. 05-380 and 05-1382, 2007), 233
Gregg v. Georgia (428 U.S. 153, 1976), 239

H
HCJ 355/79 Katlan v. Israel Prison Service [1980] IsrSC 34(3) 294, 238
High Court of Fiji at Lautoka, 235
Hope v. Pelzer et al. (536 U.S. 730, 2002), 237
Hudson v. Michigan (547 U.S. 586, 2006), 229

I
Indiana v. Ahmad Edwards (554 U.S. 164, 175, 2008), 270
Israel Supreme Court, 225, 264, 374

J
Judgment 011062, 02-002448-0369-PE, 20/10/2005, 235

K

Kennedy v. Louisiana (554 U.S. 407, 420 2008), 240
Kindler v. Canada [1991] 2 S.C.R. 779, 241

L

Law v. Canada [1999] 1 S.C.R. 497, 267, 315
Lawrence et al. v. Texas (539 U.S. 558, 2003), 229, 255
Lesbian and Gay Equality Project and Eighteen Others v Minister of Home Affairs (CCT 10/05) [2005] ZACC 20; 2006 (3) BCLR 355 (CC); 2006 (1) SA 524 (CC) (1 December 2005), 230
Let the Animals Live v. Hamat Gader Recreation Enterprises (LCA 1648/96, 22.6.1997), 247

M

Minister of Home Affairs and Another v Fourie and Another (CCT 60/04) [2005] ZACC 19; 2006 (3) BCLR 355 (CC); 2006 (1) SA 524 (CC) (1 December 2005), 230
Mohini Jain v. State of Karnataka, 243
Movement for Quality Government in Israel v. Knesset (HCJ 6427/02), 256, 263, 292
Movement for Quality Government in Israel v. The Prime Minister (HCJ 1993/03), 256, 263, 292, 374

N

National Coalition for Gay and Lesbian Equality and Another v Minister of Justice and Others (CCT11/98) [1998] ZACC 15; 1999 (1) SA 6; 1998 (12) BCLR 1517 (9 October 1998), 230, 263
Naushad Ali v. State (Criminal Appeal N° HAA 0083 of 2001 (C. P. N° 0001 of 2001L, Judgment on 21 March 2002), 235

P

Paschim Banga Khet Mazdoor Samity v. State of Bengal, 243
Planned Parenthood of Southeastern Pennsylvania et al. v. Casey, Governor of Pennsylvania et al. (505 U.S. 833, 851, 1992), 232

R

R. v. Keegstra [1990] 3 S.C.R. 697, 267
Republic of Italy v. Cambria (1996), 237, 259
Robert Maxter et al. v. State of Montana and Another (2009 MT 449), 243, 272
Robinson v. California (370 U. S. 660, 370 U. S. 666, 1962), 239
Rochin v. California (342 U.S. 165, 1952), 228
Roper v. Simmons (543 U.S. 03-633, 2004), 240, 266

S

State v Jordan and Others (Sex Workers Education and Advocacy Task Force and Others as Amici Curiae (CCT31/01) [2002] ZACC 22; 2002 (6) SA 642; 2002 (11) BCLR 1117 (9 October 2002), 270
Station Film Co. v. Public Council for Film Censorship (1994) 50 P.D. (5) 661, 271
Supreme Court of Cassation in Rome, 237, 259
Supreme Court of India, 223, 262, 274, 275, 416
Supreme Court of the State of Montana (USA), 243, 272

T

Tellis v. Bombay Municipal Corporation, 243
Texas v. Johnson (491 U.S. 397, 1989), 227
The State v. T Makwanyane and M Mchunu (CCT3/94) [1995] ZACC 3; 1995 (6) BCLR 665; 1995 (3) SA 391; [1996] 2 CHRLD 164; 1995 (2) SACR 1 (6 June 1995), 225, 240, 258, 272, 328
Thornburgh v. Am. Coll. of Obstetricians (476 U.S. 747, 1986), 232
Trop v. Dulles (356 U.S. at 356 U. S. 100), 238–240

U

USA Supreme Court, 182, 223, 227, 228, 229, 232, 237, 239, 241, 245, 246, 248, 255, 258, 262, 266, 270

V

VerfGE 12, 45 (1960), 224

W

Winston v. Lee (470 U.S. 753, 1985), 229
Women's Association for the Future of Israel v. The Broadcasting Authority (HCJ 6143/94, July 26, 1999), 265

United Nations Human Rights Committees and General Comments (GC)

C

Committee against Torture (CoAT), 125
Committee on Economic, Social and Cultural Rights (CESCR), 108, 125, 140, 141, 462
- *GC 1*, 454
- *GC 3*, 136
- *GC 10*, 142
- *GC 11*, 302
- *GC 12*, 136
- *GC 13*, 200, 234, 302
- *GC 14*, 148
- *GC 18*, 147

Committee on the Elimination of Discrimination against Women (CoEDAW), 125
Committee on the Elimination of Racial Discrimination (CERD), 125, 128, 442, 454
Committee on Enforced Disappearances (CED), 125, 127, 128
Committee on Migrant Workers (CMW), 125, 128
Committee on the Rights of the Child (CoRC), 125, 127, 128, 137, 143, 200, 233, 253, 258, 302, 357, 455
- *GC 1*, 233
- *GC 2*, 143
- *GC 5*, 137, 357
- *GC 8*, 200, 258

Committee on the Rights of Persons with Disabilities (CoRPD), 121, 123

H

Human Rights Committee (CCPR), 125, 127, 128
- *GC 6*, 241, 274
- *GC 18*, 147, 333, 473
- *GC 24*, 450
- *GC 25*, 339
- *GC 29*, 451
- *GC 31*, 135, 136

S

Subcommittee on Prevention of Torture (SPT), 125, 126, 443, 482

Countries

A

Afghanistan, 105, 221
Albania, 70, 131, 334
Argentina, 3, 57, 105, 425
Australia, 87, 92, 105, 118, 144, 145, 405
Austria, 70, 380, 384

B

Belarus, 97, 131
Belgium, 72, 87, 105, 145, 221
Bosnia and Herzegovina, 97, 142
Brazil, 92, 105, 162, 221, 425
Bulgaria, 70
Byelorussia/Byelorussian SSR, 87, 93, 96, 97, 105

C

Cambodja, 132
Canada, 78, 87, 92, 105, 118, 148, 261, 245, 267
Chile, 83, 88–90, 98, 105, 149, 184, 427
China, 27, 57, 79, 80, 84, 85, 87, 88, 93, 105, 118, 121, 176, 305, 411, 424, 427
Colombia, 83, 221, 393, 425
Costa Rica, 111, 117, 148, 162, 235, 361
Croatia, 97
Cuba, 83, 88–90, 105, 174, 213, 218
Czechoslovakia, 70, 96, 97, 105, 397
Czech Republic, 97

D

Denmark, 105, 162
Dominican Republic, 105, 162, 425

E

East Timor, 417
Ecuador, 88, 96, 105
Egypt, 57, 87, 92
El Salvador, 105
Estonia, 70
Ethiopia, 105, 221

F

Fiji, 235
Finland, 70, 218, 261, 418, 437
France, 1, 56, 60, 61, 63–67, 70, 80, 85–88, 90, 92, 93, 96, 118, 121, 130, 161, 162, 174, 209, 210, 221, 269, 270, 329, 360, 365, 375, 390, 391, 426

G
Germany, 50, 70, 71, 78, 80, 94, 194, 209, 210, 218–221, 232, 260, 262, 263, 274, 294, 300, 322, 365, 366, 376, 407, 426, 431–433, 460
Greece, 21, 30, 70, 105, 162, 201, 218, 294, 334, 335, 338, 342, 373, 384, 424
Guatemala, 105, 241

H
Haiti, 74, 105
Hungary, 70, 255

I
India, 57, 87, 88, 90, 92, 105, 118, 145, 148, 162, 186, 223, 243, 262, 274, 275, 400, 412, 416
Iran, 87, 145, 247
Iraq, 105
Ireland, 118, 218
Israel, 105, 220, 221, 223, 225, 236, 242, 247, 253, 254, 256, 263–265, 271, 292, 311, 315, 329, 374
Italy, 3, 48, 78, 202, 218, 237, 259, 376, 284, 402

J
Japan, 78, 80, 218, 407, 412

K
Kosovo, 417

L
Latvia, 70
Lebanon, 87, 90, 162, 426, 427, 433
Liberia, 105
Lithuania, 70

M
Madagascar, 221
Memel Territory, 70
Mexico, 79, 83, 92, 105, 113, 162, 218, 392, 433, 438
Montenegro, 97

N
Namibia, 221
Netherlands, 12, 74, 92, 94, 105, 117, 118, 141, 142, 223, 384
New Zealand, 84, 92, 94, 95, 105, 118

P
Palau, 121
Panama, 83, 87–90, 432
Paraguay, 425
Philippines, 87, 118, 132, 397, 432
Poland, 70, 96, 97, 105, 397
Portugal, 69, 108, 131, 218, 250

R
Republic of South Africa, 97, 221, 222, 240, 258, 262, 272, 328, 374
Romania, 70
Rwanda, 117, 152

S
Saudi Arabia, 97
Serbia, 97
Singapore, 132, 410–412
Slovak Republic, 97
Slovenia, 97
South-African Union, 97
South Korea, 133, 412
Spain, 54, 218
Sweden, 92
Swiss Confederation, 261
Syria, 105

T
Tanzania, 117
Taiwan, 412
The former Yugoslav Republic of Macedonia, 97
Trinidad and Tobago, 117
Turkey, 70, 127, 375, 380, 427

U
Ukraine/Ukrainian SSR, 87, 96, 97, 105
Union of Soviet Socialist Republics (USSR), 87, 93, 396
United Kingdom (UK), 6, 90, 91, 118, 127, 145, 174, 218, 223, 231, 233, 243, 257
United States of America (USA), 63, 79, 80, 87, 118, 131, 415, 425
Uruguay, 87, 105, 117

V
Venezuela, 105

Y
Yugoslavia, 70, 87, 93, 96, 97, 105, 107, 117, 152, 358, 381, 425

Cities and other places

A
Adriatic, 398
Aix-en-Provence, 269
Amsterdam, 265
Arusha, 117
Athens, 64, 200, 338, 342
Auschwitz, 77

B
Babylon, 57
Baltic, 131, 284, 398, 431
Bangkok, 411, 413, 415
Banjul, 111
Barcelona, 381, 383, 453
Bavaria, 219
Belgrade, 107
Berlin, 8, 32, 69, 164, 219, 286, 424
Beyrut, 426, 427
Bogota, 83, 251, 393
Bologna, 48
Boston, 76
Bremen, 219
Bretton Woods, 79
Briarcliff Lodge, 72
Bronx, 86
Buenos Aires, 4

C
Cairo, 78, 133, 414
California, 60, 227, 228, 237, 239
Cambria, 237
Chapultepec, 83, 251
Chicago, 2, 78, 79
Columbia, 262, 427
Copenhagen, 370
Crimea, 79

D
Delhi, 243, 262, 274, 275
Delphos, 30
Dijon, 74
Dumbarton Oaks, 79, 83, 84

F
Florence, 418
Freetown, 117
Freiburg, 426, 427

G
Geneva, 74, 91, 92, 97, 117, 121, 122, 125, 128, 144, 162, 175, 217, 360, 426, 431, 432
Georgia, 80
Gleiwitz, 71

H
Hamburg, 227
Helsinki, 131, 149
Hessen, 219
Hoess, 77
Hot Springs, 79

J
Jerusalem, 289, 431

K
Königsberg, 300
Kwangju, 133

L
Lake Success, 87, 89, 92, 97, 145, 162, 174, 175, 222, 277
Lautoka, 235
Lido Beach Hotel, 89
Limburg, 466, 467
Lisbon, 131
London, 79, 80, 85, 118, 119, 213, 390, 396
Los Angeles, 76, 227
Louisiana, 240

M
Maastricht, 12, 138
Manila, 132
Marseille, 269
Memel Territory, 70
Mesopotamia, 57
Mexico city, 79, 83, 113, 392, 438
Montana, 243, 272
Montevideo, 339
Montreal, 428
Montreux, 73
Morsang-sur-Orge, 269
Moscow, 78, 79, 118, 251, 286

N
New York, 4, 10, 72, 73, 76, 81, 86, 87, 97, 102, 104, 117, 120, 121, 125, 128, 149, 241, 346, 427, 434

Newfoundland, 78
Nice, 130
Nimègue, 69
Nuremberg, 52, 77, 87, 99, 118, 119, 120, 251, 375, 447

O
Ohio, 466
Oliva, 69
Oregon, 245
Ottawa, 286, 464

P
Paris, 54, 72, 73, 94, 99, 142–144, 152, 376, 395, 404, 427, 437
Passarowitz, 69
Pearl Harbour, 78
Pennsylvania, 232, 338
Persia, 57, 58
Phnom Penh, 132
Potsdam, 251
Prague, 71
Prussia, 67

R
Rome, 1, 117, 120, 146, 150, 193, 237, 251, 259, 419

S
San Francisco, 73, 78, 80, 83, 85, 89, 213, 357, 360, 392, 399, 424
San José de Costa Rica, 111, 235
Siam, 60
Stettin, 398
Strasbourg, 112, 145, 335, 377
Sumeria, 57

T
Texas, 227, 229, 255
The Hague, 73, 74, 117, 151, 169, 356, 361, 379, 381, 399, 426
Toulouse, 60, 61
Trieste, 398
Turku, 418

U
Ulm, 252
University of Cincinnati, 466
Upper Silesia, 70, 71

V
Valladolid, 55
Versailles, 70, 72, 269
Vienna, 69, 111, 121, 128, 169, 343, 411
Virginia, 62, 79

W
Westminster, 85, 398
White House, 76
Warm Springs, 80
Washington, 78, 79, 83, 245, 396
Weimar, 112, 163, 260
Westphalia, 68, 359, 465

Y
Yalta, 79, 251

CPSIA information can be obtained at www.ICGtesting.com
Printed in the USA
LVOW10*2243020414

380115LV00004B/27/P

9 783319 035659